Economic Theories
of International Politics

MARKHAM POLITICAL SCIENCE SERIES
Aaron Wildavsky, Editor

Economic Theories of International Politics

Edited by

Bruce M. Russett
Yale University

MARKHAM PUBLISHING COMPANY • CHICAGO

Acknowledgments

First I must express my gratitude to those economists from whom I learned as a student, especially to Paul Clark, Emile Despres, Kermit Gordon, William Parker, and Stanislaw Wellisz, who taught at Williams College when I was an undergraduate there; to R. F. Kahn, Nicholas Kaldor, and Robin Maris, my tutors at King's College, Cambridge University; and to Charles E. Lindblom of Yale. They stimulated in me an interest in economics that remains despite years of training in political science. Also, I must thank the economists from whom I have learned as colleagues, particularly those who commented on the manuscript during its preparation: Richard Cooper, Robert Harlow, Burton Klein, and Frederick Pryor. Perhaps the most valuable and extensive comments were those of William C. Mitchell, political scientist turned political economist. In this same class of intellectual contributors belongs Carolyn Cooper, who as my assistant worked over my prose and, in response to sometimes specific, sometimes vague guidelines, turned up approximately one-fourth of the selections ultimately used.

This project, like the others that I have engaged in during the last few years, benefitted enormously from financial support by the National Science Foundation—support which has been both generous and free of constraint. Similar thanks are due for the more recent assistance I have received from ARPA Behavioral Sciences and the Office of Naval Research. Patricia Stannard and Caroline Stancliff typed the manuscript, handled many editorial tasks, and as usual helped to make my work easier and more pleasant. Certainly there would be no book without the permission of publishers and authors to reprint the selections appearing here. I have identified them at the beginning of each paper. Finally, my thanks to Cynthia, who would always be a superior good.

Wellfleet, Massachusetts   B.M.R.
June 1968

v

Contents

Introduction

In the first three sections of this introduction are outlined basic concepts essential to a clear understanding of economic theories as they relate to international politics. In the final two sections the articles themselves, and the criteria for their inclusion, are discussed in some detail. Additional comments on the articles are included in the remarks introducing each part and also in separate notes preceding the individual papers.

1. Economics for Political Scientists

All boundaries are artificial—constructs imposed on more or less continuous distributions in order to simplify ordering the relationships on either side. This is as true of the demarcation lines between intellectual disciplines as it is of frontiers between nations. But some boundaries are more artificial than others; some nations are more tightly integrated and distinct from their neighbors than are others, and some areas of academic endeavor are more unified than others.

Political science has endured a good deal of travail in the establishment of a recognizable subject matter and method. Its roots are clearly recognizable in sociology and philosophy. In at least one major American university it still is taught in a unit labeled the Department of Public Law and Government, and in many European institutions it still is offered as a part of the law curriculum. Many colleges in the United States have only recently split a political science department away from the history department, and historical studies long comprised a most central concern of the field. Even now, with the establishment of separate departments and the general recognition that the study of politics possesses a certain distinctiveness, efforts to retain or build media for the exchange of ideas and information are evident across many of the boundaries. Many individuals refer to themselves as political sociologists, political geographers, or political philosophers. Programs in science and government, psychology and politics, law and politics, and mathematics and politics abound. And political economy has a long and continuing tradition.

If political science has experienced a cosmopolitan youth and adolescence, with both the exhilaration and the crisis of identity associated with such an origin, the field of international politics has had a history with much the same elements expressed even more strongly. Traditionally, international relations offerings have been interdisciplinary. The typical program is built upon courses in political science, diplomatic history, and international economics, with, more rarely, some bases also in psychology, sociology, and geography. Most centrally, it is rooted in political science— Hans Morgenthau, for instance, is well-known for his position that international politics is but a specific instance of a general theory of politics[1]—but the need for contributions from other disciplines is fully apparent. It is perhaps most usefully considered as a subset of political science, but intersecting also with the sets represented by history and each of the other social sciences.

The intensity of interest directed to these various intersections oscillates considerably over time; geopolitics in the Mackinder sense has been dead for some time, but renewed interest in the relevance of spatial relations is evident in a number of recent studies.[2] Lately, particular attention has gone to the contributions of psychology. Starting with the rather amorphous focus of the post-1945 "war and the minds of men" approach, there have been a great number of stimulating and increasingly sophisticated efforts to apply psychological categories and explanations to international actors. Recently, we have been given several anthologies composed of pieces addressed to international problems from a psychological or social-psychological vantage.[3] It seems to me, however, that there is at least as much available to stimulate the international relations scholar in the literature of economics, and that the opportunity has been seriously neglected.

The traditional international relations program did incorporate a course or two in economics. Almost entirely, however, such a course dealt not with international politics per se, but merely with economic factors affecting or resulting from political decisions. Decisions involving

---

[1] See, e.g., his "The Nature and Limits of a Theory of International Relations," in W. T. R. Fox, ed., *Theoretical Aspects of International Relations* (Notre Dame: University of Notre Dame Press, 1959), p. 15.

[2] See the references in B. M. Russett, *International Regions and the International System* (Chicago: Rand McNally, 1967).

[3] L. Bramson and G. W. Goethals, eds., *War: Studies from Psychology, Sociology, and Anthropology* (New York: Basic Books, 1964), R. Fisher, ed., *International Conflict and Human Behavior* (New York: Basic Books, 1964), H. Kelman, ed., *International Behavior: A Social-Psychological Analysis* (New York: Holt, Rinehart, and Winston, 1965), and J. D. Singer, ed., *Human Behavior and International Politics: Contributions from the Social-Psychological Sciences* (Chicago: Rand McNally, 1965).

tariffs, exchange rates, fiscal policy, and interest rates were at the center of attention with perhaps, in recent years, some focus on problems of economic development in poor nations. Essentially, the purpose was to provide an acquaintance with those manipulative tools of economics that can be used to serve political purposes, and sufficient terminological familiarity to permit discourse with a true expert.

Such an orientation misses the most important contributions that a knowledge of economics can make to the politics specialist. As Singer noted in the introduction to his volume on the relevance of social psychology, the scholar who would borrow from another discipline can look for a variety of elements that may be of some interest; he can borrow *data*, or *concepts*, or *methods*. None of these are implied in the traditional smattering of economics provided to the international relations curriculum. As described in the preceding paragraph, economics is hardly more than a tool—like computer programing, or a foreign language—useful for communicating information or expanding one's bag of policy tricks, but in no way entering into the scholar's personal analytical equipment for dealing specifically with political interactions.

To the degree that any of Singer's three elements have so far been important, probably the most influential has been economic *data*. Measures like Gross National Product and GNP per capita have proved useful, despite imperfections, as very crude measures of national power bases and of well-being. In my own compilation of "political and social" indicators it happens that fully 18 out of 75 indices are derived from national income accounts, with another 14 measuring the distribution of factors of production (land and labor force).[4]

The concepts and methods of economics have had some impact on the study of international politics, but only in limited areas. Bernard Brodie has said that, "Most of those who have made their mark today as theorists in strategy have been trained as economists, or at least have more than a bowing acquaintance with the concepts and principles in that field,"[5] but such a comment is deceptive. In fact, 30 percent of the specialists in problems of strategy are affiliated with political science and only 3 percent with economics.[6] While the contributions of certain economists have been absolutely central to the way the national security field has developed—one thinks most obviously of Thomas Schelling, and perhaps

[4] B. M. Russett et al., *World Handbook of Political and Social Indicators* (New Haven: Yale University Press, 1964).

[5] "The Scientific Strategists," in R. Gilpin and C. Wright, eds., *Scientists and National Policy-Making* (New York: Columbia University Press, 1964), p. 247.

[6] R. E. Licklider, *The Private Nuclear Strategists* (Yale University: Ph.D. Dissertation, 1968), p. 123.

also of Oscar Morgenstern, Klaus Knorr, and, with a belated but spreading impact, Kenneth Boulding—professional economists in the strategy field have been more important than numerous. Furthermore, the concepts and principles to which Brodie refers have been centered on only a couple of major conceptual innovations.

Most striking in their impacts are game theory and its half brother, utility theory, in which context one would want to add, to Schelling and Morgenstern, such other economist-innovators as Daniel Ellsberg, John Harsanyi, and Martin Shubik. Even here, however, the effect of the contribution has been somewhat diluted—the restrictive assumptions of game theory, in all its varieties, prevent its being used directly as an analytical device on the complex data of international politics, and the most impressive feats of Morgenstern and Schelling involve insightful analogizing, from the sight lines provided by game theory, rather than a rigorous use of that tool in its mathematical purity. And in any case, economics can lay only partial claim to the development of game theory— the work of professional mathematicians is fully as central.

The other major source of economic input to the concerns of international politics is, doubtless, systems analysis. This too is only partly attributable to economics, being rooted also in operations research. Nevertheless, the contributions of economists like Charles Hitch, Roland McKean, Alain Enthoven, and Henry Rowen are well known. But here we are already slipping into a somewhat narrow focus—systems analysis or cost-benefit analysis is most useful on restricted problems, on the assets and liabilities one acquires with a particular weapons system, rather than with broader political and social determinants of national defense postures.

It is my contention that the discipline of economics has a great deal more to offer the international politics specialist, enough to reward quite a general study of the subject, not limited to the features just discussed or to the theory of international finance. To attempt to demonstrate its relevance I have put together this volume for my own enlightenment and that of fellow scholars and advanced students. Most important for the study of international politics now, in its push toward the characteristics of a science, is the importance of formal theory in economics. The rigorous deduction of theorems from explicit assumptions, using the symbolic tools of mathematics, provides a discipline not yet widely practiced in political science. And propositions derived mathematically can often be tested quantitatively for their applicability to the real world. (I say often, but hardly always. Much of welfare economics, for example, deals with variables which are not measurable in practice.) While such mathematical tools as differential calculus and matrix algebra are now finding increasing employment in political science, economics has also long made much use of geometry, with a great variety of graphical illustrations to clarify reasoning and presentation. Faced with indifference maps or strange curves for demand, supply, cost, and profit, the international politics man is likely to be bewildered, and doubtless such bewilderment will occur more than once when looking at some of the selections included later in this volume. But the mastery of such tools can have substantial payoffs.[7] These models are, after all, merely statements of the relation of one variable to another, expressed for the sake of clarity, precision, and generalizability in mathematical or logical symbols *as well as* in English.

We are accustomed to remarking about the benefits of modern physical science, but one of the most striking successes of the century is in economics, a social science. Over the past three decades economists seem to have conquered the business cycle. In the developed Western economies we still have recessions and modest inflations, but the threat of depression or runaway inflation, so constant before World War II, has been removed. Many problems, such as stimulating and maintaining economic growth in poor societies, have not yet been solved, but control of the business cycle alone represents a saving of hundreds of billions of dollars. This success can be traced directly to the wedding of formal deductive theory, as articulated by Keynes and others, to the large body of detailed quantitative data growing out of the war and, in America, of the Full Employment Act of 1946.[8] No other social science has followed this route so determinedly, nor can any other claim even a fraction of economics' success.

2. Theories of Rational Choice

Economic theory is at heart a set of assumptions and deductions about *rational choice* on the part of individuals and organizations. It is relevant whenever actors have determinate goals but limited means of achieving those goals, and hence must allocate scarce resources. These goals may be material goods, or they may be social status or political power. In its concern with choice, economic theorizing produces principles that are fundamentally directed to behavior in general rather than merely to the allocation of material goods. Actions and choices are made under various degrees of uncertainty, and behavior involves a combination of competitive and cooperative acts. Individuals must reach agreements with

[7] An early advocate of the use of economic concepts in political analysis is G. E. G. Catlin, though his work most often took the form of terminological analogizing. See his recent *Systematic Politics* (Toronto: University of Toronto Press, 1962).

[8] See K. E. Boulding, *The Impact of the Social Sciences*, (New Brunswick, N.J.: Rutgers University Press, 1966).

others while bargaining. All parties share characteristics of both allies and competitors, in varying measure, over the *terms* of the agreements. The choices of one man are interdependent with the choices of others, and the interactions are of prime interest. Political theory must be concerned with these same phenomena.

Rationality implies the choice of different goals according to some consistent scale of preferences, with the preferences ordered by the attribution of various utilities to each goal. Preferences may, of course, change; there is no requirement to assume that they are fixed. Nor does the rational-choice focus necessarily imply any naive assumption that individuals always *are* fully rational. The rational-choice model forms an idealized set of assumptions from which propositions can be deduced and which can be tested empirically. Some of the most important contributions deal with individuals' reactions to risk and uncertainty, and others, such as those of Herbert Simon, are devoted to behavior of decision-makers under conditions of limited abilities for information processing. They ask which of an infinity of possible alternatives are actually perceived, and how new alternatives are generated.[9]

Finally, John Harsanyi suggests the dangers in labeling any behavior as "irrational," and indicates some ways in which a variety of acts may still be understood within the context of rational-choice models:

A major challenge for any rational-choice theory of social behavior is the question of how to interpret what is, or at least appears to be, "irrational behavior." Actually the term "irrational behavior" is rather misleading because it seems to prejudge the issue of whether such behavior serves any useful purposes or not. A more appropriate descriptive term is *symbolic* or *expressive* behavior....

Sometimes, what appears to be excessive preoccupation with symbolic actions is a way of making *social commitments*. For example, opposition parties may organize a protest demonstration against government policies even though they do not expect it will have any effect on the government's actions—because it will give an opportunity for the participants to commit themselves to support the anti-government camp. (Such a commitment will be particularly effective if the names of the demonstrators are likely to become publicly known, making it very hard for them to rejoin the ranks of government supporters.)

[9] See H. Simon, *Administrative Behavior* (New York: Macmillan, 1957); *Models of Man* (New York: Wiley, 1957); and "Political Research: The Decision-Making Framework," in D. Easton, ed., *Varieties of Political Theory* (Englewood Cliffs: Prentice-Hall, 1966). Note that *three* papers at the 1967 annual meeting of the American Political Science Association stressed the relevance of economic theorizing, and, specifically, rational choice models, to political phenomena. See J. Harsanyi, "Rational-Choice Models versus Functionalistic and Conformistic Models of Political Behavior;" W. C. Mitchell, "The Shape of Political Theory to Come: From Political Sociology to Political Economy," (in *American Behavioral Scientist*, 11, 2, pp. 8–37); and M. Olson, Jr., "The Relationship of Economics to the Other Social Sciences: The Province of a 'Social Report'."

In other cases, preoccupation with symbolic actions can be explained essentially as an act of *desperation*: it may simply mean that people have given up all hope of achieving their goals by reality-oriented instrumental activities, and so feel they have nothing to lose by turning to magic, ritual, ideology, and other forms of symbolic behavior. Such attitudes seem to underlie a wide variety of social movements, from some messianistic cults to some extremist political groups.

However, it may be noted that "irrational" social policies—if by this we mean highly inefficient and self-defeating policies—do not necessarily result from "irrational" behavior on the part of the individual participants. For example, some countries have been known to combine a tough foreign policy involving very low armament expenditures for reasons of economy. From a national point of view this clearly involves choosing the worst of all possible worlds. But from the point of view of the political leaders responsible for this policy it may have represented the politically most convenient compromise between the supporters of a tough foreign policy line (who presumably favored high defense expenditures) and the supporters of budget economies (who presumably would have been willing to follow a less provocative foreign policy).[10]

3. Hazards of Transference

The major problem, of course, and one which is fully as critical in the initial work in economics as in the situations to which we shall attempt to apply the approach in this volume, is whether the models, with all their rigor and, hence, simplifications, are appropriate. In abstracting to a limited number of variables and functions, have the right simplifications been made? Are the variables included really the most important ones, and are the initial assumptions fruitful? But in making the transfer from economic situations to political ones the chances for error are compounded, since even if the assumptions produced useful results in their original habitat they may be quite inappropriate to their new setting. As Boulding declared with reference to his own famous effort to apply economic theory to problems of international conflict:

Generalized models of this kind inevitably involve a degree of simplification to the point where the peculiarity of particular situations may be overlooked.... The basic model relies heavily on certain similarities between the competition of firms and of states and, indeed, of any organizations such as rival labor unions or churches that are competing in a given field. This basic similarity is fundamental to the approach of this book. Nevertheless, the differences between the various types of conflict are also very important and must be carefully examined lest we fall into the trap of making false analogy. It is one of the major tasks of science in any field to detect similarities in superficially different situations and to detect differences in superficially similar situations.[11]

[10] Harsanyi, *op. cit.*, pp. 11–13.
[11] *Conflict and Defense* (New York: Harper & Row, 1961), pp. 248–249.

And in writing a stimulating piece directed to international relations theorists, C. P. Kindleberger noted, "As one who has tried to teach that governments are not like families in the necessity to live within their income to avoid bankruptcy, I am not unaware of the danger of analogies."[12]

Many of the articles in the following collection deduce some propositions, potentially of great import for theory and policy in international politics, from some very limiting assumptions. Obviously, the professional political scientist needs to inspect and weigh those assumptions with great care. In addition, teachers who use the book as supplementary reading for advanced students in international politics theory courses should urge their students to make the same kind of critical inspection, asking under what particular circumstances, if indeed any, the models or systems of thought suggested would really have any application to the relations among nations.

Doubtless, the conditions studied in economics *are* different, often very different, from those that arise in international politics. To compare a certain kind of market situation, especially the abstract market of a given economic theory, with a particular real-world international system is sure to involve major simplifications and even distortions. But no comparison of two situations is ever strictly comparable; no man steps twice into the same river. The European balance of power in 1890 was not the same as in 1905, though that fact has not prevented historians and political scientists from drawing or applying some general principles to both. The problem always faced is to identify as clearly as possible those elements which are comparable and those which are not, and to decide whether the comparabilities are sufficient to permit useful comparison. It is impossible to say in general whether comparison will be more fruitful for the same arena over time (a nation during a five-decade period), different arenas at the same time (a market and an international system in 1968), or even different arenas at different periods.

Especially, we must beware of the verbal labels we supply to describe phenomena. An "alliance" can serve many different functions, and two such arrangements may not be at all comparable for our purposes, despite their identification by the same name. Similarly, the difference in terminology between economics and political science must not prevent us from looking behind it for possible similarities in the relationship being described. Finding analogies is not the end of the scientific process, but it may open up opportunities for more rigorous investigations. Analogy is, after all, recognized as a major mode of scientific reasoning, and the ability to recognize the utility of concepts in one area to problems

[12] "International Political Theory from Outside," in Fox, *op. cit.*, p. 76.

in another is the mark of one kind of creativity. In the end, though not necessarily at the beginning, the value of such analogies must be subject to careful test. J. David Singer sums up the problem well in considering his own interdisciplinary volume:

> However, no matter how comparable the variables may be, or how compelling the analogy, an important distinction remains to be made. Is the analogy drawn for descriptive and predictive purposes, or merely for heuristic purposes? If "heuristic" means here "suggestive" (or "productive of tentative ideas and hypotheses") it is easy to see how crucial this distinction can be. To put it another way, in the absence of better data and better models from the "real" world, the analogy may well *have to* serve as evidence, albeit evidence of a clearly interim nature. Its main value, then, is to generate reasonable hypotheses, whose confirmation ultimately requires testing in the empirical world about which we want to generalize. Until such testing, by operational, and therefore replicable, procedures occurs, we are a goodly distance from our objective of data-based theory. But given the tremendous gap which now separates us from that aspiration, it will be no great crime to treat our more sophisticated and careful analogies as a tentative variety of empirical evidence.[13]

The next problem, equally serious, involves the step from analytic models, which may be expressed in quantitative terms of price or quantity supplied or demanded, to the empirical application of these models. In some cases, economists frankly admit that their models can be only heuristic, and are incapable of being expressed in measurable units. This is especially true of much of welfare economics, where it has so far been found impossible to measure utilities on a cardinal scale, despite the need for such precision to test some (though not all) of that branch's theories. Related difficulties arise with the whole notion of subjective probabilities for unique events. We should be aware, however, that the measurement problem is especially acute in the game-theoretical application of economics to strategic questions, and this application is probably the most influential and widespread—though still highly controversial[14]—use of economic theory in the study of international politics. If despite some serious difficulties such aids to thought remain valuable, the hazards need not utterly bar our critical and judicious attempts to explore the analytical value of other elements of economics.

[13] Singer, *op. cit.*, p. 13.

[14] Trenchant broadsides, each with a scatter of shots both on and wide of the target, include A. Rapaport, *Strategy and Conscience* (New York: Harper & Row, 1964), and P. Green, *Deadly Logic* (Columbus: Ohio State University Press, 1966). The efforts of psychologists as well as economists to clarify the usage of utility and probability concepts, as well as their important laboratory work in moving toward adequate measurement, should not, however, be overlooked.

This major criticism—the impossibility of satisfactory quantification—has been leveled against attempts to introduce a highly stimulating
model, equilibrium theory, into the explanation of a variety of social
phenomena.[15] An effective response is that while we may prefer quantifiable theories, the immediate rejection of all presently nonquantifiable
models would leave us with an impoverished social theory and an impoverished social science.

Were theorists to take these criticisms to heart they might better abandon
their researches in favor of novel writing, for quantification is at present a very stern
measure of valid theory. Few social scientists dispute that mathematical formulation
is the ultimate ideal (however Utopian) of their endeavors. And, indeed, in recent
years more and more social variables have been yielding to numerical statement.
But desirable as mathematical models may be, it seems unfair to discriminate against
equilibrium because its manifest mathematical precision in the natural sciences
makes its vagueness in social thought appear distractingly unsatisfactory by comparison.[16]

It may be said that at least economic theories, when kept in their own
element, have a particular advantage that is lost when one tries to transfer
them to other arenas—economics can express its analytical units in terms
of money, a quantified instrument that is present throughout the work
of Adam Smith's descendants. Though such statements—for example,
"Politics suffers by contrast with economics in that it lacks a single,
simple basis for measurement, like money"[17]—are even sometimes made
by economists, who should of course know, I think they exaggerate.
While central and nearly ubiquitous in economics, money units no more
exhaust the possibilities for measurement in that discipline than do votes
in political science. For market analyses one measures the number of
units produced and sold, as well as cost, price, or profit. And much of
economic theorizing is, in fact, devoted to problems of comparing
utilities, of establishing indifference curves, of estimating and comparing
probabilities, and a host of other nonmonetary variables.

4. Levels of Transference

The collection that follows is a variegated lot. It attempts to illustrate some potential applications of economic theories and analytical

[15] See, e.g., D. Easton, "Limits of the Equilibrium Model in Social Research," in H.
Eulau, S. Eldersveld, and M. Janowitz, eds., *Political Behavior: A Reader in Theory and
Research* (New York: Free Press, 1956).

[16] C. E. Russett, *The Concept of Equilibrium in American Social Thought* (New Haven:
Yale University Press, 1966), p. 161.

[17] C. P. Kindleberger, "Scientific International Politics," *World Politics*, **11**, 1 (October
1958), p. 84.

techniques to major problems of international politics at a variety of levels.

The selections in the first section deal with the constitution and behavior of *subsystems* within a larger economic or political system, specifically, with questions of alliance formation and the ways in which nations combine with others to pursue common interests while at the same time retaining goals that partly conflict with those of their partners. One selection briefly notes how allies fail to observe the principle of comparative advantage within the alliance, illustrating the existence of competitive as well as co-operative interests. Another develops and applies a theory of "collective" or "public" goods to explain the patterns of burden sharing within NATO. And the next article suggests some principles for understanding the optimum size of an alliance, to explain why more or fewer nations did not join. The distribution of costs within an alliance or other collective enterprise is often determined by tacit or overt bargaining, but the bargaining solution is not necessarily either the most efficient or most "equitable" one possible. Hence, one paper considers some of the disadvantages to, and alternatives to, reliance on the bargaining process, and another discusses the implications of logrolling for surmounting the so-called paradox of voting. Both this and another selection emphasize differences in the *salience* of decision makers' preferences, as well as the usually considered differences in their preference *ordering* of various outcomes. And the final selection in the first part returns explicitly to the problem of alliance formation. Its author shows how it is possible by certain assumptions to deduce the *distribution* of benefits or costs, as discussed previously, but not in the same model to predict what actors will constitute the *membership* of a victorious alliance.

A second major portion of the book deals with the relation between the relative size and number of decision-making units to other characteristics of the system, such as its stability. There are in this respect close analogies between the structure of the international system and market structure, with similarities between nations' and firms' behavior. Hence, a number of pieces suggest the circumstances under which an essentially bipolar world (duopoly) would be stable, or offer some considerations on the consequences of a multipolar (oligopoly) situation. Further analogies could be drawn to the world dominated by a single great imperial power (monopoly) or, on the other extreme, to a globe with a substantial number of states, each of which has some, but little, influence over the international system (imperfect competition) all the way to a world of many small states, none of whom can in any way significantly affect the structure of the international system (perfect competition). Economists have studied all these situations, occasionally deriving determinate solutions from assumptions that seem relevant and plausible, more often clearing away some of the conceptual underbrush without yet being able to produce a satisfactory conclusion.

The first article in the second section discusses the effect of size on groups' behavior, suggesting, from the theory of collective goods, why a world of a few large powers might be characterized by greater stability and "responsibility" than would one composed of many smaller states. Each of the small states could by itself make little contribution to the stability of the entire system, but might reap important gains from seeking its narrow interests in a highly competitive manner. This piece introduces a series of papers about the relative advantages and disadvantages of an oligopolistic system. One considers a set of variables affecting the resource base of an actor and its ability to survive severe competition and so prevent concentration of power in the system or market from narrowing down to one or two major units. Another explores the conditions necessary for successful collusion and limitation of competition in a way that recalls the apparent conditions for a stable balance of power system. The next piece investigates empirically the relation between the degree of concentration of power in a system and the stability of individual actor's shares, and the following one considers the role of communication between the actors and the system's stability. Yet another frankly extolls the oligopolistic market as one of stability and restricted competition, where competitive instincts are turned from destructive to constructive pursuits such as scientific research and technical development to build better products rather than to sell existing ones more cheaply.

Other systems than the balance of power or oligopolistic market are explored. Two articles concern the restraints on competition in a bipolar or duopolistic system. One draws explicit analogies to arms races, but both are deeply concerned with the effect that different evaluations of attack and deterrence have on actors' behavior and on the prospects for a stable system. They are followed by a chapter, written with reference to a bipolar world, that attempts to measure the value which the gain or loss of small allies may have for a great power, suggesting the degree to which the system may be upset by a shift from one side to the other. And the paper following it presents an elegant deductive argument about bipolar competition for the allegiance of neutrals and the conditions of "peaceful coexistence." From a concern with the consequence of firms' or nations' size and number on the characteristics of the entire system, it is an obvious step then to inquire into the determinants of size. One paper deals with some hypotheses about the relation between the size of a nation (firm) and its "efficiency," and whether there may be long-term forces operating to produce an international system where power will be more heavily concentrated in a few very large states. The section concludes with a well-known theoretical treatment of some possible interactions among national size, distance, and viability.

From the system-level focus it is an obvious step to investigate other variables which affect bargaining behavior and actors' strategies. The first two papers in the third section are concerned with the relation between the interests of leaders or other authoritative decision makers and the interests of the group which they represent. One of them speculates about conditions which may bring about major divergencies of interest between the two, and the other checks some related hypotheses with empirical data on the conditions for managerial discretion in making decisions for their firms. This discussion, reminiscent of "the national interest," leads to an article applying several strands of economic theory to the ways in which nationalistic sentiments can be used to change the distribution of rewards within a nation-state, and a related selection considers some consequences of discrimination that are applicable both to international and intranational behavior. To conclude the section there are two comparative studies of collective bargaining in labor-management relations. They suggest a few of the variables which help determine whether an agreement will be reached peacefully or whether it will require a war (strike). Also, how will the bargain itself be changed by attempts to impose a requirement for peace without the credible threat of war (strike)? In these discussions we get down to the problems of comparative foreign policy, explaining the behavior of states (firms or bargaining units) in terms of their internal characteristics or previous experiences rather than by the limitations imposed by the nature of the larger system.

In the fourth and final major portion of the book we take up some insights provided by economics into the dynamic problems of system change. The initial two pieces consider, from very different theoretical perspectives, the relative merits and demerits of national states versus larger supranational entities, and some virtues and liabilities of incrementalism versus more drastic attempts to change existing systems. Together they emphasize the advantages of dealing with problems on a disaggregated small-unit level, and of refraining from efforts to transform the nation-state system into some very different form of global organization. The second of the two does not confront the size problem per se, but is concerned with problems of information and predictability in larger systems. It is followed by an example of econometric forecasting, illustrating a method whereby detailed predictions, even for very complicated systems, can be made. The volume concludes with an article explicitly stating the necessity for a comprehensive overview so as to avoid being brought, by successive small decisions, to an unwanted, unforeseen, but irreversible outcome.

5. Criteria for Inclusion

Some of the pieces reprinted here will no doubt already be familiar to some readers; for this literature, drawn from many areas within the discipline of economics, there can be no "typical" reader. With a couple of exceptions, however, especially the selection by Boulding, I have tried to omit pieces that were already widely known among international relations scholars. This means, first, that there is nothing which deals primarily with game theory, though one or two articles do touch on game-theoretical concerns, and, second, that there are no examples of cost-benefit analysis. Each of these now constitutes by itself an enormous literature and could be discussed only in the most superficial way with one or two extracts. Aside from such considerations, the criteria for inclusion were three:

1. The article or chapter should be *technically competent* by the appropriate criteria of logic or mathematical accuracy, but it would *not necessarily be the most sophisticated statement* available on the topic. As any subarea develops, the first, most innovative articles are likely to spell out their assumptions and procedures in detail. Later papers can refer to the early ones, taking the reader's basic familiarity with them for granted and providing only a highly condensed summary of relevant parts of the previous literature. Such articles may then go on to make serious modifications in the earlier material, or even to refute it. But for the reader from outside the area, who does not know its literature, the subsequent papers may be virtually incomprehensible in their condensation. Thus, despite a preference for the more recent development, I have sometimes, in the interest of this book's readers, been forced to include an earlier piece even where I knew that later writings had modified it somewhat. Economists who pick up this book will, doubtless, find many such instances. Where I felt that the later controversy or modification was important from the viewpoint of the material's relevance to international relations, I have tried to indicate this in my introduction to the piece. But if the essential point could be made by the early or simplified paper, I have not hesitated to use it.

For many readers even these "simplified" pieces will be strange and difficult, sometimes because of the unfamiliar terminology, more often because of the dependence upon symbols and geometry. Fully half of the pieces are straightforward verbal statements or, at the most, use only a few simple graphs. The rest employ either rather complicated graphs for illustration, or algebra or (rarely) higher mathematics for deriving propositions. While all will not be comprehensible to everyone, I hope the reader will not allow such treatments to discourage him. In every case he can follow the main concerns and the conclusion from the verbal statements alone, skipping the mathematics. But I have left most such presentations in for those readers whose understanding will be improved, and who would be offended by the omission of essential steps in the reasoning that brought the writer to his conclusion.[18]

2. The article or chapter should, if possible, be *empirical*; it should illustrate its conclusions with, or, better, derive them from, carefully gathered material suitable for hypothesis testing. In a few areas this criterion has been met quite successfully; some of the sections on market structure are best. But this success has been extremely uneven. Like political science, economics is not a battlefront where the whole line moves forward at the same pace with the same weapons. In many areas there simply was no good empirical material available. If there was some empirical material, the theoretical articulation was slight or nonexistent. In such cases the gaps will be obvious enough. Where possible, I tried at least to include material that was in principle subject to empirical verification with international politics material, but even here the rule had sometimes to be bent for especially stimulating presentations.

3. The article or paper should be *theoretically well articulated*, if at all possible with the original author making the transfer or analogy to the theoretical problems in international politics. If the latter were not the case, and it usually was not, then the paper should at least spell out the theoretical basis or conclusions for *economics*. The purpose of this volume, after all, is to show how economic *theory* is relevant to the concerns of international theory. Most often, the papers were written solely with economic concerns in mind, and I have indicated some of the reasons why I thought the reasoning or conclusions were important for my own substantive interests. Most readers will supply for themselves instances of relevance that I have omitted either from lack of space or from lack of the necessary insights. In that sense the book is meant to stimulate thought and not to provide ready-made models or results. In a few cases I have included materials that will seem short on theory. In such instances either I have myself supplied some thoughts toward the theoretical

---

[18] While retaining these elements essentially uncut, I have rather drastically omitted footnotes. Many such are devoted either to purely economic disputes of no interest to the present readers or to detailed qualifications and bibliographic references that seemed unnecessary. But I have retained the relevant side journeys and citations to enough related literature to get the reader started in the further pursuit of these issues.

relevance for international relations, or have, nevertheless, included them, despite my inability to account satisfactorily for the conclusions, because I thought those conclusions of great importance to analogous interests in political science.

The latter statement, however, does require me to repeat my previous more implicit comments about one more major omission. This is not a volume directed to the explanation of economic phenomena per se, however relevant those phenomena might be to international politics. Nor is it an illustration of how economic phenomena affect political phenomena or vice versa. Thus, there are no discussions of customs unions, tariff and trade policy, the inter-relationship of economic and political development, the economic roots of imperialism, or other problems in "political economy." The bridges I have tried to build here between the disciplines are from theory to theory, or possibly from method to method—not from findings to findings.

Finally, many readers will recall other articles or chapters in economics or even in international politics that are fully as stimulating and meet all the criteria specified. It would be cowardly merely to plead space limitations. While such considerations did unavoidably apply, it is all too obvious that I could not possibly be familiar with the entire literature of economic theory. I have merely dipped into certain areas that I thought would be rewarding, and continued the search to a point of satisfising rather than optimizing. My purpose is not only to indicate how these particular pieces may be relevant to the international politics scholar's interests but also to suggest where he could find many more such pieces. Economists will doubtless be able to think of any number of other articles to illustrate these and related methods of analysis. But I have written the book not for economists but for international relations scholars who may be unaware of this body of literature. Some economists may nevertheless see some new applications of their discipline to international political problems and so be stimulated to bring their skills to the effort.

I

Alliances and the Collective Pursuit of Benefits

●

Nations may cooperate to obtain benefits they could obtain alone at best with difficulty, and perhaps not at all. But they are likely to have great difficulties in agreeing on a satisfactory distribution of the gains and costs of their joint endeavor, and even in obtaining collectively as much of the benefits as they had originally intended. This has become painfully clear with the two most important international organizations to which the United States belongs, the United Nations and the North Atlantic Treaty Organization. In 1952 the members of NATO met at Lisbon and formally agreed upon a set of force goals, including most importantly a total of 96 divisions for the defense of all of western Europe from possible Soviet attack. Those force goals have never been met, with the peak accomplishment representing at best 70–75 divisions, including reserves.[1] For most of the decade following the Lisbon decisions the United States stationed in Europe all those troops that it had promised to provide, but few European states kept their commitments. In addition, the United States has devoted a much larger share of its GNP to defense expenditures than has any of its smaller allies. No amount of exhortation or diplomatic pressure exerted by the United States government has achieved notable results in producing a higher level of European contribution to the defense of Europe.

Certainly, there are major strategic considerations that have helped to bring about such a situation. Ground forces for the defense of Europe imply that a conventional or tactical nuclear war might actually be fought on European territory. While this is not a very attractive outcome for even the United States to contemplate, for the European allies, located

[1] K. Knorr, ed., *NATO and American Security* (Princeton: Princeton University Press, 1959), p. 31.

directly in the potential war zone, it is a much worse prospect. They would prefer a strategy depending upon the threat of central nuclear war which would involve most directly the territory of the United States and Russia, and thus most of the Europeans have dragged their heels in building up a force that might shift the primary scene of war to Europe. Although they had to accept the Lisbon agreement as the price for obtaining an American presence in Europe and, hence, a trip wire for the guarantee, it proved much harder to persuade them to meet the force goals as the years went on and the American commitment seemed firm.

While this explanation is helpful for understanding the European failure to produce large ground forces, it is less powerful in explaining why the European states have not made proportional (allowing for their smaller size and lower income levels) contributions to build large over-all (e.g., sea and air as well as land) forces. Most often, analysts have been reduced to other ad hoc explanations, sometimes of differing estimates of the *probability* of attack, sometimes on the level of a more fervent anticommunism in the United States or disparaging remarks about a general European tendency to shirk burdens whenever someone else can be found to pay most of the bill.

Such ad hoc explanations, however, lose much of their force in the face of so many repetitions of this pattern in other international organizations. The more recent failures of the American government to persuade its fellow members of the UN to contribute larger shares to peacekeeping operations bears some disturbing similarities to the NATO experience. Unless one is willing to accept explanations such as those which praise the Americans as a generally more conscientious and, in global matters, more civic-minded people than almost any other, the lack of a satisfactory general theoretical exposition of affairs is evident. Yet it is general, the problem is much more apparent in international matters than in situations which arise within nations, and political science has not produced the explanation. C. P. Kindleberger notes the widespread nature of the problem and its special relevance to conditions where there is no sense of community or strong political institution embracing the units which must share:

It is possible to think of the wants of a whole country, because a country, as a political and social unit committed to principles of sharing through the budgetary process, will redistribute income automatically when changes in international prices bring about changes in the distribution of income within the society. Part of the equilibrating process in interregional trade which is not present in international trade involves net taxation on some regions and net subsidies to others. The taxes and subsidies are not, as a rule, designed to be regional in their incidence, but can be regarded in this light after aggregation of their effects on individuals and local communities. Economists who object to net taxation on, say, New England, in the interest of that region, are fundamentally objecting to the basis of the federal union which is attempting to achieve equity among individuals, wherever located. To focus on the regional effect is to divide the "us" into a smaller us and a residual them. When this occurs over a significant enough series of problems, the national unit is preserved only by force, as in Spain, or in geographic terms, but as an economic and political fiction.

Since 1939 this difference between international and interregional trade has again altered. Lend-lease in wartime, and the Marshall plan in postwar reconstruction, involve international sharing which contrasts with President Coolidge's "They hired the money, didn't they?" NATO has evolved some rudimentary practice in sharing defense expenditures. Point IV and UN Technical Assistance involve certain subsidies to underdeveloped countries.

In wartime, the capacity to share is heightened by the enhanced perception of the linkage of interests. Aid for relief, as in UNRRA or disaster loans and grants, is fairly readily forthcoming either because the donor fears the unrest and disruption which would occur if he failed to take steps, or because the need is so dramatically brought home to him that the donor can imagine himself in the same position, and has compassion for others as a form of indulgence to himself. International sharing, however, is much more difficult than national, in the absence of common items of expenditure for mutual benefit.[2]

The difficulty is not limited to the failure of the collectivity to produce *enough* of the good, be it defense, poverty relief, or peacekeeping. A second aspect is that, because of failures to observe comparative advantage, whatever *is* acquired will not be obtained in what might appear to be the most efficient fashion. There is likely to be a fair amount of duplication both of production and of acquisition. The total number of some kinds of weapons will be relatively greater than is necessary for the alliance's joint aims, and they will cost more than they "should." In the following brief excerpt Malcolm Hoag states the classic economic case for comparative advantage, and laments the failure of NATO to achieve efficiency.

●

[2] "International Political Theory from Outside," in W. T. R. Fox, ed., *Theoretical Aspects of International Relations* (Notre Dame: University of Notre Dame Press, 1959), pp. 74–75.

1

What Interdependence for NATO ?

Malcolm W. Hoag

Can we afford to neglect any means of getting more defense from our limited resources? Among those means, can we neglect the advantages of an economic division of labor among allies? That we cannot neglect them is strongly indicated by the magnitude of possible savings from interallied military specialization. Even when these savings are measured only by the comparative national costs of military supplies and manpower in implementing agreed strategy—to consider briefly the relatively small economies, before turning to the possible big economies from strategic changes that are our major concern—they are not trivial. When—to take one major if somewhat academic example—the United States, the most costly producer of ships among major maritime producers, persists in building a naval fleet bigger than the fleets of the rest of the world put together, one suspects that there is gross inefficiency in the allocation of military tasks within the alliance. Where open subsidies of about one-half of construction costs are required for our merchant marine to meet foreign competition, what are the hidden subsidies implicit in the construction of our navy?

Or, to take another area of production, when the President of the United States speaks in his Budget Message of "bombers that cost their weight in gold," he refers to sophisticated planes whose enormous development costs are being spread over a very small volume of production. Such small volume and consequent high cost are not typical

Reprinted from M. W. Hoag, "What Interdependence for NATO?" *World Politics*, **12**, 3 (April 1960), pp. 370–372, by permission of The RAND Corporation.

in this country, but would be typical abroad if each ally insisted upon building its own advanced planes or missiles for small forces. For such material there are enormous economies in concentrating the final expensive stages of development and production in one place in one nation. The multiplication of production sources exemplified by British production of no less than three V-bombers, each probably only a marginal improvement over our old B-47, is a contrasting case in point of dispersion. How much more sensible might it have been had we permitted the British to earn dollars by building naval ships for us, and had they spent the dollars buying improved B-47's from us! This observation is now only a lament. But why should the British lavish money upon a Blue Streak missile because it promises to be superior to a Thor, when, by the time the Blue Streak can be operational, they could buy, much more cheaply, say, a Titan or Minuteman missile from us that also is designed for underground shelters and has far greater range than the Thor?

It is easy to understand why such dependence upon foreign supply for prestige weapons, despite the great economies it promises, arouses strong patriotic opposition. But the extent to which this opposition can be supported by rational strategic reasons has declined. Dependence upon allied sources of supply is risky, but if all-out wars must now be fought quickly with existing stocks of arms, and if peripheral national wars can be fought with but small drains upon such stocks, the risk of relying upon foreign supply becomes small. It makes more sense to buy material where it is cheapest. This reasoning applies to the United States as well as to its allies. The production of many expensive items here has been defended on mobilization base and comparative vulnerability grounds, but this argument has lost its cogency as the mobilization base has been de-emphasized and America's role as the No. 1 target of enemy attack has become apparent to all.

Nonetheless, the political barriers to purchasing foreign arms remain formidable. And achieving a less grossly uneconomic division of military manpower duties within the alliance is naturally bound to be still more difficult than for arms production. Allied forces cannot be used for military purposes that one's allies deem to be unilateral—e.g., Suez—while equipment procured from abroad obviously can be. Therefore a country will not eliminate its forces and depend totally upon the forces of others, no matter how expensive its manpower compared with that of its allies. Nor, at the other extreme, will it specialize in contributing manpower, "blood rather than treasure," even though civilians as well as military personnel are potential casualties throughout the alliance these days. Accordingly, the opportunities for manpower specialization, for substituting inexpensive Turkish soldiers for expensive American ones, are limited. Yet the limits set by these opposed political considerations are broad. There is room for substituting troops, and the place to increase relative troop contributions is clear. The United States, the expensive supplier, has consistently maintained armed forces in about as high a proportion to available manpower as any of its allies and higher than most. Measured by economic criteria, our allies are under-contributing troops. Consequently, there is great scope for economizing by greater manpower as well as material specialization in the alliance, and therefore great reason for tackling the political problems that inhibit such specialization.

●

The next selection, an extended article by Mancur Olson and Richard Zeckhauser, offers a general theoretical explanation for insufficiency and inefficiency in international burden sharing, and, especially, for the fact that the amount of defense or other good purchased is often "sub-optimal." The authors maintain that the defense bought by the United States is a "collective" or "public" good. The United States' nuclear deterrent posture provides to its allies some of the benefits of even those defense expenditures it makes purely for itself, and because the allies can thus get some defense free, without any sacrifice of their own resources, their incentive to contribute a full share is reduced. The authors' argument makes it clear why Americans cannot, despite exhortation, expect their allies to make a fully proportionate contribution so long as, (a) the purpose of the alliance is indeed to provide to the individual members more defense than they could purchase by themselves; (b) the need for defense against attack is not felt to be immediate and very pressing, and (c) there is no agreed cost-sharing arrangement whereby costs are allocated proportionately to benefits, and (d) the acquisition of such benefits cannot be made contingent, possibly by some supranational institution, upon payment of the assessment. The last condition might be exercised by some supranational institution capable of assessing fines, or conceivably by some arrangement whereby the lagging member could be excluded; that is, if it could be credibly stated that the lagging member would in no way be protected or sheltered by the alliance. Such declarations are not always observed, however, as the Prodigal's brother discovered.

●

2

An Economic Theory of Alliances

Mancur Olson, Jr., and
Richard Zeckhauser

1. Introduction

This article outlines a model that attempts to explain the workings of international organizations, and tests this model against the experience of some existing international institutions. Though the model is relevant to any international organization that independent nations establish to further their common interests, this article emphasizes the North Atlantic Treaty Organization, since it involves larger amounts of resources than any other international organization, yet illustrates the model most simply. The United Nations and the provision of foreign aid through the Development Assistance Committee are discussed more briefly.

There are some important respects in which many observers in the United States and in some other countries are disappointed in NATO and other ventures in international cooperation. For one thing, it is often argued that the United States and some of the other larger members are bearing a disproportionate share of the burden of the common defense of the NATO countries, and it is at least true that the smaller members of NATO devote smaller percentages of their incomes to defense than do larger members. There is also some concern about the fact that the NATO alliance has systematically failed to provide the number of divisions that the NATO nations themselves have proclaimed (rightly or wrongly) are

Reprinted by permission of the publishers from *The Review of Economics and Statistics*, **48**, 3 (Cambridge: Harvard University Press, August 1966), pp. 266–279. Copyright, 1966, by the President and Fellows of Harvard College.

necessary or optimal. Similarly, many nations, especially smaller nations, have failed to fulfill their quotas for UN contributions with the result that the United States contribution rises to a degree that threatens the independence of the organization. The meager level of total support for the UN and the mean and haphazard state of its finances are also sources of concern.

Some suppose that the apparent disproportion in the support for international undertakings is due largely to an alleged American moral superiority, and that the poverty of international organizations is due to a want of responsibility on the part of some other nations. But before resorting to any such explanations, it would seem necessary to ask whether the different-sized contributions of different countries could be explained in terms of their national interests. Why would it be in the interest of some countries to contribute a larger proportion of their total resources to group undertakings than other countries? The European members of NATO are much nearer the front line than the United States, and they are less able to defend themselves alone. Thus, it might be supposed that they would have an interest in devoting larger proportions of their resources to NATO than does the United States, rather than the smaller proportions that they actually contribute. And why do the NATO nations fail to provide the level of forces that they have themselves described as appropriate, i.e., in their common interest? These questions cannot be answered without developing a logical explanation of how much a nation acting in its national interest will contribute to an international organization.

Any attempt to develop a theory of international organizations must begin with the purposes or functions of these organizations. One purpose that all such organizations must have is that of serving the *common* interests of member states. In the case of NATO, the proclaimed purpose of the alliance is to protect the member nations from aggression by a common enemy. Deterring aggression against any one of the members is supposed to be in the interest of all. The analogy with a nation-state is obvious. Those goods and services, such as defense, that the government provides in the *common* interest of the citizenry, are usually called "public goods." An organization of states allied for defense similarly produces a public good, only in this case the "public"—the members of the organization—are states rather than individuals.

Indeed, almost all kinds of organizations provide public or collective goods. Individual interests normally can best be served by individual action, but when a group of individuals has some common objective or collective goal, then an organization can be useful. Such a common objective is a collective good, since it has one or both of the following properties: (1) if the common goal is achieved, everyone who shares this goal auto-

Table 1

NATO Statistics: an Empirical Test

Country	GNP 1964 (billions of dollars)	Rank	Defense budget as percentage of GNP	Rank	GNP per capita $	Rank
United States	569.03	1	9.0	1	2933	1
Germany	88.87	2	5.5	6	1579	5
United Kingdom	79.46	3	7.0	3	1471	8
France	73.40	4	6.7	4	1506	6
Italy	43.63	5	4.1	10	855	11
Canada	38.14	6	4.4	8	1981	2
Netherlands	15.00	7	4.9	7	1235	10
Belgium	13.43	8	3.7	12	1429	9
Denmark	7.73	9	3.3	13	1636	3
Turkey	6.69	10	5.8	5	216	14
Norway	5.64	11	3.9	11	1484	7
Greece	4.31	12	4.2	9	507	12
Portugal	2.88	13	7.7	2	316	13
Luxembourg	.53	14	1.7	14	1636	4

Ranks

GNP	1	2	3	4	5	6	7	8	9	10	11	12	13	14
Defense budget as % of GNP	1	6	3	4	10	8	7	12	13	5	11	9	2	14
GNP per capita	1	5	8	6	11	2	10	9	3	14	7	12	13	4

SOURCE: All data are taken from the Institute for Strategic Studies, *The Military Balance 1965–1966* (London, Nov. 1965).

matically benefits, or, in other words, nonpurchasers cannot feasibly be kept from consuming the good, and (2) if the good is available to any one person in a group, it is or can be made available to the other members of the group at little or no marginal cost.[1] Collective goods are thus the characteristic outputs not only of governments but of organizations in general.[2]

Since the benefits of any action an individual takes to provide a public or organizational good also go to others, individuals acting independently do not have an incentive to provide optimal amounts of such goods. Indeed, when the group interested in a public good is very large,

[1] See J. G. Head, "Public Goods and Public Policy," *Public Finance*, **XVII**, 3 (1962), pp. 197–219.

[2] See M. Olson, Jr., *The Logic of Collective Action: Public Goods and the Theory of Groups* (Cambridge: Harvard University Press, 1965), which treats organizations of individuals somewhat as this article treats organizations of nation-states.

and the share of the total benefit that goes to any single individual is very small, usually no individual has an incentive voluntarily to purchase any of the good, which is why states exact taxes and labor unions demand compulsory membership.[3] When—as in any organization representing a limited number of nation-states—the membership of an organization is relatively small, the individual members may have an incentive to make significant sacrifices to obtain the collective good, but they will tend to provide only suboptimal amounts of this good. There will also be a tendency for the "larger" members—those that place a higher absolute value on the public good—to bear a disproportionate share of the burden, as the model of alliances developed below will show.

2. The Model

When a nation decides how large a military force to provide in an alliance, it must consider the value it places upon collective defense and the other, nondefense, goods that must be sacrificed to obtain additional military forces. The value each nation in an alliance places upon the alliance collective good vis-a-vis other goods can be shown on a simple indifference map, such as is shown in Fig. 1.[4] ... Defense capability is measured along the horizontal axis and valued positively. Defense spending is measured along the vertical axis and valued negatively. The cost curves are assumed to be linear for the sake of simplicity. If the nation depicted in Fig. 1 were not a part of any alliance, the amount of defense it would obtain (OB) could be found by drawing a cost curve coming out of the origin and finding the point (point A) where this cost curve is tangent to the "highest" (most southeasterly) indifference curve.

In an alliance, the amount a nation spends on defense will be affected by the amount its allies provide. By moving the cost curve down along the vertical axis beneath the origin we can represent the defense expenditure of allied nations as the distance between the origin and the juncture of the cost curve and the vertical axis. If a nation's allies spend OD on defense, and their cost functions are the same as its own, then it receives OH of defense without cost. This is directly equivalent to an increase in income of OD.[5] The more defense this nation's allies provide, the further the cost

---

[3] *Ibid.*, pp. 5–52.

[4] An indifference curve is a standard tool in economics, used to summarize preference ratios between two goods or alternatives. Moving nearer one axis implies a preference for greater proportions of the good measured on that axis. The point of tangency between an indifference curve and a cost curve indicates the *amount* of each of the two goods that will be bought [Ed.].

[5] Free defense is not, however, the direct equivalent of an increase in income if the nation has already received so much defense that it would like to sell some if that were possible. This

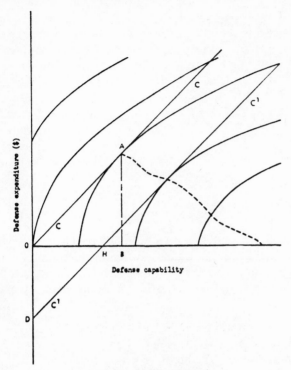

Fig. 1. Indifference map.

constraint moves to the southeast, and the less it spends on defense. By recording all the points of tangency of the total cost curve with the indifference curves, we can obtain this nation's reaction function. The reaction function indicates how much defense this nation will produce for all possible levels of defense expenditure by its allies. The amount of defense that this nation provides will in turn influence the defense output of its allies, whose reaction curves can be determined in the same way.

Figure 2 shows the reaction curves for a two-country model (which can easily be generalized to cover *N* countries). The intersection point of the two reaction curves indicates how much of the alliance good each ally will supply in equilibrium. The two reaction curves need not always intersect. If one nation has a very much larger demand for the alliance good than the other, its reaction curve may lie at every point outside that of the

---

is what an ally would want to do if the *CC* curve had shifted so far to the right that it was no longer tangent to any indifference curve. In such a case . . . the nation provides none of the collective good itself.

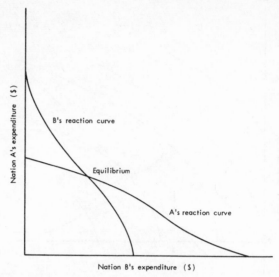

Fig. 2.   Reaction curves for a two-country model.

other, in which case it will provide all of the defense. The equilibrium output will then be the same as the isolation output of the country with the largest isolation output. Whether the reaction curves intersect or not, the equilibrium output is necessarily determinate and stable unless defense is an inferior good, in which case there may be a number of equilibria, one or more of which may be unstable.[6]

In equilibrium, the defense expenditures of the two nations are such that the "larger" nation—the one that places the higher absolute value on the alliance good—will bear a *disproportionately* large share of the common burden. It will pay a share of the costs that is larger than its share of the benefits, and thus the distribution of costs will be quite different from that which a system of benefit taxation would bring about.[7] This becomes obvious when income effects—i.e., the influence that the amount of

[6] To see this, suppose that *A* and *B* in Fig. 2 trade reaction curves. Then the equilibrium point given by the intersection point will be unstable, and there will be a tendency for one of the nations to provide all the defense. If one nation's reaction curve lies wholly outside that of the other, there will be a unique and stable equilibrium, whether or not defense is an inferior good.

[7] The authors do not advocate benefit taxation, but believe that proportionality of benefits and costs provides a useful standard of comparison, particularly in alliances which nations join to further their national interests rather than to bring about any particular distribution of income among member nations. The equilibrium outputs are not consistent with any ordinary conceptions of ability-to-pay either. They would involve a very regressive sharing if the larger nation in an alliance had the lower per capita income.

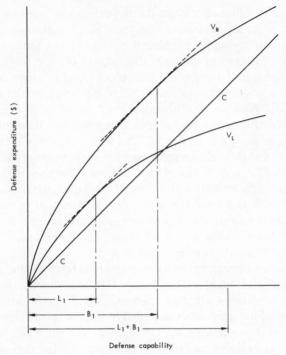

Fig. 3. Evaluation curves for two countries.

nondefense goods a nation has already forgone has on its desire to provide additional units of defense—are neglected. This is shown in Fig. 3 above, which depicts the evaluation curves of two nations for alliance forces. The larger nation, called Big Atlantis, has the higher, steeper valuation curve, V_B, because it places a higher absolute value on defense than Little Atlantis, which has evaluation curve V_L. The CC curve shows the costs of providing defense capability to each nation, since both, by assumption, have the same costs. In isolation, Big Atlantis would buy B_1 units of defense and Little Atlantis L_1, for at these points their respective valuation curves are parallel to their cost functions. If the two nations continued to provide these outputs in alliance, each would enjoy B_1 plus L_1 units of defense. But then each nation values a marginal unit at less than its marginal cost. Big Atlantis will stop reducing its output of deterrence when the sum applied by the two nations together is B_1. When this amount (or any amount greater than L_1) is available, it is not in Little Atlantis' interest to supply any defense whatever. The two nations are therefore simultaneously in equilibrium *only* when Big Atlantis provides B_1 of defense and Little Atlantis provides no defense whatever.

The disproportionality in the sharing of burdens is less extreme when income effects are taken into account, but it is still important. This can be seen most easily by supposing that Big Atlantis and Little Atlantis are identical in every respect save that Big Atlantis is twice the size of Little Atlantis. Per capita incomes and individual tastes are the same in both countries, but the population and GNP of Big Atlantis are twice that of Little Atlantis. Now imagine also that Big Atlantis is providing twice as much alliance defense as Little Atlantis, as proportionality would require.[8] In equilibrium, the marginal rate of substitution of money for the alliance good (MRS) must equal marginal cost for each of these countries, i.e., $MRS_{Big} = MRS_{Little}$ = marginal cost. But (since each country enjoys the same amount of the collective good) the MRS of Big Atlantis is double that of Little Atlantis, and (since the cost of an additional unit of defense is the same for each country) either Big Atlantis will want more defense or Little Atlantis will want less (or both will be true), and the common burden will come to be shared in a disproportionate way.

There is one important special case in which there will be no tendency toward disproportionality. That is when the indifference maps of the member nations are such that any perpendicular from the ordinate would intersect all indifference curves at points of equal slope. In this case, when the nation's cost constraint moves to the right as it gets more free defense, it would not reduce its own expenditure on defense. In other words, none of the increase in income that the nation receives in the form of defense is spent on goods other than defense. Defense in this situation is, strictly speaking, a "superior good," a good such that all of any increase in income is used to buy the good.[9]

This special case may sometimes be very important. During periods of all-out war or exceptional insecurity, it is likely that defense is (or is nearly) a superior good, and in such circumstances alliances will not have any tendency toward disproportionate burden sharing. The amount of allied military capability that Great Britain enjoyed in World War II increased from 1941 to 1944 as the United States mobilized, adding more and more strength to the allied side. But the British war effort was maintained, if not increased, during this period.

Although there is then one exception to the rule that alliance burdens are shared disproportionately, there is no equivalent exception to the rule

[8] It could be the case that even in isolation Big Atlantis would buy proportionately more defense than Little Atlantis. This would be the case if a nation's income elasticity of demand for the good were greater than one in the relevant range.

[9] Apparently the literature has neglected goods of this kind, and not made clear that they are simply the logical converse of the much discussed inferior goods. When the phrase "superior good" has been used it has usually been given an unsymmetrical and unclear

that alliances provide suboptimal amounts of the collective good. The alliance output will always be suboptimal so long as the members of the alliance place a positive value on additional units of defense. This is because each of the alliance members contributes to the point where its MRS for the good equals the marginal cost of the good. In other words, the result of independent national maximization in an alliance, when the cost function is linear and the same for all members, is that $MRS_1 = MRS_2 = \cdots MRS_N = MC$. There could be an optimal quantity of the collective good only if the total value which all of the alliance members together placed on an additional unit of the good equalled marginal cost, i.e., only if $MRS_1 + MRS_2 + \cdots MRS_N = MC$. The individual nations in an alliance would have an incentive to keep providing additional alliance forces until the Pareto-optimal level is reached only if there were an arrangement such that the alliance members shared marginal costs in the same proportions in which they shared additional benefits (that is, in the same ratio as their marginal rates of substitution of money for the good).[10] When there is such a marginal cost-sharing scheme, there need be no tendency toward disproportionality in the sharing of burdens.

3. Qualifications and Elaborations

One simplification assumed in the foregoing model was that the costs of defense were constant to scale and the same for all alliance members. Although military forces are composed of diverse types of equipment

meaning. We therefore distinguish the following classes of goods, realizing that the category to which a good belongs may depend on the level of income.

Class	Characteristic	Income elasticity of expenditure $= E$
Inferior good	Expenditure on the good decreases or is unchanged as income increases	$E \leq 0$
Inelastic good	Expenditure on the good increases, but by a smaller percent than income increases	$0 < E < 1$
Elastic good	Expenditure on the good increases by a percentage that is as great or greater than the percentage by which income increases, but by a smaller absolute amount	$1 \leq E < Y_0/S_0$[a]
Superior good	Expenditure on the good increases by as much or more than income increases	$E \geq Y_0/S_0$

[a] S_0 is the expenditure on the good when income is Y_0.

[10] A Pareto-optimal solution is defined as a situation such that no individual in the group at issue can be made better off without making someone else worse off. The possibility of dropping below the Pareto-optimal level, as well as of shifting along it, brings a mixture of competition and cooperation to the situation [Ed.].

and manpower, and thus probably vary less both in cost from one country to another and with scale of output than many single products, it is still unlikely that costs are constant and uniform. For some special types of weapon systems there are undoubtedly striking economies of large-scale production, and for conventional ground forces there are probably rising costs as larger proportions of a nation's population are called to arms. Because of this latter tendency, a small country can perhaps get a considerable amount of conventional capability with the first few percentiles of its national income. This tends to keep the military expenditures of small nations in an alliance above the very low level implied by our constant cost assumption. In any event, cross-country variations in marginal costs should not normally alter the basic conclusions deduced from the model. The differences in the amounts which member nations would be willing to pay for marginal units of an alliance good are typically so great that the cost differentials could hardly negate their effect. Even if there were very large differences in marginal costs among nations, there is no reason to assume that national cost functions would vary systematically with the valuation a country places on alliance forces.

A nation's valuation of alliance forces obviously depends not only on its national income but also on other factors. A nation on the enemy's border may value defense more than one some distance away. A nation that has a large area and long frontiers in relation to its resources may want a larger army than a compact country. On the other hand, if bomb and missile attacks are the main danger, a crowded country may wish to invest more in defense against attack by air. Similarly, a nation's attitudes or ideologies may partly determine its evaluation of defense. Many observers think that the uniformity and intensity of anticommunism is greater among the NATO countries with the highest per capita incomes, and these also happen to be the largest countries in the alliance. It also seems that many people in small and weak countries, both inside and outside of NATO, tend to be attracted to neutralist or pacifist ideologies. This pattern of attitudes may perhaps be partly explained by our model, for it suggests that small nations, which find that even large sacrifices on their part have little effect on the global balance, would often be attracted to neutral or passive foreign policies, and that large nations which know that their efforts can decisively influence world events in their own interest will continually need to emphasize the urgency of the struggle in which they are engaged. The popularity of pacific ideologies, the frequent adoption of neutralist policies in small and weak countries, and the activist attitudes and policies of the United States and the Soviet Union are at least consistent with our model.[11]

[11] One factor that might conceivably make small countries outside of an alliance spend little or nothing on defense is that they might think that the maximum force they could raise

Whatever the reasons for the different evaluations different nations have for military capabilities in an alliance, the model here still applies. If two countries in an alliance had equal national incomes, but one was more concerned about the common enemy for geographic, ideological, historical, or other reasons, the more concerned nation would not only put a higher valuation on the alliance's military capacity, but would bear a share of the total alliance costs that was even greater than its share of the total benefits. The model deals with the general case of differences in the absolute valuation that nations put upon additional units of an alliance good, whether these differences are due to differences in national income or to other reasons.[12]

Another assumption in the model developed in the foregoing section was that the military forces in an alliance provide only the collective benefit of alliance security, when in fact they also provide purely national, non-collective benefits to the nations that maintain them. When Portugal mobilizes additional forces to suppress the independence movement in Angola, a national goal unrelated to the purposes of NATO, she may at the same time be increasing the total strength of the alliance. Similarly, allied nations may be suspicious of one another, even as they cooperate in the achievement of common purposes, and may enlarge their military forces because of conceivable future conflicts with each other. In any situations in which the military forces of alliance members provide important

---

alone would not be sufficient to defeat any potential enemy, so that there would be no point in having any military forces at all. In an alliance, on the other hand, a small nation might suppose that its forces could provide the margin of victory and therefore increase their defense spending. The kink in the evaluation function that this argument implies is, however, made much less likely by the fact that even a small military force may be quite valuable to a small, unaligned country, for it might increase the costs and risks to an aggressor enough to deter him from attacking a small (and therefore probably not very valuable) country. This seems to be one argument used to support the French nuclear force.

[12] The value which a nation puts upon alliance forces may also vary with alliance policies. An alliance must sometimes choose which of two or more alternative public goods to provide, and one public good may be more valuable to some alliance members and another more valuable to others. The NATO alliance, for example, provides conventional defense as well as nuclear protection, and there have been disagreements about the proper mix between these two goods. In such a case it is possible that some nations may supply additional forces in return for more influence on alliance policy, whereas other nations may make policy concessions in order to get other members to assume a greater share of alliance costs. Such trade-offs need not change the qualitative conclusions about disproportionate burden sharing. They might simply mean that a nation can bear part of its alliance burden by making policy concessions rather than by providing additional forces. When this happens, though, the allies that obtained the policy they wanted find they value the alliance good more than before, and the opposite is true for those who have relinquished some of their control over alliance policy. This in turn makes the former set of nations provide still more defense and the latter still less.

noncollective benefits as well as alliance benefits, the degree of suboptimality and the importance of the disproportionality will decrease because the noncollective benefits give the member nations an incentive to maintain larger forces.

This fact leads to the paradoxical conclusion that *a decline in the amity, unity, and community of interest among allies need* not *necessarily reduce the effectiveness of an alliance*, because the decline in these alliance "virtues" produces a greater ratio of private to collective benefits. This suggests that alliances troubled by suspicions and disagreements may continue to work reasonably well. To be sure, the degree of coordination among the allies will decline, and this will reduce the efficiency of the alliance forces (in a sense leaving them on a poorer production function), but the alliance forces will be larger.

However important the noncollective benefits of alliances may be, there can be little doubt that above all alliances produce public goods. It is not easy to think of alliances that provide only private goods, though such alliances are perhaps conceivable. If nations simply trade sites for military bases, no common interests or public goods would necessarily be involved. An alliance might also be set up simply to provide insurance in the sense that two nations without any common purpose or common enemy would agree to defend each other in case of attack, but in which neither knew in advance which would suffer aggression. On the other hand, if these two nations thought (as they presumably would) that the fact of their alliance would make it less profitable for other nations to attack either of them, the alliance would provide a public good—a degree of deterrence that could deter an attack on either or both of these nations about as well as it could deter an attack on one alone. There is, moreover, no reason to describe a mere transaction in private goods as an alliance, and the word does not normally appear to be used in that way. A transaction in private goods would be quite as useful between enemies as between "allies," and would normally be completed by a single pair of actions or a single agreement which would not require the continuing consultation, cooperation, and organization characteristic of alliances.

Normally, an additional member can be added to an alliance without substantially subtracting from the amount of defense available to those already in the alliance, and any good that satisfies this criterion is by definition a public good.[13] Suppose two nations of the same size face a

---

[13] The number of people defended by a given military force can clearly increase without reducing the security per person. However, additional land area will normally require some additional military forces, if the area previously protected is to have the same degree of security as before, and if actual defensive conflict, rather than deterrence, is at issue. When the additional land area has no common border with the enemy, it can usually be defended

common enemy with an army larger than either of them provides by itself. They then form an alliance and maintain a level of military forces larger than either of them had before, but smaller than the sum of their two pre-alliance armies. After alliance both nations enjoy (1) more military security, and (2) lower defense costs, than they had before. This result comes about, not only because a military force can often deter attack by a common enemy against an additional nation without a substantial increase in cost but also because an alliance may make a greater level of security economically feasible and desirable, and the gains from obtaining this extra security can leave both nations better off.

Another defining characteristic that is sufficient (but not necessary) to distinguish a collective good is that the exclusion of those who do not share the cost of the good is impractical or impossible. Typically, once an alliance treaty has been signed, a member nation is legally bound to remain a member for the duration of the treaty. The decisions about how the common burden is to be shared are not, however, usually specified in the alliance treaty. This procedure works to the disadvantage of the larger countries. Often, the smaller and weaker nations gain relatively more from the existence of an alliance than do the larger and stronger powers, and once an alliance treaty has been signed, the larger powers are immediately deprived of their strongest bargaining weapon—the threat that they will not help to defend the recalcitrant smaller powers—in any negotiations about the sharing of the common burden. Even at the time an alliance treaty is negotiated, exclusion may very well not be feasible, since most alliances are implicit in an already existing danger or goal common to some group of states. That common danger or goal gives the nations that share it an incentive tacitly to treat each other as allies, whether or not they have all signed a formal agreement. A nation can only lose from having another nation with whom it shares a common interest succumb to an enemy, for that will strengthen the enemy's side at the expense of the first nation. It may well be that most alliances are never embodied in any formal agreement. Sometimes a nation may have a geopolitical position (e.g., behind an alliance member serving as a buffer state) such that it would be unusually difficult, if not impossible, to deny it the benefits of alliance protection. Then, if it regards alliance membership as a special burden, it may have an incentive to stay out of, or when legally possible to withdraw from, the alliance's formal organization.

---

without any significant extra cost. The extra cost to NATO of defending Belgium against a Soviet attack, once Germany and France are already defended, is negligible. Even when the extra land does have a common border with an enemy it is not always true that it costs much more to defend it. If the French had believed they had to defend Belgium as well as France in World Wars I and II, they might have fared better.

This paper also made the simplifying assumption that no alliance member will take into account the reactions other members may have to the size of its alliance contribution. The mutual recognition of oligopolistic interdependence can be profoundly important in small groups of firms, but in the NATO alliance at least, it seems to have been somewhat less important (except with respect to the infrastructure, which will be considered later). There are at least two important reasons why strategic bargaining interaction is often less important in alliances than in oligopolistic industries. First, alliances are often involved in situations that contain a strong element of irreversibility. Suppose that the United States were to threaten to cut its defense spending to nothing to get its allies to bear larger shares of the NATO burden. The Soviet Union, if it has the characteristics that American policy assumes, would then deprive the United States of its independence, in which case future defense savings would have little relevance. The United States threat would have only a limited credibility in view of the irreversibility of this process. The second factor which limits strategic bargaining interaction among alliance members stems from an important difference between market and nonmarket groups. In an oligopolistic group of firms, any firm knows that its competitors would be better off if it were made bankrupt or otherwise driven out of the industry. Large firms thus sometimes engage in price wars or cutthroat competition to drive out the smaller members of an oligopolistic group. By contrast, nonmarket groups and organizations, such as alliances, usually strive instead for a larger membership, since they provide collective goods the supply of which should increase as the membership increases. Since an ally would typically lose from driving another member out of an alliance, a bargaining threat to that effect may not be credible. This will be especially true if the excluded nation would then fall to the common enemy and (as we argued before) thereby strengthen the enemy at the expense of the alliance.

Even when strategic interaction is important in alliances, the advantage paradoxically still rests in most cases with the smaller nations. There are two reasons for this. First, the large country loses more from withholding an alliance contribution than a small country does, since it values a given amount of alliance force more highly. In other words, it may be deterred by the very importance to itself of its own alliance contribution from carrying out any threat to end that contribution. Second, the large country has relatively less to gain than its small ally from driving a hard bargain. Even if the large nation were successful in the bargaining it would expect only a relatively small addition to the alliance force from the small nation, but when the small nation succeeds in the bargaining it can expect a large addition to the alliance force from the large nation. There is, accordingly, no reason to expect that there is any disparity of bargaining in favor of the larger ally that would negate the tendency toward disproportionality revealed by our model.

4. Empirical Evidence

When other things are equal, the larger a nation is, the higher its valuation of the output of an alliance. Thus, if our model is correct, the larger members of an alliance should, on the average, devote larger percentages of their national incomes to defense than do the smaller nations. This prediction is tested against the recent data on the NATO nations in Table 1. The following specific hypotheses are used to test the model's predictions:

H_1—In an alliance, there will be a significant positive correlation between the size of a member's national income and the percentage of its national income spent on defense. This hypothesis will be tested against:

H_0—There will not be a significant positive correlation between the variables specified in H_1.

Since there is no assurance that the data are parametrically distributed, nonparametrical statistical tests must be used. The Spearman rank correlation coefficient for GNP and *defense budget as a percentage of GNP* is .490. On a one-tailed test this value is significant at the .05 level. We therefore reject the null hypothesis and accept H_1. There is a significant positive correlation indicating that the large nations in NATO bear a disproportionate share of the burden of the common defense. Moreover, this result holds even when the level of per capita income is held constant.

Our model predicts that there are tendencies toward disproportionate burden sharing, not only in military alliances but also in other international organizations, such as the United Nations. The test of this prediction is complicated in the case of the UN by the fact that the organization is supported primarily through assessments levied against individual members. These assessments are determined by a formula constructed by a committee of experts. The model would, however, suggest that the degree to which a member fulfills or oversubscribes its quota would be positively correlated with its size, and thus gives the following hypotheses:

H_2—In a voluntary organization with quota assessments that are not always satisfied, there will be a significant positive correlation be-

tween a member's GNP and the percentage of fulfillment or over-
fulfillment of its quota.
H_0—There will not be a significant positive correlation between the
    variables in H_2.

The Spearman rank correlation coefficient between 1961 *GNP* and
percentage total UN contributions in 1961/*normal assessment scale* was
.404. This result is significant at the .01 level. We thus accept H_2 and reject
H_0, for, as the model predicted, the larger nations in the UN did a better
job of living up to their normal assessments. The fact that members may
lose prestige and membership rights if they fail to meet their assessments,
i.e., that there are distinctly private benefits from contributions to the UN,
makes this high correlation more striking.

The foreign aid that the industrialized democracies give to the underdeveloped countries is a collective good to these aid-giving nations, at
least to the extent that they all value the development of the less developed
areas. On the other hand, individual aid-giving nations often concentrate all of their aid on particular underdeveloped areas, such as past or
present colonies, in which they have a special interest. To the extent that
different aid-giving nations are interested in different underdeveloped
areas, their aid allocations constitute private rather than collective goods.
This tends to limit any tendencies toward suboptimality and disproportionality in the provision of foreign aid. We can test for any such dispro-
portionalities with the aid of the following hypotheses:

H_3—Among a group of developed nations there will be a significant
    positive correlation between foreign aid expenditures as a percentage
    of national income and the size of the national income.
H_0—There will not be a significant positive correlation between the
    variables in H_3.

One set of data used to test these hypotheses revealed a correlation between *real national income* and *total grants and loans to underdeveloped
countries as a percentage of national income* in 1960 of .770. This figure is
significant at the .01 level. A different set of data for a different year (1962)
showed a correlation between *GNP* and *total aid as a percentage of GNP*
of .439. With the small sample of only 12 nations, this value falls slightly
short of the .05 level of significance (the borderline value is .506). Thus, both
sets of data yield correlation coefficients suggesting the expected positive
relationship, but in one case the result is clearly statistically significant
and in the other case it falls somewhat short of the .05 level of significance.
We will take the most conservative course and await further research
before finally accepting either H_3 or the null hypothesis. The most

reasonable inference at the moment is that there is some tendency toward disproportionate burden sharing, but that the private, or purely national, benefits from foreign aid are probably also very important. This is, moreover, about what might be expected from the fact that the industrialized Western nations express a common interest in the development of the poor nations generally, while at the same time many of these nations individually are interested primarily in particular underdeveloped areas with which they have special relationships.

Our model indicated that when the members of an organization share the costs of marginal units of an alliance good, just as they share in the benefits of additional units of that good, there is no tendency toward disproportionality or suboptimality. In other words, if each ally pays an appropriate percentage of the cost of any additional units of the alliance good, the results are quite different from when each ally pays the full cost of any amount of the alliance good that he provides. The costs of the NATO infrastructure (common supply depots, pipelines, etc.), unlike the costs of providing the main alliance forces, are shared according to percentages worked out in a negotiated agreement. Since each ally pays some percentage of the cost of any addition to the NATO infrastructure, we have here a marginal-cost-sharing arrangement.

Thus, our model suggests that the burdens of the NATO infrastructure should be borne quite differently from the rest of the NATO burden. There are other reasons for expecting that the infrastructure burden would be shared in a different way from the main NATO burdens. For one thing, the infrastructure facilities of NATO are all in continental European countries, and ultimately become the property of the host nation. Their construction also brings foreign exchange earnings to these countries, which for the most part are the smaller alliance members. In addition, infrastructure costs are very small in relation to the total burden of common defense, so a small nation may get prestige at a relatively low cost by offering to bear a larger percentage of the infrastructure cost. There are, in short, many private benefits for the smaller alliance members resulting from the infrastructure expenditures. Because of these private benefits, and more important because of the percentage sharing of marginal (and total) costs of the infrastructure, we would predict that the larger members of the alliance would bear a smaller share of the infrastructure burden than of the main alliance burdens.

This prediction suggests that the following hypotheses be tested:

H_4—In an alliance in which the marginal costs of certain activities are *not* shared (but fall instead upon those members who have an incentive to provide additional units of the alliance good by themselves), and in

which the marginal costs of other activities are shared (so that each
member pays a specified percentage of any costs of these activities),
the *ratio* of a member's share of the costs of the activities of the former
type to his share of the costs of activities of the latter type will have a
significant positive correlation with national income.

H_0—There will be no significant positive correlation between the variables
in H_4.

To test these hypotheses we calculated the correlation coefficient
between *national income* and *variable T* in Table 2. The Spearman rank
correlation coefficient between these variables is .582, which is significant
at the .05 level. We therefore reject the null hypothesis and conclude that
the larger members bear a larger proportion of the costs of the main NATO
forces than they do of those NATO activities for which the costs of each

Table 2

NATO Infrastructure

Country	National income 1960[a] (billions of dollars) (1)	Infrastructure % reconsidered in 1960[b] (2)	$R = (2)/(1)$ (3)	Military budget 1960 (billions of dollars) (4)	$T = (4)/(2)$ (5)
United States	411.367	36.98	.0899	41.000	1.1087
Germany	51.268	13.77	.2686	2.072	.1504
United Kingdom	57.361	9.88	.1722	4.466	.4520
France	43.468	11.87	.2731	3.311	.2789
Italy	24.950	5.61	.2248	1.076	.1922
Canada	28.178	6.15	.2183	1.680	.2732
Netherlands	9.246	3.51	.3800	.450	.1282
Belgium	8.946	4.39	.4907	.395	.0900
Turkey	4.929	1.75	.3550	.244	.1394
Denmark	4.762	2.63	.5569	.153	.0582
Norway	3.455	2.19	.6338	.168	.0767
Greece	2.684	.87	.3242	.173	.1989
Portugal	2.083	.28	.1344	.093	.3321
Luxembourg	.386	.17	.4404	.007	.0412

Ranks:

(1)	1	3	2	4	6	5	7	8	9	10	11	12	13	14
(3)	14	9	12	8	10	11	5	3	6	2	1	7	13	4
(5)	1	8	2	4	7	5	10	11	9	13	12	6	3	14

[a] United Nations, *Yearbook of National Accounts Statistics* (New York, 1964); and
Balance of Payments Yearbook, Vol. 15 (Washington: International Monetary Fund, 1964).

[b] Charles Croot, "Coordination in the Sixties," reprinted from *NATO Letter* (August
1960).

unit are shared. The difference between the distribution of infrastructure costs and the distribution of alliance burdens generally is quite striking, as the tests of the following hypotheses indicate:

H_5—In the NATO alliance there is a significant negative correlation between national income and the percentage of national income devoted to infrastructure expenses.

H_0—There is no significant negative correlation between the variables in H_5.

The Spearman rank correlation coefficient between *national income* and *variable R* in Table 2 is $-.538$, which is significant at the .05 level. Thus, not only is it the case that the larger nations pay a smaller share of the infrastructure costs than of other alliance costs; it is also true that there is a significant negative correlation between national income and the percentage of national income devoted to the NATO infrastructure, which is in vivid contrast to the positive correlation that prevails for other NATO burdens. This confirms the prediction that when there are marginal-cost-sharing arrangements, there need no longer be any tendency for the larger nations to bear disproportionately large shares of the costs of international organizations. If it happens at the same time that the smaller nations get greater than average private benefits from their contributions, they may even contribute greater percentages of their national incomes than the larger members.

5. Conclusions and Recommendations

All of the empirical evidence tended to confirm the model. In the UN there appear to be systematic forces tending to make the small nations fail to meet their quotas and leading larger nations to assume larger shares of the costs. The larger industrialized nations, moreover, seem to bear disproportionate shares of the burden of aid to the less developed countries. In NATO there is again a statistically significant positive correlation between the size of a member's national income and the percentage of its national income devoted to the common defense.

As our model indicated, this is in part because each ally gets only a fraction of the benefits of any collective good that is provided, but each pays the full cost of any additional amounts of the collective good. This means that individual members of an alliance or international organization have an incentive to stop providing the collective good long before the Pareto-optimal output for the group has been provided. This is particularly true of the smaller members, who get smaller shares of the total benefits accruing from the good, and who find that they have little or no incentive to provide additional amounts of the collective good once the larger members have provided the amounts they want for themselves, with the result that the burdens are shared in a disproportionate way. The model indicated two special types of situations in which there need be no such tendency toward disproportionality. First, in cases of all-out war or extreme insecurity defense may be what was strictly defined as a "superior good," in which case a nation's output of a collective good will not be reduced when it receives more of this good from an ally. Second, institutional arrangements such that the members of an organization share marginal costs, just as they share the benefits of each unit of the good, tend to work against disproportionality in burden sharing, and it is a necessary condition of an efficient, Pareto-optimal output that the marginal costs be shared in the same proportions as the benefits of additional units. The NATO nations determine through negotiation what percentages of any infrastructure expenditure each member will pay, and this sharing of marginal costs has led the smaller member to bear a very much larger share of the infrastructure burden than they do of the other NATO burdens. The fact that the model predicts not only the distribution of the principal NATO burdens but also the greatly different distribution of infrastructure costs suggests that the results are, in fact, due to the processes described in the model, rather than to some other cause.

The model's implication that large nations tend to bear disproportionate shares of the burdens of international organization, and the empirical evidence tending to confirm the model, does *not* entail the conclusion that the small nations should be told they "ought" to bear a larger share of the common burdens. No moral conclusions can follow solely from any purely logical model of the kind developed here.[14] Indeed, our analysis suggests that moral suasion is inappropriate, since the different levels of contribution are not due to different moral attitudes, and ineffective, since the less than proportionate contributions of the smaller nations are securely grounded in their national interests (just as the disproportionately large contributions of the larger countries are solidly grounded in their national interests). Thus, American attempts to persuade other

---

[14] We must strongly emphasize that we are *not* here questioning the fairness of the present distribution of the costs of any international undertaking. No statement about what distribution of costs ought to prevail can be made unless some (logically arbitrary) assumption is made about what income redistributions among participating nations would be desirable. Jacques van Ypersele de Strihou, in "Sharing the Burden of Defense Among Allies," an interesting PhD thesis available at Yale University, has shown that, if the British rates of progression are used as a standard of fairness, it appears that the larger European members of NATO pay an unfairly large share of the common costs, that the United States (partly because of its high per capita income) pays about the right amount, and that the smaller NATO nations (because of the same general forces explained in this paper) pay an unfairly small amount.

nations to bear "fair" shares of the burdens of common ventures are likely to be divisive and harmful even to American interests in the long run.

The model developed here suggests that the problems of disproportionality and suboptimality in international organizations should be met instead through institutional changes that alter the pattern of incentives. Since suboptimal provision is typical of international organizations, it is possible to design policy changes that would leave everyone better off, and which accordingly may have some chance of adoption. Appropriate marginal-cost-sharing schemes, such as are now used to finance the NATO infrastructure, could solve the problem of suboptimality in international organizations, and might also reduce the degree of disproportionality. Substituting a union for an alliance or international organization would also tend to bring about optimality, for then the unified system as a whole has an incentive to behave in an optimal fashion, and the various parts of the union can be required to contribute the amounts their common interest requires. Even a union of smaller members of NATO, for example, could be helpful, and be in the interest of the United States. Such a union would give the people involved an incentive to contribute more toward the goals they shared with their then more nearly equal partners. Whatever the disadvantages on other grounds of these policy possibilities, they at least have the merit that they help to make the national interests of individual nations more nearly compatible with the efficient attainment of the goals which groups of nations hold in common.

A final implication of our model is that alliances and international organizations, as presently organized, will not work efficiently, or according to any common conception of fairness, however complete the agreement and community of interest among the members. Though there is obviously a point beyond which dissension and divergent purposes will ruin any organization, it is also true that some differences of purpose may improve the working of an alliance, because they increase the private, noncollective benefits from the national contributions to the alliance, and this alleviates the suboptimality and disproportionality. How much smaller would the military forces of the small members of NATO be if they did not have their private fears and quarrels? How much aid would the European nations give if they did not have private interests in the development of their past or present colonies? How much would the smaller nations contribute to the U.N. if it were not a forum for the expression of their purely national emnities and aspirations? The United States, at least, should perhaps not hope for too much unity in common ventures with other nations. It might prove extremely expensive.

●

It could be said that within an alliance, the higher the correlation is between size and defense spending as a percentage of GNP, the greater the failure of *burden-sharing* arrangements is, and the further the association is from what would be expected within a nation-state or in a true supranational organization. Data on NATO defense contributions in other periods are relevant to this point. Jacques van Ypersele de Strihou, another author who has looked at these arrangements from the same "public good" perspective, examined relative shares both in 1963 and in 1955.[1] He found an appreciably higher correlation between size and relative defense spending in the later year than in the earlier one. In some part the higher correlation for 1963 can be traced to the rearmament of Germany. Back in 1955, as the new German army was just beginning to be formed, the Federal Republic's contribution expressed as a percentage of its GNP was one of the smallest of all the NATO allies. But by the 1960's the German share of GNP devoted to defense was greater than average for the alliance, though still below the number two position its total GNP would imply. This rise of Germany to more nearly the position that the public goods theory would predict does not, however, account for all of the better fit of the theory to the 1963 data than to the 1955 data. By this clear measure the cooperative burden-sharing aspects of NATO diminished over the decade. The explanation stems from two not unconnected factors—the decline of the apparent threat of Soviet invasion of western Europe, and the disintegration, across a broad front, of NATO cooperation and integration accompanying France's increasingly independent policy.

It is possible, however, that the alliance as a cooperative venture might fail in another way. Under some circumstances the absence of a high correlation between size and the percentage of GNP devoted to defense might indicate a failure of the alliance to provide the collective *benefits* intended. A nation which spends *more* than its size would predict is a state that feels the shelter of its bigger allies *less* than do the others, and for some reason the alliance is not providing the expected security. In this respect France's number four position in Olson and Zeckhauser's Table 1 is very instructive —despite expressed French doubts about the efficacy of American nuclear guarantees, France's defense spending does *not* put it at a higher rank than would be expected if the alliance's benefits were as intended.

[1] "Sharing the Defense Burden Among Western Allies," *Review of Economics and Statistics*, **49** (November 1967), pp. 527–536; "Sharing the Defense Burden Among Western Allies," *Yale Economic Essays*, March 1968, and "Explaining the Difference in the Relative Defense Burdens Borne by the NATO Allies," *International Studies Quarterly*, **12**, 4 (1968).

If defense was *purely* a collective good in an alliance, and there were no mechanisms to enforce contributions by the smaller members, the small states would presumably make *no* contribution. This is, of course, never the case, since the great power's guarantee of its smaller allies' security can never be perfect; its assurances can never be fully credible, and to the degree they are not, the small states will want some independent capability. Additionally, the big power may *want* to limit the credibility of its assurances, since they may carry a risk of involvement in major war for the sake of allies' objectives that may to it be trivial. In this sense the high correlation between size and relative contribution in 1963 represents a success of NATO (or at least of American military policy) in providing collective benefits. It should be noted also that van Ypersele's analysis incorporated not only the NATO allies but the European neutrals as well. They too fell on the line about where the theory would predict; the ones like Ireland and Austria with the smallest GNP's at the bottom, middle-sized Sweden toward the middle of the entire ranking. This shows that even countries not incorporated within the alliance may perceive themselves as benefiting from a good bit of its protection, and so feel able to reduce their own efforts.[2]

Several other points must be made about the assumption that military spending represents a public good. As Olson and Zeckhauser note, defense is a mixed good possessing some of the characteristics of private goods as well, and these need to be spelled out. *Deterrence* may be mostly a public good, but *defense*, should deterrence fail, is a different matter. In case an invasion does occur, difficult choices of where to mass troops, whom to defend and whom to expose, will have to be made. The collective armed forces of an alliance, in any real world strategic situation, cannot provide equal defense for all members in wartime. Thus, in anticipation of such difficulties a member may spend more for military forces which can be kept under its own command than the basic public goods theory would predict. Part of the failure of comparative advantage that Hoag noted is due to such inabilities to make defense always equally available to the members; obviously too, it represents, as well as "national pride," a lack of full confidence in the deterrence offered by the alliance's umbrella. Community (rather than individual) fallout shelters and local antimissile defenses also cease being collective goods for the whole alliance once deterrence has failed and defense is at issue. A country concerned about its defense might want these for itself.

There are other nonalliance uses of military forces that may militate against full acceptance of the principle of comparative advantage. Some

[2] See F. L. Pryor, *Toward a Positive Theory of Public Expenditure*, in press, 1969.

kinds of forces or expenditure have uses, other than simple defense or deterrence, that may make them desirable to alliance members. In this they take on more elements of private goods. For example, ground forces can be used to maintain internal security; nuclear-armed missiles do not have this function. Or some kinds of military research and development expenditures offer potential civilian benefits. French and British leaders have often expressed their unwillingness to cut themselves off from large segments of technological development as the price they would have to pay for foregoing certain kinds of weapons development. These other consider- ations, fully expressible in the language of a theory of mixed public and private goods, indicate how the simple public good prediction for defense sharing must be modified. Finally, of course, a tacit or explicit bargain is struck. Just because the United States *could* withdraw some of the collec- tive good aspects of deterrence, its European allies must pay a price to persuade their protector not to do so. That price is the provision of some troops to the enterprise.

This matter of "mixed" goods, partly public and partly private, requires more formal consideration. It concerns all those situations where an alliance or other cooperative undertaking of finite size is useful—no individual unit, acting by itself, can provide an optimal amount of the good, but still there is no need for a grouping of infinite size. At some point additional members will provide contributions that are inadequate for the benefits they absorb. In this they would be drawing upon the private goods aspect of the cooperative effort, in that there is some marginal cost to the group in serving the additional members. The next piece, by James Buchanan, represents a more formal statement of some of the considerations Olson and Zeckhauser touch upon. It deals specif- ically with this problem of how big, of the optimal scope of a club or alliance.

To apply his criteria for optimal scope to actual political situations it would be necessary to devise some means for enforcing cost-sharing arrangements, either by taxation or by excluding the laggards from the benefits of membership. Whether this would be desirable in the NATO situation is, of course, far from certain. The NATO states may regard the west European neutrals not as free-loading chiselers but as nations whom they want to protect informally without openly incorporating them in the treaty organization. It may well be in the interest of the NATO states to provide protection to such states externally, through the presence of an alliance to which the neutrals do not belong, *rather than* through major defense efforts by those neutrals. For instance, it probably is best, even for NATO, that Austria be substantially disarmed, and, hence, not seem potentially provocative to her Eastern neighbors, so long as Austria's security from attack can be assured by her Western neighbors.[3]

The following piece also illustrates some scientific and policy problems with the use of this theoretical orientation to public goods. While it alerts us to expect certain apparently disproportionate efforts by particular kinds of states, it does not provide a simple formula for predicting just what the actual distribution will be. Some of the variables Buchanan employs are very far from satisfactory measurement—how, in fact, would one operationally gauge the various benefits that members obtain from an organization like NATO? The paper indicates how far we are from moving from diagnosis to a quantitative statement of the variables for purposes of prediction.

[3] More generally, see R. Musgrave, *The Theory of Public Finance* (New York: McGraw-Hill, 1959). On several of the above points, see the comments by R. N. Cooper and J. van Ypersele de Strihou following M. Olson, Jr., and R. Zeckhauser, "Collective Goods, Comparative Advantage, and Alliance Efficiency," in R. N. McKean, ed., *Issues in Defense Economics* (New York: National Bureau of Economic Research, 1967).

3

An Economic Theory of Clubs

James M. Buchanan

The implied institutional setting for neoclassical economic theory, including theoretical welfare economics, is a régime of private property, in which all goods and services are privately (individually) utilized or consumed. Only within the last two decades have serious attempts been made to extend the formal theoretical structure to include communal or collective ownership-consumption arrangements. The "pure theory of public goods" remains in its infancy, and the few models that have been most rigorously developed apply only to polar or extreme cases. For example, in the fundamental papers by Paul A. Samuelson, a sharp conceptual distinction is made between those goods and services that are "purely private" and those that are "purely public."[1] No general theory has been developed which covers the whole spectrum of ownership-consumption possibilities, ranging from the purely private or individualized activity on the one hand to purely public or collectivized activity on the other. One of the missing links here is "a theory of clubs," a theory of cooperative membership, a theory that will include as a variable to be determined the extension of ownership-consumption rights over differing numbers of persons.

Everyday experience reveals that there exists some most preferred or "optimal" membership for almost any activity in which we engage,

Reprinted from *Economica*, **32** (February 1965), pp. 1–14.

[1] See P. A. Samuelson, "The Pure Theory of Public Expenditure," *Review of Economics and Statistics*, **36** (1954), pp. 387–389; "Diagrammatic Exposition of a Theory of Public Expenditure," *Review of Economics and Statistics*, **37** (1955), pp. 350–355.

and that this membership varies in some relation to economic factors. European hotels have more communally shared bathrooms than their American counterparts. Middle and low income communities organize swimming-bathing facilities: high income communities are observed to enjoy privately owned swimming pools.

In this paper I shall develop a general theory of clubs, or consumption ownership-membership arrangements. This construction allows us to move one step forward in closing the awesome Samuelson gap between the purely private and the purely public good. For the former, the optimal sharing arrangement, the preferred club membership, is clearly one person (or one family unit), whereas the optimal sharing group for the purely public good, as defined in the polar sense, includes an infinitely large number of members. That is to say, for any genuinely collective good defined in the Samuelson way, a club that has an infinitely large membership is preferred to all arrangements of finite size. While it is evident that some goods and services may be reasonably classified as purely private, even in the extreme sense, it is clear that few, if any, goods satisfy the conditions of extreme collectiveness. The interesting cases are those goods and services, the consumption of which involves some "publicness," where the optimal sharing group is more than one person or family but smaller than an infinitely large number. The range of "publicness" is finite. The central question in a theory of clubs is that of determining the membership margin, so to speak, the size of the most desirable cost and consumption sharing arrangement.[2]

1

In traditional neoclassical models that assume the existence of purely private goods and services only, the utility function of an individual is written

$$U^i = U^i(X_1^i, X_2^i, \ldots, X_n^i) \tag{1}$$

where each of the X's represents the amount of a purely private good available during a specified time period, to the reference individual designated by the superscript.

Samuelson extended this function to include purely collective or public goods, which he denoted by the subscripts, $n + 1, \ldots, n + m$, so that (1) is changed to read

$$U_i = U^i(X_1^i, X_2^i, \ldots, X_n^i; X_{n+1}^i, X_{n+2}^i, \ldots X_{n+m}^i) \tag{2}$$

[2] Note that an economic theory of clubs can strictly apply only to the extent that the motivation for joining in sharing arrangements is itself economic; that is, only if choices are made on the basis of costs and benefits of particular goods and services as these are confronted by the individual. Insofar as individuals join clubs for camaraderie, as such, the theory does not apply.

This approach requires that all goods be initially classified into the two sets, private and public. Private goods, defined to be wholly divisible among the persons, $i = 1, 2, \ldots, s$, satisfy the relation

$$X_j = \sum_{i=1}^{s} X_j^i,$$

while public goods, defined to be wholly indivisible as among persons, satisfy the relation

$$X_{n+j} = X_{n+j}^i$$

I propose to drop any attempt at an initial classification or differentiation of goods into fully divisible and fully indivisible sets, and to incorporate in the utility function goods falling between these two extremes. What the theory of clubs provides is, in one sense, a "theory of classification," but this emerges as an output of the analysis. The first step is that of modifying the utility function.

Note that, in neither (1) nor (2) is it necessary to make a distinction between "goods available to the ownership unit of which the reference individual is a member" and "goods finally available to the individual for consumption." With purely private goods, consumption by one individual automatically reduces potential consumption of other individuals by an equal amount. With purely public goods, consumption by any one individual implies equal consumption by all others. For goods falling between such extremes, such a distinction must be made. This is because for such goods there is no unique translation possible between the "goods available to the membership unit" and "goods finally consumed." In the construction which follows, therefore, the "goods" entering the individual's utility function, the X_j's, should be interpreted as "goods available for consumption to the whole membership unit of which the reference individual is a member."

Arguments that represent the size of the sharing group must be included in the utility function along with arguments representing goods and services. For any good or service, regardless of its ultimate place along the conceptual public-private spectrum, the utility that an individual receives from its consumption depends upon *the number of other persons with whom he must share its benefits.* This is obvious, but its acceptance does require breaking out of the private property straitjacket within which most of economic theory has developed. As an extreme example, take a good normally considered to be purely private, say, a pair of shoes. Clearly, your own utility from a single pair of shoes, per unit of time, depends on the number of other persons who share them with you. Simultaneous physical sharing may not, of course, be possible: only one person can wear the shoes at each particular moment. However, for any finite period of time, sharing is possible, even for such evidently private goods. For pure services that are consumed in the moment of acquisition the extension is somewhat more difficult, but it can be made nonetheless. Sharing here simply means that the individual receives a smaller quantity of the service. Sharing a "haircut per month" with a second person is the same as consuming "one-half haircut per month." Given any quantity of final good, as defined in terms of the physical units of some standard quality, the utility that the individual receives from this quantity will be related functionally to the number of others with whom he shares.

Variables for club size are not normally included in the utility function of an individual since, in the private-goods world, the optimal club size is unity. However, for our purposes, these variables must be explicitly included, and, for completeness, a club-size variable should be included for each and every good. Alongside each X_j there must be placed an N_j, which we define as the number of persons who are to participate as "members" in the sharing of good, X_j, including the ith person whose utility function is examined. That is to say, the club-size variable N_j, measures the number of persons who are to join in the consumption-utilization arrangements for good X_j over the relevant time period. The sharing arrangements may or may not call for equal consumption on the part of each member, and the peculiar manner of sharing will clearly affect the way in which the variable enters the utility function. For simplicity we may assume equal sharing, although this is not necessary for the analysis. The rewritten utility function now becomes

$$U^i = U^i[X^i_1, N^i_1), (X^i_2, N^i_2), \ldots, (X^i_{n+m}, N^i_{n+m})] \qquad (3)$$

We may designate a numeraire good X_r, which can simply be thought of as money, possessing value only as a medium of exchange. By employing the convention whereby the lower case u's represent the partial derivatives, we get $u_j{}^i/u_r{}^i$, defined as the marginal rate of substitution in consumption between X_j and X_r for the ith individual. Since, in our construction, the size of the group is also a variable, we must also examine, $u_{N_j}{}^i/u_r{}^i$, defined as the marginal rate of substitution "in consumption" between the size of the sharing group and the numeraire. That is to say, this ratio represents the rate (which may be negative) at which the individual is willing to give up (accept) money in exchange for additional members in the sharing group.

We now define a cost or production function as this confronts the individual, and this will include the same set of variables

$$F = F^i[(X^i_1, N^i_1), (X^i_2, N^i_2), \ldots, (X^i_{n+m}, N^i_{n+m})] \qquad (4)$$

Why do the club-size variables, the N_j's, appear in this cost function? The addition of members to a sharing group may, and normally will, affect the cost of the good to any one member. The larger is the membership of the golf club the lower the dues to any single member, given a specific quantity of club facilities available per unit time.

It now becomes possible to derive, from the utility and cost functions, statements for the necessary marginal conditions for Pareto optimality in respect to consumption of each good. In the usual manner we get

$$\frac{u_j^i}{u_r^i} = \frac{f_j^i}{f_r^i} \tag{5}$$

Condition (5) states that, for the ith individual, the marginal rate of substitution between goods X_j and X_r, in consumption, must be equal to the marginal rate of substitution between these same two goods in "production" or exchange. To this acknowledged necessary condition, we now add

$$\frac{u_{Nj}^i}{u_r^i} = \frac{f_{Nj}^i}{f_r^i} \tag{6}$$

Condition (6) is not normally stated, since the variables relating to club size are not normally included in utility functions. Implicitly, the size sharing arrangements is assumed to be determined exogenously to individual choices. Club size is presumed to be part of the environment. Condition (6) states that the marginal rate of substitution "in consumption" between the size of the group sharing in the use of good X_j and the numeraire good X_r must be equal to the marginal rate of substitution "in production." In other words, the individual attains full equilibrium in club size only when the marginal benefits that he secures from having an additional member (which may, and probably will normally be, negative) are just equal to the marginal costs that he incurs from adding a member (which will also normally be negative).

Combining (5) and (6) we get

$$\frac{u_j^i}{f_j^i} = \frac{u_r^i}{f_r^i} = \frac{u_{Nj}^i}{f_{Nj}^i} \tag{7}$$

Only when (7) is satisfied will the necessary marginal conditions with respect to the consumption-utilization of X_j be met. The individual will have available to his membership unit an optimal quantity of X_j, measured in physical units and, also, he will be sharing this quantity "optimally" over a group of determined size.

The necessary condition for club size may not, of course, be met. Since for many goods there is a major change in utility between the one-person and the two-person club, and since discrete changes in membership may be all that is possible, we may get

$$\frac{u_j^i}{f_j^i} = \frac{u_r^i}{f_r^i} > \frac{u_{Nj}^i}{f_{Nj}^i}\bigg|_{Nj=1} \qquad \frac{u_j^i}{f_j^i} = \frac{u_r^i}{f^r} < \frac{u_{Nj}^i}{f_{Nj}^i}\bigg|_{Nj=2} \tag{7a}$$

which incorporates the recognition that, with a club size of unity, the right-hand term may be relatively too small, whereas, with a club size of two, it may be too large. If partial sharing arrangements can be worked out, this qualification need not, of course, be made.

If, on the other hand, the size of a cooperative or collective sharing group is exogenously determined, we may get

$$\frac{u_j^i}{f_j^i} = \frac{u_r^i}{f_r^i} > \frac{u_{Nj}^i}{f_{Nj}^i}\bigg|_{Nj=k} \tag{7b}$$

Note that (7b) actually characterizes the situation of an individual with respect to the consumption of any purely public good of the type defined in the Samuelson polar model. Any group of finite size k is smaller than optimal here, and the full set of necessary marginal conditions cannot possibly be met. Since additional persons can, by definition, be added to the group without in any way reducing the availability of the good to other members, and since additional members could they be found, would presumably place some positive value on the good and hence be willing to share in its costs, the group always remains below optimal size. The all-inclusive club remains too small.

Consider, now, the relation between the set of necessary marginal conditions defined in (7) and those presented by Samuelson in application to goods that were exogenously defined to be purely public. In the latter case, these conditions are

$$\sum_{i=1}^{s} \left(\frac{u_{n+j}^i}{u_r^i} \right) = \frac{f_{n+j}}{f_r} \tag{8}$$

where the marginal rates of substitution in consumption between the purely public good X_{n+j} and the numeraire good X_r summed over all individuals in the group of determined size s equals the marginal cost of X_{n+j}, also defined in terms of units of X_r. Note that when (7) is satisfied, (8) is necessarily satisfied, provided only that the collectivity is making neither profit nor loss on providing the marginal unit of the public good. That is to say, provided that

$$\frac{f_{n+j}}{f_r} = \sum_{i=1}^{s} \left(\frac{f_{n+j}^i}{f_r^i} \right) \tag{9}$$

The reverse does not necessarily hold, however, since the satisfaction of

(8) does not require that each and every individual in the group be in a position where his own marginal benefits are equal to his marginal costs (taxes). And, of course, (8) says nothing at all about group size.

The necessary marginal conditions in (7) allow us to classify all goods only after the solution is attained. Whether or not a particular good is purely private, purely public, or somewhere between these extremes is determined only after the equilibrium values for the N_j's are known. A good for which the equilibrium value for N_j is large can be classified as containing much "publicness." By contrast, a good for which the equilibrium value of N_j is small can be classified as largely private.

2

The formal statement of the theory of clubs presented in Section 1 can be supplemented and clarified by geometrical analysis, although the nature of the construction implies somewhat more restrictive models.

Consider a good that is known to contain, under some conditions, a degree of "publicness." For simplicity, think of a swimming pool. We want to examine the choice calculus of a single person, and we shall assume that other persons about him, with whom he may or may not choose to join in some club-like arrangement, are identical in all respects with him. As a first step, take a facility of one-unit size, which we define in terms of physical output supplied.

On the ordinate of Fig. 1, we measure total cost and total benefit per person, the latter derived from the individual's own evaluation of the facility in terms of the numeraire, dollars. On the abscissa, we measure

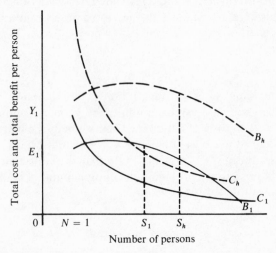

Fig. 1

the number of persons in possible sharing arrangements. Define the full cost of the one-unit facility to be Y_1, and the reference individual's evaluation of this facility as a purely private consumption good to be E_1. As is clear from the construction as drawn, he will not choose to purchase the good. If the single person is required to meet the full cost, he will not be able to enjoy the benefits of the good. Any enjoyment of the facility requires the organization of some cooperative-collective sharing arrangement.

Two functions may now be traced in Fig. 1, remaining within the one-unit restriction on the size of the facility. A total benefit function and a total cost function confronting the single individual may be derived. As more persons are allowed to share in the enjoyment of the facility, of given size, the benefit evaluation that the individual places on the good will, after some point, decline. There may, of course, be both an increasing and a constant range of the total benefit function, but at some point congestion will set in, and his evaluation of the good will fall. There seems little doubt that the total benefit curve, shown as B_1, will exhibit the concavity property as drawn for goods that involve some commonality in consumption.[3]

The bringing of additional members into the club also serves to reduce the cost that the single person will face. Since, by our initial simplifying assumption, all persons here are identical, symmetrical cost sharing is suggested. In any case, the total cost per person will fall as additional persons join the group, under any cost-sharing scheme. As drawn in Fig. 1, symmetrical sharing is assumed and the curve C_1 traces the total cost function, given the one-unit restriction on the size of the facility.[4]

For the given size of the facility, there will exist some optimal size of club. This is determined at the point where the derivatives of the total cost and total benefit functions are equal, shown as S_1 in Fig. 1, for the one-unit facility. Consider now an increase in the size of the facility. As

[3] The geometrical model here applies only to such goods. Essentially the same analysis may, however, be extended to apply to cases where "congestion," as such, does not appear. For example, goods that are produced at decreasing costs, even if their consumption is purely private, may be shown to require some sharing arrangements in an equilibrium or optimal organization.

[4] For simplicity, we assume that an additional "membership" in the club involves the addition of one separate person. The model applies equally well, however, for those cases where cost shares are allocated proportionally with predicted usage. In this extension, an additional "membership" would really amount to an additional consumption unit. Membership in the swimming club could, for example, be defined as the right to visit the pool one time each week. Hence, the person who plans to make two visits per week would, in this modification, hold two memberships. This qualification is not, of course, relevant under the strict world-of-equals assumption, but it indicates that the theory need not be so restrictive as it might appear.

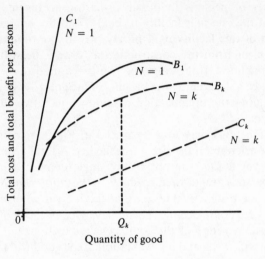

Fig. 2

before, a total cost curve and a total benefit curve may be derived, and an optimal club size determined. One other such optimum is shown at S_h, for a quantity of goods upon which the curves C_h and B_h are based. Similar constructions can be carried out for every possible size of facility; that is, for each possible quantity of good.

A similar construction may be used to determine optimal goods quantity for each possible size of club; this is illustrated in Fig. 2. On the ordinate, we measure here total costs and total benefits confronting the individual, as in Fig. 1. On the abscissa, we measure physical size of the facility, quantity of good, and for each assumed size of club membership we may trace total cost and total benefit functions. If we first examine the single-member club, we may well find that the optimal goods quantity is zero; the total cost function may increase more rapidly than the total benefit function from the outset. However, as more persons are added, the total costs to the single person fall; under our symmetrical sharing assumption, they will fall proportionately. The total benefit functions here will slope upward to the right, but after some initial range they will be concave downward and at some point will reach a maximum. As club size is increased, benefit functions will shift generally downward beyond the initial noncongestion range, and the point of maximum benefit will move to the right. The construction of Fig. 2 allows us to derive an optimal goods quantity for each size of club; Q_k is one such quantity for club size $N = K$.

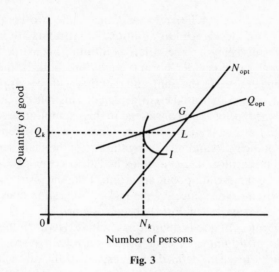

Fig. 3

The results derived from Figs. 1 and 2 are combined in Fig. 3. Here the two variables to be chosen, goods quantity and club size, are measured on the ordinate and the abscissa respectively. The values for optimal club size for each goods quantity, derived from Fig. 1, allow us to plot the curve, N_{opt}, in Fig. 3. Similarly, the values for optimal goods quantity, for each club size, derived from Fig. 2, allow us to plot the curve, Q_{opt}.

The intersection of these two curves, N_{opt} and Q_{opt}, determines the position of full equilibrium, G. The individual is in equilibrium both with respect to goods quantity and to group size, for the good under considera-tion. Suppose, for example, that the sharing group is limited to size, N_k. The attainment of equilibrium with respect to goods quantity, shown by Q_k, would still leave the individual desirous of shifting the size of the membership so as to attain position L. However, once the group increases to this size, the individual prefers a larger quantity of the good, and so on, until G is attained.

Figure 3 may be interpreted as a standard preference map depicting the tastes of the individual for the two components, goods quantity and club size for the sharing of that good. The curves, N_{opt} and Q_{opt}, are lines of optima, and G is the highest attainable level for the individual, the top of his ordinal utility mountain. Since these curves are lines of optima within an individual preference system, successive choices must converge in G.

It should be noted that income-price constraints have already been incorporated in the preference map through the specific sharing assump-tions that are made. The tastes of the individual depicted in Fig. 3 reflect

the postpayment or net relative evaluations of the two components of
consumption at all levels. Unless additional constraints are imposed on
the model, he must move to the satiety point in this construction.

It seems clear that under normal conditions both of the curves in
Fig. 3 will slope upward to the right, and that they will lie in approximately
the relation to each other as therein depicted. This reflects the fact that,
normally for the type of good considered in this example, there will exist a
complementary rather than a substitute relationship between increasing
the quantity of the good and increasing the size of the sharing group.

This geometrical model can be extended to cover goods falling at
any point along the private-public spectrum. Take the purely public good
as the first extreme case. Since, by definition, congestion does not occur,
each total benefit curve, in Fig. 1, becomes horizontal. Thus, optimal
club size, regardless of goods quantity, is infinite. Hence, full equilibrium
is impossible of attainment; equilibrium only with respect to goods
quantity can be reached, defined with respect to the all-inclusive finite
group. In the construction of Fig. 3, the N curve cannot be drawn. A more
realistic model may be that in which, at goods quantity equilibrium, the
limitations on group size impose an inequality. For example, in Fig. 3,
suppose that the all-inclusive group is of size N_k. Congestion is indicated
as being possible over small sizes of facility, but, if an equilibrium quantity
is provided, there is no congestion, and, in fact, there remain economies to
scale in club size. The situation at the most favorable attainable position
is, therefore, in all respects equivalent to that confronted in the case of the
good that is purely public under the more restricted definition.

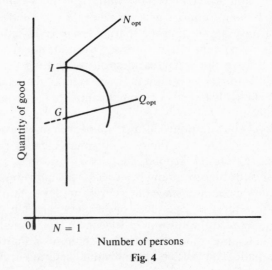

Fig. 4

Consider now the purely private good. The appropriate curves here may be shown in Fig. 4. The individual, with his income-price constraints is able to attain the peak of his ordinal preference mountain without the necessity of calling upon his fellows to join him in sharing arrangements. Also, the benefits that he receives from the good may be so exclusively his own that these would largely disappear if others were brought in to share them. Hence, the full equilibrium position, G, lies along the vertical from the $N = 1$ member point. Any attempt to expand the club beyond this point will reduce the utility of the individual.[5]

3

The geometrical construction implies that the necessary marginal conditions are satisfied at unique equilibrium values for both goods quantity and club size. This involves an oversimplification that is made possible only through the assumptions of specific cost-sharing schemes and identity among individuals. In order to generalize the results, these restrictions must be dropped. We know that, given any group of individuals who are able to evaluate both consumption shares and the costs of congestion, there exists some set of marginal prices, goods quantity, and club size that will satisfy (7) in Section 1. However, the quantity of the good, the size of the club sharing in its consumption, and the cost-sharing arrangements must be determined simultaneously. And, since there are always "gains from trade" to be realized in moving from nonoptimal to optimal positions, distributional considerations must be introduced. Once these are allowed to be present, the final "solution" can be located at any one of a subinfinity of points on the Pareto welfare surface. Only through some quite arbitrarily chosen conventions can standard geometrical constructions be made to apply.

[5] The construction suggests clearly that the optimal club size, for any quantity of good, will tend to become smaller as the real income of an individual is increased. Goods that exhibit some "publicness" at low income levels will, therefore, tend to become "private" as income levels advance. This suggests that the number of activities that are organized optimally under cooperative collective sharing arrangements will tend to be somewhat larger in low-income communities than in high-income communities, other things equal. There is, of course, ample empirical support for this rather obvious conclusion drawn from the model. For example, in American agricultural communities thirty years ago heavy equipment was communally shared among many farms, normally on some single owner-lease-rental arrangement. Today, substantially the same equipment will be found on each farm, even though it remains idle for much of its potential working time.

The implication of the analysis for the size of governmental units is perhaps less evident. Insofar as governments are organized to provide communal facilities, the size of such units measured by the number of citizens, should decline as income increases. Thus, in the affluent society, the local school district may, optimally, be smaller than in the poor society.

The approach used previously has been to impose at the outset a set of marginal prices (tax-prices, if the good is supplied publicly), translated here into shares or potential shares in the costs of providing separate quantities of a specific good for groups of varying sizes. Hence, the individual confronts a predictable set of marginal prices for each quantity of the good at every possible club size, independently of his own choices on these variables. With this convention, and the world-of-equals assumption, the geometrical solution becomes one that is relevant for any individual in the group. If we drop the world-of-equals assumption, the construction continues to hold without change for the choice calculus of any particular individual in the group. The results cannot, of course, be generalized for the group in this case, since different individuals will evaluate any given result differently. The model remains helpful even here, however, in that it suggests the process through which individual decisions may be made, and it tends to clarify some of the implicit content in the more formal statements of the necessary marginal conditions for optimality.

4

The theory of clubs developed in this paper applies in the strict sense only to the organization of membership or sharing arrangements where "exclusion" is possible. Insofar as nonexclusion is a characteristic of public goods supply, as Musgrave has suggested, the theory of clubs is of limited relevance. Nevertheless, some implications of the theory for the whole excludability question may be indicated. If the structure of property rights is variable, there would seem to be few goods the services of which are nonexcludable, solely due to some physical attributes. Hence, the theory of clubs is, in one sense, a theory of optimal exclusion, as well as one of inclusion. Consider the classic lighthouse case. Variations in property rights, broadly conceived, could prohibit boat operators without "light licenses" from approaching the channel guarded by the light. Physical exclusion is possible, given sufficient flexibility in property law, in almost all imaginable cases, including those in which the interdependence lies in the act of consuming itself. Take the single person who gets an inoculation, providing immunization against a communicable disease. Insofar as this action exerts external benefits on his fellows, the person taking the action could be authorized to collect charges from all beneficiaries under sanction of the collectivity.

This is not, of course, to suggest that property rights will, in practice, always be adjusted to allow for optimal exclusion. If they are not, the "free rider" problem arises. This prospect suggests one issue of major importance that this analysis has neglected, the question of costs that may be involved in securing agreements among members of sharing groups. If individuals think that exclusion will not be fully possible, that they can expect to secure benefits as free riders without really becoming full-fledged contributing members of the club, they may be reluctant to enter voluntarily into cost-sharing arrangements. This suggests that one important means of reducing the costs of securing voluntary cooperative agreements is that of allowing for more flexible property arrangements and for introducing excluding devices. If the owner of a hunting preserve is allowed to prosecute poachers, then prospective poachers are much more likely to be willing to pay for the hunting permits in advance.

●

Earlier, we suggested that within organizations the actual cost-sharing arrangement, when compared with certain predictions of the theory of public goods, could provide one measure of the success of collective or supranational institutions. Nevertheless, this is not the only context in which the arrangements for cost-sharing provide important information about modifications in national independence. For instance, there are often cases, within local or national economies, where the actions of one unit impose costs, disproportionate to any benefits that may be received, on other members of the economy.

A current and highly relevant example is air and water pollution. It may be cheaper for an industrial producer to dump its waste materials into the air or into a nearby river than to work out some less public means of disposal. But the costs of his action, to the society at large, may be substantially greater than the cost of an alternative waste-disposal system. The economy-wide losses in drinking water and recreational facilities may well exceed the price of a sewage-disposal plant to protect the water. In terms of the economists' efficiency argument the waste producer should be compelled to compensate the others for their losses from pollution—or, in fact, since the cost would be less, to build the sewage disposal plant and so prevent the loss. All such costs imposed on others by the producer of a good are known in economics as "external" costs (costs imposed on others external to the firm) or simply as "externalities."

So far, the case has been established in either-or terms. The economy has the sewage-disposal plant, or if the plant would cost more than what the waste destroys is actually worth, then the economy just has the sewage. This puts the argument in terms of "indivisibles," when in practice the situation is unlikely to be so clear-cut. As long as *any* external costs are imposed, the apparent price of the good produced, as indicated in the market system, understates its real use of resources and the optimum output, for the society, would be lower. The efficiency argument would demand that some means be found to impose those external costs on the producer. If it were not feasible to eliminate all the sewage, then it might be efficient at least to lower the bacterial count somewhat.

Though it may be difficult to measure the various costs, and hard, in the political process, to impose the "efficient" settlement, this principle of just compensation, often operating through government regulatory activity, is extremely common within nations. But between nations it is much less likely to operate. The efficiency argument implies an element of *justice*, that the costs should be imposed on the producer, or spread between producer and consumer, and not merely be imposed on the latter.

It assumes that the larger pie, distributed according to the efficiency criterion, is preferable to the smaller one, where externalities are not compensated. Internationally, however, such a principle is not always accepted; furthermore, even if it is, the political means for enforcing the more efficient distribution of costs often is lacking.

There are quite a number of possible situations where external costs may arise internationally, and several distinct ways for coping with the problem. Often, there may be no compensation whatever. Since World War II, and especially during the first two decades after 1945, the Soviet government erected an "Iron Curtain" around its borders, severely limiting the passage of goods, persons, and information in and out of the country. The Russian leaders deemed this necessary to maintain internal security within their own country, but, of course, the Iron Curtain restricted not only the activities of Russians, but of people in the rest of the world as well. Yet non-Russians certainly were not compensated by the Soviet government for their losses. An even more blatant case is the activities of the nuclear powers in testing their weapons in the atmosphere. No compensation was paid to children around the globe whose inherited genetic material was damaged by radiation.

Other times, compensation is paid. In an instance where the radiation damage was very direct and obvious the United States did make some compensation to the Japanese fisherman in the ship *Fortunate Dragon*. Such payments may be made by governments to individuals in another state, as happened there, or where the costs are widespread, the compensation may go from government to government. Payment by the United States to Trinidad for use of territory for air and naval bases, in recognition of the fact that Trinidadians in general have lost full use of their small territory, is an example. A more common but often overlooked situation is where two nations will strike a bargain, perhaps on tariffs and trade, or perhaps on strategic matters like military base facilities, and both feel that their nations are better off than they would be in the absence of the agreement. Particular groups in one country, however, may be seriously disadvantaged—farmers, for instance, may lose a formerly protected domestic market. In such a case the government of that state will, in its own domestic political process, work out a compensating arrangement, such as a subsidy for the disadvantaged, without any additional payments from the other government.

Usually, among nations all compensation agreements will be the result of bargaining in the international marketplace between the governments involved. Less often, as with the Japanese fishermen, the bargaining may be so implicit as to look like a unilateral gesture. Only rarely is there a supranational institution capable of administrative action to impose a regulative adjustment of the externality. The agreements entered into by members of the European Common Market, whereby there would be a joint development fund to help industries especially hard hit by new foreign competition, represents a rare example.

It is tempting to argue that an administrative or arbitration solution is the one that is preferred from the point of view of efficiency, and that the situation where it is not simply left to bargaining between governments represents a higher form of political organization. After all, in bargaining the solution arrived at will reflect the bargaining strength of the parties, and that may not, on grounds of either efficiency or some concept of equity, be the desired outcome, given all the rigidities and imperfections that are present in the international "market." This has for some time been a very common position among economists, who have reacted against the original nineteenth century eulogies of the "invisible hand," but fairly recently there has been a revived emphasis on the virtues of bargaining in the market as a means of adjusting externalities. This new view points out that judges may award excessive damages (a too-high level of compensation is as inefficient as too low a one); individuals may be encouraged to do things they would not otherwise do, only so as to receive the compensation: or the administrative costs of imposing a settlement may exceed the social value of the results. In the following selection Stanislaw Wellisz reacts in turn against what he terms this modern-old advocacy of the bargaining solution. He discusses the arguments in favor of reliance on the bargaining process and notes their hidden assumptions. Many often unexamined variables affect the bargaining outcome. In considering them he suggests some criteria for judging the most efficient means for adjusting particular externalities, and provides a partial basis for evaluating current or proposed solutions in international politics. One assumption behind complete advocacy of the bargaining solution must be that there are no legal or political impediments to bargaining. Perhaps this assumption is not too seriously violated in international affairs. But another is that there are no transaction costs or costs entailed in the bargaining process itself; to the degree that there are, including the cost of excluding freeloaders who would gain from the bargain but will not pay to bring it about, there is still a role for intervention to allocate resources.[1] Certainly, in international politics, bargaining costs, which include much of nations' expenditure on military forces and intelligence operations, are high. Thus one must ask, empirically in a given situation, what the costs of bargaining are and what costs would be incurred in the process of intervention by a supranational authority.

[1] See Guido Calabresi, "Transaction Costs, Resource Allocation, and Liability Rules—A comment," *Journal of Law and Economics*, **11** (1968), pp. 67–73.

In any case, one of the most important lessons of the recent controversy about externalities is that not all activities which produce externalities should be opposed; one cannot condemn an action merely because another party's interests are harmed by it. Economists habitually use the concept of *opportunity cost*, comparing the receipts from one activity with those that might have been obtained from alternative arrangements. If the total costs of moving people away from a smoky chimney are less than the expected costs of stopping the smoke, it is the former that should be done on efficiency grounds. This is the kind of argument by which continued nuclear testing is defended, though the measurement of costs and benefits from such activities is far more controversial than the assessment of the effects of air pollution. Similarly, an adequate analysis must be directed to the "realistically" available alternatives to an external cost, not to some ideal world.[2]

[2] See especially, R. H. Coase, "The Problem of Social Cost," *Journal of Law and Economics*, 3 (October 1960), pp. 1–44. Also, in answer to Wellisz, particularly on the ground that a centrally-administered scheme ignores the problem of information costs, see O. A. Davis and A. B. Whinston, "On Externalities, Information, and the Government-Assisted Invisible Hand," *Economica*, 33 (August 1966), pp. 303–318, and the references there.

4

On External Diseconomies and the Government-Assisted Invisible Hand

Stanislaw Wellisz

The Pigovian tradition, accepted by modern welfare economists, claims that whenever private and social costs diverge, steps should be taken to equalize the two. For instance, if sparks and smoke from a steam railway damage the surrounding land, it is appropriate to impose upon the railway costs equal to the amount of the damage. Unless such action is taken, the railway will disregard the social diseconomy and it will expand beyond the social optimum. Conversely, an activity which yields positive external effects should be encouraged to expand beyond the individual optimum which does not take into account such effects.

The modern-old economists, and especially Coase and Buchanan, challenge the established position: they claim that the private market *can* lead to a Pareto optimum, despite externalities, since it is possible to establish a market in externalities. Administrative measures, on the other hand, may cause divergences from the optimum.[1] An even stronger case is presented by Davis and Whinston.[2] The two authors consider

Reprinted from *Economica*, **31** (November 1964), pp. 347–354, 360–361.

[1] J. M. Buchanan, "Public Policy and the Pigovian Margins," *Economica*, **29**, 3 (1962), p. 17; J. M. Buchanan and W. C. Stubblebine, "Externality," *Economica*, **29** (1962); R. H. Coase, "The Problem of Social Cost," *Journal of Law and Economics*, **3** (1960).

[2] O. A. Davis and A. Whinston, "Externalities, Welfare, and the Theory of Games," *Journal of Political Economy*, **60** (1962).

two types of externalities (to be defined later): in one type, "separable externalities," it is "difficult" to reach an optimum by instituting Pigovian taxes and subsidies, while in the other, more general type, "nonseparable externalities," the task is "impossible,"[3]

Coase's vigorous and original article provides an excellent starting point for a critical appraisal of the attacks on the Pigovian tradition.

Where Pigou was anxious to compensate the victims of diseconomies, Coase concentrates his attention on the conditions under which the largest social product can be achieved:

> When an economist is comparing alternative social arrangements, the proper procedure is to compare the total social product yielded by those different arrangements. The comparison of private and social costs is neither here nor there.[4]

Coase carries his challenge right into the enemy's camp: he takes up and expands Pigou's example of a railway damaging nearby fields, and unlike Pigou, he concludes that the market is likely to yield the correct allocative solution, while judicial and administrative interference is unlikely to achieve the task. The Pigou–Coase example deserves re-examination so that we can see where the strength and the weakness of Coase's argument lie.

According to Coase, "if the railway could make a bargain with everyone having property adjoining the railway line and there were no costs involved in making such bargains, it would not matter whether the railway was liable for damage caused by fires or not."[5] If the damage suffered by the landowners is greater than the benefits reaped by the railway, the landowners will be able to pay a sum sufficient to induce the railway to curtail operations. If the damage is less than the benefit, it would be unwarranted to prevent the railway from operating because total product would thereby be diminished. Coase takes great care to show that if courts award excess damages, they are likely to curtail useful activities in order to protect the interests of the victims of external diseconomies.

The adjustment is, of course, discontinuous where the activity is discrete, but in the case of divisible activities, bargaining will lead to a true Pareto optimum. "In full Pareto equilibrium ... [the] internal benefits measured in terms of some numéraire good, net of costs, must be just equal, at the margin, to the external damage that is imposed on other parties."[6] As long as there is disequilibrium, it pays one of the sides to offer compensation to the other to achieve a modification of the

---

[3] *Ibid.*, p. 261.
[4] Coase, *loc. cit.*, p. 34.
[5] Coase, *loc. cit.*, p. 31.
[6] Buchanan and Stubblebine, *loc. cit.*, p. 381.

position. By contrast, an administrative imposition of costs will not necessarily produce an adjustment of the level of production leading to the Pareto optimum.

To clarify the reasoning underlying his conclusions in the railway case, Coase constructs the following numerical example. Assume, says Coase, that a railway faces the choice of running one or two trains per day.

> Suppose that the running of one train per day would enable the railway to perform services worth $150 per annum and running two trains a day would enable the railway to perform services worth $250 per annum. Suppose further that the cost of running one train is $50 per annum and two trains $100 per annum. Assuming perfect competition, the cost equals the fall in the value of production elsewhere due to the employment of additional factors of production by the railway. Clearly, the railway would find it profitable to run two trains per day. But suppose that running one train per day would destroy by fire crops worth $60 and two trains a day would result in the destruction of crops worth $120. In these circumstances running one train per day would raise the value of total production but the running of a second train would reduce the value of total production.[7]

The second train increases the railway's net return by $50, but causes destruction of $60 worth of crops, hence, the total product is diminished by $10. Thus, "the conclusion that it would be better if the second train did not run is correct."[8]

To prevent the second train from being run, Coase says Pigou would make the railway liable for damages. Coase cautions us, however, that if damage liability is imposed, the farmer might intensify production in order to suffer greater damages and collect greater compensation. If he does so, it might not be worthwhile for the railway to run even one train per day. For instance, if the farmer intensifies his production to such an extent that even one train per day causes $110 worth of damage, and two trains per day cause $300 worth of damage, and if the railway has to pay compensation, no trains will be run. Thus, if there is no liability, and the market is not permitted to operate, the diseconomy-producing activity is likely to be pushed beyond the Pareto-optimal point, but if there is liability, it will be curtailed below the Pareto-optimal level.[9]

In a no-liability regime the Pareto optimum will be achieved if the farmer(s) enters (enter) into a free bargain with the railway. Since the second train would cause a damage of $60 above and beyond the damage caused by the first train, the farmer(s) will be willing to pay the railway up to $60 for *not* running the second train. Since the railway gains only

[7] Coase, *loc. cit.*, p. 32.
[8] *Ibid.*, p. 32.
[9] Coase, *loc. cit.*, pp. 32–33.

$50 by running the second train, it will accept any sum above $50 for not running it. Any bargain reached between the limits of $50 and $60 benefits both sides and leads to a Pareto optimum ....

To keep within the spirit of the modern-old argument, I shall limit myself from now on to external interrelations of firms imbedded in the competitive system. Coase's railway, I shall assume, is managed along purely competitive lines, and it faces a perfectly elastic demand curve. This assumption may be difficult to reconcile with reality and also with Coase's own figures, but it is essential for the modern-old argument.

Having specified that the externalities which are under discussion arise among competitive price takers, let us consider briefly what is meant by an externality in a competitive regime: if the firms make zero profits before external costs are imposed on them, how can they bribe the would-be externality-creating units to eliminate the externality? Clearly, a brief digression on private and social costs is called for at this point.

In a perfectly competitive industry in which there are no Ricardian rents,[10] external diseconomies result in factor-use changes without creating any social costs. In such a setting, every firm operates at a zero profit level, and all the factors are paid their opportunity cost. If external costs are imposed upon one of the competitive units, that unit will make losses and, in the long run, it will go out of business. As output is curtailed and ultimately abandoned, the displaced factors find employment in alternate uses. In the initial situation the factors were employed at opportunity cost, hence the alternate-use output has the same value as the original output. Thus, there is a change in production pattern, but no social loss. Moreover, since the unit displaced by the external cost operated initially at zero profit, it has neither the incentive nor the means to bribe the externality-producing unit.

To re-create the modern-old reasoning in a competitive setting, it is necessary to postulate the existence of nontransferable resources giving rise to Ricardian rents. Consider, for instance, a case in which a smoke-stack is erected next to a farm field, and imagine that the smoke reduces the crops. If all the factors were employed at their opportunity cost, the farmer would move elsewhere, and the land would remain fallow, or it would be put to some alternative use, bringing the same rate of return to the land as the initial use. If, however, the land stays under the (now reduced) crop, or if it is put to a use in which it brings a marginal product of lesser value, a reduction of land rent will occur. The external loss

[10] Ricardian rent is a technical term for any part of the payment for the use of land (or any other factor of production) that exceeds the least amount needed to keep that factor available for use in production [Ed.].

caused by the smoke is measured not by the amount of the crop destroyed but by the decline in the difference between the value of the field's product and the opportunity cost of the movable factors, i.e., by the decline in the Ricardian rent. Thus, changes in the Ricardian rent measure the external effects of firms imbedded in a competitive setting. The net returns used in Coase's examples can thus be interpreted as net rents.

Let us now return to Coase's railway example and concentrate on the problem of losses to farmers. Coase apparently assumes that the farmers have no foreknowledge of the damage which will be done by the second train. If they had such foreknowledge, they could reduce the damage in most cases—say, by switching to crops which are less affected by smoke or by planting or sowing more sparsely.

Table 1 gives a hypothetical example of net rents accruing to farmers who have three alternative courses of action, A, B, and C, with the railway running 0, 1, 2, 3, and 4 trains daily. By stretching our imaginations we can assume that the railway operates in a competitive regime and that its net returns represent net rents. Coase's "net returns" to 1 and 2 trains are thus interpreted in Table 1, and additional numbers are made up to 3, 4, and 5 trains. Column C is consistent with Coase's assumption that no crop switching will take place (and the figures for the damage caused by 1 and 2 trains are his), while columns A and B show the hypothetical result of crop switching to reduce the damage:

Table 1

Number of trains	Net rents to the factors employed by the railway ($)	Net rents to the factors employed by alternative cropping methods ($)		
		A	B	C
0	0	50	100	150
1	100	40	80	90
2	150	30	50	30
3	170	25	20	−30
4	160	10	0	−30
5	0	0	0	−30

If the farmers have no foreknowledge of any damage, they will adopt alternative C, and if two trains are run per day, they will suffer $60 worth of damage (as in Coase's example) and have a net rent of $30, as shown in Table 1. If, however, they know that two trains will be run per day, they will adopt alternative B. This alternative would be less profitable than alternative C, if no trains were running, but it is more profitable in a two-train regime because of the lesser damage to crops.

Acting in isolation, the railway would find it profitable to run three trains per day and collect a rent of $170. The farmers would find it best to switch to alternative A, with a net rent of $25 under the three-train regime. Notice, however, that the railway would gain only $20 by running the additional train, and the farmers would lose $25. If bargaining were opened, the railway would reduce the number of trains to 2 if it received compensation larger than $20, and the farmers would be willing to pay up to $25 in exchange for a reduction of train runs from 3 to 2. Thus, it is in the interest of all parties concerned to reach a Pareto-optimal solution.

The modern-old solution as presented here is technically unexceptionable, but one may wonder whether it is mere curiosity or whether it is broadly applicable to externality problems. To obtain the solution it was necessary to assume that (1) bargaining concerns the *marginal* unit and (2) that the bargaining limits are well defined. These assumptions may or may not be satisfied in actual situations.

Consider again the railway example. To obtain the best bargain with the farmers, the railway might threaten to run five trains per day and thus destroy the entire crop. To avoid this possibility and to obtain a reduction in train runs to two a day, the farmers would be willing to pay up to $50. Conversely, if the railway company were seeking permission to run a railway, the farmers would seek to appropriate the entire rent accruing to the railway under the optimal regime, i.e., $150, even though the damage would equal only $100. Thus, the bargaining limits are set by the rents accruing to the two parties under the optimal regime, and not by the marginal rents.

It is conceivable, of course, that the modern-old economists think of situations in which large numbers of potential external-diseconomy producers compete for a large number of potential sites so that the bargaining limits are narrowed down through competition to the marginal units. If this is so, the solution is correct, but the assumptions which must be made to achieve the solution are out of harmony with the examples examined by Coase and, what is more serious, have only a faint bearing on reality.[11]

Bargaining for the entire rent accruing to the opposite party does not, in itself, preclude the possibility of reaching a Pareto optimum, for it is to

[11]When in the absence of zoning, a factory is erected, it is not usual for the factory owner to notify the nearby farmers about the amount of smoke which he intends to produce, so that the bargaining, if any, takes place after the factory is built. It is still more unusual for a number of factories to compete not only for a site but for the privilege of smoking onto nearby fields. The ex-ante bargaining would require rather unusual property relationships which would, in effect, internalize the externality.

the advantage of both parties to reach a level of joint maximum rent. Moreover, the process opens up magnificent business prospects: any activity can be turned to profit as long as it is sufficiently annoying to someone else. As long as the activity absorbs no resources, i.e., as long as the blackmailers maintain amateur standing, the economist who refrains from social judgment can find no fault with the situation.[12]

A more crucial assumption made by the modern-old school is that the parties to the bargain know how much it pays them to offer in order to induce a change in the output of the other unit. The assumption is reasonable in cases in which unit(s) "1" has (have) an external effect on unit(s) "2," but unit(s) "2" does (do) not affect externally the costs of unit(s) "1." In such situations the unit(s) determines (determine) in isolation the optimal output. The payments are determined by the benefits reaped by the "2" unit(s) when "1" output changes from the isolation equilibrium level, and the costs to "1" of such output changes. If there is a mutual externality between "1" unit(s) and "2" unit(s), neither the "1's" nor the "2's" may be able to achieve an individual optimum; hence, it may not be possible to determine the size of payments leading to a joint optimum. As Davis and Whinston have shown, the continuous case corresponds to a two-person, nonzero sum game which, in general, has no saddle point,[13] and, therefore, neither simple nor mixed strategies will yield an individual optimum. Thus, a bargain may never be reached, and even when it is reached, there will be temptation to improve one's position by violating the agreement.

The bargaining solution also breaks down, as Turvey notes, when the group suffering through (or benefiting from) an externality is too large for the members to "get together." In such cases, there is "a case for collective action to achieve optimum allocation."[14] Buchanan also

[12] Pigou took a rather dim view of the "costless bargaining" assumption: "Of bargaining proper there is little that need be said. It is obvious that intelligence and resources devoted to this purpose, whether on one side or on the other, and whether successful or unsuccessful, yield no product to the community as a whole.... These activities are wasted. They contribute to private, but not to social net product." *The Economics of Welfare*, 4th ed., 1938, p. 201. Pigou is too harsh in his judgment insofar as the bargaining process changes the pattern of resource use and provided that it is imbedded in a competitive setting, it does contribute to social product. It is quite possible, however, that just as with public regulation, the absorption of resources may be so great as to nullify the beneficial effects of improved resource use.

[13] Davis and Whinston, *loc. cit.*, p. 259 ff. Curiously enough, the numerical example given by the authors is one in which there is a stable equilibrium which will be reached with each firm acting in isolation. It is very simple, however, to construct plausible cases which do not have such an equilibrium.

[14] R. Turvey, "On Divergences between Social Cost and Private Cost," *Economica*, **30** (1963), p. 312.

recognizes the case for collective action in the case of goods which are not privately divisible, though he warns us that any political solution involves the imposition of some externalities as long as the goods are not entirely indivisible.[15]

The large-group difficulty lies in that it is to the advantage of any member of the group to refuse to bear any part of the cost of a settlement, while reaping the advantages. If there are n farmers affected by the smoke from a train, it pays any farmer to let the remaining $(n-1)$ bribe the railway and to enjoy cost-free the results of the bargain. Moreover, if the externality does not affect all the firms in a fixed proportion, it pays to form coalitions. For instance, the construction of a higher smokestack might reduce the pollution of nearby fields, but increase that of more distant areas. If this be so, one can foresee the formation of separate pressure groups, and the larger the number of possible combinations of interests, the smaller the possibility of Pareto-optimal solutions.[16]

The discussion of conditions under which the modern-old solution is valid leads to the conclusion that far from being a universal panacea, the private bargain solution to external diseconomies applies only to exceptional cases. Such cases are, moreover, of little interest to the policy maker. If a private bargain can be made to everybody's satisfaction, there is no reason for judicial or administrative interference. The policy maker must cope with situations in which "payment cannot be exacted from the benefited parties or compensation enforced on behalf of the injured parties,"[17] that is, with situations where private bargains fail. Moreover, the policy maker cannot be restricted to perfect competition but must also deal with monopolies, and private bargains involving monopolies may, as we have seen, aggravate resource misallocation instead of achieving a social optimum. . . .

1. The Pigovian Solution to the Problem of Externalities

The Pigovian prescription for externalities is: devise a system of taxes and subsidies which will modify the cost function of an externality-creating firm in such a fashion that the firm must produce at the socially optimal level if it wishes to maximize profits.

[15] Buchanan, *loc. cit.*, p. 29.

[16] To find a way out of this difficulty, one is tempted to search for a subset of units, all of which are willing to cooperate on a voluntary basis. Such a solution has no legitimate place in a purely competitive setting, for it is a basic assumption of the theory of perfect competition that all units behave exactly alike. In a large group it is in the interest of every unit to refuse to pay and to let the other units bear the entire cost; in any subset of units the same behavior must pertain.

[17] Pigou, *op. cit.*, p. 183.

The Pigovian approach may be attacked on the grounds of practicability: the cost of devising and administering a tax-subsidy scheme may exceed the benefits.... In some cases it might be preferable to use outright prohibition of certain activities (such as zoning laws), whereas in others it might be less costly to ignore the externalities and let the market function without any interference. The choice of course of action must be dictated by weighing the costs and the benefits of the alternative arrangements.

The Pigovian tax-subsidy scheme, unlike the modern-old bargains, applies to the broad spectrum of externality cases. The scheme is, nevertheless, repugnant to the modern-old economists.

Buchanan's objections to the Pigovian method are based on the observation that any administrative measure is likely to impose externalities of its own.[18] Thus, Mr. X might not feel personally threatened by fire (or he lives in an entirely fireproof building); yet he is forced to pay taxes to support the fire department. The objection is valid, alas: there is no way of constructing a nondictatorial social welfare function,[19] and there is no way of devising an equitable system of payment for public goods.[20] These points are well worth keeping in mind, and one should continuously be reminded of the dangers of administrative meddling in economic affairs. Unfortunately, however, the policy maker must choose between imperfect alternatives, and it might be well worth the economists' while to design the best available system of Pigovian taxes instead of making indignant noises when the policy makers adopt silly measures for want of expert advice.

The cost of administration and the possibility of imposition of excessive burdens on the externality-producing unit cause concern to Coase. It is true, of course, that the cost of regulation may outweigh its benefits, and that governments in general shy away from this kind of cost-benefit analysis. Public welfare would doubtless increase if we dropped the unreasonable expedient of valuing government services at cost, and if we probed into their actual value. Fear of excessive bounties is less warranted. Excessive damages work against the interests of the aggrieved parties as much as against the interests of society. If a socially useful activity is eliminated because damages are too high, no compensation will accrue to the damaged party. Farmers adversely affected by smoke are better off if they receive a steady stream of compensation from a smoke-producing factory, i.e., if they appropriate part of the rent accruing

---

[18] See Buchanan, *loc cit.*, pp. 25 ff.

[19] On this point see K. J. Arrow, *Social Choice and Individual Values*, 1951.

[20] See J. Wiseman, "The Theory of Public Utility Pricing—An Empty Box," *Oxford Economic Papers*, **9** (1957).

to the factory, than they are if the factory is forced to move away. Thus, whether cost allocation is done through bargaining or whether it is done through the judicial-administrative process, it is in the interests of all the parties to reach a social optimum, for at that point the spoils are the greatest. The problem, in either case, is how to divide the spoils; it is always in everybody's interest to make the spoils as large as possible. Unfortunately, in most types of external relations the market does not lead to a social optimum. . . .

2. Conclusions

The critics of the Pigovian tradition have done us a great service by pointing out the ambiguities and the lack of clarity in the orthodox treatment of externalities. They have done well, too, to point out how important it is to reckon the administrative cost of action taken to remedy situations in which there are externalities. Externalities may well be permitted to persist if the administrative action absorbs more resources than are lost through a deviation from a Pareto optimum. This is just common sense, but it is good to put common sense into scientific language every so often. It was also useful to point out (as Kenneth Arrow did before) that any collective action imposes the will of some on the others; hence, it too creates externalities of its own.

The mutual bargain solution proposed by the modern-old economists lacks, unfortunately, the necessary generality to be of policy importance. Pigou, as we know, was concerned with externality situations "of such a sort that payment cannot be exacted from the benefited factor or compensation enforced on behalf of the injured factors."[21] To be more precise, he should have also included cases where private bargains cannot be reached, and cases where private bargains are contrary to public interest. In the former category we must include bargains with variable-threat limits, in the latter, bargains in which monopolies are involved.

Even in the rare instances where externalities are a private matter between two parties, the superiority of private bargains over judicial arbitration is hard to accept. Whether it is reached by direct bargaining or by a judicial process, the solution to the conflict is most satisfactory to both sides if the final situation is Pareto optimal. It is clear, moreover, that even if provision is made for judicial recourse, the parties concerned may, if they wish, strike a private bargain. The fact that arbitration and other judicial methods of settling disputes is so prevalent gives proof that it is not always easy, or cheap, to reach a private bargain.

[21] Pigou, *op. cit.*, p. 183.

Finally, there is the problem of equity. To be sure, economists abandon their scientific detachment when they start moralizing. It is worth pointing out, however, that while the judicial process, rightly or wrongly, tends to compensate the victim, the bargaining process compensates the threat-making party, and one can hardly claim that threat-making deserves reward.

The last selection was concerned essentially with bilateral bargaining situations, between a party that imposes an external cost and the party or parties that initially bear the cost. A good deal of work has gone on in economics, however, with the analysis of multilateral bargaining situations. In a famous volume cited in the following paper, the economist Kenneth Arrow set forth what has become known as the "paradox of voting." He proved how, with certain assumptions in a multilateral situation, there can be no unique solution to a problem of choice among three or more options. Since the assumptions he made seem to be entirely reasonable, the paradox has come to be regarded as illustrating a serious obstacle to the achievement of collective rationality.

In the next piece sociologist James S. Coleman argues that one of Arrow's major assumptions is, in fact, not a reasonable one, and that when it is relaxed the paradox disappears. He introduces, in place of an assumption that the three or more options are rank ordered, an assumption that allows for the expression of *intensities* as well as the *order* of preferences.[1] This is done by employing the idea of the subjective probability that a given preferred outcome will actually be achieved, and, hence, of expected utility. This substituted assumption then allows for the mechanism known to political observers as logrolling, the communication of information and trading about issues other than those immediately at hand. This is tied in with previous theoretical literature stressing the importance, for maintaining the stability of a political system, of avoiding the concentration of attention on a single decision or dimension. The result is that the Arrow demonstration becomes unimportant because of its simplifications—real world situations are much more complex.

In presenting this demonstration Coleman makes a number of points that are important here. First, there is the somewhat implicit point that in the kind of rigorous deductive analysis typical of much of economics great care must be taken in the original selection of assumptions. Seemingly appropriate assumptions may actually be poorly chosen, and lead to misleading conclusions. Second, he argues that game theory is not so widely helpful as many writers assume, that in this instance the application of game-theoretical approaches only trivializes the problem by limiting the analyst to those very small systems in which game-theoretic solutions can be calculated. Finally, he indicates how his argument is related to a general theory of which the exchange of goods in a market of pure competition is a special case.

[1] For an early emphasis on the importance of intensity in politics, see R. A. Dahl, *A Preface to Democratic Theory* (Chicago: University of Chicago Press, 1956), pp. 90–123.

This demonstration is highly relevant to all those many problems of political analysis to which the Arrow voting paradox has previously been applied. Insofar as the version here applies to decision makers—especially legislators—of equal power, its importance for international politics may seem slight. Many international problems, however, do arise in situations where the nation is the unit of analysis and where the one-nation one-vote assumption is not so farfetched. Decision making in international organizations is just such a situation. Similarly, the argument can be applied to lower-level analogous processes, in legislatures, cabinets, or other collegial bodies, when analyzing comparative foreign policies.[2]

●

[2] For an argument similar to Coleman's, see G. Tullock, "The General Irrelevance of the General Impossibility Theorem," *Quarterly Journal of Economics*, **81**, 2 (May 1967), pp. 256–270, and on log rolling, J. Buchanan and G. Tullock, *The Calculus of Consent* (Ann Arbor: University of Michigan Press, 1962).

5

The Possibility of a Social Welfare Function

James S. Coleman

Ever since 1951, when Kenneth Arrow [1] published his monograph showing the paradox that social welfare functions generate, there has been interest in overcoming or bypassing this paradox. The paradox is that, given certain simple and very persuasive conditions for collective rationality, there can be no decision rule which meets these conditions. The conditions, simply stated, are these:

1. Between three alternatives, the social welfare function must give rise to a unique social ordering, no matter how individual members of the group choose to order the three alternatives.
2. The social ordering must correspond positively, or at least not negatively, to changes in the ordering of any one individual.
3. The elimination of any one alternative shall not affect the ranking of the other alternatives in the social welfare function.
4. Voters can choose freely among all alternatives.
5. No one individual's choice can dictate the social ordering independently of the choices of others.

It is easy to show that even with three voters and three alternatives, a situation can exist in which these conditions are not met by a simple majority vote. For consider three voters, X, Y, and Z, and three alternatives, A, B, and C. The rankings given by X, Y, and Z are:

Reprinted from *American Economic Review*, **56**, 5 (December 1966), pp. 1105–1122.

Rank	X	Y	Z
1	A	B	C
2	B	C	A
3	C	A	B

Now, if we eliminate alternative C, A is preferred by X and Z, and therefore wins. Thus, we say that the social welfare function generates a social order AwB (where "w" means A wins over B). When we eliminate alternative A, B is preferred by X and Y, and therefore wins. Thus, BwC. Finally, if B is eliminated, C is preferred to A by Y and Z, and therefore wins. Thus, CwA. However, this produces an inconsistent social ordering, since AwB, BwC, but CwA.

I want to suggest that this approach to a social welfare function leaves out of consideration precisely those elements which are most crucial in empirical cases of social choice, and that it is this omission which creates the apparent paradox. This omission allows the problem to be conceptualized in such a way that the third condition presented appears to be very "reasonable," while from the point of view of individual rationality, it is not.

Quite simply, I suggest that this approach, by looking at only the surface characteristics of social decision rules, neglects the most important element that nearly all such rules contain: a means for allowing the expression of relative intensities of preference, or of differences between utilities associated with alternatives. I suggest, in other words, that Arrow's impossibility theorem is relevant only to those social choice mechanisms in which it is not possible to express relative intensities, and that when it is possible to express such intensities, the third condition is inconsistent not only with "collective rationality" but with individual rationality. That is, the elimination of an alternative, though it be very low in his ordering, may change the rational individual's behavior. I will also suggest some of the most important mechanisms, in actual societies, through which individuals may express intensities.

I suggest that the appropriate way to examine such problems of individual choice and social welfare is akin to the method of studying utility under risk. That is, when the outcome of a decision is uncertain, then each individual attaches to each possible outcome a subjective probability, and, thus, to the decision an expected utility. If he has various kinds of behavior that he can carry out, then he will act in such a way as to maximize the expected utility.

In any collective decision or "social choice," the outcome is not determined by the individual's action alone. Thus, in order to behave rationally, he must estimate the expected utilities of each action open to him. These expected utilities are contingent not only on the utility of each outcome to him, but on the probability he estimates it to have under each action open to him. Consequently, the behavior of individuals in collective decisions must be governed by rationality under uncertainty or risk, not by rationality under certainty. It follows from this that the rational individual must express not only the ordering of his utilities for the possible outcomes, as he does in rationality under certainty, but also the relative sizes of utility differences between various outcomes, as he must do in rational behavior under risk.

It could be said that this approach violates the spirit of Arrow's approach, because Arrow was concerned merely with the ordering of tastes in the community, and showed that no aggregation of these ordered tastes could be consistent, in the sense of meeting his conditions for reasonableness or social rationality. The flaw in this argument is that citizen sovereignty, which is one of Arrow's conditions, implies the *expression* of these tastes or preferences, the expression that is normally embodied in voting, with the voting rule serving as the aggregation device for the society. Once this is allowed, then as indicated previously, it becomes irrational for an individual to express only his preferences, and not something more which would maximize his expected utility. This "something more" can be variously characterized as his intensity of preference or the relative sizes of utility differences between outcomes.

Thus, it is not correct to establish a relation between individual choice and social choice which uses as a model individual choice under certainty. As a subsequent example will indicate, only under a very special condition does the rational individual's behavior become like that of the rational actor under certainty.

It should be pointed out that the use of intensities of preference in relation to social choice, as derived from conceptions of utility under risk, is nothing new. Rothenberg, in his review of work subsequent to Arrow's, discusses in detail the use in social welfare functions of expected utility deriving from von Neumann–Morgenstern's definitions of utility under risk [6]. But in all these approaches, the expected utility has been imported, so to speak, from some supposed external measurement, and does not derive from the very behavior itself in the collective decision. Such an approach leads these authors to question whether it is "legitimate" to introduce intensities through use of cardinal utilities. (For example, Rothenberg says, "Assuming that we can 'measure' preference intensities with a tolerable degree of precision, is this the kind of factor which we *ought* to treat on a par with preference ordering in the context of social choice?" [6, p. 139]. This approach is a carry-over from an earlier and more naive view of social welfare, in which it was assumed that the economist, as advisor to the policy maker, could assess the tastes of individuals through some sort of measurement, and then tell the policy maker what was best for the people—always in terms of their own tastes. In fact, however, it is the political process itself which, together with the existing structure of collective decision making, expresses these tastes. Only more recently, in work like that of Duncan Black [2], Downs [4], Buchanan and Tullock [3], and Olson [5], and earlier in the individualist school of public finance stemming from Wicksell, have economists given the individual the same autonomy to express his interests in collective decisions that they have long allowed him in market behavior.

1. The Rational Individual in Collective Decisions

The simple example of three individuals and three alternatives given earlier can be used to illustrate how rational individuals may be expected to behave in collective decisions, and some of the implications for the system. We will consider the individuals in the following circumstances:

a. They can only vote, and have no information about others' votes.

b. They can vote, but they also have some information that allows them to estimate probabilities of others' votes.

c. They can not only vote on the social decision, but also have another decision on which to make a choice. They can make any agreements they desire in the negotiations preceding the vote.

A. Only Voting on a Single Issue with No Information

Let us think of a quantity U_{xa}, which is the utility of outcome A to individual X. The properties that this quantity will obey depend on the kind of behavior allowed to X. That is, although we may consider that in reality X does have some "amount of utility" which he associates with A, we will treat this "amount" as if it had only limited properties, depending on the behavior which we allow the individual. The wider the range of behavior allowed, the nearer this "amount" will come to have the properties of a real number.

If individual X does not know the preferences of Y and Z, then we can calculate the expected utility of this decision for him as follows, under a majority rule.[1] Under this complete absence of knowledge

---

[1] Such a decision rule as a majority rule would need an additional rule in case no alternative attained a majority. Such a rule we posit to be a random mechanism with probabilities for each alternative proportional to the number of votes it received. In this case, $p_a = p_b = p_c = 1/2$.

about Y's and Z's preferences, all possible combinations of Y's and Z's vote have equal subjective probability for him. Thus, a table can be set up as indicated below:

Votes of		Outcome if X	
Y	Z	votes for A	Probability
A	A	A	1/9
A	B	A	1/9
A	C	A	1/9
B	A	A	1/9
B	B	B	1/9
B	C	1/3 A, 1/3 B, 1/3 C	1/9
C	A	A	1/9
C	B	1/3 A, 1/3 B, 1/3 C	1/9
C	C	C	1/9

The outcomes are similar, but in favor of B and C, if he were to vote for B or C, respectively. If we label X's vote for A, B, or C, X_a, X_b, and X_c, respectively, the expected utility of this decision for him, if he knows nothing about Y's and Z's preference, is:

$$E(U_x|X_a) = 17/27U_{xa} + 5/27U_{xb} + 5/27U_{xc} \qquad (1)$$

$$E(U_x|X_b) = 5/27U_{xa} + 17/27U_{xb} + 5/27U_{xc} \qquad (2)$$

$$E(U_x|X_c) = 5/27U_{xa} + 5/27U_{xb} + 17/27U_{xc} \qquad (3)$$

Clearly, if $U_{xa} > U_{xb} > U_{xc}$, then subtraction will show that $E(U_x|X_a) > E(U_x|X_b) > E(U_x|X_c)$, and he will carry out action X_a if A is an available alternative and X_b if only B and C are available. Since this is the only action available to him, the only information we have concerning the utilities as a result of his behavior is an ordering. (Alternatively, the only property we need to attribute to the utilities to predict such behavior is their order.)

B. Vote on a Single Issue, with Information about Others' Preferences

If X has the same behavior alternatives available to him, but has in addition information about the ordering that Y and Z give to A, B, and C, and assumes they will vote their preference, his assessment of the situation is this:

Votes of		Outcome if he votes for			
Y	Z	A	B	C	Probability
B	C	$1/3\ A,\ 1/3\ B,\ 1/3\ C$	B	C	1

Under the belief that Y and Z will vote for B and C, respectively, his expected utilities are:

$$E(U_x|X_a) = 1/3U_{xa} + 1/3U_{xb} + 1/3U_{xc} \qquad (4)$$

$$E(U_x|X_b) = \qquad\qquad U_{xb} \qquad\qquad (5)$$

$$E(U_x|X_c) = \qquad\qquad\qquad\qquad U_{xc} \qquad (6)$$

Now, his behavior is not fully determined by the order among U_{xa}, U_{xb}, and U_{xc}. For if U_{xc} is small, relative to U_{xb} and U_{xa}, so that

$$1/3U_{xa} + 1/3U_{xb} + 1/3U_{xc} < U_{xb} \qquad (7)$$

then he will choose to take action X_b rather than X_a. This situation is exactly that of the hypothesis used in measurement of utility under risk, where his behavior in a choice between risky alternatives is used to provide information about the size of utility differences between different alternatives. Rearranging the inequality above gives the following relation, if he chooses alternative B:

$$U_{xa} - U_{xb} < U_{xb} - U_{xc} \qquad (8)$$

That is, if he chooses B although he prefers A, the utility difference between alternatives A and B is less than that between B and C.

Of course, the same analysis may be applied to the other individuals Y and Z, with the result that each person might vote for his second choice because he assumes that the others will vote their first choices. However, such a peculiar result does not make the behavior less rational for him. It means merely that he incorrectly assessed the probabilities of the others' votes. If he had knowledge, or some degree of belief, that those votes would be cast for other than alternatives B and C, respectively, then the appropriate subjective probabilities would modify the coefficients in Eqs. (4), (5), and (6). The important point is that when he no longer estimates the probabilities of others' votes to be equal for each alternative, the degenerate case of Eqs. (1) to (3) no longer holds, and his behavior will depend on the size of the utility differences between pairs of outcomes, as in (8).

Thus, even in this case of actions limited to a single vote, a comparison of utilities beyond simple ordering can come about. If he takes action X_b (a vote for B), this implies Eq. (7), or rearranged,

$$U_{xb} < 1/2U_{xa} + 1/2U_{xc}$$

under the expected utilities indicated in Eqs. (4), (5), and (6). That is, if he prefers A to B to C, but votes for B, knowing that Y will vote for B and Z for C, then this means that B is "closer to" A in utility for him than C is to B. Note that because the individual must calculate expected utilities of the outcome, no outcome is "irrelevant," so long as there is some subjective probability of its occurrence. In fact, in this case, the utility of C for X plays a crucial role in determining whether he will vote for A or B. Thus, the elimination of C might have—and legitimately so from the point of view of individual rationality as well as social welfare— an effect upon the outcome.

C. Another Collective Decision, with Vote Exchanges

The behavior available to the individual in the cases discussed previously is not enough to express much about the utilities that various alternatives have for him. Neither does it correspond to the behavior available to members of decision-making bodies, such as city councils, legislatures, town meetings, or social groups. In any such body, the individuals, in attempting to maximize their expected utilities, will use whatever power they possess. The principal kind of behavior that is available to them in nearly all cases is a sequence of decisions. The essential properties that such a sequence introduces are shown by introducing a single new decision, with alternatives labeled similarly to the first. The orders by X, Y, and Z are:

Rank	X	Y	Z
1	A'	B'	C'
2	B'	C'	A'
3	C'	A'	B'

Now, considering again individual X in the situation where he knows the various orders of the others (that is, there is full communication, obtained through discussion), he has expected utilities under a wide range of possible actions. For now he has the power to induce an action on the part of another person in response to an action on his part. For example, suppose for him the utility differences between A', B', and C'

are very small, while the utility differences between A, B, and C are very large. Then he might consider an exchange of votes with Z such that A and C' would win.[2] His utility under this possible action could then be compared with his expected utility under the conditions of no exchange (assuming his subjective probabilities are 1 that Y and Z will vote for B and C respectively):

$$U_{xa} + U_{xc'} \overset{?}{>} 1/3U_{xa} + 1/3U_{xb} + 1/3U_{xc} + 1/3U_{xa'} + 1/3U_{xb'} + 1/3U_{xc'}$$
(9)

Rearranging,

$$U_{xa} - U_{xb} + U_{xa} - U_{xc} \overset{?}{>} U_{xa'} - U_{xc'} + U_{xb'} - U_{xc'} \qquad (10)$$

If the indicated utility differences for A, B, and C were greater than the indicated ones for A', B', and C', then he would indeed prefer to make the exchange, rather than not. Similarly, he could consider an exchange with Y, to give outcomes A and B'. If inequality (10) holds, then he will also want to compare the two possible exchanges:

$$U_{xa} + U_{xc'} > U_{xa} + U_{xb'}$$

This inequality does not hold if $U_{xb'} - U_{xc'} > 0$, as the initial order implies. Thus, for him the bargain with Y has highest utility. But it may be a bargain which he cannot make, since Y would have to accept the utility of his least preferred alternative, A. That is, $U_{ya} + U_{yb'}$ may not be large enough, compared to the alternative actions, for Y to make this exchange. Considering the possible alternatives for Y as exchanges with X or Z (for in the general case of unequal utility differences between alternatives, some action which involves exchange will always have a higher utility for an individual than an equal chance of all alternatives), there are two cases: B and C', or B' and C. Thus if either

$$U_{yb} + U_{yc'} > U_{ya} + U_{yb'}$$
(11)

or

$$U_{yb'} + U_{yc} > U_{ya} + Y_{yb'}$$
(12)

then Y will prefer to make an exchange with Z. But Y's initial preference ordering gives $U_{yc} > U_{ya}$, so that at least (12) will hold. This will not insure, of course, that Z will be satisfied with such a trade.

This kind of behavior need not lead, of course, to a stable solution which, in a game-theoretic sense, dominates all others. The outcome

---

[2] The one explicit recognition of such vote-exchange behavior by economists is in Buchanan and Tullock [3, Ch. 10]. However, political scientists are so fully aware of this behavior that they have common names for it: "horse trading," "logrolling," "making a deal," and other terms that would be appropriate in economic markets.

may depend on many chance factors, such as who talks first to whom. However, the basic point is that each person will attempt to maximize his expected utility. He will do so by taking that action for which the increment in expected utility—the analog to marginal utility for a situation of this type—is greatest. Ordinarily, this action will be one of exchange: increasing his control over a decision for which control makes a great deal of difference in his expected utility, and in return giving up to another person control over a decision for which control makes little difference in his expected utility. If we consider, in the first analysis, his actions to be limited to pairwise exchanges of control, then he will order decisions i in terms of $\Delta U_{xi} = E(U_{xi}|v_{ix}) - E(U_{xi})$, where v_{ix} is an additional vote gained by X on decision i by this action. The relative sizes of ΔU_{xi} for all issues i express his *interest* in gaining a vote on each issue. He will also order possible actions in terms of the decrement in expected utility that the loss of his vote to a given individual k on a given decision j would mean: $\Delta U_{xkj} = E(U_{xj}|v_{jk}) - E(U_{xj})$, where v_{jk} is the transfer of control over his vote on decision j to individual k. Thus, with such a situation and limited to pairwise exchanges, each rational individual will try to carry out an exchange increasing control over decision i in return for losing control over decision j such that ΔU_x is maximized:

$$\Delta U_x^* = \max_{\substack{i,j,k \\ i \neq j}} (\Delta U_{xi} - \Delta U_{xkj})$$

It is useful to consider a particular example of utilities associated with different alternatives which would generate exchange attempts in the case of the 2-decision system just presented. Assume the following utilities associated with each alternative by each person. (These numbers are to be compared only for a given individual; the scaling for different individuals is arbitrary, since no interpersonal comparison of utility is implied. Also, the full properties of an interval scale are not assumed, but only the "distances" between utilities associated with different alternatives in the same decision. It is more convenient, however, to use specific numbers, even though all the properties of these numbers are not required for the behavior under discussion.)

	X	Y	Z
U_a	10	8	9
U_b	5	10	8
U_c	1	9	10
$U_{a'}$	10	8	9
$U_{b'}$	9	10	6
$U_{c'}$	8	9	10

In this situation gaining control of the first decision clearly has higher expected utility increment for X than does gaining control over the second decision. For if his assessment of the probabilities of A, B, and C is $1/3$ each without control, then if we call ΔU_{x1} his utility increment in decision 1 through gaining control over it,

$$\Delta U_{x1} = U_{xa} - (1/3 U_{xa} + 1/3 U_{xb} + 1/3 U_{xc})$$
$$= 10 - 5.33 = 4.67$$

and

$$\Delta U_{x2} = U_{xa'} - (1/3 U_{xa'} + 1/3 U_{xb'} + 1/3 U_{xc'})$$
$$= 10 - 9 = 1.0$$

The loss of utility through giving up his vote to Y or Z can be evaluated as follows, where ΔU_{xy1} is his increment (or decrement) in utility from decision 1 through giving up his vote to Y:

$$\Delta U_{xy1} = 5.0 - 5.33 = -0.33$$
$$\Delta U_{zz1} = 1.0 - 5.33 = -4.33$$
$$\Delta U_{xy2} = 9 - 9 = 0$$
$$\Delta U_{zz2} = 8 - 9 = -1$$

Thus, in evaluating the interest in X in particular exchanges (the expected utility of the exchanges) by $\Delta U_{xi} + \Delta U_{xkj}$, two exchanges have sharply higher utility than any others:

$$\Delta U_{x1} + \Delta U_{xy2} = 4.67 - 0 = 4.67$$
$$\Delta U_{x1} + \Delta U_{xz2} = 4.67 - 1 = 3.67$$

A similar evaluation would show that for Y both decisions 1 and 2 are of equal interest, and a trade with Z on either will maximize Y's expected increment (at 1.0). For Z, control over decision 2 is of most interest, and an exchange with X gives highest expected increment in utility (at 1.67). Thus, in this situation, X and Z would make an exchange, giving X control over decision 1 and Z control over decision 2. The outcomes would be A for decision 1, and C' for decision 2.

This discussion should be sufficient to show that when individuals are released from restrictive conditions upon behavior and information (i.e., voting on only one issue and complete absence of information about others' behavior), then rational behavior demands that every alternative which has some subjective probability of occurrence can affect their behavior, though it may be least preferred. As a consequence, when such behavior is allowed, the condition which Arrow states, independence of outcome from "irrelevant" alternatives, can hardly be imposed. For since no alternatives are irrelevant in the expected utility calculations which govern behavior, it is hardly reasonable to expect that any will be irrelevant to the outcome.

Given, then, the freedom from Arrow's impossibility theorem, we can proceed to investigate the structural conditions that will allow expression of more than the simple preferences that voting on a single issue implies.

The principle theoretical approach in the literature makes use of successive adjustments on a single proposal. Knut Wicksell [7] introduced this conception into public finance by asking how taxes could be assessed in such a way that the optimum amount of public services would be provided, and the allocation would be such that marginal benefits equaled marginal costs for each. Wicksell's solution was theoretically most elegant, though it had flaws which made it impossible to carry out in practice. His thesis was: (a) always to vote on a combined proposal which included not only the amount and mode of public expenditure, but also the distribution of taxes or other means of paying for the expenditure; (b) then to require the measure to pass not by majority but by unanimous vote. In this way, the amount of expenditure and distribution of burden would be so adjusted that those who value the activity least would pay least (otherwise they could not be induced to vote for it), and more generally, the amount and distribution would be continually adjusted until each voter's marginal costs equaled his marginal benefits. Such a measure would be approved unanimously, and only such approval, Wicksell held, would assure that benefits were greater than costs for all. Such a principle assumes, of course, that all persons have perfect calculating ability, that there is some means of efficiently carrying out the multiple adjustments in a proposal necessary to reach this state of perfect adjustment, and perhaps most important of all, that people will reveal true preferences. That is, it assumes that all persons are constrained, by fear of retaliation in kind, from understating their interest in the public activity.

However, Wicksell, and all those who have followed in this direction (with the exception of Buchanan and Tullock, in *Calculus of Consent*, Chapter 10), limit their attention to the single issue, and limit the resources available to the individual to his vote on this issue. Yet an economic man will be willing to spend various other resources, such as votes on other issues, etc., in proportion to his expected utility gain from their expenditure. Thus, if those who are not interested in the decision can extract from the former such resources, down to the last bit that the former are willing to give, the latter will be recompensed, through a much simpler and more efficient mechanism than an attempt to adjust the tax or the expenditures so that it fits perfectly the utility structure of the population. This implies, at the extreme, that it is not important if there are tax loopholes, if these loopholes are made evident to all at time of passage of the bill, and those who will gain from them are made to pay, in terms of other legislation, the full amount that they are willing to pay in order to gain the loopholes.

Thus, it becomes fruitful to develop further the possibilities which arise as a consequence of an expanded range of behavior among persons involved in collective decisions—a range of behavior which includes the employment of various resources, especially control over other issues, in the form of votes on other decisions which involve this collectivity. To be sure, such an approach would be academic if the proposed behavior was uncommon or impossible in decision-making bodies. But exactly the contrary is true. Numerous observers of legislative bodies have suggested that the very essence of legislative behavior is exchanges which bring about support on different issues; and there is evidence to suggest that when a single decision dominates a political or social system, so that its importance makes such exchanges impossible, the decision-making process breaks down; and not only is there no "social welfare function," there is overt conflict. Often, in actual collectivities, such as legislatures, there are a number of other resources that various legislators have, and can use in exchanges. One of these is partial control of positions within the legislature, such as committee membership. All these resources are used in the same way that goods are used in a barter market: in exchange for control over those events whose outcome one is most interested in. Many of these resources act to make unequal the power of different legislators, and thus give unequal degrees of power to their constituents. It is useful to conceive, however, of an ideal simple collectivity in which each actor's only resources are his votes on other collective decisions. With such a conception, one can raise the question of what conditions would allow the system of exchange to approach more nearly the free markets which in pure economic competition allow individuals to maximize their utility, relative to their initial resources.

2. Extensions to Many Decisions and Many Individuals

From the three-person, two-decison example presented previously, two kinds of extensions are possible, affecting the result in different ways. One is an extension to a greater number of decisions, and the other is an extension to a greater number of individuals. I shall consider first the former.

In this example, it was worth a great deal, in X's private utility calculations, to gain alternative A rather than B; and worth still more to gain A rather than C. In contrast, it was worth little to Y, relative to his other utility comparisons, to gain B rather than C, or C rather than A. Yet, for the very small gain of C in place of A, Y could make an offer to Z which might overcome X's potential agreement with Z. For a gain to Y that was a smaller gain than several others for him, he could counter an agreement of X's which would make most difference to X of all possible agreements. Thus, even though this agreement was of utmost importance to X, he had no way of implementing his feelings, though it would obviously be worth more to him relative to his other interests to gain control of this decision than to either Y or Z (again, relative to Y's and Z's other interests).

An extension in number of decisions destroys this inequity, by giving each of the persons a large amount of resources which he can employ or fail to employ on a decision, depending on its importance to him. For example, assume that there were a hundred other issues, each with three alternatives, A_i, B_i, C_i, and each ranked as in the first decision by X, Y, and Z. Suppose also that the relative utilities were in each case except the first, 10, 9, and 8, for each of the three members. Then individual X, to whom the first decision is of such importance, could offer to Z enough to express this importance. He could, for example, offer Z his vote on decisions 2 and 3, an offer which would be impossible for Y to counter and still make an expected profit, but one which would still leave X with an expected gain on these decisions considered all together.

More generally, the extension from two decisions to a great many allows even more flexibility of adjustments in exchange than this example indicates. In the extreme case, it approaches in one sense a market situation, in which persons have various resources, divisible into small units, and also many different wants. Each person's wants, of course, are scaled by the totality of his resources; but he can pay out various quantities of resources in order to get those things he wants most. In terms of political preferences, this means that those decisions for which the alternatives differ most for him in utility are the ones over which he can gain control through giving up his partial control over those of less importance to him. It allows, in short, an expression of "intensity" such that the outcome of the decision will tend to be the one which maximizes aggregate utility.[3]

---

[3] It must be clearly understood that the aggregating function is one in which the sum of each person's utility differences between outcomes over all decisions are weighted by his power over the decisions. Thus, the total sum of each person's utilities as used in aggregating is proportional to the sum of his power. The precise definition of this power is given later in this analysis.

This extension from a few decisions to a great many leads toward a market in one way, but not in another. With a very small number of persons, there can still be a large difference between the "price" paid for a vote (in terms of other votes) and its value to the purchaser. If the decisions that are of great interest to him are of little to the other persons, he can gain control over them with little sacrifice on his part, and then tend to gain more in utility from the set of decisions than his power would warrant. He, in effect, would be in the role of monopsonist, who can drive the price down to what he is willing to pay.

An extension in the direction of a great number of other individuals engaged in the set of decisions moves this in the direction of a free market, in which prices are established by competition among both buyer and seller.

A large and complex society, where there is a complex web of interdependence among various activities, tends to generate both the extensions discussed here. The extension of decisions occurs simply through the extension in time of the society; the extension in number and utility-variations of individuals occurs through the complexity of the economic and social structure. It is true, of course, that the particular form of government distributes power of particular decisions in special ways, which may neglect the interests of some persons and give great weight to the interests of others. But that is a matter which can be more fully studied when the fundamental points discussed in the paper are better understood. The major point to be made here is that, just as a free market with pure competition can be conceived in economic exchange, and used as a theoretical model from which actual systems can be examined, a similar model of pure competition can be conceived in collective decisions. Although actual social systems deviate from this model, it can nevertheless serve as a basis from which the deviations can be studied.

3. An Ideal System of Collective Decisions

The system of collective decisions differs in several important respects from economic markets. One respect, which we shall not investigate, is that occasioned by time: collective decisions are made in a sequence, over an extended period of time, while in some economic markets, time need not be taken into account. Though time, together with discounting, mechanisms of credit-extension, insurance, etc., must play an important part in the further development of the present theory, the elements will be left unexamined here.

Another way in which this case differs from economic markets is in the lesser flexibility in exchange—for example, the relative absence of successive exchange of the same goods. Since the entities being exchanged are promises of an action, these promises are not as negotiable as economic goods, or money by which such goods are counted. Another aspect of the lack of flexibility is the fact that in this case, power leads to realization of interests; but the interest gained cannot be reconverted to power in the same way that economic goods, once gained, can be reconverted in a perfect market to the money which bought them. As a consequence of this last point, and of the lack of a measure of value such as money, it is necessary to devise a different way to express the value of power over a particular issue. The equation to be presented below is consistent with the framework of economic markets, but it is applicable in collective decisions as well, which do not generate their own measure of value.

Let us first define a quantity which is analogous to ΔU_{xi} given previously, which was the interest of X in gaining a vote on decision i. It was defined as the difference in expected utility due to that vote. Now, let us define analogously r_{ix} as the difference in expected utility given that the decision is under his control (which is merely the utility of the most-preferred alternative), and the unconditional expected utility:

$$r_{ix}^r = U_{xa} - E(U_{xi}) \tag{13}$$

where A is the alternative most preferred by X in decision i. This we will call, for heuristic purposes, X's *interest* in the decision. This is assumed to be exogenously given, dependent on the structure of social and economic activities, and the content of decision i.

Also exogenously given is the formal control structure over the issue. In the case of m decisions decided by a vote among n individuals, each person has control of $1/n$ on each of the m decisions. This will be labeled c_{ij}, the control of individual j over issue i. The total resources of individual j consist of his control over all issues, but weighted by the value of "importance" of each decision. If the value of each decision is v_i, then the power of individual j is

$$p_j = \sum_{i=1}^{m} v_i c_{ij}$$

where

$$\sum_{j=1}^{n} c_{ij} = 1$$

The total control over each decision is 1, that is, $\Sigma_{j=1}^{m} c_{ij} = 1$. Now, given these definitions, the value of a given decision where there is pure competition is the sum of each actor's interests times the power of that actor:

$$v_i = \sum_{j=1}^{n} r_{ij} p_j \tag{14}$$

or

$$v_i = \sum_{j=1}^{n} \sum_{k=1}^{m} r_{ij} v_k c_{kj} \tag{15}$$

This recursive definition says in effect that the value of a decision is equal to the sum of the interests of each individual in the decision, but weighted by the power of the individual. In turn, the individual's power depends upon the value of those issues over which he has some control.

Solution of Eq. (15) for the set of v_i can give the value or price which any individual should have to pay to gain control over each decision. Such prices would not be exact in imperfect competition, but where there are enough competitors and enough decisions, the price should come to that point. This gives both the value of an individual's resources (i.e., votes) in the market, and the price he can expect to pay for decisions he wants. It establishes the rate of exchange which should obtain as the market approaches rationality.

4. More Fundamental Revision

In a sense, this discussion has gone at the problem backwards, showing how a framework of exchange in a free market is possible in collective decisions just as in the exchange of economic goods. This is necessary for historical reasons. But having done so, it is more profitable to attempt to restate the general theory in a way that is appropriate to collective decisions and then show that exchange of private goods is a degenerate case. The basic elements of such a theory will be indicated later, but only to show the way in which such a generalization could proceed.

Consider the world as consisting of a set of *events*. Each event has two or more possible outcomes, and these outcomes have consequences for individuals, which the individuals evaluate differently. Each event is also characterized by a distribution of control over the outcomes. The sum of such control is less than or equal to 1.0, and it may be conceived as the probability that the person holding the control can determine the outcome.

Then in a market of exchange of economic goods, the goods themselves are the events. Consumption of the good by a given individual is one outcome of the event. Possession of the good constitutes control over the event. Thus, this is a simple situation in which the consequences of a given outcome are zero for all individuals other than the individual who consumes it, and control over the event is always 1.0 for the person in whose possession the goods lie, and 0 for all others.

The fact that makes some events come under multiple control in collective decisions is their multiple consequences, or "externalities." Whatever outcome is chosen, it will have consequences for many individuals. Thus, many have an interest in gaining control of it, and various forces (in *other* collective decisions) move such events into the area of collective decisions, with a certain structure of control (such as one vote for one person). Thus, collective decisions are events in which control is formally distributed over more than one actor (though it may come into the hands of a single actor, through exchanges). They tend also to be events in which any outcome has consequences for many actors. Because of the divided control, a much more extensive calculation—using expected utility, rather than certain utility—is necessary in carrying out rational behavior. Nevertheless, the structure is the same, and the private-goods exchange case can be treated as a special case in which the control over an event is always 0 or 1. The equations of exchange in the collective decision case should thus reduce to those of the private goods case when the matrix of control takes on a special form.

5. Conclusion

One might be tempted to develop these ideas further in a game-theoretic direction, since, obviously, game-theoretic considerations are relevant. One referee has suggested that the points developed here are more relevant to game-theoretic analysis of political behavior than to Arrow's and subsequent work on a social welfare function. This, however, misses the major import of the discussion. Arrow's work, by attempting to derive social choice as a function of individual preference, begins to shift the idea of a social welfare function away from a normative concept to a positive one. I. M. D. Little and others of a normative persuasion have recognized this danger and rejected Arrow's approach as irrelevant to welfare economics. Having begun the shift, however, one cannot stop halfway, but must incorporate in the theory that behavior which the rational actor would carry out. Arrow's theorem depends upon individual rationality under certainty, which allows no expression of intensity of preference, but only ordering among alternative outcomes. It is clear, however, first, that rational behavior in collective decisions requires rationality under uncertainty or risk, which opens the possibility of expression of intensity of preference; and second, that in actual groups, the existence of a sequence of decisions gives actors the resources that allow the expression of such intensity, even if imperfectly and incompletely.

When one takes this perspective, political behavior can be viewed as a generalization of market behavior, and the functioning of legislatures or other bodies in collective decisions as an extension of a market. In this "market," each actor has only partial control over any given outcome, rather than complete control over a goal, thus requiring the more complex calculations of rational behavior under risk. This extension of rationality has been developed as part of game theory; but to categorize the present results as work in game theory trivializes them by limiting their use to microsystems, in which game-theoretic solutions can be calculated. It would be as if the indeterminacy of outcome in a two-person bargaining situation had constrained economists from developing the concept of a perfect market, and the power that brings to economic analysis.

Similarly, in collective decisions, disregarding the confusion and indeterminacy of game-theoretic solutions in a microsystem (for small-number interaction cases are always the most difficult for analysis), one can develop an idea of a perfect system of collective decisions, and thereby derive the value of control over a given decision, and the power of a given actor, and can ultimately develop for such decisions the tools of economic analysis.

References

1. K. J. Arrow, *Social Choice and Individual Values* (New York: Wiley, 1951).
2. D. Black, *A Theory of Committees and Elections* (Cambridge: Cambridge University Press, 1958).
3. J. M. Buchanan and G. Tullock, *The Calculus of Consent* (Ann Arbor: University of Michigan Press, 1962).
4. A. Downs, *An Economic Theory of Democracy* (New York: Harper & Row, 1957).
5. M. Olson, Jr., *The Logic of Collective Action* (Cambridge: Harvard University Press, 1965).
6. J. Rothenberg, *The Measurement of Social Welfare*, Englewood Cliffs: Prentice-Hall, 1961.
7. K. Wicksell, "A New Principle of Just Taxation," in R. A. Musgrave and A. T. Peacock, eds., *Classics in the Theory of Public Finance* (New York: Macmillan, 1958), pp. 72–118.

●

The next selection is reprinted from an article by Duncan Black. The article was later incorporated as a chapter in Black's stimulating book *The Theory of Committees and Elections*,[1] which provides a fuller treatment of the underlying assumptions and some further consequences of the analysis and to which the reader is referred for further study. Black's concern is not so very different from the kind of problems that were discussed by Coleman in the previous piece. Here we begin with a substantial number (more than three) of decision makers and with also a fairly large number of issues or parliamentary motions, each of which must be accepted or rejected and which each of the decision makers is capable of ordering from most to least preferred. Like Coleman, Black builds his analysis not just upon the ordering of preferences but upon the assumption that intensities of preference can be measured; he requires that measurement on an interval scale.

The key concept is dependent upon this interval assumption, and is a variation on the idea of demand elasticity from market theory. A demand elasticity measures the percentage change in the quantity of a good that will be sold for a given percentage change in price. Formally, it is defined as $(\Delta Q/\Delta P) \times (P/Q)$, where Q is the quantity sold, P is the price at which the units are sold, and Δ is the standard symbol for "amount of change in."[2] A calculated value of less than one is referred to as unresponsive or *inelastic*; values greater than one indicate an *elastic* market situation.

The article demonstrates how different distributions of preference greatly affect the stability of the system. If most members are concentrated toward the middle of the distribution and the intervals between their most preferred positions are thus slight, the shift of a few votes from one side to the other (a small change in price) will make little difference in the actual policy outcome (the quantity "sold"). But if most members are crowded into the extremes, so that the intervals between the preferred

---

[1] (Cambridge: Cambridge University Press, 1958). Except for Figs. 1 and 2, the graphs in the following selection are reproduced from the book rather than from the article.

[2] The formula is equivalent to

$$\frac{(\Delta Q/Q)}{(\Delta P/P)}$$

and also to the reciprocal of the slope of the demand curve, times P/Q. An important extension of the idea is that of "cross-elasticities" measuring the substitutibility of one product for another, or

$$\frac{(\Delta Q_A/Q_A)}{(\Delta P_B/P_B)}$$

policies of those few near the center are great, the shift of just a few votes will result in a marked change in policy as measured on the interval scale. In short, if the entire distribution of voters by preference is essentially normal or bell-shaped, the demand elasticity for the vote of a single "voter" or nation in an international organization will be low, and the system will be stable; if it is bimodal, the system is likely to be quite unstable. There is some reason to think that most salient preference distributions manifested in the United Nations have in recent years been bimodal.[3] It may also be true in international politics more generally, though outside of one-nation one-vote representative bodies like the General Assembly, the neutralists are relatively weak in power bases such as wealth or military strength. Their weakness makes a bipolar system fairly insensitive to the neutralists' shifts, and, hence, less unstable than it would be if many of the middle countries represented a potential major increment to the power of either side.

This concept of elasticity is a valuable one with many applications to political and economic problems. Economists also speak of other elasticities, such as the supply elasticity (the additional proportion of a good that will be supplied by producers in response to a given percentage change in price), and the income elasticity (the percentage change in the quantity of a particular good that will be consumed in response to a given percentage change in income), and import and export elasticities for foreign trade. In the *World Handbook of Political and Social Indicators*[4] we illustrated one limited (cross-sectional) way of estimating income elasticities for developing countries—for example, the increased amount of mass communication and medical facilities that would be consumed for given rises in income levels. Actually, the elasticity is the same as the

[3] Cf. H. R. Alker and B. M. Russett, *World Politics in the General Assembly* (New Haven: Yale University Press, 1964), Ch. 10. A. Downs, *An Economic Theory of Democracy* (New York: Harper & Row, 1957), also makes valuable use of conclusions drawn from different preference distributions. He is primarily concerned, however, with the consequent distribution of political party positions and whether the parties will be highly differentiated and antagonistic, or Tweedledum and Tweedledee. Despite the great importance and interest of Downs' work, I have not reprinted any selections from it in this book because I assume that most political scientists are by now familiar with it. Also, some of his assumptions are very restrictive in the application to empirical systems. See D. Stokes, "Spatial Models of Party Competition," *American Political Science Review*, **57** (1963), pp. 368–377. Major predecessors for Downs' work are H. Hotelling, "Stability in Competition," *Economic Journal*, **39**, 1 (1929), pp. 4–57, and A. Smithies, "Optimum Location in Spatial Competition," *Journal of Political Economy*, **49** (1941), pp. 423–439. Gordon Tullock, in *Toward a Mathematics of Politics* (Ann Arbor: University of Michigan Press, 1967), pp. 50–61, adapts the Downs argument to cases where voters differ on two issue dimensions.

[4] B. M. Russett et al., *World Handbook of Political and Social Indicators* (New Haven: Yale University Press, 1964), pp. 299–301.

B-weight in a regression analysis, measuring the slope[5] of the regression line (the change along the vertical axis in response to a given change along the horizontal axis). While elasticities are sometimes treated as though they were linear functions, the same whatever the point along the supply or demand schedule one touched, this is of course an oversimplification. As in familiar regression analysis, the assumption of a curvilinear relationship is often more realistic.[6] A virtue of Black's article is the use of such a relationship.

●

[5] Actually, the reciprocal of the slope times P/Q.

[6] While we often use linear demand curves, this does not mean that elasticity is linear also. Actually, a linear demand curve has a constantly changing elasticity.

6

The Elasticity of Committee Decisions with Alterations in the Members' Preference Schedules

Duncan Black

1. The Fundamental Notions

The technique of orthodox economics can be employed to find what the decision of a committee will be. We have shown this elsewhere, but for the sake of making the present discussion self-contained, we will briefly recapitulate the nature of our findings.

The assumptions are that in a committee with a given number of members, say n members, a given number of motions, say m motions, have been put forward. The motions can be denoted by $a_1, a_2, \ldots, a_n$. Each member of the committee is assumed to rank the motions in some definite order of preference: this order of preference can be different for each member of the committee, and we assume that the committee is reaching its decision by the use of a simple majority.

If in a particular committee four motions a_1, a_2, a_3, and a_4 have been put forward, and the member "A" prefers a_3 to any of the others, is indifferent as between a_1 and a_4, and prefers either a_1 or a_4 to a_2, his scale of valuations can be represented by a vertical schedule as in Fig. 1. In this schedule, the point denoting a_3 is placed higher than the point

Reprinted from *South African Journal of Economics*, **17**, 1 (March 1949), pp. 88–100.

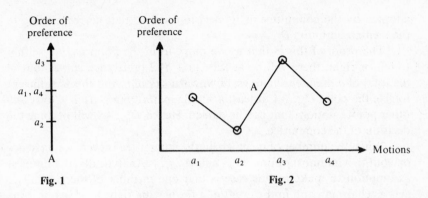

Fig. 1   Fig. 2

denoting a_1 or the point denoting a_4; the points denoting a_1 and a_4 are placed at the same level; and the point denoting a_2 is placed at a lower level. The member's name "A" is placed below the schedule. Or we may represent the same scale of valuations on a two-dimensional diagram such as Fig. 2. In this diagram, the motions a_1, a_2, a_3, and a_4 are represented by points on a horizontal axis, while order of preference is again shown in a vertical direction. In drawing a diagram of this type, the rule observed is that if, of any two motions a_h, a_k, a given member prefers a_h to a_k, then a_h must stand at a higher level on his preference curve than a_k. Or, if the member should be indifferent, as between a_h and a_k, the two motions must stand at the same level on his preference curve. It will be seen that Figs. 1 and 2 are equivalent to each other.

Either of the schedules that we have given will not only be a schedule of valuations but also a voting schedule. The member "A," for instance, prefers a_3 to a_1; and if a_1 were to be put in a vote against a_3, he would vote for a_3 which he prefers. Or, if a_1 and a_4 should meet in a vote, being indifferent between the two, he would abstain from voting.

We have already argued that in some important types of problem, particularly in economic problems, it will often be possible to arrange the motions on the horizontal axis in such a way that the preference curve of every member becomes single peaked. In these circumstances it will be true of any member that there is one motion—i.e., an optimum value— that he prefers to any other; and the further any motion lies from his optimum, either to right or left, the less preferred to him will it be.

Let us take a committee in which n, the number of members, is odd, and in which the preference scale of each member can be represented by a single-peaked curve. And let us name the optima of the members $O_1, O_2, \ldots, O_n$ in the order of their occurrence as we move along the horizontal axis from left to right. In these circumstances the motion adopted by the committee as its decision will be that corresponding to the median optimum $O_{(n+1)/2}$.

The proof of this is that as we move from the point $O_{(n+1)/2}$ either to left or right, there will be at least $(n+1)/2$ preference curves, out of the total of n preference curves, downward sloping. And this is sufficient to give the point $O_{(n+1)/2}$ at least a simple majority $(n+1)/2 : n$ over any other point (motion) that can be named. Hence, $O_{(n+1)/2}$ will become the decision of the committee.

When the number of members in the committee is even, we have not one but two midmost optima, $O_{n/2}$ and $O_{(n/2)+1}$. Analytically, the simplest assumption to make in this case is that one member of the committee acts as chairman and in the event of a tie, has the right to a casting vote. Then, if the optimum of the chairman's curve lies at or to the left of $O_{n/2}$, $O_{n/2}$ becomes the decision of the committee; or, if the chairman's optimum lies at or to the right of $O_{(n/2)+1}$, $O_{(n/2)+1}$ becomes the decision of the committee. Proof is almost identical with that for the preceding case. When we know which member acts as chairman of the committee, the result again becomes determinate.

To give examples, the upper part of Fig. 3 (discussed later) depicts the preference curves of the seven members A–G of a committee. The curves are of the single-peaked type, each curve having attached to it the name of the member whose curve it is; but, since the decision of the committee depends only on the location of the peaks of the curves, only the peaks are shown, and the remainders of the curve have been omitted. The optima of the curves, each corresponding to the peak of the curve for the member in question, are $O_1 \ldots O_7$. We have proved previously that the decision adopted by the committee will be O_4. When there is an even number of members in the committee, as in the circumstances represented in the upper part of Fig. 4 (discussed later), the decision adopted by the committee will be O_3 or O_4, according as the chairman's optimum lies at or to the left of O_3, or else at or to the right of O_4.

These explanations have been somewhat condensed, but will, I hope, be enough to carry the reader through the subsequent argument. To begin with we will consider the case in which the members' preference curves are all of the single-peaked variety; and in the concluding section we will deal briefly with the more complicated case where the members' preference curves can be of any sort whatever.

2. When the Members' Preference Curves Are Single Peaked

To illustrate the type of problem which we wish to consider, we may take the example of a cartel. Let us suppose that price-fixing in this cartel is

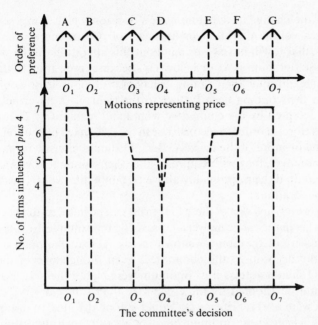

Fig. 3

done once a year by a committee which uses a simple majority. And let us suppose that at a meeting of this committee, the basic phenomena—the demand for its product and its cost position—leave the position of each firm identical with what it had been at the corresponding meeting a year earlier. The preference schedule of each firm in regard to price will be identical with its preference schedule of the earlier date. Unless some new source of change is introduced, the same price as before will be selected. One or more of the firms, we may suppose, are pondering the chance of being able to influence the decision of the cartel by inducing others, through enticement or threat, to alter their voting behavior at the next meeting of the committee. The enticement may be the offer of some trading or business advantage, or the threat may be to leave the cartel and enter into competition with the remaining members. The particular concern here is to examine and, if possible, to measure the effect on the committee's decision when some of the members alter their voting.

First we take the case when the number of members in the committee is odd. Let us suppose that there are seven firms, A, B, . . . , G, in the cartel voting on price, each with a single-peaked scale of preferences. When each voted in accordance with its scale of preferences, the decision accepted would be O_4, correspond to the median optimum. (See upper part of Fig. 3). Now, if a firm whose optimum is above O_4, is considering the extent of the change in the committee's decision which it can secure by inducing a voting alteration on the part of one or more other firms, it is clear that it will have to bring about this alteration on the part of a firm whose optimum is at or below O_4, because, even though the firms E, F, G should alter their voting behavior, voting as they would have done had their optima been further to the right of O, nevertheless, the decision accepted by the committee would still remain O_4. The requirement, therefore, in order to secure a rise in the price fixed by the committee, is that one or more of the firms A, B, C, D should alter their manner of voting; moreover, they will require to alter their voting to the extent that they would do if their optima lay above O_4; only thus will O_4 cease to be the median optimum.

If, however, any one of these four firms can be induced to vote as if its optimum lay in the range between O_4 and O_5, for example, to vote as if its optimum were at the point a shown in Fig. 3, then the point a would become the decision of the committee. Even though one of the firms A, B, C, D should vote as if its optimum were higher than O_5, no higher price would be adopted by the committee than if it had voted as if its optimum were at O_5, because O_5 would still be the median optimum.

Thus, a firm whose optimum lies at or above O_5 can alter the decision of the committee to the point a, where $O_4 < a \leq O_5$, by inducing one firm whose optimum lies below O_5, to a vote as if it had an optimum at a.

To bring into existence a decision higher than O_5, it is sufficient if two of the firms whose optima lie at or below O_5 are induced to vote as if their optima lay at some point between O_5 and O_6. By getting two of the firms A, B, C, D, E to vote as if they have common optima at the point b, say, where $O_5 < b < O_6$, the committee's decision can be altered from O_4 to b.

Similarly, the committee's decision can be brought to a point such as c, where $O_6 < c \leq O_7$, if three of the firms with optima below O_7 can be brought to vote as if they have common optima at c.

If a firm with optima below O_4 wishes to move the committee decision from O_4 to some lower point, corresponding conclusions will apply.

The effect produced on the committee decision by influencing the voting behavior of 1, 2, 3 firms, so that they vote as if they had common optima, is represented in the lower part of Fig. 3. In this diagram, along the horizontal axis the decision of the committee is shown, and along the vertical axis four *plus* the number of firms whose voting behavior must be altered in order to produce the result shown in the horizontal axis. This diagram is a summary of the entire position. It is to be read in conjunction with our finding that if the decision of the committee is to be raised to the point h, say, where $h > O_{(n+1)/2}$, the members whose voting

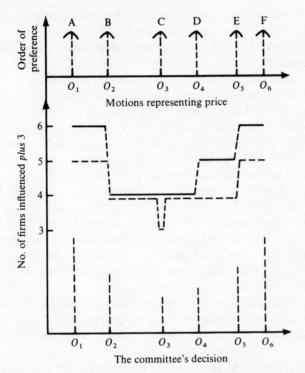

The broken curve applies if B, the chairman, is among the members influenced.
The continuous curve applies if B is not among the members influenced.

Fig. 4

behavior must be influenced, will be those with optima below h; or, if the decision is to be altered to a point k, where $k < O_{(n+1)/2}$, the members influenced must have optima above k.

(Throughout this part of the discussion our supposition is that the members influenced to alter their voting behavior vote as if they all have their optima at a common point. In practice this might not be so, and the members may be influenced so that they vote as if their optima were displaced, and located at different points on the horizontal axis. The effect which this produces in altering the decision of the committee could then be got by comparing the median optimum among the final curves with the original position of the median optimum.)

When the number of members in the committee is even, the effects are similar. Let us suppose that there are six members in the committee, with optima situated as in the upper part of Fig. 4; and let B be the chairman. The decision of the committee, if the members voted in accordance with the preference curves shown, would be O_3.

The members A and B can bring the decision of the committee to any point between O_2 and O_3 (the point O_2 included), provided they can induce one of the other members to vote as if his optimum lay at this point.

A can bring the committee's decision to any point between O_1 and O_2 (the point O_1 included), provided he can induce B, the chairman, and any one of the other members C, D, E, F to vote as if they had their optima at this point; or if he is unable to influence B, provided he can induce any three of the members C, D, E, F to vote as if their optima lay at this point. Influencing two members other than B to vote as if their optima lay at a point between O_1 and O_2 would not be sufficient to make this point the decision of the committee, because there would then be three optima effective to the left of B's optimum O_2, and three effective at or above O_2. With B as chairman this would leave O_2 as the decision.

To raise the committee's decision to a point between O_3 and O_4 (O_4 included), it would be sufficient to induce one of the members A, B, or C to vote as if his optimum lay at such a point.

To raise the decision to a point between O_4 and O_5 (O_5 included), it would be sufficient to induce any two of the members A, C, or D to vote as if their optima lay there, or to induce B alone to vote as if his optimum lay there.

The decision could be brought to any point between O_5 and O_6 (O_6 included), by inducing either three of the members A, C, D, E to vote as if their optima lay there, or by inducing one of these members and B to vote as if their optima lay there.

The position is set out in the lower part of Fig. 4, where the decision adopted by the committee is shown along the horizontal axis, and along the vertical axis we show 3 *plus* the number of members influenced. To the left of the chairman's optimum, and again to the right of O_4, the curve is double-branched, and the branch which applies depends on whether or not the chairman has been among the members influenced. When the chairman has been influenced, it is the curve shown as a broken line which applies.

Sometimes, as in the instances just presented, it would be possible to apply the theory to compare the movement as between one recorded decision of the committee and another. Or the theory might sometimes cover the phenomena which occur where there is only a single recorded decision. For example, trade union representatives who are deciding on hours of labor or wage rates, may be influenced late in the meeting, after their preference schedules have already been formed, by another speaker; and their preference schedules may be formed anew. The comparison

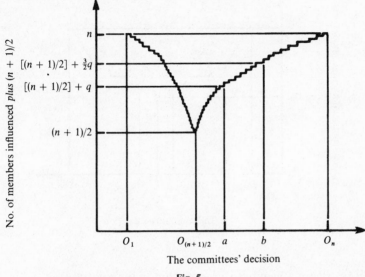

The committees' decision

Fig. 5

used by our theory now would be, not between one recorded decision and another but between the decision reached after this speaker has addressed them and the decision which would have been reached had the representatives voted before his speech was made. Similarly, the theory would apply where a member was addressing Parliament late in the debate and influencing the preference schedules, as so far formed, of the other members of the House. The comparison would be between the decision reached in a vote after the member's speech has influenced the preference schedules of the members and the decision which would have been reached in a vote before his speech was made.[1]

Let us now consider further the type of curve that appears in the lower part of Figs. 3 and 4. The properties of such a curve can be better examined from the instance shown in Fig. 5. In this diagram, for simplicity, n is taken as odd. From O_1 to the point a lying to the right of $O_{(n+1)/2}$, the curve is comparatively rigid; and to the right of a is comparatively elastic. The significance of this is that if a member of the committee whose optimum is to the left of $O_{(n+1)/2}$ (being, say, in the neighborhood of O_1), is able to influence a given number of members with optima to the right of $O_{(n+1)/2}$ so that they vote as if their optima were lower than this, the decision of the committee would alter comparatively little. The same

---

[1] Like the firms in the cartel, the members of Parliament can influence the decision by preaching "not to the converted but to the unconverted."

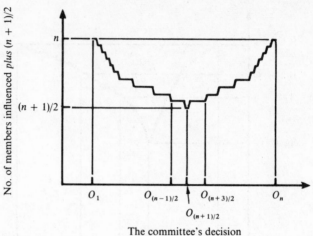

The committee's decision

Fig. 6

would be true of a member with optimum to the right of $O_{(n+1)/2}$ (being, say in the neighborhood of O_n), as regards the first members whose voting he managed to influence: in the diagram he would have to influence b members to alter the committee's decision from $O_{(n+1)/2}$ to a. But after this each increase in the number of members whose voting was influenced would bring a comparatively large change in the decision of the committee; and influencing an additional $b/2$ members would shift the decision considerably to the right to the point c. If it were found readily possible to influence b members, the member instigating the change might exert himself strenuously to influence still more of them.

A case which may easily arise in practice is that in which the bulk of the members have optima lying toward the extremities of the range, and only a few have optima in the region between. The diagram would then tend to be like that shown in Fig. 6. In these circumstances there is a very precarious balance ready to swing violently in favor of whichever side manages to influence the voting of a few members with optima at $O_{(n+1)/2}$ or beyond it. Mathematically it is of no consequence whether the members influenced are those with optima in the center of the range or not; but the shift needed in their voting behavior to alter the balance is less than that for other members, and in practice it might be mainly they who were subjected to inducement or threat. They would be in the position too, to make the change less obtrusively than other members, and they would run less risk of ostracism. Thus, the small center parties in a committee or coalition will sometimes be subject to extreme pressure from the wings; and at the same time they will sometimes hold the key to power. The diagram has possibilities that might have interested Machiavelli.

With the balance thus precarious, it would sometimes be easier for one of the parties of the extremities to bring about a change in his favor by introducing new members; or, less easy than this as a rule, by eliminating some of the existing members. New allies with a community of interests would be more dependable than those whose support had to be won, and they would be cheaper. Strictly speaking, however, this consideration is extraneous to the present discussion, in which the number of members is assumed constant.

Let us now suppose that the number of members in the committee becomes sufficiently large, with their optima sufficiently evenly distributed, so that the curve of the lower part of Fig. 3 can be regarded as smooth, or the two curves of Fig. 4 can be regarded as smooth and coincident. And as before, let us assume that the committee is discussing the size of some measurable variable such as price.

Granted this, we can introduce an index of the shape of the curve at each point, that will show the proportionate extent to which the committee's decision alters in response to a given increase in the proportion of members influenced. Let us denote the number of members influenced by N and the committee's decision by a. A suitable index to show the effect is:

$$e = \frac{+da}{-dy} \cdot \frac{y}{a}$$

where

$$y = \frac{n+1}{2} + N$$

for n odd, $\{O \leq N \leq [(n-1)/2]\}$, or

$$y = \frac{n}{2} + N$$

for n even, $[O \leq N \leq (n/2)]$; the *plus* or *minus* sign to apply according as a is increasing or diminishing when N increases. This is, in fact, a measure of point elasticity, precisely similar to that used in economics to show the alteration in quantity sold in response to an alteration in price.

If we chose, we could take one value of the coefficient, namely, unity, as the critical case, and regard curves with elasticity less than unity as being rigid and those with elasticity greater than unity as being elastic. Cournot, the first economist to investigate the matter, saw that the case in which elasticity is equal to unity has an exact and important meaning when we are dealing with economic phenomena : but when we are dealing with committee decisions, less importance attaches to unit elasticity, and it becomes more necessary to specify the numerical measure of the elasticity of the curve in question. That is, the broad distinction of curves into elastic and rigid, such as is employed in economics, would be less useful in politics.

The general interpretation of the index that we have given will be familiar from economics. If for a particular point on a curve the measure of elasticity is, say, 2, then a 1 percent increase in y will give rise to an alteration of 2 percent in the size of the variable that represents the committee decision. Other values of the coefficient would be similarly interpreted. Also, it is clear that, *ceteris paribus*, the greater the elasticity of a curve, the greater will be the inducement to some members of the committee to bring about alterations in the voting of others. The members who will be keenest to alter the voting will be those whose optima lie toward the extremities of the range. This is the practical significance of the coefficient and the ideas underlying it.

Quite a number of recent works, in international politics and in empirical political theory more generally, have explored the problems of coalition-building and alliance formation.[1] The Olson and Zeckhauser piece dealt with how costs and benefits might be distributed within an alliance, and the article by Buchanan touched upon the question of the ultimate size of the alliance. But in both papers the basic composition of the alliance, or at least its core, was already given. A general theory of alliance formation will have to deal with all of these variables at once. In the next article, John Cross indicates some of the difficulties in building such a general theory, but shows the outlines of how it can be done with either of two alternative sets of assumptions. He refers briefly to the potential contribution of game theory but on the whole relies upon the more traditional tools of economic analysis.

In one of his models it is possible to derive a determinant solution for the payoffs (benefits) accruing to each member of a winning coalition. Since there is only one possible distribution of payoffs with the assumptions, analysis of the bargaining process is unnecessary. But this procedure is not able to tell *which players* will be incorporated in the winning alliance, only the distribution of payoffs among members in the abstract. The other model does provide an answer to the question of who will be in the victorious coalition, though the solution is complex and the membership is not at all obvious to casual perusal. This model does not, however, solve for the distribution of the payoffs, since the distribution depends, in this formulation, on the characteristics of the bargaining process that must be known. The article helps to indicate both some of the opportunities available to political analysis and the substantial task remaining before a generally useful theory can be built.

---

[1] In international politics see G. Liska, *Nations in Alliance* (Baltimore: Johns Hopkins University Press, 1962): H. J. Morgenthau, *Politics Among Nations* (New York: Knopf, 3rd ed., 1960), Part 4: and R. Dawson and R. Rosecrance, "Theory and Reality in the Anglo-American Alliance," *World Politics*, **19**, 1 (1966), pp. 21–53. For more general theoretical statements see, *inter alia*, W. A. Gamson, "Theory of Coalition Formation," *American Sociological Review*, **26**, 3 (1961), pp. 373–382, "An Experimental Test of a Theory of Coalition Formation," *American Sociological Review*, **36**, 4 (1961), pp. 565–573, and "Coalition Formation at Presidential Nomination Conventions," *American Journal of Sociology*, **58**, 2 (1962), pp. 157–171: M. Leiserson, *Coalitions in Politics: A Theoretical and Empirical Study* (New Haven: Yale University, Ph.D. Dissertation, 1966): W. Riker, *A Theory of Political Coalitions* (New Haven: Yale University Press, 1962) and B. M. Russett, "Components of an Operational Theory of International Alliance Formation," *Journal of Conflict Resolution*, **12**, 4 (1968), in press.

7
Some Theoretic Characteristics of Economic and Political Coalitions

John G. Cross

This paper represents an attempt to make use of a few postulates which are frequently found in economic theory, and to achieve thereby some insights into an important problem in the theory of political interactions—the formation of coalitions. It is suggested that the same competitive process which constrains market behavior has, in reality, an equally important role in the determination of alliances, and that the search for a "best" alliance is no different in principle from the search for a lowest price. The resulting analysis will be found to apply to a wide variety of alliance situations provided that two fundamental premises are satisfied: (1) alliance members are motivated by a desire to maximize the value (to themselves) of their membership,[1] and (2) membership in one grouping *precludes* membership in another, that is, choice among alternatives must be a dominant problem.[2]

Reprinted from *Journal of Conflict Resolution*, **11**, 2 (June 1967), pp. 184–195.

[1] The theory itself requires only existence of preferences and preference maximization, but if its predictions are to be confirmed or rejected, some means must be found to *observe* the values of coalition membership. In some cases, this is becoming possible: the value of an international trade agreement might reasonably be approximated by the consequent increase in trade volume, the value of a political agreement may be associated with the number of times one's own position prevails, or even by one's share of the pork-barrel, and so on.

[2] Most cases of alliances—military coalitions, voting blocs, economic transactions,

We postulate that each party will attempt to gain for himself the most that the situation will allow. Thus, we imagine that the potential member of a military alliance would normally prefer a stronger defense force to a weaker one, the member of a voting bloc would prefer to win rather than to lose, the firm would prefer higher profits to lower, and so on.[3] No one will join or remain a member of a coalition if he feels that he can do better elsewhere, or, indeed, if he feels he would be better off alone, outside all coalitions. This seeking of a "best" alliance makes possible the dynamic process of competition. If a coalition finds that the value of a potential ally exceeds the payoff which he is currently receiving elsewhere, it is possible to make him a bid which will induce him to join, other things being equal. Conversely, the members of any coalition which finds that a crucial member is likely to transfer to some other alliance can attempt to retain his membership, if possible, by increasing his share of the value of the agreement. In general, increasing the payoff to any member will entail reductions in the shares (or expected shares) of the other members.[4] The process of competition does *not* require that any individual be able to measure the gains which are realized by any other; it requires only that one be able to formulate an offer and then observe whether or not it is accepted.

It is generally true in the simplest economic models that the outcome of the competitive process will satisfy the condition of "Pareto optimality": that is, coalitions will not yield expected gains to any member which are lower than those which would be warranted (i.e., made available) by the expected gains of the other allies.[5] In the case of members for whom there is continuing competition, the outcome must possess this property because no coalition will waste bidding power by bidding less than it can,

---

etc.—do seem to have the property of excluding coalitions which would be possible otherwise. France can join NATO, the Warsaw Pact, or neither, but once one of these three alternatives is chosen, the other two are out of the question, at least for the time being.

[3] One might, of course, wish to qualify the "stronger defense force" with the notion of a "minimal winning coalition": that coalition which yields the greatest gains to its members. This simply inserts another objective for that of over-all force, a substitution which is perfectly compatible with the theory.

[4] It may be, of course, that other allies can be induced to lower their own expected gains through subsequent negotiations, increasing the payoff to the new member. Expectations of such modifications of payoff would be taken into account in calculating the value of membership.

[5] In other words, if George and Sidney are dividing a ten-dollar bill and George receives $6, Sidney will not receive $3 (which wastes $1) but $4. Another definition of Pareto optimality may be a "condition in which it is impossible to make one member of a given coalition better off (e.g. by increasing George's share) without making another worse off (e.g., by decreasing Sidney's share)." The two definitions are perfectly equivalent. See Baumol (1965), pp. 376–377.

after satisfying the demands of the other members. Without competition, Pareto optimality is not so easily satisfied: if Sidney has no alternative alliance possibilities, George could conceivably divide $10 with him by keeping $5, giving Sidney $3, and throwing away the rest. Our model contains no incentives for such behavior, however, and we rely upon George's good will (and upon Sidney's insistence on the best return he can get) to give us a Pareto-optimal split in this case as well.[6]

Despite the close relationship between a party's desire to maximize his return and the presence of a competitive bidding process, it is important to keep the distinction between these two hypotheses clear. The first states that each individual will select from the whole set of feasible coalitions that one which will give him the highest possible return *given* the demands or payoff expectations of the necessary allies. The coalitions which would have to form in order to yield these maximal returns to all individuals, however, may be incompatible with one another. The association which would yield the highest return to Albert may require the membership of Sidney, and Sidney may also be essential to Bill's alliance; hence the satisfaction of the expectations of both Albert and Bill is impossible. The second hypothesis deals with the *response* of individuals to such incompatible expectations, suggesting that competition will arise for "scarce" members (e.g., Sidney). Careful specification of this relationship is important because, as is well known in the literature on the theory of games, coalition problems have the property that *there may not exist any set of coalitions and associated maximal payoff expectations which are compatible with one another.*[7] To the economist, this is an unfamiliar conclusion. His models of simple competitive markets have generally represented situations in which every individual was able to buy or sell whatever he wished at going prices.[8] Unfortunately, as we shall see, these situations arise only as special cases of our system.

1. Solution of the Coalition Model—an Example

The purpose of this theory is to determine as nearly as possible (a) which coalitions are likely to form in a given situation and (b) what

---

[6] The reader may be interested in the theory of the "bargaining set," which contains an approach to the coalition problem which is rather different from this one. The major contrast between the two is that the bargaining set payoffs are not Pareto-optimal. See Aumann and Maschler (1964).

[7] In game-theoretic terms, the "core" of the game—the set of all *feasible* payoff configurations which satisfy the maximum demand hypothesis—may be empty. See Luce and Raiffa (1957), pp. 192–196.

[8] Many analyses have been performed of so-called "market games" (which, unfortunately, have relatively little to do with markets). The cores of these games are not empty. For example and further references, see Shapley (1959).

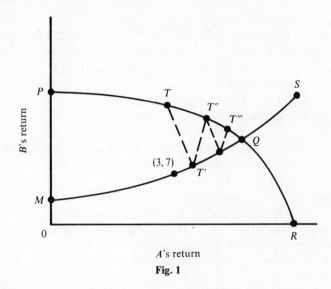

Fig. 1

payoffs (expected gains) are likely to accrue to the members of those alliances. As in the case of economic models which make use of competitive processes, we expect these factors to be determined within an "equilibrium" framework. There will prove to be a set of coalition configurations which can be called "stable"; that is, any deviation from one of these configurations will set up (competitive) forces tending to restore it (or some other stable configuration). The set of all stable coalition configurations with their associated payoffs to members will be called our "solution."

Figure 1 represents diagrammatically a simple three-person situation in which any two individuals may form a coalition. The two axes in the diagram represent the returns to A and to B, respectively. These may be measured in whatever units are relevant to the problem: dollars, political power, expected number of political or military victories, expected increase in trade volume, etc. The curve PQR bounds the distribution of possible gains to members of the two-person coalition $[A, B]$. The set represented here is convex and continuous, but these conditions impose no serious restrictions on the model.[9] Any distribution of returns within the boundary PQR is possible, but if we employ our Pareto optimality assumption (i.e., that the players will not "throw away" value) we must use the frontier PQR itself as the only set of outcome alternatives relevant to the alliance $[A, B]$.

[9] The curve PQR is defined only in the positive quadrant. We consider nonmembership in any alliance always to be an available alternative to a player, and we consider all benefits from other agreements to be measured from this as an origin. The curve PQR is a graphic representation of the set of Pareto-optimal payoffs from the coalition $[A, B]$.

The positively sloped line MQS represents combinations of returns to A and to B which would leave the third potential ally indifferent between the two coalitions $[A, C]$ and $[B, C]$ (assuming Pareto optimality in these cases also). For example, a demand of \$10 on the part of C may leave a maximum possible return to A of \$7 from the coalition $[A, C]$ and a maximum possible return to B of \$3 from the coalition $[B, C]$. Thus, the curve MQS must pass through the point $(3, 7)$. The gain to the third player diminishes as we move away from the origin along MQS. The curve MQS may or may not pass through the origin: it is perfectly possible for $[B, C]$ to be capable of a maximum return to C which exceeds the capacity of the alliance $[A, C]$.

As the figure is drawn, the payoff to the third player, C, is determined implicitly, while the payoffs to the other two players can be read off the diagram directly. This asymmetry arises only because it leads to the simplest possible diagram. Any two of the three players could have been represented on the axes and no asymmetry whatever is intended in the following analysis.

Suppose that A and B have tentatively settled on the coalition $[A, B]$ with their returns divided as shown at point T in Fig. 1. This agreement, of course, leaves C out altogether. The latter, however, can make a better offer to A through the coalition $[A, C]$ if the split is described by some point such as T'. Now, suppose that A and C have tentatively settled on the coalition $[A, C]$ with their returns divided as shown at Point T'. B can respond to this alliance by attempting to bid away either A or C. Since in this case A is making a relatively low bid, we expect B to try to form the alliance $[A, B]$ again and not to unite with C; given the current demand of C, $[B, C]$ could yield only a much lower return to B. For the same reason, C will retaliate by again bidding for $[A, C]$. Thus, since A happens to be making the relatively low bid, the other two compete for his allegiance, increasing his payoff in the process. This sequence (or *tâtonnement*) will follow a path such as that which is described by the dashed line $T\ T'\ T''\ T'''\ldots$, and which will eventually converge to the intersection at Q.

The model described by Fig. 1 may be characterized by a number of features. First, the sequence $T\ T'\ T''\ldots$ leads to a *unique* intersection at Q. The model implies that the gains to be realized from coalition membership are completely determined by the environment (which determines the values of the alliances). The conclusion may come as something of a surprise, for it contrasts sharply with many other analyses of examples similar to this (e.g., examples of three-person constant-sum games) which have concluded that the payoffs to coalition members are completely indeterminate. Indeterminacy is often suggested because any player who is left out can attempt to join an alliance simply by asking for a payoff lower than that shown at point Q and bidding away one of the other two players.[10] In this model, however, such a reduction will simply lead to competition for that player, restoring his higher payoff.

Second, we find ourselves in complete uncertainty as to which coalition will form. The gains associated with Q are compatible with any one of three possible alliances, and hence at this point each of the three individuals is totally indifferent between the two alternatives which are available to him. Even after the players have settled on the demands determined at Q, we might expect the coalition-formation process to include oscillation among feasible groupings before a final alliance is settled upon. In practice, we still expect such oscillations to have their limits: the costs associated with making and breaking agreements are presumably sufficient to inject some stability into most alliance systems. On the other hand, the potential of the model for easy rearrangements of the coalitions is an important property of the "solution."

Third, we observe that by the very nature of the situation, one of the three players must receive nothing at all. The odd man may attempt to ensure his own membership through a reduction in his bid, but this will simply set the other two to competing for his allegiance, bidding his return back up again. At best, he can displace one of the other two, but then we simply have a different player as "odd man." Thus, despite perfectly reasonable bids—that is, despite each player's ability to point to a possible coalition which would yield to him his own bid—the situation arbitrarily reduces one man's gain to zero. This is an example of the possibility which was brought up at the end of the last section: the optimum demand hypothesis has been satisfied, but the competitive process, although it does determine the distribution of gains to coalition members, can *never* lead to a set of expectations which are mutually consistent. Although this case may seem disturbing at first, the phenomenon is quite common, a fact to which anyone who has ever been odd man in the choosing of childhood baseball teams could probably testify.

The conclusion that one potential member must be excluded is a simple result of the arithmetic of the example. If only one two-party alliance is permitted in a group of three, obviously somebody must be left out. It is important to recognize that this property is quite inessential

[10] For examples, see Rapoport (1960), pp. 198–210. The original treatment of such problems by von Neumann and Morgenstern (1953, pp. 288–290) concluded that the payoffs are indeterminate, although they chose to distinguish two different classes of outcomes, associating all coalition structures other than that corresponding to our point Q with social discrimination. This distinction, however, was not a consequence of any a priori differences in the two cases, but simply a description of the appearances of the two possible kinds of coalition configuration.

to the main conclusions of the model. Had a four-person game which permitted only two-person coalitions been used, there would be no odd man, and if this new situation were otherwise identical to the three-person case, the solution would have the same properties as before. (The curve PQR becomes a surface in three-dimensioned space, and the line MQS is again positively sloped and passes through this surface at some point Q.) Gains from coalition membership are uniquely determined, and again we have no notion as to *which* coalitions actually form.

A final feature of the example in Fig. 1 is the absence of any use for the bargaining process in the determination of a solution. It is widely accepted that within any alliance there is some room for negotiation among members over the division of the benefits of agreement. Thus, the United States has often attempted, through negotiation, to decrease its share in the expense of NATO, to improve its international trade position, to exert its influence in Latin America, and so on. It is tempting to conjecture that the frequent failure of such efforts is due to the fact that these alliances are imbedded in larger systems (such as that in our example), themselves composed of relatively similar participants, so that the distribution of payoffs is virtually determined already. Certainly, many such political coalitions should be looked upon as subject to a deterministic equilibrium rather than in terms of the bargaining process.[11]

2. Indeterminate Models and the Relevance of Negotiations

In Fig. 1, the line MQS moves away from the origin as the return to the third party, C, falls. This line always has a limit at some point S which corresponds to a zero return to C; that is, given the demands of A

[11] The term "bargaining process" here is meant to describe the distribution of payoffs through a voluntary sequence of bids and concessions *which are not prescribed already by the presence of alternative agreement possibilities*. If an automobile salesman lowers his price because I have received a lower bid from his competitor, that is not a bargaining concession, but a response to a market force. The dealer in this case has no choice. Unfortunately, this is a much more restrictive definition than those which frequently appear in the literature. In some cases the term has been used so loosely that it would be possible to refer to the sequence $T\,T'\,T''\ldots$ as a "bargaining process" despite the fact that it is forced upon the parties (in our theory) by the existence of alternative agreement possibilities. We would prefer to avoid using the term for any situations of this sort.

We have other reasons for suggesting that the international alliance system offers some good examples of this model. Not only are there several instances in which the bargaining process seems to be ineffective, but there is little evidence that alliances are predetermined by any established environmental conditions. Thus (admittedly casual) evidence suggests that international alliances shift far more frequently than changing cultures or even "national interests" would seem to justify, reflecting the "oscillatory" property which we discovered formally. Note that any possible "side payments" must be included in the specification of the payoff possibilities.

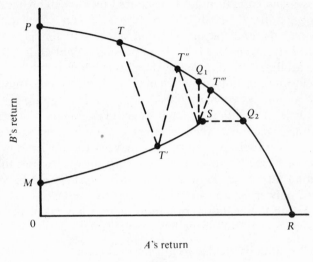

Fig. 2

and *B*, which are represented by the point *S*, the third player is indifferent among joining either of the two coalitions [*A*, *C*] and [*B*, *C*] and remaining alone. In the example used to construct Fig. 1, this point was placed out beyond the boundary *PQR*. Suppose that, as in Fig. 2, this is not the case. At first, the coalition-formation process will proceed just as before, the sequence of bids following the dashed path $T \ T' \ T''$, etc. At some point T''', however, within the range from Q_1 to Q_2, this sequence stops, for here the third participant is cut out altogether with an expected gain of zero (or less). Since alliance with *A* or *B* now would leave *C* with no gain, he can have no further influence over the choice of coalitions. Here the bargaining process certainly does become important, and we would have to turn to variables relevant to negotiation to determine the players' payoffs.[12] We have certainly lost the unique payoff determination which was implied by the first model. In return, however, some new information has been gained, for we can now predict *which* of the three possible coalitions will form! This determinism will always arise when bargaining ranges are possible, because, by definition, once the two (or more) players are within that range, there are no nonmembers who could profitably bid for their allegiance.

[12] Within the range Q_1Q_2 *any* set of payoffs is possible, no alternative agreement possibilities exist, and hence, in the terms of footnote 11, distribution is performed by the bargaining process. Some theories of the bargaining process do exist. See Cross (1965) and the references therein.

This second case, then, is characterized by a much higher degree of certainty regarding the coalition structure itself, less information on the value of payoffs, and the introduction of the bargaining process. We might add that in this case there is no possibility that an individual will be forced arbitrarily to receive less than his equilibrium expected payoff. Such exclusion can only arise when there is still competition among coalitions at our "solution" point(s), and this is not the case here.

This type of coalition structure is certainly common in experience. It can arise, for example, whenever some coalition is obviously preferred to others: geographic proximity may make a certain military alliance "natural" or I may buy from a certain supermarket because there is no other within fifty miles. However, such coalitions should be viewed as prominent only in an *ex post facto* sense; they may not be nearly so obvious before the coalition-formation process has taken place. As an example, consider the following five-person game:

1. All coalitions yield a fixed sum in dollars to be divided among members as they choose.
2. All coalitions are two-person coalitions.
3. The coalition (2, 4) pays \$14.
4. The coalitions (1, 2), (1, 4), (1, 5), (2, 5), and (4, 5) all pay \$12.
5. The coalitions (2, 3) and (3, 4) pay \$10.

Is it obvious to the reader which of these coalitions is "prominent" in the sense that it must always form? (The solution is in footnote 13 below.)

It is hoped that the example just presented has successfully pointed out an important analytical pitfall. It is very common to see particular alliances pointed out as "natural" ones which "obviously should have been expected to form." We are suggesting here that this "obviousness" has arisen largely as a *consequence* of the process of coalition formation. Moreover, if, as one might expect, the bargaining process generates a distribution of payoffs which is somewhere near the midpoint of the range $Q_1 Q_2$, an observer might conclude empirically that any third party who is unable to form a worthwhile alliance with either A or B is completely irrelevant to the system and hence could be disregarded totally; in fact, however, the determination of the range over which two allies may bargain is as important as the determination of the payoffs themselves, and thus the third individual must still play a critical role in the analysis.

A minor problem arises with regard to the end points Q_1 and Q_2. If A and B tentatively agreed upon a coalition with a division of payoffs

---

[13] The necessary coalition is (1, 5) with the payoffs $5 \leq P_1 \leq 7$; $P_1 + P_5 = 12$. One of the other three players is an odd man, and their equilibrium payoff demands are uniquely determined: $P_2 = 7$; $P_4 = 7$; $P_3 = 3$.

determined as at the point Q_1, then A could *threaten* B, maintaining that unless B reduced his return, A would join in the still possible alliance with C. This introduces a new process, different from simple competition, but whose plausibility is quite compelling. If we accept the effectiveness of this threat we must conclude that A's gain will always be higher than that represented at Q_1 and always lower than that represented at Q_2. As a consequence of eliminating these end points from our solution set, however, the bargaining range has the rather undesirable mathematical property of being open. Conceptually, this poses no problems, but in some cases, for the sake of simple mathematical solutions, this conclusion may have to be revised.

The two solutions depicted in Figs. 1 and 2 stand in strong contrast to one another. Characteristics relating to (1) the determinateness of the gains from membership, (2) the choice of the final coalition, and (3) the relevance or irrelevance of the bargaining process are sufficiently different to justify their classification into two separate cases.[14] Mixed cases, however, are still possible. Coalition systems can be constructed which contain a bargaining range for some parties and which determine the payoffs completely for others (a case in point is the example given on page 122 and in footnote 13). These cases can arise only in examples involving more than four players, and for these our simple diagrammatic approach is no longer satisfactory. Techniques do exist for solving larger problems, however, and one of these is given in the next section.

3. A Linear Analysis

The theory presented in the preceding sections is intended to be a perfectly general one and should not be restricted to three-person cases. The purpose of this section is to show by means of one particular solution

[14] This distinction, however, differs markedly from that which appears most commonly in the literature of game theory. There, the existence problem which was mentioned at the end of the first section (that is, whether or not there exists a set of coalitions and payoff expectations such that each player can receive his demand) takes on great interest. This problem arose in the first example simply as a piece of arithmetic which had no impact on the returns from coalition membership or on the other major features of the solution. There are two reasons for this difference in emphasis. First, we are looking at a somewhat different problem; our concern lies more with describing what the outcome of the coalition-formation process may be expected to be than with the normative problem of discovering what "strategies" may be most appropriate to a given situation. The existence of certain kinds of solutions would be of much greater importance to this latter type of study than it is to ours. Second, we have placed more emphasis upon the alliance structure itself. Since the existence problem has heretofore been a major stumbling block in theoretical studies of coalition problems, it is gratifying to be able to suggest that perhaps it is not of such central interest for the description of individual behavior.

technique (1) that the theory is general and not dependent upon the particular sequences of bids used for the examples, (2) that it is possible to apply the theory to specific problems which involve very large numbers of participants, and (3) that the theory may be fitted easily into the existing framework of the theory of games, deriving its "solution" directly from the characteristic function.[15]

The technique outlined here can be applied only to a certain class of problems: those in which all payoffs are expressed in common units (such as dollars) and in which these physical payoffs are fully transferable among members *within* one coalition.[16] Satisfaction of these conditions enables us to express the value of any coalition in terms of a fixed quantity of the payoff good and to compare directly the payoffs which a player can obtain from various alternative alliances (these are the properties of the "characteristic function" as well).

Define the constant V_k as the total value of the kth coalition and u_i as the payoff "demand" of the ith participant. The maximal return hypothesis states that each person will demand *at least* the largest payoff for himself which is consistent with the set of possible alliances and all the other players' demands. That is, for each player j:

$$u_j \geq \max_k \left(V_k - \sum_{\substack{i \in k \\ i \neq j}} u_i \right)$$

From this it follows immediately that

$$\sum_{i \in k} u_i \geq V_k \qquad \text{for all } k \tag{1}$$

The competitive process will tend to increase the payoff offers to any scarce player who is essential to two or more coalitions, and simultaneously it will tend to reduce the payoff expectations of other members of those coalitions. It is also true that competition will tend to reduce the arithmetic sum of *all* payoff demands.

Proof: Suppose two coalitions K and L both require the membership of a player (or group of players) m before they will be complete. If these coalitions are to form at all, and if Pareto optimality is to be

---

[15] For the definition and description of the characteristic function, see von Neumann and Morgenstern (1953), pp. 238–245, or Luce and Raiffa (1957), pp. 182–191.

[16] Thus if "side payments" are possible between two coalitions X and Y, we must define the possibility of a "grand coalition" $[X, Y]$. The conditions presented here are often satisfied in practice, especially when the problem has a predominantly economic dimension. They also characterize most empirical experimentation with coalition-formation behavior.

satisfied, we must have:

$$\sum_{\substack{i\in K \\ i\neq m}} u_i + u_m = V_k \qquad \sum_{\substack{i\in L \\ i\neq m}} u_i + u_m = V_L$$

(If there are several individuals who are essential for the formation of both K and L, u_m represents a summation of their payoffs.) Competition must *decrease* the two summation terms as it increases the payoff u_m. If we add the two equations together, we obtain:

$$\sum_{\substack{i\in K \\ i\neq m}} u_i + \sum_{\substack{i\in L \\ i\neq m}} u_i + 2u_m = V_K + V_L$$

The right-hand side of this equation is constant, and the competitive process increases u_m; therefore the expression:

$$\sum_{\substack{i\in K \\ i\neq m}} u_i + \sum_{\substack{i\in L \\ i\neq m}} u_i + u_m$$

must be decreasing. Since this expression represents the sum of the payoff demands of all (relevant) players, the proof is complete. (Note that no individuals are represented in both summation terms; all potential members of both K and L are included in the "player" m.)

Define M as the *maximum* sum of payoff demands of which the coalition situation is capable; that is, choose that set of *disjoint* coalitions (i.e., they could all exist simultaneously) which will generate the largest value for $\Sigma_{\text{all }i} u_i$ and represent that sum by M. The corresponding set of disjoint coalitions may be represented by the symbol N. By definition, if $\Sigma_{\text{all }i} u_i > M$, some payoff expectations are incompatible with one another, competition must ensue, and the sum of all payoff demands must fall as shown previously. Moreover, it is easy to show that if $\Sigma_{\text{all }i} u_i < M$ then there exists some coalition k whose members are asking *less* than V_k; i.e., we would have a contradiction to conditions (1).

Proof: By hypothesis, we would have the sum of all players' demands falling short of the sum of the values of all the disjoint coalitions in N. That is,

$$\sum_{\text{all }i} u_i < \sum_{k\in N} V_K \qquad (2)$$

We may proceed to remove coalitions from N one by one and examine them. Suppose we remove coalition k'. If $\Sigma_{i\in k'} u_i \geq V_{k'}$, the inequality in (2) above must be preserved for the remaining coalitions. Thus, we may delete coalitions from the sum until either a violation of (1) is found, or only one coalition remains: that last coalition must preserve the inequality in (2). This would then provide our contradiction of (1).

In conclusion, we find that the competitive process will always tend to reduce $\Sigma_{all\,i}\, u_i$ so long as that sum does not fall below M or, what we have shown to be the same thing, so long as conditions (1) are never violated. As it happens, a particularly simple means of expressing this fact is available through a linear programing model. The whole set of possible equilibrium payoff demands may now be described as all of the possible solutions to the linear program:

$$\min \sum_{all\,i} u_i$$

subject to:

$$\sum_{i \in k} u_i \geq V_k \qquad \text{for all } k$$

(Recall that when k contains only one member, $V_k = 0$.)

This model will generate the same solutions as will the models described in the previous sections. For example, in any experiment in which any coalition containing just two members receives $10, the program will yield a *unique* solution with all possible members demanding $5. If it is arithmetically possible, of course, everyone will receive $5 as a payoff; otherwise, as we have pointed out before, somebody will be left out. This unique solution may be characterized as one for which the objective function is minimized at a *vertex* of the constraint set. On the other hand, we may imagine a four-person example in which all pairs yield $10 except the pairs $[A, B]$ and $[C, D]$; these two return nothing at all. It is easy to show that the solution now yields a multitude of possible payoffs, all subject to the condition[17]

$$0 \leq u_a \qquad u_b = u_a \qquad 0 \leq u_c \qquad u_d = u_c$$

and

$$u_a + u_c = \$10$$

This solution arises when the minimum of $\Sigma_{all\,i}\, u_i$ occurs on a *facet* (rather than an intersection point alone) of the constraint set defined by (1).

It is a straightforward matter to construct the dual to the linear program which we have described.[18] The dual is a maximization model

[17] Note that u_a cannot fall below u_b because then players C and D will both shun player B and attempt to ally themselves with A instead—raising u_a and lowering u_b. Moreover, A and B no longer have the protecting coalition $[A, B]$ to prevent the sum of their two demands from falling below $5. The same two points apply to C and D.

[18] For the definition and construction of the dual program, see Baumol (1965), pp. 103–128.

which assigns weights W_k ("shadow prices") to the various possible coalitions in such a manner as to reflect the extent to which an increase in the value of the kth coalition would increase the value of $\Sigma_i u_i$. Naturally, these weights are positive with their values constrained between zero and one. Four possible situations may arise for each weight W_k:

1. $W_k = 1$ for all possible solutions to the dual: This condition implies that the coalition k must form.
2. $W_k = 0$ for all possible solutions to the dual: The coalition k never forms.
3. W_k can range from 0 to 1 (and some other weights $W_1, \ldots, W_m$ correspondingly range from 1 to 0): The coalition k may form; if it doesn't, some coalition(s) $1, \ldots, m$ will form instead.
4. $0 \leq W_k < 1$ and W_k is unique for all possible solutions to the dual: W_k may form. However, the fact that increasing V_k does not increase $\Sigma_i u_i$ correspondingly implies that in this solution some players not in k are depending upon potential members of k as allies—thus some players must be excluded in the solution.

In cases 1, 2, and 3 the coalitions never exclude players from the solution; in case 4, some players must be excluded.[19]

Case 1 represents the situation in which negotiation will occur; $W_k = 1$ if and only if k must form and, as we have seen, this will only arise in a solution for which no members of k have alternatives which are as attractive as k itself. For this case, there is one weakness of the linear programing solution: it includes the end points of the bargaining range (Q_1 and Q_2 in Fig. 2) as possible payoffs. The program, of course, deals only with closed sets, and hence the threat process which we introduced to exclude Q_1 and Q_2 cannot be incorporated into the model. In practice, however, the bargaining ranges should be readily identifiable, and exclusion of the end points would not be difficult.

The examples in Figs. 1 and 2 were used to characterize two different classes of solution. In more complex situations, of course, we may have mixed solutions, the payoffs of some alliances determined at a unique point, while other groups must participate in negotiations before dividing the returns. In terms of the dual of our linear program, some W_k may be fixed at 1 (negotiated outcome) while others are fixed at fractions or vary between zero and one (uniquely determined payoffs).

[19] Note that this dual program may be used to determine whether or not the "core" of the original game is empty—if the solution of the dual can be constructed with integer values (0 or 1) for all W_k, the core is not empty; otherwise it is.

4. Conclusions

The preceding analysis has used a few simple assumptions to generate relatively well-defined models. That this is not the whole story is clear from the need in one case for a theory of the bargaining process and in the other case for a theory to describe the choice of a final coalition. The reader will also note that the possibility of higher-order alliances has been disregarded. For example, in a game in which the coalitions [A, B] and [A, C] each would receive $10, and [B, C] would receive nothing, our model predicts the solution $u_a = \$10$; $u_b = u_c = 0$. This is the "competitive solution." On the other hand, if the payoffs were freely transferable among the players, it would be perfectly possible for B and C to combine with one another, choose one of their pair to deal with A alone and thus bargain with A on noncompetitive terms. In fact, one experimenter has observed precisely this behavior.[20] In principle, such a combination can be treated simply as another coalition possibility. However, the important question, as in economic theories of oligopoly, is not how such a coalition should behave but under what circumstances it will form at all. This question we must still leave unanswered.

Our final comment relates to the hypothesis that individuals will attempt to achieve the maximum possible objective gain. Situations immediately come to mind for which this is not a reasonable assumption. For example, if Albert, Bill, and Charles are to divide $3.00 among themselves, the distribution to be decided by majority vote, one is more likely to find each receiving $1.00 than two of the three receiving $1.50. The reason for this, of course, is that an important social ethic, that of equity, is probably too powerful to be disregarded. Moreover, equity is easy to implement in cases such as this where the payoff is so easily measured. It is in more complex situations, in which the gains to be expected from coalition membership are less easily measured and compared and in which individual and political "nationalism" are more apparent, that we expect the theory to apply.

References

1. R. J. Aumann and M. Maschler, "The Bargaining Set for Cooperative Games," in Dresher, Shapley, and Tucker, eds., *Advances in Game Theory* (Annals of Mathematics Study No. 52) (Princeton: Princeton University Press, 1964), pp. 443–476.
2. W. J. Baumol, *Economic Theory and Operations Analysis* (Englewood Cliffs: Prentice-Hall, 2nd ed., 1965).

[20] Maschler (1961). In this case, the payoffs were made transferable—by the players themselves and under their own initiative—by means of a probabilistic device: the toss of a coin to determine who was to negotiate with a player A.

3. J. G. Cross, "A Theory of the Bargaining Process," *American Economic Review*, 55 (March 1965), pp. 67–94.
4. R. D. Luce and H. Raiffa, *Games and Decisions* (New York: Wiley, 1957).
5. M. Maschler, "An Experiment on N-Person Cooperative Games," in *Recent Advances in Game Theory*, privately printed for members of a Princeton University conference held October 4–6, 1961, pp. 49–56.
6. A. Rapoport, *Fights, Games, and Debates* (Ann Arbor: University of Michigan Press, 1960).
7. L. S. Shapley, "Solutions of a Symmetric Market Game," in A. W. Tucker and R. D. Luce, eds., *Contributions to the Theory of Games*, Vol. 4 (Princeton: Princeton University Press, 1959), pp. 145–162.
8. J. von Neumann and O. Morgenstern, *Theory of Games and Economic Behavior* (Princeton: Princeton University Press, 3rd ed., 1953).

II

Markets and International Systems

●

Just as much of international politics theory concerns the behavior of nations in different kinds of international systems, so is much of economic theory directed to the behavior of firms in different kinds of market situations. This branch of economics considers the effect of the market environment on firms' decisions about how much they will produce and the price at which they will offer their goods. The market imposes certain limits, often quite restrictive ones, on firms' behavior, but usually that behavior is not solely determined by the condition of the market. Most theories leave a range of indeterminacy within which a firm's decisions depend upon an interaction between the goals and characteristics of the firm itself on the one hand and the behavior of the other firms in the market on the other. Their choices are limited by the number of firms, their relative size, and the number and size of firms or individuals who serve as buyers. This idea of interaction between determinants at the level of characteristics of the firm (nation) and the market (international system) is, of course, familiar to the theorist of international politics. A president's foreign policy acts will depend in large part on the domestic support he can muster and the number and resources of other nations that can challenge or support him.

The parallels can be made specific to various systems with different numbers of firms. Economists characterize as *perfect competition* a market situation in which there are so many firms of similar size that the actions of any one seller do not perceptibly affect the quantity of goods sold in the market or the price at which they will be sold. A typical example is the market for a standardized agricultural commodity like wheat or cotton. Whereas the price at which wheat will be sold certainly depends in large part upon how much all farmers, in sum, decide to produce, no single farmer can raise the selling price of his own wheat merely by restricting his own output.

Imperfect competition and *monopolistic competition* are terms used to describe a market where there are many sellers, but not as many as in perfect competition. More important, the goods are not perfectly homogeneous, with one farmer's produce being perfectly substitutable for another. It is as though each farmer specialized in producing a different variety of apple, and consumers built up mild and differing preferences for Mackintosh or Greening or Delicious. Under these circumstances each farmer would have a modest degree of control over the marketing conditions for the apple over which he had a "monopoly" within the general apple market. He could restrict his output somewhat, and attempt to sell that output at a slightly higher price. Perhaps he might undertake a bit of advertising in order to hold most of his customers' loyalty to Mackintosh even at the higher price. But his ability to manipulate price and quantity while retaining any expectation of selling his whole output would be limited. Too much manipulation, and people would buy other kinds of apples.

Imperfect competition, with its element of product differentiation, shades easily into the category of *oligopoly*, or a market which is dominated by only a few large sellers. Here, the actions of one firm clearly affect the others. When one lowers his price, the others must also lower theirs if they are to retain their previous shares of the market. If one raises his price and the others do not, his share of the market will contract. But unlike the market of perfect competition, his price-raising action will be fully apparent to the other producers. Instead of holding their prices and taking up larger shares of the market they may, as a result either of tacit agreement or of open communication, decide to raise their prices also. If they match the "leader's" price, market shares will stay the same and total output will be reduced. Their goal will be, with the collusive price increase, to limit the reduction in quantity sold and so substantially increase their total revenues. If so, the firms may end up each with higher overall profits than at the lower price and larger output. Under these circumstances different assumptions about the goals of the firms produce very different patterns of interaction among them—collusive and competitive behavior, stable and unstable prices.

Duopoly is a special case of oligopoly—a market dominated by only two large firms. Again, their interactions will be very different under various possible assumptions, and the range of indeterminacy is usually great. Finally there is *monopoly*, in pure form, where there is only a single seller, or slightly diluted, where the giant is, nevertheless, so much bigger than any of the other firms which he may allow to exist on sufferance that he can completely dominate their marketing behavior.

Obviously, there are corresponding international systems that can be described by the variables of size and number of nations. For monopoly there is the dominant world empire; for duopoly, the bipolar system with two big states, much more powerful than any other state or combination of states, competing for the allegiance and resources of people in the small states but at the same time sharing a common interest in restraining that competition. In unrestrained competition between them they will vie vigorously for the neutrals' favor, with foreign aid and other support for the neutrals' own goals. But if they can collude, or agree to limit their competition, they can avoid "price war" and the risk of ultimate "bankruptcy" for one or even both. Similarly, a balance-of-power system bears many resemblances to oligopoly, where there are several (more than two, upper limit unclear) large nations who compete but also share cooperative interests in controlling their competition.

Analogies to imperfect competition are harder to think of, though the current international system exhibits the "product differentiation" that is typical both of it and of oligopoly. Each of the states offers a somewhat different mix of rewards to its "customers;" some emphasize material well-being, some, different kinds of freedoms under varying forms of political institutions, etc. Possibly, without the two superpowers in the current world, power would be sufficiently widely distributed, even despite the existence of now second-rank powers like Britain and China, that the parallel to imperfect competition would be close. Finally, a world resembling perfect competition would be one where all the existing states were broken up into units no larger, say, than current states of the United States. Possibly, a universal international system, providing that it were based on direct popular representation rather than a federation employing unit votes as in the UN Security Council, would contain elements of such a system. The perfect competition model could then be applied to a world legislature, *except* for blocs which are made possible by communication and the various sources of influence members have over each other.[1] As it is, game-theoretical investigations on the marginal cost of the last vote at the decision point are more promising than the simple competitive model.

The analogies to market behavior are frequently deceptive, however, if they merely stop with the crude similarities between the number of firms in a market and the number of states in an international system. The mere fact that the number of units is the same does not establish a

---

[1] See also K. Boulding's comparison, in *Conflict and Defense* (New York: Harper & Row, 1962), pp. 273–276, of market systems with M. Kaplan's six international systems in *System Process in International Politics* (New York: Wiley, 1957).

useful parallel. The situation needs to be spelled out in a little more detail. One way would go as follows:

A firm buys goods and services from individuals and other firms. These raw materials, including land and labor, are processed and the firm then must sell its products in competition with other firms. It is, thus, a three-stage model, with seller, firm, and buyer, and the one firm interacting with other firms by way of their competition for sales to the third-stage buyer. Firms may also compete as buyers of inputs, in which case terms such as "monopoly" and "oligopoly" are replaced by "monopsony" and "oligopsony." Who, then, are the buyers and sellers in international politics?

Let us consider the national government as equivalent to the firm. It buys goods and services (e.g., labor) principally, but not exclusively, from the people within its political boundaries. It also sells—in exchange for taxes—goods and services, again principally, but not exclusively, to its own populace. In addition to all the domestic benefits we citizens are accustomed to "buying" (health, welfare, education, police security, etc.) we obtain some measure of security from foreign threats. The government also sells some of these products outside its boundaries; the government-firm does not make only a single "product." Some are occasionally sold to other peoples as individuals or subnational groups, some, especially security in the form of military protection in a tacit or explicit alliance, are sold to other firms or governments. Its costs of operation are what it pays, in money or in some less tangible form, to its domestic and international suppliers; its profit could (in principle, if not in practice) be measured by the government's security in tenure, its probability of remaining in power against the twin threats of internal overthrow and external subjection. This is the difference (assuming both could be measured in the same coin) between its intake and the value of the services it provides. Because the firm is both buyer and seller, it will sometimes be selling to the very individuals or other firms from which it buys: e.g., General Motors sells Chevrolets to its employees. There is no contradiction here, though the limited number of firms in the entire economy (nation-states in the system) and the high degree of autarchy (self-reliance) in the international system imply a great difference in internal dependence between the nation and even the largest firms.

In an oligopolistic world, where there are a few large firms or governments that among them account for a large fraction of the total output of power and employ a large fraction of the resources as well (oligopsony), these governments are likely to be the most secure and to provide themselves with above-average profits. But even smaller governments can produce at some profit, and occasionally a substantial one. The game is not zero-sum, and even the small powers can stay in business under most conditions. It is important to remember that the governments do *produce* useful goods and services, and that the black ledger of one firm does not automatically imply red ink for another. Small firms are able to stay in business for a variety of reasons. In part it is a consequence of restraint among the largest ones, who, for the sake of avoiding "cutthroat" competition among themselves, allow the smaller firms to retain small segments of the market. A large firm's attempt to increase greatly its access to such markets would threaten the access of the other big firms, and the addition to its own market strength would raise their fears of dominance. Anyway, the smaller firms are usually left with the less lucrative markets.[2]

These analogies do, of course, have their limits, and I hope not too many readers will feel I have pushed past those limits into absurdity. The readings which follow should demonstrate the usefulness of this approach. First, we shall look at some materials on oligopolistic markets. Two quite different normative outlooks exist in the literature regarding oligopolies. Both rest on some factual descriptions that have been or could be tested empirically, but each is addressed to maximizing different values. One puts basic emphasis on efficiency; the other stresses the virtues of stability.

One viewpoint maintains, with the classic economic argument, that oligopoly represents a situation of probable restraint on competition, especially price competition, and, hence, is *inefficient*. We have said that in perfect competition no single firm can affect the market price for its product. It has no incentive to lower its prices below those being offered by other firms, because by definition the free-market price in perfect competition is just that necessary to equate supply and demand. The firm is already selling its full output at the prevailing price, and even if it wants to expand, its impact upon the entire market will be so infinitesimal that it will not have to lower its price to sell the increased output. But in an oligopoly, the action of one of the big firms will affect marketing conditions. An individual firm can increase its own sales by lowering price, and, unlike perfect competition, its share of the market is already big enough that its increased sales would come in large part at the expense of its competitors' expected sales and its price-cutting actions would be fully visible. They would be met by retaliatory price-cutting as its competitors

---

[2] Although we would *not* translate the whole discussion of government's product into wealth, it is notable that GNP and GNP per capita are correlated with a moderate .53 (B. M. Russett et al., *World Handbook of Political and Social Indicators* (New Haven: Yale University Press, 1964), p. 276).

tried to hold their shares of the market, perhaps quickly degenerating into price war. To avoid this, in a stable oligopoly prices will be maintained at a higher level than they would be in the atomistic market of perfect competition. Competition will instead be manifested in heavy advertising budgets and attempts to make their basically very similar products look different through various superficial attributes. In the latter way a firm can obtain and hold customers by "brand loyalty," and by its advertising and subtle differentiation hope incrementally to expand its share of the market without presenting to its competitors any clear-cut competitive act that would provoke price retaliation. In crude form this is the situation that is deplored by those who disapprove of oligopolies—they stifle price competition, consumers pay more than they "should," and competition is channeled into forms that are of little social utility. By this argument the economist who values efficiency regards oligopoly and its tacit agreements as bad.

But there is another point of view that, without contradicting most of this theoretical argument, stresses the virtues of oligopoly. It is this point of view that seems to have a good deal of attraction for many international relations theorists, and it seems, in fact, to be made more often by political scientists than by economists. They identify not with the consumer's interest in obtaining the product at the lowest price, but with the consumer's interest, and, more directly, with the firm's interest, in maintaining a high degree of stability in the market. By these arguments even collusion for stability and the avoidance of price competition (and they often read *price* war, in an effort to punish or even bankrupt another firm, as equal to international *armed* war) is good. These advocates see perfect competition as analogous to a world composed of many small states, and are alarmed at what they view as one of the consequences of perfect competition—substantial price fluctuations and other instabilities in the market, with a high rate of bankruptcy for the firms. They are likely to point to the bankruptcy rate of small restaurants or to the gyrations in agricultural prices before government price supports were instituted.[3]

The first selection in this section is a rather brief passage from a book by Mancur Olson, Jr. It does not rely explicitly upon oligopoly theory at all, but draws instead largely upon the theory of public goods. Nevertheless,

---

[3] R. D. Masters, *The Nation is Burdened* (New York: Knopf, 1967), pp. 50–59. I am grateful both to Masters' book and to our conversations for introducing me to several of the pieces reproduced in this volume, though I have not drawn from them the same conclusions as he has. Sten Sparre Nilson uses the cobweb theorem from economics—a model of time-lagged interactions—to analogize about international politics of the eighteenth century. See "Measurement and Models in the Study of Stability," *World Politics*, 20, 1 (1967), pp. 1–30.

it deals with some of the same variables, and makes a case for the relative ease with which public goods can be obtained in a *small* group rather than a large one. Obtaining the collective good, he says, depends upon informal coordination; without means of communicating information about each others' actions this coordination cannot be achieved. Thus, visibility, which is most readily available in a small group, is crucial, though he does recognize that visibility is to some degree an independent variable that can be deliberately manipulated by organizational characteristics of the group. Size also militates against successful joint action because the larger the group the smaller the share of any total benefit going to a single member, and, hence, the less the incentive for members to seek the collective good rather than possible private goods. Yet another variable introduced is organization costs, which are likely to be directly related to the size of the group. Although such organization costs are not relevant to an oligopoly operating under the Sherman Anti-Trust Act, where overt collusion is prohibited, they may be very important to nations that want to pursue a collective benefit.

While perusing this section, it will be useful to think of stability, or the avoidance of war, as the relevant collective good to be sought. In so doing some slightly more general applications than those that might apply strictly to oligopoly theory may appear. This perspective suggests, for instance, why small powers may behave more "irresponsibly" than big powers in promoting foreign revolutions, warring with their neighbors, seeking nuclear weapons, or perhaps being prone to begin catalytic war— their actions are less "visible" than a great power's would be, and they are likely to have less impact on the stability of the entire system. For them, general international peace may be the collective good which they can, individually, do little to promote, and yet, again thinking in terms only of themselves in isolation, do little to damage either. Under such conditions their own apparent private interests in war may take precedence.

8

A Theory of Groups and Organizations

Mancur Olson, Jr.

In a small group in which a member gets such a large fraction of the total benefit that he would be better off if he paid the entire cost himself, rather than go without the good, there is some presumption that the collective good will be provided. In a group in which no one member got such a large benefit from the collective good that he had an interest in providing it even if he had to pay all of the cost, but in which the individual was still so important in terms of the whole group that his contribution or lack of contribution to the group objective had a noticeable effect on the costs or benefits of others in the group, the result is indeterminate. By contrast, in a large group in which no single individual's contribution makes a perceptible difference to the group as a whole, or the burden or benefit of any single member of the group, it is certain that a collective good will *not* be provided unless there is coercion or some outside inducements that will lead the members of the large group to act in their common interest.

The last distinction, between the group so large it definitely cannot provide itself with a collective good, and the oligopoly-sized group which may provide itself with a collective good, is particularly important. It depends upon whether any two or more members of the group have a perceptible interdependence, that is, on whether the contribution or lack of contribution of any one individual in the group will have a perceptible

Reprinted by permission of the publishers from M. Olson, Jr., *The Logic of Collective Action: Public Goods and the Theory of Groups* (Cambridge: Harvard University Press, 1965), pp. 44–52. Copyright, 1965, by the President and Fellows of Harvard College.

effect on the burden or benefit of any other individual or individuals in the group. Whether a group will have the possibility of providing itself with a collective good without coercion or outside inducements therefore depends to a striking degree upon the number of individuals in the group, since the larger the group, the less the likelihood that the contribution of any one will be perceptible. It is not, however, strictly accurate to say that it depends solely on the number of individuals in the group. The relation between the size of the group and the significance of an individual member cannot be defined quite that simply. A group which has members with highly unequal degrees of interest in a collective good, and which wants a collective good that is (at some level of provision) extremely valuable in relation to its cost, will be more apt to provide itself with a collective good than other groups with the same number of members. The same situation prevails in the study of market structure, where again the number of firms an industry can have and still remain oligopolistic (and have the possibility of supracompetitive returns) varies somewhat from case to case. The standard for determining whether a group will have the capacity to act, without coercion or outside inducements, in its group interest is (as it should be) the same for market and nonmarket groups: it depends on whether the individual actions of any one or more members in a group are noticeable to any other individuals in the group.[1] This is most obviously, but not exclusively, a function of the number in the group.

It is now possible to specify when either informal coordination or formal organization will be necessary to obtain a collective good. The smallest type of group—the group in which one or more members get such a large fraction of the total benefit that they find it worthwhile to see that the collective good is provided, even if they have to pay the entire cost —may get along without any group agreement or organization. A group agreement might be set up to spread the costs more widely or to step up the level of provision of the collective good. But since there is an incentive for unilateral and individual action to obtain the collective good, neither a

[1] The noticeability of the actions of a single member of a group may be influenced by the arrangements the group itself sets up. A previously organized group, for example, might ensure that the contributions or lack of contributions of any member of the group, and the effect of each such member's course on the burden and benefit for others, would be advertised, thus ensuring that the group effort would not collapse from imperfect knowledge. I therefore define "noticeability" in terms of the degree of knowledge, and the institutional arrangements, that actually exist in any given group, instead of assuming a "natural noticeability" unaffected by any group advertising or other arrangements. This point, along with many other valuable comments, has been brought to my attention by Professor Jerome Rothenberg, who does, however, make much more of a group's assumed capacity to create "artificial noticeability" than I would want to do. I know of no practical example of a group or organization that has done much of anything, apart from improve information, to enhance the noticeability of an individual's actions in striving for a collective good.

formal organization nor even an informal group agreement is indispens-able to obtain a collective good. In any group larger than this, on the other hand, no collective good can be obtained without some group agreement, coordination, or organization. In the intermediate or oligopoly-sized group, where two or more members must act simultaneously before a collective good can be obtained, there must be at least tacit coordination or organization. Moreover, the larger a group is, the more agreement and organization it will need. The larger the group, the greater the number that will usually have to be included in the group agreement or organiza-tion. It may not be necessary that the entire group be organized, since some subset of the whole group may be able to provide the collective good. But to establish a group agreement or organization will, nonetheless, always tend to be more difficult the larger the size of the group, for the larger the group the more difficult it will be to locate and organize even a subset of the group, and those in the subset will have an incentive to continue bargaining with the others in the group until the burden is widely shared, thereby adding to the expense of bargaining. In short, costs of organization are an increasing function of the number of individuals in the group. (Though the more members in the group the greater the total costs of organization, the costs of organization per person need not rise, for there are surely econo-mies of scale in organization.) In certain cases a group will already be organized for some other purpose, and then these costs of organization are already being met. In such a case a group's capacity to provide itself with a collective good will be explained in part by whatever it was that originally enabled it to organize and maintain itself. This brings attention back again to the costs of organization and shows that these costs cannot be left out of the model, except for the smallest type of group in which unilateral action can provide a collective good. The costs of organization must be clearly distinguished from the type of cost that has previously been considered. The cost functions considered before involved only the direct resource costs of obtaining various levels of provision of a collective good. When there is no preexisting organization of a group, and when the direct resource costs of a collective good it wants are more than any single individual could profitably bear, additional costs must be incurred to obtain an agreement about how the burden will be shared and to coordin-ate or organize the effort to obtain the collective good. These are the costs of communication among group members, the costs of any bargaining among them, and the costs of creating, staffing, and maintaining any formal group organization.

A group cannot get infinitesimally small quantities of a formal organization, or even of an informal group agreement; a group with a given number of members must have a certain minimal amount of organization or agreement if it is to have any at all. Thus, there are significant initial or minimal costs of organization for each group. Any group that must organize to obtain a collective good, then, will find that it has a certain minimum organization cost that must be met, however little of the collective good it obtains. The greater the number in the group, the greater these minimal costs will be. When this minimal organizational cost is added to the other initial or minimal costs of a collective good, which arise from its previously mentioned technical characteristics, it is evident that the cost of the first unit of a collective good will be quite high in relation to the cost of some subsequent units. However immense the benefits of a collective good, the higher the absolute total costs of getting any amount of that good, the less likely it is that even a minimal amount of that good could be obtained without coercion or separate, outside incentives.

This means that there are now three separate but cumulative factors that keep larger groups from furthering their own interests. First, the larger the group, the smaller the fraction of the total group benefit any person acting in the group interest receives, and the less adequate the reward for any group-oriented action, and the farther the group falls short of getting an optimal supply of the collective good, even if it should get some. Second, since the larger the group, the smaller the share of the total benefit going to any individual, or to any (absolutely) small subset of members of the group, the less the likelihood that any small subset of the group, much less any single individual, will gain enough from getting the collective good to bear the burden of providing even a small amount of it; in other words, the larger the group the smaller the likelihood of oligopolistic interaction that might help obtain the good. Third, the larger the number of members in the group the greater the organization costs, and, thus, the higher the hurdle that must be jumped before any of the collective good at all can be obtained. For these reasons, the larger the group, the farther it will fall short of providing an optimal supply of a collective good, and very large groups normally will not, in the absence of coercion or separate, outside incentives, provide themselves with even minimal amounts of a collective good.

Now that all sizes of groups have been considered, it is possible to develop the classification of groups that is needed. In an article that was originally part of this study, but which has been published elsewhere, this writer and his co-author argued that the concept of the group or industry can be given a precise theoretical meaning, and should be used, along with the concept of pure monopoly, in the study of market structure. In that article the situation in which there was only one firm in the industry was called pure monopoly. The situation where the firms are so few that the actions of one firm would have a noticeable effect on some one other firm or group of firms was called oligopoly; and the situation where no one firm had any noticeable effect on any other firm was called "atomistic competition." The category of atomistic competition was subdivided into pure competition and monopolistic competition within the large group, and oligopoly was also divided into two subdivisions according as the product was homogeneous or differentiated.[2]

For inclusive or nonmarket groups the categories must be slightly different. The analog to pure monopoly (or pure monopsony) is obviously the single individual outside the market seeking some noncollective good, some good without external economies or diseconomies. In the size range that corresponds to oligopoly in market groups, there are two separate types of nonmarket groups: "privileged" groups and "intermediate" groups. A "privileged" group is a group such that each of its members, or at least some one of them, has an incentive to see that the collective good is provided, even if he has to bear the full burden of providing it himself. In such a group there is a presumption that the collective good will be obtained, and it may be obtained without any group organization or coordination whatever. An "intermediate" group is a group in which no single member gets a share of the benefit sufficient to give him an incentive to provide the good himself, but which does not have so many members that no one member will notice whether any other member is or is not helping to provide the collective good. In such a group a collective good may, or equally well may not, be obtained, but no collective good may ever be obtained without some group coordination or organization. The analog to atomistic competition in the nonmarket situation is the very large group, which will here be called the "latent" group. It is distinguished by the fact that, if one member does or does not help provide the collective good, no other one member will be significantly affected and, therefore, none has any reason to react. Thus, an individual in a "latent" group, by definition, cannot make a noticeable contribution to any group effort, and since no one in the group will react if he makes no contribution, he has no incentive to contribute. Accordingly, large or "latent" groups have no incentive to act to obtain a collective good because, however valuable the collective good might be to the group as a whole, it does not offer the individual any incentive to pay dues to any organization working in the latent group's interest, or to bear in any other way any of the costs of the necessary collective action.

Only a *separate and "selective" incentive* will stimulate a rational individual in a latent group to act in a group-oriented way. In such circumstances group action can be obtained only through an incentive that

[2] Mancur Olson, Jr., and David McFarland, "The Restoration of Pure Monopoly and the Concept of the Industry," *Quarterly Journal of Economics*, **76**, 4 (1962), pp. 613–631.

operates, not indiscriminately, like the collective good, upon the group as a whole, but rather *selectively* toward the individuals in the group. The incentive must be "selective" so that those who do not join the organization working for the group's interest, or in other ways contribute to the attainment of the group's interest, can be treated differently from those who do. These "selective incentives" can be either negative or positive, in that they can either coerce by punishing those who fail to bear an allocated share of the costs of the group action, or they can be positive inducements offered to those who act in the group interest. A latent group that has been led to act in its group interest, either because of coercion of the individuals in the group or because of positive rewards to those individuals, will here be called a "mobilized" latent group. Large groups are thus called "latent" groups because they have a latent power or capacity for action, but that potential power can be realized or "mobilized" only with the aid of "selective incentives."

In the following chapter Martin Shubik presents some highly suggestive empirical studies of actual market behavior, in which he specifies a
number of the variables affecting firms' behavior and, thus, the system's
stability, and in an approximate way measures their importance. The
chapter employs some aspects of game theory, but the presentation is most
interesting for the specification of the variables. The static theory of non-
cooperative games is utterly insufficient for such a situation, but a good,
dynamic *n*-person theory containing elements both of competition for
markets and cooperation in avoiding great instabilities is still lacking.
Shubik, however, continues to work on the project in laboratory experiments incorporating some of these variables.

Essentially, the problem is: what are the conditions for "workable"
competition—what is necessary to provide a stable market? He postulates
five sets of variables for measuring the vulnerability of one firm to the
actions of a competitor. These are given at the beginning of the article;
some analogous international relations variables that may help in illustrating the usefulness of the system are:

1. *Short-run market vulnerability.* This is a function of the kind and
quantity of the nation's (firm's) assets and the military capabilities of the
other—what damage can be done to it in a surprise attack; how much can
its revenue or income be reduced by various kinds of attack of which the
opponent is capable? In the international politics analogy, how many of its
strategic retaliatory vehicles could the enemy destroy in an attack with a
given striking force and the precautions, in the way of hardening, mobility,
dispersion, and concealment that the nation has taken? What is the exchange ratio of incoming missiles to missiles in silos? How many people
would not be likely to survive an attack, given the opponent's capabilities
and the nation's ballistic missile defenses for cities and fallout shelter
system?

2. *Short-run financial vulnerability.* This is a function of what damage
could be done to it (short-run market vulnerability) and the resources it
would have to sustain such a loss. What are its forces-in-being? How many
strategic retaliatory vehicles would be left after an attack? What proportion
of its population and industry would survive, and how much would have to
survive to keep the economy and social system viable? What is the quality
of its political and military leadership? How well trained and equipped are
the troops?

3. *Long-run market vulnerability.* Which of its assets could be destroyed not in a relatively short war, but in either an extended war of attri-

tion or a long period of cold war? What measure of protection does distance or terrain provide from invasion? Which of its foreign investments are subject to nationalization by the opponent or its allies? Which of its sources of imports, or raw materials, manufactured goods, or spare parts, can be cut off by blockade or embargo? Which of its foreign markets could be closed by hostile naval action?

4. *Long-run financial vulnerability.* To counter the losses that could be inflicted upon it, what resources could the nation muster? How *dependent* is the economy on those foreign investments that could be nationalized or trade that *could* be cut off? What is the GNP, and what stockpiles, natural resources, what physical plant and equipment exist? What is the nation's growth potential? Does the country import most of its food and raw materials, or is it autarchic? What, overall, is its ratio of foreign trade to GNP? What are the skill and educational attainments of the population, and what is its potential for learning or devising solutions to new challenges? Can the political system be geared to both innovation and concentration over a sustained effort?

5. *Control vulnerability.* How susceptible is the regime to overthrow by domestic opponents supported from abroad? How popular is the government? What domestic minorities might oppose it? Are there former immigrants from the opposing state, and how loyal are they now? What is the potential for subversion or guerrilla warfare? How good is national morale?

In short, these are questions that involve the basic problems of measuring the power of nations—what damage can be done to them, and to the various resources they have for immediate response and for long-term change. They are not susceptible to easy measurement in a single composite index, or even as separate variables. Doubtless satisfactory measurements are harder to devise for international behavior than for predicting the behavior of industrial firms. Nevertheless, Shubik's piece suggests the great potential of such variables for explaining market behavior, and the possibility of applying some such analysis, even if crude, to international problems is intriguing.

The chapter is stimulating as an illustration of two markets, for automobiles and cigarettes, where the industry is relatively stable. The largest firms, though not the few weak, small ones, are fairly secure, their shares of the market fluctuate but within definable limits, and price competition is very rare. The conditions for producing this stability, however, are very complex and depend upon much more than just the number of firms in the industry and their size. Hence, the conclusions one draws about the desirability of oligopoly, even just from the viewpoint of stability and the avoidance of price war, must be very carefully hedged. Shubik lists a number of moves available to the firm's managers. Research and innovation is, of course, one with a direct counterpart in international politics. Other analogies that might be suggested behind the verbal labels include a similarity between advertising and ideological propaganda. If price changes are equated with war or other military action, then there are also analogies to other national instruments of foreign policy such as the use of foreign aid or vote trading in international organizations. The reader can supply many of these for himself. Bankruptcy conditions for a firm are essentially the conditions under which the nation would be no longer viable as an independent state.

9

Strategy and Market Structure

Martin Shubik

Here we tentatively suggest five different types of "rule of thumb" measures of *vulnerability*, some of which are associated *damage exchange rates*. These proposed measures are directly related to the theoretical construct of a game of economic survival. After we have defined them, their relevance to the definition and measurement of competition or collusion will be discussed.

1. *Short-run market vulnerability* is a measure of the amount of damage that can be done to a firm by short-run market action of an opponent or by a shift in a market parameter. It is related to the nature and size of inventory positions, the immediate effect of price changes, advertising maneuvers, and style shifts upon immediate profits. A different measure can be given for each variable considered. Thus, the short-run market vulnerability with respect to price is measured by the loss of profit to a firm caused by a price cut of an opponent.

The revenue of firm i in the single period t is given by the market matrix $R_{i,t}(a; s_1, s_2, \ldots, s_n)$ where a is a random variable (i.e., it is the move controlled by the exogenous features of the market), and the $s_j, j = 1, 2, \ldots, n$ are the strategies of the players in this single-period subgame.[1] The short-run market vulnerability of firm i with respect to an action by firm j is given by

$$\frac{\Delta R_{i,t}}{\Delta s_j}$$

Reprinted from M. Shubik, *Strategy and Market Structure* (New York: Wiley, 1959), pp. 293–324.

[1] The strategy s_j will, in general, be multidimensional, involving price, production, advertising, and many other factors. Further specification is needed in order to be able to define an incremental change in s_j. In some cases, in which we limit the strategy of a player to a single variable, such as price, the meaning of a small change is clear.

The short-run market damage exchange rate is given by

$$\frac{\Delta_j R_{i,t}}{\Delta_j R_{j,t}}$$

where the Δ_j indicates that the increment is defined with respect to a change in s_j.

2. *Short-run financial vulnerability* relates to current asset and liability position, to the nature of the firm's capitalization, especially the leverage present, to the credit rating of the firm, and to the state of the money markets. It is given by the ratio of the largest amount of money that a firm can lose in a single period (determined by the short-run market vulnerability) to the amount of losses that force bankruptcy or possibly takeover or other financial reorganization.

3. *Long-run market vulnerability* depends upon the structure of overhead costs, flexibility of product-variation, and the state of long-run demand. The long-run market vulnerability of firm i against a change in strategy by firm j for τ periods is given by

$$\frac{\sum_{t=0}^{\tau} \Delta R_{i,t}}{\Delta S_j}$$

The long-run market damage exchange rate is given by

$$\frac{\sum_{t=0}^{\tau} R_{i,t}}{\sum_{t=0}^{\tau} R_{j,t}}$$

Practically, this measure is not very satisfactory, since we face considerable difficulty in specifying what is meant by an incremental change in strategy by player j. However, at least in theory, it is possible to calculate the resulting revenues over a number of periods caused by the employment of any set of strategies ....

4. *Long-run financial vulnerability* depends upon the total assets and credit that a firm can muster in a struggle for survival. It can be measured by the ratio of the largest amount of money that a firm could stand to lose over a specified number of periods to the amount of losses that the firm is able to sustain before it is forced into liquidation or some other form of reorganization. This is not quite adequate because the amount that a firm can lose over several periods is, in general, determined by the time path through which it converts frozen or fixed assets into liquid assets available to avoid short-run disaster.

5. *Control vulnerability* depends upon the way stockholdings are fractionated, the size of the stock issue, and the debt structure. It is

measured by the size of resources required by an "invading group" to capture the corporation through gaining stockholding allies, buying in the open market, exerting pressure through credit control, or fighting for proxies, using an optimal combination of these tactics. A short- and long-run control vulnerability can be defined. The first is the cost to an invading group on the assumption that no countermeasures are taken. The second is the cost to an invading group on the assumption that defenders attempt to prevent the capture.

The indices described are suggested merely as a means of examining the strategy spaces and revenues of a group of firms. If the firms are at an efficient point equilibrium, the short-run damage exchange rate will be unfavorable to a firm that cuts price. The financial vulnerabilities play a role in an economy in which only long-term individual financial considerations may overrule technological efficient allocation conditions. If we are able to measure the strategic vulnerabilities of firms or groups of firms, it then becomes possible to form estimates of the varieties of $\{k_i\} - \{r_j\}$ stability that are consistent with the state of the market. It is the strategic interconnection of firms and the behavior exhibited under various conditions of this interconnection that form a central part of the theory and measurement of oligopolistic power.

1. The Automobile Industry

A. *Description of the Automobile Industry*

In this and the succeeding section we present a brief sketch of two industries up until the end of 1955 in order to indicate the relationship between the theoretical construct of a game of economic survival, the measures of interdependence suggested, and the type of empirical investigation envisioned as necessary to reconcile our knowledge of market forms more closely with a theory of oligopoly.

The automobile industry has an oligopolistic structure with three major and two minor firms and an amount of foreign competition. Its products reach the consumer via many thousands of distributors.

The nature of the industry has changed considerably since its early days. At the turn of the century automobile manufacturers contracted with other firms for most of their parts and, in the main, merely did the assembling. Because of this system capital requirements were small, and entry was correspondingly easy. In 1899 there were fifty-seven producing establishments in the industry, and by 1904 this number had increased to

121. As the industry grew, the more successful firms began to integrate, and the numbers thinned.

At present the diversification and complexity of the corporate structure of the remaining firms is considerable. Although the mere counting of the number of corporations controlled by a single business entity does not necessarily supply information about the diversity of its activities, it may serve as a crude index of diversification and may suggest natural subdivisions of a large corporation. In some cases more or less semi-independent sections are organized as divisions with no separate corporate existence.

The consolidated financial statement of General Motors includes approximately seventy corporations. It controls several hundred other corporations. In some cases the control is split with another large corporation. For instance, it owns 50 percent of the Ethyl Gas Corporation, with Standard Oil of New Jersey owning the other 50 percent, and $33\frac{3}{10}$ percent of the International Freighting Corporation, with du Pont owning the rest. In 1955, 91 percent of its sales, exclusive of defense contracts, were automobiles and trucks.

American Motors consists of Hudson and Nash and about twenty other companies, including Kelvinator. Sixty-seven percent of its sales in 1955 were automobiles. Ford Company's diagram of corporate structure has about forty companies, including 50 percent of the Humboldt Mining Company, the Fordson Coal Company, and Ford Tractor and Equipment Sales Company of Canada. Over 90 percent of its sales were automobiles and trucks. Chrysler is split into divisions rather than many separate corporations, except for a few subsidiaries such as the Chrysler Corporation of Canada. However, its business is diversified.

Even Kaiser Motors, which has now gone out of the automobile business, did so by ceasing to make utility vehicles and becoming part of Kaiser Industries Corporation, which operates directly through controlled corporations or partially through minority stockholding in the sand and gravel, engineering, construction, aluminum, chemical, steel, and cement businesses.

In 1955 General Motors sold over 50 percent of all the automobiles sold in the United States, 80 percent of the buses, 43 percent of the trucks, a considerable proportion of the diesel locomotives and refrigerators, 20 percent of all wheel-type farm tractors, as well as other defense material. Chrysler sold approximately 17 percent of all cars sold, around 9 percent of the trucks, as well as medium tanks, guided missiles, air conditioning, marine engines, Oilite powdered metal products, and Cycleweld adhesives.

With the exception of Ford, the control of the automobile firms appears to lie with the officers. The stock issues are large and the holdings fractionated. In the Ford Company the Ford family controls 40 percent of the votes, hence just about all the power. Table 1 indicates the size of the stock issues and number of stockholders. Du Pont owns about 23 percent of General Motors. Leaving out antitrust considerations, it is the only financial concentration in a position to capture control of General Motors, if it wished to do so. The largest individual shareholder of Chrysler in 1955 held $1\frac{15}{100}$ percent. The long-term debt structure is not very important in this industry. Most financing has utilized earnings or the sale of common stock.

The ratio between current assets and current liabilities has varied between 1.7 and 4 for the firms. The two smallest companies have tended to have the worst ratios. They are also heavily dependent on bank loans.

As automobiles are a consumer durable, demand depends upon the size and age distribution of previous stocks as well as upon prices and income levels. It has been variously estimated that the price elasticity for automobiles in the United States is between $-.5$ and -1.0. Even given a $200 to $300 cut in automobile prices, it appears to be highly unlikely that more than 8,500,000 cars can be sold per annum for several years to come.

Little is known for certain about the relative efficiencies of the various firms in the automobile industry. The industry is of the break-even type. Heavy overhead costs must be met, and, therefore, profits are very sensitive to volume. Table 2 gives the production figures for the main line of automobiles for four of the companies.

The mere presence of high rates of profits for the larger firms does not establish a criterion to measure and compare inherent manufacturing efficiencies.

Styling and advertising are important components of competition in the automobile industry. A wrong guess by a small firm can spell disaster. The demand fluctuations for Studebaker and Chrysler products appear to be heavily related to styling and "sales competition" rather than price. There are no estimates available of the cross-elasticities of demand between different makes of automobiles. Product differentiation and consumer loyalty obviously play a major role in automobile demand. However, in the low-priced range it appears reasonable to assume that a price cut of over $100 by Chevrolet would seriously eat into the markets of the other firms if it went unanswered.

An indication of the importance of the automobile industry to the economy is given by the following figures: In 1955 there were approximately 51,000,000 passenger cars and 10,000,000 trucks and buses in the United States. The Automobile Manufacturers Association calculated in 1953 that 700,000 businesses could be classified as automotive. Among these were 50,000 new- and used-car retailers, 17,000 used-car dealers, 60,000 general repair establishments, 188,000 gasoline stations, and 210,000 for-hire trucking firms. These amounted to approximately one-sixth of all the firms in the United States. In that year automotive retailer sales (dealers, parts, and gasoline) amounted to $44 billion. The 1954 employment figure in highway transport industries was placed at 9,800,000.

Production and financial information for five years of operation is given in Tables 3 through 9.

Table 1

Control Structure

	Shares	Stock-holders	Control
General Motors	276,000,000 common 1,800,000 preferred 5 percent 1,000,000 preferred 3.75 percent	600,000	Directors and officers
Ford	53,500,000 common	310,000	Ford family
Chrysler	8,700,000 common	88,000	Directors and officers
American Motors	5,700,000 common	55,000	Directors and officers
Studebaker-Packard	6,400,000 common	110,000	Directors and officers

Table 2

Production (in millions of popular cars)

	Chevrolet	Buick	Ford	Plymouth	Studebaker
1951	1.118	.404	.902	.623	.233
1952	.878	.321	.775	.475	.173
1953	1.477	.485	1.181	.663	.190
1954	1.414	.531	1.396[a]	.472	.085
1955	1.830	.781	1.764[a]	.815	.112

[a] Includes Thunderbirds.

Table 3

Production (in millions of automobiles)

	Total	General Motors	Ford	Chrysler	American Motors	Studebaker-Packard	Kaiser
1951	5.3	2.27	1.17	1.229	.254[a]	.298[b]	.100
1952	4.3	1.78	1.00	.953	.228[a]	.225[b]	.075
1953	6.1	2.80	1.54	1.246	.212[a]	.268[b]	.022
1954	5.6	2.88	1.69	.776	.011	.113	.005
1955	7.9	3.99	2.24	1.464	.162	.182	.005

[a] American Motors was formed in 1954 as a combination of Nash Kelvinator and Hudson Motors.

[b] Studebaker-Packard was formed in 1954 as a combination of Studebaker and Packard.

Table 4
Production (in millions of trucks and buses)

	Total	General Motors	Ford	Chrysler	American Motors[a]	Studebaker-Packard
1951	1.42	.562	.320	.169		.052
1952	1.21	.453	.235	.162		.059
1953	1.20	.476	.315	.105		.032
1954	1.04	.412	.303	.107		.015
1955	1.25	.499	.374	.116		.019

[a] None.

Table 5
Sales (in millions of dollars)

	General Motors	Ford	Chrysler	American Motors	Studebaker-Packard
1951	7,466	2742	2547	582[a]	682[b]
1952	7,549	2640	2601	573[a]	879[b]
1953	10,028	4211	3348	672[a]	930[b]
1954	9,824	4062	2072	400	650[b]
1955	12,443	5594	3466	441	480

[a] Estimated, exact data not published.
[b] Studebaker-Packard was formed in 1954 as a combination of Studebaker and Packard.

Table 6
Assets (in millions of dollars)

	General Motors	Ford	Chrysler	American Motors	Studebaker-Packard
1951	3672	1469	758	279[a]	265[b]
1952	4001	1584	914	321[a]	228[b]
1953	4405	1758	898	340[a]	294[b]
1954	5130	1895	1035	267	246
1955	6176	2585	1363	260	230

[a] Estimated, exact data not published.
[b] Studebaker-Packard was formed in 1954 as a combination of Studebaker and Packard.

Table 7

Net Profit (in millions of dollars)

	General Motors	Ford	Chrysler	American Motors	Studebaker-Packard
1951	506	126	72	15[a]	24[b]
1952	559	117	79	21[a]	25[b]
1953	598	166	75	4[a]	13[b]
1954	806	228	19	−11	−26
1955	1189	437	100	−7	−30

[a] Estimated, exact data not published.

[b] Studebaker-Packard was formed in 1954 as a combination of Studebaker and Packard.

Table 8

Dividends (in millions of dollars)

	General Motors	Ford	Chrysler	American Motors	Studebaker-Packard
1951	350	35	65	—	—
1952	349	35	52	—	—
1953	349	52	52	—	—
1954	437	90	39	4	0
1955	592	175	35	0	0

Table 9

Income Retained (in millions of dollars)

	General Motors	Ford	Chrysler	American Motors	Studebaker-Packard
1951	143	92	7	—	—
1952	197	82	27	—	—
1953	236	114	23	—	—
1954	357	138	−20	−15	−26
1955	584	262	65	−7	−30

B. *Competition in the Automobile Industry*

The previous description provides the information for setting up a crude model of the automobile market as a game of economic survival. Although insufficient detail has been given to merit setting up a completely formal model, we can relate this information to the general structure of the game... and use the indices of vulnerability to estimate the type of competition in the automobile industry.

1. There are five major *players* (the domestic firms), several minor players (foreign competition, primarily German and British), and apparently no firms-in-being or potential entrants, since there does not appear to be a financial and engineering group available with the necessary ante.

2. The *personal moves* of the players which are of importance in this industry include advertising, styling, innovation, pricing, production and inventory scheduling, the payment of dividends, and investment (labor-union and industry bargaining is highly important to all firms).

3. The *chance moves* involve probabilities of technical success in research and innovation, the vagaries of consumer taste, and the fluctuations in national income.

4. The *positional payoffs* are determined by the distribution of the corporate net income, as are the *corporate asset positions.*

5. The *bankruptcy conditions* are determined by the various firms' ability to lose money and still be able to meet their obligations. Both Studebaker-Packard and American Motors barely have a quarter of a billion dollars each; hence, even under the most optimistic assumption that they could afford to lose all, they could still be driven into bankruptcy or merger in one or two poor years.

6. The *liquidation* or *ruin values* depend upon the degree of specialization of the equipment being sold. The two small automobile companies could realize their best values if they sold out to the others. Such a sale to General Motors or Ford would probably be declared illegal. At the end of 1955 General Motors evaluated its real estate, plants, and equipment at $4354 million, less $2001 million for depreciation. In order to evaluate its liquidation worth, we would have to calculate the effect of such a sale on the market.

7. The *information conditions* are such that at the end of every year the firms are completely informed of most of the moves made by their opponents, although they may lack information about some of the long-term development and planning actions. As an outsider's guess, we may assume that they are equally and fairly well informed about each other's costs and that they are equally adept or inept at "crystal-ball gazing" at outside events or factors exogenous to the industry.

8. *The utility function and motives for maximization* ... The profit maximization motive suggested by the simple static theory of the firm is not adequate in a dynamic corporate setting. Without having to resort to complex psychological theories, it is not difficult to observe that even if all directors and officers were motivated solely by monetary goals, the

institutional structure of a large corporation is such that the corporate goal, although in general it will be positively correlated with immediate money income, will involve many other considerations. The aims of a corporation are sometimes stated generally in terms of duties towards stockholders, employees, consumers, and even the government.

A direct relation between the welfare of the salaried employees and the net income of the firm may come about through a fixed bonus scheme. Thus, the General Motors bonus plan calls for at most 12 percent of net earnings after deducting 5 percent on net capital. This amount must not exceed the amount paid out as dividends.

The automobile industry has been very heavily self-financing, as can be seen by the small size of long-term debt as well as the size of retained earnings (see Table 9). This may relate to the cyclical nature of the industry, since a heavy debt structure would magnify the variance in yearly earnings. Thus, it appears that the lessening of revenue fluctuation is taken into consideration in the aims of the firms. We continue the discussion of motivation later.

Competition between the automobile firms can proceed along several lines. As we have already noted, advertising, styling, innovation, investment, production and inventory scheduling, and pricing all may enter as components of a strategy. Using the measures suggested previously, we examine the payoffs associated with some of the strategies available to the firms.

There are at least two types of policy which would, if adopted by General Motors, spell doom to American Motors and Studebaker-Packard and could possibly ruin even Chrysler. General Motors could cut prices drastically. A $300 cut across the board would appear to be sufficient; or a larger cut, say, $400, off Chevrolet might be more effective. Alternatively, it could take a gamble and introduce nine-month or even six-month styling in order to take away product acceptance from other cars. As the cost of setting up new production lines is very high, the three smaller firms would be unable to counter with the same tactics.

The effectiveness of the latter policy would depend upon consumer reaction to an increased tempo of change in styling and might misfire on the company attempting it. The effect of a major price cut is easier to predict. A very rough index of the ability of the firms to compete via price can be obtained by dividing profits by the number of automobiles and trucks sold. This leaves out of consideration other product diversification and the different profitability of various automotive lines; however, it supplies a crude estimate of the ability to maneuver in the automobile market. This calculation is in Table 10.

Table 10

Profit[a] per Automotive Unit

	General Motors	Ford	Chrysler	American Motors	Studebaker-Packard
1951	522	316	108	75	180
1952	674	280	244	121	191
1953	503	329	148	19	187
1954	500	249	24	Deficit	Deficit
1955	608[b]	371	142	Deficit	Deficit

[a] Profit before income tax.
[b] Includes overseas production.

An evaluation of the payoffs resulting from the employment of the strategies noted can be obtained by examining the vulnerability criteria. The *short-run market vulnerability* of Studebaker-Packard and American Motors is such that a $300 price cut by General Motors would certainly keep them operating in the red unless they happened to capture a style market. If the cross-elasticity of demand between different makes of automobiles were moderately high, then on the assumption of a market for around 8,000,000 automobiles Ford could meet the price cut of General Motors and still make a profit. If Chrysler met the price cut and maintained only its market share (even in a slightly expanded market), then it would probably operate in the red. If it did not meet the price cut and if market cross-elasticity were high enough to reduce its market share by 50 percent or more, it would operate in the red. *Short-run market vulnerability* for all firms is unlikely to be larger than one per automobile[2] and is probably not smaller than .5 per automobile for the small firms, i.e., a $100 price cut by General Motors should cause a drop in profit of at least $50 per automobile for the small companies.

As leverage is low in the automobile industry, the dangers of *short-run financial vulnerability* are not important to the three larger firms. Studebaker-Packard, which lost $14.3 million in the first three months of 1956, could be forced out within a year. Its danger level is at best of the order of $100 million. However, even without action by General Motors or Ford, a downturn in the market would be sufficient to wipe out the two smaller firms.... If there are random elements present, a stationary state may remain in equilibrium only with some probability. A "run of bad luck" against a particular firm might weaken it sufficiently to render it unable to

[2] For instance, at the worst a firm can meet a price cut of an opponent and thereby maintain the same share of the market as before (on the assumption that income effect is negligible).

enforce an equilibrium it had previously been able to maintain. As the small firms become poorer, their credit ratings deteriorate; hence their financial vulnerability increases cumulatively.

Unless a small company is able to protect itself by successful product differentiation sufficient to offset even major price cuts, then in the automobile industry *long-run market vulnerability* is high, since there is little chance to retrench and cut down overhead.

We have seen from Table 1 that the financial structure of the automobile industry is such that "takeovers" and raids on the three large firms are virtually impossible.[3] Voting control is fractionated and common stock predominates. The directors and officers are in control of the automobile companies. With the exception of Ford, no members of a controlling group hold a significant amount of stock.

At best the short-run damage exchange rate via price competition for General Motors is not better than ten for one sustained by the small firms. Even if cross-elasticities were infinite between the products, if the other firms met a price cut on, say, just Chevrolet, the difference in volume would cause General Motors by far the greater absolute loss.

In order to demonstrate the effect of different corporate goals upon the various strategies, we assume two different (and highly simplified) sets of motivation for the directors of General Motors. We first assume that they wish to maximize the discounted (expected) value of the monetary income of General Motors. Second we assume that their only interest is to see that the public is offered automobiles at as cheap a price as is consistent with paying stockholders a "fair" return from investment and employees, including officers, a "reasonable incentive" rate of remuneration.

In the first case, in which we assume that the directors are interested in maximizing expected monetary income to the corporation, they can compute two different types of income streams. The first is one in which they maximize their expected discounted income subject to the restraint that the other firms are able to survive. The second income stream consists of two parts, the profits made in carrying out a policy designed to put its competitors out of business and the extra profits obtained after it has been successful in this policy. There are several reasons why an all-out price war should not be fought. It would take so long to drive Chrysler out of the market that at a discount rate of 4 or 5 percent the profits foregone could never be recouped, unless the price of automobiles were doubled after the market struggle. Even then, it is fairly certain that General Motors could not put Ford out of business, no matter what strategy were utilized. Another reason why a market fight would not be employed is that public

---

[3] The two small firms lie within the range of raid feasibility.

opinion and legal action would be taken against General Motors long before Chrysler were bankrupted. Furthermore, in a cyclical industry even General Motors might be loath to expand its capacity to a size sufficient to cope with the whole industry demand. Thus, if profit maximization is the motivation, a strategy of heavy price cutting will not be adopted.

In the second case, in which we assume that the directors wish to serve the public, they may feel that a 5 percent return to capital is a "fair" yield to stockholders. The 1955 stockholders' equity was a $4255 million; hence, approximately $213 million would be required for dividends. Even if a bound of one million dollars per annum were taken as a "reasonable incentive" rate for an officer, General Motors still appears to be in a position to indulge in price cuts which only Ford could survive with a high degree of certainty. The antitrust division could then descend upon General Motors with a Sherman Act accusation of attempting to monopolize which would in fact be based upon the motivation of the directors of General Motors to sell automobiles as cheaply as possible. Thus, even though "public service" were the motivation, the directors of General Motors could not cut prices heavily for fear of the antitrust laws.

C. Numbers and Stability in the Automobile Industry

Entry of new firms, exit or merging of existing firms, and competition by means of many different weapons characterize the state of a market. The cost of entry into the automobile industry is so large that it appears reasonable to assume that there are no firms-in-being. Joe S. Bain has estimated that at present the capital requirement for a minimum optimal firm in the automobile industry, exclusive of shakedown losses, is of the order of $250 to $500 million.[4] This estimate is based on a range running between 5 and 10 percent of the volume of the low-price field (Ford, Chevrolet, and Plymouth). He has also suggested that about $250 million more would be needed for shakedown losses in order to give a firm an even chance of becoming established.

Even without any aggressive tactics on the part of the larger firms, mere chance fluctuations are sufficient to ruin the two smaller firms. Possibly the number of competitors could be preserved if the small firms merged with strong outside corporations.

Given the present economic background of the automobile industry, we must expect that there will be no wide divergence in pricing policies, even with no explicit cooperation between the directors of the firms. High competition in styling, innovation, efficiency, and advertising can go on.

[4] J. S. Bain, *Barriers to New Competition* (Cambridge: Harvard University Press, 1956), pp. X, 329.

The more approximately constant sum are the effects of a competitive weapon, the stronger the competition will be. In other words, weapons which fight for market share in which one firm's gain is approximately the other firm's loss will be used extensively. When one firm puts out an innovation the probability that an opponent can retaliate with an equally effective innovation before the costs have been at least covered is by no means as great as the probability that a price cut can be replied to fast enough to make it unprofitable. As the techniques of advertising and styling become more and more routine, the effectiveness of one firm's threat to take action against another is greater and the employment of these weapons becomes more jointly detrimental; hence, we must eventually expect a limitation on the percentage of expenditure in these areas.... The market is not $\{0\} - \{1\}$ stable [i.e., no player is motivated to change strategy— Ed.]; hence, it is not competitive in the pristine sense. As the threat of counteraction by General Motors is sufficiently large to make any sizeable downward pricing action by a group of all the other firms unprofitable, General Motors is the dominant firm with respect to price... Healthy competition does not necessarily mean the preservation of unhealthy competitors. However, in an oligopolistic market with few large firms efficiency becomes difficult to define. Inherently, American Motors might be far more efficient than Ford, but in any emergency it would fail first. Although competition via increased technical efficiency and innovation may remain high, there is little that can be said a priori about the optimality of resource utilization in the automobile industry because of the size and structure of the firms and the importance of financial conditions to survival in an imperfect market.

2. The Cigarette Industry Today

The cigarette industry today is dominated by three of the four major companies [American Tobacco, Liggett and Myers, R. J. Reynolds] formed ... in 1911, with the fourth company, Lorillard, and two newcomers, Philip Morris and Brown and Williamson, being the only other competitors of substantial size. Competition in the industry is characterized by a heavy stress on advertising and product differentiation. This has run the gamut from slogans to king-sized, cork-tipped, filtered, mentholated, or oval-shaped cigarettes. Machinery for the production of cigarettes is fairly well standardized, and, although no data is available, it appears safe to assume that the costs of production of cigarettes of similar quality and size are approximately the same to any producer who uses the machines at the same intensity. In 1949, 95 percent of the cigarette production was carried out in twenty-one plants. The major blocks to entry are the sizes of advertising expenditures and the cost of carrying a sufficiently large inventory necessary to allow the tobacco to age. (See Table 12).

Each firm produces a variety of products. American Tobacco Company produces "Lucky Strike," "Pall Mall," "Herbert Tareyton," "Filter Tip Tareyton," and eight other brands of cigarettes. It produces "Half and Half," "Blue Boar," and "Genuine 'Bull' Durham" smoking tobaccos, as well as approximately twenty other brands and six brands of chewing tobacco. Its cigar brands include "La Corona" and "El Roi-Tan." Reynolds' products include "Camel," "Winston," and "Cavalier" cigarettes, "Prince Albert," "Stud," and "George Washington" smoking tobaccos, as well as other smoking tobaccos and several brands of chewing tobacco. Liggett and Myers makes sixty-three different kinds of cigarettes and smoking and chewing tobaccos, including "Chesterfield" and L. & M. Philip Morris sells "Marlboro," "Parliament," "Dunhill," "Spud," "English Ovals," "Virginia Rounds," "Player's Navy Cut," and "Philip Morris" cigarettes, as well as smoking tobaccos and Benson and Hedges cigars. Lorillard produces "Old Gold," "Kent," "Embassy," "Murad," and "Helmar" cigarettes, several smoking and chewing tobacco brands, and little cigars. The products of Brown and Williamson include "Avalon," "Kools," "Raleigh," "Viceroy," and "Wings."

The consumer is reached via many thousands of distributors who in turn deal through approximately 1,500,000 retail outlets. This introduces numerous difficulties in the study of the effect of pricing and other moves among the manufacturing firms.

A. Control

In their book,[5] Berle and Means included a statement of control of the 200 largest corporations in 1929. At that time they listed American, Reynolds, and Liggett and Myers as controlled by the legal device of non-voting common stock. The holdings of power in Lorillard were believed to be widely distributed.

The Temporary Natural Economic Committee report shows that in 1938 the twenty largest stockholders held 20.5 percent of American, 35.9 percent of Liggett and Myers, and 59.7 percent of Reynolds common stock, although Tennant has noted that several of the large holders were banks, brokers, and insurance companies. The 1954 share structure of the firms is given in Table 11. Control is presumed to be with the directors and officers only because no evidence to the contrary is in the possession of this writer.

There is a considerable overlap between directors and officers. American has eight directors out of nineteen who are officers; Liggett

[5] A. A. Berle, and G. C. Means, *The Modern Corporation and Private Property* (New York: Macmillan, 1933), pp. 95–116.

Table 11

	Shares	Stock-holders	Control
American	6,513,000 common	81,000	Directors
Tobacco Company	528,000 preferred	7,000	and officers
Reynolds	396,000 common	79,000	Directors
Tobacco Company	9,604,000 common class B		and officers
	490,000 preferred 3.6 percent	12,000	
	260,000 preferred 4.5 percent		
Liggett and Myers	3,912,000 common		Directors
	225,000 preferred 7 percent cumulative	44,000	and officers
Philip Morris	2,887,000 common		
	180,000 preferred 4 percent		Directors
	124,000 preferred 3.9 percent	28,000	and officers
Lorillard	2,853,000 common		Directors
	98,000 preferred 7 percent cumulative	28,000	and officers
Brown and	Wholly owned		
Williamson	subsidiary of British-American		
	Tobacco Co. Ltd.		

and Myers, six out of twelve; Philip Morris, five out of ten; Lorillard, seven out of thirteen; and at Reynolds almost all directors are officers or counsel.

B. Maximization and Control

As the officers are not major stockholders, their personal fortunes are not necessarily highly correlated with the size of the dividends declared (see Tennant for a discussion of bonus plans). In fact, since this is an industry which needs heavy financing because of inventory loads and tobacco taxes, there is an incentive to retain earnings in order to attain greater long-run strategic flexibility without complete dependence on outside financing. In the last ten years the percentage of earnings paid out in dividends has varied from almost 100 per cent down to less than 50 percent.

As a crude first approximation, it appears that the directors attempt to maximize long-run expected income to their firms, subject to bounds on risk and to the necessity of paying out sufficiently large dividends to make their stock attractive at prices above book value.

C. Asset Structure

The long-term debt structure is large in the cigarette industry, and preferred stock also plays an important role in the financial structure. This

Table 12

Current	American Tobacco	Reynolds	Liggett and Myers	Philip Morris	Lorillard
(1)	3.15–4.61	3.96–5.17	3.56–7.53	2.23–3.24	2.30–5.23
(2)	88.97–91.06	91.21–91.84	90.05–93.16	88.71–91.30	83.61–88.34
(3)	35.20–41.20	25.38–35.78	31.67–40.81	17.96–29.50	28.40–40.01
(4)	10.11–8.50	15.86–17.89	5.76–6.66	16.39–20.72	7.54–12.13

(1) Assets/liabilities
(2) Inventories/current assets
(3) Long-term debt
(4) Preferred issues

gives a leverage to the earnings of the common shares. This particular capital structure of the industry appears to be caused mainly by the need for large inventories of tobacco. Table 12 shows that in the years 1948–1954 inventories have made up approximately 90 percent of current assets. This table also lists the ranges in the percentages of long-term debt and preferred stock equity to ownership and long-term debt. The first set of figures is the ratio of current assets to current liabilities. These serve as an index of short-run vulnerability.

An index of the importance of the tobacco industry and the major firms in it is given by their net sales in the national market. Table 13 shows the net sales for five of the six largest firms for the period 1951–1955 (in units of $1000).

The total assets of the firms in the same period are shown in Table 14 (in units of $1000).

D. The Demand for Tobacco

Although the per capita demand for cigars and other forms of tobacco has fallen in the last fifty years, the per capita demand for cigarettes

Table 13

	Tobacco	Reynolds	Liggett and Myers	Philip Morris	Lorillard
1951	942,552	814,217	539,947	305,804	188,447
1952	1,065,738	881,424	603,081	306,698	214,508
1953	1,088,380	876,189	586,499	314,895	253,933
1954	1,068,579	814,274	548,862	294,902[a]	231,047
1955	1,090,845	866,426	546,965	283,219[a]	228,268

[a] Philip Morris Incorporated and Benson & Hedges Consolidated.

Table 14

	American Tobacco	Reynolds	Liggett and Myers	Philip Morris	Lorillard
1951	734,480	577,886	479,794	253,586	135,485
1952	783,154	591,641	488,288	265,025	160,844
1953	798,870	598,609	497,229	240,305	173,991
1954	775,364	617,636	491,309	255,131[a]	184,210
1955	801,725	611,641	458,592	261,593[a]	186,366

[a] Philip Morris Incorporated and Benson & Hedges Consolidated.

has risen almost without break. In 1954 there was a slight decline over 1953. The "cancer scare" appeared to be strong enough to change temporarily the secular trend in the consumption of cigarettes. Table 15 gives the per capita consumption of tobacco products in the United States for the years 1945–1954.

Tennant gives a multiple regression of per capita consumption on real national income and on "time" (i.e., a trend factor). This is done for the years 1913–1945. He obtains

$$X_1 = -.446 + .460X_2 + .00156X_3$$

where X_1 is the logarithm of consumption in hundredths of a pound, X_2 is the logarithm of income in dollars, and X_3 is the year of observation numbered according to its last two digits.

This gives an income elasticity of $+.460$ for tobacco.

Table 15
Per Capita Consumption (in pounds)

	Cigarettes	Cigars	Tobacco	Total
1945	7.76	1.23	2.10	11.09
1946	8.75	1.36	1.58	11.69
1947	8.76	1.29	1.51	11.76
1948	9.13	1.31	1.46	11.90
1949	9.15	1.16	1.44	11.75
1950	9.16	1.18	1.42	11.76
1951	9.64	1.18	1.31	12.13
1952	9.94	1.25	1.25	12.48
1953	10.03	1.26	1.19	12.48
1954	9.48	1.23	1.15	11.86

Table 16

Net Income before Dividends and Rate Earned on Net Worth, Less Good Will

	Net income (millions of dollars)					Net income (as percentage of net worth)				
	American Tobacco	Liggett and Myers	Reynolds	Lorillard	Philip Morris	American Tobacco	Liggett and Myers	Reynolds	Lorillard	Philip Morris
1936	20.1	24.2	29.3	3.5	2.4	12.0	17.3	20.6	8.2	31.2
1937	26.2	21.4	27.6	2.3	3.6	15.8	15.1	19.6	5.4	25.5
1938	25.4	20.6	23.7	4.0	5.7	15.6	14.2	16.8	9.3	34.4
1939	26.4	20.7	25.6	3.8	6.6	16.2	13.9	17.7	8.9	25.0
1940	27.7	20.3	25.5	3.9	7.4	16.9	13.4	17.2	8.7	25.1
1941	23.3	17.9	23.2	3.4	7.4	14.7	11.7	15.2	7.5	15.8
1942	22.3	16.8	19.9	3.9	7.8	13.5	10.1	12.8	8.5	15.8
1943	22.5	16.7	18.6	3.6	6.9	13.2	9.9	11.7	6.9	11.1
1944	19.9	14.8	17.8	3.6	6.8	11.7	9.2	11.0	6.9	10.5
1945	19.7	14.9	19.7	3.5	6.1	11.4	9.1	9.3	6.7	10.5
1946	29.9	18.4	28.0	3.5	5.0	16.1	10.9	12.7	6.5	9.0
1947	33.8	22.9	32.1	5.5	6.0	13.6	13.1	13.9	10.0	7.1
1948	43.9	29.3	34.6	5.6	6.0	16.3	15.8	12.9	9.9	8.6
1949	45.7	29.6	40.5	6.8	12.5	15.7	12.7	14.0	11.6	16.3
1950	41.7	29.1	40.3	6.7	15.3	13.6	12.0	13.2	10.7	18.3
1951	33.1	21.8	32.1	5.1	16.7	10.5	9.0	10.2	7.7	13.9
1952	34.1	21.4	31.9	5.7	12.6	9.0	9.0	10.0	8.4	10.2
1953	41.2	23.0	34.1	7.2	11.3[a]	10.5	9.3	10.2	9.2	9.0[a]
1954	43.1	22.2	44.8	6.3	12.4[a]	11.0	9.0	13.0	8.0	9.1[a]
1955	51.7	26.7	53.2	6.6	11.5[a]	12.2	10.3	14.2	8.1	8.0[a]

[a] Consolidated with Benson & Hedges.

It is suggested that the price elasticity of cigarettes is low, although no formal verification is given.

E. Advertising and Demand

From his study Tennant concludes that we may be nearly certain that the advertising elasticity of total cigarette demand is very small, although no attempt has been made to impute any of the long-run trend in tobacco consumption to advertising.

The elasticity of demand for different cigarette brands depends heavily upon the size and success of individual advertising campaigns. The company reports list selling, advertising, and administrative expenses together. In 1955 these amounted to approximately 10 percent of the total net sales of Liggett and Myers; 6 percent of the sales of Reynolds, and 10.5 percent for Philip Morris. Nicholls presents a table of advertising expenditures for the six main firms for the years 1939–1949, and Tennant shows change in market share between Camel, Lucky Strike, and Chesterfield. The considerable fluctuation in market share contrasts with the fairly steady increase in the overall demand for cigarettes.

The 1955 report of the American Tobacco Company notes that: "Trade estimates of national advertising expenditures again indicated, as they have for the last fifteen years, that your Company's traceable advertising costs per pack of cigarettes are substantially lower than the industry average."

It appears that advertising efficiency grows with size, hence, advertising expenditures are a factor working to the disadvantage of the small-sized firm. However, no formal study of the fluctuation of individual brand sales has been made.

F. Strategies and Profits

Both Nicholls and Tennant present an analysis of the price behavior of the firms in the market for cigarettes. The pricing policy has for the most part been one of follow the leader, with Reynolds instigating the majority of the changes. American next, and Liggett and Myers the least. Both upward and downward price changes have been followed with a few exceptions. Although the price increase in the early 1930s may have helped to make 1930, 1931, and 1932 exceptionally profitable years, it appears to have been a tactical blunder. This can be seen by the plummeting of profits in the following years, due to the loss of market shares to new firms and the drastic price cuts to stem the growth of new entries in the cigarette industry. Table 16 gives the net income figures for five companies in the period 1936–1955, as well as net income calculated as a percentage of net worth.

These firms maintain almost the same percentage of inventory to current assets, and their buying tactics in the tobacco markets appear to be similar.

G. Indices of Vulnerability, Stability, and Strategies

The *short-run market vulnerability* of all firms in the cigarette industry is high. Since they all have approximately the same product line, if any firm wished to cut prices across the board and its reductions were not met, it appears that the cross-elasticity between different brands is high enough that the other firms would lose more revenue than if they met the cut. If they met the cut, then the damage exchange rate would be proportional to the volume of trade done, i.e., it might cost a very large firm several dollars of lost profits to cause a dollar loss to a small firm if it had to take action on a national basis. On the other hand, the damage exchange rate might be better if the small firm were confined to a regional market.

The *short-run financial vulnerability* of the six largest firms does not appear to be of great importance to fraternal warfare between them. They all have sufficient resources to weather several bad years, hence, there is no payoff to be gained by indulging in fight-to-the-death struggles. The short-run financial vulnerability of a new entrant would be great unless he could come in with sufficient resources to take high losses for several years and establish a market via pricing and advertising in order to gain product acceptance.

Long-run market vulnerability is hard to characterize, since it contains a large random component due to the unpredictability of the success of advertising campaigns and innovation. The successes of Reynolds after World War I and the recent successes and failures of Philip Morris and of Lorillard would have been hard to predict.

In a market even with a secular increase in demand but with rising costs of production small firms may have a high long-run market vulnerability. This could be caused by a policy which leaves the competitive products of the major firms at prices such that the small firms are unable to raise prices without losing markets and are forced to work on diminishing margins as costs rise. This appears to be the policy followed by the major firms to limit the inroads of the economy brands during the 1930s. Such a policy has long-run profit maximization justification if the costs of containment are less than the costs of possible loss of markets owing to the permanent establishment of new firms.

The long-run financial vulnerability of the major firms with the possible exception of Lorillard appears to be small. In order for ruin conditions to play a role the attacking firms would have to wait so long that the war costs would be more than the expected value of future extra profits, even if antitrust legislation did not interfere. This is not the case for minor firms. If a sufficiently low ceiling is established by the major firms, then random fluctuations may be enough to take care of small competitors.

The costs of carrying inventory, the dependence upon debt financing, the costs of prepaid tobacco tax, and the flat-rate feature of the tax, regardless of the final price of the cigarettes, as well as the apparent increasing returns to scale in advertising, are all factors which work in the favor of large, established firms in the cigarette industry.

Control vulnerability is not important for the large firms. The capture of a large firm would take a considerable amount of money under the present capital structure. Even if this were possible, given the state of the antitrust laws, any merger among the six largest firms would probably be declared illegal. For the small firms this is not so. Thus, it is not surprising that the American Tobacco Company acquired the American Cigarette and Cigar Company on December 31, 1953, and that Philip Morris consolidated with Benson & Hedges.

The form of strategy that approximates the behavior of the major firms in the cigarette industry can be described as follows:

Firm i accepts a price $p_{i,t}$ in the tth period for its mth product and a range of advertising expenditures $A_{i,t} \leq a_{i,t} \leq \bar{A}_{i,t}$ for its mth product, provided the other major firms charge certain equivalent prices for comparable products and keep their advertising expenditures within given ranges. If any major firm j inaugurates a price increase, then the decision to meet the increase depends upon the state of information of i at that time. If the increase is met and no other firms meet the increase, and if business falls off as a result, then the old price will be resumed. If firm i initiates a price raise and is not followed sufficiently within a specified time, it will resume its previous price. If any major firm cuts prices, the ith firm will meet this cut if it observes that its market will be sufficiently affected to make it more profitable to do so. If any firm exceeds some bound in advertising expense, and this apparently has an important effect on the market of i, the campaign will be met. If any marginal firm or small competitor begins to take more than some percentage of the market, determined by the costs of fighting a containing action at that level, the ith firm will cut prices and/ or increase advertising on the relevant products or, depending upon financial and legal conditions, attempt to absorb the competitor.

If we consider this type of strategy as a threat strategy, then ... it appears that price in the cigarette industry is stable against downward cuts (given the present state of demand) if each of the big three were to use this type of strategy against any violator or group of violators (i.e., the subset consisting of the largest three firms is sufficient to deter price cuts by any other firm or group of firms). The fluctuation in demand for brands has been so considerable that any stability will be of the conditional type. . . .

H. Conclusions

. . . Because of lack of information, it was not possible to evaluate the effect of different policies upon the payoffs to the firms. However, even without doing so, it is fairly evident that because of the high state of information and common technology, the ease of retaliation, the difficulties in hiding price cuts or other major policy changes, and the large investment of the firms, the conscious parallelism which results from following the type of strategy outlined is highly probable and needs no cooperative mechanism to bring it about.

The variability in demand for specific brands or types of cigarettes is large enough to be an important source of danger to a small firm. Hence, advertising and product variation present a formidable barrier to entry. Possibly the biggest threat to any change in the industry structure (barring any great change in the overall demand for cigarettes) would be caused by the success of a brand of an already existing small cigarette firm which had established a small specialized market and was not immediately financially vulnerable to demand fluctuations for or price cuts affecting other types of cigarettes.

As there does not appear to be very much scope for technological improvements in the manufacture of cigarettes (as compared with the manufacture of automobiles or other durables), the oligopolistic pressures to avoid intensive price competition force competition to be channeled into advertising and product variation. In consumer durable industries the desire to avoid price competition may switch the competitive forces to technological research and new methods. In the cigarette industry, under its present structure, the social disadvantages of next-to-no price competition are hardly counteracted by dynamic innovation features. This appears to be caused by the combination of an oligopolistic structure with the technological conditions in the production of cigarettes.

Although we have attempted to link theory and investigation for two industries, considerably greater detail is required. Possibly after the simulation of several complex models of industries we will be able to validate economic theories of solution to n-person games.

Another set of analogies may be examined briefly before going on to some other useful empirical work. There are certain similarities between the nuclear "club," especially the United States, Britain, and the Soviet Union, and an oligopolistic cartel. In the international political arena, as in many European economies or some international markets, formal collusion for the restraint of competition, in the formation of cartels, is not forbidden by higher edict. The three major nuclear powers, beginning before the acquisition of usable atomic weapons by France and China, have groped their way toward a set of tacit and overt restrictions which would limit the ability of other powers to obtain their own nuclear capabilities either through transfer or through self-development. Some of the slowness with which nuclear weapons have, in fact, proliferated is doubtless due to the success of these efforts, though that success is still modest enough, and the restraints have many loopholes. But to the degree that this analogy is appropriate—from the cartel to the nuclear club trying to prevent further entry and "ruinous competition" from other powers—a brief listing of the barriers to entry that have been found relevant in market situations will be instructive. Most of these are the result of the industrial structure and are not necessarily erected by collusion among the firms. Circumstances creating barriers to entry in industry:[1]

1. Circumstances giving an absolute cost advantage to some or all established firms.
    a. Control of production techniques by established firms, via patents or secrecy, which permits exclusion of entrants from optimal techniques or the levying of a royalty charge for their use [technical secrets for the manufacture of bombs and delivery vehicles].
    b. Imperfections in the markets for hired factors (including materials) which favor established firms, or ownership or control by agreement of strategic factor supplies by such firms [access to uranium ore, availability of nuclear scientists].
    c. Requirement by the entering firm of enough factors to cause market price to rise significantly (linked to the need for large scale to gain efficiency) [the economic and social costs of bidding scientists and engineers away from their previous occupations].

[1] J. S. Bain, "Conditions of Entry and the Emergence of Monopoly," in E. H. Chamberlin, ed., *Monopoly, Competition, and Their Regulation* (New York: Macmillan, 1954), pp. 226–227. The international relations analogues in brackets at the end of each statement are my own; the preceding material is quoted verbatim.

    d. Money-market conditions imposing higher interest rates or more severe rationing of investible funds on potential entrant firms [discriminatory access to foreign aid].

2. Circumstances giving a product-differentiation advantage to some or all established firms.
    a. Patent control of superior product by established firms [a variant of 1a].
    b. The possible accumulative preference of buyers for established brand names and company reputations [a sense, in the rest of the world, that the existing nuclear powers are more "responsible" or "legitimate" than newcomers would be].
    c. Ownership or contractual control of favored distributive outlets by established firms [foreign air and missile bases].

3. Circumstances discouraging entry because of the size of an economical increment of entry.
    a. Real economies to the large-scale firm such that the optimal and possibly smaller-scale firm will supply a significant share of the market [need for a large industrial base, need for testing sites, the high cost of effective intelligence services].
    b. Strictly pecuniary economies of the same order [bargaining power based on size].

4. Absolute legal prohibitions on entry.

This list suggests a variety of ways in which collusion among the nuclear powers might be exercised against potential entrants short of "absolute legal prohibitions."

If oligopoly *can* produce a stable market structure, it is now clear that this is hardly a consequence that can always be expected merely from the fact that only a few firms dominate the industry. It is essential to dig still further into the question of precisely what conditions favor stability. Fortunately, there is now a rather large body of empirical material in economics on which a variety of propositions have been tested. Two such studies follow. The first is an article by George Stigler, which develops a theory of oligopoly and provisionally tests it on some data on market conditions in the United States. The paper is of interest because of its rigorous empirical investigation, its tentative conclusions about some of the conditions that favor stability, and not least because some of its assumptions are strikingly similar to some of those often made for "balance of power" systems internationally. He notes, for example, "It is a well-established proposition that if any member of the agreement can secretly violate it, he will gain larger profits than by conforming to it." ("Act to increase capabilities; fight rather than pass up an opportunity to increase capabilities.")[2] "All agreements whose violation would be profitable to the violator must be enforced." ("Act to oppose any coalition or single factor which tends to assume a position of preponderance with respect to the rest of the system.") As with balance-of-power theory, however, it is not always clear from what quarters the enforcement must come: national or supranational, collusive or institutional at a higher level. Also, one major difference between balance of power theory and Stigler's propositions must be noted. There is nothing akin to the proposition "Stop fighting rather than eliminate an essential national actor," unless one assumes either the presence of antitrust pressure and governmental assistance to failing firms, or a very sophisticated sense that the market will be more stable with the existing number of firms than with fewer and that this would compensate the other firms for passing up the opportunity to expand their market shares. (For some arguments that this might be true see the discussion later on the instabilities of duopoly.)

In the following discussion, note again the crucial role played by information and the possibilities of keeping violation secret. The idea of fixed market shares, where each oligopolist is expected to sell only to his established customers, is reminiscent of "spheres of influence," and here too, a venture beyond accepted customers or spheres is a highly visible and provocative act. Note too the major conclusion—the frequency of price-cutting is positively related to the degree of concentration of *buyers* (the greater the potential of a single market, the greater the pressures to violate the collusive agreement). Here, it is perhaps more useful to consider price cutting as analogous to subversion or supporting local guerrillas rather than necessarily to the more overt forms of military action.

●

---

[2] All parenthetical quotations here are from M. A. Kaplan, *System and Process in International Politics* (New York: Wiley, 1957).

10

A Theory of Oligopoly

George J. Stigler

1. The Task of Collusion

A satisfactory theory of oligopoly cannot begin with assumptions concerning the way in which each firm views its interdependence with its rivals. If we adhere to the traditional theory of profit-maximizing enterprises, then behavior is no longer something to be assumed but rather something to be deduced. The firms in an industry will behave in such a way, given the demand-and-supply functions (including those of rivals), that their profits will be maximized.

The combined profits of the entire set of firms in an industry are maximized when they act together as a monopolist. At least in the traditional formulation of the oligopoly problem, in which there are no major uncertainties as to the profit-maximizing output and price at any time, this familiar conclusion seems inescapable. Moreover, the result holds for any number of firms.

Our modification of this theory consists simply in presenting a systematic account of the factors governing the feasibility of collusion, which, like most things in this world, is not free. Before we do so, it is desirable to look somewhat critically at the concept of homogeneity of products, and what it implies for profit-maximizing. We shall show that collusion normally involves much more than "the" price.

Homogeneity is commonly defined in terms of identity of products or of (what is presumed to be equivalent) pairs of products between which the elasticity of substitution is infinite. On either definition it is the

Reprinted from *The Journal of Political Economy*, 72, 1 (February 1964), pp. 44–59, by permission of the University of Chicago Press. Copyright, 1964, by the University of Chicago Press.

behavior of buyers that is decisive. Yet it should be obvious that products may be identical to any or every buyer, while buyers may be quite different from the viewpoint of sellers.

This fact, that every transaction involves two parties, is something that economists do not easily forget. One would, therefore, expect a definition of homogeneity also to be two-sided: if the products are what sellers offer, and the purchase commitments are what the buyers offer, full homogeneity clearly involves infinite elasticities of substitution between both products and purchase commitments. In other words, two products are homogeneous to a buyer if he is indifferent between all combinations of x of one and (say) $20 - x$ of the other, at a common price. Two purchase commitments are homogeneous to a seller if he is indifferent between all combinations of y of one and (say) $20 - y$ of the other, at a common price. Full homogeneity is then defined as homogeneity both in products (sellers) and purchase commitments (buyers).

The heterogeneity of purchase commitments (buyers), however, is surely often at least as large as that of products within an industry, and sometimes vastly larger. There is the same sort of personal differentia of buyers as of sellers—ease in making sales, promptness of payment, penchant for returning goods, likelihood of buying again (or buying other products). In addition, there are two differences among buyers which are pervasive and well recognized in economics:

1. The size of purchase, with large differences in costs of providing lots of different size.
2. The urgency of purchase, with possibly sufficient differences in elasticity of demand to invite price discrimination.

It is one thing to assert that no important market has homogeneous transactions, and quite another to measure the extent of the heterogeneity. In a regime of perfect knowledge, it would be possible to measure heterogeneity by the variance of prices in transactions; in a regime of imperfect knowledge, there will be dispersion of prices even with transaction homogeneity.

The relevance of heterogeneity to collusion is this: it is part of the task of maximizing industry profits to employ a price structure that takes account of the larger differences in the costs of various classes of transactions. Even with a single, physically homogeneous product, the profits will be reduced if differences among buyers are ignored.... Disregard of differences among buyers proves to be equivalent to imposing an excise tax upon them, but one which is not collected by the monopolist.

A price structure of some complexity will usually be the goal of collusive oligopolists.

2. The Methods of Collusion

Collusion of firms can take many forms, of which the most comprehensive is outright merger. Often, merger will be inappropriate, however, because of diseconomies of scale, and at certain times and places it may be forbidden by law. Only less comprehensive is the cartel with a joint sales agency, which again has economic limitations—it is ill suited to custom work and creates serious administrative costs in achieving quality standards, cost reductions, product innovations, etc. In deference to American antitrust policy, we shall assume that the collusion takes the form of joint determination of outputs and prices by ostensibly independent firms, but we shall not take account of the effects of the legal prohibitions until later. Oligopoly existed before 1890, and has existed in countries that have never had an antitrust policy.

The colluding firms must agree upon the price structure appropriate to the transaction classes which they are prepared to recognize. A complete profit-maximizing price structure may have almost infinitely numerous price classes: the firms will have to decide upon the number of price classes in the light of the costs and returns from tailoring prices to the diversity of transactions.... There are net profits to be obtained by catering to differences in transactions. The level of collusive prices will also depend upon the conditions of entry into the industry, as well as upon the elasticities of demand.

Let us assume that the collusion has been effected, and a price structure agreed upon. It is a well-established proposition that if any member of the agreement can secretly violate it, he will gain larger profits than by conforming to it. It is, moreover, surely one of the axioms of human behavior that all agreements whose violation would be profitable to the violator must be enforced. The literature of collusive agreements, ranging from the pools of the 1880's to the electrical conspiracies of recent times, is replete with instances of the collapse of conspiracies because of "secret" price cutting. This literature is biased: conspiracies that are successful in avoiding an amount of price-cutting which leads to collapse of the agreement are less likely to be reported or detected. But no conspiracy can neglect the problem of enforcement.

Enforcement consists, basically, of detecting significant deviations from the agreed-upon prices. Once detected, the deviations will tend to disappear because they are no longer secret and will be matched by fellow conspirators if they are not withdrawn. If the enforcement is weak, however—if price-cutting is detected only slowly and incompletely—the conspiracy must recognize its weakness: it must set prices not much above the competitive level so the inducements to price-cutting are small, or it must restrict the conspiracy to areas in which enforcement can be made efficient.

Fixing market shares is probably the most efficient of all methods of combating secret price reductions. No one can profit from price-cutting if he is moving along the industry demand curve,[1] once a maximum profit price has been chosen. With inspection of output and an appropriate formula for redistribution of gains and losses from departures from quotas, the incentive to secret price-cutting is eliminated. Unless inspection of output is costly or ineffective (as with services), this is the ideal method of enforcement, and is widely used by legal cartels. Unfortunately for oligopolists, it is usually an easy form of collusion to detect, for it may require side payments among firms and it leaves indelible traces in the output records.

Almost as efficient a method of eliminating secret price-cutting is to assign each buyer to a single seller. If this can be done for all buyers, short-run price-cutting no longer has any purpose. Long-run price-cutting will still be a serious possibility if the buyers are in competition: lower prices to one's own customers can then lead to an expansion of their share of their market, so the price-cutter's long-run demand curve will be more elastic than that of the industry. Long-run price-cutting is likely to be important, however, only where sellers are providing a major cost component to the buyer.

There are real difficulties of other sorts to the sellers in the assignment of buyers. In general, the fortunes of the various sellers will differ greatly over time: one seller's customers may grow threefold, while another seller's customers shrink by half. If the customers have uncorrelated fluctuations in demand, the various sellers will experience large changes in relative outputs in the short run. Where the turnover of buyers is large, the method is simply impracticable.

Nevertheless, the conditions appropriate to the assignment of customers will exist in certain industries, and in particular the geographical division of the market has often been employed. Since an allocation of buyers is an obvious and easily detectible violation of the Sherman Act, we may again infer that an efficient method of enforcing a price agreement is excluded by the antitrust laws. We therefore turn to other techniques of enforcement, but we shall find that the analysis returns to allocation of buyers.

[1] More precisely, he is moving along a demand curve which is a fixed share of the industry demand, and, hence, has the same elasticity as the industry curve at every price.

In general, the policing of a price agreement involves an audit of the transactions prices. In the absence or violation of antitrust laws, actual inspection of the accounting records of sellers has been employed by some colluding groups, but even this inspection gives only limited assurance that the price agreement is adhered to. Ultimately, there is no substitute for obtaining the transaction prices from the buyers.

An oligopolist will not consider making secret price cuts to buyers whose purchases fall below a certain size relative to his aggregate sales. The ease with which price-cutting is detected by rivals is decisive in this case. If p is the probability that some rival will hear of one such price reduction, $1 - (1 - p)^n$ is the probability that a rival will learn of at least one reduction if it is given to n customers. Even if p is as small as .01, when n equals 100, the probability of detection is .634, and when n equals 1000, it is .99996. No one has yet invented a way to advertise price reductions which brings them to the attention of numerous customers but not to that of any rival.

It follows that oligopolistic collusion will often be effective against small buyers even when it is ineffective against large buyers. When the oligopolists sell to numerous small retailers, for example, they will adhere to the agreed-upon price, even though they are cutting prices to larger chain stores and industrial buyers. This is a first empirical implication of our theory. Let us henceforth exclude small buyers from consideration.

The detection of secret price-cutting will, of course, be as difficult as interested people can make it. The price-cutter will certainly protest his innocence, or, if this would tax credulity beyond its taxable capacity, blame a disobedient subordinate. The price cut will often take the indirect form of modifying some nonprice dimension of the transaction. The customer may, and often will, divulge price reductions, in order to have them matched by others, but he will learn from experience if each disclosure is followed by the withdrawal of the lower price offer. Indeed, the buyer will frequently fabricate wholly fictitious price offers to test the rivals. Policing the collusion sounds very much like the subtle and complex problem presented in a good detective story.

There is a difference: In our case the man who murders the collusive price will receive the bequest of patronage. The basic method of detection of a price-cutter must be the fact that he is getting business he would otherwise not obtain. No promises of lower prices that fail to shift some business can be really effective—either the promised price is still too high or it is simply not believed.

Our definition of perfect collusion, indeed, must be that no buyer changes sellers voluntarily. There is no competitive price-cutting if there are no shifts of buyers among sellers.

To this rule that price-cutting must be inferred from shifts of buyers there is one partial exception, but that is an important one. There is one type of buyer who usually reveals the price he pays, and does not accept secret benefices: the government. The system of sealed bids, publicly opened with full identification of each bidder's price and specifications, is the ideal instrument for the detection of price-cutting. There exists no alternative method of secretly cutting prices (bribery of purchasing agents aside). Our second empirical prediction, then, is that collusion will always be more effective against buyers who report correctly and fully the prices tendered to them.

It follows from the test of absence of price competition by buyer loyalty—and this is our third major empirical prediction—that collusion is severely limited (under present assumptions, excluding market sharing) when the significant buyers constantly change identity. There exist important markets in which the (substantial) buyers do change identity continuously, namely, in the construction industries. The building of a plant or an office building, for example, is an essentially nonrepetitive event, and rivals cannot determine whether the successful bidder has been a price-cutter unless there is open bidding to specification.

The normal market, however, contains both stability and change. There may be a small rate of entry of new buyers. There will be some shifting of customers even in a regime of effective collusion, for a variety of minor reasons we can lump together as "random factors." There will often be some sharing of buyers by several sellers—a device commending itself to buyers to increase the difficulty of policing price agreements. We move then to the world of circumstantial evidence, or, as it is sometimes called, of probability.

3. The Conditions for Detecting Secret Price Reductions

We shall investigate the problem of detecting secret price-cutting with a simplified model, in which all buyers and all sellers are initially of equal size. The number of buyers per seller—recalling that we exclude from consideration all buyers who take less than (say) .33 percent of a seller's output—will range from 300 down to perhaps 10 or 20 (since we wish to avoid the horrors of full bilateral oligopoly). A few of these buyers are new, but over moderate periods of time most are "old," although some of these old customers will shift among suppliers. A potential secret price-cutter has then three groups of customers who would increase their patronage if given secret price cuts: the old customers of rivals; the old customers who would normally leave him; and new customers.

Most old buyers will deal regularly with one or a few sellers, in the absence of secret price-cutting. There may be no secret price-cutting because a collusive price is adhered to, or because only an essentially competitive price can be obtained. We shall show that the loyalty of customers is a crucial variable in determining which price is approached. We need to know the probability that an old customer will buy again from his regular supplier at the collusive price, in the absence of secret price-cutting.

The buyer will set the economies of repetitive purchase (which include smaller transaction costs and less product testing) against the increased probability of secret price-cutting that comes from shifting among suppliers. From the viewpoint of any one buyer, this gain will be larger the larger the number of sellers and the smaller the number of buyers, as we shall show later. The costs of shifting among suppliers will be smaller the more homogeneous the goods and the larger the purchases of the buyer (again an inverse function of his size). Let us label this probability of repeat purchases p. We shall indicate later how this probability could be determined in a more general approach.

The second component of sales of a firm will be its sales to new buyers and to the floating old customers of rivals. Here, we assume that each seller is equally likely to make a sale, in the absence of price competition.

Let us proceed to the analysis. There are n_0 "old" buyers and n_n new customers, with $n_n = \lambda n_0$ and n_s sellers. A firm may look to three kinds of evidence on secret price-cutting, and, therefore, by symmetry, to three potential areas to practice secret price-cutting.

1. *The behavior of its own old customers.* It has, on average, n_0/n_s such customers, and expects to sell to $m_1 = pn_0/n_s$ of them in a given round of transactions, in the absence of price-cutting. The variance of this number of customers is

$$\sigma_1{}^2 = \frac{(1 - p)pn_0}{n_s}$$

The probability of the firm losing more old customers than

$$\frac{(1 - p)n_0}{n_s} + k\sigma_1$$

is given by the probability of values greater than k. The expected number of these old customers who will shift to any one rival is, say,

$$m_2 = \frac{1}{n_s - 1}\left[\frac{(1 - p)n_0}{n_s} + k\sigma_1\right]$$

with a variance

$$\sigma_2{}^2 = \frac{n_s - 2}{(n_s - 1)^2}\left[\frac{(1 - p)n_0}{n_s} + k\sigma_1\right]$$

The probability that any rival will obtain more than $m_2 + r\sigma_2$ of these customers is determined by r. We could now choose those combinations of k and r that fix a level of probability for the loss of a given number of old customers to any one rival beyond which secret price-cutting by this rival will be inferred. This is heavy arithmetic, however, so we proceed along a less elegant route.

Let us assume that the firm's critical value for the loss of old customers, beyond which it infers secret price-cutting is

$$\frac{(1 - p)n_0}{n_s} + \sigma_1 = \frac{(1 - p)n_0}{n_s}\left[1 + \sqrt{\left(\frac{p}{1 - p}\frac{n_s}{n_0}\right)}\right]$$

$$= \frac{(1 - p)n_0}{n_s}(1 + \theta)$$

that is, one standard deviation above the mean. Any one rival will on average attract

$$m_2 = \frac{1}{n_s - 1}\left[\frac{(1 - p)n_0}{n_s} + \sigma_1\right]$$

of these customers, with a variance of

$$\sigma_2{}^2 = \frac{n_s - 2}{(n_s - 1)^2}\left[\frac{(1 - p)n_0}{n_s} + \sigma_1\right]$$

Let the rival be suspected of price-cutting if he obtains more than $(m_2 + \sigma_2)$ customers, that is, if the probability of any larger number is less than about 30 percent. The joint probability of losing one standard deviation more than the average number of old customers and a rival obtaining one standard deviation more than his average share is about 10 percent. The average sales of a rival are n_0/n_s, ignoring new customers. The maximum number of buyers any seller can obtain from one rival without exciting suspicion, minus the number he will on average get without price-cutting ($[1 - p]n_0/n_s[n_s - 1]$), expressed as a ratio to his average sales, is

$$\frac{[\theta(1 - p)n_0/(n_s - 1)n_s + \sigma_2]}{n_0/n_s}$$

This criterion is tabulated in Table 1.

Table 1

Percentage Gains in Sales from Undetected Price-Cutting by a Firm

$$Criterion\ I: \frac{1}{(n_s - 1)}\left[\theta(1 - p) + \sqrt{\frac{n_s(n_s - 2)(1 - p)(1 + \theta)}{n_0}} \right] \qquad \theta = \sqrt{\frac{p}{1 - p}\frac{n_s}{n_0}}$$

Probability of repeat sales (p)	No. of buyers (n_0)	No. of sellers					
		2	3	4	5	10	20
$p = .95$	20	6.9	11.3	11.3	11.4	11.8	12.7
	30	5.6	8.9	8.8	8.8	9.0	9.6
	40	4.9	7.5	7.4	7.4	7.5	7.9
	50	4.4	6.6	6.5	6.4	6.5	6.8
	100	3.1	4.4	4.3	4.3	4.2	4.4
	200	2.2	3.0	2.9	2.8	2.8	2.8
	400	1.5	2.1	2.0	1.9	1.8	1.8
$p = .90$	20	9.5	14.8	14.7	14.6	14.8	15.7
	30	7.8	11.7	11.5	11.4	11.4	12.0
	40	6.7	10.0	9.7	9.6	9.5	9.9
	50	6.0	8.8	8.6	8.4	8.3	8.6
	100	4.2	6.0	5.8	5.6	5.4	5.5
	200	3.0	4.1	3.9	3.8	3.6	3.6
	400	2.1	2.8	2.7	2.6	2.4	2.4
$p = .80$	20	12.6	19.3	18.9	18.7	18.6	19.4
	30	10.3	15.4	15.0	14.7	14.5	15.0
	40	8.9	13.1	12.7	12.5	12.2	12.5
	50	8.0	11.6	11.2	11.0	10.6	10.8
	100	5.7	8.0	7.7	7.4	7.1	7.1
	200	4.0	5.5	5.3	5.1	4.8	4.7
	400	2.8	3.8	3.6	3.5	3.2	3.2
$p = .70$	20	14.5	22.3	21.8	21.5	21.2	21.9
	30	11.8	17.8	17.3	17.0	16.6	16.9
	40	10.2	15.2	14.8	14.5	14.0	14.2
	50	9.2	13.5	13.1	12.8	12.3	12.4
	100	6.5	9.3	9.0	8.7	8.2	8.2
	200	4.6	6.5	6.2	6.0	5.6	5.5
	400	3.2	4.5	4.3	4.2	3.8	3.7

The entries in Table 1 are measures of the maximum additional sales obtainable by secret price-cutting (expressed as a percentage of average sales) from any one rival beyond which that rival will infer that the price-cutting is taking place. Since the profitability of secret price-cutting depends upon the amount of business one can obtain (as well as upon the excess of price over marginal cost), we may also view these numbers as the measures of the incentive to engage in secret price-cutting. Three features of the tabulation are noteworthy:

a. The gain in sales from any one rival by secret price-cutting is not very sensitive to the number of rivals, given the number of customers and the probability of repeat sales. The aggregate gain in sales of a firm from price-cutting—its total incentive to secret price-cutting—is the sum of the gains from each rival, and, therefore, increases roughly in proportion to the number of rivals.

b. The incentive to secret price-cutting falls as the number of customers per seller increases—and falls roughly in inverse proportion to the square root of the number of buyers.

c. The incentive to secret price-cutting rises as the probability of repeat purchases falls, but at a decreasing rate.

We have said that the gain to old buyers from shifting their patronage among sellers will be that it encourages secret price-cutting by making it more difficult to detect. Table 1 indicates that there are diminishing returns to increased shifting: The entries increase at a decreasing rate as p falls. In a fuller model we could introduce the costs of shifting among suppliers and determine p to maximize expected buyer gains. The larger the purchases of a buyer, when buyers are of unequal size, however, the greater is the prospect that his shifts will induce price-cutting.

In addition it is clear that, when the number of sellers exceeds two, it is possible for two or more firms to pool information and thus to detect less extreme cases of price-cutting. For example, at the given probability levels, the number of old customers that any one rival should be able to take from a firm was shown to be at most

$$(1 - p)\frac{n_0(1 + \theta)}{n_s + 1}$$

with variance

$$\frac{(n_s - 2)(1 - p)(1 + \theta)}{(n_s - 1)^2}n_0$$

At the same probability level, the average number of old customers that one rival should be able to take from T firms is at most

$$\frac{T(1 - p)n_0}{n_s - T}\left(1 + \frac{\theta}{\sqrt{T}}\right)$$

with the variance

$$\frac{(n_s - T - 1)}{(n_s - T)^2}(1 - p)\left(1 + \frac{\theta}{\sqrt{T}}\right)n_0 T$$

Each of these is smaller than the corresponding expression for one seller when expressed as a fraction of the customers lost by each of the firms pooling information.

There are, of course, limits to such pooling of information: not only does it become expensive as the number of firms increases but also it produces less reliable information, since one of the members of the pool may himself be secretly cutting prices. Some numbers illustrative of the effect of pooling will be given at a later point.

2. *The attraction of old customers of other firms is a second source of evidence of price-cutting.* If a given rival has not cut prices, he will on average lose $(1 - p)(n_0/n_s)$ customers, with a variance of σ_1^2. The number of customers he will retain with secret price-cutting cannot exceed a level at which the rivals suspect the price-cutting. Any one rival will have little basis for judging whether he is getting a fair share of this firm's old customers, but they can pool their information and then in the aggregate they will expect the firm to lose at least $(1 - p)(n_0/n_s) - 2\sigma_1$ customers, at the 5 percent probability level. Hence, the secret price-cutter can retain at most $2\sigma_1$ of his old customers (beyond his average number), which as a fraction of his average sales (ignoring new customers) is

$$\frac{2\sigma_1}{n_0/n_s} = 2\sqrt{\frac{(1 - p)pn_s}{n_0}}$$

This is tabulated as Table 2.

Table 2
Old Customers that a Secret Price-Cutter can Retain,
as a Percentage of Average Sales

$$\text{Criterion II: } 2\sqrt{\frac{p(1 - p)}{2}\frac{n_s}{n_0}}$$

Probability that old customer will remain loyal (p)	No. of old customers per seller (n_0/n_s)			
	10	20	50	100
.95	13.8	9.7	6.2	4.4
.90	19.0	13.4	8.5	6.0
.85	22.6	16.0	10.1	7.1
.80	25.3	17.9	11.3	8.0
.75	27.4	19.4	12.2	8.7
.70	29.0	20.5	13.0	9.2
.65	30.2	21.3	13.5	9.5
.60	31.0	21.9	13.9	9.8
.55	31.5	22.2	14.1	10.0
.50	31.6	22.4	14.1	10.0

If the entries in Table 2 are compared with those in Table 1,[2] it is found that a price-cutter is easier to detect by his gains at the expense of any one rival than by his unusual proportion of repeat sales. This second criterion will therefore seldom be useful.

3. *The behavior of new customers is a third source of information on price-cutting.* There are n_n new customers per period, equal to λn_0. A firm expects, in the absence of price-cutting, to sell to

$$m_3 = \frac{1}{n_s} \lambda n_0$$

of these customers, with a variance of

$$\sigma_3{}^2 = \left(1 - \frac{1}{n_s}\right)\frac{\lambda n_0}{n_s}$$

If the rivals pool information (without pooling, this area could not be policed effectively), this firm cannot obtain more than $m_3 + 2\sigma_3$ customers without being deemed a price-cutter, using again a 5 percent probability criterion. As a percentage of the firm's total sales, the maximum sales above the expected number in the absence of price cutting are then

$$\frac{2\sigma_3}{n_0(1 + \lambda)/n_s} = \frac{2}{1 + \lambda}\sqrt{\frac{(n_s - 1)\lambda}{n_0}}$$

We tabulate this criterion as Table 3.

Two aspects of the incentive to cut prices (or, equivalently, the difficulty of detecting price cuts) to new customers are apparent: the incentive increases rapidly with the number of sellers and the incentive increases with the rate of entry of new customers. As usual, the incentive falls as the absolute number of customers per seller rises. If the rate of entry of new buyers is 10 percent or more, price-cutting to new customers allows larger sales increases without detection that can be obtained by attracting customers of rivals (compare Tables 1 and 3).

Of the considerable number of directions in which this model could be enlarged, two will be presented briefly.

[2] For example, take $p = .95$. The entry for 10 customers per seller is 13.8 in Table 2— this is the maximum percentage of average sales that can be obtained by price reductions to old customers. The corresponding entries in Table 1 are 6.9 (2 sellers, 20 buyers), 8.9 (3 and 30), 7.4 (4 and 40), 6.4 (5 and 50), 4.2 (10 and 100), etc. Multiplying each entry in Table 1 by $(n_s - 1)$, we get the maximum gain in sales (without detection) by attracting customers of rivals, and beyond 2 sellers the gains are larger by this latter route. Since Table 1 is based upon a 10 percent probability level, strict comparability requires that we use $1.6\,\sigma$, instead of $2\,\sigma$, in Table 2, which would reduce the entries by one-fifth.

The first is inequality in the size of firms. In effect, this complication has already been introduced by the equivalent device of pooling information. If we tabulate the effects of pooling of information by K firms, the results are equivalent to having a firm K times as large as the other firms. The number of old customers this large firm can lose to any one small rival (all of whom are equal in size) is given, in Table 4, as a percentage

Table 3

Maximum Additional New Customers (as a percentage of average sales)
Obtainable by Secret Price-Cutting

$$Criterion\ III : \frac{2}{1 + \lambda}\sqrt{\frac{\lambda(n_s - 1)}{n_0}}$$

Rate of appearance of new buyers (λ)	No. of old buyers (n_0)	No. of sellers					
		2	3	4	5	10	20
1/100	20	4.4	6.3	7.7	8.9	13.3	19.3
	30	3.6	5.1	6.3	7.2	10.8	15.8
	40	3.1	4.4	5.4	6.3	9.4	13.6
	50	2.8	4.0	4.8	5.6	8.4	12.2
	100	2.0	2.8	3.4	4.0	5.9	8.6
	200	1.4	2.0	2.4	2.8	4.2	6.1
	400	1.0	1.4	1.7	2.0	3.0	4.3
1/10	20	12.9	18.2	22.3	25.7	38.6	56.0
	30	10.5	14.8	18.2	21.0	31.5	45.8
	40	9.1	12.9	15.8	18.2	27.3	39.6
	50	8.1	11.5	14.1	16.3	24.4	35.4
	100	5.8	8.1	10.0	11.5	17.2	25.1
	200	4.1	5.8	7.0	8.1	12.2	17.7
	400	2.9	4.1	5.0	5.8	8.6	12.5
1/5	20	16.7	23.6	28.9	33.3	50.0	72.6
	30	13.6	19.2	23.6	27.2	40.8	59.3
	40	11.8	16.7	20.4	23.6	35.4	51.4
	50	10.5	14.9	18.3	21.1	31.6	46.0
	100	7.4	10.5	12.9	14.9	22.4	32.5
	200	5.3	7.4	9.1	10.5	15.8	23.0
	400	3.7	5.3	6.4	7.4	11.2	16.2
1/4	20	17.9	25.3	31.0	35.8	53.7	78.0
	30	14.6	20.7	25.3	29.2	43.8	63.7
	40	12.6	17.9	21.9	25.3	38.0	55.1
	50	11.3	16.0	19.6	22.6	33.9	49.3
	100	8.0	11.3	13.9	16.0	24.0	34.9
	200	5.7	8.0	9.8	11.3	17.0	24.7
	400	4.0	5.7	6.9	8.0	12.0	17.4

of the average number of old customers of the small firm; the column labeled $K = 1$ is of course the case analyzed in Table 1.

The effects of pooling on the detection of price-cutting are best analyzed by comparing Table 4 with Table 1. If there are 100 customers and 10 firms (and $p = .9$), a single firm can increase sales by 5.4 percent by poaching on one rival or about 50 percent against all rivals (Table 1).

Table 4
Percentage Gains in Sales from Undetected Price-Cutting by a Small Firm

$$Criterion\ IV: \frac{1}{n_s - K}\left[\theta(1 - p)\sqrt{K} + \sqrt{\frac{n_s K(1 - p)(n_s - K - 1)(1 + \theta/\sqrt{K})}{n_0}}\right]$$

$$\theta = \sqrt{\frac{p}{1 - p}\frac{n_s}{n_0}}$$

Probability of repeat sales (p)	No. of firms $(n_s - K + 1)$	Buyers per small seller (n_0/n_s)	Size of large firm (K)			
			1	2	5	9
$p = .9$	2	10	9.5	13.4	21.2	28.5
		30	5.5	7.7	12.2	16.4
		50	4.2	6.0	9.5	12.7
	3	10	11.7	15.8	23.9	31.4
		30	6.3	8.7	13.3	17.6
		50	4.8	6.6	10.2	13.5
	4	10	9.7	13.1	19.7	25.7
		30	5.2	7.1	10.9	14.4
		50	4.0	5.4	8.3	11.0
	10	10	5.4	7.2	10.7	14.0
		30	2.9	3.9	5.9	7.7
		50	2.2	2.9	4.5	5.9
$p = .8$	2	10	12.6	17.9	28.3	37.9
		30	7.3	10.3	16.3	21.9
		50	5.7	8.0	12.6	17.0
	3	10	15.4	21.0	32.1	42.3
		30	8.4	11.6	18.0	23.9
		50	6.4	8.9	13.8	18.4
	4	10	12.7	17.3	26.3	34.7
		30	6.9	9.5	14.7	19.5
		50	5.3	7.3	11.3	15.0
	10	10	7.1	9.5	14.4	18.9
		30	3.8	5.2	8.0	10.6
		50	2.9	4.0	6.1	8.1

If 9 firms combine, the maximum amount the single firm can gain by secret price-cutting is 28.9 percent (Table 4). With 20 firms and 200 customers, a single firm can gain 3.6 percent from each rival, or about 30 percent from 9 rivals; if these rivals merge, the corresponding figure falls to 14.0 percent. The pooling of information, therefore, reduces substantially the scope for secret price-cutting.

This table exaggerates the effect of inequality of firm size because it fails to take account of the fact that the number of customers varies with firm size, on our argument that only customers above a certain size relative to the seller are a feasible group for secret price-cutting. The small firm can find it attractive to cut prices to buyers which are not large enough to be potential customers by price-cutting for the large seller.

The temporal pattern of buyers' behavior provides another kind of information: What is possibly due to random fluctuation in the short run cannot with equal probability be due to chance if repeated. Thus, the maximum expected loss of old customers to a rival in one round of transactions is (at the 1σ level)

$$\frac{n_0}{(n_s - 1)n_s}(1 - p)(1 + \theta)$$

but for T consecutive periods the maximum expected loss is (over T periods)

$$\frac{T}{n_s - 1}(1 - p)\frac{n_0}{n_s}[1 + \theta\sqrt{T}]$$

with a variance of

$$\sigma_s^2 = \frac{(n_s - 2)}{(n_s - 1)^2}T(1 - p)\frac{n_0}{n_s}[1 + \theta\sqrt{T}]$$

This source of information is of minor efficacy in detecting price-cutting, unless the rounds of successive transactions are numerous—that is, unless buyers purchase (enter contracts) frequently.

Our approach has certain implications for the measurement of concentration, if we wish concentration to measure likelihood of effective collusion. In the case of new customers, for example, let the probability of attracting a customer be proportional to the firm's share of industry output (s). Then the variance of the firm's share of sales to new customers will be $n_n s(1 - s)$, and the aggregate for the industry will be

$$C = n_n \sum_1^r s(1 - s)$$

for r firms. This expression equals $n_n (1 - H)$, where

$$H = \sum s^2$$

is the Herfindahl index of concentration. The same index holds, as an approximation, for potential price-cutting to attract old customers.

The foregoing analysis can be extended to nonprice variables, subject to two modifications. The first modification is that there be a definite joint profit-maximizing policy upon which the rivals can agree. Here, we may expect to encounter a spectrum of possibilities, ranging from a clearly defined optimum policy (say, on favorable legislation) to a nebulous set of alternatives (say, directions of research). Collusion is less feasible, the less clear the basis on which it should proceed. The second modification is that the competitive moves of any one firm will differ widely among nonprice variables in their detectability by rivals. Some forms of nonprice competition will be easier to detect than price-cutting because they leave visible traces (advertising, product quality, servicing, etc), but some variants will be elusive (reciprocity in purchasing, patent licensing arrangements). The common belief that nonprice competition is more common than price competition is, therefore, not wholly in keeping with the present theory. Those forms that are suitable areas for collusion will have less competition; those which are not suitable will have more competition.

4. Some Fragments of Evidence

Before we seek empirical evidence on our theory, it is useful to report two investigations of the influence of numbers of sellers on price. These investigations have an intrinsic interest because, so far as I know, no systematic analysis of the effect of numbers has hitherto been made.

The first investigation was of newspaper advertising rates, as a function of the number of evening newspapers in a city. Advertising rates on a milline basis are closely (and negatively) related to circulation, so a regression of rates on circulation was made for fifty-three cities in 1939. The residuals (in logarithmic form) from this regression equation are tabulated in Table 5. It will be observed that rates are 5 percent above the average in one-newspaper towns and 5 percent below the average in two-newspaper towns, and the towns with one evening paper but also an independent morning paper fall nearly midway between these points. Unfortunately, there were too few cities with more than two evening newspapers to yield results for larger numbers of firms.

The second investigation is of spot commercial rates on AM radio stations in the four states of Ohio, Indiana, Michigan, and Illinois. The basic equation introduces, along with number of rivals, a series of other

Table 5
Residuals from Regression of Advertising Rates
on Circulation[a]

No. of evening papers	n	Mean residual (logarithm)	Standard deviation of mean
One	23	.0211	.0210
With morning paper	10	−.0174	.0324
Without morning paper	13	.0507	.0233
Two	30	−.0213	.0135

[a] The regression equation is

$$\log R = 5.194 - 1.688 \log c + .139(\log c)^2$$
$$\quad\quad\quad (.620) \quad\quad (.063)$$

where R is the 5 M milline rate and c is circulation.

SOURCE: American Association of Advertising Agencies, *Market and Newspaper Statistics*, **VIIIa** (1939).

factors (power of station, population of the county in which the station is located, etc.). Unfortunately, the number of stations is rather closely correlated with population ($r^2 = .796$ in the logarithms). The general result, shown in Table 6, is similar to that for newspapers: the elasticity of price with respect to number of rivals is quite small (−.07). Here, the range of stations in a county was from 1 to 13.

Table 6
Regression of AM Spot Commercial Rates (26 Times) and
Station Characteristics, 1961 ($n = 345$)

Independent variables[a]	Regression coefficient	Standard error
1. Logarithm of population of county, 1960	.238	.026
2. Logarithm of kilowatt power of station	.206	.015
3. Dummy variables of period of broadcasting		
a. Sunrise to sunset	−.114	.025
b. More than (a), less than 18 hours	−.086	.027
c. 18–21 hours	−.053	.028
4. Logarithm of number of stations in county	−.074	.046
$R^2 = .743$		

[a] Dependent variable: logarithm of average rate, May 1, 1961 (dollars).
SOURCE: "Spot Radio Rates and Data," *Standard Rate and Data Service, Inc.*, **XLIII**, 5 (May 1961).

Both studies suggest that the level of prices is not very responsive to the actual numbers of rivals. This is in keeping with the expectations based upon our model, for that model argues that the number of buyers, the proportion of new buyers, and the relative sizes of firms are as important as the number of rivals.

To turn to the present theory, the only test covering numerous industries so far devised has been based upon profitability. This necessarily rests upon company data, and it has led to the exclusion of a large number of industries for which the companies do not operate in a well-defined industry. For example, the larger steel and chemical firms operate in a series of markets in which their position ranges from monopolistic to competitive. We have required of each industry that the earnings of a substantial fraction of the companies in the industry (measured by output) be determined by the profitability of that industry's products, that is,

Table 7

Profitability and Concentration Data

| Industry[a] | Concentration (1954) | | Average rate of return (1953–1957) | | Ratio of market value to book value (1953–1957) |
	Share of top 4	H^b	All assets	Net worth	
Sulfur mining (4)	98	.407	19.03	23.85	3.02
Automobiles (3)	98	.369	11.71	20.26	2.30
Flat glass (3)	90	.296	11.79	16.17	2.22
Gypsum products (2)	90	.280	12.16	20.26	1.83
Primary aluminum (4)	98	.277	6.87	13.46	2.48
Metal cans (4)	80	.260	7.27	13.90	1.60
Chewing gum (2)	86	.254	13.50	17.06	2.46
Hard-surface floor coverings (3)	87	.233	6.56	7.59	.98
Cigarettes (5)	83	.213	7.23	11.18	1.29
Industrial gases (3)	84	.202	8.25	11.53	1.33
Corn wet milling (3)	75	.201	9.17	11.55	1.48
Typewriters (3)	83	.198	3.55	5.39	.84
Domestic laundry equipment (2)	68	.174	9.97	17.76	1.66
Rubber tires (9)	79	.171	7.86	14.02	1.70
Rayon fiber (4)	76	.169	5.64	6.62	.84
Carbon black (2)	73	.152	8.29	9.97	1.40
Distilled liquors (6)	64	.118	6.94	7.55	.77

[a] The number of firms is given in parentheses after the industry title. Only those industries are included for which a substantial share (35 percent or more) of the industry's sales is accounted for by the firms in the sample, and these firms derive their chief revenues (50 percent or more) from the industry in question.

[b] H is Herfindahl index.

Table 8
Rank Correlations of Measures of Profitability and Measures of Concentration

	Measure of profitability		
Measure of concentration	Rate of return on all assets	Rate of return on net worth	Ratio of market value to book value
Share of output produced by four largest firms	.322	.507	.642
Herfindahl index (*H*)	.524	.692	.730

that we have a fair share of the industry and the industry's product is the dominant product of the firms.

Three measures of profitability are given in Table 7: (1) the rate of return on all capital (including debt), (2) the rate of return on net worth (stockholders' equity), (3) the ratio of market value to book value of the common stock.

In addition, two measures of concentration are presented: (1) the conventional measure, the share of output produced by the four leading firms; and (2) the Herfindahl index *H*.

The various rank correlations are given in Table 8. The various concentration measures, on the one hand, and the various measures of

Table 9
Prices of Steel Products, 1939, and Industry Structure, 1938

Product class	Prices, 2nd quarter, 1939 (percent)		Herfindahl index	Output in 1939 relative to 1937
	Average discount from list price	Standard deviation		
Hot-rolled sheets	8.3	7.3	.0902	1.14
Merchant bars	1.2	4.5	.1517	.84
Hot-rolled strip	8.5	8.3	.1069	.56
Plates	2.6	4.8	.1740	.85
Structural shapes	3.2	4.3	.3280	.92
Cold-rolled strip	8.8	9.8	.0549	.88
Cold-rolled sheets	5.8	5.0	.0963	1.14
Cold-finished bars	0.9	3.4	.0964	.83

SOURCE: Prices: "Labor Department Examines Consumers' Prices of Steel Products," *Iron Age* (April 25, 1946); industry structure: 1938 capacity data from *Directory of Iron and Steel Works of the United States and Canada*; output: *Annual Statistical Report, American Iron and Steel Institute* (New York, 1938, 1942).

profitability, on the other hand, are tolerably well correlated. All show the expected positive relationship. In general, the data suggest that there is no relationship between profitability and concentration if H is less than .250 or the share of the four largest firms is less than about 80 percent. These data, like those on advertising rates, confirm our theory only in the sense that they support theories which assert that competition increases with number of firms.

Our last evidence is a study of the prices paid by buyers of steel products in 1939, measured relative to the quoted prices (Table 9). The figure of 8.3 for hot-rolled sheets, for example, represents an average of 8.3 percent reduction from quoted prices, *paid by buyers*, with a standard deviation of 7.3 percent of quoted prices. The rate of price-cutting is almost perfectly correlated with the standard deviation of transaction prices, as we should expect: the less perfect the market knowledge, the more extensive the price-cutting.

In general, the more concentrated the industry structure (measured by the Herfindahl index), the larger were the price reductions. Although there were no extreme departures from this relationship, structural shapes and hot-rolled strip had prices somewhat lower than the average relationship, and cold-finished-bars prices somewhat higher than expected, and the deviations are not accounted for by the level of demand (measured by 1939 sales relative to 1937 sales). The number of buyers could not be taken into account, but the BLS study states:

> The extent of price concessions shown by this study is probably understated because certain very large consumers in the automobile and container industries were excluded from the survey. This omission was at the request of the OPA which contemplated obtaining this information in connection with other studies. Since a small percentage of steel consumers, including these companies, accounts for a large percentage of steel purchased, prices paid by a relatively few large consumers have an important influence upon the entire steel price structure. Very large steel consumers get greater reductions from published prices than smaller consumers, often the result of competitive bidding by the mills for the large volume of steel involved. One very large steel consumer, a firm that purchased over 2 pct of the total consumption of hot and cold-rolled sheets in 1940, refused to give purchase prices. This firm wished to protect its suppliers, fearing that "certain transactions might be revealed which would break confidence" with the steel mills. However, this company did furnish percent changes of prices paid for several steel products which showed that for some products prices advanced markedly, and in one case nearly 50 pct. The great price advances for this company indicate that it was receiving much larger concessions than smaller buyers.[3]

[3] See "Labor Department Examines Consumers' Prices of Steel Products," *op. cit.*, p. 133.

These various bits of evidence are fairly favorable to the theory, but they do not constitute strong support. More powerful tests will be feasible when the electrical equipment triple-damage suits are tried.[4] The great merit of our theory, in fact, is that it has numerous testable hypotheses, unlike the immortal theories that have been traditional in this area.

[4] For example, it will be possible to test the prediction that prices will be higher and less dispersed in sales on public bids than in privately negotiated sales, and the prediction that price-cutting increases as the number of buyers diminishes.

●

The next selection is an article by Michael Gort which examines some evidence on the possible causes of industrial concentration and on its consequences for the stability of market shares. *Concentration* is simply the degree to which a small proportion of the firms in an industry account for a large proportion of the sales; *stability* in this context is the degree to which individual firms' shares of the market remain constant over time.

At least three conclusions should be noted : First, stability is, indeed, related to the degree of concentration, as is predicted by most theories of oligopoly and which would tend to support analogous propositions favoring the concentration of international power in a few large nations. Second, stability is positively related to the degree that products are differentiated—ideological competition, which fosters clear preference for the "product" of one large nation over that of a competitor, would here be seen as a factor for "brand loyalty" and stability of shares or spheres of influence. Finally, stability is *negatively* related to the overall growth rate of the industry—periods of rapid technological development and social change produce many opportunities for a unit to grow at the expense of others through vigorous competition.[1]

●

[1] It should be recognized that these findings, as applied to firms by Gort, are still tentative. It has been pointed out, for instance (by Stephen Hymer in a personal communication), that Gort's use of the product-moment correlation coefficient may be misleading. A high correlation between the market shares of firms at the beginning and at the end of different periods indicates not that the shares were essentially the same, but merely that the shares at the end represented some linear transformation of the shares at the beginning. That is, the correlation would be unity if each firm's sales grew by some fixed amount, but the *shares* of the big firms would, nevertheless, have been reduced. The data need further analysis before firm conclusions can be drawn even from them.

11

Analysis of Stability and Change in Market Shares

Michael Gort

In recent years, much effort has been invested in measuring the concentration of industry output or sales in a few leading producers. While there is some intrinsic interest in the relative size of leading firms, the usefulness of this information depends largely on the adequacy of concentration measures as at least a rough gauge of market control. That is, it depends on the existence of a relation between the extent to which the largest producers can exercise control over prices, output, or quality of product, and concentration in sales. One of the chief objections to "concentration ratios"[1] as descriptions of market structure is that high ratios may be consistent with considerable instability in the market shares of individual firms. In judging the intensity of competition in an industry, the ability of leading firms to maintain their relative position in a market is probably more significant than the extent of concentration at a single point in time. While concentration ratios for American manufacturing industries are now available for several years, historical changes in these ratios are severely deficient as measures of stability in shares. First, since the ratios show only the proportion of industry sales contributed by a group of leading firms (typically, four or eight) they obviously tell us nothing

Reprinted from *The Journal of Political Economy*, **71**, 1 (February 1963), pp. 51–60, by permission of The University of Chicago Press. Copyright, 1963, by The University of Chicago Press.

[1] Concentration ratios, as computed for American manufacturing industries, show the proportion of an industry's output or sales that is contributed by a group of leading producers (four, eight, or twenty).

about the distribution of shares, or changes in this distribution within the groups. Second, the concentration ratio for a group of the largest four or eight firms can remain highly stable notwithstanding changes in the firms that compose these groups.

This discussion has three objectives. First, it presents new information on stability and change in the market shares of leading firms. Second, it examines some of the reasons for stability in shares and, in particular, the relation between stability and other aspects of market structure. Finally, it explores the consquences of stability for industry profit rates.

1. Measures of Stability

The measures of stability were based on data that showed the market shares of the same leading firms in two years (1947 and 1954) in each of 205 manufacturing industries. The data were drawn from the 1947 and 1954 Censuses of Manufactures and showed the percentage of industry shipments contributed by each of the firms in the two years. The list of 205 industries included all those in manufacturing for which comparisons of market shares were not precluded by technical deficiencies in the data.

Analysis was restricted to the firms that were among the leading fifteen in either or both of the years 1947 and 1954. Thus, the sample included firms that generally grew faster than average (those that entered the class of leading fifteen in 1954) as well as those that on the whole grew less than average (firms that left the class of leading fifteen). The maximum number of observations for any industry was twenty-six, and the modal number nineteen. The data employed restrict the analysis to firms which might be considered either large or medium-sized for their industries, but fortunately it is in this size range that stability in shares is most relevant for analysis of competitive structure.

Two measures of stability were used. The first was the correlation coefficient for the relation of 1947 and 1954 market shares. These coefficients tell us the extent to which the shares at one point in time are dependent on those at another point. Thus, they indicate how well we can predict future market shares from a knowledge of present or past shares. The second measure used was the geometric mean of the regression of 1954 on 1947 shares and the reciprocal of the regression of 1947 on 1954 shares.[2] The measure is designed to overcome the bias that affects either of the two regression coefficients taken separately—a bias that arises from the

[2] The measure was the geometric mean of $\Sigma x_0 x_1 / \Sigma x_0^2$ and $\Sigma x_1^2 / \Sigma x_0 x_1$ when x_0 stands for the deviations from the mean share in 1947 and x_1 the deviations from the mean share in 1954. . . .

general tendency of firms that are largest at the end of a period to have grown more than average, and of those that are largest at the outset to grow less than average in the future. Accordingly, coefficients of more than unity signify on the average a growth in the market shares of large firms at the expense of the smaller ones, while coefficients that are less than unity signify the opposite. For convenience, throughout most of this discussion the correlation coefficient is referred to as "stability coefficient A" and the regression coefficient (computed by the method just described) as "stability coefficient B."

How stable are the market shares of leading firms? The adjectives one is likely to select depend partly upon what one expected to find. Most of the A coefficients (correlations) were quite high. One hundred and fifty-two of the 205 industries had a coefficient of .8 or higher, 111 a coefficient of .9 or higher, and 74 a coefficient of at least .95. . . . On the other hand, the selection of industries for the coefficients was, as previously explained, biased in the direction of stability; the interval of time was fairly short, being only seven years; and a fair dispersion of coefficients is nonetheless in evidence . . . In any event, our data do show that, generally, high market shares for individual firms are not the consequence of transitory events such as brief lags in the adjustment of competitors' output to changes in the level or composition of demand. Also, they suggest that [these] industries represent meaningful markets in the sense that there is substantial mobility of resources among the individual products incorporated in the categories. Otherwise, differences in rate of growth of demand for the various products would have necessarily led to wide shifts in observed "market" shares. That is, the relative importance of individual products differs widely within the output (in a given industry) of various firms. Accordingly, if the resources of individual firms are immobile, unevenness in the growth in demand for these products will lead to changes in the relative sizes of firms.

The B coefficients (regressions) were roughly evenly divided between those that were below and above unity. Many of them, however, deviated from unity only negligibly, 78 of the 197 falling between the limits of .9 and 1.1. There were 78 that were less than .9 and 53 that were higher than 1.1. Thus, this body of data certainly would not support a conclusion that, on the whole, concentration has been increasing in manufacturing industries.

When all the industries are cross-classified on the basis of coefficients A and B, a strong relation emerges between the two (Table 1). Of the seventy-eight industries in the stable class on the basis of the B measure (those in the .9–1.1 class) fifty-one were in the upper two quartiles with respect to A.[3]

Table 1
Relation of Stability Coefficient B and Industry Variables

Variables[a]	No. of industries with coefficient of		
	Less than .9	.9–1.1	More than 1.1
Growth:			
1st quartile	18	18	14
2nd quartile	11	22	16
3rd quartile	17	20	12
4th quartile	20	18	11
	66	78	53
Concentration, leading 4 firms			
1st quartile	18	10	22
2nd quartile	20	17	12
3rd quartile	17	19	13
4th quartile	11	32	6
	66	78	53
Concentration, leading 5–8 firms			
1st quartile	19	16	14
2nd quartile	20	20	9
3rd quartile	13	18	18
4th quartile	14	23	11
	66	77	52
Firm size:			
1st quartile	21	10	17
2nd quartile	17	19	12
3rd quartile	14	22	11
4th quartile	13	23	11
	65	74	51
Stability coefficient A:			
1st quartile	19	11	20
2nd	18	16	15
3rd	13	26	10
4th	16	25	8
	66	78	53

[a] Quartiles are in ascending order with respect to variables.

High stability in the sense of strong dependence of market shares in one year on those in an antecedent one is clearly a more serious problem from the standpoint of maintaining competition if it is associated with increasing concentration. In this respect, Table 1 shows that there were only eighteen industries in the two upper quartiles for coefficient A that were characterized by increasing concentration as measured by coefficient B (industries for which the coefficient was more than 1.1). The data also point to an absence of relation between stability and a more commonly used measure of increase in concentration. When the A coefficients were correlated with the percentage change from 1947 to 1954 in the concentration ratio for the leading four firms, the simple correlation was $-.143$ (with 202 observations).

2. Sources of Stability

Stability in market shares can be expected to occur primarily under two sets of conditions. The first is an absence of disequilibrating forces such as a high rate of growth in demand or rapid change in technology. The second is the presence of concentration in the size distribution of firms. The relation of concentration to stability stems, however, partly from the fact that both are affected by the same variables.

Rapid growth generates instability in two ways. First, given imperfect foresight, some firms adjust their scale of production to anticipated growth faster than others and this leads to shifts in market shares. Second, assuming there are recurrent lags in the adjustment of supply to rapid changes in demand, earnings will recurrently rise above a "normal" (opportunity-cost) rate of return. This should lead to entry of firms in the industry— hence, to changes in market shares. Entry with its consequent shifts in shares can also be expected to occur when changes in technology lead to a reduction in costs compared to prices. Moreover, technical innovations are unlikely to be introduced simultaneously by all producers, with the result that they alter the competitive position of firms and, thus, their market shares.

Concentration can affect the stability of market shares directly to the extent that fewness of large sellers permits collusive agreements. Also, as sometimes alleged, with high concentration sellers may adjust to the

---

[3] When the χ^2 test was applied, the frequencies in Table 1, with industries cross-classified by both coefficients A and B, differed significantly from those expected in the absence of a relation between the two measures. The value of χ^2 was 15.74, which, with six degrees of freedom, is acceptable at the .05 level of significance.

interdependence of their sales by limiting the extent of competition in price. In part, however, a relation of concentration to stability arises from the effect on both of barriers to entry in an industry.

Barriers to entry limit increases in the number of firms in an industry in response to growth in demand. Consequently, they reduce the chance that the market shares of the older producers will decline as the industry grows. Moreover, the principal barriers to entry (product differentiation, scarce resources, and legal restrictions such as patent rights) also make it harder for one firm to capture a part of the market in which another firm has an established position. Since barriers to entry also tend to lead to concentration, a positive relation between concentration and stability should be present.

3. Concentration and Stability

High concentration occurs with a variety of market structures. There are markets in which a few producers account for substantially all industry output and virtually no small producers exist (for example, electric turbogenerators or alkalis and chlorine). There are others in which a number of firms of intermediate size account for a significant proportion of total output, notwithstanding fairly high concentration in the leading four firms (for example, steel works and rolling mills). Alternatively, there are markets in which the leading four producers contribute a sizable proportion of industry output with the rest divided among a large number of small firms (for example, meat packing), and still others in which there are a dozen or so important producers with the rest of output contributed by many small firms (for example, petroleum refining). The important question that this raises is: what is the relation between stability in shares and the specific type of size distribution that characterizes an industry? More concretely, is stability primarily a function of the relative size of the several largest producers or does it make a difference if there is also a group of fairly important producers of intermediate size? A priori, more than one answer is possible. On the one hand, the shares of the several largest firms may be more vulnerable if there are a number of other important producers. On the other, given the same degree of concentration for the leading four firms, competition is easier to restrict when a large proportion of the remaining market is divided among only a few producers.

The A coefficients showed a strong positive relation to 1947 concentration ratios for the leading four producers. When the industries were classified by deciles on the basis of these ratios, the average stability coefficient for the lowest concentration decile was only .478, as compared with .959 for the highest. (The average coefficients were .705 and .715 for the second and third lowest deciles, respectively, as compared with .936 and .935 for the eighth and ninth.) In contrast, the concentration ratios for the next four firms (those ranked fifth through eighth in terms of size in the industry) showed virtually no relation to the coefficients, and neither did the ratios for the sixteen firms ranked fifth to twentieth. If we denote the A coefficients by the subscript 1, and the concentration ratios for firms one to four, five to eight, and five to twenty, by the subscripts 2, 3, and 4, respectively, we have the following sets of correlations:

$$r_{12} = \quad .523 \qquad R_{1.23} = .523$$

$$r_{13} = \quad .097 \qquad R_{1.234} = .529$$

$$r_{14} = \ -.049$$

$$r_{23} = \quad .218$$

$$r_{24} = \quad .130$$

The evidence presented here indicates that stability in market shares is strongly related to the relative size of the several largest producers in an industry, but variations in the way the rest of the market is divided (at least to the extent that these variations were captured by concentration ratios) appear generally to make little difference. Since this result may have stemmed from the dominant role of the several largest producers in industries characterized by a wide dispersion in firm sizes, we proceeded to test the same hypothesis for the industries that were in the lower third in terms of a measure of dispersion in firm size.

For manufacturing industries in general, high barriers to entry should lead not only to a high concentration for the leading four producers but also to concentration in the remainder of the market. However, if concentration for the first four firms is high, the remaining market is smaller, with the result that there is less to be divided among the next group of firms. Thus, the correlations presented show little relation between the ratios for the leading four firms and those for either the next four or the next sixteen. In contrast, for the low-dispersion industries the correlations (using the same subscripts as before) were $r_{23} = .889$, and $r_{24} = .840$. Consequently, since the measure of stability was again strongly correlated with concentration for the largest four producers ($r_{12} = .529$ for the sixty-three observations), it was not surprising that there was also a significant relation between stability and the two other concentration ratios $r_{13} = .426$, $r_{14} = .411$). However, with the concentration ratio for the leading four firms as one variable, the addition of the other two ratios as independent variables contributed virtually nothing to explaining the variance in our measure of stability ($R_{1.23} = .538$, and $R_{1.234} = .539$).

The results are substantially the same for Coefficient B. Moreover, both the positive and the negative deviations of the coefficient from unity appeared to have the same relation to concentration. From Table 1 it is apparent that Coefficient B is strongly related to the concentration ratio for the leading four firms. Among industries that were stable as judged on the basis of B (those for which the coefficient was in the .9–1.1 class) there were more than three times as many in the highest as in the lowest concentration quartile. Conversely, for industries for which there was a shift in favor of either the large or the small firms, the frequencies in the lowest concentration quartiles were substantially greater than in the highest. As for coefficient A, there was no clear relation between B and the concentration ratio for the fifth through eighth firms. In short, once again the results tend to show that such forces as contribute to stability in market shares are reflected almost entirely in the extent of concentration of output in the several largest producers. Whether, in addition, firms of intermediate size for the industry have a significant or a minor share of industry output appears to make little difference.

4. Scale Economies and Stability

Earlier, it was argued that the same forces that operate as barriers to entry contribute to stability in market shares. We now examine in this connection the role of two factors commonly cited as barriers to entry, namely, scale economies and product differentiation.

No direct measures of economies of scale exist at present for any broad list of industries. Assuming there is pressure for firm sizes to move in the direction of optimum size, a higher average firm size in an industry will tend to be associated with greater economies of scale. Because of lags in the adjustment process, and also because mergers affect firm sizes though they may be initiated for reasons unrelated to economies of scale, average firm size is only roughly related to most efficient size. Regardless of this relation, however, the influence of firm size on stability in market shares is of significance in itself. To what extent is absolute firm size a relevant variable as distinct from the relative size of leading firms or other characteristics of size distribution? To examine this question, average size of shipments in 1947 was computed for each industry for the firms in our sample. If scale of output contributes to stability in market shares, high stability should be positively correlated with average size of shipments, at least for those firms on the basis of which measures of stability were computed. It will be noted that size was measured on the basis of output within the industry rather than by conglomerate firm size. Output within the industry seems, on the whole, more relevant for production and marketing economies of scale, while conglomerate size is more pertinent to economies of scale in financing.

Although the absolute size of a firm is frequently cited as a source of "market power," size did not prove to be an important variable in explaining stability. The simple correlation between coefficient A and average size, while statistically significant, was only .222 (with 188 observations.) With concentration for the leading four firms as an independent variable in the equation, the net contribution of average shipments size to explaining the variance in stability, though statistically significant at the .05 level, was very small. For the 188 observations, $r = .521$ with the concentration ratio alone, while $R = .537$ when size was introduced as a second independent variable. In short, with respect to coefficient A, it is the relative size structure of firms in an industry that is important rather than absolute size of producers.

Probably in part because of the relation of average firm size to concentration, Table 1 discloses a pattern in which there are more industries in the lower quartile with respect to firm size for industries with B coefficients of either less than .9 or more than 1.1. More stable industries (those with coefficients of .9–1.1) were classified least frequently in the first or lowest quartile. However, the variation in frequencies above the first quartile was modest for all three classes of industries. For the three-class breakdown of industries on the basis of B (as in Table 1) the value of χ^2 was not significant at the .10 level. However, when industries with coefficients of less than .9 and more than 1.1 were combined and a two class breakdown was examined (the other class being that of industries with B values of .9–1.1), the value of χ^2 was significant at the .05 level.

Using a different method of analysis, there was no significant relation between coefficient B and firm size. The method consisted of taking the deviations from unity in the values of B (without reference to whether these deviations were positive or negative) and correlating them with firm size. The correlation was $-.158$.

5. Product Differentiation and Stability

For the role of product differentiation only a simple test was possible. On the basis of judgment and qualitative information, we divided the industries into those with relatively high and those with moderate or low degrees of product differentiation. Seventy-one industries were classified in the former category and ninety-two in the latter, while forty-two industries defied classification on the basis of information available to us. Of the seventy-one, there were thirty-one cases of A coefficients of .95 or higher (Table 2). Of the ninety-two industries with a lower degree of

Table 2
Relation of Stability in Market Shares to Product Differentiation

	No. of industries with high differentiation	No. of industries with moderate or low differentiation
Stability coefficient A:		
.95 and over	31	27
.8–.949	25	41
Less than .8	15	24
	71	92
Stability coefficient B:		
More than 1.1	18	24
.9–1.1	35	29
Less than .9	18	35
	71	88

differentiation, there were only twenty-seven with A coefficients of .95 or over. When a two-class breakdown for stability was used—industries with coefficients of .95 or over and those with coefficients of less than .95—the χ^2 test pointed to a significantly higher proportion of cases in the high-stability class among industries with high product differentiation. However, with the three-class breakdown shown in Table 2, the value of χ^2 did not indicate a significant difference between the observed frequencies and those expected on the null hypothesis.

Industries for which the size distribution of firms was stable were somewhat more numerous in the category of high product differentiation; conversely, those in which either the large or the small firms grew faster than average were more numerous in the category of moderate or low product differentiation (Table 2). Thus, the results for coefficient B are similar to those for coefficient A and our relatively crude test, on the whole, appears to support the hypothesis that stability in market shares occurs more frequently when products are highly differentiated.

6. Industry Growth and Stability

As indicated earlier, disequilibrating forces, such as sharp movements in the level of demand, should reduce the stability in market shares. With industry growth measured by change in production indexes from 1947 to

1954, the simple correlation between stability and growth, though certainly not very strong, was statistically significant at the .01 level. Also, consistent with the hypothesis, the relation was negative ($r = -.255$, with 205 observations). With the concentration ratio for the leading four firms as one variable, the net contribution of growth to reducing the unexplained variance in coefficient A was still significant ($F = 21.24$, with $n_1 = 1$ and $n_2 = 202$) and the regression coefficient was again negative.

In short, as anticipated, there is evidence of a negative relation between stability in market shares as measured by A and industry growth. . . . The simple correlation for coefficient A and the concentration ratio for the leading four firms was .618 (with 205 observations). When growth was introduced as a second explanatory variable, the regression coefficient for growth was negative again and $R = .653$. The introduction of growth as a second variable once again significantly reduced the unexplained variance; $F = 16.27$ with $n_1 = 1$ and $n_2 = 202$.

As Table 1 shows, there was no discernible relation between industry growth and coefficient B. This was contrary to what might have been expected, not only because growth in demand should lead to entry and thus exert a downward influence on concentration but also in the light of some evidence that concentration is inversely related to industry size.

So far these discussions of oligopoly have been in static terms, asking what are the values of the variables that characterize existing market situations, whether stable or unstable. The following article by Oliver Williamson represents a theoretical attempt to establish some of the conditions under which a stable distribution of market shares may become unstable, or, from the other side, how stability may be created. The model first assumes, on the basis of empirical evidence reported by others, that the condition of the market importantly influences the degree of cooperation that will be possible among the firms. In times of prosperity where demand is strong, competitive price-cutting will be infrequent, but in periods of recession, either general or specific to the industry, pressure to increase one's share of the diminished market will be keen. An analogy here, in addition to international economic conditions, may be periods of general social and political upheaval versus stability as influences on nations' external aggressiveness.

Another key element in the theory is again the level of communication and interaction among the firms, with stability positively related to communication. These two independent variables then interact in the theory as follows: a much more favorable environment is required to move the system from a highly competitive to a collusive situation than is required to maintain collusion once it has been established. Similarly, as the collusive situation will survive serious deteriorations in the environment, once it does shift to competitive behavior, it will stay there even despite modest environmental improvements. In developing this model the author draws heavily on the basic equilibrium and feedback models, developed in other social sciences, that will probably be familiar to many international relations scholars as well. Some international relations research also has discussed related "conflict absorbing" or "accommodation absorbing" mechanisms that make it hard to move away from an equilibrium position.[1]

As in earlier selections, the role of communication is stressed. Note the emphasis, in slightly different form than before, on the greater difficulties of collusion for stability as the number of units in the system increases. In their article Deutsch and Singer employed communication theory to

---

[1] O. R. Holsti, "The Belief System and National Images: A Case Study," *Journal of Conflict Resolution*, **6**, 3 (1962), pp. 244–252, and C. E. Osgood, *An Alternative to War or Surrender* (Urbana: University of Illinois Press, 1962).

suggest some virtues in the fact that a greater number of actors in international politics meant a lower average attention to each unit;[2] here, the implication is not consoling.

[2] K. W. Deutsch and J. D. Singer, "Multipolar Power Systems and International Stability," *World Politics*, **16**, 3 (1964), pp. 390–406.

12

A Dynamic Theory of Interfirm Behavior

Oliver E. Williamson

The phenomenon that occupies our attention in Sections 1 and 2 is the widely reported tendency for certain classes of oligopolistic industries to alternate between competitive and collusive solutions. Boulding has characterized this behavior in the following terms:

... it is of some interest to note that under conditions of perfect oligopoly there is some tendency for price wars to break out, and then we are apt to have rather curious fluctuations around some equilibrium, with prices falling in the price war and then rising again in what I suppose we ought to call a price peace, in which a happy state of collusion, gentlemanliness, or just plain political organization prevails.[1]

Based on this recurrent cycle of cooperation and conflict, we take as our preliminary objective the following paradigm suggested by Simon: "given the description of some natural phenomena, ... find the differential equations for processes that will produce the phenomena."[2] This accomplished, the basic model is extended in Section 3 to investigate the influence of market structure on inter-firm behavior, and to study the effects of (and adaptations to) regulatory restraints. The advantages of the proposed approach are summarized in Section 4.

Reprinted by permission of the publishers from *The Quarterly Journal of Economics*, **79**, 4 (Cambridge: Harvard University Press, November 1965), pp. 579–607. Copyright, 1965, by the President and Fellows of Harvard College.

[1] K. E. Boulding, "The Uses of Price Theory," in A. R. Oxenfeldt, ed., *Models of Markets* (New York: Columbia University Press, 1963), p. 156.

[2] H. A. Simon, "The Architecture of Complexity," *Proceedings of the American Philosophical Society*, **106** (December 1962), p. 479.

1. A Gross Description

The factor that appears to be mainly responsible for shifting the firms in an oligopoly between cooperative and conflict solutions is the condition of the environment. Thus, although oligopolists can be assumed to be continuously aware of their interdependency relationship and of the collective advantages of pursuing a qualified joint profit maximization strategy,[3] adherence to a joint profit maximization agreement may be made difficult during times of adversity by current pressing demands that cause short-run own-goals of one or more of the members to override collective considerations. Assuming that when adversity is experienced by one it is experienced generally, deviation by one member of the coalition is likely to induce defensive responses by others and the entire relationship tends quickly to deteriorate into one of conflict and active competition. As the condition of the environment improves, however, the oligopolists are likely to perceive own-needs as less pressing and, hence, a return to a cooperative solution becomes feasible.

The description just presented appears to characterize the primary factors that influence the recurrent cycle of cooperation and conflict that we have taken as the dynamic phenomenon requiring explanation. Similar descriptions have been reported elsewhere. Thus, Kaysen observes that

... in a general environment of declining demand for the product of the group, ... each [oligopolist] has a poor income prospect.... Since any gain by one oligopolist can be made only at the expense of his rivals, all changes in prices are likely to be viewed as aggressive, and lead to retaliation.... Tacit agreements are unlikely to last. [Hence, oligopolists] are more likely to maintain agreements, and thus act monopolistically, in periods of rising ... demand.[4]

Similarly, Mitchell's observation of interfirm behavior led him to conclude that

... pools, working agreements, and combinations of other kinds become far more difficult to sustain in face of a buyer's market, and many of them go to pieces because their members suspect one another of secret undercutting of rates.[5]

In terms of more specific examples we have Bain's description of price behavior in the steel industry in the 1920's and 1930's. Thus, he observes:

---

[3] See W. J. Fellner, *Competition Among the Few* (New York: Knopf, 1949), for a discussion of the factors that influence qualified joint profit maximization.

[4] C. Kaysen, "A Dynamic Aspect of the Monopoly Problem," *Review of Economics and Statistics*, **31** (May 1949), p. 112.

[5] W. C. Mitchell, *Business Cycles and their Causes* (Berkeley and Los Angeles: University of California Press, 1941), pp. 134–135.

... the steel industry had long been the scene ... of a fairly elaborate tacitly collusive system of price determination.... The major evident imperfection is that of secret price shading.... The incidence of this shading ... was apparently variable with the state of the market, or the relation of demand to available capacity. In the first half of the 1920's, and again in 1941 and 1942, for example, with relatively good demand, price concessions were very infrequent and on the average extremely small. But in 1939 and 1940, when there was considerable excess capacity ..., significant price shading affected as much as 70 or 80 percent of all steel tonnage sold.... For most of the decade of the 1930's, ... detailed findings are not available, but ... [with] much unutilized capacity, a high incidence of price shading was probably experienced.[6]

A more recent (and more spectacular) example is afforded by the electrical equipment conspiracy in the 1950's. Indeed, at one stage or another of their histories, this alternating pattern of behavior appears to be representative of a wide variety of oligopolies.

In addition to the influence of the condition of the environment on interfirm relations, are there any other salient features of this process that require attention? If we are to take seriously the argument that socialization influences are important, explicit concern for the communications process by which interfirm agreements are achieved and maintained may be essential. Obviously, the effectiveness of the electrical equipment conspiracy rested on the coordinated exchange of information, and presumably this is true more generally. Thus, Simon inquires "What corresponds, in the social sciences, to the postulate of 'no action at a distance'? I think the direct analogue is 'no influence without communication'."[7] And Kaysen and Turner observe that "parallel price changes by a large number of firms will almost inevitably require ... [an extensive] machinery of intercommunication.... Even industry of small numbers will typically require agreement."[8] Hence, in addition to a mechanism that transmits changes in the condition of the environment through the system, a communication mechanism may also be warranted.

2. A Dynamic Model

The first part of this section identifies the basic variables, describes the relationships that exist between them, and provides a preliminary mathematical interpretation of the relations proposed. The second part develops, in a *qualitative* sense, the equilibrium and dynamic properties of the resulting system.

[6] J. S. Bain, *Industrial Organization* (New York: Wiley, 1959), pp. 309–310.

[7] H. A. Simon, *Models of Man* (New York: Wiley, 1957), p. 7.

[8] C. Kaysen and D. F. Turner, *Antitrust Policy* (Cambridge: Harvard University Press, 1959), p. 145.

A. The Interfirm Relationships

The most important question to raise in attempting to develop a model that possesses the indicated properties is: what are the critical endogenous variables? Once these have been specified, a connected framework with which to investigate them can be devised and this can then be augmented to include a variety of exogenous influences. The endogenous variables that I have chosen for this purpose are: (1) a performance variable; (2) an adherence to group goals variable; (3) an interfirm communication variable. The values that these variables take on are not independent but are mutually determined as part of a simultaneous system.

The performance variable is an index of the level of achievement of the firms in the industry. Ordinarily, this will be a profits measure, and, obviously, it will depend, among other things, on the condition of competition that prevails in the industry. Such a variable is essential to transmit the influence of changes in the condition of the environment that occupied an essential role in the description of interfirm behavior in Section 1. We shall also use it in our analysis of the effects of structural conditions and regulatory restraints.

Adherence to group goals is a measure of what Lange has called the "discipline" of the group, which he defines as the "degree to which the individual firms are willing to act in unison as members of the group."[9] The group goal will be taken to be one of qualified joint profit maximization, and the willingness of firms to place such a long-run collective goal ahead of short-run own goals is a measure of the strength of adherence.

The interfirm communication variable is a measure of the amount of valid information transfer between firms within the industry. Explicit treatment of the role of communication is frequently omitted from economists' descriptions of the interfirm coordination process. It is obvious, however, that communication is essential to coordinated response, and it is our contention that the amount of communication both affects and is affected by the level of adherence.

To these three endogenous variables we need to add the condition of the environment as an exogenous variable. The direct effect of an increase in demand is to improve the level of performance and a deterioration leads to a decline.

In a gross sense, these are the basic variables and relationships that the proposed model rests on. Our objective now is to elaborate the description of the qualitative relations that exist between the variables

[9] O. Lange, *Price Flexibility and Employment* (Bloomington, Ind.: Principia Press, 1944), p. 41.

by resorting to the organization theory and social psychology literature on small group interaction. With this completed, we will be in a position to develop a model that possesses the indicated attributes.

The proposed relationships between the endogenous variables are the following:

1. The level of collective performance varies directly with the degree of adherence to group goals and with the condition of the environment

2. the degree of adherence varies directly with the amount of interfirm communication and with the level of performance

3. the amount of communication varies directly with the degree of adherence, at least initially

The proposition that the level of collective performance increases as the member firms adhere more closely to the group goal of qualified joint profit maximization follows from the definition of terms. It similarly follows that the direct effect of an improvement in the condition of the environment is to increase the level of performance. The second and third relations are perhaps less obvious (although neither are they counter-intuitive), and, thus, deserve additional elaboration.

The observation that communication tends to enhance adherence has been widely recorded. It can be found in the organizational studies of Barnard, March and Simon, Thompson, and Cartwright and Zander, among others.[10] Although the precise statement of the relation varies slightly, the general proposition that intragroup communication promotes shared goals appears to be a well-established empirical finding. That the level of performance also has a positive influence on the degree of adherence has been less widely observed. However, March and Simon argue that a deterioration in performance (due to an unfavorable change in the condition of the environment) causes the group to reinterpret the relationship between the membership as being more competitive than cooperative, and conflict is apt to result.[11] Barnard also observes that cooperation is conditional on the capacity of the environment to produce satisfaction,[12] and, thus, adversity poses a threat to an adherence relationship which had been quite stable under more favorable conditions.

The proposition that the influence of communication on adherence is reciprocated has been made by March and Simon[13] and constitutes

[10] C. I. Barnard, *The Functions of the Executive* (Cambridge: Harvard University Press, 1962), p. 89; J. G. March and H. A. Simon, *Organizations* (New York: Wiley, 1958), pp. 60, 66; V. A. Thompson, *Modern Organization* (New York: Knopf, 1961), p. 105; D. Cartwright and A. Zander, *Group Dynamics* (New York: Harper & Row, 1960), p. 80.

[11] March and Simon, *op. cit.*, pp. 120, 126.

[12] Barnard, *op. cit.*, pp. 60–61.

[13] March and Simon, *op. cit.*, p. 66.

one of the basic linkages in Homans' observations of group activity.[14] That is, not only does communication promote adherence, but adherence in turn induces communication.

In a very general sense, therefore, we emerge with the following basic relations:

$$\pi = \pi(A\,;E) \qquad \pi_A > 0 \qquad \pi_E > 0 \tag{1}$$

$$A = A(\pi, C) \qquad A_\pi > 0 \qquad A_C > 0 \tag{2}$$

$$C = C(A) \qquad C_A > 0 \tag{3}$$

where π, A, and C are performance, adherence, and communication, respectively, and E refers to the condition of the environment. Our objective in the next part of this section will be to consider the effects of lagged responses on the dynamic behavior of this system, to examine the equilibrium relations that obtain, and to develop the dynamic response of the system to changes in the condition of the environment.

B. A Differential Equations Model

We hypothesize that the changes in the level of performance in response to changes in either adherence or the condition of the environment occur very rapidly, but that the adjustments in the attitude of the group (adherence) and in the interaction between group members (communication) take time. That is, the social processes that characterize group behavior are assumed to require time to come into adjustment, whereas the economic response of the system is assumed to occur relatively quickly. Considering the inertia that is generally associated with making social adjustments, as compared with the immediacy with which changes in demand or in the degree of interfirm competition affect prices and output, this view seems plausible. Thus, we reformulate our system as follows (where (t) designates the time period to which the measures apply):

$$\pi(t) = \pi[A(t)\,; E(t)] \qquad \pi_A > 0 \qquad \pi_E > 0 \tag{1}$$

$$\frac{dA(t)}{dt} = g[\pi(t), C(t), A(t)] \qquad g_\pi > 0 \qquad g_C > 0 \qquad g_A < 0 \tag{2'}$$

$$\frac{dC(t)}{dt} = \psi[A(t), C(t)] \qquad \begin{aligned} &\psi_A > 0 \text{ for low } A \\ &\psi_A < 0 \text{ for high } A \\ &\psi_C < 0 \end{aligned} \tag{3'}$$

[14] G. C. Homans, *The Human Group* (New York: Harcourt, Brace & World, 1950), p. 101.

The first two expressions are completely consistent with our discussion of the connections between the variables in Section 1 and in the response relations indicated previously. The last expression is likewise consistent with the preceding discussion with one exception. It indicates that the directional influence of adherence on communications may depend on the level of adherence, whereas previously it was assumed that this influence was always positive. Certainly at low levels of adherence an increase in adherence will tend to promote more complete transfer of information so that the amount of communication will increase in response. At very high levels of adherence, however, the consensus becomes so widely shared and highly articulated that the degree of understanding which prevails may reduce both the urge and the necessity to communicate. That this latter seems plausible is our reason for introducing it into the system. It is not, however, essential to the analysis.

By substituting Eq. (1) into Eq. (2') we obtain:

$$\frac{dA(t)}{dt} = g\{\pi[A(t); E(t)], C(t), A(t)\}$$

This can be re-expressed as

$$\frac{dA(t)}{dt} = \phi[C(t), A(t); E(t)] \tag{2''}$$

which, together with Eq. (3'),

$$\frac{dC(t)}{dt} = \psi[A(t), C(t)] \tag{3'}$$

reduces our system to a pair of differential equations for the determination of $A(t)$ and $C(t)$.

The system represented by Eqs. (2'') and (3') can be represented graphically in the C–A plane. At any point in the plane, the direction of adjustment can be obtained from the equation of the trajectory, namely

$$\frac{dA}{dC} = \frac{dA/dt}{dC/dt} = \frac{\phi[C, A; E]}{\psi[A, C]}$$

This gives the rate of change of A relative to C for each possible pair of (C, A) values. To each point there corresponds one and only one possible response and connecting consecutive points along the direction of indicated response yields an integral curve. The collection of such curves provides the direction field of the system. Several such curves are shown in Fig. 1 by the curved arrow constructions.

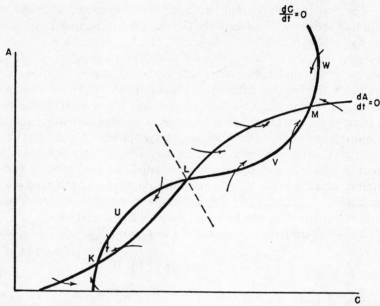

Fig. 1.

The character of the direction field depends on the nature of our partial equilibrium relationships. That is, consider the set of points at which the level of adherence is in equilibrium, namely, where

$$\frac{dA}{dt} = \phi(C, A; E) = 0 \tag{4}$$

At any point on this curve there is no tendency for the level of adherence to the group goal to adjust. Hence, the trajectory, dA/dC must be horizontal everywhere along this curve, moving to the right or to the left according to whether ψ is positive or negative at the point in question. Similarly, the set of points where

$$\frac{dC}{dt} = \psi(A, C) = 0 \tag{5}$$

defines a curve in the C–A plane along which there is no tendency for the level of communication to change. The trajectory at every point along this curve will thus be vertical, moving up or down depending on whether ϕ is positive or negative.

At the points where (4) and (5) intersect, that is, where both relations are satisfied simultaneously, the system will be in equilibrium. The stability of these points depends on the character of the direction field in the neighborhood of the equilibrium. As shown in Fig. 1, points K and M are stable equilibrium positions while L is an unstable equilibrium.

Although the basic assumptions that are embodied in Fig. 1 have already been stated, some additional comments on the relationships shown are warranted.

First, consider the curve along which the adherence to group goals variable is in equilibrium. It is drawn with a positive slope, to reflect the assumption that the equilibrium level of adherence increases in response to increases in communication, and the slope goes through an increasing then decreasing phase. Only the second phase is essential to the analysis and it is due to a saturation phenomenon. That is, given the condition of the environment, the effect of increasing the amount of communication is assumed eventually to encounter a diminishing response region where subsequent increases in communication produce successively smaller increases in the equilibrium level of adherence. This can result from the combination of two effects. First, the early communications may be concerned with more essential matters for obtaining coordination among the rivals than are later ones. In addition, the susceptibility to influence is almost certainly going to reach a saturation point as long as a difference between individual and group goals exists. This latter is related to Fellner's argument that, short of merger, rivals are apt to achieve only a qualified joint profit maximization position; agreements to advance group goals are subject to significant constraints.[15]

The increasing slope region shown in the lower ranges of the adherence equilibrium curve is due to assumed economies of scale in communication. Thus, a little bit of communication produces only a negligible response, but as communication cumulates, a much sharper definition of group goals becomes possible. Although this condition seems highly plausible, it is not essential to the argument.

Consider next the curve along which the amount of communication is in equilibrium at every level of adherence. Initially, this curve also has a positive slope but, in addition to passing through a region of increasing then decreasing returns, it becomes backward bending at very high levels of adherence. The reasons for this have been given already. It follows from the assumption that the felt need to communicate declines when the agreement on group goals becomes thoroughly shared. This backward bending property is not essential to the analysis, however. It is sufficient that saturation conditions set in so that the communication

---

[15] Fellner, *op. cit.*, pp. 223–232.

equilibrium curve need merely approach a vertical asymptote rather than turn back on itself at very high levels of adherence.

As drawn, the curve $dC/dt = 0$ has its intercept along the C axis to the right of the intercept $dA/dt = 0$. That is, at zero adherence the equilibrium level of communication exceeds the level of communication required to maintain zero adherence. As a result, a system initially in a position of very low adherence will, due to a felt need to communicate even when every member is motivated to attend solely to his own interests, tend to move to an equilibrium level of adherence that exceeds zero (to a position such as K). In other words, a completely fractionated industry is an unnatural condition; the level of dealings necessary to transact business in an orderly way generally promotes an identity of interest that exceeds zero. Under extreme conditions this relationship between the two intercepts might be violated, in which case the system would then possess only a single equilibrium position. It would be at the intercept of the communication equilibrium curve with the C axis.

So much, then, for the shapes and positions of the curves. As indicated earlier, the intersections K and M are stable equilibria. Should the system start out at any point above the dashed line through L, it would move toward the high level equilibrium at M, while if it should start out anywhere below, it would move (asymptotically) to the low level equilibrium at K. The high level equilibrium being a position of substantial communication and adherence will, through the mechanism of Eq. (1), lead to a high level of performance while the low level equilibrium, being one where independent rather than joint actions are preferred, yields a lower level of individual and collective achievement.

More interesting than the equilibrium properties of the system, however, is the dynamic response of the system to changes in the condition of the environment (E). A change in the condition of the environment has a direct effect on performance via Eq. (1). But performance in turn influences the level of adherence through Eq. (2). Thus, the environment has an effect on adherence and acts as a shift parameter on this relation [Eq. (2″)]. The communication relation, however, is not directly influenced by the environment. Hence, the curve $dC/dt = 0$ remains fixed as changes in E occur, while the curve $dA/dt = 0$ is shifted by changes in the condition of the environment.

More precisely, a decline in E tends to produce a condition of excess supply (evaluated at normal price) and the curve $dA/dt = 0$ is shifted down. Thus, at every level of adherence, a higher level of communication is necessary in order to maintain equilibrium with respect to the adherence relation when the environment deteriorates than when the environment is favorable. The unfavorable environment tends to amplify differences between own and group goals so that, in order to encourage collective rather than independent action, a higher level of information exchange is required. Thus, although from the point of view of the industry the economic incentive to act collectively and maximize joint profits is always operative, a tendency for disparity to develop in the attitudes of the individual members during periods of adversity makes a policy of collective action difficult to sustain. An improvement in the condition of the environment reverses these forces and the curve $dA/dt = 0$ is shifted up.

Consider the system initially at a high level equilibrium position when a decline in the environment begins. If the point M is above the point W in Fig. 1 (the maximum value of C on the curve $dC/dt = 0$), the first effects of the decline will be to increase communication but decrease adherence. If the deterioration continues, the curve $dA/dt = 0$ will pass through W; beyond this point both A and C will decline. As the curve $dA/dt = 0$ continues to shift down, the points L and M will begin to converge. When the point V is reached, tangency between the two partial equilibrium relations occurs, L and M will have become identical, and the equilibrium will be unstable from below but stable from above. Thus, any further decline in E will send the system to a low level (stable) equilibrium at K.

As soon as an improvement in the environment begins, the adherence equilibrium curve will shift up. However, the system will tend to persist at its low level equilibrium position, K. Thus, even after the system re-establishes tangency at V and moves back toward its original position (as shown in Fig. 1), there will only occur a modest increase in adherence and communication. Not until the curve $dA/dt = 0$ moves so far as to obtain tangency with the curve $dC/dt = 0$ at U (at which position L and K converge) and the equilibrium becomes stable from below but unstable from above will the system be ready to move to a new high level position. If improvements in the condition of the environment shift the curve $dA/dt = 0$ beyond tangency at U, a new high level equilibrium will be re-established. The cyclical sequence of adjustment is shown in Fig. 2.

The movements between V and K and between U and M occur very rapidly, since they are movements from disequilibrium to equilibrium positions, whereas the movements between M and V and K and U occur only in response to continuing changes in the condition of the environment. Thus, the system has the property that once a low level equilibrium is achieved, there will tend to be persistence at a low level, whereas once a shift to a high level occurs, persistence at a high level will develop.

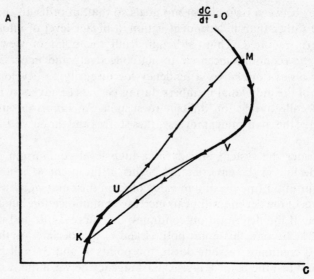

Fig. 2.

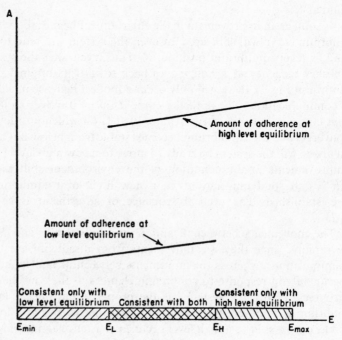

Fig. 3.

In other words, if the system is operating at a low level of adherence and communication (i.e., the competitive solution), a substantial improvement in the environment will be necessary before the system will shift to a high level of adherence and communication. *Indeed, the condition of the environment required to drive the system to the collusive solution is much higher than the level required to maintain it once it has achieved this position. Similarly, a much more unfavorable condition of the environment is required to move the system from a high to a low level equilibrium than is required to maintain it there.* These conditions are displayed graphically in Fig. 3.

The cross-hatched area reveals that there is a wide range of environmental conditions over which the system can be in either high or low level equilibrium, depending on where it originates. Thus, if the system is in a low level equilibrium position, the condition of the environment must exceed E_H before the system will shift to a high level equilibrium position. But once it has shifted to a high level equilibrium, the condition of the environment must fall to E_L before a low level equilibrium will be restored.

This is not an intuitively obvious property for such a system to possess and is a refutable implication. Indeed, we find that not only is the dynamic model capable of reproducing the cyclical behavior that was taken as the immediate objective of the analysis, but, in addition, it displays persistence properties that were not included in the original description. Although after the fact it seems reasonable to expect the system to have such persistence properties, that they were not detected before the fact suggests that one of the merits of attempting more than a naive formulation is that the model itself will frequently not merely yield the principal properties of the system, but will provide refinements as well. . . .

3. Extensions

The proposed model can be extended to include a self-recovery mechanism that is capable of partially restoring the system to a high level equilibrium without an attendant improvement in the condition of the environment, to examine the influence of a variety of structural conditions, and to study the effects of regulatory restraints.

A. A Self-Recovery Mechanism

The only endogenous means by which adherence is secured in the proposed model is through interfirm communication. Since the

communication equilibrium relationship is assumed to be independent
of the condition of the environment, the system develops no internal
response to adversity, but depends on an improvement in the condition
of the environment to restore it to a high level equilibrium position.
Although this formulation of the model is useful for purposes of detecting
the basic dynamic properties of the system, a more complete model would
take into account the increased incentive to communicate that occurs
when the difference between maximum performance attainable and
actual performance realized becomes great. Thus, the communication
relationship [Eq. (3′)] should probably be reformulated with a step
mechanism as follows:

$$\frac{dC}{dt} = \tilde{\psi}(\tilde{\pi}, A, C) \tag{3″}$$

where

$$\tilde{\pi} = \frac{\pi^* - \bar{\pi}}{\pi^*}$$

$\pi^* =$ maximum profit rate attainable

$\bar{\pi} =$ average profit rate realized

and

$$\tilde{\psi}_{\tilde{\pi}} > 0 \text{ when } \tilde{\pi} > k$$
$$= 0 \text{ when } \tilde{\pi} \leq k$$
$$0 < k < 1$$

As long as the difference between maximum profits attainable (π^*) and
actual profits realized ($\bar{\pi}$) is not great, changes in the condition of the
environment have no direct influence on communication. If, for example,
the system were initially operating in the high level equilibrium region,
changes in E that shifted the adherence equilibrium relationship insufficiently to move the system out of the high level equilibrium region
would probably have no effect on the locus $dC/dt = 0$; the values of π^*
and $\bar{\pi}$ would tend to move together and the incentive to communicate
would not be directly affected. If, however, the condition of the environment deteriorated sufficiently to drive the system to a low level equilibrium
position, the difference between π^* and $\bar{\pi}$ would become relatively large
and an attempt to restore the system to a higher level equilibrium position
via the communication mechanism could be expected. Thus, the communication equilibrium locus $dC/dt = 0$ would be shifted to the right
as a result of the widening gap that develops between π^* and $\bar{\pi}$ when the
system moves from a high to a low level equilibrium, and a partial recovery

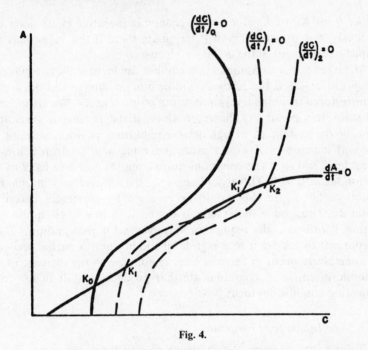

Fig. 4.

will set in without any attendant improvement in the condition of the environment. The recovery will occur with a lag (the communication equation is expressed as a differential equation) and may or may not be sufficient to restore the system to a high level equilibrium position. The possible types of adjustments are shown in Fig. 4.

The position K_0, where the adherence equilibrium relationship intersects the locus $(dC/dt)_0 = 0$, represents the initial position to which the system moves as a result of the deterioration in demand. Since at this position the value of $(\pi^* - \bar{\pi})$ is relatively great, the recovery mechanism built into the communication relation is brought into play and the locus $dC/dt = 0$ is shifted to the right. But since the low level equilibrium is stable, the system will tend to remain in this region despite the shifting of the communication equilibrium locus, *unless* the shift is so substantial that the only intersection between the two loci is a high level equilibrium one. In terms of the relations shown in Fig. 4, a shifting of the communication equilibrium locus from $(dC/dt)_0 = 0$ to $(dC/dt)_1 = 0$ will shift the system from K_0 to K_1 but not to K'_1. The latter position, although a stable equilibrium position consistent with the shift, would not be attained since the system originated at K_0 and will persist in the low level region as long as a low level stable equilibrium exists. Thus, the system will recover from K_0 to K_1 due to the economic incentive effect described previously, but the recovery will terminate there if this represents the complete adjustment of the $dC/dt = 0$ locus.

If, however, the communication equilibrium locus shifts to a position such as $(dC/dt)_2 = 0$, the recovery will be more complete and the system will be restored to a high level equilibrium position at K_2. We are inclined to dismiss this possibility, however, since, if the process is reversible, restoring the system to a high level equilibrium position without an attendant increase in E would cause the value of $\tilde{\pi}$ to drop below its critical level and shift the communication equilibrium curve back to the position $(dC/dt)_0 = 0$. This would again set the self-recovery mechanism in motion, but again this would be reversed by the forces described previously. Thus, once the system is driven to a low level equilibrium position, it will generally require an improvement in the condition of the environment to restore it to a high level equilibrium. A partial recovery will nonetheless occur at the low level region due to the increase in the economic incentive to communicate that produces a shift in the communication equilibrium locus.[16]

B. The Influence of Structure

Taking into account the influence of structural conditions in the industry should permit us to examine the dynamic behavior under study with more precision. Thus, we want to investigate the influence of number of rivals, the condition of entry, the history of the industry, and the nature of the product. Letting

$$N = \text{number of rivals}$$
$$B = \text{barriers to entry}$$
$$T = \text{economic age of the industry}$$
$$D = \text{differentiability of product}$$

the model presented in Eqs. (1), (2'), and (3') can be augmented as follows:

$$\pi = \pi[A; E, B, D] \qquad \pi_E > 0 \qquad \pi_B > 0 \qquad \pi_D = ? \qquad (6)$$

$$\frac{dA}{dt} = g[C, \pi, A; N, T, D] \qquad g_N \leq 0 \qquad g_T > 0 \qquad g_D < 0 \qquad (7)$$

$$\frac{dC}{dt} = \psi[A, C; N, T] \qquad \psi_N < 0 \qquad \psi_T \geq 0 \qquad (8)$$

[16] If the improvement in the condition of the environment is long in coming, it seems reasonable to suppose that the system might drift back toward the position K_0. The persistent failure of groups to realize their objectives frequently produces this sort of frustrated response.

Lest the analysis appear ad hoc, it might be useful to consider the heuristic that we have employed for introducing the parameters into the model. With respect to the performance equation, which is fundamentally an economic relation, the question that we posed was: indirect socialization influences aside, does the parameter have a direct economic effect? If the answer was negative, the parameter was omitted from the performance equation. If the answer was affirmative, the parameter was introduced into the performance relation and the appropriate sign of its associated partial derivative was designated. In considering the communication expression, which is basically a social relation, the question was: Indirect economic effects aside, does the parameter in question have a direct socialization influence? Again, if the answer was negative, the parameter was omitted, whereas if it was affirmative, the parameter was included and the appropriate sign of its partial derivative attached. The adherence relation has both economic and social parts and here the question was: does the parameter influence perceptions? The process for inclusion or omission described previously was again repeated.

Despite the fact that we make only gross distinctions in separating the parameters into mainly social or mainly economic types, the partitioning seems worth the effort. It permits us to introduce each parameter into the system through the relation that is directly responsive to the type of influence in question, and its direct and indirect effects can then be traced out. In a naive model, where no differentiation between social and economic influences is attempted, the process of imputing directional effects to each of the parameters is much more conjectural, relying on an intuitive juggling of the direct and indirect effects of the parameters in question to obtain some net evaluation.

Ceteris paribus, we have the following propositions:

a. As the number of rivals (N) increases, the locus $dC/dt = 0$ shifts to the left. That is, although the total amount of communication between rivals may increase as N increases, we hypothesize that the *average* amount, at every level of adherence, will decline; each firm will receive less of a transmission concerning the intentions of each of its rivals as the number of rivals increases.[17]

[17] As the number of rivals increases, the volume of transmissions necessary to keep each rival in touch with every other (assuming each transmits to every other) increases in proportion to $[(N - 1)N]/2$ or, approximately, as $1/2$ the square of N. Thus, even allowing for a reorganization of the network to achieve a more efficient configuration, it is likely that the *average* communication, as defined earlier, will decline as N increases. For a similar view of the influence of N on interfirm communication, see Phillips, *Market Structure, Organization, and Performance, op. cit.*, pp. 29–30. W. J. Baumol likewise agrees that combinatorial diseconomies of scale develop despite hierarchical organization designed to

In addition, the locus $dA/dt = 0$ will either remain unchanged or will fall at every level of communication as N increases. It will fall if, as seems likely, the incentive to advance own rather than group goals increases as N increases. But it is not obvious that the *direct* effect of an increase in the number of rivals necessarily shifts the adherence equilibrium locus down in this way. The incentives to coordinate may be substantially unchanged, in which case the curve $dA/dt = 0$ would be unaffected.

In either case, the ultimate (as contrasted with the immediate) effect of an increase in N will, as a result of the shift in the communication equilibrium locus, lead to a lower level of adherence than existed previously. This behavior is also hypothesized by Kaysen and Turner, who observe that "the larger the number, the greater is the likely diversity among firms.... These diversities... increase the probability that some of the firms in the oligopoly group will find independent action rather than joint action advantageous."[18] Although they indicate that this decrease in adherence is a direct effect, for our purposes it is sufficient to observe that be it direct or indirect, a decline is predicted, and to point out that the precise mechanism can presumably be investigated in the laboratory.

The decline in adherence leads to a reduction in the level of aggregate performance. The amount of communication will necessarily decrease if the locus $dA/dt = 0$ remains fixed, and will ordinarily decline in any case.

Restated in concentration ratio terms (of which N is a proxy), a decrease in concentration leads to a decrease in the level of adherence. Indeed, as concentration declines, the system may be shifted into what becomes effectively a permanent low level equilibrium position: the relation between the curves $dA/dt = 0$ and $dC/dt = 0$ becomes such that changes in the condition of the environment are able only to shift the system within the low level equilibrium region.[19]

---

reduce the communication load in systems where otherwise everyone must communicate with everyone else. "Urban Services: Interaction of Public and Private Decisions," in H. G. Schaller, ed., *Public Expenditure Decisions in the Urban Community* (Baltimore: Johns Hopkins Press, 1963), p. 7.

[18] Kaysen and Turner, *op. cit.*, p. 115. See also March and Simon, *op. cit.*, p. 127.

[19] Two pieces of evidence can be adduced in support of the behavior described. First, we have Bain's analysis of the profit rates in a 42 industry sample over the period 1936–1940. He finds that industries in which the concentration ratio for the 8 largest firms exceeded 70 percent averaged an 11.8 percent rate of return on the stockholders' equity, whereas in industries in which the concentration ratio was less than 70 percent the average profit rate was only 7.5 percent, the difference being statistically significant. Moreover, *within* either group he was unable to detect a significant association; only *between* groups did it appear. (J. S. Bain, "Relation of Profit Rate to Industrial Concentration: American Manufacturing,

b. A higher entry barrier (B) provides existing firms with a differential advantage over potential rivals and thus leads to an increase in performance. Whether the barrier is due to economies of large scale production or large capital requirements, the insularity that it provides permits existing firms to increase price and realize larger profits. That is, assuming that the entry preventing price is below the short-run monopoly price, an increase in the height of the barrier to entry increases the joint profit maximizing price ($p*$). With adherence held constant, the direct (or immediate) effect of an increase in B is to increase the level of prices and profits in the industry.

· The increase in performance has an indirect effect on the adherence relation (since $g_\pi > 0$), shifting it upward at every level of C. Thus, an increase in B leads to an increase in the equilibrium level of adherence. . . .

c. As the industry accumulates experience (i.e., as T increases), the equilibrium level of adherence shifts up at every level of communication and the equilibrium level of communication shifts to the right at every level of adherence. Unambiguously, experience leads to a higher level of adherence and, since $\pi_A > 0$, the performance level of the industry also increases. Whether the passage of time increases the level of communication depends on the initial position under comparison.

d. A differentiable product (D) leads to analytical difficulties. It is not clear, for example, what aggregate industry performance means in these circumstances. The performance measure that we described previously indicates that an increase in the dispersion of firm profits around a specified mean leads to a decrease in aggregate performance. But if differentiation is responsible for the high profits of one group of firms, and if differentiation effectively insulates these firms from their rivals, these firms are apt to be unconcerned over the disparity between their profits and those of their rivals insofar as this influences the adherence relation. Thus, differentiation renders our notion of an aggregate performance measure somewhat inappropriate.

With respect to adherence we are on surer ground. The direct effect of differentiation here is to shift the equilibrium level of adherence

---

1936–1940," *Quarterly Journal of Economics*, **65** (August 1951), pp. 293–324.) On conventional market structure analysis, this discontinuity is difficult to explain. On the basis of our model, however, we see that in order to reach the high level equilibrium region the industry may have to exceed some threshold level of concentration. Below this level the industry operates continuously in the low level equilibrium region. Above this level it alternates between high and low level equilibrium positions in response to changes in the condition of the environment. Industries in this latter category would be expected to earn higher average profits than industries below threshold. . . .

down at every level of communication. For one thing, as we have just indicated, differentiation tends to widen the conflict between own and group goals. For another, as March and Simon have observed, "it is extremely difficult to communicate about... non-standardized objects." Thus, more communication is required to sustain any given level of adherence. Put differently, the locus $dA/dt = 0$ falls. Whatever the effect on profits, we would expect that the equilibrium level of adherence and communication will decline....

4. Conclusions

The proposed model attempts to merge the principal social and economic factors that appear to be responsible for an important class of oligopoly behavior into a system of simultaneous equations within which these influences work themselves out. Since the phenomenon of alternation between competitive and cooperative solutions that provided the original stimulus for the analysis involves a process of dynamic adjustment, the proposed model was formulated as a system of differential equations. Upon examination, the model was shown to display: (1) multiple equilibria, for which the stability of each was evaluated; (2) a capacity to generate the alternation phenomenon in question in response to changes in the condition of the environment; (3) persistence behavior that went undetected in the original description of the dynamic characteristics of the system. Thus, the model not only reproduced the gross characteristics of the behavior under examination but it suggested refinements as well.

In addition, the dynamic model lent itself to a variety of extensions. First, a "self-recovery" mechanism was built in. Examination of this mechanism led us to conclude that probably only a partial recovery from a low level equilibrium position would result from internal responses; a complete recovery would await an improvement in the condition of the environment. Second, the influence of industry structure was investigated. It was shown that the social and economic influences of structural variables could be traced through the model with comparative ease. In the usual treatments, where no attempt is made to discriminate between social and economic influences or between direct and indirect effects, the process of assigning directional effects to structural parameters is much more conjectural and therefore highly uncertain. Finally, the effects of regulatory constraints were investigated. The dynamic model displayed further versatility by revealing what types of conditions are necessary for enforcement to be effective. It also suggested a natural extension of the argument to consider adaptive responses to regulation and possible surveillance strategies.

So far in this section we have been exploring, for their possible relevance to theories of international stability, some of the conditions under which an oligopolistic industry might exhibit stable market shares. The next selection, a chapter from John Kenneth Galbraith's book, *American Capitalism*, discusses not the conditions that produce stable oligopoly, but one of its alleged virtues.[1] Galbraith takes issue with the economic efficiency view outlined previously, and chastises his colleagues for having overlooked a major social benefit that stems from the abnormally high profit margins that clearly are available in such industries—the very substantial investments in research made possible by a combination of the high rates of return and the diversion of competition into product differentiation. To this great expenditure on research and development he traces much of the dynamism of the entire American economy. (The chapter was written at a time when government expenditures on research and development were little more than a tenth of what they were in the mid-1960's.) By analogy, the competition among a few major states in an international system would promote large-scale and beneficial research and development activities in the attempt, by each state, to improve its relative status in the system.[2]

Despite the stimulating character of the chapter, several somewhat critical points can be made:

1. The case would be stronger if the relation of expenditures on research and development to the degree of concentration of industries had been investigated systematically rather than illustrated anecdotally.[3]

[1] Galbraith develops this argument again in his recent book, *The New Industrial State* (Boston: Houghton Mifflin, 1967).

[2] The nearly four-fold expansion of research and development expenditures in the United States between the early 1950's and the mid-1960's has sometimes been attributed to the expectations of long-term political competition with the Soviet Union. (Data from U.S. Bureau of the Census, *Statistical Abstract of the United States, 1966* (Washington: U.S. Government Printing Office, 1966), p. 543, and *Statistical Abstract of the United States, 1962* (Washington: U.S. Government Printing Office, 1962) p. 542).

[3] There are, in fact, many exceptions. See C. Wilcox, *Public Policies toward Business* (Homewood, Ill.: Richard D. Irwin, Inc., 3rd ed., 1966). At the international level, the size of the scientific enterprise in the United States is not greater than what one would "expect" from the total American GNP. For example, the United States produces about one-third of total world income, and contributes approximately the same proportion of physics and chemistry papers in journals. Several second-rank powers, however, contribute notably more to the scientific enterprise than their GNP would lead one to expect. This is especially true of Japan and the United Kingdom, for whom the proportion of world journal articles is twice and three times, respectively, their shares of world income. (Data from Derek J. de Solla Price, "Nations Can Publish or Perish," *International Science and Technology*, October 1967, pp. 85–91.)

2. Following from the first point, anecdotal exceptions to the rule can also be found. As was illustrated in Shubik's review of the highly concentrated cigarette industry, the substitute for price competition is sometimes almost *exclusively* advertising, with little or no socially useful scientific research. In other industries, such as steel, the major innovations often originate with the small firms, not the large ones, which may be reluctant to upset a stable market division painfully arrived at.

3. High rates of expenditure on research and development may not, in international politics rather than industrial competition, always be so desirable. This is especially so when the motive is indeed competitive, to maintain or possibly increase one's share of the "market." Research on public health, or even research directed toward prestige-building spectaculars, may be relatively benign, but military research and development on a large scale carries with it the risk of a qualitative as well as a quantitative arms race. Innovation, as for example with the development of an antiballistic missile system, may threaten to upset a delicate balance between protection and vulnerability for retaliatory vehicles, or force the introduction of new weapons of mass destruction when they become technically feasible, even if no one really wants them.[4] Research and development thus may have two quite different kinds of consequences. It may bring forth new products that are desirable from the point of view of the consumer, but at the same time become a means of destroying competing firms through offering a more "attractive" product on the market than they can match. The two must be kept analytically separate since "security" in international politics is a product ultimately accruing to the individual not merely as a consequence of a single nation's (firm's) exertions, but also of the *interaction* of the major producing and selling units in the system.

●

[4] See W. R. Schilling, "The H-Bomb Decision: How to Decide Without Actually Choosing," *Political Science Quarterly*, **71**, 1 (March 1961), pp. 24–26.

13

The Economics of Technical Development

John Kenneth Galbraith

A benign Providence who, so far, has loved us for our worries, has made the modern industry of a few large firms an almost perfect instrument for inducing technical change. It is admirably equipped for financing technical development. Its organization provides strong incentives for undertaking development and for putting it into use.[1] The competition of the competitive model, by contrast, almost completely precludes technical development.

There is no more pleasant fiction than that technical change is the product of the matchless ingenuity of the small man forced by competition to employ his wits to better his neighbor. Unhappily, it is a fiction. Technical development has long since become the preserve of the scientist and the engineer. Most of the cheap and simple inventions have, to put it bluntly, been made. Not only is development now sophisticated and costly but it must be on a sufficient scale so that successes and failures will in some measure average out. Few can afford it if they must expect all projects to pay off. This was not the case in the late eighteenth and the nineteenth century. Then, in the beginning stages of the applications of science and technology to industry and agriculture, there was scope for the

Reprinted from *American Capitalism: The Concept of Countervailing Power* (Boston: Houghton Mifflin, 1952; and London: Hamish Hamilton Ltd., 1952), pp. 91–99.

[1] This point has been much overlooked by economists. A major exception was the late Professor J. A. Schumpeter in whose system the innovating role of large enterprises is strongly emphasized. See his *Capitalism, Socialsim and Democracy* (New York: Harper & Row, 2nd ed., 1943), pp. 79 ff. While my analysis is in a tradition of economic theory different from his, and one of which he was frequently critical, the conclusions on this point are similar.

uncomplicated ingenuities of a Hargreaves or a Franklin. The competition of the competitive model encouraged such ingenuity and assured the spreading of its fruits. As elsewhere, the competitive model had great appropriateness to the industrial society which it was designed to interpret. Its designers were not abstruse theorists or dolts. It is the society they interpreted that has changed.

Because development is costly, it follows that it can be carried on only by a firm that has the resources associated with considerable size. Moreover, unless a firm has a substantial share of the market, it has no strong incentive to undertake a large expenditure on development. There are, in practice, very few innovations which cannot be imitated—where secrecy or patent protection accords a considerable advantage to the pioneer. Accordingly, the competitor of the competitive model must expect that his innovation will be promptly copied or imitated. Whether it be a new product or a new way of reducing the costs of producing an old one, the change will be dispersed over a market in which he has only an infinitely small share. The imitators, who haven't stood the cost of development, profit along with the pioneer. And, presently, prices will adjust themselves to remove entirely the advantage of the innovator. He is thus restored to a plane of equality with his imitators. Thus, the very mechanism which assures the quick spread of any known technology in the purely competitive market—and which was a strong recommendation of that market— eliminates the incentive to technical development itself. It leaves to the pioneer, apart from the rare case of effective patent protection, only the fleeting rewards of a head start. Where the costs of development are considerable, there is no reason to suppose that the returns to the pioneer will be sufficient to compensate for the cost. On the contrary, as the costs of development increase—and with time and progress toward more sophisticated innovation they must increase—there is a diminishing likelihood that they will be recovered. The higher the level of science and technology required for change, the more nearly static an industry which conforms to the competitive model will become.

In the industry that is shared by a relatively small number of large firms, the convention that excludes price competition does not restrain technical innovation. This remains one of the important weapons of market rivalry. The firms, typically, are large. Hence, resources are available on a scale appropriate to the modern requirements of technical development. Some of them in fact are the fruits of market power—of monopoly gains. And, while imitation must be assumed and expected, the convention which limits price competition also insures that the returns, whether to a new product or from cost-reducing innovation, will acrue to the innovator as well as to its rivals for a period of time. The presence of market power makes the latter time period subject to some measure of control.

Thus, in the modern industry shared by a few large firms, size and the rewards accruing to market power combine to insure that resources for research and technical development will be available. The power that enables the firm to have some influence on prices insures that the resulting gains will not be passed on to the public by imitators (who have stood none of the costs of development) before the outlay for development can be recouped. In this way market power protects the incentive to technical development.

The net of all this is that there must be some element of monopoly in an industry if it is to be progressive. This, at first glance, is shockingly at variance with accepted notions. Economists have long excoriated the comfortable domination of an industry by a single firm in the belief that such a firm will sit not only on production but on progress as well. So, far from spending money on innovation, it may even suppress patents in order to protect existing investment in plant and machinery.

Such a view of the behavior of a monopoly may not be entirely in error although as Schumpeter has argued, it may be somewhat improbable in a world where there are always potential substitutes and where innovation is proceeding elsewhere. The error has resulted from generalizing from what may be the plausible behavior of a single firm in possession of the entire output of an industry to the consequences of the monopoly power of a few firms sharing the output of an industry. Because stagnation is a plausible counterpart of monopoly in the first case it has been thought to be a likely counterpart of the monopoly power that undoubtedly exists in the second case. This generalization, so far from being valid, would appear to be almost completely in error.

To be sure, some room must be left for exceptions. One can imagine that the convention against price competition could be extended, in the industries of small numbers, to innovation. And, as in the well-publicized instances of patent suppression, this has undoubtedly happened. But to maintain a convention against innovation requires a remarkably comprehensive form of collusion. This is difficult as well as legally dangerous. While it would be going too far to say that oligopoly insures progress, technical development is all but certain to be one of the instruments of commercial rivalry when the number of firms is small. Like advertising and salesmanship—and unlike price competition, which is unique in this respect—technical development is a safe rather than a reciprocally destructive method by which any one firm can advance itself against its few powerful rivals.

Moreover, in a community which sets great store by progress, technical progress is an important source of business prestige. An American business concern simply cannot afford the reputation of being unprogressive. If it has no laboratories, it must imagine some; an annual report that makes no reference to research is unthinkable. Such an environment is highly unfavorable to any systematic restraint on innovation.

Thus, there can be little doubt that oligopoly, both in theory and in fact, is strongly oriented toward change. There can be no serious doubt at all that the setting for innovation, which is so favorable in this market structure, disappears almost entirely as one approaches the competition of the competitive model.

These propositions can be readily verified by experience. The American farmer, the producer who most closely approaches the competitor of the model, does almost no research on his own behalf. It was the foresight of genius that caused this to be recognized at an early stage in our history, with the result that technical development within this field has been almost completely socialized. We now take for granted that technical development in agriculture as such will come from the State Experiment Stations and from the United States Department of Agriculture. Not minimizing for a moment the well-publicized efforts of the men of literature who have invested their royalties in land, there would be little technical development and not much progress in agriculture were it not for government-supported research supplemented by that of the large corporations who devise and sell products to the farmer. The individual farmer cannot afford a staff of chemists to develop an animal protein factor which makes different proteins interchangeable as feeds. So many would appropriate the innovation so quickly, without having contributed to the cost of development, that it wouldn't profit any farmer to try.

The other industries which are distinguished by a close approach to the competitive model are also distinguished, one can almost say without exception, by a near absence of research and technical development. The bituminous coal industry, apart from a handful of very large operators, the cotton textile industry, apart from a few very large groups of mills, the clothing industry, the lumber industry, and the shoe industry do very little research. None of them are thought of as technically progressive industries. All of them (apart always from the few large firms they contain and which help prove the case) roughly meet the specifications of the competitive model. They also conform to the ideal which the American economists has had anciently in mind. No firm in these industries (the few special cases again excepted) has appreciable influence on prices; each is forced by circumstances which it cannot control to search for the greatest efficiency of operation; in most of them entry and exit are admirably free; few of the firms in these industries engage in extensive competitive advertising and salesmanship. Yet almost no one would select them as a showpiece of

American industrial achievement. The showpieces are, with rare exceptions, the industries which are dominated by a handful of large firms. The foreign visitor, brought to the United States by the Economic Cooperation Administration, visits the same firms as do attorneys of the Department of Justice in their search for monopoly.

The reductions in cost, and the consequent increases in efficiency from technical change can be of a wholly different order of magnitude from those sacrificed as the result of the exercise of market power. Thus, it comes about that a slight continuing loss of efficiency, as compared with ideal performance, from the possession of market power is regularly offset and more than offset by large gains from technical development. Economists, aided by the new market theory, have fixed their attention on the loss and have overlooked the offset. In concentrating on the inefficiency of the steam engine—specifically, the fact that it is not being worked to ideal capacity—they have failed to notice that the owner was designing a gas turbine.

A comparison of the oil with the bituminous coal industry usefully illustrates the point being emphasized. The oil industry is an unquestioned oligopoly; in any market area there are a few large firms and the characteristic fringe of independents. Over the years it has been under repeated attack for violation of the antitrust laws; it has rarely been free of suspicion of holding prices above the level that would be associated with more vigorous price competition. Profits have generally been excellent. Yet few would be inclined to trade the oil industry for the bituminous coal industry, which, abstracting from the stabilization operations of John L. Lewis, approaches the competition of the model.

The oil industry is clearly progressive—almost as progressive, perhaps, as the uncommonly attractive brochures of its member companies unreluctantly concede. As the result of its enterprise in petroleum exploration and recovery, in developing new products, and in engineering new methods of transporting both petroleum and products, the consumer of gasoline and fuel oil has been a far more fortunate man than the consumer of coal. The continuing shift of customers from the admirably competitive coal industry to the dubiously competitive oil industry emphasizes the point.

Thus, while the incentives in the American economy do not, at any given moment, act to encourage the largest possible production at the lowest possible price, this is not the tragedy that it appears to be at first glance. The market concentration of American industry that is affirmed by the statistics and condemned by the competitive model turns out on closer examination to be favorable to technical change. To get the ideal equilibrium of price and output of the competitive model, we should almost certainly have to forego the change. Life might be simpler were we to do so, but progress, as it is called, is a wheel to which we are all bound.

It seems reasonable to suppose that if the same technical talent that has been devoted to the search for oil, or to its utilization, had been brought to bear on coal mining in the last half-century, the coal industry would be very different from what it is today. New techniques of recovery might long since have been developed. Men would no longer toil like moles in mining operations that "under the most favorable conditions are hazardous and highly inefficient ... an unpleasant, uninspiring and none too healthy occupation."[2] It is significant, by way of verifying the technical limitations of competition, that recent efforts to raise the technology of coal production have required the cooperative effort of the industry—some three hundred operators, railroads, and equipment suppliers now jointly support Bituminous Research, Inc.—and that the significant work on the hydrogenation of coal has been under government sponsorship. One of the country's experienced research administrators has observed of the coal industry that "An industry with 6000 little units has made a terribly difficult pattern on which to develop modern industrial research programs."[3]

---

[2] "Coal I: The Industrial Darkness," *Fortune* (March 1947). Quoted from *Industrial Engineering and Chemistry* (August 1946).

[3] Frank A. Howard, *ibid.*, p. 87. It must be observed that the anthracite industry, the ownership of which is considerably more concentrated than bituminous mining, has not, at least until recent times, been credited with any strongly progressive tendencies. There appear, however, to have been special reasons, relating generally to character of ownership, for this.

●

I have not attempted in these selections and in my brief comments upon them to develop anything like a full theory of the relation of market theory to the operation of the international political system, but a variety of useful parallels and insights do emerge. Having examined some of the arguments (and some of their limitations) for an oligopolistic international system rather than one resembling perfect competition, we must now ask whether more of an alleged good thing (concentration) would be even better. Would a duopolistic world, with only two great powers, be even more stable?

Many articles in international politics have examined aspects of the case for and against the bipolar system, either in the abstract or with specific attention to the historical experience of the 1950's. There have also been several rigorous though limited analyses of the stability conditions, using mathematical models derived from the natural sciences—many are related to what are now known as Richardson processes. The following two selections deal with the problem, using the tools and theoretical orientations that have been employed in economics. The first, by Martin McGuire, deals explicitly with an attempt to develop the analogy between duopoly and arms races in a bipolar world. His book *Secrecy and the Arms Race* proceeds from a discussion of the actions taken by one side in isolation to their interactions when each takes account of the other's moves. This latter part, which is of course the more realistic, is further divided into sections allowing for (1) perfect information about each other's procurement decisions and (2) imperfect information or secrecy. While the second is more relevant to international politics, the section assuming perfect information is sufficiently complicated and, even with its limitations, sufficiently interesting to merit reprinting here on its own. Note also that the discussion is limited to a pure provocation and deterrence situation involving only missiles—a very limited set of assumptions, but still able to provide useful insights. Like Shubik he is concerned with the resources and vulnerabilities of the unit, and assumes that there is a breaking point, a level of resource availability or utility below which a state cannot in the long run survive. Extended periods below that utility level will result in political collapse or upheaval.

Within the limits of his assumptions, two of his conclusions are: If each side is interested in both deterrence and a potential for attacking the other, the level of armaments maintained will be greater than if it were interested in either deterrence or attack only; partial mutual disarmament reduces deterrence but increases attack potential. The assumptions behind these and other conclusions should be analyzed with care.[1]

●

[1] Another work illustrating the uses and limitations of deductive economic models for analyzing duopolistic arms races is M. D. Intrilligator, "Some Simple Models of Arms Races," *General Systems: Yearbook of the Society for General Systems Research*, 9 (1964), pp. 143–150. See also E. A. Deagle, Jr., "The Politics of Missile-making: A Dynamic Model," *Public Policy*, Vol. 16 (Cambridge: Harvard University Press, 1967), who emphasizes the importance, in interactive arms races, of good intelligence and, occasionally, of deliberate information leakage to prevent the opponent from embarking on a stepped-up procurement policy based on mistaken estimates of one's strength. See also T. C. Schelling, "The Strategy of Inflicting Costs," and M. McGuire, "The Structure of Choice between Deterrence and Defense," in R. N. McKean, ed., *Issues in Defense Economics* (New York: National Bureau of Economic Research, 1967).

14

The Arms Race:
An Interaction Process

Martin McGuire

1. The Arms Race as Economic Theory

One main purpose of this study is to present a theory of the arms race. And the theory devised herein is essentially an economic theory, although many may wonder how it is possible to utilize theoretical economics for such a purpose. This can be done because abstract economics deals with the science of choice—choice between alternative ends (and how much of each) when the resources available for securing these ends are limited. The arms race can legitimately be viewed, also, as a sequence of choices made by antagonists, both of whom are seeking security and power. In this way, as a science of choice, economic theory is validly applied to more than the conventional problems of economics—to the arms race, for example.

In addition, the economist brings some useful concepts to a consideration of the arms race. He is accustomed to thinking in terms of costs, benefits, and prices. The division of arms-race phenomena into considerations of cost and benefit itself will result in valuable insights into the problem. Beyond that, the notion of price has particular utility as a result of its role in summarizing the great and complex varieties of information that are required for the making of rational, best choices—of incurring costs so as to achieve benefits. The information summarized is essentially of two sorts: that which describes the preferences of the decision maker and that which describes the technology available for attaining a desired result. To know the price that some element in a nation's military force structure commands is to have a rule for accepting or rejecting proposed alternatives in that military posture *without having to calculate out the total effects of a change*. Thus, the economist is inclined to seek out rules for facilitating choice, and, thereby, for advancing the study of arms races....

An arms race may be viewed as an interacting sequence of decisions by two sides, in which each side in making any single decision makes the choice of employing given resources for the acquisition of arms, thereby exchanging for what those resources might have otherwise produced the contribution to national objectives that these arms may make. The problem is clearly within the realm of economics. Thus, in keeping with sound economic practice, we shall formulate and analyze the logic of a single choice by a single side—what we shall call the "one-sided" element in the problem—and only then proceed to the interactive sequence—the "two-sided" aspect, which is made up of a number of one-sided choices. Information also has been singled out as having a special relevance to the arms race. Accordingly, we further divide the problem into treatment with perfect versus imperfect information. This, therefore, gives us a four-part theory. Each part will be treated in turn, in order of its complexity with respect to the choice of armaments by (1) one sided : perfect information ; by (2) one side : imperfect information ; by (3) two sides : perfect information ; by (4) two sides : imperfect information.[1]

2. The Prerequisites for an Economic Model

Why are weapons of war accumulated? A thoroughgoing answer to this would require extensive study of war itself, its initiation, and progress to conclusion. Our purpose here is less ambitious—namely, to fashion a set of plausible behavioral assumptions which, though not exhaustive, are sufficient to generate an arms race, thereby allowing us to proceed with the main study.

Suppose the two sides in an arms race are called side X and side Y, and that each possesses x and y missiles, respectively. Either side can, potentially, strike the other first. Call the number of X's surviving missiles if Y were to strike first z_x, and the number of Y's if X were to strike first z_y. Our model of the arms race centers about these four variables, x, y, z_x, z_y. Side X has as its decision variable the value of x. Side Y has as its decision variable the value of y. Each combination (x, y) results in some potential outcome (z_x, z_y). The numbers of surviving missiles on either side if the other attacks are of fundamental importance throughout our theoretical

[1] These excerpts deal only with point (3); the book considers all of them in sequence [Ed.].

description. They hold a central place in our account, best likened to the position of a "good" in economic thought. The outcomes z_x and z_y are similar to economic goods in that they are sought as enhancing a side's utility—which is to say, as advancing that side's national purposes. But z_x and z_y are achieved only at a cost, the cost of other goods and other utilities foregone—which is to say, at the sacrifice of other national purposes.

Let it first be asked : How do z_x and z_y advance national objectives? In this study we make the assumption that the utility deriving from the allocation of resources to missiles is embodied entirely in the consequent potential increase in one's own surviving missiles if the enemy attacks, and potential *decrease* in the opponent's number of surviving weapons if one attacks first one's self. . . . In summary, what is said there is as follows : each side knows that if it attacks the other's missiles, there is some fixed (by assumption) probability that the victim will retaliate upon the attacker's cities, even though this would be an irrational decision for the victim to make. It would be irrational for the victim because he would destroy most of the attacker's incentive to capitulate in the face of the *potential* destruction to his population from the *threat* of retaliation. But the initiation of a missile war puts such pressures on the victim that he knows and the attacker knows that rational control may be lost. Nevertheless, even knowing this, a side might begin the war with a counterforce strike. It might do so if it were provoked or challenged—short of being attacked—to the point that the loss consequent upon accepting the provocation or losing the challenge would exceed the uncertain destruction in the form of retaliation, following its first strike. The attacker would in all probability not fire all his missiles in his first, counterforce blow; else he should encourage irrationality in the victim. (By firing all his missiles the attacker would also leave himself helpless in the face of the rational response—the *threat* of retaliation—by his victim.) According to our assumption, the attacker, therefore, holds back a fraction of his arsenal of missiles, the percentage being fixed regardless of the size of the stock.

Such a view of the nature of international conflict and potential war supports the assumption that utility can be measured in terms of own and enemy potentially surviving missiles. For if I can reduce my enemy's potential residual, then he must be less provocative, since he will know that I am now more easily decided to attack. Having less to lose from his uncertain retaliation, I will attack at a lower level of his provocation. At the same time if I can build up my own residual from a possible initial counterforce attack by the enemy, I then can be more provocative. *A fundamental axiom of this study is that the utility accruing to either partner in the arms race derives from these two sources.* An argument is offered in the text to show that the marginal utility to a side decreases as its own residual stock of missiles grows larger, and increases as its opponent's residual declines in size.

The theory just enunciated is supposed to be factually descriptive and not in any way ethically prescriptive. I do not wish to recommend that any nation accumulate missiles so that it can be more provocative, but I do think that, ceteris paribus, the more missiles a side has, the better off it considers itself to be. The deterrent motive for possessing missiles can be explained in various ways, as can the diminishing marginal utility from increases in one's surviving force. But if one says an enemy is deterred from attacking one's own country, that must imply that he is deterred for some degree of one's provocation. I can always substitute surrender, retreat, or capitulation for deterrence. Since an enemy must have some reason for attacking me—something to gain from doing so—presumably, I can bribe him not to attack. Conversely, the more deterrence I have, the less conciliatory need I be to remain out of war. From this it follows that when one side increases its first-strike counterforce potential, the other must become less provocative or build up its own deterrence again.

"Provocation" here should be understood as any act which challenges an adversary's interests, other than the act of altering the balance of strategic weaponry. Hence, it is the desire to be able to confront an opponent with nonnuclear challenge and to be able to thwart his nonnuclear initiatives *with minor risk of nuclear war* that drives the accumulation of strategic nuclear weapons on both sides.

It is to be emphasized that this view is restricted in that it refers to a world with only two sides. No pretense is made to include third or Nth powers with independent interests, nor to analyze the place of allies or proxies in mutual deterrence. No special attention is given to the deterrence of limited wars; but this is consistent with our theory, since a side's deter-

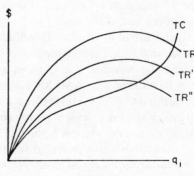

Fig. 1.

rence potential only establishes the maximum in provocation it can undertake. Any level of provocation short of that maximum is open to either side—is not deterred. Hence, the need for limited-war capabilities and so on. . . .

3. The Missile Race and Duopoly Theory

To the reader familiar with the economist's explanation of duopolistic markets, the similarity between this theoretical structure and our arms races is striking. The point of this section is to set forth an explicit comparison of the two, and to explore the possibilities for "solutions" in arms races as suggested by duopoly theory.

A. Essentials of Economic Duopoly

The theory of oligopoly is meant to describe the principles behind and the results of the behavior of a profit-maximizing firm that buys its inputs and/or sells its outputs in markets in which its influence over price is more than negligible. Duopoly refers to a special case in which only two firms sell a single homogeneous good to a large number of buyers. Duopsony refers to the special case in which only two firms buy a single homogeneous input from a large number of sellers. Thus, duopoly (duopsony) theory is taken normally as referring to the firm as the decision unit. Further, the two firms, if duopolists (duopsonists), are limited by a single market-demand (supply) schedule.

Consider the duopoly case. Assume a downward sloping market-demand schedule for the single good produced by both firms; therefore, the greater the total quantity offered for sale by both firms combined, the lower the unit price at which the market is cleared. Both firms receive this price for each unit they have offered for sale. It is characteristic of duopoly that a single market-demand schedule is posited, over which neither firm has control. Figure 1 shows the total cost curve, TC, of firm number one, and the total revenue curve, TR, indicating gross sales when the second firm produces nothing. Costs are assumed to remain unchanged, regardless of the action of the second firm, but the possibilities for revenue decline as the second firm increases its output. The total revenue curves TR', TR'', . . . , denote the first firm's revenue possibilities as the second firm produces and offers increasing quantities of the good in question.

Profit equals revenue less costs. Figure 2 shows the profit contours derived by making this subtraction in Fig. 1. In Fig. 2, q_2^i indicates all combinations of output and profit attainable by the first firm when the second firm's output is fixed at q_2^i. In the figure, $q_2^0 < q_2^1 < q_2^2$; profit $= \pi$.

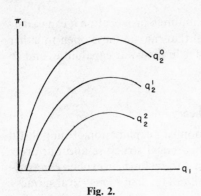

Fig. 2.

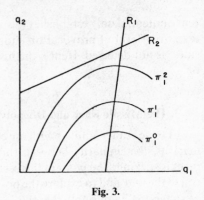

Fig. 3.

In Fig. 3 the same information is transferred to $q_1 - q_2$ axes, with the profits of the first firm denoted by $\pi_1{}^i$, and $\pi_1{}^0 > \pi_1{}^1 > \pi_1{}^2$. Suppose the first firm maximizes its profit for every value of q_2 which the second, for reasons not yet explained, happens to choose. The locus of such maxima connects the highest points on all the curves $\pi_1{}^i$. This is the first firm's reaction curve, and is denoted by R_1. The reaction curve of firm number two is derived by an analogous procedure. It is labeled R_2 in the figure (isoprofit curves not shown). Such is our account of duopoly presented in this abbreviated fashion to allow for comparisons with the interactive aspect of arms races.

B. Duopoly and the Arms Race Compared

... The major difference between the duopoly model outlined and the interactive model of the arms race developed beforehand would seem to be the existence and central position of a market-demand schedule in the duopoly case (or supply schedule in the case of duopsony). No such corollary exists in our account of arms races. The reason for this, however, is not difficult to find.

Duopoly theory is a special branch of the theory of the producer, whereas our account of the arms race reduces as an economic theory, to a special case of the theory of the consumer, or of one who exchanges one good (money in this case) for another (security, or intimidating power). Duopoly and oligopoly theory have been very largely occupied with the behavior of the firm for the simple reason that as a decision unit within the realm of conventional economics the consumer is taken as having an imperceptible and, therefore, negligible effect upon the price or exchange ratio at which he must trade. The consumer of received economic theory has at his disposal an income or wealth denoted by, say, $\overline{M}$. His preferences, as revealed by a hypothetical experiment, are summarized by a set of indifference contours between money, M, and good Q. The consumer must trade along the price line, whose slope is fixed by the price of the good in question. While the price is determined by the aggregate preferences of all consumers plus the profit-maximizing behavior of all firms, the individual consumer is powerless to affect this price. The idea of monopoly, partial or total, does not ordinarily arise within the context of consumer choice. . . . In a theory of the contest to accumulate missiles as presented here, on the other hand, there are only two "consumers," each wishing to maximize its own utility, and each having a direct effect upon the terms on which the other can buy the "good" in question. *In other words, our theory of the arms contest, in particular of the missile duel, reduces to an extension of duopoly theory into the region of consumer behavior,* a region which in general is considered the preserve of "perfect competition." In speaking of the arms race or the missile duel we are speaking of a class of *economic* problems and not of a unique problem foreign to economics. Our "consumer" is indeed limited by an exchange line which determines the price he must pay in exchange for the good he acquires, in this case missiles surviving (of his own or the enemy). But the position and shape of this exchange line is determined by the expenditures of the second party. In economic duopoly the source of interdependence between rivals is a market, exterior to both. In our duopolistic theory of consumption the interdependence is direct; one rival's "consumption" influences his opponent's utility directly, proceeding through no market intermediary. Formally, the decisions as to how much of a good to produce and how much deterrence to buy are identical.

4. Duopoly Solutions to the Arms Race

For years economists have amused one another with proposed solutions to duopoly situations. The purpose of this section is to explore the applicability of such notions to the particular sort of interactive process typified by our arms race, and to develop an idea of the implications of such solutions to arms races, to a country's security and strategic posture. We begin with the definition of solution.

A solution is achieved wherever a pair of decision-variables (x, y) attain certain values—say (x_0, y_0)—from which neither side is inclined to move once achieved. Different combinations of (x, y) will appear to exhibit this characteristic under different assumptions as to the psychology, behavior, intercommunication, and the legal limits of the situation. Whatever these assumptions, the feature common to all solutions is that for the values obtaining at the solution, each side is confirmed in its expectations about the behavior of the opponent and, therefore, has no need to change

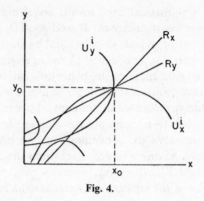

Fig. 4.

the value of its decision-variable. The values comprising a solution, in other words, are mutually self-confirming. If each side takes the other's decision as given, and adjusts to it, the outcome of the adjustment is the same values each started with. Figure 4 and figures to follow will be used to illustrate a number of such solutions.

A. The Cournot Duopoly Unrelenting-Arms-Race Solution[2]

First, consider the case in which both sides X and Y derive utility only from the capability to deter. Figure 4 shows two reaction curves R_x and R_y for side X and Y, respectively. It will be recalled that the reaction curve is the locus of points denoting the maximum utility available to one side for every value of the decision-variable of the opponent. Thus, the curve R_x connects the peaks of all X's utility contours (which are concave to the x-axis), and R_y connects the peaks of all Y's utility contours (which are concave to the y-axis). The two curves R_x and R_y intersect at the point (x_0, y_0). At this point side X is faced with y_0 missiles; X's best position or maximum utility is achieved when he maintains just x_0 of his own missiles. In doing this X confronts side Y with x_0 missiles. Side Y now maximizes his utility by choosing y_0 missiles—just the number which led X to select x_0. Thus, both sides' expectations are confirmed at the value (x_0, y_0).

[2] In Cournot's model each duopolist sets his output at that quantity which will maximize his profits on the assumption that his competitor will *not* change *his* output in response. The assumption is not likely to be well-founded, but the model may, nevertheless, describe certain duopolists' behavior—perhaps more in politics, where it is harder to obtain firm measures of gain and loss than in business. For an important argument that oligopolists make their day-to-day decisions with *only the most cursory* thought about the probable reactions of competitors see W. J. Baumol, *Business Behavior and Growth* (New York: Macmillan, 1959), Ch. 4, passim [Ed.].

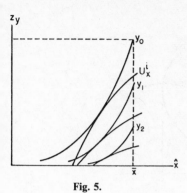

Fig. 5.

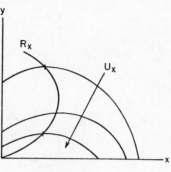

Fig. 6.

Now turn to the case in which each side is not interested in deterrence and, therefore, not in surviving missiles with which to retaliate, but rather is interested in striking first or in making a credible threat of striking first and is occupied, therefore, with the numbers of enemy surviving missiles. Figure 5 shows a set of cost curves for various enemy numbers of missiles, $y_0, y_1, y_2, \ldots$, and a utility function consistent with the properties

$$U_x = U_x(\hat{x}, z_y)$$

$$\frac{\partial U_x}{\partial \hat{x}} > 0, \qquad \frac{\partial^2 U_x}{\partial \hat{x}^2} < 0$$

$$\frac{\partial U_x}{\partial z_y} < 0, \qquad \frac{\partial^2 U_x}{\partial z_y^2} > 0$$

Figure 6 then shows these utility contours transformed into x–y space. The contours have all a positive y-intercept, are all concave from below, and reach maxima in y first at increasing, and then at decreasing, values of x.

It was shown elsewhere that linear utility functions result in a trivial equilibrium at the origin, whether stable or unstable. If, in contrast to the linear assumption, this utility function is assumed, reaction curves are as shown in Fig. 7, where the curvature of R_x at high values of x indicates the increasing pain-cost of giving up money to buy missiles, and the decreasing benefits of *reducing* enemy survivors as the enemy's total force increases. A stable equilibrium exists at (x_0, y_0).

Now imagine that each side in the arms competition is interested in both deterrent and attack potential. Clearly, *the level of armaments obtaining at a Cournot solution will be greater than if either deterrent or attack potential alone figured in a side's preferences.* Since utility derives from two sources, it will pay each side to accumulate missiles beyond the

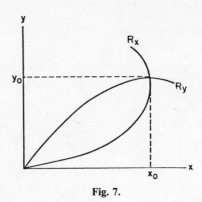

Fig. 7.

point at which marginal utility from one source alone equals marginal utility of money.

The major criticism of the solution at the intersection of the reaction curves in the case of economic duopoly is that it imputes too great a naïvete to the firm. The firm acts on the assumption its rival will hold its output constant, yet this assumption is repeatedly proven false. It would seem plausible to assume the firm learns to anticipate its rival's reaction. This criticism can be leveled at our model of the arms race also, but Cournot's behavior assumption should continue to have appeal. To suppose a country's leaders have explicit knowledge of their own preference function is a step with which many would quarrel; to suppose explicit knowledge of the rival's preferences is perhaps too heroic; yet this is required if one is to anticipate his reactions. Further, the simple naïve assumption leading to an equilibrium—if any is to be found at all—at the intersection of either side's reaction functions has appeal in that it describes a blind behavior,

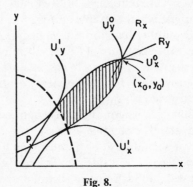

Fig. 8.

not strictly irrational, merely shortsighted. It is, of course, true that one major element in deciding how many missiles or bombers to build should be our guess at the number now possessed or to be possessed by the enemy. Postponing considerations of uncertainty, the relevant question within the context of a duopolistic description of the arms race is whether included in our guess of an enemy's missile force are estimates of his reaction to *our* missiles. If we ignore the fact that how many missiles to build depends upon how many the enemy builds, which in turn depends on how many we build, and so on, we conform to the behavior of the naïve duopolist.

B. The Pareto-Optimal Mutual-Disarmament Solution

If both X and Y were concerned solely with deterrence, and if both were able to observe the rival's as well as their own utility functions, then the classic Pareto-optimal solution shown in Fig. 8 would appear to be attainable.[3] In this figure the broken curve joins all points in the $x-y$ plane from which no movements can be made without damaging the position or reducing the utility of at least one of the two sides. The reader should recall that utility contours closer to the x-axis represent greater utilities for X, and contours closer to the y-axis greater utilities for Y. Starting from the Cournot solution (x_0, y_0), for example, by moving along curve $U_y{}^0$ side X could improve its own position to U'_x while Y suffers no loss, or by moving along curve $U_x{}^0$ side Y could improve its position to U'_y while side X suffers no loss. Within the cigar-shaped, shaded area it will be seen that both X and Y can improve over $U_x{}^0$ and $U_y{}^0$, respectively, simultaneously.

Of the possible types of behavior and the ensuing "solutions," that of Cournot duopoly seems best as a description of the arms-build-up process early in the contest. The complexity involved in maximizing under the assumption the enemy remains unchanged is in itself a formidable task. To do better than the Cournot duopolist requires reflection on the nature of the two-sided process, a grasp of the opponent's position and motivation, and no little introspection about one's own ends and means. All of this is least likely to materialize early in an arms race.

The possibility of duopolistic solutions for which one or both sides must anticipate the reaction of the adversary does, however, seem genuine later in an arms contest. With a substantial accumulation of weapons, and lapse of time, a learning process should be expected to occur. In particular,

---

[3] There may also be something to recommend the point P in Fig. 8 as a point to seek in a disarmament negotiations. At P arms are greatly reduced from (x_0, y_0) with *no loss* in utility on either side. At P both X and Y have greatly reduced deterrence and, therefore, may be less likely to be provocative. But as discussed later in this section, at P both X and Y are very vulnerable to attack.

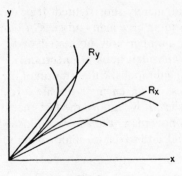

Fig. 9.

if an equilibrium point such as (x_0, y_0) in Fig. 8 were reached, it is plausible to suppose a lapse of time would result in reflection on both sides over the benefits of cooperation. The appeal of Fig. 8 as a diagram of the gain possible with limited disarmament is strong. The most preferred, or Pareto-optimal, section of the cigar-shaped area of improvement for both sides is the Von Neumann Morgenstern solution to the duopoly problem, and it is toward that contract curve we should hope disarmament negotiators might strive.

Insofar as our model of the arms race reflects reality, certain features of the Pareto-optimal solution are worthy of mention. The first is that complete and total disarmament is not likely to be the best solution. Only if the utility curves are of the shape shown in Fig. 9 is the *origin* the best position, from which neither side can move without damaging the other. In other words, *to the extent that the arms race is conceived to be a deterrent race, the belief that total disarmament is the best solution implies belief that there is no equilibrium short of the unstable equilibrium of the origin.* This is

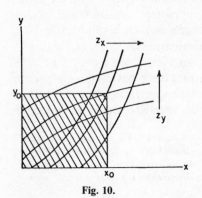

Fig. 10.   Fig. 11.

shown by the necessarily diverging (or converging only beyond attainable bounds) reaction curves of Fig. 9. The second point to remark is that to reach the contract curve solution both sides must restrain their accumulation of arms below what the intersection of reaction curves would dictate. In other words, disarmament must result in less money being spent on strategic weapons by each side. A third point is that in such an arms-limitation scheme as that diagramed in Fig. 8 at least one side would have to accept a lower level of security via deterrence, that is, a lower own z, than obtains at the naïve duopolist solution. This loss of utility via less deterrence would be more than compensated for by an increase in utility deriving from resources retained for other uses.

The fact that for mutual partial disarmament at least one side must forego some security arising from its retaliation potential can be proven most easily by plotting equal z_y and z_x contours. Figure 10 shows many such contours for z_x and for z_y, with the arrow in each case indicating the direction of increase in the z.[4] Suppose some point in the x–y plane was the naïve equilibrium at the intersection of X's and Y's reaction curves. Remember, both X and Y are deterrers only. The shape of the utility contours through that point determines the cigar-shaped area in which simultaneous improvements (increases in utility) for both sides are possible. This is shown again in Fig. 11. A movement toward the contract line within the shaded area of Fig. 11 and starting from (x_0, y_0) must be a south-west movement. (The utility contours determine the limits of the direction of movement, and the cigar-shaped area must lie in a NE-SW direction, as dictated by the construction that at the intersection of reaction curves each utility contour reaches a maximum.) Therefore, returning to Fig. 10 the southeast direction of movement requires that at least one of the two values z_x or z_y must decline. Therefore, at least one side must lose potential for deterrence by having its own z decline.

Now consider the situation when both X and Y seek only an attack potential. Figure 12 shows X's and Y's utility maps for this case. Observe that no contract curve exists; the origin itself is the only point from which no movements can be made to make one side better off without diminishing the utility of the other side. From every other point in x–y space both sides can be improved simultaneously. We suggested aforegoing that a Pareto-optimal contract curve implies that partial disarmament is preferable to total disarmament. That conclusion, however, depends upon the shapes of the utility contours, which, in turn, depend on the assumption

[4] z_x is the number of X's missiles that will survive if Y fires all his missiles, and varies with the number of missiles each side has. Along *one* contour $z_{const.}$, sides X and Y compensate for each other's strategic inventory just to the extent that the surviving number of missiles (say z_x) remains unchanged in the face of (Y's) attack [Ed.].

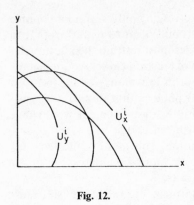

Fig. 12.

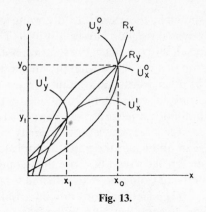

Fig. 13.

that both sides are retaliators only. This inference is absent from an account of a two-sided contest to acquire first-strike potential. If each side operated solely from this aggressive motive, then, indeed, the best (joint-utility-maximizing) solution would be complete and total disarmament.

We can now approach the case in which each side derives utility both from an ability to deter and from an ability to attack. A Cournot equilibrium solution obtains at some combination of missiles on either side (x_0, y_0). Corresponding to (x_0, y_0) is a combination (z_x^0, z_y^0) and two indices of utility U_x^0 and U_y^0. Imagine now that both sides begin to disarm. As demonstrated by Figs. 10 and 11, at least one side must suffer a decline in its own z. It seems plausible to suppose in the interests of equity of symmetry that each of the two rivals will allow its own z to decline. Suppose, for the sake of argument, that this is so. Then as disarmament progresses, both sides will suffer a decline in their own z, but will be more than compensated by the resource savings allowed. Imagine the two rivals stopped somewhere on a contract curve as in Fig. 11 (where the assumption of deterrence only is made). At such a point money savings would no longer justify further reductions in z_x and z_y, if X derived utility only from z_x and Y only from z_y. But in the case being considered here, X also gains utility from lower z_y and Y from lower z_x. Therefore, both X and Y can beneficially disarm further—until the possible savings in resources plus the decrease in the opponent's z are just balanced by the utility lost from the reduction in one's own z. In other words, not only does the introduction of a desire to threaten attack tend to increase arms on both sides at a Cournot solution, it also tends to decrease armaments at a Pareto-optimal, partial disarmament solution over and above the reductions allowed when both sides wish only to deter.

It should be noted that subject to the assumptions maintained thus far, partial mutual *disarmament reduces deterrence potential* of at least one and probably of both sides, while it *increases attack potential* of at least one and probably both sides.

Once the restriction of a duopoly solution, wherein numbers only are variable, is relaxed, it is possible that a disarmament arrangement whereby both sides improve their retaliatory capacity and decrease their first-strike potential may be reached. If both sides agree to reduce the accuracies or the yields of their missiles, this has the effect of making each a less potent attacker, and, therefore, each a more potent defender.[5] Numbers could then be reduced on both sides without reducing the deterrent power of either side from the initial number-yield-accuracy combination. There is, however, a disadvantage to disarming via reducing the accuracy or yield of one's weapons, but the disadvantage cannot be explained within the structure of our model. The disadvantage is that with very inaccurate missiles, if one is attacked first and wishes to retaliate, one can only retaliate against cities, or one is pushed in that direction. Our model is limited by the assumption that what deters a potential attacker is the fixed probability that a retaliatory strike is not counterforce, but rather counter-city. The point remains, however, that insofar as disarmament is restricted to limitations in numbers of missiles, the gain to either side is not in "security" via retaliatory capability, but in a money savings, utility-wise, greater than the loss in this potential for retaliation.

C. The Leader-Follower: Unilateral Disarmament Solution

If one of the two adversaries in our arms race can anticipate the preferences and, therefore, the reactions of the second, while the second can or does not do the same, then a leader-follower type of solution can be found. Figure 13 shows such a solution at (x_1, y_1). Side X is the leader; by choosing the value x_1, rather than x_0, X can induce Y to choose y_1. At (x_1, y_1) both X and Y are better off than at (x_0, y_0) since $U_y^1 > U_y^0$ and $U_x^1 > U_x^0$. The point (x_1, y_1) is on side Y's reaction curve. Both sides improve their positions because of X's ability to anticipate Y's reaction to his decision.

The rationale for suggesting such a solution for duopolistic, market-oriented, profit-maximizing firms centers about the idea of a disparity in size between the two firms. There is a large firm and a small one; the small one conforms to the policies of the large one, allowing the larger firm to determine price or quantity. The large firm foresees this and in effect controls output of the two-firm industry.

The argument from a disparity in sizes would not seem to apply to arms races as imagined here. The leader-follower argument does, nevertheless,

[5] If the war is a sequence of pure counterforce blows, lower yields and accuracies would diminish deterrent capability as well.

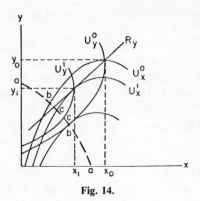

Fig. 14.

seem to find a reflection in the position of the "unilateralist" for disarmament, of those who argue for disarmament by the West with no
agreement with the Soviets. The assumption here is surely that the Soviets
would react to our one-sided disarmament by reducing their own weapons
inventory. It is interesting that the much simplified assumptions about
the nature of war used to generate this arms race seem reasonably close to
the "unilateralist's" pre-occupation with the all-out-attack-all-out-
retaliation form which war with missiles could take. To the extent that
those assumptions are true, the analysis of this discussion lends some
support to a partial unilateral disarmament (by X in Fig. 13 from x_0 to x_1).
The argument lends none, however, to the case for *total* unilateral disarmament. This analysis provides some rationale for the idea that one should
begin negotiations for an arms-control agreement by voluntarily and
unilaterally *partially disarming*. Figure 14 illustrates this.

Suppose our current position were (x_0, y_0). If disarmament negotiations are undertaken from (x_0, y_0) with a view toward reaching the contract curve $a–a$, the range of possible solutions is $b–b$. Within the range $b–b$
both sides can improve over U_x^0 and U_y^0, and the exact division of utility
is assumed to depend upon cunning at negotiation, bargaining strength,
chance, and so forth. If now side X is considering an initial unilateral
reduction in arms, as a gesture (perhaps to get negotiations moving), he, X,
can only move along Y's reaction curve, since Y is not yet playing the game.
Suppose X disarms to x_1. Side Y follows, disarming to y_1. Side X is now
on U_x^1 and Y is on U_y^1. From the point (x_1, y_1) negotiations over further,
mutual, disarmament can lead to the contract curve in the range $c–c$. As
between beginning negotiations from (x_0, y_0) and (x_1, y_1), two things have
happened to the range of possible outcomes: (1) the range has narrowed,
and (2) in a sense, the range $c–c$ is more favorable to Y than to X. It may be,

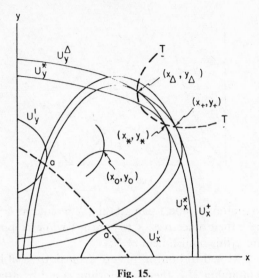

Fig. 15.

however, that the move is useful to X if X wishes to raise the lower limit of his negotiating position, for example, or if a narrow bargaining range is deemed necessary for any ultimate agreement at all.

D. Maximin Threat: Survival-Extinction Solutions

There is another analogy between arms races and duopoly worth making, in which each side considers the possibilities for threatening its rival or for punishing him. It will be seen that the threat is in the nature of a blackmailer's threat, for if the threatener must carry out his threat, he too will suffer. Figure 15 shows the situation with which we propose to deal. Point (x_0, y_0) denotes the point of equilibrium if each side were to maximize its own utility for every choice made by the opponent and were to assume that the opponent does not change his choice variable in response to one's own decision—that is (x_0, y_0) is the naïve duopoly solution. Suppose now, for reasons soon to be discussed, that side X wishes to punish Y by reducing Y's utility. Side X can do so by increasing his armaments, that is, by increasing x. In doing so he, X, must decrease his own utility as well. This follows from the fact that the point (x_0, y_0) is a utility maximum for both sides. The same is true of side Y, which can punish X by increasing y, but in doing so must harm itself as well. If X is doing the threatening and Y is assumed to respond by maximizing its own utility, and if X is determined not to allow its utility to drop below U_x^*, but *is* prepared to *maintain* that lower utility, then X can reduce Y to U_y^*,

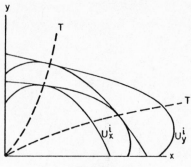

Fig. 16.

which is the maximum U_y side Y can attain if X maintains U_x^*. At (x_*, y_*) both sides achieve their objectives, X to punish Y while keeping $U_x = U_x^*$, and Y to minimize this punishment at U_y^*.

If instead Y wished to punish X, and X maximized utility, and if Y insisted on maintaining U_y^Δ, then equilibrium could be attained at (x_Δ, y_Δ) where X attains U_x^*. Again, if X threatened a minimum utility of U_x^+ and Y's utility maximizing response were U_y^Δ, then the point (x_+, y_+) would be a solution. In fact, an entire set of such points exists and is described by the curve TT in Fig. 15. In the parlance of economics this is known as a threat curve. There is, of course, no logical reason for supposing, if both sides X and Y can fulfill threats, that the minimum utility one side will deliberately choose is the same as the maximum utility it can attain in response to the threat from its rival to choose its own minimum. For example, X may deliberately choose U_x^+, forcing Y to U_y^Δ, while Y, as a threatener, would only choose U_y^*, allowing X a utility greater than U_x^*.

To carry this analysis a step further suppose sides X and Y are at (x_0, y_0) as a start, that bargaining over disarmament is under way, and that each side can threaten to punish the other, but would do so only to improve his own prospects for a favorable outcome. If side X can threaten Y with U_y^Δ by choosing U_x^+, then side Y should be pleased with any level of utility greater than U_y^Δ. Similarly, if Y can threaten X with U_x^*, then X should gain if a bargain is struck giving him anything greater than U_x^*. In short, the possibilities of making threats by one side or by both expand the range of possible outcomes—the assumption remaining that the final outcome will be on the contract curve. In Fig. 15, if X can threaten Y with U_y^Δ and Y can X with U_x^*, then the range of final outcomes is over a–a on the contract curve, as shown.

Implicitly, we have assumed each side is a deterrer only. Now imagine both sides are potential attackers. A first-strike two-sided model, while it alters the contract curve, does not seem to alter the characteristics of the threat curve; and the analysis of the foregoing sections on a two-sided deterrence model would seem to apply, with one peculiarity—the threat curve passes through the origin. Figure 16 shows the two branches of the threat curve. The left-hand branch shows the locus of points at which side Y will elect to maintain a certain U_y and X will react so as to maximize U_x, subject to the constraint imposed by Y. The right-hand branch of the threat curve shows the locus on which Y maximizes utility subject to the fixed utility constraint established by X—the opposite of the left-hand branch.

E. Viability Analysis of the Arms Race

There is a considerable body of literature on the subject of how, given the maximum threats of either side, the division of utility should proceed in arriving at a solution. Such proposed solutions as may be found in the literature on duopoly should have some application to the problem of arms negotiation. Suppose the arms race is viewed as a long struggle of attrition. If one side is considerably more wealthy than the other, it may try to bludgeon the other into ultimate submission simply by outspending the other. If Y is less able to withstand a low level of satisfaction, X may count on being able to strike a favorable bargain at a later date. It may be that side Y is indeed richer than is X, but politically less capable of laying out money with little visible security in return. For any reason whatever one or both sides in the arms race may have its "breaking point." One measure of such a "breaking point" might be some absolute limit on the amount of resources which a side can devote to defense. Another could be an absolute lower limit to the number of survivors from a first strike by an enemy which one side can allow. There may be an upper limit on the numbers of enemy missiles to survive one's own first attack. Some limitation may exist as to the ratio of attacking to defending forces. Or there may be some minimum utility which a side is prepared to accept.

Figure 17 shows the last of the possibilities suggested. Each side is supposed to have some level of utility below which it cannot survive. Its government may fall, its people may revolt, its army defect, or, in general, the country forced to such a low level of utility, may accommodate and adjust to the role of being dominated. In Fig. 17 the area with vertical shading is the area in which Y cannot survive: the area of horizontal shading is the region in which X cannot survive; the unshaded region is one of joint survival, and the cross-hatched area one of joint extinction.

This leads us to concentrate upon the survival-extinction dichotomy posed in Figs. 17 through 21 as distinct from the optimum decision, utility-

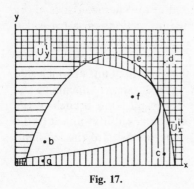
Fig. 17.

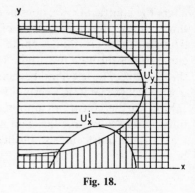
Fig. 18.

maximizing sequence, characteristic of previously considered solutions to arms race models. If the curves of minimum utility for survival are as drawn in Fig. 17, then both sides can indeed survive under all conditions. That is, side X cannot choose x so as to preclude (1) Y's choosing a y which will place both in the region of mutual survival or (2) Y's choosing a y which will force X to change, returning Y to a region of survival. If an initial point is a, for example, by increasing y, Y can reach, say, b. If the initial point is c, Y can increase y to d, whence X will decrease x to at least e and Y, in turn, can reach f. Figure 18 now shows a case in which one side can preclude the survival of the other. In Fig. 18 side Y can keep X in X's extinction region and survive, while X cannot do the same to Y. But to force nonviability on Y, X must accept nonviability for itself.

Thus far, we have considered a low utility accruing to one side as a limitation on "survival," over the long run. We now wish to introduce into the analytical apparatus constraints on the region of survival in addition to minimum utility. The introduction of constraints other than a minimum-utility constraint is not strictly rational. The utility or preference function is supposed to compare all combinations of security and wealth with all others so as to rank every position conceivable against every other. It makes sense to introduce a *minimum* utility acceptable because utility may be conceived as short-run. Deliberately choosing a low present utility may be worthwhile if it forces the enemy to change, to concede, and in the long run to raise our own utility. The justification for introducing other constraints independent of utility can only be that, as a matter of fact, within the decision-making machinery disagreements over the value of security versus money result in other arbitrary limits being established.

As an example of such an additional constraint, let us assume that some minimum number of one's own missiles surviving an enemy first strike is "required." Figure 19 then shows that the possibilities for reaching

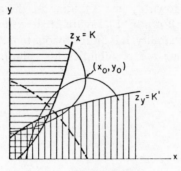

Fig. 19.

the contract curve may be narrowed by the additional constraint. Other values on z_y and z_x could eliminate the contract curve solution. In the figure the area to the left of $z_x = K$ is nonviable for X, and the area below $z_y = K'$ is nonviable for Y. It can be seen that this additional constraint could in principle (1) eliminate all solutions at arms levels below (x_0, y_0) (2) limit the range on the contract curve at which a solution is possible, or (3) have no effect upon equilibria points or on the possibilities for negotiated solutions.

Suppose, as a different example, that some maximum defense budget exists, regardless of the opponent's position. Such a limitation is most likely to affect the possibilities for making threats. If the limits on defense expenditure are as indicated by B_x and B_y, in Fig. 20 the entire maximin threat curve is eliminated, and with this the applicability of the utility contours through threat points to possibilities for negotiated agreement.

A third and last type of outside constraint to be considered here is the minimum ratio of one's own forces to the enemy's and vice versa. Suppose side X refuses under all conceivable circumstances to be outnumbered by

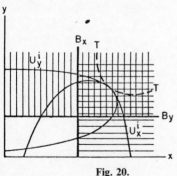

Fig. 20.

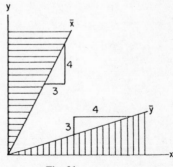

Fig. 21.

more than 4 to 3 (shown by line $\overline{X}$). Suppose the enemy has the same absolute constraint (shown by Y). Figure 21 shows us the unshaded area, the region of mutual viability. It is quite obvious that this type of constraint can drastically change the possibilities for solutions within a utility-maximizing context.

●

Overall, neither the McGuire piece nor the other articles cited on page 238 present a set of conditions that allow one to be very sanguine about the prospects for stable equilibrium in duopoly. This is because none of them fully allow for the possibility that each firm will take its rival's probable reactions into account before making its own moves. In the following article Irvin M. Grossack develops what we may call a "peaceful coexistence" model, in which neither rival has as his goal the ruin of the other. Both firms are aware that what they do affects the other, but the possibility of collusion does not enter into the model as developed. He shows how, assuming that each rival has the same intelligence and initiative (a useful stress on symmetry for foreign policy analysts who might rather attribute to their own state a slightly larger share), it still is possible to avoid infinite regress. Furthermore, he shows that under reasonable assumptions the appropriate response to an aggressive "leader" is for the responding unit to adopt a "stayput" strategy, and settle on an output quantity where the resulting price at which he must sell imposes smaller losses on him than the same price does on his rival. Since this "stayput" strategy is not simply a *lex talionis* response to his rival's aggressive strategy, it does not imply degeneration into arms race or self-exacerbating price war. So long as the two rivals are of very approximately the same size, the defensive strategy can in time force the leader, even though he may be larger, to abandon his aggressive efforts to expand his share of the market. If the leader is very much larger than his rival, however, or if some other less plausible conditions apply, then the defensive strategy may not succeed.

A major element in this paper which has not appeared in our earlier selections is the discount rate a firm applies to future earnings, or the relative value it places on long-run rather than short-run maximization of profits. A standard assumption of economists, akin to—though rather more rigorously defined than—the political science notion that a nation maximizes its "national interest," is the assumption that a firm maximizes its profit. Most often it is assumed that the firm maximizes its short-run profits. But as will be apparent on recalling Shubik's discussion, under favorable conditions of market and financial vulnerability a sacrifice of short-run profits may pay handsomely in long-run profits if it enables one to eliminate a weaker competitor. In other circumstances firms will refrain from tempting grabs at short-run profits because such moves would endanger their long-run position. Here, Grossack assumes that both the leader and his rival adopt long-run profit maximizing strategies.

Neither the role nor, especially, the measurement of short-run versus long-run maximizing has been well developed in economics, nor, of course,

in international politics, but it would seem absolutely central to many of
the most important real-world concerns of both. What kinds of actors are
likely to prefer either strategy? What are the conditions which are most
likely to bring these latent preferences into action? If the system is composed largely of long-run maximizers but there are several short-run
maximizers in it, how much of the latter's "disruption" can the system
stand?[1] Decision makers surely do have different preferences for short-
and long-term gains; that is, they do have, implicitly at least, subjective
discount rates.[2] Long-run gains may never accrue to me, only to my descendants, and how much am I willing to give up for them? The prospect of
long-run gains involves an element of risk, as they may never come
through any way. For these reasons a lender is able to command a rate of
interest on his loan. But just how, in international politics, would one go
about measuring those rates? How does one even go about sorting out his
own preferences? In the summer of 1967 problems of just this sort seemed
to be bringing agony to the members of the Israeli government. How do
they weigh the various advantages and disadvantages of the acquisition of
territory versus a more magnanimous settlement? Not only does each
solution imply different long- and short-run consequences, and, hence,
different discount rates, it is so difficult even to see what the long-run
consequences of either general approach would be. But despite the formidable nature of these analytical obstacles, a way around if not over them
must be found if we are to be able to make satisfactory statements about
some of the most central choices of our time.

[1] For some experimental evidence on the importance of perspectives in affecting the
way players actually behave in duopoly see H. L. Johnson and A. M. Cohen, "Experiments in
Behavioral Economics: Siegel and Fouraker Revisited," *Behavioral Science*, **12**, 5 (September
1967), pp. 353–372. In games, theology students were markedly more cutthroat than were
business students, who tended to play cooperative strategies.

[2] On some of these points see the two essays by C. P. Kindleberger cited earlier in this
volume.

15

Duopoly, Defensive Strategies, and the Kinked Demand Curve

Irvin M. Grossack

Despite a long and distinguished history, the Cournot duopoly model generally serves only as an introduction (after which it is usually demolished) to modern discussions of duopoly and extensions into oligopoly. One reason for the decline of the Cournot model is surely our never-ending search for more realistic models; as a result, recent advances in duopoly theory stress the importance of variables other than price and output, together with the possibilities inherent in partial or full collusion and predatory practices. But perhaps the more important reason for the lack of general acceptance of the Cournot solution is its patently unacceptable assumption that each duopolist accepts his rival's output as given datum and takes no account of the influence his own output can have upon the output of his rival. When this assumption is relaxed—that is, when the duopolists are allowed to engage in what has become known as conjectural variation[1]—noncollusive output-competing duopoly theory is embarrassingly enriched by a large number of possible solutions instead of merely one.

The possibility of conjectural variation behavior has, in effect, provided a roadblock to the development of noncollusive, nonpredatory,

Reprinted from *Southern Economic Journal*, 32, 4 (April 1966), pp. 406–416.

[1] "Conjectural variation" is the term commonly used to describe the process whereby a duopolist (or oligopolist) takes the reaction of his rival to his own policies into account when formulating these policies.

duopoly theory in which price and output are the only variables. This blocking has probably had much to do with the channeling of research in this area toward "game-theoretic" models which focus upon collusion, threats, side payoffs, and so forth as the relevant variables for the duopolists. Realistic and useful as these models may be, there is a great deal to be said for the development of models where collusion and predacity play no part since, at a minimum, it appears desirable to have models that can serve as a norm against which inherently unlawful activity can be assessed. Furthermore, the game-theoretic approach has not been a marked success when it comes to extending duopoly solutions into the general oligopoly case, whereas the approach to be proposed here has great promise in this direction.

The main purpose of this discussion is to demonstrate that conjectural variation possibilities need not be a drawback to the development of noncollusive, nonpredatory duopoly models with stable solutions that appear to reflect the real world. Progress has been hampered, I believe, because duopoly models have traditionally assumed that each duopolist adopts a single strategy that is maintained throughout all phases of the analysis. But if we allow duopolists to change their strategies in order to counter aggressive moves by their rivals, simple and quite reasonable solutions emerge. Such solutions can take place, it will be argued, because a number of defensive strategies are generally available that can inhibit aggressive behavior. One of these defensive strategies in particular—the continuance of some "best" level of output by a non-leader, despite aggressive moves by a "leader"—will receive most of our attention because of its inherent simplicity and plausibility. Interestingly, when this strategy is employed, the leader's demand curve has a kink at the same price and output of the Cournot duopoly solution.

This discussion is confined to a pair of duopolists, each producing a single undifferentiated product. Let us assume that the market·is such that only one price can prevail, so that the duopolists can compete only by varying their outputs. Let us also consider only the case of a linear industry demand curve, known to both duopolists, together with zero production and marketing costs. The following behavioral assumptions are necessary to the argument:

1. The duopolists will not collude in any way.
2. Both duopolists are aware that their own outputs put pressure upon the profits of their rivals, and are prepared to take this pressure into account in selecting their outputs. Yet, neither duopolist has as his intent the ruin of his rival. (The difference between trying to pressure or ruin a rival is admittedly difficult to determine.)

3. Both duopolists are fully aware of the alternatives open to their rivals, although they may not be sure which alternative will be selected.

4. Both duopolists are willing, if need be, to sacrifice short-run profits on behalf of possible higher future profits.

1. Cournot Duopoly and Conjectural Variation

This section gives an outline of the Cournot duopoly solution together with the changes that come about when conjectural variation is introduced. Let us designate

$$P = a - b(X_1 + X_2) \tag{1}$$

as the industry demand curve, where P is the market price, X_1 and X_2 are the outputs of Duops I and II, respectively, and a and b are parameters. The total revenue functions for each of the duopolists will then be

$$R_1 = X_1 P = X_1[a - b(X_1 + X_2)] \tag{2}$$

and

$$R_2 = X_2 P = X_2[a - b(X_1 + X_2)] \tag{3}$$

Since costs are zero, each duopolist can find his profit-maximizing output by setting the partial derivative of his own revenue function with respect to his own output equal to zero, and then solving for his output. This procedure yields the following profit-maximizing outputs for the duopolists:

$$X_1 = \frac{a - bX_2}{2b} \tag{4}$$

and

$$X_2 = \frac{a - bX_1}{2b} \tag{5}$$

From (4) and (5) it is clear that the profit-maximizing output for each duopolist depends upon the output of his rival.

Equations (4) and (5) are commonly known as reaction curves. The major behavioral assumption of Cournot is that each duopolist takes his rival's output as given datum, and continuously adjusts his own output to the datum in accordance with (4) or (5), as the case may be. With this assumption, it can be shown that there will be movement toward an equilibrium that has the following values:

$$X_1 = \frac{a}{3b}$$

$$X_2 = \frac{a}{3b}$$

$$P = \frac{a}{3}$$

$$\pi_1 = \frac{a^2}{9b}$$

$$\pi_2 = \frac{a^2}{9b}$$

where the π's represent the respective profits.

The possibility of conjectural variation enters into the picture when one, or possibly both, of the duopolists perceives that he can increase his profits by learning how his rival behaves and then uses this information to select his output. To illustrate how this works, let us designate Duop I as the "leader," who is "alive" to possibilities, i.e., he does *not* behave à la Cournot. He notices that Duop II behaves in accordance with (5) and that it may be possible to determine Duop II's output through his own output policy. In this event, X_2 is not datum to Duop I in his revenue function, (2); instead, Duop I (in effect) substitutes the right-hand side of (5) in (2), obtaining a total revenue curve that depends only upon his own output as follows:

$$R_1 = X_1 \left[a - b \left(X_1 + \frac{a - bX_1}{2b} \right) \right] \tag{6}$$

If Duop I uses (6) to select his profit-maximizing output, and if Duop II *does in fact* behave à la Cournot, the new equilibrium solution will be as follows:

$$X_1 = \frac{a}{2b}$$

$$X_2 = \frac{a}{4b}$$

$$P = \frac{a}{4}$$

$$\pi_1 = \frac{a^2}{8b}$$

$$\pi_2 = \frac{a^2}{16b}$$

A comparison of this equilibrium with the Cournot equilibrium shows that conjectural variation pays off for Duop I since he can increase his profits by about 11 percent over what "Cournot behavior" would have yielded. Duop II, on the other hand, suffers almost a 50 percent decline in profits.

There is nothing contrived about the conjectural variation solution so far as we have gone. In fact, about all that we have assumed about Duop I's behavior is that he perceived his own demand curve (and revenue function) which, in turn, depended upon his ability to anticipate Duop II's mode of behavior. The Cournot solution, in contrast, basically requires complete lack of knowledge by both duops of their own demand curves.

2. Defensive Responses to Leadership

The equilibrium solution just shown depends, of course, on Duop II actually behaving as a "follower"; that is, his simply taking his rival's output as given and then adjusting his own output to the amount that maximizes his profits. But such a solution requires the assumption that one of the duopolists has all the initiative and intelligence, while the other is a bit of a clod. An assumption such as this is not one that is capable of supporting a tenable theory.

If the assumption is granted that Duop II has the same intelligence and initiative as Duop I, the natural inclination of some analysts has been to also allow Duop II to engage in conjectural variation. But when this is carried on, and we entertain the possibility of double or triple conjectural variation (I know that he knows that I know...), it is soon discovered that the model has no solution; and little, if anything, can be said about the stable prices and outputs we see about us in oligopolistic industries. It is at this point that I think we have tended to give up on the noncollusive, nonpredatory duopoly solution.

Where did the analysis go wrong? I think it was with a basic misunderstanding of aggressive leadership, a misunderstanding that in turn was conditioned by our traditional blind spot that the firm always maximizes short-run profit. Thus, it was assumed that Duop I, the supposed leader, would cut back his output in order to maximize short-run profits if Duop II did not behave à la Cournot. When we grant Duop II the intelligence to perceive this weakness on the part of Duop I, then he (Duop II) would produce the leadership output, expecting Duop I to cut back his output. But then again, Duop I notices once more that Duop II, in order to maximize profits, will cut back if he (Duop I) adopts a leadership output. And so it goes....

I would think that short-run profit maximizing is completely inconsistent with what we mean by leadership. A true leader, in this case as in others, would be prepared to sacrifice short-run profits if necessary in order to obtain greater profits in the future. He would first use conjectural variation to select the output most favorable to himself. Then he would *preempt* this output, communicating the "fact" to Duop II that he has every intention of continuing at this output. In effect, as leader, Duop I presents Duop II with a fait accompli. With this notion of a short-run-profit-sacrificing-if-necessary leader, the analysis takes a completely different path.

Faced with a leader who has preempted an output favorable to himself, we could then inquire into Duop II's response. One possible response by Duop II is to actually be the follower Duop I thought he might be. Duop II would, in this case, continue to use (5) to select his profit-maximizing output. But, although Duop II would, in fact, be maximizing his short-run profits, he *permanently* ends up with profits smaller than they would be if Duop I had not preempted. Even more important, followership by Duop II provides no incentive whatever for Duop I to give up his leadership output.

Assuming this situation is not satisfactory to Duop II, he could be expected to adopt some sort of a "defensive strategy" which may induce Duop I to forego leadership. This entails trying to impose leadership costs upon Duop I. Any strategy for Duop II along these lines in essence requires a sacrifice of some short-run profits in the hope of higher future profits.

One possible defensive strategy is that of counterleadership, where Duop II, say, could match Duop I's output. In our case this means Duop II also produces $a/2b$, which would result in zero profits for both duopolists. Basically, counterleadership is an extreme strategy which, though perhaps providing a great inducement to Duop I to give up his leadership, also imposes high, and possibly intolerable, costs upon Duop II. The result in this case will generally depend upon who can outlast whom, which would probably be a function of the relative financial resources of the duops. We can tentatively conclude that counterleadership would be chosen by Duop II only if his resources are substantially greater than those of Duop I.

The other possible defensive strategy is one that I will call "stayput"— and will try to argue that in most instances the stayput strategy is a very plausible and effective response by Duop II, the nonleader. In the stayput strategy, Duop II selects an output that will make the leadership strategy much more costly to Duop I than the stayput strategy is to Duop II. He also communicates the "fact" to Duop I that he intends to stay put at this output rather than react to Duop I's output. In this way, Duop II seeks to induce Duop I away from leadership by placing himself in a position where he can outlast Duop I in the event Duop I persists in leadership.

Is there some optimal stayput for Duop II? To investigate this question, let S be the optimal stayput output when Duop I produces some leadership output L. Also, let M_1 be the profit-maximizing (leadership given up) output for Duop I when Duop II produces S, with M_2 the profit-maximizing (follower) output for Duop II when Duop I produces L. Equations (4) and (5) give the values of M_1 and M_2 as follows:

$$M_1 = \frac{a - bS}{2b} \tag{7}$$

$$M_2 = \frac{a - bL}{2b} \tag{8}$$

The opportunity cost of leadership to Duop I (up to the point Duop II follows, if he does) is the difference between his profits at his profit-maximizing output of M_1 and his leadership output of L. This we can designate as $C_1 = \pi_1(M_1) = \pi_1(L)$. Similarly, the opportunity cost of the stayput strategy to Duop II (up to the point Duop I foregoes his leadership, if he does) is his profits at his profit-maximizing output of M_2 minus his profit at the stayput output of S. Similarly, we can designate this cost as $C_2 = \pi_2(M_2) - \pi_2(S)$. Using the industry demand function (1), we can find the four profit figures as follows:

$$\pi_1(M_1) = M_1[a - b(M_1 + S)] \tag{9}$$

$$\pi_1(L) = L[a - b(L + S)] \tag{10}$$

$$\pi_2(M_2) = M_2[a - b(L + M_2)] \tag{11}$$

$$\pi_2(S) = S[a - b(L + S)] \tag{12}$$

all subject to the constraints placed upon M_1 and M_2 by (7) and (8).

We can define the optimal stayput output, S as that output which is most likely to induce Duop I to forego his leadership output. What conditions are likely to achieve this objective for Duop II? I think the main condition is that the leadership cost to Duop I be much greater than the stayput cost to Duop II. With this condition, Duop II is in a good position to "outlast" Duop I and, if this fact is communicated to Duop I, Duop I would probably realize that leadership is not likely to become profitable.

A very simple decision rule is therefore available to Duop II to implement his stayput strategy. He should produce that output S such that the difference between the cost of the leadership strategy to Duop I and the cost of the stayput strategy to Duop II is maximized. Symbolically, if D is this difference, so that

$$D = C_1 - C_2 = [\pi_1(M_1) - \pi_1(L)] - [\pi_2(M_2) - \pi_2(S)] \qquad (13)$$

Duop II should produce the value of S that maximizes D.

Using Eqs. (7) through (12) to substitute in (13), D can be found in terms of S, L and the parameters. With the help of the calculus we then find that the value of S that maximizes D works out to $a/3b$, which, very interestingly, is also the output obtained by the Cournot duopoly model. Perhaps even more important is the fact that the value of S selected by this criterion is completely independent of L, the leadership output of Duop I. This independence suggests that an output of $a/3b$ is in some ways a "natural" level of output with which to achieve "security" when faced with an aggressive rival. Whether the stayput strategy itself is optimal in some sense to Duop II is a question that is reserved for the next section.

Before turning to this section, however, we can obtain a picture of the possible demand curves facing a duopolist under our set of assumptions. Let us continue to regard Duop II as a nonleader (although he may respond in a number of ways to Duop I's leadership), so that we can concentrate upon the demand curve(s) facing Duop I as the potential leader. From (1), we can specify Duop I's demand curve as

$$\bar{R}_1 = (a - bX_2) - bX_1 \qquad (14)$$

seeing that it depends upon X_2, the output of Duop II. A value of X_2 for each of Duop II's strategies follows:

$$X_2 = [a - bX_1]/2b$$
(follower profit-maximizing strategy)

$$X_2 = a/2b$$
(counterleadership)

$$X_2 = a/3b$$
(defensive stayput strategy)

Corresponding to these strategies, there are three different demand curves facing Duop I as follows:

$$\bar{R}_1 = a/2 - .5bX_1$$
(Duop II a follower) $\qquad (15)$

$$\bar{R}_1 = a/2 - bX$$
(Duop II a counterleader) $\qquad (16)$

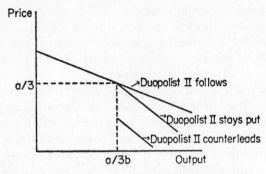

Fig. 1.   Set of possible demand curves facing a duopolist.

$$\bar{R}_1 = 2a/3 - bX_1 \tag{17}$$
(Duop II a stayputter)

If Duop II considers the counterleadership and stayput strategies only when Duop I becomes a leader by producing beyond $a/3b$, (16) and (17) would face Duop I only when he produces beyond $a/3b$. The set of possible demand curves confronting Duop I is shown in Fig. 1.

According to Fig. 1, Duop I's demand curve is continuous only if Duop II is a "follower," or, alternatively, a short-run profit maximizer. But if Duop II employs a defensive strategy, Duop I's demand curve will either have a kink (stayputter strategy for Duop II) or a discontinuity (counterleadership by Duop II). Both the kink and discontinuity take place at the "Cournot output" of $a/3b$, and a study of the marginal revenue curves would show that $a/3b$ is the short-run profit-maximizing output for Duop I. The kink or discontinuity arises, of course, because Duop II's choice between short-run profit maximization and strategies designed to impose leadership costs upon Duop I changes with Duop I's output. The analysis is completely symmetric for the demand curve(s) of Duop II, the nonleader, except for the possibility that the equivalent of (16)—that is, when Duop I exercises leadership—would be extended over the complete range of Duop II's output.

3. Likelihood of the Defensive Strategies

This section suggests that not only are the defensive strategies possible but that one of them—probably the stayput strategy—is reasonably likely to be chosen by a duopolist confronted by a leadership output on the part of his rival. The reasonableness of these strategies will be viewed from both the short and long run, and the analysis assumes some uncertainty by each duopolist about the strategy of his rival. It should be borne in mind that a follower role, which maximizes short-run profits, is always available to both duopolists.

With Duop I designated as the potential leader, and with Duop II continuing in his role of nonleader, Table 1 presents the output, price, and profit results of various strategy pairs.[2]

Some simple comparisons of the figures show how unattractive leadership to Duop I and followership to Duop II can be once the possibility of the stayput strategy is admitted. Duop I, it can be seen, can increase his profit by at most 11 percent if he selects leadership to followership behavior—and this is only if Duop II is kind enough to passively maximize his current profit. On the other hand, leadership can cost Duop I either $33\frac{1}{3}$ percent, or 100 percent, of his obtainable profit of $a^2/9b$ if Duop II adopts one of his defensive strategies. Evidently, Duop I should rate the probability of Duop II being a follower quite high before adopting leadership.

The stayput strategy is almost intuitively appropriate to Duop II once Duop I has produced the leadership output. Compared to his profit-maximizing follower profit of $a^2/16b$ (given Duop I's leadership), Duop II's stayput output only reduces his profit by 6 percent—from $a^2/16b$ to $a^2/18b$. Yet, with this small sacrifice, Duop I possibly may be induced to return to his follower output, and Duop II's profit as a result would be almost double the profit he obtains if he simply "follows"; that is, Duop I's profits could be $a^2/9b$ rather than $a^2/16b$. The crux of the matter is that Duop I, by his leadership outputs, places Duop II in a position where Duop II has little to lose and possibly much to gain, by opting for the stayput output.

Counterleadership by Duop II places a maximum cost of leadership upon Duop I—but it also imposes a high cost upon himself. Of course, there may be conditions in which counterleadership may be preferable to the stayput strategy for Duop II—primarily, when it substantially

Table 1
Results of Strategy Pairs

Strategies		Outputs			Profits	
Duop I	Duop II	Duop I	Duop II	Price	Duop I	Duop II
Follower	Follower	$a/3b$	$a/3b$	$a/3$	$a^2/9b$	$a^2/9b$
Leader	Follower	$a/2b$	$a/4b$	$a/4$	$a^2/8b$	$a^2/16b$
Leader	Stayputter	$a/2b$	$a/3b$	$a/6$	$a^2/12b$	$a^2/18b$
Leader	Counterleader	$a/2b$	$a/2b$	0	0	0

[2] I assume here that once a strategy is adopted, it is carried forward to its logical end.

raises the likelihood that Duop I will be induced to give up his leadership. However, it seems incorrect to conclude that Duop I would generally be more likely to forego leadership if faced with counterleadership rather than Duop II's stayput strategy. Duop I, of course, could be aware that counterleadership is expensive to Duop II; as a result, he may be more inclined to try to "outlast" Duop II than if he knows Duop II has adopted a strategy that can be inexpensively maintained for a long time.

The desirability of the defensive strategies to Duop II can be studied through short-run valuations of the various strategies. Let us assign p as the probability as viewed by Duop II that Duop I will forego leadership if Duop II adopts the stayput strategy, and p' as the probability as viewed by Duop II that Duop I will be induced to forego leadership if Duop II counterleads. Then $(1 - p)$ and $(1 - p')$ are the probabilities that Duop I will not give up his leadership output. Using the figures in Table 1, the follower, stayput, and counterleader strategies can then be valued (designating them as $V(F)$, $V(S)$, and $V(C)$) as follows:[3]

$$V(F) = a^2/16b \qquad (18)$$

$$V(S) = p(a^2/9b) + (1 - p)(a^2/18b) \qquad (19)$$

$$V(C) = p'(q^2/9b) + (1 - p')(0) \qquad (20)$$

By equating (18) and (19) and solving for p, we can find the value of p at which Duop II is indifferent between the follower and stayput strategies. This works out to $p = .125$, and can be interpreted as follows: whenever Duop II is convinced that the probability is greater than $\frac{1}{8}$ that his stayput strategy will induce Duop I to forego leadership, he should select the stayput strategy. Put another way, Duop II should normally prefer the stayput to the follower strategy unless he has very strong reasons for believing that Duop I intends to persist in leadership despite the costs imposed upon him by Duop II's stayput strategy.

An equation of (18) with (20) and a solution for p' gives $p' = \frac{9}{16}$ as the point of indifference for Duop II for his counterleader strategy. Duop II should, therefore, prefer counterleadership to followership only if he is convinced the chances are good (better than one-half) that Duop I will, as a result of Duop II's counterleadership, forego leadership. A comparison of p with p' shows that, if Duop II has very little information on Duop I's pattern of behavior, counterleadership is much riskier to Duop II than the stayput strategy. Duop II should select counterleadership over the stayput strategy only when he thinks that the probability of Duop I foregoing leadership due to the increased pressure on his profits is

[3] $V(F)$ is fixed because there is no inducement to Duop I to forego leadership.

sufficiently enhanced so as to compensate for his (Duop II's) greater sacrifices.

Assessing the defensive strategies in a long-run context appears especially proper since all three nonfollower strategies—leadership, counterleadership, and stayput—basically require a sacrifice of short-run profit opportunities in the hope or expectation of receiving greater long-run profits. The element of the rivals being able to "outlast" each other also implies the necessity to bring time into the analysis. In this framework, the foregone profits can be considered a "cost stream," with the increased (expected) profits a "benefit stream." By subtracting the discounted cost stream from the discounted benefit stream, we can obtain the "present value" of a strategy in much the same manner that one would follow for valuing an investment.

Let us evaluate the stayput strategy for Duop II as a response to leadership by Duop I. If Duop II is willing to be a follower and maximize his short-run profits, he can obtain profits of $a^2/16b$. If, however, he adopts the stayput strategy, the immediate effect is that his profits would only be $a^2/18b$. The difference between these profits, $a^2/16b - a^2/18b$, then becomes the cost of the stayput strategy to Duop II per period of time. We turn now to the benefits. If Duop I is induced away from leadership, and returns to his profit-maximizing output, then Duop II's profits would be $a^2/9b$ instead of $a^2/16b$. The difference, $a^2/9b - a^2/16b$, then represents the benefits per period of time to Duop II that could be attributed to the stayput strategy. The cost stream takes place over the time period running from the present to the future time period *when and if* Duop I foregoes leadership. The benefit stream starts at the time when Duop I foregoes leadership (if he does) and extends to Duop II's time horizon.

We can now determine the subjective present value of the stayput strategy given the following additional information: i, the rate at which Duop II discounts the future; t', the year in which Duop II "expects" Duop I to give up his leadership; n, the number of years that Duop II expects to stay in business. If we make the simplifying assumption that, if and when Duop I foregoes leadership he does so permanently, we have the following expression for the present value of the stayput strategy:

$$PV(S) = [a^2/9b - a^2/16b] \int_{t'}^{n} e^{-it} \, dt - [a^2/16b - a^2/18b] \int_{0}^{t'} e^{-it} \, dt \quad (21)$$

It is possible to evaluate the desirability and reasonableness of the stayput strategy to Duop II by inquiring how long he should be willing to maintain it in order to induce Duop I away from leadership. If (21) is set equal to zero and solved for t', t' becomes the maximum number of years it would pay Duop II to continue the stayput strategy if he presently thinks that, before that time, Duop I will give up his leadership. With the simplifying assumption that n is very large, $t' = 2.08/i$. If Duop II's discount rate is as high as .1 per annum, the following interpretation is possible: as a response to a leadership output by Duop I, Duop II should be prepared to adopt and maintain the stayput output if he thinks it will induce Duop I to forego his leadership output within 20.8 years. Of course, this length of time becomes somewhat smaller if n is not infinity and the possibility is introduced that Duop I may return to leadership after he foregoes it—but it is sufficiently impressive to show how attractive the stayput strategy can be.

A similar analysis can be made of counterleadership for Duop II. The benefits will be the same as those in (21), but Duop II gives up all his possible short-run profits as the cost of this strategy. Using the same symbols and assumptions we obtain

$$PV(C) = [a^2/9b - a^2/16b] \int_{t'}^{n} e^{-it}\,dt - [a^2/16b] \int_{0}^{t'} e^{-it}\,dt \qquad (22)$$

Setting (22) equal to zero, and solving for t', yields $t' = .575/i$. Thus, if i is again .1, Duop II should prefer counterleadership to followership if he thinks that its effect will be to induce Duop I away from leadership within 5.75 years. Although counterleadership appears preferable to followership, it is again inferior to the stayput strategy, unless it is markedly more effective in inducing Duop I away from leadership.

The leadership strategy for Duop I can be evaluated with the same techniques under the conditions of each of Duop II's defensive strategies. If Duop I is willing to be a short-run profit maximizer, the profits of $a^2/9b$ are always available to him. He employs the leadership strategy with the hope of raising his profits to $a^2/8b$, so that $a^2/8b - a^2/9b$ represents the benefits of leadership per period of time. The cost of leadership depends on the defensive (if any) strategy selected by Duop II. If Duop II selects the counterleader strategy, Duop I's profits are zero, and the cost of leadership is the $a^2/9b$ foregone. But if Duop II selects the stayput strategy, the cost of leadership to Duop I is only $a^2/9b - a^2/12b$. Both costs are per periods of time.

Let us now designate θ as Duop I's discount rate, m as the number of years Duop I expects to stay in business, and τ' as the years by which Duop I expects Duop II to forego his defensive strategy permanently. Let us also use τ as the time subscript. The present value of the leadership strategy for Duop I can then be evaluated for each of Duop II's defensive strategies as follows:

$$PV(L) = [a^2/8b - a^2/9b] \int_{\tau'}^{m} e^{-\theta\tau}\, d\tau - [a^2/9b - a^2/12b] \int_{0}^{\tau'} e^{-\theta\tau}\, d\tau \quad (23)$$

(Duopolist II stays put)

$$PV(L) = [a^2/8b - a^2/9b] \int_{\tau'}^{m} e^{-\theta\tau}\, d\tau - [a^2/9b] \int_{0}^{\tau'} e^{-\theta\tau}\, d\tau \quad (24)$$

(Duopolist II counterleader)

If (23) is set equal to zero and solved for τ', and if we assume that m is a very large number, then $\tau' = .406/\theta$. For (24) the solution is $\tau' = .202/\theta$. The desirability of leadership to Duop I then depends upon the defensive strategy he thinks Duop II will adopt, by when he thinks Duop II will forego his defensive strategy, and his own discount rate. If Duop I expects Duop II to be a stayputter, and if Duop I's discount rate is also .1, he should adopt leadership only if he has reason to believe that Duop II will permanently forego the stayput strategy within 4.06 years. If Duop I expects Duop II to counterlead, the leadership strategy becomes desirable only if Duop II will forego counterleadership within two years.

Although other possible combinations of strategies can be evaluated with these tools, we are in a position to draw some conclusions. If the discount rates are the same for both firms, and if Duop II selects the stayput strategy, he is prepared to "outlast" Duop I by continuing his strategy five times as long as Duop I is prepared to continue his leadership. Duop II is also prepared to "outlast" Duop I by more than twice as long if he (Duop II) adopts counterleadership. In effect, Duop II has much more to gain from his defensive strategies than Duop I has to gain from leadership, and Duop II should therefore be expected to "fight harder" than Duop I. This fact alone serves to make the defensive strategies relatively attractive to Duop II, while making leadership relatively unattractive for Duop I.

Although the defensive strategies are generally both more attractive to Duop II than followership, we have still to use this framework to determine whether the stayput strategy is superior to counterleadership. One way of approaching a comparison of the two defensive strategies is to allow the discount rates for the duopolists to differ. The values of t' and τ' found previously show that leadership could become relatively more attractive to Duop I than a defensive strategy is to Duop II only if his discount rate is substantially lower than Duop II's. This could be the case if (contrary to our initial assumptions) Duop I is perhaps larger than Duop II in some way, or can borrow more cheaply, and is perhaps diversified. Duop I may then be prepared to outlast Duop II when the latter adopts the counterleader strategy if Duop I's discount rate is a little less than half of Duop II's discount rate. But Duop I should expect to "outlast" Duop II when the latter adopts the stayput strategy only when Duop I's discount rate is about one-fifth that of Duop II. From these figures we can see that the stayput strategy is especially appropriate for Duop II when he is considerably smaller than Duop I. Since leadership basically makes little sense to Duop I, except if he is substantially larger than Duop II, and since the stayput strategy gives the smaller firm its greatest advantage, we can tentatively conclude that the stayput defensive strategy is the one that should generally be adopted against leadership.

4. Concluding Remarks

The main thrust of this discussion is that, to a duopolist facing a "leader," adoption of one of the defensive strategies is generally almost mandatory. Of the two defensive strategies, the stayput strategy is especially appropriate, since it costs the stayputter little and as a consequence increases his chances of outlasting a persistent leader. We can also conclude that, in general, leadership would not pay against the defensive strategies. The main exception to these conclusions would stem from the leader having the advantages associated with much greater relative size when compared to his rival. Only then could even the stayputter strategy be unattractive to the nonleader, with leadership subsequently attractive to the leader. Other exceptions basically depend on the leader being more intelligent than the nonleader, or able to bluff the nonleader, or when the leader consciously tries to hurt the nonleader, even at great expense to himself.

From this I would also conclude that "conjectural variation leadership" should not be a blanket objection to the development of noncollusive duopoly and oligopoly theory, but rather should be reserved for the exceptional cases where the resources of the firms are very unequal and for when one or more of the firms are prepared to engage in predatory behavior. Even though the analysis has made nongeneral assumptions with regard to costs, a single homogeneous product, a single price, two firms, and so forth, casual observation suggests that firms in oligopolistic markets tend to be stayputters. When a firm increases its output, I do not think that other firms usually decrease their outputs accordingly, or increase their outputs as counterleaders. Rather, they often do not change their outputs at all. The stayput strategy suggests that these firms make calculations as to what portions of the market "belongs" to them and to their rivals, where these calculations are made with an eye to "automatically" penalizing aggressive firms who deviate from their "proper" shares.

●

    If two powers are competing in a substantially duopolistic or bipolar (but not tight bipolar) world, a variety of useful questions can be asked about the way they will evaluate their interests in various areas. Only after evaluating how much a particular country or "market" is worth can a decision be made on whether or not to defend it from the other duopolist. To some degree such an evaluation is based on an estimate of revenue foregone, or opportunity cost, but in his paper Charles Wolf, Jr., depends also on examining what it would cost to replace the benefits, especially the military security contribution, that had been provided by a country that might be "lost." It should be noted, however, that the utility of opportunity costing depends on a careful assessment both of the *probability* that the cost will be incurred and, especially, on a careful assessment of that cost *in the larger context of still other opportunities.* For example, in his article Wolf discusses the value of Laos in terms of how its loss would increase the vulnerability of the other countries of Southeast Asia. Building explicitly on the falling dominoes analogy, he suggests that those costs would be very high. But the policy maker deals not with a certainty that the failure to take certain action will result in the loss of Laos, but only with a probability that a marginal increment or decrement from an existing expenditure will produce or avert the loss of Laos. Hence, that marginal change in expenditure has to be weighted by the probability that the domino will fall and some new expenditure will be "required" to keep the next domino from falling, etc. Also, Wolf says that by this opportunity-cost and falling-domino calculation, Southeast Asia, or even Laos alone, may be "worth" much more than all of Southeast Asia together would be worth in a central war! As a result, one must fall back from the strictly military considerations to the economic aspects of value which he discusses, and to less easily measurable political consequences.

●

16

Some Aspects of the "Value" of Less-Developed Countries to the United States

Charles Wolf, Jr.

If one thinks seriously about any of the major international trouble spots in the world today, one soon confronts the problem of what really is the "value" of, for example, Cuba, Berlin, or Laos to the United States. The view put forward in this article is that, while the question is unanswerable in a rigorous and precise sense, some useful things can be said in approaching it, and in trying to distinguish between more and less unsatisfactory answers to it. In principle, of course, the value of other countries to the United States includes that of the advanced countries, and, most significantly, of western Europe. The present article, however, will be primarily concerned with ,the value of less-developed countries to the United States, and with their value in certain extreme contingencies over a time period that is relatively short from the standpoint of history, though somewhat longer from the standpoint of economics.

Let me begin by clarifying some terms and concepts that will be employed. The first concept concerns the distinction between the *direct* and the *indirect* value of a country to the United States. By direct value is meant those aspects which can be immediately related to US interests. By

Reprinted from C. Wolf, Jr., "Some Aspects of the 'Value' of Less-Developed Countries to the United States," *World Politics*, **15**, 4 (July 1963), pp. 623–634, by permission of The RAND Corporation.

indirect value is meant those aspects of a particular country's value which relate to *other* countries that, in turn, are of direct value to the United States.

The second point concerns a distinction between value to the United States, and value to the Soviet Union or to communist China. Particular countries may well differ in their cardinal and ordinal values to the United States, the Soviet Union, and to China; this article will be mainly concerned with relating value to *United States* interests.

The third point concerns the obvious distinction between the value of a particular country in connection with local wars, and its value in various central war contingencies. A further distinction can be made between the value of a country to the United States in connection with wars involving China, and wars involving the Soviet Union, or with those involving both communist powers.

Finally, there is a distinction between values, or components of value, that can be *quantified*, and those components which, at best, can only be *qualified*. The components of value that can be quantified are those for which an alternative cost can be estimated, or at least those aspects for which the concept of alternative cost has meaning. *Where it is possible to estimate the cost of achieving some given and constant consequence or outcome in two different ways, the value of one way can be considered to be defined, as an upper bound, by the cost of obtaining the same result in the alternative way.*

For some aspects of the value of a particular country, the notion of alternative costs can be usefully applied to give a rough indication of magnitudes involved in the quantifiable components of a country's value. For both the military and economic components of value, this approach has merit and applicability.

However, for other components of value this approach fails to make sense. When we discuss the political, psychological, and ideological components of a country's value to the United States, alternative cost does not help very much. For these aspects of value, we simply have to rely on opinions, discussion, and judgments. Moreover, these qualitative aspects of value may well dominate the ones that can be quantified. This does not mean, however, that we should refrain from trying to identify the relevant numbers wherever we can. Nor does it mean that all ways of expressing the qualitative components of a country's value to the United States are equally clear, comprehensive, and useful. One can be qualitative in better and worse ways, just as one can be quantitative in better and worse ways.

Let us first consider those aspects of the value of other countries which can be approached quantitatively. My aim here is to give some idea of a method that might be employed, as well as a rough indication of some of the numbers that might enter into this work. Incidentally, when I use the adjective "large" or "substantial" to characterize my conjectures about these numbers, I will have in mind five-year costs that are, say, over $1 billion, while "small" will mean a guess that the figure would be below this threshold.

1. Military Aspects of Value

The military value of a country or area can be upper-bounded by assuming the "loss" of the particular area, formulating a number of different war scenarios, and then asking what costs the United States would have to incur to make the expected outcome in these contingencies indifferently preferred, or equivalent, to the expected outcome without the loss of the country or area concerned. (In this context the term "loss" is used in a complete and unsophisticated sense to mean simply the inclusion of the country within the communist bloc so that the bloc is enabled to derive whatever military benefits the area might confer on it. In making this purposely extreme assumption, the implication is not that such a "loss" is the *only*, or even the *most likely*, alternative to an existing relationship between the United States and the particular country. The implication is simply that the assumption of "loss," in this complete sense, provides a useful means for upper-bounding the military components of that country's value to the United States.)

The notion of value that I am trying to convey is depicted in Fig. 1. S_1 is the assumed "present" status of a country. Moving to S_2—a hypothetical "loss" status—is assumed to require that additional military costs would have to be incurred by the United States to offset the military benefits derived by the communist bloc from this change of status. The discontinuous "Z" line and the convex dotted line represent possible shapes of a

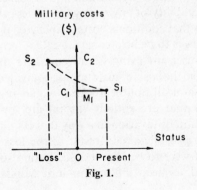

Fig. 1.

resulting "equal military-effectiveness" or "indifference" curve. The *upper bound* to the military value of the given country or area is represented by C_2-C_1 on the diagram. Only if we are prepared to assume that the United States *would, in fact, be willing* to incur these incremental costs can we assert that this upper bound represents the *actual* military value of the given country or area.

Let me illustrate this notion of value more correctly. To pick a hypothetical case, consider a scenario involving the buildup by North Vietnam, China, or the Soviet Union of a consequential capability within South Vietnam and Thailand for waging guerrilla war against the present governments in those countries. Now, assume the "loss" of Laos in the sense in which I am using that term. Given this assumption, we could then estimate the military "value" of Laos by examining several different kinds of "costs" that would have to be incurred in order to maintain an equivalent *counter*-guerrilla capability in Vietnam and Thailand after this assumed "loss." One kind of cost would be that associated with maintaining enough additional surveillance along the 700-mile common border between Laos and Thailand, and the 200-mile common border between Laos and South Vietnam, so that the support or buildup of guerrilla manpower, training, supplies, and equipment would be as difficult (i.e., as costly) as it would have been *without* the loss of Laos.

As an alternative, or supplement, to these surveillance costs, we could attempt to estimate the increase in Thai and Vietnamese para-military forces of the civil guard type that would be necessary to restrain the level of guerrilla, insurrectionist incidents to some "acceptable" maximum, even allowing for some increase in the flow of guerrilla manpower and supplies across the common Thai and South Vietnamese borders with Laos....

The value of Laos is related to contingencies involving countries other than Laos itself. It is in this sense that the "stack of cards" or "dominoes" analogy, which has sometimes been applied to the countries of Southeast Asia, makes a certain amount of sense. A "loss" of Laos increases the vulnerability of environing countries; stated another way, such a loss requires that additional costs be incurred if the vulnerability of environing countries is to be held constant....

For contingencies involving island countries like the Philippines, Taiwan, or Australia, the costs of maintaining equivalent military effectiveness, given the loss of all Southeast Asia, would probably not be substantial. Countries that are entirely littoral are, by that fact, already exposed to infiltration or invasion in a way that is unlikely to impose any additional exposure on them as a result of the loss of other mainland areas. If Indonesia were to be lost, it is likely that some additional cost would be required to keep infiltration into Mindanao and the Sulu

Archipelago in the Phillippines to a constant level, but in general, such incremental costs would be relatively modest. On the other hand, for countries like India and Pakistan, whose accessible land borders (with Burma) would be extended by the loss of Southeast Asia, the incremental costs of maintaining equivalent defensibility might be appreciable.

The value of all of Southeast Asia in central war contingencies could be taken as minor. Such value as the area has in central war scenarios relates primarily to central war targets that might be assigned to Air Force units based in or staging through the area. Inasmuch as reaching these targets from other sources, or through the use of other weapons systems not having such basing requirements, should not entail heavy incremental costs, the value of the region in central war is small.

It should be evident that in principle the same approach could be applied in North Asia to a consideration of the value of South Korea, Japan, and Taiwan, and to a consideration of the value of other under-developed areas, as well.

In the North Asian context, for example, we would want to consider the effect of a loss of each of the three countries in turn on the costs of achieving an indifferently preferred defense posture in the other two. It should be emphasized again that I am referring here only to military costs. The psychological and political costs . . . could well be both more significant and more difficult to overcome than the strictly military costs.

In a local war context, the loss of Japan would substantially increase the costs of maintaining equivalent defense capabilities in Korea, but this relationship is (from a military point of view) asymmetrical. In both the local war and central war contexts, the military value of Japan would be by far the greatest of the three. In central war (through the mid-1960's, at least), a loss of Japanese bases would involve appreciable incremental costs to obtain an outcome with equivalent expected damage to major com-munist targets. Moreover, the "loss" of Japan could increase potential communist nuclear capabilities, as well as the communist recuperation base. To offset these effects would clearly entail substantial costs for the United States and the free world.

Of all the underdeveloped countries, those whose value in a central war context would probably be the greatest by far would be the under-developed countries in Latin America. Pursuing the analysis just presented, we might envisage a central war scenario with communist missile sites in Cuba, Mexico, and the Dominican Republic. Given such "losses," the problem would be to ascertain the incremental costs of maintaining an indifferently preferred military posture. Such costs, in connection with a bilateral counterforce strategy, for example, would involve the increased requirements for protecting our retaliatory capabilities against weapons of higher accuracy (and with lesser warning time) that could be delivered from such nearby sites. In the context of a strictly retaliatory or finite deterrence strategy, one would also want to look at the value of particular areas like Latin America from the standpoint of overcoming the loss of credibility that might be involved for the United States, owing both to the expansion of the recuperation base afforded the Soviet Union, and the relatively greater vulnerability of the United States to a continuation of the conflict as a result of the forward location of communist bases.

It should be evident that, in principle, the same sort of analysis is applicable to investigating the military value of western Europe as well as of the underdeveloped countries. In fact, a strong case can be made for extending the analysis to western Europe, because, as in the case of Japan, there are important interdependencies, both military and nonmilitary in nature, that link western Europe to the less-developed areas.

2. Economic Aspects of Value

The economic aspects of a country's value to the United States can be divided into three components; the value of investments owned by American residents in the country; and the value of (or "gains" from) imports from and exports to the particular country or area. As in the case of military aspects of value, the economic components can be approached in terms of the foregone benefits (or opportunity costs) of the hypothetically "lost" investments, imports, and exports. (Incidentally, it should be noted that "loss" in a military context does not necessarily imply "loss" in an economic sense. A country might become a part of the communist bloc, or even a communist military base, and still continue to trade with the free world. Conversely, a country might expropriate foreign assets, and forego trading with the United States, while still refusing to permit communist military installations on its territory).

1. The value of American investments in a particular country is the discounted value of the income stream associated with those investments. Though the concept is fairly clear, measurement is quite difficult because of the uncertainty connected with the income stream, and with the appropriate discount rate to use in calculating present value. However, as a practical matter, a number might be attached to this component of value by taking the average income received in the last four or five years from US investments in particular foreign areas as a basis for estimating the income stream over, say, a twenty-year useful life, and calculating present values by using three or four alternative, but plausible, discount rates. Alternatively, and still more simply, this component of value might be quantified by making a suitable upward adjustment in the book value of American

assets in particular countries or areas (and perhaps supplementing this estimate with a further upward adjustment in the book value of similar assets, both direct and portfolio, of western Europe and Japan in these areas). As an indication of the orders of magnitude that are involved here, the following figures on US private direct investments abroad in 1959 are of interest:

Latin America	$ 8.2 billion
Europe	5.3 billion
Africa	.8 billion
Asia (excluding the Middle East)	1.0 billion
Middle East	1.2 billion
Canada	10.2 billion
Other	3.0 billion
	$29.7 billion

These figures are, of course, understated because they reflect book value rather than present or market value. They are also understated, from the standpoint of the "value" problem, because they do not include the value of European investments in, say, the Far East and the Middle East, which are frequently greater than those of the United States, yet which are of indirect value to the United States. Anyhow, they give some indication of the general orders of magnitude that are involved.

2. The value of a country as a source of US imports can be represented not by the *value* of imports from that country, but rather by the *difference* between the money value of imports and the cost of buying the same imports, or the next best substitutes, from alternative sources, including domestic sources. The value of a country as a source of imports can be less than, equal to, or greater than the actual money value of imports from that country. In effect, the *value* that is involved here is the *loss* of consumers' surplus resulting from a shift in the supply curve due to exclusion or loss of the particular country as a source of imports.

In Fig. 2, S_1 and S_2 represent world supply of exports to the United States of a particular product, "pre-" and "post-loss," respectively. D is the total US demand for imports of the product. Q_3Q_1 is the amount of world exports to the United States provided by the particular country at the "pre-loss" equilibrium price P_1. P_2 and Q_2 are, respectively, the price and the quantity of world exports to the United States post-loss.

The net value of the foregone imports is, in effect, represented by the shaded portion of the diagram. If demand is inelastic, if the country's share of world supply is large (and, hence, the shift in the supply function is considerable), or if the new supply curve is inelastic, the loss of consumers' surplus which results can be greater than the value of the original

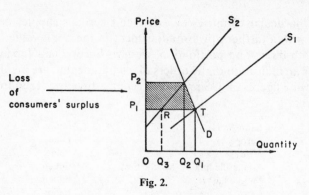

Fig. 2.

imports from the country concerned.[1] This will, however, not generally be the case, and will fairly definitely not be the case for those imports for which the particular import source is only a minor source of supply, or for which domestic substitutes are available whose supply is relatively elastic.

To give a rough idea of the orders of magnitude involved, US imports in 1960 from the less-developed areas were $5.9 billion, or 40 percent of total US imports of $14.6 billion. Imports from the less-developed countries by the United States plus Canada, western Europe, Australia, New Zealand, South Africa, and Japan were about $19.6 billion or 24 percent of their total imports of $81 billion in 1960.

3. The value of a particular country as a market for exports is the fall in US export prices, or the reduction in earnings realized by US factors of production producing for export markets, due to that country's "loss" and the resulting fall in demand for US exports. The amount of this reduction will depend both on the extent of the shift in, and the elasticity of, the resulting demand curve, as well as on the elasticity of the US export supply curve.

In Fig. 3, D_1 and D_2 represent world demand for US exports of a particular commodity, "pre-" and "post-loss," respectively. S is the US supply of exports of the same commodity. Q_3Q_1 is the amount of US exports bought by a particular country at the pre-loss equilibrium price P_1. The shaded portion represents the loss of producers' surplus or rent, resulting from the fall in world demand. Under unusual conditions, this loss of producers' rent can exceed the money value of the original exports to that country,[2] but usually it will be well below the initial export value.

Again, to give a rough idea of the order of magnitude involved, exports by the United States in 1960 to the less-developed areas of Asia,

---

[1] That is, the shaded quadrilateral may exceed the rectangle Q_1Q_3RT.
[2] That is, the shaded quadrilateral may exceed the rectangle Q_1Q_3RT.

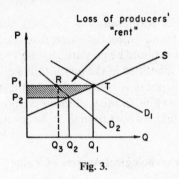

Fig. 3.

Africa, the Middle East, and Latin America were $6.5 billion, or about 32 percent of total US exports of $20 billion. Exports to the less-developed areas, excluding communist countries, by the United States plus Canada, western Europe, Australia, New Zealand, South Africa, and Japan were $21 billion in 1960, or about 25 percent of their total exports of $85 billion.

It should be noted that the economic aspects of a country's value to the United States are easier to identify conceptually than empirically. However, with some reasonable simplifying assumptions, it should be possible to make fairly acceptable quantitative estimates. . . .

Even if it were possible to quantify the military and economic aspects of a country's value in the manner I have been describing, this would not necessarily imply that we should be prepared to incur costs equivalent to this value in order to prevent the "loss" of the particular country. To draw this inference, we would have to know something about the effects of such costs on the likelihood of the loss taking place. From this standpoint, all that the quantitative components of a country's value tell us is the upper bound to the costs we should be willing to incur to reduce the likelihood that the more costly alternative will occur.[3]

[3] Consider a program (e.g., economic or military aid) costing X. Associated with X is a probability of "loss" of P. In the absence of X, the probability of loss is estimated as II, with $II > P$. Assuming the "value" of the country concerned is V, X is only justifiable if:

$$X + PV < IIV \qquad (1)$$

$$X < V(II - P) \qquad (2)$$

In the case most favorable for the contemplated program, $(II - P)$ approaches unity, so that V provides the upper bound for a justifiable X. Generally, however, $(II - P)$ will be less than unity, because P will seldom approach zero. *Hence, a justifiable X ought to be appreciably less than V.* It is easy to adapt this formulation to allow for the fact that if "no-loss" occurs, with or without X, some further costs may subsequently have to be incurred to support the country under consideration. Under this circumstance, X will be less attractive the greater the subsequent "no-loss" costs are likely to be. Denoting these subsequent costs by S, (1) can

Actually, the latter formulation is not fully acceptable either. The important nonquantitative aspects of value, discussed below, would tend to raise the cost that we should be prepared to incur to prevent a country's loss *beyond* the limits identified in the quantitative military and economic aspects of value. The point is, simply, that while the investigation of quantitative aspects of value in this instance may provide some illuminating orders of magnitude, its operational implications are ambiguous.

3. Political and Psychological Aspects of Value

As previously mentioned, some, and perhaps most, important aspects of value, in this context, are nonquantitative. This does not mean that a serious attempt to fill in the numbers should not be made, where possible. But it does mean that the qualitative aspects must be borne prominently in mind before reaching conclusions on the basis of the economic and military components alone.

The first major qualitative consideration arises from the political-psychological interdependencies among countries and areas. Some interdependencies (for example, those I have referred to between Laos on the one hand, and Vietnam and Thailand on the other) can be identified in military and/or economic terms, costed, and compensated for, or simply accepted. But there are others, relating more to attitudes which can be described in terms of phrases like "wave of the future," or "march of history," or "inevitable trend," that cannot be readily compensated for or accepted. Even though attempts can be made to take measures that will compensate for the apparent military and economic consequences of a particular country's loss, it is more difficult to find ways to compensate for the effect of even a dimly perceived notion of trend on the loyalties and confidence of other people and countries. While this applies particularly to the underdeveloped areas, it extends beyond them. We would be wrong to think that the "loss" of a country like India might not have nearly as profound a psychological impact on the United Kingdom and western Europe, as, for example, the loss of Laos may have on confidence and loyalties in Thailand and South Vietnam; or that the loss of South Korea might not have an equivalent impact on Japan....

---

be restated:

$$X + PV + (1 - P)S < V\text{II} + (1 - \text{II})S \qquad (3)$$

$$X < V(\text{II} - P) + S(P - \text{II}) \qquad (4)$$

In this case a justifiable X must be less in relation to V than in (2) because of the higher probability that additional cost will be required after X, i.e., since $P - \text{II} < O$.

When we try to relate the value of other countries to the character of US society, the connections become more tenuous and certainly more difficult to measure, but not necessarily less important. If we consider any consequential subset of countries, clearly the military and economic consequences of their loss would probably be to raise the US defense budget, including that part devoted to foreign military assistance, and to lower somewhat our real national product as well as its rate of growth. Notwithstanding some prophets of gloom, a 20 percent, or a 50 percent, or even a 200 percent increase in the size of our defense budget would not "bankrupt" the United States, nor would a 2 percent annual rate of growth in national product, rather than a 5 percent growth rate, mean national doom. But it is probably fair to say that substantially increased defense budgets maintained over a protracted period, if associated with a relatively slow rate of growth in the economy, would be likely to have significant effects on the character and quality of US society domestically; on the extent of bureaucracy, on the control of information, on the sense of tension and vigilance in daily living....

●

The difficulties faced by a small power in balancing off two competing major powers lend themselves well to the tools of economic analysis. In the next selection Albert O. Hirschman considers the situation where two powers (Usonia and Russonia) compete by "selling" foreign aid in return for political alignment as expressed by votes in the UN. The outcome is not simply a matter of who can pay the highest price, however, because he assumes that the sought-after country (Thirdonia) will have its own preferences, independent of the monetary price offered, for alignment with one side or the other. Specifically, it will have a preference for more or less political neutralism (it may prefer, independent of its aid choice, to vote more often with one side or the other, or may prefer a middle position) and for more or less economic independence (a preference as to the relative amounts of aid it would prefer to receive from each side—it may prefer equality, commitment to one side, or merely maximizing total receipts, regardless of their sources). Similarly, the competing powers may respond in various ways to the small country's behavior—they may give constant amounts of aid, regardless of alignment or, more likely, reward favorable political alignment in various degrees. By examining the possible interactions among these different behaviors Hirschman is able to set forth the conditions under which alignments shift and those conditions which produce stable patterns of association. In classical fashion he progressively relaxes his initial assumptions to bring the theoretical model closer to conditions that actually operate in a bipolar world of "peaceful coexistence." In doing so he makes some far from obvious points—for example, how a more generous aid-giving policy can under some conditions encourage a recipient country to move politically *away* from the donor toward a more neutralist position.

Hirschman's model has the great virtue of being fully operational. Its key variables, aid flows and UN voting alignments, are entirely measurable, and one could trace the shifts in aid and voting patterns over time for quite a number of countries to investigate their actual preferences and the explanatory power of the theory.

I have also included, in addition to Hirschman's paper, a communication by David Barkin that followed it, and Hirschman's reply. Barkin makes the very useful comment, in elaborating on the model's implications, that a country may want to maintain its "nonalignment" in two domains that may conflict. It may want both economic independence, to avoid external control through the commercial lever, and political neutralism on issues that arise in the UN. Both of these goals may have intrinsic, not immediately instrumental value. Hirschman's reply, "After all, it is largely the desire to appear neutral which makes Thirdonia wish to distribute its receipts of a given total of aid as equally as possible between Usonia and Russonia," is thus not really satisfactory empirically nor even in terms of his model. But this does not make the model less important or less valuable.

17

The Stability of Neutralism: A Geometric Note

Albert O. Hirschman

Suppose two powerful, industrialized countries, called Usonia and Russonia, compete by means of capital exports and other forms of "aid" for influence in various underdeveloped countries, typified by Thirdonia. We are interested in exploring whether anything can be said about the resulting relations between total aid, the proportions of the total supplied by each of the powers, the political position of Thirdonia, and, particularly, about the stability of that position. Usonia and Russonia, even though antagonistic over a wide range of issues, may come to perceive a community of interest in such stability, or at least in the avoidance of utter instability, for sudden large-scale changes in alignment on the part of Thirdonia could increase the risk of war between the two powers to a point not desired by either.

Aid from each of the two powers is likely to be influenced by the political alignment of Thirdonia as expressed, for example, by the proportion of votes it casts in the United Nations General Assembly in line with Usonia's or Russonia's wishes. Aid received from Usonia may be assumed to be the larger, the more closely aligned Thirdonia is with Usonia, with a similar aid-giving behavior holding for Russonia. For the time being, we shall suppose that complete alignment with Usonia yields the same flow of aid as does complete alignment with Russonia.

Reprinted from *American Economic Review*, **54**, 2 (March 1964), pp. 94–100. "Comment" and "Reply" reprinted from *American Economic Review*, **54**, 5 (December 1964), pp. 1069–1073.

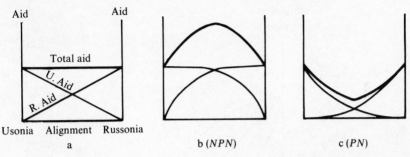

Fig. 1. Types of symmetrical aid-giving behavior by Usonia and Russonia.

Figures 1a, 1b, and 1c portray some of the principal resulting possibilities when political alignment is shown on the horizontal axis and the amount of aid received on the vertical axis. In Fig. 1a aid from Usonia declines linearly and aid from Russonia increases in the same fashion, as Thirdonia takes up political positions farther removed from Usonia and closer to Russonia; in Fig. 1b aid from both decreases little as Thirdonia moves toward neutralist middle ground; while in Fig. 1c aid is cut to the bone as soon as Thirdonia ceases to be a faithful camp-follower. The total aid flow available to Thirdonia results from adding up the two individual aid flows from Usonia and Russonia and is shown as the heavy line or curve in the figures: It is invariant with respect to political alignment in 1a, and exhibits either a maximum or a minimum for the neutralist position depending on whether the aid-giving behavior of the powers corresponds to the one portrayed in 1b or in 1c.

We have just derived the transformation curve or opportunity set available to Thirdonia if aid-from-Usonia and aid-from-Russonia are considered as two commodities which can be "produced" in differing combinations, depending on the country's position between the two powers. The three possibilities just discussed are shown along traditional lines in Fig. 2, where one of the two commodities is measured along the horizontal and the other along the vertical axis. Aid-giving behavior of Fig. 1b which does Not Penalize Neutralism (*NPN*) is now seen to result in the traditionally shaped transformation curve, while 1c-type insistence on substantial identification on the part of the aid-givers results in the opposite shape (labeled *PN* for Penalization of Neutralism).

Consider next the preference functions of Thirdonia for aid from Usonia and Russonia. Again, we may distinguish between three principal possibilities shown in Fig. 3. First, Thirdonia may be exclusively interested in maximizing aid: in this case its indifference map will consist of straight lines such as *MM* (for Mercenary Maximization of aid) forming a 45°

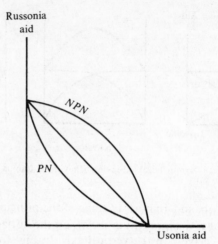

Fig. 2.   Thirdonia's opportunity sets.

angle with the axes along which the two aid flows are measured. The next possibility is that a country puts a high value on independence as well as on aid and feels that, for any given total, its independence is the greater, the more the ratio of Usonia aid to Russonia aid approaches unity. Such a preference would result in the traditionally shaped indifference curve, labeled *AI* (for Aid plus Independence).

A third conceivable preference pattern exists. Thirdonia could prefer complete alignment with one of the two superpowers to a middle position,

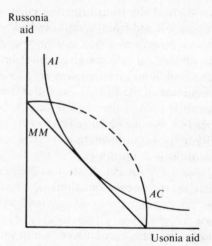

Fig. 3.   Thirdonia's indifference functions.

either because it has a liking for a strong, ideological stance or because it does not wish to be suspected of playing Usonia off against Russonia for the sake of material advantage or for some other reason. Given any fixed amount of aid, the country prefers getting it all from one source rather than through any combination of the two aid-givers. The resulting shape of the preference pattern is shown in the curve labeled *AC* (for Aid plus Commitment); the middle portion of this curve is dotted to indicate that, at any point of time, a country exhibiting this preference pattern is likely to find itself on one or the other end of the curve and is likely to visualize only immediately adjacent positions.

We can now join our "transformation" and "indifference" curves (Figs. 2 and 3), and one important result follows immediately. The traditional point of stable equilibrium is achieved by joining the *NPN* curve of Fig. 2 with the *AI* curve of Fig. 3. In other words, if Thirdonia's preference pattern is such that it values both aid and independence, a stable point is best achieved through aid-giving behavior on the part of Usonia and Russonia that does not penalize neutralism. Should aid be reduced strongly as soon as Thirdonia ceases to be wholly aligned with one or the other aid-giving powers (curve *PN* of Fig. 2), then a potentially unstable situation results from the *AI*-type of preference. The highest *AI* curve could touch the *PN* curve at two widely distant points, between which the aid-receiving country would be indifferent. Even if there is only one point of tangency, small real or imagined shifts in the position of the two similarly shaped curves could produce a drastic shift of the optimal point, i.e., a sudden switch in Thirdonia's position in relation to the two superpowers. Hence, if an underdeveloped country is known to have the Aid-plus-Independence type of preference and if both Usonia and Russonia, in the interest of reducing the risk of war, are intent on preventing sudden shifts in the world power balance through shifts of positions on the part of less developed countries, then they ought to adopt the aid-giving behavior of Fig. 1b, which does not penalize neutralism.

Looking at some of the other conceivable combinations of the transformation curves of Fig. 2 and of the indifference curves of Fig. 3, we find that Mercenary Maximization (*MM*) of aid is compatible with stability only if neutralism is not penalized (*NPN* curve of Fig. 1). Small real or imagined shifts in the supply curve of aid of a linear or *PN* type could produce a complete flip-flop on the part of a country that is only interested in squeezing the maximum aid out of the two competing powers.

What happens if a country puts a positive value on ideological commitment to one of the aid-giving powers and, hence, has a preference function of the *AC* type? In this case, the more stable situation appears to result from the transformation curve following the *PN* rather than the *NPN* type. In other words, if Thirdonia likes commitment, the most stable situation is created through the aid-giving countries responding to and reinforcing this attitude by penalizing decisively any straying from the commitment path. It is possible to speak of stability in this situation only if Thirdonia, which is by definition aligned with one of the aid-giving powers at the outset, does not visualize a switch all the way to the other camp (its preference curve is defined at any one time only for one or the other end of the *AC* curve of Fig. 3).

At this point in our reasoning we perceive that, in contrast to the usual assumption of economic theory, the shapes of the transformation and indifference curves in our model are *not* independent: clearly, the *NPN* and *AI* curves, on the one hand, and the *PN* and *AC* curves, on the other, "belong" together and generate each other. A Thirdonia with the *AI*-type preference will see its behavior rewarded and its correctness confirmed by finding that its opportunity set is, in fact, *NPN*; and the realization on the part of Usonia and Russonia that Thirdonia is *not* "playing off one against the other," but is genuinely interested in keeping at an equal distance from both, may induce them to adopt the kind of aid-giving behavior that does not penalize neutralism. On the other hand, the *AC*-type of preference on the part of Thirdonia will generate expectations of unbending loyalty on the part of the country to which it professes to be committed; should these expectations be disappointed ever so little, aid is likely to be reduced drastically, in accordance with the *PN* pattern.

Unstable situations exist, nevertheless, and can now be viewed as a result of transitional departures from the two basic stable situations, *NPN-AI* and *PN-AC*. Suppose we start out with preference system *AC* and opportunity set *PN*. An unstable situation can then arise because Thirdonia shifts its preference pattern to *AI*, while Usonia and Russonia hold fast to *PN* instead of switching to *NPN*. A potentially unstable situation results, in other words, if a previously committed country shifts to a neutralist or independent position and its previous mentor cannot reconcile itself to the loss of its dominant influence and attempts to coerce the country back to the fold. The possible, and, indeed, likely, result is that the country will move even farther away.

Another case of instability would occur in the following situation: Suppose Thirdonia has the neutralist *AI*-type of preference, but the aid-giving countries have adopted the *NPN* aid-giving behavior simply as a means of cajoling Thirdonia into becoming a satellite: after a while they may then tire of waiting for this hoped-for event and try a more coercive policy of the *PN* type—Thirdonia's choice would be unpredictable.

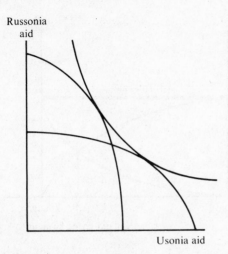

Fig. 4. Two equally neutralist Thirdonias with different opportunity sets.

The model could no doubt be complicated considerably in various ways, for example, by introducing time more explicitly into the analysis. Suppose that the longer Thirdonia continues as Usonia's or Russonia's satellite, the more it will tend to be taken for granted with a consequent decline in aid received—such aid-giving behavior could easily be shown to give rise to instability.

Another realistic complication of the model may be briefly discussed. Suppose that the maximum aid flow that can be obtained by Thirdonia I from Usonia is larger than that which Russonia can be expected to provide, while the opposite holds for Thirdonia II. This means that the opportunity set facing these two countries is no longer symmetrical with respect to the coordinates. Figure 4 assumes that the relevant opportunity sets are of the *NPN* type and that both Thirdonias have the same neutralist *AI*-type preference pattern. It is clear then that the two countries will select different foreign policy positions and would receive their aid in different proportions from the two superpowers, even though they have basically the same neutralist attitude. For this reason, it is impossible to detect (to "read off") the extent or sincerity of their neutralism merely from the proportion of total aid received from one of the two contenders for influence (or from the proportion of votes cast in the UN General Assembly in line with the wishes of either Usonia or Russonia).

Thus far, we have assumed (see Figs. 1a, 1b, and 1c) that the aid-giving behavior of Usonia and Russonia is symmetrical. Naturally, this need not be—indeed, is not likely to be—the case. An interesting combination results if Usonia exhibits the *NPN* behavior of Fig. 1b and Russonia

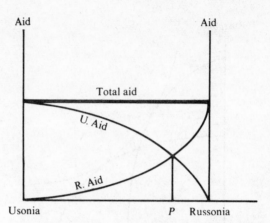

Fig. 5. Asymmetrical aid-giving behavior.

the *PN* behavior of Fig. 1c. The outcome could well be, as shown in Fig. 5, that total aid will once again be invariant with respect to Thirdonia's political alignment. If Thirdonia is neutralist and therefore has the *AI*-type preference function, it will now select the political position that will equalize aid from both camps and will therefore tend to take up the political position *P* on Fig. 5, rather close to Russonia. This situation will be exasperating to Usonia, whose contribution to Thirdonia's development equals that of Russonia. As a result, Usonia will now be tempted to imitate Russonia and withdraw to the *PN*-type of aid-giving behavior. This sequence would lead to the unstable *AI-PN* combination we have already discussed. Suppose, however, that instead of Usonia adopting Russonia's behavior, Russonia, for some reason, goes over to Usonia's *NPN*-type behavior; we would now be back to the stable *NPN-AI* combination, and Thirdonia would assume a truly neutralist position, equidistant from both blocs. The irony would be, in this case, that Russonia's more generous aid-giving policy would have led Thirdonia to move politically away from Russonia.

Another step toward the real world is taken if we allow for multi-lateral aid agencies or for aid-giving countries other than Usonia and Russonia. Taking the most worrisome unstable case, where a neutralist country faces aid-giving behavior that penalizes neutralism (the *AI-PN* combination), it appears that the function of multilateral aid or of aid from countries other than the two superpowers may well be to restore stability by stepping up aid from these sources as Thirdonia moves to neutralist ground. In this way the total aid available to Thirdonia from all three sources of aid could approximate the *NPN* rather than the *PN* shape and stability would be restored. It is conceivable that Usonia and

Russonia, realizing the domestic policy constraints under which they operate, find it difficult in their bilateral relations with Thirdonia to adopt anything but the *PN*-type of aid-giving behavior; it would then make good sense for them to foster deliberately multilateral aid or aid from other industrial countries in such a way as to compensate for their inability to make their own bilateral aid-giving behavior conform to the requirements of stability.

Finally, it might be tempting to analyze how the behavior of each of our three principal actors is shaped by expectations about that of the other two. But before the resulting complications are explored, it was perhaps worthwhile to show that a simple static model can account satisfactorily for a variety of real-life situations and can even yield some suggestions for policy.

Comment

David Barkin

Professor Hirschman's refreshing treatment of "The Stability of Neutralism" suggests the type of contribution that economic tools can make to the solution of problems in the other social sciences. However, such an excursion into interdisciplinary analysis requires a high degree of precision, especially when new concepts are introduced. When using new concepts, care must be taken not to revert to their often imprecise and confusing colloquial connotations; in this instance lack of care resulted in an error in reasoning.

Two concepts—economic independence and political neutrality— were introduced, and lack of differentiation between them led to conflict. In his diagrammatic presentation Hirschman represented economic aid on the ordinate and political alignment on the abscissa. Aid is available from both Russonia and Usonia, and each is willing to give a maximum of OT tons of gold (Fig. 1) to a fully committed nation; *economic independence* may be defined as equal aid for Thirdonia from each of the two big powers. On the other hand, political alignment is measured by the proportionate distribution of the underdeveloped land's votes in the UN General Assembly; *political neutrality* is achieved at ON when its votes are distributed equally between the two superpowers.

The true meaning of the concepts may best be demonstrated in the case where Russonia and Usonia act symmetrically and do Not Penalize Neutrality. No conflict between the two ideas arises; Thirdonia can maximize the volume of bullion it receives by behaving like a neutralist and demanding economic independence. Referring to Fig. 1b in the article,... we find that political neutrality can be achieved without

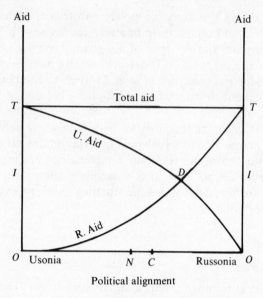

Fig. 6.

sacrificing economic independence; OA tons of gold will be forthcoming from each donor if ON votes are delivered to Russonia and Usonia at appropriate times in the General Assembly. In Hirschman's framework this is a stable solution—the concave opportunity locus determined by the policies of the two powerful, industrialized nations will be tangent to a convex indifference curve of the independent and neutralist Thirdonia.

A pitfall in the use of the two concepts arises when one of the powers attempts to take advantage of this stable equilibrium. A change by one of the rich nations (say, Russonia) from a policy of Not Penalizing Neutrality to one of Punishing Neutrality leads to paradoxical situation that by giving less aid a country can secure more votes in the U.N. This is illustrated in Fig. 6 by a slightly modified version of Professor Hirschman's fifth figure.

In this case, Russonia and Usonia are each contributing OI tons of gold for the development of Thirdonia, while Russonia is receiving a larger share of the votes. Clearly, Thirdonia is not politically neutral as Professor Hirschman suggested when he said "If Thirdonia is neutralist . . . it will now select the political position that will equalize aid from both camps and will therefore tend to take up the political position . . . rather close to Russonia." Economic independence and political neutrality are conflicting goals in this example; a move to distribute votes more equally in the General Assembly will force Thirdonia to become economically dependent on Usonia. Therefore, Thirdonia's position will not be as simple as indicated in the note. Although the country cannot influence the total volume of bullion it receives because the policies of the two richer nations determine its opportunity locus, Thirdonia can determine the amount of aid it receives from each donor by its voting behavior. The poor country will be torn between two positions of political neutrality and economic independence, represented by N and I, respectively, in Fig. 6. Thirdonia, with a preference for both political neutrality and economic independence, will be as unhappy about remaining in position D as Usonia will be about its loss of support in the UN. A move to an intermediate position (C) involves a trade-off of less political alignment with Russonia (more neutrality) for more economic dependence on Usonia (less independence).

Whatever position the neutrally and independently inclined country opts for, the paradoxical situation alluded to by Hirschman persists: Thirdonia favors Russonia as a direct result of its reduction in aid. This, of course, would last only until Usonia reacts to Russonia's policy by adopting a policy Penalizing Neutrality; in this event the world would conform to the unstable combination of Aid plus Independence (or more precisely, Independence plus Neutrality) and Penalizing Neutrality of Hirschman's schema, that is, minimum development assistance for Thirdonia.

Reply

Albert O. Hirschman

Mr. Barkin's point is a useful elaboration of my note. The non-symmetrical aid-giving behavior I portrayed in Fig. 5 is indeed likely to set off a conflict between a neutralist aid-receiving country's desire to remain politically equidistant between the superpowers and its propensity to distribute its receipts of aid as equally as possible between them, with the result that some compromise between these two conflicting urges would emerge. Unfortunately, his eagerness to convict me of "an error in reasoning," while achieving for himself a "high degree of precision," obliges Mr. Barkin to surround his argument with an air of unreality by unhelpfully "precise" definitions of neutralism and economic independence. These two concepts cannot be distinguished as neatly as he proposes to do; it would be more realistic, so it seems to me, to speak of two behavioral dimensions of neutralism (or of both neutralism and independence): one could term them the equidistance propensity and the equidistribution (of aid) propensity. After all, it is largely the desire to appear neutral which makes Thirdonia wish to distribute its receipts of a given total of aid as equally as possible between Usonia and Russonia.

I neglected one of these dimensions (and quite a few more, I suspect) and am happy to see that my model can handle it with ease.

I take this opportunity to point out that the move of one of two aid-giving powers from a policy Not Penalizing Neutralism (*NPN*) to one that does (*PN*)—see my Figs. 1b and 5 or Barkin's 6—bears a striking similarity to the attempt on the part of a trading country to improve its terms of trade by imposing a tariff. A unilateral transition of one of the aid-giving powers from the *NPN* to the *PN* policy permits it to reap better "terms of aid"—the country that lowers its aid schedule will paradoxically achieve a political gain. One limitation of this gain lies in the likelihood of retaliation; but, even in the absence of retaliation— and this is a further parallel to the tariff argument—there is an *optimum* point in the unilateral shift from the *NPN* to a *PN* policy beyond which Thirdonia is likely to turn away from the aid-policy-shifting power and back toward the country which maintains an *NPN* policy. Suppose Russonia suddenly decides that, short of complete alignment, no aid whatever will be forthcoming. Then the total aid curve would have the shape of a distorted *V* (somewhat like a square root without the horizontal portion) and, if Thirdonia is neutralist, we would be essentially back at the unstable *AI-PN* combination: Thirdonia may go all the way back to Usonia, but this is uncertain. A more determinate result is obtained if we follow Barkin and let the equidistance propensity come into play: Thirdonia would then most likely end up at a point somewhere between complete alignment with Usonia and the midpoint on the alignment scale, thus achieving its minimum requirements of nonalignment at the smallest possible sacrifice of aid. In this fashion, it can be shown that a *radical* policy of penalizing neutralism is self-defeating even, and perhaps especially, in the absence of retaliation.

●

So far we have been examining the *consequences* of different distributions of firm, by size and number, within the market. If, indeed, certain consequences are more likely from one kind of distribution than another, it becomes equally necessary to understand the *causes* of that distribution.[1] Are there any long-run trends toward or away from the concentration of economic power in the hands of only a few firms for each market and, if so, do those trends suggest any important lessons for the size distribution of nations in the international system? In the following chapter I discuss some of the ways inferences can be generated, using an approach which has been rather widely applied to the study of economic market structure.

●

[1] For several detailed studies of the relation between national market size and economic efficiency see E. A. G. Robinson, ed., *Economic Consequences of the Size of Nations* (New York: St. Martin's Press, 1960).

18

Is There a Long-Run Trend Toward Concentration in the International System?

Bruce M. Russett

1. National Size in Historical Systems

Many theories of international politics draw major propositions from the structure of the international system; that is, from the number and relative size of the nations that go to make up the system, the degree to which population or other power bases are concentrated in a few states. We have theories that a bipolar system is or is not more "stable" than a balance of power system, or, extending the argument, that a world with very small nations would or would not be less prone to severe wars than would a multipolar world with only a few major powers.[1] These theories are not at the moment entirely satisfactory for making reliable statements about the contemporary world. Either they rest upon unrealistic assumptions, or they require many qualifications. Yet, some preliminary efforts to test alternative hypotheses do suggest that over the past century and a half the structure of the system has been a moderately good predictor to the amount and nature of violent conflict in the system.[2] These theories have a long and for the most part honored place in the history of international relations theory, and contain at least the seeds of important

Reprinted from *Comparative Political Studies*, 1, 1 (1968), pp. 103–122.

[1] See, e.g., M. A. Kaplan, *System and Process in International Politics* (New York, Wiley, 1957), Part I; K. W. Deutsch and J. D. Singer, "Multipolar Power Systems and International Stability," *World Politics*, 16, 3 (April 1964); K. Waltz, "The Stability of a Bipolar World," *Daedalus*, (Summer 1964), pp. 881–909; and R. N. Rosecrance, "Bipolarity, Multipolarity, and the Future," *Journal of Conflict Resolution*, 10 (September 1966), pp. 314–327.

explanations. By analogy, similar theories have substantial explanatory power in economics for the behavior of firms—in a number of significant ways one can specify "the difference it makes" whether a market is basically duopolistic (only two firms, or at least two firms very much bigger than any others), oligopolistic (several large firms), or approximating perfect competition (many small firms, none of them large enough in isolation to affect the price or quantity of goods sold).

If it is conceded that there is something relevant, for policy as well as for theory, in the structure of the international system, it behooves us to devote some effort to description—to get some sense of the *current* distribution of nations by size—and to test some hypotheses about what that distribution *has been* in the past so as to be able to offer some further hypotheses, however speculative, about what that distribution may *be becoming*. In this article we shall look at the evidence available as to trends in the distribution of nations by population size. The data include information on the "birth" and "death" of nations of various sizes, population growth rates, and static data for the distribution of nations by size at particular points in time and from which we can test some inferences about random processes that might have generated those distributions. To anticipate, we find that the available data are ambiguous, but at least there is no good evidence that the distribution is changing or that there are forces at work which are notably increasing or weakening the degree of concentration.

While population alone is not a good index of power in current international politics, the data for population are very much better than for indices such as military capability or economic strength that might be theoretically more preferable. Furthermore, the number of people is a relevant measure of size for many purposes, and in the long run it may be a more important dimension of power than it seems at present. Its current disabilities stem from the power that Western organization and capital accumulation conveys in the industrialized countries, but over most of history the differentials across the globe were far less than they are at present. And they may become less again at some time in the future. Hence, we shall limit our empirical investigation to concentration of population, while acknowledging that a study of the distributions of power more generally would cover other variables also.

The first crude bit of evidence suggests that over the *very* long run the relative size of the largest nations has not changed greatly. For virtually all of recorded history the largest state in the world has been China.

---

[2] J. D. Singer and M. Small, "Alliance Aggregation and the Onset of War," in J. D. Singer, ed., *Quantitative International Politics: Insights and Evidence: International Yearbook of Political Behavior Research*, Vol. VI (New York: Free Press, 1968).

Currently, China's population of 700 million represents approximately 21 percent of the people of the world; its estimated 1939 population of 452 million was also about 21 percent of the world's people then. On a much longer time scale, a census in the second century AD turned up 59.5 million Chinese; estimates for world population at the time are roughly 210–250 million. This would put China at about 25 percent—a remarkably constant proportion, all things considered.

The picture is not much different if we look at heterogeneous empires rather than units that more nearly approximate nation states. The United Kingdom and the non-self-governing parts of the British Empire in 1939 amounted to possibly 524 million people, or about 24 percent of the then-current world population, and estimates of the extent of the Roman Empire contemporary with the census for ancient China put it at around 55 million, or perhaps just under 25 percent of the total. So however we choose to define the appropriate political unit for long-term comparison, it would seem that over at least a 2000-year period the largest has contained on the order of one-fifth to one-fourth of the entire world's population.[3]

2. Growth Rates and Economies of Scale

Pure description of present and past distributions by itself offers little guidance in suggesting what may occur in the future. Fortunately, however, it is possible from the descriptive material on the size distribution of nations to make some inferences about how the distribution got that way. Essentially, the problem is: do large nations have any particular advantages of scale, so that big states are likely to grow faster than small ones (and, hence, become proportionately bigger), or, on the contrary, do big countries face diseconomies of scale so that they typically grow at slower rates than smaller ones? This brings to mind traditional economic explanations for the relative size of firms, explanations that depend upon assumptions about the structure of costs.

One such explanation is that the larger a firm is, the more efficient it will be, i.e., it will be able to produce at a lower cost per unit of output. Obvious examples stem from the contrast of production-line to hand-crafted techniques of manufacture. If there are efficiencies that can be achieved only with a very great output relative to the size of the market, then small firms will have difficulty competing with large ones, and the likely result will be an oligopolistic industry. But another explanation contends that per unit costs do not decline indefinitely as the size of firm

[3] W. S. Woytinsky and E. S. Woytinsky, *World Population and Production* (New York: Twentieth Century Fund, 1953), pp. 33–34.

increases, that eventually there comes a point where unit costs begin to rise again and the larger firm becomes inefficient.

Clearly, very small firms do suffer real disadvantages, but it seems unlikely that *dis*economies of scale can be traced simply to production methods or that over a long enough time span to allow for plant and staff expansion there is, even for a particular industry, any "optimum" firm size. It is possible, however, that the size of firms may be limited by organizational difficulties and problems of management control of very large firms.[4] There are a variety of theories about loss of control in large institutions, especially those that are hierarchically organized.

There is evidence, however, that for many industries long-run costs are stable once some minimal firm size has been reached. Except for the costs of entry that keep very small firms out entirely, size would otherwise be irrelevant to a firm's prospect of success. The *proportionate* growth rate would thus be a random variable in the sense of being uncorrelated with the absolute size of a firm or with its relative performance in the previous time period. Size would then be determined by the statistical "law of proportionate effect," sometimes named "Gibrat's law" for its maker. The assumption that proportionate growth is independent of size means not that the distribution of firms by size will be normal, but that it will be highly *skewed*, with a clustering of most firms toward the left-hand (small-size) side of the scale and a sharply decreasing number as one looks further to the right. If Gibrat's law holds, the resulting distribution will be a *lognormal* one. That is, if for the numbers representing the firms' size we were to substitute their logarithms, *then* the distribution of the logarithms would be normal (bell-shaped).

A normal curve is generated when a large number of small, independent, random forces act on a variate in an additive manner; and a lognormal curve can be generated if they act multiplicatively. In the present context this means that the determinants of the growth of firms tend to change the size of firms by randomly distributed *proportions....*

The first implication of this simple model is that large, medium and small firms have the same *average* proportionate growth. The second implication is that the *dispersion* of growth rates around the common average is also the same for large, medium and small firms. The third implication is that the *distribution* of proportionate growth rates is also lognormal. Thus if in any period firms on average stay the same size, so that average proportionate growth is unity, just as many firms double as halve their sizes.... Since this applies to all firms, it follows that if x percent of large firms *double* their size, x percent of small firms *halve* their size. Therefore a fourth implication of the simplest lognormal model is that the relative dispersion of the sizes

[4] J. Williamson, "Profit, Growth, and Sales Maximization," *Economica*, 33, 1 (February 1966), pp. 1–16; and O. E. Williamson, "Hierarchical Control and Optimum Firm Size," *Journal of Political Economy*, 75, 2 (April 1967), pp. 123–138.

of firms tends to increase over time. In this analysis the disparity of the sizes of firms increases over time, in spite of the fact that large firms have the same average proportionate growth as medium and small firms; this is so because 50 percent of large firms with above-average growth include firms which were formerly among the smallest in the class of large firms but which enter the ranks of the very largest firms and overtake some of the former leaders.[5]

Thus, a lognormal curve is circumstantial evidence that costs are constant and that large firms have no particular efficiency advantages. The fact that several investigations have turned up highly skewed and in some cases lognormal distributions has been cited as evidence against the existence of economies of scale.

It is essential to note that this entire subject—both on the empirical evidence and the theoretical explanations—is a matter of considerable dispute among economists. The wide range of empirical phenomena to which such distributions can be fitted, however, together with the accuracy of the causal explanations in many cases where they can be fully tested, indicates that the appearance of similar phenomena in international politics would deserve very careful study, despite the skepticism which "curve fitting" may initially provoke.[6] Short-run projections of concentration would, of course, be done more effectively through the aggregation of demographers' single-country models of individual birth and death rates. The question to be investigated here is more general and more fundamental.

3. The Size Distribution of Nations

This discussion is relevant to the international system not simply because of any crude analogy between the distribution of firms and the

[5] P. E. Hart, "The Size and Growth of Firms," *Economica*, **29**, 113 (February 1962), p. 30. For the basic paper, see G. U. Yule, "A Mathematical Theory of Evolution Based on the Conclusions of Dr. J. C. Willis, F.R.S.," *Philosophical Transactions of the Royal Society of London*, **213** (1924), pp. 21–87.

[6] I do not pretend to know this literature thoroughly, but in addition to the references cited previously and in the following pages, see, among many others, Stephen Hymer and Peter Pashigian, "Turnover of Firms as a Measure of Market Behavior," *Review of Economics and Statistics*, **44** (February 1962), pp. 82–87; E. Mansfield, "Entry, Gibrat's Law, Innovation, and the Growth of Firms," *American Economic Review*, **52** (December 1962), pp. 1023–1051; R. E. Quandt, "On the Size Distribution of Firms," *American Economic Review*, **56** (June 1966), pp. 416–432; and T. R. Saving, "The Four-Parameter Lognormal, Diseconomies of Scale, and the Size Distribution of Manufacturing Establishments," *International Economic Review*, **6** (January 1965), pp. 105–114. Y. Iriji and H. A. Simon, "Business Firm Growth and Size," *American Economic Review*, **54** (March 1964), p. 79, have shown that the law of proportionate effect does not require that the percentage change in size of a unit from one period to another be independent of the unit's size, but only that the change in size of *the totality of firms in each size stratum be independent of stratum.*

distribution of nations, but because some of the causal hypotheses advanced about the size of firms and of nation-states are so similar. There is, of course, the proposition that only rather large nations are "efficient" and can provide necessary or desirable services to their people at minimum cost. Rather powerful are the arguments that recall economists' points not about efficiencies, but about the market power of large firms—big states, because of their power, can coerce smaller ones so as to obtain a more favorable cost-to-revenue ratio. Or it is contended that very large nations are inefficient, that they must incorporate such diverse peoples, and incur so many bureaucratic costs from hierarchy, that they are ill-suited to survive.

In fact, the distribution of nations by population size in three different years, for which we have reasonably good data, *is* highly skewed and provides a very good fit to the lognormal distribution. Figures 1a, 1b, and 1c show graphs for the size distribution for nation-states in 1967, 1957, and 1938. The skewness has been removed by substituting logarithms for the original figures for population in thousands. The actual distribution is shown as the number of nations in each of a number of uniform (by logarithms) size classes, and the curve superimposed illustrates what the ideal normal distribution would be.[7]

Allowing for the effects of grouping, the fit is, indeed, very close, and for each of the three years. Employing a chi-square goodness-of-fit test to test the null hypothesis that the distribution is *not* normal, we obtain values of about 3.6, 7.0, and 6.6, respectively, for 1938, 1957, and 1967. For 1967 this is statistically significant only at the .88 level, meaning that almost nine-tenths of the time we would correctly *reject* the null hypothesis in favor of the alternative hypothesis of normality. For 1938 and 1957, when the range was narrower and the total number of nations was less, I used fewer size classes and, hence, there are fewer degrees of freedom.

[7] Data are from B. M. Russett et al., *World Handbook of Political and Social Indicators* (New Haven: Yale University Press, 1964), pp. 18–20; United Nations, *Demographic Yearbook, 1966* (New York: United Nations, 1967); United Nations, *Demographic Yearbook, 1962* (New York: United Nations, 1963); United Nations, *Demographic Yearbook, 1958* (New York: United Nations, 1959); and *World Almanac and Book of Facts, 1944* (New York: World Telegram and Sun, 1944). Some data are estimated. "Sovereign state" is defined in 1957 and 1967 to include all members of the UN, plus Switzerland and the nations excluded by cold-war politics, whose existence is acknowledged if not always recognized. Byelorussia and the Ukraine, however, are not counted, despite their formal UN membership. Ministates that are not members of the UN (e.g., Andorra, Monaco) are not counted because they are too small (below the minimum firm size) to carry on even the minimal activities of international politics that the small UN members do. The 1938 country list is compiled from B. M. Russett, J. D. Singer, and M. Small, "A Standardized List of Political Entities in the Twentieth Century," *American Political Science Review,* **62**, 3 (September 1968), applying UN memberships retroactively, and including the Baltic states.

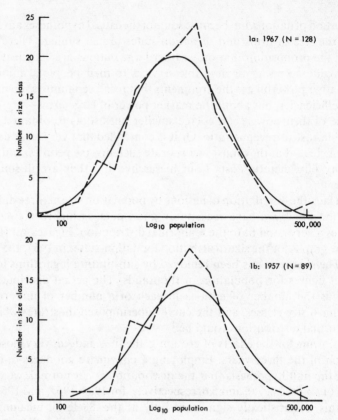

Fig. 1. Log$_{10}$ population distribution of nations by size classes (thousands).

Their chi-square-values are both significant at the .73 level, meaning that one properly would reject the hypothesis of nonnormality only about three-quarters of the time. But all three of these figures together indicate a strikingly good and consistent fit.[8]

The three separate years are given to show the effect of adding so many ex-colonies to the international system during the past three decades. As is apparent, the effect has not been great. There has been an increase in the dispersion (as the lognormal model of efficiency uncorrelated with size would predict), and despite world population growth, the mean size of

[8] If significance levels of .88 and .73 don't seem very impressive, bear in mind that we are reversing the normal procedure where one takes a theoretical distribution such as the normal one, and sets the *null* hypothesis that the distribution is normal. One typically hopes to find evidence that the null hypothesis can be rejected and the alternate hypothesis of non-normality can be accepted, but to do so one must have rather high confidence that the departure from normality is not induced by chance alone. Since one would usually demand

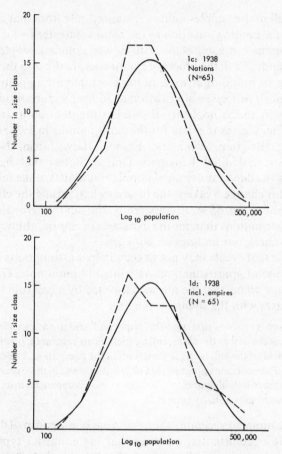

Fig. 1. (continued) Log_{10} population distribution of nations by size classes (thousands).

nation has shifted slightly downward, from the logarithm for almost 7 million to just over $5\frac{1}{2}$ million. But the overall fit has remained good throughout the period.

A problem arises, however, as to how we should treat colonial empires. Are we concerned with the growth or shrinkage of the national

a significance level of .05 before rejecting the hypothesis of normality, levels of .88 and .73 look pretty good for the reverse procedure.

In calculating the chi square, I collapsed the last two-size classes at each tail into a single category so as to raise the expected frequency in that class above 1. With expected frequencies below unity the chi-square test is not appropriate. Some statisticians would insist on frequencies of at least 5, but this seems too conservative. See W. G. Cochran, "Some Methods for Strengthening the Common X^2 Tests," *Biometrics*, **10** (December 1954), pp. 417–451.

core, or of all of the peoples under centralized rule from that core? There are reasons for limiting attention to the nation-state itself—for instance, if we are concerned in some sense with power, colonial people are rarely as great an addition to the power of a nation as are those in the metropole —but doing so would omit some of the most interesting political (rather than biological) processes of growth and so lose important information. Accordingly, it seems necessary to present the data both ways, and so part 1d of Fig. 1 gives the data for the same nations in 1938, except that for the ten (Belgium, Denmark, France, Italy, Japan, Netherlands, Portugal, Spain, United Kingdom, United States) that had colonial empires I have added the colonies' population to that of the metropolitan territory. This change weakens the fit somewhat, raising the chi square to 4.2, significant at the .65 level. Apparently, the random growth model fits better for core-nations than for the dynamics of empire, although we shall continue to check our findings on both sets.

While actual events may not fit the model's assumptions precisely, it serves as a useful approximation. As Iriji and Simon note, Galileo's law of the inclined plane, that the distance traveled by a ball rolling down the plane increases with the square of the time

... does ignore variables that may be important under various circumstances: irregularities in the ball or the plane, rolling friction, air resistance, possible electrical or magnetic fields if the ball is metal, variations in the gravitational field—and so on, ad infinitum. The enormous progress that physics has made in three centuries may be partly attributed to its willingness to ignore for a time discrepancies from theories that are in some sense substantially correct.[9]

For the moment accepting the hypothesis of a lognormal distribution, we have the circumstantial evidence that big countries typically grow neither more nor less rapidly than smaller ones, and there is no overall tendency for either a decline or an increase in concentration in the international system. This corresponds fully with what poor evidence we cited earlier for millennia-long periods. Of course, if one thinks of nations as growing in population only by the biological processes of birth and death among their citizenry, then such a finding is not surprising. On that basis there would be few plausible hypotheses that big nations would have an advantage except by some rather involved mechanisms, such as a correlation between size and per capita income and, consequently, faster (or slower) natural rates of population increase in the larger and, thus, richer countries. But this hypothesis, at least, is poorly supported empirically,[10] and in any case natural life processes certainly do *not* provide the only

[9] Iriji and Simon, *op. cit.*, p. 78.
[10] See Russett et al., *op. cit.*, p. 277, where the correlation is shown to be below .20.

way that nations grow or shrink. Nations accept immigrants and provide emigrants. Furthermore, they annex other areas, fission, or, in turn, are annexed. When these processes are recalled, various alternative hypotheses about the advantages (or handicaps) accruing to big countries in international competition are not so implausible. They just do not seem to meet with much support here.[11]

4. Some Alternative Models

Yet this rather neat fit to the lognormal distribution, with the consequent deductions we can make for speculating about how the distribution might have been generated is, unfortunately, complicated by some alternative models and hypotheses that cannot easily be rejected. Herbert Simon, for example, has suggested that if in addition to random growth rates one assumes a process of birth for new firms, the consequence is the Yule distribution, which looks like the lognormal one except that there are a few more very large firms:

Let us assume that there is a minimum size, S_m, of firm in an industry. Let us assume that for firms above this size, unit costs are constant. Individual firms in the industry will grow (or shrink) at varying rates, depending on such factors as (a) profit, (b) dividend policy, (c) new investment, and (d) mergers. These factors, in turn, may depend on the efficiency of the individual firm, exclusive access to particular factors of production, consumer brand preference, the growth or decline of the particular industry products in which it specializes, and numerous other conditions. The operation of all these forces will generate a probability distribution for the changes in size of firms of a given size. Our first basic assumption (the law of proportionate effect) is that this probability distribution is the same for all size classes of firms that are well above S_m. Our second basic assumption is that new firms are being "born" in the smallest-size class at a relatively constant rate.... What distinguishes the Yule distribution from the lognormal is not the first assumption—the law of proportionate effect—but the second—the assumption of a constant "birth rate" for new firms. If we assume a random walk of the firms already in the system at the beginning of the time interval under consideration, with zero mean change in size, we obtain the log-normal. If we assume a random walk, but with a steady introduction of new firms from below, we obtain the Yule distribution.[12]

[11] Data on nations' size by measures such as total GNP are, as indicated earlier, less reliable than population data, especially for changes over time. A test of the distribution of nations' GNP in 1957, nevertheless, powerfully supports the major hypothesis of this article; it fits a lognormal distribution with a chi square of 4.5 at a significance level of .92, even higher than any test of the population data. This needs to be examined further. Data from Russett et al., *op. cit.*, pp. 152–154.

[12] H. Simon and C. P. Bonini, "The Size Distribution of Business Firms," *American Economic Review*, **48** (September 1958), pp. 607–617. Note some of the analogies between reasons for the growth or shrinkage of firms and those for nations.

Simon has also developed an alternative model, allowing for the death of small firms at the same rate as the birth of some new small firms, that again produces a Yule distribution.[13] A distribution more like the Yule than the lognormal can also be produced when there are some efficiency advantages to be gained only by extremely large size.

One analyst has reconciled the basic proportionate effects model with what many economists have described *empirically* as a *progressing* degree of concentration in quite a number of industries. He does it by assuming that the average firm does grow some, and by distinguishing between average *growth* rates and *survival* rates. He attributes lower survival rates to the smaller firms. The analysis recalls a variety of phenomena in international politics—large nations' attempts to secure safety through control over foreign sources of vital supplies, the coercive market power of big countries in international politics, and the alleged greater caution and "responsibility" or conservatism which many observers attribute to great powers.

The fact that mortality decreases with size, that firms—at least in free enterprise conditions—are subject to high infant mortality but that very large firms rarely succumb, is well established.... Now if big firms have a better chance of survival than firms of smaller size, this will readily explain why, in the course of time, they obtain more scope for themselves, as a group, than the others....

Simultaneously, the difference in the chance of survival can also offer an explanation of... what becomes of the advantage of big firms in large-scale economies of operation—what do they do with it? They use it, not to earn more and to grow faster, but to survive better than the smaller firm.

It will be appreciated that a firm can use its advantages over its competitors in either of two ways: either to earn more, or to have more safety—that is, either to increase the mathmatical expectation of the profit rate or to decrease the variance of it.... A firm may increase its chances of survival at the expense of the rate of profit by holding more reserves of various kinds, such as financial reserves in the form of liquid assets, government bonds, etc, but in many cases also as stocks of raw material. It may also acquire sources of raw materials, not very profitable, but essential for operation in certain contingencies. Or again, it may diversify its production programme in a way which will entail a sacrifice in efficiency (higher cost) but will reduce the impact of a failure in any one line....

Thus the greater profit and growth rate of "bigness" exists—at least to a large extent—only potentially, and is not realized owing to the preference of big firms for safety.[14]

    [13] H. A. Simon, *Models of Man* (Wiley: New York, 1957), Ch. 9.

    [14] J. Steindl, *Random Processes and the Growth of Firms* (New York: Hafner, 1965), pp. 218–221. W. J. Baumol suggests that the managers of firms may prefer to avoid even moderate risk so as not to antagonize their shareholders. Losses attributable to risk taking may provoke immediate shareholder dissaffection, and even windfall gains from successful risk taking may provoke ultimate dissatisfaction if they lead to expectations of *continued*

These models mean that there are several different mechanisms by which an increasing degree of concentration could arise in a system such as the international system. They are relevant because, in fact, the Yule distribution does fit our empirical distributions of nations at least as well and perhaps a bit better than the lognormal one, and because of our interest in finding the *why* behind the *is*. From the graphs it is apparent that the number of very big countries at the upper tail is slightly greater than predicted by the normal model. This evidence must be taken with a good deal of skepticism, however, since it is based on the deviations of only one or two countries from their "expected" point in the distribution. As some of the analagous controversies in economics have indicated, it is often virtually impossible to decide just which of several hypothetical distributions actually provides the best fit to a set of data and, even after obtaining a fit, to decide which variant of the law of proportionate effect offers the proper causal description. We cannot differentiate among them with purely static data.

5. Four Hypothetical Sources of Concentration

An international system is *concentrated* to the degree that a high proportion of the total population is contained in a small proportion of the countries. There are several ways in which increasing concentration could occur:

1. More rapid growth rates for the very largest nations than for smaller ones.

2. The "death" of small nations by annexation or merger at the same or greater rate as new ones were being born, while large nations retained high survivor rates.

3. A great increase in the number of very small nations (births in the lowest size class).

4. The birth of one or two very large nations, either by merger or by entry into the list of sovereign nations from a former state of colonial dependency.

The finding of a perfectly lognormal distribution would have been strong disconfirmation of the first hypothesis, but the suggestion that a

---

high gain that cannot be met. Cf. *Business Behavior, Value, and Growth* (New York: Macmillan, 1959), esp. Chs. 6, 7, and 10. Governments similarly may wish to avoid risk taking for fear of reprisal from their constituents. Marshall Hall and Leonard Weiss, "Firm Size and Profitability," *Review of Economics and Statistics*, **49**, 3 (August 1967), pp. 319–331, show that the rate of profit *is* higher for large firms than for smaller ones even controlling for the degree of concentration of the industry.

Table 1
Mean Growth Rates of Nations' Population, 1939–1965 by Quartile

	Top quartile, %	Second quartile, %	Third quartile, %	Bottom quartile, %	Overall mean, %
Nation-states	142	143	149	183	154
Nations and empires	104	151	149	183	147

Yule distribution fits equally well limits the confidence with which that hypothesis can be rejected. What is now required for further differentiating among these plausible alternatives, or for rejecting all in favor of a finding that concentration is not increasing, is to look at the actual data on observed *growth rates* as well as the size distribution. We must also have data on the *births* and *deaths* of nations. This can be done successfully only with data spread over quite a long time period, measured in several decades as an absolute minimum. Unfortunately, such information is not very accurate even for the Western developed nations, let alone for the underdeveloped world. Population censuses have not been sufficiently reliable for a long enough time to permit the fine measurement really demanded here.

We can, however, go a bit farther. First, we have nearly complete information, if of less than desirable accuracy, on national population growth rates over the period 1939–1965.[15] We can divide the distribution into several subsets and see if big countries have, in fact, grown faster than smaller ones. The first row of Table 1 shows the average growth rate for the countries in each quartile of the distribution. The second row in the table allows for the decline of empires, giving the quartile means of the growth rates for the same units except that for the empires I have combined the population of the colonies with that of the metropolitan territory in the prewar year, and in 1965 for those that still had colonies.

1. The hypothesis that big nations have been growing faster than smaller ones is unambiguously rejected. This finding is not merely an artifact of the grouping by quartiles, nor does it hide higher growth rates for the few nations at the very high end. Of the eight largest states, only China, and that barely (155 percent), had a growth rate higher than the

[15] The data are for 1939–1965 population growth, but it seemed relevant to do the analysis for the political units that existed in January 1938, before the largely temporary elimination of a number of independent states from the international scene immediately before and during World War II. Data are from United Nations, *Demographic Yearbook, 1958* (New York: United Nations, 1959), Table 4, and United Nations, *Demographic Yearbook, 1965* (New York: United Nations, 1966), Table 4. The prewar population estimates for Afghanistan, Liberia, Saudi Arabia, and Yemen were too crude to use here.

Table 2
Standard Deviation of Growth Rates of Nations' Population, 1939–1965 by Quartile

	Top quartile	Second quartile	Third quartile	Fourth quartile
Nation-states	48.6	33.6	35.1	35.1
Nations and empires	59.8	33.9	35.1	35.1

rate achieved by the average nation overall (154 percent). Size does make some differences in growth, but opposite from the way expected. Growth rates for the *smallest* quartile of nations have been well above the average for nations as a whole. This is even more true if empires rather than nation-states are included in the computations, and there, reflecting the breakup of colonial holdings after World War II, the *largest* quartile shows by far the *least* growth.

Incidentally, there are other reasons for questioning whether the law of proportionate effect is the source of the size distribution of nations. According to the second and third implications of the law as drawn by Hart, the *standard deviation* of growth rates should be the same for small nations as for large ones, and the distribution of growth *rates* should itself be lognormal.

Investigation turns up little evidence of these properties. Table 2 shows the standard deviations of nations' 1939–1965 growth rates for each quartile of the distribution. For the three lowest quartiles the dispersion is virtually the same, but for the top quartile, whether one looks at nations only or at nations and colonial empires, the measure of dispersion is much *higher* than for the other quartiles. Thus, it not only appears that the proportionate effects model does not strictly apply for the largest states, but that big countries are prone to more risky behavior than are smaller ones. Apparently, a nation or empire has to *take chances in order to grow big* and to stay big, and is likely as a result to expand or shrink by a greater proportional amount than most countries.[16] Note, however, that this

[16] This finding in a way complements that of Stephen Hymer and Peter Pashigian, "Firm Size and Rate of Growth," *Journal of Political Economy*, **70** (December 1962), pp. 566–569, who looked at the standard deviations of growth rates of firms in different size classes. Because of the possibilities large firms have for diversification to spread their risks, they predict a *sharply inverse* relation between size and the variation in growth rates. Although they do find a somewhat inverse relationship, the fact that the standard deviation for large firms' growth rates is greater than predicted (though less than for smaller firms) brings them to conclude that large firms are also prone to greater risk-taking behavior. While all the *assumptions* of their model are not appropriate for transferring an expectation of an inverse relationship from firms to nations, the *finding* is nevertheless relevant.

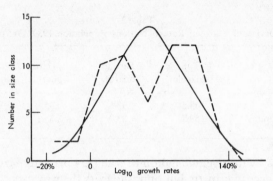

Fig. 2.   Log$_{10}$ distribution of nation's population growth rates, 1939–1965.

seemingly more risk-prone behavior was not reflected in lower *survival* rates for big countries. Shrinkage rates are not so sharp, or the "cushion" available to a big country is large enough, that over the time period studied no states above the smallest size class actually dropped out of the international system of sovereign entities (see point 2).

As for the implication that the distribution of proportionate growth rates should be lognormal, it too is not borne out in the crude data available. Figure 2 shows the actual distribution superimposed on the hypothetical normal curve. The curve is vaguely normal with bunchings toward the middle, but more nearly bimodal. The chi square for goodness of fit is 9.8, significant at the .13 level. We probably would *reject* the hypothesis of normality, though with a .13 probability of error and, hence, without much confidence. [The curve for empires is an even poorer fit (slightly skewed) and not shown.] It is true that the data for time changes are rather gross for a procedure requiring fine measures, and also that they are incomplete in a way that may be relevant. There are four nations with missing data (Afghanistan, Liberia, Saudi Arabia, and Yemen), and from what crude information that is available it is clear they would fall somewhere in the middle of the distribution. Should most or all of them belong in the middle category, they would moderately improve the worst aspect of the fit. The significance level and the problem of data error do leave open the possibility that some implications of the proportionate effects model may not be so inapplicable as they appear here.

2. Another of the four possible sources of concentration listed previously was that large nations would have substantially lower death rates (Steindl) or, ideally, that all "deaths" of nations would be in the smallest size class (Simon). On the whole, the differential death rate models simply do not apply—only four permanent deaths by annexation or merger have occurred since 1938. The Baltic states of Estonia, Latvia, and

Lithuania were absorbed into Soviet Russia in 1940, and Zanzibar joined Tanganyika in 1964, shortly after achieving independence. It is true that these few deaths all involved nations with populations under three million, so they are not inconsistent with the hypothesis; but they were so few compared with the number of births (67) as to be essentially irrelevant to the characteristics of the distribution.

3. We said that a great increase in the number of very small states could produce a Yule distribution. That is a substantial oversimplification of what has actually happened. True, a much larger proportion of new than of old states *do* fall in the very small size class. The smallest four—Maldive Islands, Iceland, Barbados, and Gambia—are all post-1938 nations, and of the 15 under one million only Luxembourg was in existence at the beginning of the period. But above that level there is no relation between size and post-1938 independence. And the new sovereign states of the past twenty years include India, Pakistan, and Indonesia, each now with over 100 million people. Thus, attributing part of the departure from lognormality to the introduction of new small states is plausible, but incomplete. In addition to the large new nations that do not fit the model, the process of introduction has not been "at a relatively constant rate." Forty percent of the countries that became independent over the entire 30 year period did so between 1960 and 1962.

4. A single very big country—India—was born during the time period in question. Its birth would, with the other birth and death patterns noted previously, in large part account for the departure from lognormality in the upper tail observed earlier, and its position in the number two ranking has tended to increase the degree of concentration. But it is difficult to generalize from the single case to any longer-term trends in the system. India is the first state to join the community of nations near the top of the size distribution since Germany did so a century ago.

6. Stable Concentration, 1938–1967

Having checked out the various mechanisms by which concentration might have increased in the post-1938 era, we can now return to the actual data on what did happen. Figure 3 shows the Lorenz curves for the distribution of nation-states by population in 1938 and 1967. A Lorenz curve is drawn by ranking nations from smallest to largest and computing the percentage of the total *population* held by various percentages of the *total number* of nations, starting at the lower end. The further the curve is from the line of equality bisecting the square from lower left to upper right, the greater the degree of concentration.[17]

[17] H. R. Alker and B. M. Russett, "Indices for Comparing Inequality," in R. L. Merritt and S. Rokkan, eds., *Comparing Nations* (New Haven: Yale University Press, 1966).

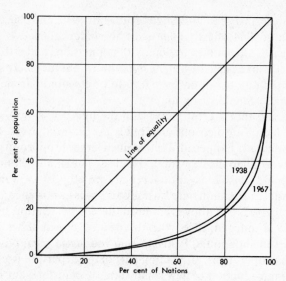

Fig. 3. Lorenz curves of population concentration by nations, 1938 and 1967.

The two curves are similar, but not identical, with some indication of an increase in concentration over the period. The Gini index of concentration (which measures the area between the Lorenz curve and the line of equality) increased from .746 to .776. Virtually all that difference occurred between 1957 and 1967, since the 1957 curve (not drawn) is almost identical with the 1938 one and has a Gini index of .748. If we look at the extent of colonial empires as well as of nations, however, we find that the curve has been effectively unchanged. For 1938, empires and nations together the Gini index is .785, or very *slightly more* concentrated than the distribution in 1967. By this interpretation the post-World War II end of empire has not really varied the distribution of a major power base, population, from what is was three decades ago. The results of those events do not offer any support for a prediction of greater concentration in the future.

7. Summary

We examined the size distribution of nations at several points in time and explored several possible mechanisms by which that distribution might change. Some questions were resolved; others remain open.

1. There is no evidence that the largest states are proportionately either larger or smaller than 2000 years ago.

2. The *size distribution* for recent years is nearly lognormal, and

hence consistent with a random growth model implying no correlation between size and proportionate growth.

3. The *size distribution* also, however, departs slightly from lognormality in a way that leaves open the possibility that the very largest states may be growing faster.

4. The *size distribution* also departs slightly from lognormality in a way that is consistent with a Yule distribution that could be generated by various models employing random growth and certain birth and death rates.

5. Over recent decades large nations have *not grown faster* than smaller ones, contrary to the possibility suggested by item 3.

6. The *distribution* of observed *growth rates* does not fit the requirements of the random growth model (item 2) well, but the data are not highly reliable for the fine measurements required.

7. A combination of the *death* and especially the *birth* patterns for nations in recent decades could have produced a departure from lognormality roughly in the direction suggested by item 4.

8. The actual change in the degree of *concentration* in the system over the past three decades has been very small.

●

The final selection for this portion of the book is from the work of Kenneth E. Boulding, who is well known for his applications of economic theories to problems of international politics. Here, he takes a basic model of conflict and discusses its relations to international problems, while carefully noting some of the limitations of that analogy. It too concerns the number of nations that will be "viable" in an international system and is relevant to the concern with concentration. The model is derived, however, from location theory and other aspects of the theory of the firm rather than from oligopoly models.

It is an intriguing source of insights and hypotheses and, in principal, the variables, such as distance, are measurable. But in practice, the obstacles to measurement are extremely serious—what is at stake is not simply distance, but the function by which national power declines over distance. For some forms of strategic power in a nuclear world the decline may be quite nonlinear. Neglecting opposition by the defense (which is ignored in the formal model), the costs of delivering weapons at intercontinental ranges are very much greater than over short distances. Here the Boulding model needs to be modified. With conventional power the problem is much more complex and dependent on differing technical capabilities and topographical features of the relevant surface of the earth.[1]

●

[1] See A. Wohlstetter and R. Rainey, "Distant Wars and Far-Out Estimates," paper presented to the American Political Science Association Meeting, Washington, September 1966, and Wohlstetter, "Theory and Opposed System Design" in M. Kaplan, ed., *New Approaches in International Relations* (New York: St. Martin's, 1968).

19

The Theory of Viability

Kenneth E. Boulding

The first problem to be considered is that of *viability*. By this, we mean the ability and the willingness of one party to destroy or eliminate another. A party that cannot be absorbed or destroyed as an independent source of decisions is said to be *unconditionally viable*. A party that can be absorbed or destroyed by another is *conditionally viable* if the party that has the power to destroy it refrains from exercising this power. The party that can absorb or destroy another is said to be the *dominant* party. Thus, a party that is conditionally viable survives only at the will of the dominant party. Perhaps two kinds of conditional viability should be distinguished. There are some situations in which it does not pay the dominant party to extinguish the other; this might be called *secure* conditional viability. There are other situations in which it would pay the dominant party to extinguish the other but in which the dominant party refrains through goodwill toward the dominated. This might be called *insecure* conditional viability.

Where we have a situation in which both parties are unconditionally viable or in which there is secure conditional viability, we have what Strausz-Hupé has called *protracted conflict*,[1] where the problem is how to control the conflict process rather than to resolve it; the resolution may come eventually through change in the character of the parties or through the growth of a sense of community between them, but it cannot come through the absorption or destruction of one party. Where we have insecure conditional viability, there is a strong tendency for the weaker

Abridgement of pp. 58–59, 230–245, 259–264, from K. E. Boulding, *Conflict and Defense*. Copyright © 1962 by Kenneth E. Boulding. Reprinted by permission of Harper & Row, Publishers.

[1] R. Strausz-Hupé, *Protracted Conflict* (New York: Harper & Row, 1959).

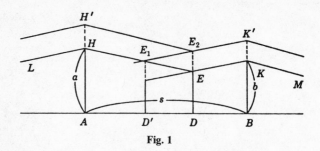

Fig. 1

party to be absorbed or destroyed by the stronger. This may be bad—
making a desert and calling it peace—or it may be good—the integration
of organizations that are too small to be useful or serviceable into larger
and more inclusive organizations. The value judgments here are not easy;
it is not always true, for instance, that absorption is good and extinction is
bad, though we may reasonably have a certain prejudice in this direction.
It should be observed also that, when a party is absorbed into another,
it frequently retains some identity within the larger organization and
that absorption may, in fact, mean the setting up of a larger organizational
framework that actually increases in some sense the viability of the component parts. Thus, the several states within the United States are much
more viable as states than they would be as independent countries.
Whatever value judgments we apply to these processes, it is clear that
they form an important element of the field of study of conflict.... We
want to find the conditions under which one state can conquer or overcome the other. This is a problem formally similar to that of the conditions
under which one firm can overcome another. Thus, suppose, in Fig. 1,
we have two states, A and B, with the home bases located at A and B,
respectively. For the moment, we shall suppose that their home bases
are points rather than areas, but this assumption can easily be relaxed
later. $AB(= s)$ is the distance between the two states. We suppose for
simplicity a world that consists only of the line AB and its projections.
Now let us suppose a variable called *national strength* or, more simply,
strength. The measurement of this is a difficult problem. Military strength
is a multidimensional quantity, composed not only of the number of
men in the armed forces and the equipment that they carry but also of
subtle psychological variables such as the will to fight. For the present
argument, however, we shall suppose that some index of strength can
be constructed, the only condition being that at any point where A can
beat B, A's strength must be larger than B's, and vice versa. We shall
then suppose that each nation's strength is a maximum at its home base;
this we call its *home strength*. It is measured by AH for A and BK for B

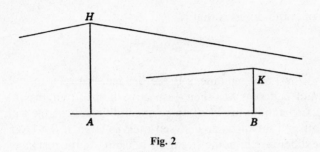

Fig. 2

in Fig. 1. We suppose, furthermore, that each nation's strength declines as it moves away from its home base, following the lines HE and HL for A and KE and KM for B. In the figure, we assume these to be straight lines; their slope may be called the *loss-of-strength gradient*, a very important quantity, which we might name for short the LSG. In fact, the strength lines will not always be straight, and the LSG will vary from place to place even under the most ideal conditions, as is shown in the appendix (omitted here); however, this is a minor amendment, as the deviations from linearity are not likely to be great. The law of diminishing strength, then, may be phrased as *the further, the weaker*; that is, the further from home any nation has to operate, the longer will be its lines of communication, and the less strength it can put in the field.

In Fig. 1, then, with home strengths $AH(= a)$ and $BK(= b)$, there is a boundary of equal strength at D, where the strength lines intersect at E. To the right of D, B is dominant and is stronger than A; to the left of D, A is dominant and is stronger than B.... The area where each country is dominant may be called its *sphere of influence*. Suppose now that country B is not satisfied to have so small a sphere of influence and wishes to push the boundary of equal strength farther away from its home base. It may be able to do this by raising the amount of resources devoted to the means of coercion, so that its home strength rises from BK to BK'. The boundary of equal strength is pushed from D to D'. If now A is not satisfied with this position, A may likewise increase its home strength by devoting more resources to arms, and the point of equal strength is moved back to D again (E_2). This is the pattern of the arms race and also of the price war. Following its distinguished theoretician, we have called this a Richardson process.

Considering now merely the statics of viability, we see, as in the case of the firm, that both nations will be unconditionally viable only if each is stronger than the other at home. This is clearly the case in Fig. 1. In Fig. 2, however, A is dominant, and B is only conditionally viable, for A is stronger than B, even on B's home base. The condition for unconditional viability of both nations is that

$$\frac{b - a}{s} < c > \frac{a - b}{s} \tag{1}$$

where c is the LSG per mile, s is the distance between the two power centers, and a and b are their respective home strengths. As before, therefore, two nations are likely to be unconditionally viable with respect to each other if the distance between them is large, if the LSG is steep, and if the difference in home strengths is slight. As the distance becomes smaller, the LSG's less, and the differences in home strength greater, the chance of unconditional viability diminishes.

There is a concept of maximum home strength that corresponds to the economic concept of minimum average cost. This maximum home strength depends much more directly on the absolute size of a nation than does the average cost on the absolute size of a firm. It may be measured roughly by the total number of men who can be devoted to war. This depends first on the total population and second on the proportion of the population that can be devoted to war. This latter ratio depends mainly on the general level of technique of the nation and especially on its efficiency in the production of food and other basic necessities. A nation that must devote 90 percent of its people to food production in order to feed itself obviously cannot devote more than a small proportion of its manpower to war without disaster from starvation. A nation that can feed itself, like the United States, with 10 percent of its population can devote a much larger percentage of its labor force to war. The efficiency of the war industry is also an important element in the home strength; 100 men well equipped may be worth 10,000 men without equipment. The factor of morale is also of enormous importance; there must be a will to war before resources can be devoted to it. These factors, especially the latter, are strongly susceptible to fluctuation. Nevertheless, under given circumstances, the concept of a maximum home strength is meaningful. These are the significant a and b quantities of Eq. 1.

The problem of *returns to scale* presents peculiar difficulties in the case of the nation-state—difficulties that are by no means absent from the firm, but seem to be less pressing. One difficulty is that the area of influence, that is, the area within the nation's boundary of equal strength, may include two parts: the nation proper and its dependencies. The situation of the nation, therefore, is more complex than that of the firm, where the expansion of its field of influence simply means an extension of its market and its sales; the customers are not thought of as part of the firm. In this sense, all the firm's field of influence consists of dependencies.

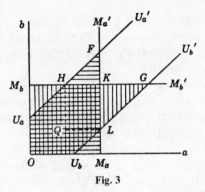

Fig. 3

In the case of the nation, however, the distinction between the core of people who identify with the nation and the dependents, who are merely subjects of the nation, is an important one. The subjects, if they are dissident enough, may be a source of weakness to the nation rather than a source of strength and may diminish rather than increase its home strength. As a nation expands its field of influence, then, it is almost certain sooner or later to run into diminishing returns to scale, that is, a decrease in its home strength with each successive increase in the field of influence. This phenomenon may have a different set of causes from the somewhat similar phenomenon that is observed in the case of the firm, where it arises mainly out of the difficulties of maintaining communications systems and a good decision making process as the scale of the enterprise increases. This factor applies also to the nation or the empire, but there is, in addition, the further factor of heterogeneity and conflicting loyalties. This may sometimes come into the picture of the expansion of a firm as it develops new products; there are diseconomies of heterogeneity in the firm as well as in the state, but they are peculiarly striking in the case of the imperial state....

In Fig. 3, we plot the home strengths of the two nations a and b along the horizontal and vertical axes, respectively.... The competitive strength of the party increases as we move away from the origin.... We then postulate two viability boundaries $U_a U_a'$ and $U_b U_b'$ with equations $b - a = sc$ and $a - b = sc$. These are analogous to market extinction lines.... Only within these lines is Eq. 1 fulfilled. Above and to the left of $U_a U_a'$, nation B is stronger than A at A's home base; below and to the right of $U_b U_b'$, A is stronger than B at B's home base. Now let us suppose that, for each nation, there is a maximum level of home strength, OM_a for A and OM_b for B, dependent on their resources, their will to strength, and so on. In this figure, we suppose that this maximum home strength is constant and that it is independent of the area of influence of each nation and, therefore, independent of the home strength of the other nation. We have, therefore, maximum-home-strength boundaries $M_aM'_a$ for A and $M_bM'_b$ for B. A is not viable anywhere to the right of $M_aM'_a$, and B is not viable anywhere above $M_bM'_b$.

These boundaries now define viability areas for each nation. The viability area for A is the horizontally shaded area OM_aFU_a, shaded horizontally to suggest that A can move horizontally by its own choice, but not vertically. Similarly, the viability area for B is the vertically shaded area OM_bGU_b. The cross-hatched area OU_aHKLU_b, where these two viability areas overlap, is the area of *mutual viability*. Then we have two triangles U_aM_bH and LKG where B is viable but A is not and two triangles U_bLM_a and HKF where A is a viable and B is not. In the unshaded area, neither part is viable.

These boundaries do not, of course, give us any equilibrium solution to the home strengths. This depends, if it exists, on the Richardson equations and the Richardson processes outlined [elsewhere]. If the Richardson processes of arms-race reaction give an equilibrium within the area of mutual viability, this, presumably, is a stable condition as long as the assumptions and coefficients underlying the equations remain constant. There are strong reasons in the case of Fig. 3 for supposing that, in fact, the Richardson process must result in an equilibrium within the area of mutual viability. Suppose, for instance, that the equilibrium of the Richardson process is in the triangle HKF, where B is not viable; B can always move vertically downward into the area of mutual viability. Similarly, from any point outside the area of mutual viability, one or other of the parties has the power to move within it. Unless, therefore, one or other of the parties deliberately seeks suicide, the Richardson process must be limited to the area of mutual survival. Where, within this area, the equilibrium will lie depends on the initial hostilities and reactivities of the two parties. If we have two very hostile and reactive parties, the probability is that, in the absence of the restriction placed on the Richardson equations by the necessity for reaching a solution within the area of mutual viability, there would be either no equilibrium or an equilibrium somewhere beyond K. In this case, the equilibrium is likely to be at K, where both parties are at their maximum home strength. If the parties are somewhat less irrational and quarrelsome, the position Q is a kind of minimax, which would represent a solution imposed by a condition that might be called that of rational quarrelsomeness. Thus, if the parties are at K, it may occur to B that, if he reduced his home strength from M_aK to M_aL, he is really no worse off militarily, as A still cannot really beat him, and he may be better off economically, as he does not have to waste all these resources on defense. The same thing

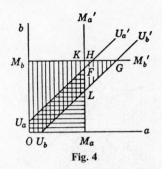

Fig. 4

may occur to A, in which case he moves to H, and the joint move lands the parties at Q. Below Q, B might feel uneasy, as A could move him into the area U_bLM_a, where he would be wiped out; similarly, to the left of Q, A might be uneasy over B's power to move him into the area U_aM_bH.

The most advantageous situation of all, of course, would be an equilibrium at O. This might be called the equilibrium of rational co-operativeness, as it is the position of which both parties are clearly best off on condition that they can trust each other. If they cannot trust each other, however, the position may be unstable, for, at this position, each party could wipe out the other by an appropriate move.

Consider now what will happen in this model if the viability boundaries U_aU_a' and U_bU_b' move closer together, as they will if either c, the LSG, or s, the distance between nations, diminishes. We recall that $OU_a = OU_b = cs$, so that a decline in c or s reduces OU_a and OU_b without changing the slope of the lines. The area of mutual viability becomes smaller and slenderer: H, L, and Q move toward K. If the home strengths of the two nations are not exactly equal, then, at some point, either H or L will coincide with K, which will then be the minimax. As c or s declines farther, we have a situation, as in Fig. 4, where there is no longer a minimax and the weaker party, in this case A, is no longer unconditionally viable. B can establish a level of home strength greater than M_aF against which A has no recourse: there is no level of home strength available to A at which B is not stronger than A at A's home base. This does not mean that A may not survive and may not be conditionally viable. The equilibrium of the Richardson process may lie in the area of mutual viability OU_aFLU_b. This, however, is either because B wills to keep A alive and presumably feels better off within this area than outside it or because B is rather unreactive and has low initial hostility.

Now let us relax the very unrealistic assumption that the home strength of each nation is constant. In Fig. 5, we suppose that the home strength of each nation is at a maximum at its greatest extent of influence where the home strength of the other is zero. Then we suppose that, for

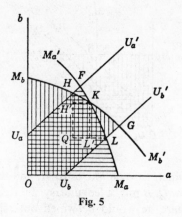

Fig. 5

each nation, as the home strength of the other nation rises, the maximum home strength of the first declines. We have, therefore, a maximum-home-strength curve for A, M_aM_a', and a similar curve for B, M_bM_b'. There will again be a viability area for A, shaded horizontally, OU_aFM_a, and a similar area for B shaded vertically, OM_bGU_b. Where these overlap is the area of mutual viability OU_aHKLU_b. The analysis is not very different from that of Fig. 3. There will be a minimax solution at Q, for, below Q, either country can be wiped out by an appropriate move of the other into region U_bLM_a or U_aHM_b, respectively. Now, however, we notice a certain difference; if B ventures above H', A can render him nonviable by moving into the area FHK, where A is viable but B is not. Similarly, if A ventures to the right of L', B can move into KLG. We have, therefore, a kind of minimax quadrilateral $QL'KH'$, within which neither party can move to ruin the other without ruining himself. If we suppose that the parties try to get away with the least amount in

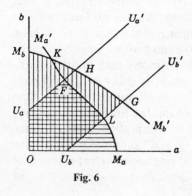

Fig. 6

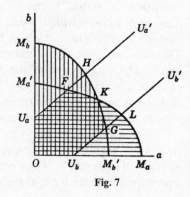

Fig. 7

defense expenditures while still remaining within this safe area, we shall end up at Q as before. In Fig. 3, of course, the minimax quadrilateral is $QLKH$.

Now suppose that we rotate the line M_aM_a' counterclockwise, indicating that the loss of home strength with loss of dominated area operates more strongly than before. The point K approaches H; the minimax quadrilateral shrinks until, when K and H coincide, it has disappeared. Beyond this, we get a condition like Fig. 6. Here, A is no longer unconditionally viable; if B increases its home strength above F, there is no move that A can make that can make it stronger than B at home. There is no minimax; A's only hope for survival is the lack of will on B's part to exterminate it. This lack of will may be rationally based, in which case we have a secure conditional viability..., or it may be a result of ignorance and inertia.

If both home strength curves bend steeply, we may get a situation like Fig. 7. This is, in fact, a not implausible system. The assumption is that the maximum home strength of any country diminishes very rapidly in the neighborhood of the viability boundary with increase in the home strength of the competitor. What is happening here is that the enemy is pushing its dominance deep into the home territory; the weaker power has less and less resources to draw upon, and its ability to resist rapidly disintegrates as the enemy pushes in. This situation is assumed to hold for both countries. We then get a situation in which neither country is unconditionally viable. There is an area of mutual conditional viability OU_aFKGU_b, but, from any point within this area except K, either country can take a move that will eliminate the other. A can move to the right into the area KGU_bM_aL, or B can move upward into the area KHM_bU_aF. The point K is a curious kind of quasi-equilibrium. If the parties are actually at K, they are likely to stay there; neither party can increase its home strength, and if either decreases its home strength, it exposes

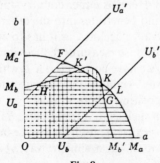

Fig. 8

itself to extinction from the other. On the other hand, if the parties are not at K, there is no sure way of getting there, for below K there is no sure way of preventing one of the parties from expanding its home strength to the point where it can overcome the other. It is possible, of course, that a Richardson process might yield an equilibrium at K, but this would be a pure accident; there is nothing inherent in the nature of the system that would give this result. This is, therefore, a very unstable relationship; it will almost always result in one of the parties gobbling up the other.

The instability of this situation may be resolved not only by conquest but by changes in the home-strength boundaries. Suppose, for instance, that A is able to make things very difficult and costly for B as B tries to advance close to A's home base. As we approach A's viability boundary $U_a U_a'$, B's home strength, then, will diminish, as in the curve $M_b HK'$ in Fig. 8. This means, in a sense, that A is concentrating on defensive weapons close to home. Not surprisingly, this restores A's unconditional viability. At any level of A's home strength within the area FHK', B can only move, vertically, we recall, to points of mutual viability or to points where B is not viable. In Fig. 8, however, B is only conditionally viable. At any level of B below K, A can move horizontally from the area of mutual viability into the area $KGU_b M_a LK$ and so can exterminate B; at any level of B above H, A can exterminate B by moving into the area FHK'. We may note that, if the line $M_b HK'$ is somewhat less steeply sloped, indicating a smaller degree of effectiveness of A's defensive measures, the point H may be above the point K, in which case we get the rather surprising result that a defensive measure on the part of one country restores unconditional viability to both, as there is a minimax area restored in which values of a and b can be found in which neither party can exterminate the other.

In Fig. 8, we suppose that only one party took these highly defensive measures; usually, however, what is open to one is also open to the other, so that Fig. 9, where both parties take highly defensive measures, is likely to develop out of Fig. 8. Here, as either country approaches the viability boundary of the other and penetrates into the other's home territory, the home strength of the invader declines, as it has to absorb a dissident and hostile population and defense measures reduces its capacity for inflicting damage. In Fig. 9, then, we have an area $QHK'L$ which is a minimax area, within the area of mutual viability in the sense that, within it, neither power can move to a position where it alone can survive. Suppose, for instance, from a position such as R, A tries to lure B into the area HFK' by disarming; B can always extricate itself and move into the area of mutual viability by disarming itself. In a similar way, A can always extricate itself from the area $LK'G$.

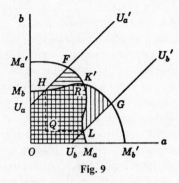

Fig. 9

In these models, we have assumed implicitly that the various boundary lines and functions were independent and that, for instance, the unconditional-viability boundaries were not affected by the position of the system on the home-strength boundaries and that the home-strength boundary of one country was not affected by the position of the home-strength boundary of the other. In fact, this assumption may not be true, and the models should be modified accordingly, even though the detailed analysis of this type of modification requires mathematical analysis well beyond the scope of this discussion. . . . For instance, a fall in the cost of transport would affect not only the viability boundaries but also the boundaries of minimum net return, which correspond, in the case of the firm, to the home-strength boundary in the models of the present discussion. Similarly, we must recognize that home strength is not a simple quantity but a complex of many factors and that a change in the structure of the defense organization of one nation may affect the home-strength boundaries of both nations. In simple cases, it is not too difficult to make the appropriate modifications in the present models, and, in any case, these interrelationships are likely to be of a second order of magnitude and do not affect the usefulness of the first-order models.

In all these cases, it is clear that a decline in LSG (*c*) or in the distance between the national centers (*s*) will bring the two viability lines closer together and will lessen the chances for a stable solution. A further condition of stability can now be added: the less powerful the principle of increasing returns to scale, or of increasing home strength with increase of area dominated, and the more powerful the opposite principle of diminishing returns to scale, the more likely are we to find stable equilibriums of national defense. The recipe for stability is to have high cost of transport of violence, countries a long way apart, and rapidly diminishing efficiency with increase of scale. It is because of a failure of all three of these conditions that we face an acute breakdown of the system of national defense in the world of today.

The question of the number of firms that, in a stable system can occupy a given closed area such as a sphere has been discussed [elsewhere] and the solution given there is generally applicable to the problem of how many nations can stably occupy a similar closed surface such as the earth. The problem does not seem to be capable of simple mathematical solutions without introducing extremely limiting assumptions; however, the broad lines of the solution are clear. The stability of the system depends on the attainment, for each contiguous pair of nations, of a certain critical value of cs. This critical value depends in part on the shape of the maximum-home-strength functions, in part on the nature of the Richardson process equations, and in part on the preference functions of the nations themselves. Given this critical value of cs, however, it is clear that any decline in c must increase the minimum value of s, the distance between the national centers, at which a stable system is possible. On a circle, the relation between s and n, the number of nations, is very simple: on a circle with circumference k, we have $n = k/s$. The larger s, the fewer nations there can be. On a homogeneous sphere, the mathematical relation is much more complicated, as we noted earlier; however, with the possibility of unimportant exceptions, the same rule follows: the farther apart the national centers, the fewer nations there can be. With every diminution in the LSG, therefore, the maximum number of independent national units consistent with stability of a system of national defense diminishes. The only possible exception to this principle would be if a diminution in the LSG resulted in a diminution in the critical value of cs. This might happen, for instance, if a general decline in the cost of transport enabled more people to travel abroad and so led to a decline in xenophobia, a more tolerant and sympathetic attitude toward other countries, and general spirit of live and let live. Even though a decline in the cost of transport will almost always cause a decline in the number of countries that can coexist in unconditional viability, it may also lead to an increase in the stability of conditional viability. This is not, one should add, a certain result; sometimes better communications corrupt good manners and travel makes people all the more self-centered and hostile to foreigners. It is, however, a possible result that should always be considered.

In this model, we have thought of the earth as a uniform globe, which, of course, it is not. The geographical heterogeneity of the earth's surface, however, in no way destroys the value of the model we have developed; indeed, as we shall see, it can be used to develop some important interpretations of the course of history.

We should not leave this theoretical model without calling attention to the modifications that may be introduced into it by the recognition of the dynamic character of the processes involved. Up to this point, we have assumed that the home strength of a nation is a function only of its area of dominance and, therefore, of the home strength of the competing nation. In fact, of course, the home strength is also a function of time. If it is below the maximum value, it can grow only at a certain maximum rate. It takes time to raise armed forces, supply them with equipment, and train them. Furthermore, a nation may be able to maintain a level of home strength for short periods that it cannot maintain indefinitely. This is somewhat analogous to the distinction made in the theory of the firm between average variable cost, which must be covered by average revenue if the firm is to survive in the short run, and the (greater) average total cost, which must be covered if it is to survive in the long run. By putting forth a great national effort, a nation may be able to sustain a very high level of home strength for a while, but the effort will exhaust it, and, inevitably, as weariness and exhaustion set in, its home strength will decline. The static theory that we have been elaborating in this chapter is essentially a theory of the long-run equilibrium of national defense; in the short run and in the dynamic course of the system, we cannot assume given levels of home strength and given boundaries of equal strength.

Nevertheless, the static theory illuminates the dynamic process. At the beginning of a war, for instance, one nation is frequently better prepared, that is, with its home strength at a higher proportion of the maximum, than its opponent. Consequently, it is able to drive deep into what previously had been its enemy's territory or dominated area. As it advances, however, the great law of diminishing strength with distance (the further, the weaker) not only comes into play to weaken the invader at the boundary of contact of the two forces but serves to strengthen the defender. Now, however, the dynamics of the situation comes into play; if the initial push of the invader is not sufficient to reach the defender's home base, as time goes on, the defender is able to mobilize his resources, and his home strength rises faster than that of the invader, who is closer to his maximum and has fewer unutilized resources to mobilize. If the invader has been exceeding his long-run home strength, then, as time goes on, exhaustion and weariness will set in, and his home strength may even decline. If his will to invade depends on the success of the invasion, then, if the initial push is halted and a stationary front established for a while, the morale element in his home strength will diminish. The defender's morale, on the other hand, is likely to increase; the halting of the invasion is a sign that the defender is, in fact, viable—something that must be a little in doubt while the invasion is proceeding—and he will have a positive image of the outcome of the conflict, with the invader repulsed and humiliated. As the invader's home strength declines and the defender's grows, the temporary equilibrium gives way; the invader starts to retreat, and, once this process begins, it may lead to a disastrous collapse in the invader's morale. It is true that, as the invader is pushed back, he gets closer to his base and his lines of communication get shorter; however, he may still be operating in hostile territory, which is a source of weakness rather than of strength, and his lines of communication can be harried by the defender's people, while the defender's lines, being in his own territory, are quite secure. Once the invasion turns back, then, it is likely that the retreat will continue right back to the old frontiers and beyond; the retreat may even turn into a rout. If the countries are big enough, of course, the erstwhile invader may rally himself as he is pushed back into his own country, as in the model of Fig. 9. Now it is the other country who is the invader and who suffers the disadvantages of invasion, and it will not be surprising if the war ends with the parties in much the same relative position in which they started.

The inference is that the static solution may be a fairly stable one, in the sense that it can survive large disturbances, if the countries are large and are both unconditionally viable. If the countries are small and close together, the static theory may give little clue to the dynamic course of history, for an initial aggression may be total, in the sense that the defending country is overrun and subjugated before it has time to reach its maximum home strength. Once this has happened, a country that is potentially viable may be suppressed or may never come into existence because of the dynamic factors in the situation. There may be an initial hump that the country finds impossible to get over by its own efforts. A general war, however, in which the dominant countries weaken each other may lower the threshold of formation of a dormant country and permit its reformation as an independent state. . . .

It is a commonplace of military history that military technology has usually exhibited a race between the offensive and the defensive armaments: each new offensive weapon has rendered obsolete the old defensive armament but has, in turn, stimulated the development of new defenses. The arrow and the spear produced the shield and the wall; the cannon and the rifle eventually produced the tank and the ironclad. The increased technical efficiency of offense generally seems to precede that of defense, perhaps because the payoffs to the innovator are greater in the case of offensive weapons. This is because offensive weapons always have a defensive aspect, through their power to destroy the offensive weapons of the enemy, whereas defensive weapons seldom have an offensive aspect. For the innovator, therefore, the development of a more efficient offensive weapon kills two birds with one stone: it

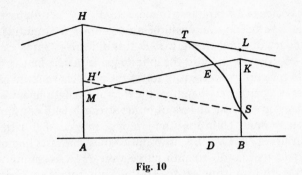

Fig. 10

makes his own threats more effective, by increasing his capacity to injure his enemy, and it makes the enemy's threats less effective, for it diminishes the enemy's power to injure by reason of the increased power of the innovator to injure the enemy's offensive weapons. The improvement of a defensive weapon from a situation of rough parity with the offensive weapons has, by contrast, very little payoff; it may slightly diminish the power of the enemy to injure the innovator, but it does little or nothing to increase the power of the innovator to injure a potential enemy. It is not surprising, therefore, that the dynamics of weapon development has always favored a constant increase both in the power and the range of offensive weapons and that the improvement in defensive weapons, where it has taken place, has been a catching up rather than a leading change....

A unilateral improvement in offensive weapons is likely to lead to a situation like Fig. 6, where the lagging party is deprived of unconditional viability.

If, now, the innovator does not take immediate advantage of his opportunity to conquer the other party, this party will imitate the innovation, and we shall have a situation like Fig. 7, in which neither of the parties is unconditionally viable and a very unstable situation results. Now there is a strong incentive to develop defensive weapons, even for one of the parties, as in Fig. 8, as this may restore his unconditional viability, and if the other party follows suit, as in Fig. 9, this may restore unconditional viability for both parties.

The distinction between defensive and offensive weapons can also be made in terms of their effects on the LSG. Thus, in Fig. 10, as in Fig. 1, *AH* is the maximum home strength of country *A* and *BK* of *B*. If there are uniform LSG's, as in the lines *HTL* and *KEM*, country *B* is clearly not unconditionally viable. Now suppose that *B* can develop defensive weapons that will change *A*'s strength line from *HTL* to *HTES*. The effect of B's defensive weapons is to increase A's LSG as A approaches B. If the effect is sufficient, there will be an equilibrium of mutual viability and a boundary of equal strength at E. It is difficult to translate changes in the loss-of-strength line into the infinite-game matrix figures of Figs. 3 to 9. A little device, however, easily solves the problem; instead of supposing that the defensive weapon alters the loss-of-strength line, we suppose that it creates an equivalent loss of home strength with constant linear, loss-of-strength lines. Thus, the strength of country A at B with the loss-of-strength curves $HTES$ is BS; it would be the same if its home strength were AH' and its loss-of-strength curve were $H'S$. Assuming a decline in home strength of A from AH to AH', moving from T to S with a fixed imaginary LSG is equivalent to the actual decline in the strength curve from T to S. This is essentially, the approach of Figs. 8 and 9; these can be interpreted as implying either a loss in its real home strength as one nation invades another's heavily defended territory or an increase in the LSG, which is the slope of the loss-of-strength curve, as the invasion proceeds, with a corresponding decline in the virtual home strength such as AH'.

This leads to a very important distinction that corresponds roughly, though not exactly, to the usual distinction between offensive and defensive weapons. This is the distinction between innovations that diminish one's own LSG (aggressive) and innovations that increase the opponent's LSG (defensive). The first type of innovation has the effect of making existing nations less viable and the existing equilibrium, if it exists, more precarious; the second has the effect of increasing the viability of the existing nations and system. We have seen, however, that, from a situation of equilibrium, the aggressive innovation is much more likely to pay off to the innovator, especially if he can take advantage of it quickly, before it is imitated. This is one reason for the observed phenomenon of the secular decline through history of the LSG and the secular rise in the minimum size of the viable nation; defense weapons are always fighting a rear-guard action. In addition, there is the phenomenon of technical development in general making for cheaper transport; the payoffs for improvements in transport are high in all fields, whereas there are seldom payoffs for increasing costs of transport except through highly artificial means like tariffs, which appear in this analysis as a thoroughly defensive weapon. General improvement in means of transport are nearly always reflected in a decline in the LSG, simply because the transport of violence always involves the transport of men and things.

The possibility of reversing the LSG, at least for a certain distance, is illustrated in Fig. 11. This is the problem of the effect of *bases*, or secondary centers of home strength. By establishing a base at G, the

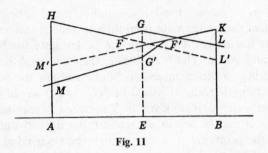

Fig. 11

country *A* may actually raise its on-the-spot strength between *F* and *G*, and this raises it above what would have been everywhere beyond *G*. The naval bases of Britain and the air bases of the United States are good examples of the attempt to overcome the factor of loss of strength with distance. In the special sense in which we have used the terms, the off-territory base may be both defensive and offensive. Insofar as it raises the country's strength line, as in *FGL* of Fig. 11, above what it would have been without the base (*FL'*), it is clearly an offensive weapon, making mutual viability more difficult. A base may also have the effect of lowering the strength line of the opponent. With *A*'s base located at *E* in Fig. 11, *B*'s loss-of-strength line may well be *KF'G'M* instead of *KM'*. The base requires an effort to circumvent, and this reduces *B*'s strength at all points beyond it; the reduction, in fact, probably begins as soon as the effective range of the base is reached at *F'*. In this sense, therefore, the base is defensive. It is this offensive-defensive character of a base which makes bases so touchy a subject in international negotiations; it is easy for the owner of a base to see only its defensive aspects and for the other party to see only the offensive aspects.

This model also serves to illustrate the theory of the buffer state. Thus, in Fig. 12, suppose we have a buffer state C_1C_2 between the two main centers of power. The strength gradient of each of the two main

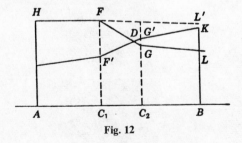

Fig. 12

centers dips as it passes through the buffer state, indicating that the organization of the buffer state is enough to reduce the power of main centers in its territory, even though the buffer state itself may not be unconditionally viable. The buffer state, therefore, may restore unconditional viability to the main centers; thus, without the buffer state in Fig. 12, A's strength gradient would be HL', and B would no longer be unconditionally viable. It is clearly in B's interest, therefore, to establish a buffer state. It may be less in A's interest, but if the dynamic situation is such that the positions of A and B might be reversed at some future date, the maintenance of the buffer state may be in B's interest also. The fact that the point of equal strength (D) between A and B may lie within the boundary of the buffer state also may reduce tension, as there is less gain to either party in trying to move the position of D. Hence, there will be less chance of an arms race, and the whole situation is more stable than it would be in the absence of the buffer state. The buffer state must however, have enough inner coherence in its own right not to be dominated by either of the major powers; otherwise, fear of domination by one may lead the other to extinguish it or lead the major powers to divide it. Poland in the eighteenth century was a good example of a buffer state that failed; Belgium, Holland, Luxembourg, and perhaps Switzerland are examples of states which have perhaps never been unconditionally viable but which have survived because of their buffer situation.

III

Internal Determinants of National Behavior

●

The preceding section dealt primarily with the ways in which the structure of the international system limited or otherwise affected the behavior of national governments, using the activity of the firm in the market as the analogue. Economists have to develop detailed hypotheses about the behavior of various decision-making units—the individual consumer, the firm, the labor union, or the nation in foreign trade. Often choice is sharply circumscribed by market conditions, but in other circumstances actions depend heavily on internal decision-making processes. The analytical problem is almost identical with the "level of analysis" problem in international politics, where we are faced with the need to weigh and evaluate numerous internal and external influences on foreign policy.

Few analytical efforts devote themselves solely either to the systemic (market) level or to subsystemic determinants, although the emphasis in the last section was on the former. Here, we shall look at several papers that give more attention to "internal" analysis—the characteristics of the firm or of its particular personnel which influence decision making. The first paper, by R. Joseph Monsen, Jr., and Anthony Downs, lies on the border line between organization theory and economics proper. In attempting to develop a theory to explain firms' organizational and market behavior, the authors distinguish between different kinds of ownership and managerial structures. Managers do not necessarily have the same interests as owners, and when the two functions are separated, the firm may develop in ways quite inconsistent with what the majority of stockholders might consider to be in their best interests.

Traditionally, economic theory has assumed that entrepreneurs act to maximize their profits. Managers, however, may be concerned primarily not with the firm's profit but with maximizing their own income. This will require certain satisfactions for the owners, but, the authors contend, the managers' security of tenure may best be served by avoiding behavior that may *seem* risky or result in sharp fluctuations in the firm's earnings. The punishment for grievous error, they suggest, is greater than is the reward for outstanding success. Where ownership is widely diffused, these divergencies of interest are likely to be especially severe because of difficulties in obtaining and distributing to the stockholders accurate information on the use of the firm's resources. Furthermore, the managers at all levels within the firm may go to great lengths to manipulate *other managers or shareholders* through their control over information. Large size particularly results in delegation and in consequent vulnerability, by the top managers, to manipulation of their information sources by subordinates.

The implications for national foreign-policy making are not hard to perceive. The notion of a "national interest" in maximizing power is directly analogous to the idea that firms maximize profits, but, in fact, there is no uniform national interest for all strata and elements of the population. There are some interests, say in the mere survival of the state, that are shared throughout it, but particular goals will be ranked differently by various subgroups. Leaders may be more interested in extending their own tenure in office than in pursuing a course that would offer the greatest hypothetical increment of national power, especially if such a course involves high risks and high stakes. Subordinates' security concerns may run counter to those of their superiors—they may avoid difficult decisions or high-risk innovations that may be necessary for the welfare of the nation or for maintaining the leadership's long-term domestic power base. And certainly the manipulation of information, both within governmental structures and from government to voters (shareholders), is not unknown in any political system, though it clearly is more common in some than in others. If a policy a leader cherishes goes badly, his subordinates may not tell him of its failure.

Just as Monsen and Downs can distinguish among various types of firms according to the relationship between owners and managers, we can make the same sort of distinctions among types of national political systems, between governmental structures providing relatively close popular control of the leadership and those where the men at the top of the pyramid are able more effectively to pursue private goals that diverge from the general ones. Thus, the interests perceived as central will vary not only within nations but across nations according to different types of decision-making systems subjected to different types and degrees of popular control. The national interest as a unique set of goals that are (or ought to be) pursued by a government is not a powerful explanatory variable, and this article helps to suggest why it fails.

●

20

A Theory of Large Managerial Firms

R. Joseph Monsen, Jr., and Anthony Downs

1. Types of Firms

In most economic theory, questions regarding the relationships among different parts of the firm simply do not arise. Instead, economists generally assume that the firm can be treated as a single person, with a unified and integrated set of motives and the ability to carry out its goals without any wasted effort except that imposed by the technical limitations of production and distribution. There are some exceptions to this viewpoint, but those holding other views have not succeeded in shaking the dominance of the traditional concept. For example, A. A. Berle, Jr., and Gardiner Means long ago pointed out that the separation of ownership from management created situations which traditional theory was not adequate to deal with.[1] In sociology, a sizable literature has grown up concerning bureaucracy in large organizations, and much of it is applicable to large-scale firms. However, thus far the theory of bureaucracy and the theory of the firm have not been successfully integrated.

There are so many different kinds of firms in the real world that any method of classifying them is bound to be arbitrary. Nevertheless, we have developed several categories of firms based on two variables:

Reprinted from *The Journal of Political Economy*, **73**, 3 (June 1965), pp. 222–236, by permission of The University of Chicago Press. Copyright, 1965, by The University of Chicago Press.

[1] *The Modern Corporation and Private Property* (New York: Macmillan, 1932). A later work on the same subject is Berle's *Power without Property* (New York: Harcourt, Brace & World, 1959).

size, and the relationship between the owners of the firm and those who manage it. We have concentrated solely upon these two because they have a direct relationship to the question of whether or not the firm maximizes profits.

Our purpose in using size as a criterion for distinguishing among firms is to separate those with bureaucratic management structures from those that do not have such structures. Therefore, we will consider any firm *small* if it has less than 1000 employees, and *large* if it has 1000 or more employees. This boundary line between small and large firms is admittedly arbitrary, but it will serve our purposes in the present analysis.

There are also many different relationships between the owners of firms and those who actually manage them (that is, the highest-ranking men in the management structure). As a start toward categorizing these relationships, we propose the following catalogue of firms:

1. *Owner-managed firms* are those managed by the people who own controlling interests in the firm (whether it is a corporation, a partnership, or some other type of organization).

2. *Managerial firms* are those managed by men who do not own anywhere near a controlling interest in them (or any interest at all). Such firms can be further divided into:

a. *Diffused ownership managerial firms* in which no one person or organized coalition of persons owns a controlling interest in the firm.

b. *Concentrated ownership managerial firms* in which one person or an organized coalition of persons owns a controlling interest in the firm and (presumably) exercises control over the management. For all purposes of our analysis, such firms are nearly identical with owner-managed firms. Therefore, we will use the term *managerial firms* to refer only to diffused ownership managerial firms.

3. *Nonownership firms* are those legally considered nonprofit organizations. "Ownership" of such firms does not include the legal right to receive earnings from them. Moreover, such firms are usually entirely controlled by trustees or directors with no ownership relation to them at all.

4. *Fiduciarily owned firms* are those whose "owners" are persons making capital payments into the firms primarily for purposes other than receiving income or capital gains therefrom. Examples of such firms are mutual insurance companies and pension funds. The managers of such firms are normally similar to trustees and usually have no significant ownership in the firms themselves.

It seems clear from the catalogue presented that the traditional theory of the firm does not apply equally well to all types of firms. For example, it is not obvious that nonownership firms maximize profits, since they are by definition nonprofit organizations. Moreover, fiduciarily owned firms probably have a much stronger orientation toward tempering profit maximization with considerations of security than owner-managed firms. However, our analysis will not deal with these types of firms any further, but will instead concentrate on managerial firms. Our only point in introducing this catalogue of firms—which could undoubtedly be improved and, we hope, will be—is to illustrate our beliefs that (1) different principles of behavior should be formulated for different types of firms, and (2) the traditional principle of profit-maximization really applies to only a limited number of types—even though they may be extremely important.

2. The Basic Theory

A. *Background Structure*

This article advances a theory about the way that certain firms make decisions under relatively realistic conditions. Specifically, the following conditions will be assumed:

1. The firms involved are large corporations with ownership divided among a great many stockholders. No one stockholder has anywhere near a controlling interest.

2. Each firm has a board of directors elected by its stockholders. This board has ultimate power over the firm's policies and can replace any of its executives (though in some cases it is effectively controlled by those executives).

3. Each firm is operated by a set of managers arranged in a hierarchical pyramid. This pyramid contains at least the following three layers:

a. Top management consists of those few key executives who are involved in making the basic policy and planning decisions.

b. Middle management consists of those operating executives under top management who are responsible for carrying out various specialized tasks within the firm. There may be several horizontal layers within the middle management structure. The lowest level of middle management has direct authority over lower management.

c. Lower management consists of supervisory personnel at the foreman or comparable level. Lower management has direct authority over production or lowest-level clerical personnel.

4. Managers (especially top managers) may own stock in their respective firms. However, the proportion of stock which any one manager or group of managers in a firm controls is so small that it does not

constitute anywhere near a controlling interest in the firm. Moreover, the stock dividends of each manager comprise a relatively small part of his income in relation to his salary and bonuses.

5. Each firm operates in a world of uncertainty and risk in which knowledge is costly and perfect knowledge normally unobtainable. These conditions prevail regarding both the firm's relations with the rest of the world, and relations among various parts of the firm itself.

6. The degree of oligopoly or monopoly prevalent in each firm's industry is not specified. Our theory does not offer any solution to the oligopoly problem. However, we will assume that (*a*) each firm operates in a market which contains enough competition so that the firm can conceivably face some risks regarding its long-term survival, but (*b*) it enjoys enough of a monopolistic position so that it can usually earn profits larger than the "normal" level associated with a perfectly competitive industry.

Under these conditions, there are three classes of decision makers who can potentially affect a firm's policies and behavior: owners, members of the board of directors, and managers. Since managers are usually represented on the board of directors by the very top executives of the firm, there are really only two autonomous groups in the firm's decision-making structure: owners and managers. Where ownership is extremely fragmented and no large stockholders exist, the managers often effectively control the board of directors through proxy agreements. However, we assume that the board is sufficiently independent of the managers to punish extremely poor management performance and reward very good performance.

B. Central Hypotheses

The central hypotheses of our theory concern the *motivations* of owners and managers. We believe that traditional theory is correct in assuming that the people who operate business firms are primarily motivated by their own self-interest. But pursuit of self-interest is a characteristic of human persons, not organizations. A *firm* is not a real person, even when incorporated; hence, it really cannot have motives or maximize anything. When traditional theorists stated that *firms* maximize profits, they really meant that the *people who run firms* make decisions so as to maximize the profits of the firms. As long as firms were operated by their owners, this assumption was consistent with the self-interest axiom, because the profits of the firms were the main incomes of their owners.

But in most of the largest and most significant modern firms, ownership and management are functions carried out by two entirely separate groups of people. Even management itself is really a combination of functions carried out by different groups. Thus, the entity normally referred to as *the firm* has, in fact, become a number of different subentities. The people in each of these subgroups within the firm are still primarily motivated by self-interest. However, their changed relationship to the firm as a whole has changed the way in which their self-interest leads them to behave regarding the firm's profits. Therefore, our theory is really nothing more than the application of the self-interest axiom in traditional theory to a new type of firm: one in which ownership is separate from management; and management itself consists of a bureaucratic hierachy containing several layers.

Our two central hypotheses can be stated as follows:

1. *Owners desire to have each firm managed so that it provides a steady income from dividends and gradual appreciation of the market price of the stock.*
2. *Managers act so as to maximize their own lifetime incomes.*

Since these two hypotheses are the foundations of our whole analysis, we will examine each in detail.

C. The Motivation of Owners

Although every stockholder certainly prefers a rapid rate of advance in the price of his stock to a slow rate, most owners also prefer a slow but steady rise to an erratic combination of rapid rises and equally rapid declines. This is probably true even if the total rise would be slightly higher in the case of erratic movement. A slow but steady rise preserves each owner's ability to get back his original investment plus a profit at any time, whereas up-and-down price movements create uncertainty in his mind about the future price of the stock, thereby creating an apparent risk that he might suffer a loss if he had to sell at a certain moment. Since stockholders typically know far less about the firm's situation than managers, such uncertainty can exist in the minds of stockholders even if the managers know the erratic short-run movements of the stock's price result from factors which will work out favorably in the long run.

Another important characteristic of owners is their ignorance of the alternative policies available to the firm. Since owners are remote from the firm's actual decision making, they learn about the firm's performance only ex post, and then only through "official" reports from top management (unless the firm has so blundered that its mistakes have been publicly reported). As a result, owners have no reliable way of determining whether the firm is maximizing its profits and the growth of its stock prices or not. Their only yardstick consists of comparisons with other similar firms. Even this yardstick is an imprecise one, for no two firms are ever exactly alike, and the performance of every firm in any one year is usually conditioned by some unique events applicable to it alone. Therefore, owners can assess the performance of their own top management only by a relatively general comparison with other similar firms and with the stock market as a whole.

The ignorance of stockholders drastically reduces the amount of marginal switching they do from one stock to another that appears to be enjoying better performance. They simply cannot accurately judge small differences in quality of performance. Moreover, the capital gains tax "rakes off" 25 percent of all value appreciation every time a stockholder switches from one stock to another. Thus the force of competition among different stocks, which would in theory be expected to put pressure on top management to *maximize* the rate of growth of its stock price, is in fact severely weakened by both ignorance and the tax structure.

As a result, owners tend to act as "satisficers" instead of "maximizers." *In our interpretation "satisficers" differ from "maximizers" only in capability, not in intention.* They would like to maximize, but the limitations of their ignorance and their finite capacity cause them to adopt behavior different from that of a theoretical maximizer. Consequently, if the price increases of the firm's stock meet some minimal criterion of "satisfactory growth" in comparison with alternative investments, and dividends do not fall, they will approve of the firm's top management. If the performance of the firm is so poor that these results are clearly not being attained, they will disapprove of the firm's top management.

Owners express their approval or disapproval of managers in the annual elections of the board of directors. However, because of the diffusion of ownership, it takes an extraordinarily poor management performance to trigger a real uprising among stockholders—an uprising violent enough to elect directors who will remove or drastically discipline the top managers. Normally, top management controls the board of directors through proxy agreements; hence the key executives are self-perpetuating, unless they radically disappoint the owners.

Nevertheless, fear of potential rebellion among stockholders imposes a latent check on the actions of the incumbent management. This fear is increased by the operations of professional "outside raiders" who specialize in rallying dissident owners against incumbent managers. The

New York Central Railroad over the years has provided a number of examples of revolts sparked by such "outsiders."

Moreover, although a very poor management performance may result in a rebellion, a very good one does not usually cause a powerful movement among stockholders to reward their managers with lavish bonuses. Hence, *the punishment for grievous error is greater than the reward for outstanding success.* This asymmetry between failure and success tends to make the managers of a diffused-ownership firm behave differently from the managers of the type of owner-managed firm envisioned by traditional theory.

Although a majority of stock owners in the United States seek "safe growth" as described previously, a certain minority are far more interested in rapid appreciation of stock prices. They are the buyers of so-called growth stocks. However, we are excluding these owners from our analysis because (1) Most of the large corporations in the United States with widely diffused ownership are not "growth" corporations. But our theory applies only to diffused-ownership firms. (2) "Growth" stocks comprise a small minority of all stocks (although they receive a great deal of publicity).

D. The Motivation of Managers

Our second central hypothesis is simply the application of self-interest to the managers of large firms. Today the largest, most significant firms in the United States are owned by thousands of individual stockholders who are remote from actual management and decision-making. Conversely, the men who really run these firms are professional managers. Although they may own some stock, their ownership is usually a *result* of their executive positions rather than the *cause* of their holding such positions. Also, their incomes are not identical with the firm's profits, and may not even vary in any strict relation to the firm's profits. As a result, when managers act in their own self-interest, they do not always act in the interest of the owners.

What *is* in their self-interest is maximizing *their own* incomes. As prudent men, they consider their (discounted) incomes over the course of their *entire working lives*, not just in the current year, or while working for their current employer. These incomes include both *monetary elements* (salaries, bonuses, capital gains from stock options, etc.) and *nonmonetary elements* (leisure, prestige, power, etc.). The non-monetary aspects of income can be equated at the margin with dollars; hence, we can conceive of the managers as maximizing the present value of their lifetime incomes in dollar terms.

The pursuit of self-interest by managers also has important repercussions upon relationships *among managers* within the firm itself. Just as it is not always in the interest of top management to maximize the returns to the owners, it may not always be in the interest of the middle management to carry out the orders of top management. It is necessary, therefore, to break the firm down into component parts in order to discover the levels on which individual motivations actually operate.

It should be pointed out that the self-interest of individual managers has definite limits. We certainly do not mean to depict corporate managers as avaricious, grasping individuals willing to break every moral law in their ruthless drive to success—as the jackets of some business novels have put it. We do not impute any more self-interest to managers as a group than to the members of other social or economic groups. We merely assume that an important fraction of all managers is sufficiently motivated by self-interest to count its own long-run welfare as more important than the welfare of either the owners of the firm or the other managers therein.

3. Impact of Bureaucracy on Behavior of Firms

In order to analyze in more detail the way in which managers in very large firms make decisions, it is first necessary to examine the *context* of managerial decision making. Each manager occupies a certain position in the organizational pyramid formed by the corporate hierarchy. Above him are his *superiors*, who have control over his promotions, salary, bonuses, and other elements of his success. Below him are his *subordinates*, whose promotions and income he analogously influences and whose efforts he depends upon to produce results pleasing to his superiors. Alongside him at other positions on the same level of the hierarchy are his *peers*. They are engaged in specialized tasks different from his own, but they are competing with him for eventual promotion to higher levels. *The basic problem which each manager faces is the necessity of pleasing his superior to attain advances in income* (either through promotion to higher-paying jobs or higher salary in his existing job). In the case of top management, the superiors involved are represented by the board of directors and the stockholders.

From the point of view of each firm's owners, the function of managers and employees is to make the greatest possible contribution toward achieving the objectives of the owners. But whatever the owners' objectives may be, we believe that *the bureaucratic structure of large firms will cause management to deviate systematically from achieving ownership objectives.* This will occur because (1) the motives of managers are not identical with the motives of owners, as we have pointed out, and (2) in large companies, the nature of the administrative structure makes it impossible for the owners to control the behavior of managers completely—or even for top managers to control the behavior of those below them completely.

The following specific factors may cause managerial behavior to deviate from ownership objectives:

1. It is often very difficult to measure accurately the contribution made by each individual employee to profits, stock-price gains, or any other financial objectives. In such instances—which may cover a majority of management personnel in a large corporation—superiors are driven to use subjective impressions or irrelevant objective tests they have set up as means of deciding whom to promote. Therefore they must promote men who somehow make the most favorable impression on them, and these may not necessarily be the men who actually contribute most to ownership (or top management) objectives.

2. The superiors themselves may not be pursuing policies which are identical with those of the firm's owners. If so, they might tend to promote men who carried out the policies they were pursuing rather than men who carried out policies which maximized the owners' objectives.

Insofar as either of these factors is in effect, managers on the middle and lower levels of the corporate bureaucracy will find themselves best served by actions which create the most favorable impression upon their superiors, regardless of the impact of such actions upon corporate profits or other ownership gains. Of course, the subjective impressions of their superiors will by no means be divorced entirely from factual evidence; hence, no manager can completely ignore the possible objective measureable effects of his behavior upon corporate prosperity. But the tools which measure individual contributions to profits or stock-price increases are often very imprecise, especially regarding such nonselling and non-production jobs as public relations, personnel management, and advertising. Therefore, an individual manager may be able to choose among several alternative actions which will affect profits or stock prices in the long run, but which will have no differing effects upon the objective indexes which his superiors must rely on to rate the quality of his performance. If a number of executives in a firm select among such policies so as to please their superiors rather than to maximize ownership objectives, the cumulative effect of such choices may in the long run cause a substantial loss of potential benefits to the firm's owners.

Even more important are the long-run effects of certain actions managers may take to advance their own interests which reduce the firm's efficiency. Since the managers are motivated by the advancement of their own incomes, they will perform acts which impair the firm's efficiency if (1) those acts tend to advance their own interests, and (2) it is impossible or very difficult for their superiors to discover these acts. Gordon Tullock has presented an ingenious and persuasive theory of political bureaucracies which encompasses a number of such actions.[2] Among those applicable to corporate bureaucracies are the following:

1. *Managers at every level of the corporate pyramid tend to screen information in their possession so that only data favorable to them are passed upward to their superiors.* Insofar as cost accounting and other auditing techniques administered by outsiders are available to the superiors, this cannot be done. But there is always a considerable element of judgment in information flowing through the corporate hierarchy. Hence, managers can screen out judgment factors unfavorable to them before they pass data upward to those who have authority over their own incomes and appurtenances. Also, in order to please superiors, managers may tend to pass to them only information that verifies the desires of the superiors, or proves that their decisions were wise.

If the corporate hierarchy has many levels, the cumulative effect of this screening process may become substantial. For example, assume that the top level of a corporation is designated the A level, the next level, the B level, etc. and that there are five levels in all. Each A executives has a number of B-level men (say, three) under him; each B executive has a similar group of C-level men under him; and so on, down to the lowest or E-level, which consists of men "in the field" who receive information "first hand." In theory, each man passes on information to his superior, who winnows the most important data from the many reports made to him and passes those upward to *his* superior. This process is repeated up to the A level, where the top men make decisions based on the information emerging from the hierarchy below them. Thus, screening information is a legitimate part of each manager's job. But he may deliberately (or even unconsciously) suppress some of the information which his superiors need to know because that information is either unfavorable to himself or displeasing to his superiors. If each manager thus suppresses only 10 percent of the data, he should pass upward if top management is to be properly informed, then managers at the A level will receive only 66 percent of the important data fed into the pyramid at the E level ($.9^4 = .656$).

Thus, the tendency for managers to screen information may cause top management to be systematically misinformed through (*a*) failure

---

[2] "A General Theory of Politics" (undated and unpublished mimeographed manuscript).

to learn vital facts, especially ones adverse to lower management levels, and (*b*) a tendency to be told only what they want to hear.

2. *Managers at every level tend to carry out only part of the orders given to them.* Since the personnel of each corporation are pursuing their own interests instead of the firm's, they will be reluctant to carry out any orders which would reduce their income, power, prestige, or chances of advancement. To some extent, they must obey such orders because they will be fired for insubordination if they flatly refuse. However, the vigor with which they execute such policies, their attention to proper follow-up procedures, and their imaginative application of these policies in new situations may be minimized without any actual insubordination. The technique of "kicking it around until it disappears" is well known in all large organizations.

The cumulative effects of such partial failure to execute orders can be very great if a corporation has many layers in its organization hierarchy. In the case of the five-level organization cited previously, a failure by each layer of managers below level A to carry out just 5 percent of the orders they receive from their superiors would result in only 81 percent of the top management's orders being carried out by the lowest level personnel ($.95^4 = .814$). Moreover, some allowance must also be made for inefficiency in carrying out orders due to incompetence, inertia, and misunderstanding.

It is true that cost accounting, auditing, and other objective performance reports can significantly reduce the ability of subordinates to practice undetected insubordination. Nevertheless, no large corporation actually carries out the policies established by its leaders in precisely the manner originally envisioned by those leaders.

We realize that there are many techniques that owners and top managers can use to counteract the inefficiences discussed. Corporate spies, peer-group pressures, personal ties between members of top management and lower management, random inspections, and a host of other devices are often used to produce closer conformance of subordinates' behavior to the desires and policies of owners and top managers. Nevertheless, we believe that all of these remedies are only partially successful in very large organizations. As a result, the inefficiencies described cause large firms to deviate systematically and significantly from the course of action that would in fact maximize attainment of the owners' objectives—or even the objectives of top management.

These inefficiencies are inherent in all *large* organizations. Hence, they will exist not only in large managerial firms with diffused ownership but also in large nonprofit organizations, large owner-managed firms, and even large government agencies. Therefore, even if we agreed with traditional theory that the owners of a firm wish to maximize profits (and we do agree in the case of owner-managed firms), we would contend that the difference between *owner* motivation and *managerial* motivation will cause systematic deviations from profit-maximizing behavior as long as the firm is large enough so that the owners themselves cannot supervise all facets of its activities.

When such large size exists, the owners must yield some discretion over the firm's behavior to managers whose goals are not identical with the goals of the owners. The manager at the top of a large firm, or the owner in a profit-maximizing firm, must delegate authority to others (that is, permit screening of information and give some discretion to his subordinates in carrying out his orders) because his own personal *capacity* to handle information and decisions is limited at a level below the amount of information and problems generated by the organization. This is a function of *size*. However it does not *necessarily* create inefficiency. *Inefficiency* arises whenever such delegation of authority leads to results other than those which are optimal from the viewpoint of the top man. But nonoptimal results may occur because the *goals* of the persons to whom he has delegated authority are different from his own. If these subordinates had goals precisely identical to his own, then they would act as mechanical extensions of his own capacity. That is the implicit assumption of the classical literature on the firm to which we object.

Thus, in essence, some behavior which is nonoptimal from the viewpoint of the top man arises because of *both* size and goal divergence. Large size is what requires him to delegate authority in the first place; but goal divergence can cause that delegation to create nonoptimal results.

Even if the top man had subordinates whose goals were exactly identical to his own, some inefficiencies of a *technical* nature might arise, again due to the limited capacity of each individual decision maker in the firm. For example, specialists working in different parts of the firm whose activities had unforeseen overlapping effects might not realize this fact until some uncoordinated behavior had taken place; that is, until the behavior of one somehow impeded the plans of the other, unbeknown to the first. This kind of inefficiency is due *entirely* to the size of the firm; that is, to the fact that individuals have limited capacities and the firm is larger than their capacities. But behavior of the firm which is not optimal from the viewpoint of the top man can be caused *either* by size alone (technical inefficiency) or by a combination of size and divergent goals (technical plus motivational inefficiency). Screening, of course, arises because of size. But screening per se is not necessarily a form of inefficiency. It can lead to inefficiency without any difference in motives, but it does not *always* lead to inefficiency, *unless* a difference of motives is also present. Then screening will always create inefficiency to some extent.

4. Implications of the Theory Regarding Behavior of Management

Now that we have set forth our basic theory and examined the bureaucratic context of managerial decision making, we will explore the theory's implications regarding the behavior of managers at various levels within the firm.

A. Top-Management Behavior

1. *The organizational setting.* The top managers in a large firm are those few key executives who are involved in making basic policy and planning decisions. They are normally paid for their performance in three ways: (a) by salaries and bonuses, (b) by stock options, and (c) by expense accounts and other untaxed perquisites. However, high personal income-tax rates limit the amount of their salaries and bonuses they can retain, and they cannot *retain* any wealth from expense accounts and other similar untaxed benefits. Therefore, top managers normally regard stock options as a very significant form of compensation. Hence, top management normally has a direct and powerful interest in the *market price* of the firm's stock. Clearly, creation of such an interest is the primary justification of the stock-option arrangement from the owners' point of view, although the nature and size of the arrangement is usually determined by the managers themselves.

An important part of top management's environment consists of groups outside the firm's administrative structure who are in a position to challenge the quality of top management's performance. They include labor unions, government officials, and the public at large. Strong criticism from any of these groups can seriously tarnish the general public image of all-around competence which top management seeks to foster by "getting along well" with all important groups. This type of public image is far ... more significant to top management in a diffused-owner-ship firm than in an owner-managed firm or a concentrated-ownership firm. When ownership is diffused among thousands of stockholders, the owners are almost indistinguishable from the general public insofar as top management is concerned; hence, the public image of the firm is very likely to be the owner's image too. Moreover, stockholders have so few contacts with management that any widely circulated criticism of top management is likely to convince many stockholders that "where there's smoke, there's fire." Therefore, top management is often highly sensitive to criticism from major groups outside the firm.

2. *Top management's promotional strategy.* The best way for top management to maximize its own lifetime income is to "keep the stockholders happy." This normally involves three basic policies:

a. *Carefully screening all information which is forwarded to stockholders or the public at large* so that it reflects an outstanding management performance. The results of this policy can be readily seen by reading a typical annual report or attending an annual stockholders' meeting. Of course, professional reporting agencies like the *Wall Street Journal* provide some objective check on management's ability to suppress unfavorable information. However, it is quite easy for managers to conceal a great deal of inefficiency from such "outsiders," especially since only outstanding blunders make good news copy.

b. *Directing the firm toward achievement of constant or slightly rising dividends plus steadily increasing stock prices.* However, top management need only attain a "satisfactory" rate of stock-price growth, not a "maximum" one.

c. *Maintaining a "public image" of competence by avoiding controversy and criticism.* Public criticism of the firm or controversy about its policies tends to contradict this "image" and raise doubts in the minds of the stockholders about the wisdom of retaining the existing top management.

3. *Implications of top-management behavior.* The result of top management's employing the policies presented here is that the firm (a) is more likely to avoid risky decisions, (b) will have less variability of earnings, (c) may grow more slowly, and (d) will be less likely to go bankrupt than it would if the managers sought to maximize profits. Top management will avoid highly risky decisions because they might cause the earnings of the firm to fluctuate instead of growing steadily, even if the total profits of the firm would be larger with fluctuating earnings. Top management abhors fluctuating earnings for the following reasons:

a. If the earnings in a given year decline, the price of the stock may fall. This would be repugnant to all owners—including the top managers themselves—and might cause the owners to throw out top management, especially if the stock market in general has risen.

b. Stocks with fluctuating earnings generally have lower price-earnings ratios than those with steadily rising earnings. It is clearly in the interest of all owners—including top managers with stock options—to maintain high price-earnings ratios.

Thus, the attention of management is focused on stock *prices* rather than *earnings* (profits), which are viewed as means to obtain higher stock prices rather than as ends in themselves. Therefore, if top management must choose between (*a*) maximizing profits over a given period by accepting fluctuating earnings, or (*b*) achieving total profits by maintaining steadily rising annual earnings, it will normally choose the latter. Therefore, diffused-ownership firms will experience less *variability of earnings* than firms which try to maximize profits.

In our opinion, this relatively conservative attitude by top management would lead to slower growth than a "pure" policy of profit maximization *among those firms which survive*. Other implications of our hypothesis and forecasts consistent with it concerning top management behavior are as follows:

a. Research and development expenditures are more likely to be budgeted for steady yearly growth than for "crash" expansion of promising innovations.

b. Diffused-ownership firms will exhibit a strong predilection for diversification of products, especially through merger, as a means of reducing risks taken on any one product or line of products. Since diversification through merger tends to reduce the rate of return on capital, owner-managers would be less likely to adopt such policies.

c. Financing rapid expansion through additional stock offerings is less likely to be used by top management in diffused-ownership firms than by owner-managers. In many cases, the original owners of a firm which expands rapidly use sales of common stock to "buy themselves out" of the corporation, thus capitalizing on their original ownership interest. Managers whose only stock comes from stock options are more likely to adopt internal financing, bank borrowing, or bond issues for such financing so as not to dilute their own interests. Among long-established firms, both owner-managed and managerial types will probably avoid additional equity financing with equal distaste because of its dilution effects. However, managers may be willing to finance through stock offerings if they feel that the additional capital will enable the firm to rapidly expand sales. The work of McGuire, Chiu, and Elbing has shown that executive incomes are significantly correlated to firm sales.[3] Under the circumstances given, then, professional management will have to decide which course of action will most likely maximize their lifetime incomes—raising less capital from internal financing or obtaining greater financing (and stock dilution) from stock offerings.

d. Top management will be much more sensitive to public, union, and government criticism than owner-managers would be. Hence, top managers will be more conciliatory in their public dealings than might be required for profit maximization.

[3] J. W. McGuire, J. S. Y. Chiu, and A. O. Elbing, "Executive Incomes, Sales and Profits," *American Economic Review* (September 1962).

e. Top managers will use their roles in the firm to enhance their own personal prestige and stature. As a result, they will contribute to local causes and participate in community affairs more than they should from a purely profit-maximizing point of view.

f. In order to stabilize future profits, avoid controversy, and prevent adverse publicity, top management may make concessions to labor unions more readily than owner-managers would. This will tend to reduce profits below the level which would be attained by a truly profit-maximizing firm.

g. Expense accounts are likely to be more extravagant in managerial firms than they would be if managers really maximized returns to owners. Although expense-account benefits and salaries are both deductible, salaries are a much more visible and easily checked form of management compensation. Therefore, managers will seek to expand expense-account benefits in order to raise their total compensation without attracting the attention of owners. This will result in greater total compensation for them than is required to retain their services. The fact that such non-salary benefits will influence their choices among firms (and, hence, may appear to be a necessary part of their compensation by each firm) does not destroy this argument. Managers *as a group* are probably extracting rent because of inflated expense accounts; that is, they are compensated more in *all* managerial firms than is necessary to keep them from becoming nonmanagers. Thus, what may appear as true costs to individual firms are still an excessive reduction of profits among all managerial firms compared with what profits would be if truly maximized.

h. Managerial firms are likely to respond more slowly to declines in profits than they would if they really pursued profit maximization. Since managers wish to preserve their personal prerogatives (such as large expense accounts) and do not suffer directly from lower profits, they will be willing to "ride out" a sudden decline in profits without cutting back expenditures in the hope that it will be temporary. In contrast, true profit-maximizers would exhibit no such inertia but would immediately alter their existing behavior patterns. However, if lower profits continue, even managerial firms will adjust their behavior so as to avoid having lower yearly earnings cause any decline in stock prices (if possible).

B. Middle-Management Behavior

1. *The organizational setting.* Middle managers are those operating executives under top management who are responsible for carrying out various specialized tasks within the firm. Middle managers are normally

paid for their performance primarily by salaries and bonuses and second-arily by expense accounts and other untaxed perquisites.

2. *Middle management's promotional strategy.* The best way for middle managers to maximize their lifetime incomes is to increase the size of those incomes by being promoted to higher-paying positions within the firm or in other firms. Since their promotions are determined by the recommendations of their superiors, their efforts to obtain promo-tion consist essentially of doing whatever will most please and impress their superiors, regardless of the effects of their actions upon the profits of the firm.

We have already pointed out several ways in which this type of motivation will cause deviations from "pure" profit maximization. In addition, middle managers must get along well with their subordinates, since they must rely upon the performance of the latter to assist them in impressing top management. This dual need for pleasing superiors and cooperating with subordinates places middle managers in a somewhat different position from top managers. Top management can employ cost accounting, personal ties with lower management, peer-group informants, and numerous other devices to keep well informed about what middle managers are doing. This means that middle managers have much less scope for covering up mistakes than do top managers—even though the magnitude of the errors which top managers might make is much greater.

3. *Implications of middle-management behavior.* Middle managers will normally tend to be risk avoiders in making decisions. A certain degree of advancement can be obtained merely by surviving, doing daily tasks, and not committing any outstanding blunders. This tendency, plus the desire of middle management to initiate those ideas which reflect the preconceived notions of their superiors, may produce an excessive lack of creativity and innovation at the middle-management level. Con-sequently, the firm may pass by many profit-increasing possibilities on the middle-management level which would be taken up by a truly profit-maximizing firm.

Insofar as middle managers are entrusted with labor relations, they may also tend to grant concessions to unions more readily than owner-managers would. Since strikes always involve more risks due to uncer-tainty than do settlements, risk-avoiders will have a built-in bias toward achieving settlements through concessions. Again, the result may be lower profits than would be attained by more aggressive and tougher owner-manager firms.

In highly decentralized firms, middle managers may be entrusted with far more responsibility than in centralized firms. In such cases, middle managers will undertake much riskier actions because the potential rewards will be higher. In fact, the position of middle management in such firms is riskier than the position of top management, because, as noted, middle managers are more closely scrutinized by their superiors than are top managers. Thus, the attitude of middle managers toward risks depends largely upon the structure of costs and rewards associated with different types of behavior on their part. The middle managers at General Electric and Westinghouse involved in price-fixing litigation were apparently willing to take on extraordinary risks in order to gain entry into the ranks of top management.

C. Lower-Management Behavior

1. *The organizational setting.* Lower managers are those supervisory personnel at the foreman or comparable level who have direct authority over production or lowest-level clerical personnel. They are normally paid for their performance by salaries and bonuses. Their salaries are partly based on seniority and longevity in the firm, and their bonuses are based on achieving production or quality goals. Normally, lower managers have little expectation of being promoted in middle or top management because the educational standards for those higher echelons are beyond their capabilities.

2. *Lower management's promotional strategy.* The best way for lower managers to maximize their lifetime incomes is to seek promotions up to the highest attainable lower-management level and then to hold on to what they have achieved. Often, their performances can be accurately measured objectively by means of production quotas, quality checks, costs accounting, etc. Thus, the efforts of lower management are more intensively directed at meeting objective performance criteria than is the case with middle and top management.

3. *Implications of lower-management behavior.* Lower managers are risk avoiders of a high order. Their aim is primarily to retain their present positions by meeting quotas and avoiding gross errors. In this echelon are the classic bureaucrats who never violate the rules and fear to "stick their necks out." As with middle management, the result is undoubtedly a lower level of creativity, innovation, and risk taking than would occur in a firm perfectly organized to maximize profits.

D. Nonmanagement Personnel: The Workers

In our analysis of the firm into several parts, we have deliberately ignored those workers who are not part of the firm's management structure. They are normally distinguished from management personnel because they are paid hourly rates instead of salaries. In most large, diffused-ownership firms, these workers are members of labor unions which represent them in collective bargaining with management. It is already a well-accepted tenet in economic theory that union leaders and members are not motivated by profit maximization for the firm which employs them. For this reason, we believe that unionized workers (and perhaps even nonunionized workers) should be considered as factors of production hired by the firm rather than constituent parts of it.

5. Summary

1. We have proposed a modified theory of the firm to explain the behavior of large, diffused-ownership firms, which we refer to as *large managerial* firms. This theory assumes that ownership and management are essentially separate, and that each such firm is so large that its management hierarchy contains at least three types of managers: top, middle, and lower. We postulate that both owners and managers act in their own self-interest by pursuing the following goals:

a. Owners are basically *satisficers* who desire uninterrupted dividends and a steady rise in the price of the firm's stock. Their remoteness from the firm's actual affairs makes it impossible for them to press for profit-maximizing behavior.

b. Managers are "economic men" who *desire to maximize their own lifetime incomes* (which includes both monetary and nonmonetary elements), principally by obtaining rapid promotions as a result of pleasing their superiors in the firm.

2. The behavior of large managerial firms deviates from the profit maximization posited by the traditional theory of the firm for the following reasons:

a. The large size of such firms requires them to develop *bureaucratic management* structures which cannot be perfectly controlled by the men in charge of them. In particular, these structures tend to (i) provide biased information to top management which reflects its own desires and ideas too strongly and (ii) only partially carry out the orders issued by top management. These tendencies cause systematic deviations from whatever goals the organization is ostensibly pursuing. They exist in large owner-managed firms as well as large managerial firms, since they result from sheer size. In essence, such deviations are caused by divergences of goals *within* management; that is, between middle and lower management on the one hand, and top management on the other. These goal divergences are able to influence the firm's behavior because large size both compels top managers to delegate authority to their subordinates and prevents them from checking up completely on how that authority is used. This behavior of the firm which is not optimal from the viewpoint of the top man may be caused *either* by size alone (technical inefficiency) or by a combination of size and divergent goals (technical plus motivational inefficiency).

b. The separation of ownership and management limits owners to being satisficers instead of maximizers; hence, managers aim at achieving steady growth of earnings plus gradually rising stock prices instead of maximum profits. As a result, large managerial firms are more cautious; spend less on "crash" research programs; experience less variability of profits; have larger expense accounts; evidence more conciliation in dealings with government, unions, and the public; and probably grow more slowly than they would if they sought to maximize profits. In essence, these outcomes result from the divergence of goals *between* owners and top management set forth previously. The size and structure of the firm both compel owners to delegate authority to top management and prevent them from checking up fully on its performance or imposing their own goals upon top management.

●

Some of the same interests pursued in the previous piece are carried on in an article by Oliver E. Williamson that not only presents a stimulating deductive argument but also tests some hypotheses empirically. It too is centrally concerned with the differences of interest between managers and owners, and explores some of the conditions under which managers are likely to obtain wider latitude (less stringent controls) to pursue their particular interests as they differ from those that might characterize the firm more generally. The author investigates this chiefly with a multiple regression equation to weigh the influence of several variables on differences in executive compensation in firms. We may take executive compensation, including both salaries and fringe benefits, as an approximate indicator of the degree to which managers or government leaders are able to gratify their own interests. In government, of course, salaries and even monetary fringe benefits are likely to constitute only a small portion of the largely intangible rewards accruing to officials, much more so than in business. Thus, to measure officials' decision latitude we would need a different indicator or set of indicators, but the question is essentially the same and, with some ingenuity, researchable.[1]

The dependent variables that Williamson uses to "explain" executive compensation are size of staff, outside (nonmanagement) representation on the board of directors, the degree of concentration characteristic of the industry, and barriers to entry inhibiting other firms from coming into the industry. The first variable corresponds, in national decision making, to the size of the government bureaucracy or to the financial resources available to the government. It could be measured rather easily by either government employee totals or budgetary figures, or perhaps best by a combination of the two. The precise counterpart for composition of the board of directors is less easy to discover; clearly it has to do with the formal structure of government and the controls available to the governed.[2] Another aspect, however, is the degree of control from outside the nation. Just as some members of the board of directors might not be either managers *or* substantial shareholders in the company, so all governments, but especially those of the smaller countries, are subject to external control from allies, states whose nationals have heavy trading

[1] Decision latitude is a basic variable in the Inter-Nation Simulation devised by Harold Guetzkow and his associates, and the continuum is related to Morton Kaplan's dichotomy of system-dominant versus subsystem-dominant in *System and Process in International Politics* (New York: Wiley, 1957).

[2] Perhaps there is a partial analogue in pressure groups and the use of ad hoc committees appointed to investigate problems and recommend governmental action.

interests or financial investments in the small countries, and a host of other formal or informal levers for influence. Several indices would be required to cover even the most important facets of this.

The last two variables are essentially systemic ones. Williamson found that industrial concentration was positively associated with executive compensation; we have seen suggestions earlier in this book about why higher concentration is associated with higher profit rates, few price wars, and greater stability in market shares. The obvious analogy is that national decision makers would have more latitude in bipolar situations than in multipolar ones, and in multipolar worlds than where there were *no* very large states. It is not hard to imagine ways in which decision makers, particularly of great powers, would have freedom of choice in bipolar or multipolar situations, and there is especially the argument we cited by Masters that individual states may be more stable where "competition" is far from perfect. But there are also good points to be made on the other side. Certainly, countries have much greater freedom to shift alignments when international concentration is low than when it is high. Here, we have two contradictory hypotheses, and it would be necessary to apply a two-tailed rather than a one-tailed test for statistical significance. The final variable, barriers to entry, is an attempt to take into account the dynamic element of system concentration, with some of the same problems as are encountered with the static measure. For a similar study of national foreign policies additional variables would be required, and perhaps one or two of these would have no close analogues, but the insights and basic approach seem applicable.

●

21

Managerial Discretion and Business Behavior

Oliver E. Williamson

The importance of managerial discretion in the operations of the large corporation has been widely recognized. Carl Kaysen has recently characterized the large corporation as one "in which the constraints imposed by market forces are loose, and the scope for managerial choice is considerable" [7, p. 90], and R. A. Gordon holds that the development of the large corporation has led

to a greater emphasis on the non-profit goals of interest groups other than the stockholders. Almost certainly, the personal and group goals of ... executives are a part of the total value system—the desires for security, power, prestige, advancement within the organization, and so on. ... Profits are viewed as the basic constraint subject to which other goals can be followed [6, p. xii].

Although there is substantial support for these views, it is by no means universal, and before general acceptance can be attained, a number of questions need to be answered. Can operational significance be provided to these managerial goals? Can such a translation of managerial objectives be integrated into a theory of the firm from which meaningful theorems can be derived? What is the evidence that discretion has an important and systematic impact on business behavior? Specifically, what influence does competition in the product market, managerial tastes, and the diffusion of stockholder control have on the allocation of resources in the business firm? How do regulatory or other constraints influence nonprofit behavior?

Reprinted from *American Economic Review*, **53**, 5 (December 1963), pp. 1032–1057.

My purpose in this discussion is to show that the first two of these questions can be answered in the affirmative, that the preliminary evidence tends to support the proposition that the opportunity for discretion does have a systematic effect on resource-allocation decisions, and that regulatory constraints are apt to produce particularly strong manifestations of nonprofit behavior. Part 1 introduces the notion of "expense preference" for translating managerial goals to an operational form, develops the implications of a model constructed around these objectives, and contrasts these with those obtained from the profits-maximization hypothesis. Part 2 examines some of the preliminary evidence on discretionary behavior.

1. Some Models of Business Behavior

My purpose in this section will be to show how managerial objectives can be introduced into a theory of the firm, to develop the implications of a model responsive to what appears to be the salient motives of managers, and to contrast these with those obtained from short-period and multi-period versions of the profits-maximization hypothesis.

A. A Managerial Discretion Model

1. *Managerial Objectives.* The following list represents a (largely overlapping) composite of the managerial motives identified as the result of the experiences and insights of the organization theorists Chester I. Barnard [3] and Herbert A. Simon [12] and the study of business leadership of R. A. Gordon [6]: salary, security, power, status, prestige, professional excellence. That they are neither equally significant nor entirely independent should be obvious. Rather than attempt a finer discrimination, however, it seems more fruitful to inquire into the behavior such motives produce.

The usual objection to introducing nonpecuniary elements into the theory of the firm is that such considerations, if not unimportant, are analytically evasive. Since their importance is an empirical question, it can hardly be dismissed so easily. In order, however, to assess their influence, an analytical basis for examining them must be devised. Shifting attention from the motives to the *means* by which the motives are realized provides the necessary connection. That is, rather than attempt to introduce security, power, prestige, and so forth into the theory directly, we ask instead: to what activities do these motives give rise? These activities, rather than the motives, are then made a part of the model.

The essential notion that we propose in order to connect motives with behavior is that of *expense preference*. That is, the management does not have a neutral attitude toward costs. Directly or indirectly, certain classes of expenditure have positive values associated with them. In particular, staff expense, expenditures for emoluments, and funds available for discretionary investment have value additional to that which derives from their productivity.

Expansion of staff is an activity that offers positive rewards, the benefits of which can be enjoyed quite generally [9, pp. 321–322]. Indeed, since promotional opportunities within a fixed-size firm are limited, while increased jurisdiction has the same general effect as promotion but simultaneously produces the chance of advance for all, the incentive to expand staff may be difficult to resist. Not only is it an indirect means to the attainment of salary [11] but it is a source of security, power, status, prestige, and professional achievement as well.[1]

We use the term "emoluments" in a somewhat special sense. They refer to that fraction of managerial salaries and perquisites that are discretionary. That is, emoluments represent rewards which, if removed, would not cause the managers to seek other employment. They are economic rents and have associated with them zero productivities. Thus, they are not a return to entrepreneurial capacity but rather result from the strategic advantage that the management possesses in the distribution of the returns to monopoly power. Being a source of material satisfaction and an indirect source of status and prestige, they are desirable as a means for satisfying goals in each of these respects.

The management would normally prefer to take these emoluments as salary rather than as perquisites of office since, taken as salary, there are no

[1] As has been observed among organization theorists, "the modern organization is a prolific generator of anxiety and insecurity" [14, p. 24]. This insecurity is partly due to uncertainty with respect to the survival of the organization as a whole and, more important (and more immediately relevant to its individual members), of the parts with which the individuals identify. Attempts to reduce this condition can be expected; indeed, the direction these efforts will take can be anticipated. If the surest guarantee of the survival of the individual parts appears to be size, efforts to expand the separate staff functions can safely be predicted.

That staff contributes to power, status, and prestige should be self-evident. This is true within the organization as well as in the manager's business and social relationships outside the firm. The vast influence that executives in large industrial organizations enjoy arises much more from the perceived control over resources that they possess than from the personal wealth which they have attained.

The "professional" inducement to expand staff arises from the typical view that a progressive staff is one that is continuously providing more and better service. An aggressive staff will therefore be looking for ways to expand. Although in choosing directions for expansion the relative contribution to productivity will be considered, the absolute effect on profits may be neglected. As long as the organization is able to satisfy its performance requirements, there is a predisposition to extend programs beyond the point where marginal costs equal marginal benefits. The incentive to increase staff, having both natural and legitimate elements, is exceptionally difficult to resist.

restrictions on the way in which they are spent, while, if withdrawn as corporate personal consumption (such as expense accounts, executive services, office suites, etc.), there are specific limitations on the ways these can be enjoyed. However, there are two considerations that make perquisites attractive. First, for tax purposes it may be advantageous to withdraw some part of discretionary funds as perquisites rather than salary. Second, perquisites are much less visible rewards to the management than salary and, hence, are less likely to provoke stockholder or labor dissatisfaction. Hence, a division of emoluments between salary and perquisites is to be expected.

Although it is difficult to specify what fraction of salary and perquisites is discretionary in the sense defined, it is possible, as we show in Part 2, to test for the relation of these rewards to competition in the product market and managerial tastes. Thus, they can be identified ex post even if not ex ante.

The existence of satisfactory profits is necessary to assure the interference-free operation of the firm to the management. Precisely what this level will be involves a complicated interaction of the relative performance of rivals, the historical performance of the firm, and special current conditions that affect the firm's performance. Management, however, will find it desirable to earn profits that exceed the acceptable level. For one thing, managers derive satisfaction from self-fulfillment and organizational achievement, and profits are one measure of this success. In addition, profits are a source of discretion (indeed, we define "discretionary profits" as the difference between actual profits and minimum profits demanded). Discretionary profits represent a source of funds whose allocation may be importantly determined by managerial, in addition to economic, considerations. As with the expansion of staff, the expansion of physical plant and equipment provides general opportunities for managerial satisfaction and for much the same reasons.

2. *The Model.* Since these notions will be introduced explicitly into a mathematical model, it will be useful to define them more precisely. The relationships that we shall use are:

R = revenue = $P \cdot X$; $\partial^2 R/\partial X \partial S \geq 0$
P = price = $P(X, S; \varepsilon)$; $\partial P/\partial X < 0$; $\partial P/\partial S \geq 0$; $\partial P/\partial \varepsilon > 0$
X = output
S = staff (in money terms) or (approximately) general administrative and selling expense
ε = the condition of the environment (a demand-shift parameter)
C = production cost = $C(X)$
M = managerial emoluments
π = actual profits = $R - C - S$

π_R = reported profits = $\pi - M$
π_0 = minimum (after tax) profits demanded
T = taxes where t = tax rate and $\overline{T}$ = lump-sum tax
$\pi_R - \pi_0 - T$ = discretionary profits
U = the utility function

From our statement of the firm's objectives, the firm is operated so as to

maximize: $U = U[S, M, \pi_R - \pi_0 - T]$
subject to: $\pi_R \geq \pi_0 + T$.

As formulated, the constraint is of the same form as the last term in the utility function. Hence, assuming that second order conditions are satisfied and disallowing corner solutions, the constraint becomes redundant so that we can treat the problem as one of straightforward maximization. Substituting the functional relationships for profits into the expression we have:

maximize: $U = U[S, M, (1 - t)(R - C - S - M) - \pi^0]$.

The following first-order results are obtained by setting the partial derivatives of U with respect to X, S, and M equal to zero.[2]

$$\frac{\partial R}{\partial X} = \frac{\partial C}{\partial X} \tag{1}$$

$$\frac{\partial R}{\partial S} = \frac{-U_1 + (1 - t)U_3}{(1 - t)U_3} \tag{2}$$

$$U_2 = (1 - t)U_3 \tag{3}$$

From Eq. (1) we observe that the firm makes its production decision in the conventional fashion by equating marginal gross revenue to the marginal costs of production. However, Eq. (2) reveals that the firm will employ staff in the region where the marginal value product of staff is less than its marginal cost. This equation can be rewritten as:

$$\frac{\partial R}{\partial S} = 1 - \frac{1}{(1 - t)} \frac{U_1}{U_3}, \qquad \text{where } \frac{U_1}{U_3}$$

is the marginal rate of substitution between profits and staff. In the profit-maximizing organization, staff has no value other than that associated with its productivity, so that this exchange rate is zero, and the equality of marginal costs and value products obtains. Equation (3) discloses that the firm will absorb some amount of actual profits as emoluments—the amount being dependent on the tax rate.

[2] In these expressions, U_1 is the first partial of the utility function with respect to S, U_2 is the first partial with respect to M, and U_3 is the first partial with respect to $\pi_R - \pi_0 - T$.

Table 1

Responses to Displacements from Equilibrium
for the Managerial Model

Variable	Parameter		
	ε	t	$\overline{T}$
X^0	+	+	−
S^0	+	+	−
M^0	+	+	−

Having established the equilibrium conditions, the comparative statics properties of the model remain to be developed. That is, we want to find how the system adjusts to a change in the condition of the environment (the demand-shift parameter ε), a change in the profit tax rate (t), and a lump-sum tax ($\overline{T}$).

The results for a displacement by each of the parameters are shown in Table 1. The direction of adjustment of any particular decision variable to a displacement from its equilibrium value by an increase in a particular parameter is found by referring to the row and column entry corresponding to this pair.

Actually, the response to a change in the profits tax rate is not unambiguous. It can be shown that this response is separable into a net substitution effect and the equivalent of an income effect, where the net substitution effect is always positive and the income effect is always negative. The gross substitution effect is the combination of these two separate effects and, hence, depends on their relative magnitudes. Under reasonable assumptions, the gross substitution effect will be positive, as shown in the table.[3]

B. Entrepreneurial Models

The significance of these responses can best be discussed by comparing them to the corresponding results obtained from profit-maximizing models. Consider first the usual or single-period profit-maximizing model. As is well known, the equilibrium relations for this model require that the firm be operated so as to equate marginal gross revenue with the marginal costs of production and the marginal value product of staff with its marginal cost. The comparative statics responses are shown in Table 2.

The differences between the models are more numerous than their similarities. Indeed, it is only with respect to the demand-shift parameter (ε) that the two return the same results, and even here the result is not

[3] Only when the firm is pressed very hard to satisfy its minimum-profits constraint is a reversal apt to occur.

Table 2

Responses to Displacements from Equilibrium
for the Short-Run Profits-Maximizing Model

Variable	Parameter		
	ε	t	$\overline{T}$
X^0	+	0	0
S^0	+	0	0

identical. In addition to the increases in staff and output that the profit-maximization model shows, the managerial model also indicates that spending for emoluments will increase as ε increases. Moreover, while the qualitative differences with respect to ε are not great, quantitative differences may produce sharper discriminations. In general, a profits-maximizing firm will adjust to changes in business conditions within narrower bounds than the utility-maximizing firm. The absence of slack in its operations, as contrasted with the calculated accumulation (and decumulation) of slack by the utility-maximizing firm, is responsible for these quantitative differences.

A more general entrepreneurial model can be obtained by devising a multiperiod or discounted version of the profits-maximization hypothesis. The variables are subscripted by time periods by i, where $i = 1, 2, \ldots n$, and n is the planning horizon. Letting r be the discount rate, profits in year i will be discounted by $1/(1 + r)^{i-1}$. Let this be represented by α^{i-1}. We make the assumption that production decisions in period k affect costs in no other period or, if there are effects, that these are offsetting. However, staff expenditures in period k are assumed to have a positive influence on future-period revenues over the entire planning horizon. Indeed, the length of the "period" can be defined as the interval beyond which current production decisions have no effect and the length of the planning horizon as the number of such periods for which current staff expenditures have a positive effect.

Letting π represent the discounted value of profits, the objective is to maximize:

$$\pi = \sum_{i=1}^{n} (1 - t)(R_i - C_i - S_i - \overline{T}_i)\alpha^{i-1}$$

First-order conditions for a maximum are obtained by setting the partial derivatives of π with respect to X_1 and S_1 equal to zero. Thus, we have:

$$\frac{\partial R_1}{\partial X_1} = \frac{\partial C_1}{\partial X_1} \tag{4}$$

Table 3
Comparative Statics Responses for the Discounted Profits-
Maximizing Model

Variable	Parameter			
	ε	t'	t''	$\bar{T}$
X_1^0	+	+	0	0
S_1^0	+	+	0	0

$$\frac{\partial R_1}{\partial S_1} = 1 - \sum_{i=2}^{n} \frac{\partial R_i}{\partial S_1} \alpha^{i-1} \tag{5}$$

Inspection of Eq. (4) reveals that the firm chooses that value of output for which the marginal gross revenue is equal to the marginal costs of production. Equation (5), however, shows that the current marginal value product of staff is less than its current marginal cost.[4] These equilibrium conditions are thus similar to those obtained from the managerial model.

Since the effects when the tax is levied for a period less than the planning horizon are different from those when the tax covers the entire horizon, the tax-rate effect is split into "temporary" (designated tax rate t') and "permanent" (designated tax rate t'') types. The comparative statics responses for this model are displayed in Table 3.

Whereas the qualitative responses to a "temporary" change in the profits tax rate are identical to those obtained from the managerial model, a change in the "permanent" profits tax or the levy of a lump-sum tax (or bounty) produces no effect in the profits-maximizing organization. A response to both is predicted by the managerial model. Hence, a discrimination between the hypotheses on the basis of comparative statics properties is potentially achievable.

2. Some Evidence

Changes in either the profits tax or a lump-sum tax provide the most direct basis for distinguishing between the utility and profits-maximization theories. Testing the effects of a profits tax, however, requires that a rather advanced type of simultaneous-equations model be devised, while lump-sum taxes are hard to come by. The first of these carries us beyond the range of the present analysis, and only preliminary evidence on the effects of the lump-sum tax is available.

[4] Over the entire horizon, however, the marginal value product of staff equals its marginal cost.

Fortunately, other tests of a less direct but nonetheless meaningful sort can be devised. For one thing, the comparative statics implications are limited to qualitative responses; quantitative differences are neglected. If, therefore, significant quantitative differences between the two theories can be shown to exist, these can be used for making a discrimination where qualitative properties are identical.

Secondly, tests of particular behavior are available. Thus, the utility-maximizing theory is based on the proposition that opportunities for discretion and managerial tastes will have a decided impact on the expenditures of the firm. More precisely, those expenditures that promote managerial satisfactions should show a positive correlation with opportunities for discretion and tastes. The profit-maximizing theory is somewhat ambiguous on this question. Interpreted as a theory which attends entirely to the stockholders' best interests, it clearly implies that expenditures which, under the utility-maximizing hypothesis, will be positively correlated with measures of discretion and tastes, will instead be uncorrelated with these relationships. Interpreted somewhat more loosely, closer agreement with the utility-maximizing hypothesis can be obtained. Thus, it is possible that the management first selects that physical combination of factors that maximizes profits and then absorbs some amount of actual profits as cost. These absorptions may be correlated with the same measures of discretion and taste as would be expected under the utility-maximizing theory. Hence, evidence that managers respond to opportunities for discretion is not inconsistent with the profit-maximizing theory, but neither is evidence to the contrary; the theory is simply silent on this question. However, the failure of firms to respond to opportunities for discretion constitutes a contradiction of the utility-maximizing hypothesis, while observations that firms do display expense-preference behavior supports it.

The executive compensation and retained-earnings analyses reported later are designed to test for the effects of discretion and taste in management expenditure decisions. The summary of the field studies (omitted here) is concerned with the question of physical magnitudes of adjustment to adversity and provides some indication of what criteria are involved in making expense adjustments as well as what effects a lump-sum tax has on business behavior.

A. Principal-Firm Analysis

If the firm is operated so as to attend to managerial interests, then the classes of expenditures for which expense preference was indicated should be expanded beyond the levels called for by strictly profit considerations. The amount by which such expansions occur should be positively related to the opportunity for discretion and the tastes of the management. More precisely, if X is an expenditure for which a positive expense preference exists, I_1 is an index of the absence of competition, I_2 is an index of management taste, I_3 is an index of stockholder diffusion, and $f(\pi)$ is the level of X which would be supported solely by profit considerations, then under the utility-maximization hypothesis:

$$X = f(\pi)g(I_1, I_2, I_3)$$

where

$$\frac{\partial X}{\partial I_i} > 0$$

Under the stockholder version of the profits-maximization hypothesis, the partial derivative of X with respect to each of the I_i will be zero.

Since it is in the large corporation that manifestations of discretionary behavior are alleged to be important, and as complete data are most readily available among larger industrial firms than their smaller counterparts, the tests are restricted to those firms that clearly qualified as "principal firms." Among the 26 industries included in the analysis, selection was limited to the two largest firms, ranked according to sales, in each. The tests performed are cross-section tests for the years 1953, 1957, and 1961.

1. *Executive Compensation.* George Stigler has observed that the estimation of the effect of monopoly on profit may be complicated by the absorption of some fraction of "true" monopoly profits as cost. In particular, "the magnitude of monopoly elements in wages, executive compensation, royalties, and rents is possibly quite large" [*13*, p. 35]. Our interest here is limited to testing only a part of this hypothesis. Specifically, we examine the effects of discretion on compensating the top executive.

Focusing on a single representative of management might appear to restrict severely the relevance of our results. If the compensation of the rest of the management group were determined independently of that of the chief executive, this would certainly be the case. However, payments between executive levels are carefully scaled [*2*, p. 181] [*8*, p. 320] [*11*]. Hence, the factors that influence compensation to the top executive can be presumed to affect the level of staff compensation generally.

Under the utility-maximizing hypothesis, a positive expense preference toward emoluments exists. In particular, executive salaries should be correlated with the opportunities for discretion. Letting W_a be the actual salary of the management and W_c be the competitive salary, we have: $W_a = W_c + (W_a - W_c)$, where $W_a - W_c$ is a measure of the monopoly returns withdrawn by the management (by virtue of its advantageous position) as economic rent.

As indicated previously, the hypothesis that discretion influences expenses takes the form $X = f(\pi)g(I_1, I_2, I_3)$, where $f(\pi)$ is the expense incurred strictly on a profit-maximizing basis, and I_1, I_2, and I_3 are indices of the absence of competition, the tastes of the management, and the diffusion of the stockholders, respectively. Specifying $f(\pi)$ for purposes of studying executive compensation is somewhat difficult. A measure of hierarchical activity over which the executive in question has responsibility, together with the special abilities required for the position, probably measures this approximately. For the top executive, the level of hierarchical activity is effectively the entire staff structure. Thus, let $f(\pi) = f'(S, Z)$, where S is the level of staff (general administrative and selling expenses) and Z is an index of special ability.

We assume that the index of competitive pressure (I_1) is reflected by the concentration ratio and the entry barrier in each industry. The concentration ratio reflects the influence of realized interdependencies between rivals. Where concentration ratios are high, interdependencies will generally be intimate, and behavior between rivals will at least be circumspect and may involve explicit agreements. In either case, the influence of competition will be consciously controlled. Hence, an increase in the concentration ratio will tend to widen the opportunities for managerial discretion. Obviously, this measure is defective and there will be exceptions. However we are content merely to account for average rather than exceptional behavior.

The barrier to entry measure, as developed by Joe S. Bain [1], is explicitly designed to estimate the extent to which firms are insulated from the effects of competition. Although concentration and entry conditions are correlated, they are by no means identical. In combination they provide a particularly good measure of the opportunities for discretion. High concentration together with a high barrier to entry will tend to produce substantial discretion, for not only is potential competition limited, but existing rivals are few enough to appreciate their conditions of interdependence. Low values for each of these measures will tend to produce the reverse effect, while mixed values, presumably, give rise to mixed effects.

To allay any suspicion that the concentration ratio and entry barriers are merely another measure of size, it might be noted that the product moment correlations between the logarithm of sales and the logarithms of "staff," concentration, and barriers (for the firms included in the sample) are about .75, $-.13$, and $-.14$, respectively. Quite clearly, these latter two correlations are small enough that if concentration and barriers have an effect on compensation, it is not primarily due to their relationship to size.

A sharp measure of managerial tastes (I_2) is not available. However, the composition of the board may act as a proxy measure of the extent to which management desires to operate the firm free from outside interference. Although low proportional representation of the management on the board of directors need not reflect a "taste" for active outside participation in the affairs of the firm, clearly, a high internal representation does reflect the intent of the management to conduct the affairs of the firm free from such outside influence. We hypothesize that, as the management representation on the board increases, there tends to be a subordination of stockholder for managerial interests. In this sense, the composition of the board reflects management's attitude toward discretionary resource allocations and a voluntary change in composition reflects a change in these "tastes."

An estimate of stockholder diffusion (I_3) was not obtained. Such a measure would probably be correlated with the composition of the board variable. However, the association may not be great. Where substantial concentration of ownership exists, there is frequently a tendency towards nepotism. This, in turn, may produce high internal representation rather than the high outside representation that would otherwise be predicted. If, in fact, the correlation were zero (and there were no other neglected variable to consider), our estimate of the composition effect would be unbiased. As it is, some bias may result from the lack of a diffusion measure.

The effects of each of the independent variables on executive compensation should be positive. In addition, they are assumed to be multiplicative. Thus, we assume that:

$$X_i = \alpha_0 S_i^{\alpha_2} C_i^{\alpha_2} H_i^{\alpha_3} B_i^{\alpha_4} U_i \tag{6}$$

where

X_i = compensation of the top executive
S_i = administrative, general, and selling expense (i.e., "staff")
C_i = concentration ratio in the industry
H_i = height of the barrier to entry in the industry
B_i = composition of the board
U_i = a random error term[5]

and the subscript i refers to the ith firm in the sample.

Taking logarithms of both sides of the equation and using these data to obtain least-squares estimates of the net regression coefficients, we obtain the results shown in Table 4.

The signs for each of the parameters in all three years are as predicted by the expense-preference hypothesis. Moreover, with the exception of the

[5] U_i includes the effects of special abilities (the Z variable mentioned previously), the omitted stockholder-diffusion variable, numbers of years the top executive has held that position, and other neglected factors.

Table 4
Regression of Executive Compensation on "Staff," Concentration
Ratio, Composition of the Board, and Barriers to Entry

	Year		
	1953	1957	1961
"Staff"			
Coeff.	.228^a	.240^a	.218^a
S.E.	.061	.052	.054
Partial	(.564)	(.610)	(.614)
Concentration			
Coeff.	.503^a	.513^a	.422^b
S.E.	.157	.143	.152
Partial	(.517)	(.517)	(.470)
Composition			
Coeff.	.137	.139	.053
S.E.	.118	.101	.120
Partial	(.213)	(.224)	(.084)
Entry Barriers			
Coeff.	.446^a	.221^b	.200
S.E.	.110	.114	.126
Partial	(.606)	(.307)	(.290)
Coeff. of Correl.			
(adjusted)	.786	.724	.687

[a] Significant at the .1 percent level
[b] Significant at the 2.5 percent level

composition of the board coefficient, which is significant at the 10 percent level only in 1957, all of the regression coefficients are highly significant—two-thirds being significant at the 2.5 percent level. Whereas the relation of executive compensation to general administrative and selling expense (i.e., "staff") is almost certain to be positive and significant, there is no reason to believe that the measures of taste and discretion that we introduce should have the effects shown (unless one endorses the view that management responds to opportunities for discretion in the ways indicated). Since the compensation of the chief executive generalizes to the entire staff structure, these results have broad significance for the resource-allocation process within the business firm. Furthermore, we would expect that these same measures of discretion would produce similar effects over the entire range of expenditures on emoluments.

Of course it could be argued that the concentration ratio and entry-barrier variables have positive regression coefficients because they are correlated with the profit rate—that this profitability effect is responsible for the results obtained. But obviously, the causality runs from concentration and entry barriers to profits rather than the reverse. Thus, by focusing on the market structure, the model directs attention to the ultimate determinants of discretionary behavior (competition in the product market) rather than the apparent determinant (the profit rate). Although these market variables might not perform as well as the profit rate among the smaller firms in the industry, it does not seem inappropriate to use them for studying the behavior of the two largest firms where the relationship between market structure and behavior is probably reasonably direct. Indeed, it is of interest to note that : (1) if the profit rate on the stockholders equity is substituted for the concentration ratio and entry-barrier variables, the coefficient of determination (R^2) falls to two-thirds of the value obtained using these market variables in 1953 and 1961, and yields less than a 10 percent increase in R^2 in 1957; (2) if the profit rate, concentration ratio, and entry-barrier variables are all included, the profit rate is significant only in 1957 and has the wrong sign in 1961, while the concentration ratio and entry-barrier variables remain significant at the 10 percent level or better in every year.

Although the profit rate might perform better if a weighted average were used instead of current values, the argument offered previously that this is an apparent rather than the ultimate determinant of behavior still applies. Moreover, the appropriate estimate of the profit rate is the actual rather than the reported rate. But the actual rate is unknown if, as the evidence above suggests, some fraction of actual profits is absorbed as salary and perquisites.

Some feeling for the responsiveness of salary to the independent variables in the regression equation can be obtained by taking the median of the estimates for each parameter and finding the effect on salary of increasing each individual independent variable by a factor of two. In some gross sense we can expect that executive salaries will possibly increase on the order of 17 percent if the level of staff activity were to double, on the order of 41 percent if the concentration ratio in the industry were to double, on the order of 10 percent if the internal representation on the board were to double, and on the order of 25 percent if the industry of which the firm was a part had a substantial or high barrier to entry rather than a low one. Thus, not only are the signs as predicted by the theory, but the magnitudes are sufficiently large to render somewhat doubtful the contention that discretionary effects are unimportant.

2. *Earnings Retention.* The composition of the board variable was used in the executive compensation model to reflect the "tastes" of the management for discretion. Internal representation on the board acts as a proxy for the attitude of the management toward outside influence.

As the proportional representation of management on the board increases, it is assumed that stockholder interests tend to be subordinated to managerial objectives. This was manifested in the executive compensation regression by the positive regression coefficient associated with the composition of board variable.

A second test for this effect is to examine the relationship between composition of the board and earnings-retention policy. Consistency with our model requires that the earnings-retention ratio be directly related to the composition of the board. This follows, since retained earnings are a source of discretion and a high internal representation provides the opportunity for management to shift the dividend policy to its advantage.

Alternative theories of the firm that regard managerial objectives as unimportant implicitly predict that there will be no association between the composition of the board and retention policy. Thus, our hypothesis of a direct association is tested against the null hypothesis of no association.

Earnings retention will, of course, be responsive to a number of considerations other than that of the composition of the board. Most important, investment opportunities will differ between industries and these could easily be overriding. If it can be assumed that the firms in the same industry have identical opportunities, however, these effects can be neutralized.

A paired-comparison technique was used to neutralize the industry effects. That is, between the two principal firms in each of the 26 industries we compare the composition of the board and earnings-retention ratio. The random variable can take on either of two values: 1 if the higher internal representation is paired with the higher earnings-retention ratio, and 0 otherwise. Hence, it is distributed as a binomial. Under the hypothesis that no association exists, the expected number of times the positive association will occur, divided by the total number of observations, is one-half. Thus, the null hypothesis is that the binomial parameter p is .50. Our model, however, predicts that the positive association will occur more than one-half of the time—i.e., that p exceeds .50.

The results for each of the three years as well as the pooled results for all three years are shown in Table 5. The proposition that internal representation has no effect on the earnings-retention policy between pairs of firms in the same industry is unsupported by the data. In every year the proportion of positive observations exceeds .50. In 1953 and 1957 the probability that a value as high as that observed if the null hypothesis were true is .34 and .13, respectively, and in 1961 this drops to .02. Clearly, we are inclined to reject the hypothesis in favor of the alternative suggested. That is, due to the discretion associated with the retention of earnings and the opportunity to influence the retention policy which arises from

Table 5
Binomial Test for Association between Composition of Board and
Earnings-Retention Policy

	1953	1957	1961	All years
Number of observations	25	26	26	77
Expected number of positive occurrences under the null hypothesis	12.5	13	13	38.5
	$(p = .50)$	$(p = .50)$	$(p = .50)$	$(p = .50)$
Actual number of positive occurrences	13.5	16	18	47.5
	$(\hat{p} = .54)$	$(\hat{p} = .62)$	$(\hat{p} = .69)$	$(\hat{p} = .62)$
Probability that value as high as observed would occur if the null hypothesis were true[a]	.34	.13	.02	.02

[a] Normal approximation to the binomial was used to obtain the probabilities that the null hypothesis would produce the results observed.

representation on the board, the relation that we suggested (namely, that between pairs of firms in the same industry, the higher the internal representation, the higher the earnings retention rate) is supported by the data. Although it is possible that the composition of the board is acting only as an intervening variable and that the real explanation for this association lies elsewhere, no simple connection suggests itself.

The strongest evidence in favor of our hypothesis is provided by the pooled results for all three years. Here, the observed number of positive occurrences would appear by chance under the null hypothesis with a probability of only two times in a hundred. Before the pooling of the observations can be justified, however, it is first necessary to establish that the observations are independent and that the association observed in one period is simply not carried over to the following period. Since the composition of the board and earnings-retention decisions reflect policy considerations that exhibit continuation in consecutive years, lack of independence between consecutive years would be expected. On the other hand, our observations are separated by a period of four years. The association between consecutive years may well be eliminated over this interval. Since the issue can scarcely be resolved on a priori grounds, we submit the hypothesis that the observations are independent to test.

A chi-square test for association was used. A low value of χ^2 is consistent with the hypothesis that the observations between successive four-year intervals are independent. The value of χ^2 between 1953 and 1957 is .0065, and between 1957 and 1961 is .62. Sampling randomly from independent populations, values as high or higher than this would occur 95 percent and 45 percent of the time, respectively. Hence, the hypothesis of independence is supported, the pooling of the observations is justified, and the best test for the composition of the board effect is that of all three years combined. Here, the possibility that the positive association observed has occurred by chance is only .02. Indeed, among pairs of principal firms we can expect that the firm with the higher internal representation on the board of directors will have a higher earnings-retention ratio about three-fifths of the time.

The results just presented are limited to directional effects only and say nothing about the magnitudes involved. This is probably all that the data justify. However, a crude estimate of the quantitative effect is available by an application of the general model suggested previously for studying discretionary expenditures. Thus let

R_{ik} = the retained-earnings ratio

ρ_k = the rate of return on investment available to principal firms

C_k = the concentration ratio

H_k = the entry barrier

B_{ik} = the composition of the board of directors

V_{ik} = a random-error term

The subscript i refers to the firm, and the subscript k refers to the industry of which the firm is a part. Then, assuming the relation is multiplicative, we have:

$$R_{ik} = \beta_0 [f(\rho_k)]^{\beta_1} C_k^{\beta_2} H_k^{\beta_3} B_{ik}^{\beta_4} V_{ik} \tag{7}$$

Taking the ratio of retained earnings between the ith and jth principal firms in the same industry yields:

$$\frac{R_{ik}}{R_{jk}} = \left(\frac{B_{ik}}{B_{jk}}\right)^{\beta_4} V' \tag{8}$$

Taking logarithms of both sides of the equation, the value of β_4 can be estimated by least squares. The resulting estimates for 1953, 1957, and 1961 are .17, .17, and .16, respectively, but only the 1957 estimate is significant at the 10 percent level. These estimates suggest that the retained-earnings ratio would increase by about 12 percent if the internal representation on the board of directors were to double.

A tenuous connection between the composition of the board and the investment policy of the firm can be obtained by noting the results obtained by Myron Gordon and M. Fg. Scott in their recent studies of investment financing. Gordon remarks that

"The really surprising result is produced by return on investment.... In both industries there is a statistically significant tendency for the retention rate to fall as the corporation's rate of return increases. We must conclude that either [our estimate] is a poor measure of rate of return on investment or that corporations are not primarily influenced by the price of their stock in setting dividend rates" [5, pp. 231–232].

And Scott, in a somewhat more broadly based study of dividend policy, observes that the

"negative correlation of − .30 between undistributed profits ... and the subsequent growth of earnings ... is somewhat surprising. It suggests that stockholders ... might benefit from more generous dividend distributions" (*10*, p. 244].

For a theory that makes the firm's objectives identical with those of the stockholders, such a result is somewhat disquieting. For an approach such as ours, however, which allows for the subordination of stockholder to managerial objectives, a possible explanation for these results based on the composition of the board analysis can be easily provided.

As was suggested previously, high internal representation on the board of directors favors attention to managerial objectives, and this is manifested in a high earnings-retention rate. The funds thus provided are available to the management for the pursuit of expansionary objectives, and the resulting investment, being based on a combination of profit and expansionary goals, will exceed the amount dictated by profit considerations alone. As a result, the average rate of return in firms whose management is inclined to subordinate stockholder objectives can be expected to fall below that in firms where management interests are more nearly those of the stockholders. Thus, the tastes of the management, as revealed originally in the composition of the board, make their influence felt through the earnings-retention policy and, thence, on the return on investment. Where these tastes favor expansion, there is an adverse effect on the rate of return on investment. This indirect implication of our theory is precisely the result that Gordon and Scott report. Although conjectural, it suggests the value of including a "taste" variable, of which the composition of the board is a somewhat imperfect proxy, in future studies of the investment decision.

3. Conclusions

Based on the twin assumptions of self-interest and rational behavior, a general approach for introducing managerial objectives into a theory of the firm has been suggested. The notion of expense preference constitutes a critical part of the argument. It provides the essential connection for relating managerial objectives to operating behavior.

In addition to the comparative statics properties that were investigated, the managerial model also provides identical qualitative responses to those of the profits-maximizing model with respect to a sales tax (of either the specific or ad valorem variety). Thus, the utility-maximization hypothesis preserves the main theorems of the profits-maximization hypothesis with respect to shifts in demand and application of a sales tax. Indeed, since there is little dispute concerning the general validity of these implications of the classical theory, it would be distressing to have the managerial model predict differently. However, when it comes to matters where the qualitative implications of the profits-maximizing model have been somewhat suspect, namely, the effects of a profits tax and a lump-sum tax, the managerial model registers responses that contradict the classical theory.

The evidence presented is clearly suggestive rather than definitive. Such as it is, it generally supports the implications of the utility-maximization approach. Although it is not strong enough to provide a discrimination between the utility- and profits-maximizing theories, it does suggest that either firms are operated as indicated by the managerial model or, if "actual" profits are maximized, that reported profits are reduced by absorbing some fraction of actual profits in executive salaries and possibly in perquisites of a variety of sorts. This raises a serious question whether studies of monopoly power based on reported profits provide an accurate estimate of the effects of monopoly. It is possible that a nonnegligible part of true monopoly profits is absorbed internally.

If subsequent results confirm the present findings concerning the effects of internal representation on the board of directors on executive compensation and dividend policy, the case for an independent board becomes much more compelling. Although Gordon has already argued this position persuasively [6, pp. 343–351], the reasoning has lacked empirical support and there is little indication that his views have been heeded.

A continuing investigation of the effects of discretion on managerial behavior would appear to be warranted. Indeed, we could not agree more with Becker's view that the economist *can* provide nonpecuniary motives with economic content and that "progress in this field has been hindered not so much by an intractable concept as by the economists' reluctance to take the concept seriously" [4, p. 179].

References

1. J. S. Bain, *Barriers to New Competition* (Cambridge: Harvard University Press, 1962).
2. J. C. Baker, *Executive Salaries and Bonus Plans* (New York: McGraw-Hill, 1938).
3. C. I. Barnard, *The Functions of the Executive* (Cambridge: Harvard University Press, 1962).
4. G. S. Becker, "Competition, Monopoly, and the Pursuit of Pecuniary Gain: Comment," in *Aspects of Labor Economics* (Princeton: Princeton University Press, 1962).
5. M. J. Gordon, *The Investment, Financing and Valuation of the Corporation* (Homewood, Ill: Richard D. Irwin, Inc., 1962).

6. R. A. Gordon, *Business Leadership in the Large Corporation* (Berkeley: University of California Press, 1961).

7. C. Kaysen, "The Corporation: How Much Power? What Scope?," in E. S. Mason, ed., *The Corporation in Modern Society* (Cambridge: Harvard University Press, 1960).

8. H. Koontz and C. O'Donnell, *Principles of Management* (New York: McGraw-Hill, 1955).

9. A. Marshall, *Industry and Trade* (London: Macmillan, 1919).

10. M. Fg. Scott, "Relative Share Prices and Yields," *Oxford Economic Papers*, **14** (October, 1962), pp. 218–250.

11. H. A. Simon, "The Compensation of Executives," *Sociometry*, **20** (March 1957), pp. 32–35.

12. H. A. Simon, *Administrative Behavior* (New York: Macmillan, 1961).

13. G. J. Stigler, "The Statistics of Monopoly and Merger," *Journal of Political Economy*, **64** (February 1956), pp. 33–40.

14. V. A. Thompson, *Modern Organization* (New York: A. A. Knopf, 1961).

●

Nationalism as an influence on states' foreign policy behavior has received a great deal of attention from historians and political scientists, but not so much from economists. In the next article, however, Harry G. Johnson shows how a number of theoretical models from economics can suggest explanations of the behavior of peoples and governments. Nationalism actually is an especially appropriate phenomenon for economists to study because nationalistic actions so often appear incompatible with narrowly defined economic interests of states. The expropriation of foreign owned industry by a nationalist government, for example, frequently is undertaken only at great cost for acquisition if compensation is paid to the former foreign owners, or with great and rather predictable political and, ultimately, economic costs if fair compensation is not provided. And it will involve heavy losses in efficiency when there are not enough skilled nationals available to run the newly acquired organizations without stripping old ones of key personnel. Or an autarchic self-sufficient trade policy, involving the imposition of quotas or tariffs on foreign merchandise to discriminate in favor of domestically produced goods, will result in hidden losses that may easily more than match whatever long-term gains may accrue from building up infant industries.

In his essay Johnson notes three different strands of thought by economists that individually and woven together make up a set of stimulating hypotheses about why nationalistic actions are nevertheless undertaken. One strand is represented by a theory of discrimination developed by Gary Becker, relying chiefly on a psychological concept of "taste" for discrimination, where the nonpecuniary rewards that an individual obtains by discriminating are worth foregoing material gains.

A second stems from Anthony Downs' ingenious effort to construct "an economic model of democracy." Some difficulties with this part of the presentation are likely to be more apparent to a political scientist than they would be to an economist. For example, Down's theory relies heavily on some assumptions about the distribution of voters' preferences, and especially whether those preferences are unimodal or multimodal. This strand of thought comes, ultimately, from location theory in economics, but it is severely circumscribed in political problems because political issues can so seldom be described in unidimensional terms. That is, while attitudes on some policy positions will be highly correlated with each other, others will be unrelated to the first set, though perhaps they may, in turn, be highly correlated with each other. The fact that two, three, or more dimensions may be required for even a summary description of voter's preferences severely weakens the Downs application. Economic location theory can be extended to two-dimensional situations (e.g., location on a north-south as well as an east-west axis). But with more than two dimensions (e.g., plus altitude) the analytical problems are much more severe, and determinate solutions seem to be virtually unattainable. Another difficulty in applying the Downs' model as Johnson attempts to do is the assumption that proportional representation tends to produce a multiparty system. While this has, indeed, long been part of the folklore of politics, the empirical evidence behind it is not unanimous. But these are relatively minor flaws that should not detract from the general utility of the suggested way of thinking.

The third and final element Johnson employs comes from a theory of nationalism set forth by Albert Breton. Generalizing from his observations about the origins and support of French-Canadian separatism, Breton notes that the middle classes contain a much higher proportion of enthusiasts for separation than do the working classes. His evidence is drawn from survey data dividing the French Canadians into three income classes: below $2000 a year, $2000–$6000, and over $6000. Endorsement of separatism is positively correlated with income at these levels, being 20 percent, 24 percent, and 34 percent, respectively.[1] The reason, he suggests, is that nationalism usually becomes a vehicle not for increasing the total income of a nation—the difficulties cited above militate against that occurring—but for a *redistribution* of income from the lower classes to the politically influential middle class. Nationalism, and, specifically, its economic manifestations such as the take-over of foreign-owned industry and the imposition of barriers to imports, provides white-collar jobs for those with some skills, replacing the foreign managers, technicians, and artists who formerly held the positions within the country or who provided the goods and services that were formerly imported. He supports this observation with some evidence of cases where restrictions on the utilization of foreign-produced goods clearly stemmed from the material interests of domestic *producers* rather than from any desire on the part of domestic *consumers* to have a home-grown product available. For instance, he notes that in Canada the demand for United States television is very high, as shown by the number of viewers who turn to American stations in preference to Canadian ones and, especially, by the number who go to a substantial expense ($5.00 per month) to take cable services providing American programs. Yet, a recent Canadian government ruling required that 55 percent of television programs broadcast by the CBC during certain hours must be of Canadian origin. This, he says, is obviously a subsidy for Canadian artists at the expense of the rest of the population, and not

[1] A. Breton, "The Economics of Nationalism" *Journal of Political Economy*, **72** (1964), p. 381.

consonant with the consumer's wishes.[2] Thus, a society's "investment in nationality" serves the immediate interests of particular classes of citizens not only at the expense of some others but at the expense of the average "welfare" of the society as a whole.

This focus on differential rewards from a foreign policy is a useful accompaniment to the earlier pieces which helped break down the notion of a monolithic "national interest." Johnson does note at the end of his essay, however, that in the long run the initially disadvantaged classes may gain from nationalism if the creation of a substantial middle class is essential to developing a stable society and democratic government.

●

[2] *Ibid.*, p. 385.

22

A Theoretical Model of Nationalism in New and Developing States

Harry G. Johnson

Nationalism in new and developing states is a complex problem of increasing concern to both political scientists and economists. To the political scientist, nationalism appears, on the one hand, as an integrative ideological force facilitating the establishment of a viable and cohesive nation-state; on the other hand, ethnic groupings, especially when they coincide with geographical, linguistic, and religious differences, generate the phenomenon of nationalism within the state and constitute a threat to the political stability of the state and the prospects for its survival. In addition, nationalism is a factor fundamental to the understanding of the ideological role of the concepts of "colonialism" and "imperialism" in the political life of ex-colonial states. Equally, to the economist, nationalism appears, on the one hand, as a driving force responsible for the urge of less developed countries (of which the majority are new states) to accelerate their economic development by economic planning, and, on the other hand, as the major political influence responsible for the fact that many features of the policies, concepts, and methods of economic development planning in such countries either do not make economic sense or else would make economic sense only in certain specific and rather exceptional economic circumstances the actual presence of which no one has felt it necessary to establish by empirical economic research.

Reprinted with permission from the *Political Science Quarterly*, **80**, 2 (June 1965), pp. 169–185.

This last point may be illustrated by a variety of examples. In the first place, both public pronouncements in developing countries and the literature on economic development are pervaded by an emphasis on industrialization as the necessary path to economic development, despite the fact that many economists, looking either to past economic history or to the current situation in the less developed countries, have concluded that the development of agriculture or of exports of certain natural resource products constitutes their logical path to economic development. Secondly, in regard to the choice of industries to be fostered by development policy, there is a marked tendency to regard certain industries as strategic, almost regardless of the size of the country, its location, or its available skills. Which industries these are depend in large part on the stage of development. In the earliest stages of development, a steel industry is generally regarded as the *sine qua non* of economic development, even though steel requires a massive investment of capital and the world steel industry has tended to suffer from chronic overcapacity rather than excessive pressure of demand. In more advanced countries, such as Canada, Australia, the Union of South Africa, Mexico, and Argentina, the *sine qua non* of development is a domestic automotive industry, even though the establishment of such an industry involves, essentially, the local production of American or European models at costs substantially above the prices of imports. In countries that are generally regarded as advanced, other than the United States, a comparable emphasis has been placed on the production of atomic energy, even though the commercial profitability of that form of power is not yet firmly established. As indicated, an economic justification for regarding the specific industrial activities mentioned as strategic is difficult to provide; instead, the selection of what activity is strategic seems to be governed by rivalry with and imitation of other nations that are regarded in some sense as superior.

A third example, different in nature, is the almost universal prevalence of a preference for public enterprise over private enterprise. Such a preference is not necessarily a question of nationalism—it may be a consequence of political philosophy—but it frequently seems to be dictated by nationalism rather than by socialist political principle. The problem for the economist here is to explain what, if any, advantage a country with limited managerial skills and limited administrative capacity derives from organizing industrial activities under governmental control rather than through reliance on the competitive marketplace.

Two other examples are drawn from the area of international economic relations. In commercial policy, developing countries generally place great emphasis on policies of substituting domestic production for imports, when the economics of the situation would indicate that economic efficiency would best be served by reliance on the principle of comparative advantage. And in almost all the developing countries and new nations, there is strong opposition to the investment of foreign capital and to the employment of foreign scientific, technical, and managerial personnel, even though capital and professional people are scarce and their scarcity frequently constitutes the major bottleneck in the process of economic development. Both phenomena are clearly derived from nationalism.

The problem these examples pose for the economist as social scientist is to explain the tenacity with which these policies are followed and the regularities of behavior that can be discerned among countries, in terms of an underlying logical connection running from nationalism to economic policy. The purpose of this article is to provide such an explanation, in the form of a theoretical model of economic nationalism in new and developing states; the intention is not to pass judgment on the wisdom or otherwise of nationalist policies, but rather to explain such policies as a rational and economic response to certain types of situations.

1

The theoretical model presented derives primarily from three recent applications of economic theory to problems hitherto not generally considered to fall within its range.

The first of these is Gary S. Becker's study of discrimination against Negroes in the United States.[1] The key concept of this work is the "taste for discrimination," the notion that people who discriminate are willing to sacrifice material gain—by paying higher prices or accepting lower prices in their economic transactions—in order to enjoy a psychological gain derived from avoiding contact with the group discriminated against. The model of nationalism presented here adopts from Becker's work the notion that individuals seek—in accordance with the postulates of economic theory—to maximize their satisfaction, but that this satisfaction includes enjoyment of both psychic income and material income; it simply substitutes for the taste for discrimination a taste for nationalism.

The second source of the model is Anthony Downs' application of economic theory to the processes and practices of democratic government.[2] Downs' basic hypothesis is that political parties seek to maximize their gains from office; but that they win office by catering to the preferences of the voters, and can only continue in office by satisfying the voters'

[1] G. S. Becker, *The Economics of Discrimination* (Chicago: University of Chicago Press, 1957).

[2] A. Downs, "An Economic Theory of Political Action in a Democracy," *Journal of Political Economy*, **66** (1957), pp. 135–150, and *An Economic Theory of Democracy* (New York: Harper & Row, 1957).

preferences for various types and quantities of governmental activity. In other words, power is exchanged for desired policies in a political transaction between party and electorate. A strategic element in Downs' theory of the workings of democracy is the cost of acquiring information. Downs uses this cost to explain the reliance on persuasion in arriving at political decisions; the inequality of political influence; the role of ideology; electoral apathy; and the bias of democratic government toward serving producer rather than consumer interests.

The third source of the model is Albert Breton's analysis of the economics of nationalism.[3] Breton identifies nationality with ownership by nationals of various types of property, and regards it as a type of collective consumption capital that yields an income of utility and can be invested in by spending public funds on the acquisition of such capital. Using this framework, Breton produces a number of specific and testable propositions about nationalism: nationalist policy is mainly concerned with redistributing income rather than increasing it; specifically, the redistribution is from the working class to the middle class; consequently, where the working class is poor, there will be a tendency to resort to confiscation rather than purchase of property. Furthermore, nationalism will tend to favor investment in national manufacturing, since manufacturing jobs and ownership are preferred by the middle class; its collective nature will appeal to socialists; and its emergence will be correlated with the rise of new middle classes who have difficulty in finding suitable career opportunities.

2

The development of the model of economic nationalism starts from Downs' model of the working of democracy. It is posited that political parties are engaged in the business of exchanging governmental policies and services, from which a party in power derives benefits in the form of psychic and material gains of various kinds, for votes from the electorate. The party's success in gaining and keeping power depends on its success in furnishing what the electorate desires from the government in exchange for its votes. The main obstacle to efficiency in this exchange stems from ignorance on both sides about the prospective gains from the policies offered, and the cost of acquiring the information necessary to make the change efficient. This obstacle forces the political party to depend for its information about voter preferences on pressure groups and lobbyists, and on the communications media. Also, though Downs does not develop the point because he is primarily concerned with established democracies, this

[3] A. Breton, "The Economics of Nationalism," *Journal of Political Economy*, **72** (1964), pp. 376–386.

dependence gives the political parties a strong incentive to establish control over communications media as a means of establishing political control.

The average voter, however, is motivated by his own rational self-interest not to acquire much knowledge about the policies of political parties and their consequences for his economic welfare, because whether or not he is well informed, he will have a negligible influence on which party is elected. It is this that gives ideology a crucial role in political life. The establishment of a distinctive party ideology simplifies the party's problem of communicating to the electorate by enabling the party to summarize all of its policies in one general symbolism; and it simplifies the problem of the voter, who can vote by ideology instead of being obliged to weigh up each party's record and promises on the whole range of specific policy issues. Parties will, therefore, compete largely through their ideologies.

In well-established democracies, the type of party system that emerges from this competition will depend on a variety of features, including the distribution among voters of ideological preferences, whether election is by proportional representation or by plurality, and the geographical distribution of voter preferences. Proportional representation will tend to foster a multiplicity of ideologically differentiated parties, whereas plurality election will promote a two-party system, except where ideological difference is associated with geographical region. Actual policy in a multiparty system will, however, represent a compromise among ideologies, owing to the necessity of forming coalitions to command power. In a two-party system, the relation of party ideologies will be determined by the distribution of voter preferences for ideologies: if voters tend to group around a central ideological position (the distribution of voter preferences is unimodal), party ideologies will tend to be virtually indistinguishable. If, on the other hand, voter preferences group around two or more typical positions (the distribution of voter preferences is multimodal) and voters refrain from voting if party ideology departs too far from their own ideological preferences, party ideologies will be significantly differentiated; such a situation, however, may make the country politically unstable, and threaten political disintegration.

Where democracy is not well established, there will be a strong incentive for a party to attempt to create a comprehensive and preclusive ideology to enable it to enjoy exclusive control of government; this will be especially so in an underdeveloped economy and society. The change of office from party to party in a normal democracy is an economically wasteful process, and relies on the capacity of the sociopolitical and economic system to reabsorb ousted political officeholders without imposing great private losses on them. In an economically underdeveloped country, the

change of office between parties is likely to impose substantial economic
losses on the individuals who have to wait their turn in office, by comparison with the power and the material gains they would enjoy if they controlled the government permanently. The acceptance of normal democracy
depends on acceptance of the rules of the game; but the acceptance rests
not only on a democratic tradition but also on an economic and sociopolitical system that does not impose severe economic losses on political
losers.

Nationalistic feeling provides a foundation for the establishment of a
preclusive ideology as a prerequisite for one-party government; and there
is an evident connection between the stridency of nationalism in the new
nations and their propensity to establish one-party government. Even
where the two-party system is maintained, the competition in ideology
would tend to make both parties stress nationalism and nationalistic
policies if there were widespread nationalistic sentiment among the
electorate. Only if there were a sharp division of voter preferences, some
voters envisaging advantages in nationalistic policies and others envisaging
serious disadvantages, would there be significant political division on
the issue; and in this case the political stability of the country would be
seriously threatened.

Finally, one of Downs' important conclusions is that the working of
political democracy will display an asymmetry with respect to economic
issues. This asymmetry arises from the concentration of producer interests
and the dispersion of consumer interests, which makes it easy to organize
lobbies for producer interests and difficult to organize them for consumer
interests. The relevance of this asymmetry for nationalism is that nationalist policies tend to concentrate on specific producer interests, whereas
their costs are dispersed thinly over the mass of consumers, so that it is not
too difficult for nationalist policies to win political support on the basis of
the producer gains they promise, even though the net benefits, taking
consumers and producers together, are negative.

3

The foregoing argument has outlined an approach to the working of
political democracy and party government and has attempted to integrate
nationalism in developing countries with it. The next problem is the nature
of nationalism as an ideology, and of its political action program.

As an ideology or state of political feeling, nationalism can be conceived of, along the lines of the Becker analysis of discrimination against
Negroes, as attaching utility or value to having certain jobs held or certain
property owned by members of the national group rather than by nonmembers of the national group. (The difference between the two concepts,

though this is a difference largely of degree rather than of kind, is that the utility accrues to members of the national group whether or not they themselves hold the jobs or the property in question; the consequences of this difference are elaborated subsequently.) In this context, it is most useful to employ a broad definition of property ownership, one including in property not merely the ownership of physical or financial assets but also rights to certain kinds of jobs, since job opportunities are property in the sense of yielding a stream of income to the holder. Nationalism can accordingly be conceived of as a state of social psychology or political sentiment that attaches value to having property in this broad sense owned by members of the national group.

The question that immediately arises is: To what kinds of property does this utility of nationality become attached? Clearly, in some sense it is the "important" or prestigious or socially relevant kinds of property that acquire this added value. One such, obviously, is the result of cultural and artistic activities—the national literature, music, and drama. Another is positions of authority in the governmental apparatus and in the social structure. Still another comprises particular types of economic activity and economic roles that carry superior status (and usually superior income also).

A related question is: What determines which specific items of property acquire added value from nationalism? There seem to be two major ways in which nationalistic utility can be acquired. One is internal, through observation within the country of foreign operations there; the property yielding income and status to the foreigner becomes the property valued by the nationalists. This mechanism of generating nationalistic utility is particularly important in ex-colonial countries or countries where foreign investment and alleged "economic imperialism" have been significant, where nationalism seeks particularly to replace the officialdom of the colonial power and the executives and shareholders of the foreign enterprises with nationals. The other mechanism is external, through contact with and observation of other nations, which provides knowledge of what forms of property are highly regarded in such societies.

Both of these mechanisms involve the determination of the nationalistic values of specific form of property by imitation or emulation of other countries, either of their actual practices or of the "image" of themselves they project abroad. The importance of international emulation in determining nationalistic objectives is evident in a variety of areas. Examples in the field of economic policy have already been provided. Examples in other fields readily spring to mind, such as the importance frequently attached to the winning of Olympic medals by a country's athletes, or the tendency of the allocation of resources for scientific research in the more advanced countries to be dominated by the spectacular accomplishments of other countries.

4

The next step in the analysis is to recognize that the benefits from the gratification of nationalist sentiment are of two sorts, particular and general, or tangible and intangible. The particular benefits are the incomes and prestige that accrue to those nationals who acquire the property rights or the offices and employment opportunities in which nationalism invests. The general benefits consist of the psychic satisfaction derived by the community at large from gratification of the taste for nationalism. It is important to notice here the concentration of the tangible benefits on the subgroup of nationals that is eligible to hold the property or to fill the positions, as distinguished from the dispersion of the intangible benefits, which presumably accrue to the whole national society insofar as its members share the taste for nationalism. It is the intangible benefits that give national ownership of property the character of a collective consumption good—one for which consumption by one individual does not preclude consumption by another—and for the economist raises the difficult problem of how to determine the optimal quantity to supply.

The tangible benefits are directly or indirectly economic, and are of considerable value to the individuals who may receive them; thus, the bias of the democratic process toward producer interests becomes relevant. These individuals have an economic incentive to pursue these prospective benefits through the cultivation of nationalism. Further, given the mechanisms by which nationalistic utility become attached to specific items of property, these items will tend to be such as to yield tangible benefits primarily to the educated, the entrepreneurially qualified classes, some at least of the wealthy, and other elite groups, so that there is an inherent class slant to the economic interest in pursuing nationalism.

There is, moreover, a natural consilience of the strictly economic interests in nationalism and the cultural interests in nationalism. Both the intellectuals engaged in cultural activities and the owners and managers of communications media have an interest in nationalism, particularly when it can be combined with a linguistic difference, but even when it cannot, because nationalism creates a monopolistic barrier to competition from other countries' purveyors of the same sorts of cultural products. Thus cultural nationalism complements economic nationalism, both involving tangible benefits in the form of protection of the market for the services of individuals. This consideration suggests also that the strength of economic and cultural interests in nationalism will vary with the threat of competition and the need for protection of the market. One would expect to find nationalist sentiment strongest where the individuals concerned are most vulnerable to competition from foreign culture or from foreign economic activities; conversely, one would expect to find that the nations that are leading culturally and economically will tend to be internationalist and cosmopolitan in outlook, because this would tend to extend the market area for their cultural and economic products. These expectations accord broadly with experience.

5

We now turn from nationalism as a political ideology to nationalism as an economic program. As such, nationalism seeks to extend the property owned by nationals so as to gratify the taste for nationalism. There are a variety of methods available for accomplishing this objective.

One obvious method is confiscation, that is, the forced transfer of property from foreign owners to nationals. Here it is important to notice a certain ambiguity in the concept of confiscation, extremely useful to nationalists, which arises because what appears to be confiscation may not really be confiscation in the fundamental economic sense of the term. For example, nationalizing the civil service, or nationalizing the administrative and executive jobs in a particular enterprise, may appear to transfer property of value from the foreigners to the nationals. But insofar as the foreigners were receiving a fair price for their skilled qualifications, and nationalization involves replacing them with nationals of inferior skills at the same salaries, the effect is primarily to transfer income within the national group toward the individuals favored with promotion at the expense of the general community which must bear the costs of poorer administration, inferior economic efficiency, or deterioration of the quality of the service that results.

The result of nationalizing jobs is not, of course, necessarily merely a transfer of income among nationals. If previously there has been genuine discrimination against nationals, for example, where the civil servants have been of a foreign nationality even though their jobs could be performed as efficiently or more efficiently by nationals available at lower salaries, there will be a genuine transfer of income from foreigners to nationals, since discrimination against nationals in employment gives foreigners a source of monopoly gain at the expense of nationals. It is always difficult to determine, however, whether the employment of non-nationals represents discrimination against nationals or reflects their inferior quality; under competitive conditions there is a presumption in favor of the latter assumption. The possibility of discrimination apart, nationalizing jobs is a matter of transferring income among members of the national group, with side effects in reducing aggregate real income by reducing the efficiency of performance. Genuine confiscation, which transfers valuable property from foreigners to nationals, is therefore largely confined to property in the narrow sense, that is, to the tangible wealth—cash, securities, real property, and enterprises—owned in the country by foreigners.

The alternative to confiscation is investment of resources or purchase, that is, the use of wealth or savings that otherwise would be available for other purposes to purchase material property or job opportunities for nationals. This may be effected directly through public investment, or indirectly through various policies influencing private investment. The public investment method includes both the nationalization of existing foreign enterprises with fair compensation, and the use of development funds or public revenue to create new enterprises. The method of influencing private investment involves using tariffs and related policies to stimulate industries of the kind desired; these policies also entail public investment, in the sense that the use of the tariff, for example, involves imposing a tax on the consumer in the form of higher prices, the revenue from which goes to subsidize the creation of the protected enterprises by the private entrepreneurs who then receive the higher prices.

6

It must be recognized, of course, that nationalism is not the only reason why a government may choose to adopt any of these policies. There are many economic arguments as to why such policies might be beneficial in terms of increasing the national income, rather than serving purely to gratify the taste for nationalism. The relevant economic analysis is quite elaborate. It runs in terms of divergences between the private and the social costs of or returns from various kinds of investment, and includes such possibilities as rationalizing the system of production by consolidation of control, training the entrepreneurial and laboring forces and so obtaining social benefits that private competition would not produce if left to itself (the infant industry argument), and obtaining cost reductions through exploiting economies of scale. These arguments are frequently effective in attracting support for nationalistic policies from nonnationalists, and especially socialists, who are inclined to believe implicitly that competition is inherently inefficient and susceptible of improvement by governmental action. The real question, however, is whether the facts of the situation conform to the possibilities of theoretical reasoning. Typically, little or no effort is devoted to confirming that this is so, the theoretical possibilities being employed instead to provide a plausible and apparently scientific defense of policies that are adopted for essentially nationalistic reasons.

With respect to the method of nationalization, it is necessary to realize that, provided compensation is fair, there is no transfer of wealth from foreigners to nationals, and no net gain in national wealth, because fair compensation involves paying the previous owner the present value of the future income he would have earned from the enterprise. The only exception occurs when nationalization permits efficiency-increasing changes in production methods that the previous owner would not have introduced. The gain (or loss) from nationalization does not result from the mere fact of nationalization; instead, gains or losses are the result of changes in management methods and policies introduced after nationalization. Insofar as the objective of nationalization is to provide jobs for nationals, presumably people are employed in large numbers or are of a lower quality than previously were employed, and this obviously involves economic waste.[4] Alternatively stated, potential national output is sacrificed in return for the psychic income obtained from greater employment of nationals. The same is true of public investment in the creation of new industries when such investment is influenced by the desire to provide high-income and high-status jobs for nationals.

The desire to provide more, and more worthy, jobs for nationals will influence the selection of industries for nationalization in certain ways, and this may incidentally provide a means of distinguishing nationalistic from socialistic nationalization. "Nationalistic" nationalization, aside from the obvious tendency to concentrate on industries employing a high proportion of foreigners, will tend to be aimed at industries with a well-established and fairly static technology that can be managed by bureaucratic routine, and at industries that enjoy a monopolistic position in the domestic market rather than competing actively in the domestic or especially the foreign market, since these characteristics will permit the employment of larger total numbers, and the substitution of lower-quality nationals for higher-quality foreigners, without risking the breakdown and bankruptcy of the industry. In any case, public ownership of industry, whether achieved by nationalization or new investment, permits losses incurred in consequence of the pursuit of nationalistic policies to be underwritten, within limits, by the taxing and borrowing powers of the government.

The alternative to investment or purchase of industry is the use of tariffs, tax concessions, and special privileges to promote the establishment of the kinds of industries that are desired. This method involves a much more clear-cut possibility of economic loss, through higher costs of production paid for by consumers in the form either of higher prices or of

---

[4] Again, there may be an economic gain rather than a loss, if, previously, nationals were discriminated against in the employment practices of the nationalized industry.

lost tax revenue that has to be made up either by other taxes or by reduced governmental services, and an overt transfer from the general consumer, who pays the higher prices or taxes or loses governmental services, to the favored producers who are given a protected position in the market. The use of the tariff or of tax concessions to induce the local establishment of particularly desired industries, however, frequently has the paradoxical result of increasing nationalist dissatisfaction rather than contributing to satisfaction, by inducing the foreign producer of a product previously imported to establish domestic production facilities in the country, with the result that the country exchanges the dissatisfaction of not having the industry in the country for the dissatisfaction of having its industry owned and staffed by foreign enterprises.[5]

7

The major implications of the theory of nationalist economic policy presented in this discussion may now be briefly summarized.

One implication is that nationalism will tend to direct economic development policy along certain specific lines; these lines might represent economic optimality, and would do so if the conditions posited by some familiar economic arguments were present. Failing empirical validation of those arguments, however, the consequence will be a reduction of material production below the economy's potential.

In the first place, nationalist economic policy will tend to foster activities selected for their symbolic value in terms of concepts of "national identity" and the economic content of nationhood; in particular, emphasis will be placed on manufacturing, and, within manufacturing, on certain industries possessing special value symbolic of industrial competence (such as the steel and automotive industries). Secondly, nationalist economic policy will foster activities offering prestigious jobs for the middle class and/or the educated class; the nature of such activities varies with the stage of development, very underdeveloped countries favoring bureaucratic jobs offering steady incomes for routine work, more advanced countries favoring managerial and professional jobs suitable for the products of the educational system, fairly mature countries favoring jobs in higher education and research.[6] Thirdly, nationalism will tend to favor both extensive state control over and extensive public ownership of

---

[5] This consequence of the tariff has been an important factor in the exacerbation of nationalist sentiment in Canada in recent years. The formation of the European Economic Community similarly has fostered American investment within the Community's boundaries and thereby provoked nationalist complaints.

[6] The emphasis on education in contemporary development tends to produce a rat race in which a country first invests a great deal of scarce capital in educating people, and then is obliged to invest a great deal more in providing suitable employment opportunities for them,

economic enterprises: state control provides employment for the educated directly, in the central control system, while both the control system and public ownership give the government social control over the allocation of jobs to nationals.

A second implication is that nationalism will tend to direct economic policy toward the production of psychic income in the form of nationalistic satisfaction, at the expense of material income. If attention is confined to material income alone, a third implication is that nationalism will tend to redistribute material income from the lower class toward the middle class, and particularly toward the educated middle class; in this respect, nationalism reinforces the trend of modern society toward the establishment of a class structure based on educational attainment.

This last implication relates to material income only, and does not necessarily imply that the lower classes are worse off because of nationalism when both real and psychic income are reckoned into the account. It is quite possible that the psychic enjoyment that the mass of the population derives from the collective consumption aspects of nationalism suffices to compensate them for the loss of material income imposed on them by nationalistic economic policies, so that nationalistic policies arrive at a quite acceptable result from the standpoint of maximizing satisfaction. It may even be that nationalistic policies are the cheapest and most effective way to raise real income in less developed countries; in some cases, one suspects, the prospects for genuine economic growth are so bleak that nationalism is the only possible means available for raising real income.[7]

It would seem, however, from the economic analysis of government presented earlier, that the lower classes are unlikely to be net gainers from economic nationalism, due to the effects of ignorance and the costs of acquiring information in concentrating political power in the hands of pressure groups, and the general tendency for producer interests to dominate over consumer interests that results from the natural response of voters to the high cost and negligible value of acquiring political information. The tendency for the mass of the population to suffer losses from economic nationalism is probably reinforced in the new nations by the prevalence of systems of one-party government, in which the party is based largely on

the consequence being a double waste of resources. Sometimes needs both for more education and for better jobs for the educated are urged simultaneously, despite the implicit economic contradiction.

[7] Field research by members of the Committee for the Comparative Study of New Nations suggests that this may in fact be the case in some of the new African nations. Nationalism may itself create such a situation, nationalistic economic policies blocking economic growth so effectively that it becomes necessary to resort to ever more extreme nationalistic sentiment and policy to maintain the illusion of economic development.

urban support and frequently exercises a virtual monopoly over the country's communications system.[8]

Even though nationalism may involve a substantial redistribution of real income toward the middle class at the expense of the mass of the population, this redistribution may perform a necessary function in the early stages of forming a nation, in the sense that the existence of a substantial middle class may be a prerequisite of a stable society and democratic government. In other words, an investment in the creation of a middle class, financed by resources extracted from the mass of the population by nationalistic policies, may be the essential preliminary to the construction of a viable national state. This problem, however, belongs in the spheres of history, sociology, and political science rather than economics.

[8] Both dependence on urban support and control over communications media are logical consequences of the economic theory of government as applied to such countries. Dependence on urban support in turn reinforces the bias of development policy toward promotion of manufacturing, and in general fosters policies favoring the city-dweller at the expense of the agricultural population. A particular aspect of this, important especially in Latin America, is the maintenance of low urban transport rates by direct or indirect subsidization, which in its turn fosters urban population growth and increases the political importance of urban residents.

●

Racial discrimination, like nationalism, is a phenomenon with important economic consequences and often deep economic roots as well. Part of the preceding article by Johnson was built upon a book by Gary Becker, in which the author contended that much discriminatory behavior could be explained by a "taste" for discrimination, a taste that induced whites to prefer working with other whites even at the cost of somewhat lower economic returns. By this theory the discriminators do not gain materially, and the impetus to their actions stems from a variety of cultural preferences rather than a self-interested maximization of economic gain.

In the following selection Anne O. Kreuger takes off from this analysis, but contends that under certain conditions it is not necessary to assume an underlying "taste" for discrimination, but that discrimination can be consonant with strictly economic motivations and that the discriminators do, in fact, benefit materially from their course of action. She shows the assumptions under which *white* real income would be maximized by discrimination, even though the total income of whites and non-whites combined must always be less with the "inefficient" allocation resulting from discrimination rather than the mechanisms of a fully competitive free market.[5] At the same time, however, she demonstrates that white *capitalists'* income would be less with discrimination than without it, so it is not the entire white community that would benefit. Unlike Johnson's discussion, which had behind it some scraps of evidence showing how nationalism benefited the middle class at the expense of workers, there seems to be no empirical data that indicates whether white workers really do gain from discrimination at the expense of white capitalists as well as non-white workers. Note too that there is little that non-whites can profitably do in the way of purely economic counterdiscrimination. A very small amount of retaliation will raise their incomes slightly, but much "black power" discrimination will take them beyond the optimal point and reduce their incomes still further, while of course reducing white incomes too. It is conceivable, however, that the threat of retaliation, with the damages it would inflict on both parties, could become a source of bargaining advantage for nonwhites, in which case a variety of quite different models would become applicable. And certainly this basic model could be applied to cases of initial discrimination not by a majority, but by an entrenched privileged minority like the south African whites. There,

---

[1] According to the Council of Economic Advisers, *Economic Report to the President, January 1965* (Washington: US Government Printing Office, 1965), p. 167, "It is estimated that Society loses up to $20 billion per year of potential production as a result of employment discrimination and poorer educational opportunities for non-whites."

the potential economic gains, even leaving the bargaining possibility aside, would be greater for the colored majority that was being discriminated against.

In the form presented, the Kreuger article seems to apply almost entirely to domestic politics rather than to foreign policy concerns. But the same kind of theoretical orientation is applicable to international trade discrimination, for example, by industrial countries against the underdeveloped states which produce raw materials and are populated by colored peoples. Furthermore, there is overwhelming evidence not only that countries discriminate in favor of their own nationals (through tariffs and quotas) but by often subtle means in favor of some partner nations against others. Trading patterns are heavily determined by political and cultural ties as well as by mere considerations of cost and comparative advantage. An evaluation of the distribution of net gains and losses from international discrimination could follow much the same course as the Kreuger article.

●

23

The Economics of Discrimination

Anne O. Kreuger

In his *Economics of Discrimination*,[1] Professor Gary Becker develops a useful model for analyzing the economic effects of discrimination. Treating Negro and white sectors as if they were separate countries in an international trade model, he analyzes discrimination under the assumption that the white sector owns a higher ratio of capital to labor than does the Negro sector. If no discrimination existed, whites would export capital (or import labor) to the point where the marginal products of capital (and, hence, labor) are equal in both sectors. With a "taste for discrimination," whites prefer to use their capital with white labor, and can be induced to export capital only at a higher return than they can get at home. The "taste for discrimination coefficient" t_c implies that factors owners (in this case white capitalists) require a return $(1 + t_c)$ times as great as they earn at home in order to induce them to work with Negro factors of production.

Since the extra return earned by exported white capital in the Becker model is a payment to offset the "cost" to white capitalists of working with Negro labor, Becker defines the "net income" of whites as being equal to the marginal product of capital in the white sector times all white-owned capital (exported and domestically used) plus the white wage bill. Thus, the difference between the white return on capital in the two sectors is not treated as additional net income. If whites have a taste for discrimination

Reprinted from *The Journal of Political Economy*, **71**, 5 (October 1963), pp. 481–486, by permission of The University of Chicago Press. Copyright, 1963, by The University of Chicago Press.

[1] Chicago: University of Chicago Press, 1957.

their net income is maximized by imposing this differential, because as an argument of their utility function whites have preferences for working with other white factors of production. While this is a plausible hypothesis, other interpretations of discrimination are possible in which the motive for discrimination is economic rather than one of mere taste. Becker's analysis requires that a taste for discrimination must be an argument of the utility function. In what follows, it is shown that several white utility functions could lead to discrimination, with whites having no taste for discrimination (in the sense of preferring to work with other white-owned factors of production) whatsoever.

Section 1 demonstrates that white real (money) income will be maximized by an appropriate degree of discrimination. Section 2 considers the kinds of white utility functions that could generate such a result. Section 3 shows why, given plausible empirical magnitudes, Negro gains from counterdiscrimination are likely to be negligible. Last, plausible empirical values of white and Negro factor ownership are used to estimate the quantitative impact of discrimination.

1. Maximization of White Income

Becker assumes that white and Negro sectors have identical production functions and that competition prevails within each sector. Then

$$Y_w = f(L_w, K_w - E) + f_{k_n}E \tag{1}$$

$$Y_n = f(L_n, K_n + E) - f_{k_n}E \tag{2}$$

Y is the total real income of a sector, f the common production function, L the quantity of labor used in a sector. The subscripts w and n denote white and Negro variables, respectively. K_w is the white-owned capital stock, K_n the Negro-owned capital stock, and E represents the quantity of capital exported by the white sector. White and Negro factors are assumed to be perfect substitutes.

The production function is assumed to be first-order homogeneous, twice differentiable; f_l and f_k, the marginal products of labor and capital, are positive; f_{ll} and f_{kk}, the second partial derivatives of output with respect to the inputs, are negative.

Real white income is total output produced in the white sector plus the payment received by exported white capital used in the Negro sector. Since there is only one good in the system, there is no need for a price unit, and both incomes are expressed in terms of units of output. Negro income is equal to output produced in the Negro sector less the payment to white capital used in production in that sector.

Equations (1) and (2) together assure that all white and Negro factors of production will be used, and that trade between the two sectors will balance.

As Becker clearly indicates, the sum of white and Negro incomes Y_t is maximized when the marginal product of capital in one sector equals that in the other:

$$Y_t = Y_w + Y_n = f(L_w, K_w - E) + f(L_n, K_n + E) \tag{3}$$

$$\frac{\partial Y_t}{\partial E} = -f_{k_w} + f_{k_n} = 0 \tag{4}$$

If the marginal product of capital is equal in the two sectors, the marginal product of labor must also be equal, since both are functions of the ratios of the inputs only. To maximize white income, differentiate partially with respect to capital exports:

$$\frac{\partial Y_w}{\partial E} = -f_{k_w} + f_{k_n} + f_{kk_n}E \tag{5}$$

Thus, for a maximum,

$$f_{k_w} = f_{k_n} + f_{kk_n}E \tag{6}$$

Since $f_{kk_n} < 0$, the marginal product of capital in the white sector should be lower than the marginal product of capital in the Negro sector for maximum white income.[2]

The demand for capital in the Negro sector is implicit in the assumption that capital will be paid its marginal product. The elasticity of demand for imported capital in the Negro sector, n_d, will be the elasticity of demand for capital weighted by the inverse of the proportion white capital represents of total capital used in the Negro sector. Defining n_k as the elasticity of demand for capital, and recalling that f_k is the price of capital,

$$n_k = \frac{1}{f_{kk}} \frac{f_k}{K} \tag{7}$$

Since $K = K_n + E$

$$n_D = \frac{1}{f_{kk}} \frac{f_k}{E} = \frac{1}{f_{kk}} \frac{f_k}{K} \frac{K_n + E}{E} = \frac{n_k}{r} \tag{8}$$

where

$$r = \frac{E}{K_n + E}$$

---

[2] This will maximize total real white income. In general, however, white capital income will be lower than when the marginal returns are equalized, because white workers are gaining intramarginally by working with more capital; see Table 1.

Substituting into Eq. (6)

$$f_{k_w} = f_{k_n}\left[1 + \frac{1}{n_D}\right] \tag{9}$$

Since $n_D < 0$, whites will maximize their incomes by having a lower price (marginal product) of capital at home than in the Negro sector. The symmetry with international trade theory should be clear. If whites behave as perfect competitors in their allocation of capital, they will do less well than if they impose an optimum tax, just as a country faced with a less than perfectly elastic offer curve can improve its own welfare by imposing an optimum tariff.

If whites are concerned only with maximizing their own incomes, the optimal differential between home and foreign returns (a "tax") will be

$$t_w = \frac{-1}{n_D + 1} \tag{10}$$

2. The White Welfare Function

It has so far been seen that white money income may increase by appropriate discrimination against Negroes. However, although aggregate white income would increase through such a practice, white capitalists' incomes would be lower, and white labor income higher, than were discrimination not practiced. Hence, white capital owners would not discriminate if they were maximizing their own incomes and had no taste for discrimination.

There are several possible ways in which discrimination against exporting capital to the Negroes might occur even if white capitalists had no personal taste for discrimination. For example, white capitalists may aim at maximizing income of the whole white community rather than white capitalists income only. A welfare function of this kind would be quite similar to Becker's, except that discrimination would be directed at maximizing white real income rather than avoiding the distastefulness of working with Negro factors of production. If the distribution of capital ownership among whites were relatively equal, the direct income losses of white capitalists would be relatively small. That such relative equality might exist is more plausible when it is recalled that human capital is, within this model, treated as similar to physical capital (since otherwise Negro and white labor cannot be treated as homogeneous).

A second possible way in which nonoptimal allocation of capital might occur would be in the allocation of publicly owned capital. Investment in education, for example, could be particularly important in this regard. Optimal investment of public capital would, from the viewpoint of the entire community, equalize the return on investment in both the white and Negro sectors.

Since decisions on the direction of public investment are made through the ballot box, white labor might, through its majority position, attain effective decision-making power. Since, in educational investment, the recipient of education collects the returns on his skills, it would be in white labor's interest to invest as much public capital in itself, and as little in Negroes, as possible. The return to educational investment in white labor would be lower than that to Negroes. This case violates the model of Section 1, in that exported white capital would not receive the value of its marginal product in the Negro sector. It would, however, lead to too much capital in the white sector, and too little in the Negro sector, with non-equalized rates of return to capital and labor in the two sectors.

Because recipients of investment in education collect the returns on it, there would be no incentive for white labor to allocate any public capital to the Negro sector. This raises the possibility that white labor might, if it had this power, distort the allocation of capital sufficiently in the interest of maximizing its own income, so that white real income was not maximized. It is also possible that it might use its voting power to maintain a monopoly on skills, and could conceivably use this power to discourage the exportation of white physical capital.

To the extent that this possibility has empirical validity, measurement of the degree of discrimination should not make allowance for skill differentials between Negroes and whites, at least to the extent that these differentials arise because of the distribution of public capital.

It is beyond the scope of this paper to attempt to test whether Becker's hypothesized utility function or one of the explanations of discrimination suggested previously, or some combination of them, more nearly approximates reality. It should be noted, however, that the welfare implications of the alternative functions are somewhat different. With Becker's utility function, for example, discrimination is Pareto-optimal in the sense that Negroes cannot be better off without whites being worse off, given that they have a taste for discrimination. If one of the alternatives suggested previously were the case, discrimination would be non-Pareto optimal, since an end to discrimination could be so managed as to give both whites and Negroes more income.

3. Maximization of Negro Income

Since whites could increase their money incomes by the imposition of an appropriate tax on exported capital, it is of interest to inquire whether, in general, Negroes could, for any given rate of discrimination by whites, improve their position by retaliation.

In order to investigate this, the white supply of capital to the Negro sector must be considered.

Let whites demand a return on capital invested abroad $(1 + t_w)$ times higher than the home rate of return on capital. They will then export capital until $(1 + t_w)f_{k_w} = R$, where R is the payment they receive per unit of capital exported to the Negro sector.

The white supply of capital to the Negro sector is then a function of the marginal productivity of capital in the white sector. The higher R, the more capital will be forthcoming. The elasticity of supply of capital to the Negro sector will be

$$n_s = \frac{-1}{f_{kk_w}} \frac{f_{k_w}}{E} = \frac{-n_K}{\rho} \rho = \frac{E}{K_w - E} \tag{11}$$

By reasoning similar to that in Section 1, Negro income may now be written:

$$Y_n = f(L_n, K_n + E) - ER \tag{12}$$

where ER now describes the movement along the white supply of capital schedule.

$$\frac{\partial Y_n}{\partial E} = f_{k_n} - R - E\frac{\partial R}{\partial E} \tag{13}$$

where $\partial R/\partial E$ is the increase in the Negro payment to white capital necessary to induce a small increase in capital imports. To maximize Negro incomes, then,

$$f_{k_n} = R\left[1 + \frac{1}{n_s}\right] \tag{14}$$

and an optimal Negro tax on inputs of white capital t_n, will maximize Negro income when

$$t_n = \frac{1}{n_s} \tag{15}$$

It will be shown in the following section, however, that the white elasticity of supply of capital will, in general, be so high that the optimal Negro "taste for discrimination" will be negligible.

That the Negro optimal tax rate is not independent of the white rate of taxation may be seen by recalling that the elasticity of supply of white capital to the Negro sector is the elasticity of demand for capital in the white sector divided by the ratio of total white capital in the Negro sector to white capital used in the white sector. The change in the optimal Negro tax with respect to a change in the white tax rate will be

$$\frac{\partial t_n}{\partial t_w} = \frac{\partial t}{\partial n_s} \frac{\partial n_s}{\partial \rho} \frac{\partial \rho}{\partial t_w} = \frac{-n_{K(1-p)} \dfrac{\partial E}{\partial t_w}}{n_K{}^2 (K_w - E)} \tag{16}$$

which is negative, since n_k and $\partial E/\partial t_n$ are negative and ρ is less than unity.

Similarly, the change in the optimal white tax rate with respect to a change in the Negro tax will be

$$\frac{\partial t_w}{\partial t_n} = \frac{n_K \dfrac{\partial E}{\partial t_n}(1 - r)}{r^2 \left(\dfrac{n_k}{r} - r\right)^2 (K_n + E)} \tag{17}$$

which will also be negative, since the level of white capital exports will decrease with an increase in the Negro tax rate. Hence, if there were a parallel to tariff retaliation in the case of discrimination, the process would be convergent to stable "tastes for discrimination."

4. Estimation of Gains and Losses with Discrimination

It is instructive to recompute Becker's estimates of the cost of discrimination in terms of the present analysis.[3] Taking his illustrative numbers, and recomputing on the basis of his values, $Q = L^{2/3}K^{1/3}$, $L_w = 9$, $L_n = 1$, $K_n = 1$, $K_w = 150$, Table 1 gives the results for representative values of E.

As Becker's computations indicate, total money income of whites and Negroes would be a maximum when 14.1 units of capital are exported

Table 1
Effects of Varying Degrees of Discrimination

E	White income	Negro income	White MP_k	Negro MP_k	White capital income	White labor income	White n_s	Negro n_D	Optimal White tax (%)	Optimal Negro tax (%)
0	22.989	1.000	.051	.333	7.66	15.32	—	—	—	—
2	23.207	1.122	.052	.160	7.94	15.26	111.0	−2.25	—	—
3	23.232	1.191	.052	.132	8.01	15.22	73.5	−2.00	—	—
4.1	23.239	1.260	.052	.113	8.05	15.19	53.0	−1.86	116	1.9
5.0	23.235	1.312	.052	.101	8.07	15.16	43.5	−1.80	—	—
8.0	23.189	1.464	.053	.076	8.14	15.05	26.6	−1.68	—	—
14.1	23.014	1.702	.055	.055	8.19	14.83	14.4	−1.60	—	—

[3] Becker, pp. 20 ff.

to the Negro sector. Moreover, he is correct in his assessment that white money income is not significantly affected by capital exports to Negroes: at its maximum, white money income would increase by about 1 percent over the no-trade position; free-trade white income is not significantly greater than no-trade white income.

However, white income would be maximized by capital exports of 4.1 units (to the nearest tenth of a unit), as compared with free trade exports of 14.1 units. The elasticity of Negro demand for capital at that optimal white level is 1.86, and hence a return 116 percent higher in the Negro sector would have to be required by white capitalists. At the point Becker believes may be more representative, capital exports of 8, white income is only about 0.87 percent higher than with no trade, and three-quarters of 1 percent higher than it would be at free trade. A differential return of about 43 percent would have to exist on the part of whites to maintain this degree of higher income. It should be observed that if this estimate approximates reality, aggregate income of Negroes and whites would increase, by ending discrimination, about one-fourth of 1 percent.

The more interesting element in the computations for present purposes, however, is that the optimal Negro "discrimination" is exceedingly small. Given their minority position, the elasticity of supply of capital to them (or demand for labor if one takes the alternative model) is quite high and gains from counterretaliation will be limited.

5. Summary

The major point of this analysis has been to establish that, under certain circumstances, a majority group may gain economically if it discriminates against a minority group. In this case, undesirable as the social and political results of discrimination may be, whites may increase their own income at the expense of the minority. Moreover, in plausible empirical circumstances, the opportunity for the minority to retaliate will, in general, be very limited. To the extent that the majority gains through discrimination, however, such gains will be small and income of the entire community will be less than would occur with no discrimination.

●

Just as students of international politics are centrally concerned with identifying the causes of war, economists and sociologists interested in industrial relations have developed a variety of explanations, of greatly differing plausibility and explanatory power, for the causes of strikes. And just as there is an enormous amount of folklore but little firm comparative evidence about why wars occur, the level of knowledge about the causes of strikes is not especially high—despite the enormous costs that wars have inflicted upon mankind and the far from trivial economic and human costs borne by societies as a result of industrial conflict.[1] The comparative study of political systems and their conflicts has frequently been termed an exercise in historical sociology; in much the same way a similar approach to labor-management conflict is on the borderline between economics and sociology.

We could not, of course, simply transfer findings about the causes or correlates of strikes to the origin of wars, and in this case there is, in fact, little in the way of reliable findings about strikes. But the similarities in the kind of explanations that are suggested are so striking as potentially to offer a number of useful insights. Some industries clearly are more strike prone than are others, and some firms and unions within particular industries have been more strike prone than have others. Again, we have a combination of potential systemic and subsystemic determinants. Explanations can be offered in terms of the *market* conditions faced by the industry as a whole, about the character of the *interactions* between the decision-making units (firm and union), about the nature of the *decision-making systems* themselves, or about the idiosyncratic characteristics of the *individuals* who happen to hold key decision-making positions within those units.

The first article, by E. R. Livernash, reviews quite a number of possible explanations. Unfortunately, the empirical references are illustrative and anecdotal rather than rigorous presentations of evidence; nevertheless, the piece is based on great familiarity with strike conditions and usefully illustrates the very wide variety of possible hypotheses about causes that could be tested in a rigorous manner. Two kinds of questions are asked.

---

[1] If anything, it would appear that the international relations literature is, in fact, better than the industrial relations material. We do, at least, have the large-scale comparative studies of L. F. Richardson, *Statistics of Deadly Quarrels* (Chicago and Pittsburgh: Quadrangle and Boxwood Presses, 1960): P. Sorokin, *Social and Cultural Dynamics*, Vol. III (New York: American Book Company, 1937); and Q. Wright, *A Study of War* (Chicago: University of Chicago Press, 1965, 2nd ed.) and have the promise of J. D. Singer and M. Small, *International War, 1815–1965: A Statistical Handbook* (New York: Wiley, 1969).

First what conditions contribute to the *readiness* of a firm or a union to take a strike; that is, what conditions make them less willing to accept an unfavorable bargain and more prepared to carry out the threat of a strike (or, for a firm, to permit the strike rather than settle). Second, what determines the *intensity* of the strike, measured here as its duration. Although Livernash separates the two discussions, we may combine them here for the sake of sorting out the different types of explanation.

One of the most important influences, he contends, has to do with the nature of the bargaining units—what are their *resources* for riding out a strike, and their relative abilities to inflict damage? Here we have some close analogies to the analysis of national power, and to the kinds of variables identified by Shubik as influencing the competitive behavior of firms in oligopolistic markets. Short- and long-run market vulnerability relate to the amount of damage each party can do to the other, especially, in this case, the consequences of a strike for the firm's market position. Will the loss of production during a strike result in a permanent loss of customers? The political variables we postulated to be appropriate for market vulnerability are relevant here again. Similarly, short-run financial vulnerability has to do, for firms, with their cash positions and their inventories of produced goods. For unions it is a combination of the individual members' liquid assets and the union's strike fund, which determines the level of sacrifice that will be required while the men stay out of work. Long-run financial vulnerability would be the firm's credit position and, somewhat less relevant perhaps, union members' ability to obtain loans. Again, the previous analogies apply, and again it is the *balance* of relative strengths between the two parties, more than the absolute value of either in isolation, that affects the outcome.

Resembling Shubik's variable of control vulnerability is Livernash's concern with the political instabilities within the union. He notes that the management usually attempts to establish direct communications with the employees and to reduce their willingness to tolerate strike-prone leaders. A corresponding option is seldom open to the union in its effort to manipulate management, though occasionally there are efforts to persuade stockholders that management's intransigence is reckless and endangers the firm's viability. On the international level, however, this kind of informal penetration, and communication directed to several levels of the opponent's decision-making system, is well known. It is widely believed in international politics that the internal stability of a regime importantly influences its readiness to engage in foreign conflict, but there is little evidence as to what the regularities are. Under some conditions an unstable regime will resort to war in an effort to unify the populace, to distract it from domestic difficulties, or to provide an excuse for repressing opposition.

Under other circumstances domestic weakness and the fear of collapse under further strain will deter a regime from foreign adventures, but no one knows very surely just when and how these influences operate. Similarly, Livernash suggests the vulnerabilities to which a weak union leadership is exposed *during* a strike, but it is also often argued that a weak leadership may be more prone to *initiate* a strike—so as to prove its militancy to a demanding rank-and-file. And again good evidence on these hypotheses is lacking. Management and, especially, union *morale*, covering a vague but obviously important set of variables, also must be included here.

Another set of influences has to do with the *interaction* process itself, both currently and in the past. A high level of hostility in the relationship, perhaps born of earlier strikes or near-strikes, may impede "rational" calculation and make agreement difficult, even though in less highly charged circumstances the parties' interests in an agreement might be fully apparent. Various structural conditions concerning the bargaining process may affect the quality of communication that takes place. Additionally, firms' and unions' negotiating *tactics* vary among themselves and over time just as do national leaders' tactics. They may shift between "firm" and conciliatory. The author also notes that the negotiating process is a continuous one, not a discrete set of events that begins only at contract-expiration time or that lasts only through the strike period. This calls to mind the famous dictum about the continuity between diplomacy and war.

Livernash emphasizes that the labor-management bargaining process does not occur as an isolated act between just two parties any more than an international war affects only the participants. The terms of the contract settlement and the fact of a strike, if it develops, will have major consequences for other firms and unions in this and in related industries, and for consumers throughout the economy. If it is the first of a prospective series of negotiations in an industry, the initial firm and union local will be under pressure, and will be supported by, other companies and union groups. Especially if market conditions make one or the other party vulnerable to a one-sided settlement, corresponding agents are likely to fear, and to take steps to prevent, a "domino effect."

In addition, Livernash repeatedly mentions the parties' calculations about the possibility of intervention by the government, and the prospect of such intervention affects their readiness to initiate or accept a strike. In international politics nations must weigh the possibilities for intervention by the "government"— the UN—but of course that actor is relatively weak. The chance of great power intervention to restrain or tip the conflict, in the "interest of the wider international community," is often very real, however. That intervention can range, in labor-management conflicts as well as in international clashes, from mediating "good offices" to adjudication or compulsory arbitration. In what would be, if applied to international politics, a very controversial position, the author warns about the dangers of intervention or its anticipation by the parties directly involved. He says that if the weaker party expects external intervention to save it from the consequences of a long strike (war), the likelihood of overt conflict may go up. Not only will strikes (or wars) thus become more frequent but the intervening party may find itself involved in future interventions much more often than it would if it had not encouraged the expectation that such intervention would be available. The author recognizes that often some external intervention in industrial disputes may indeed be necessary for the interests of the economy as a whole, just as the absence of supranational or great power intervention could have far more serious consequences than would any future undesirable expectations. But to limit the latter, he suggests the use of partial injunctions, requiring only that particular plants or firms return to production, while the rest of the industry remained idle. This could provide sufficient production to meet the essential (particularly national security) needs of the economy without relieving the conflicting parties of the unpleasant consequences of their dispute. Clearly this would often be a harsh counsel in international relations, but there sometimes are occasions when it would be desirable to limit external intervention in local conflicts very carefully. The intervention might be confined to seeing that nuclear weapons were not used, that international waterways were kept open, or that neighbors were not sucked into the war, but the central battle might be permitted to go on for some time.

In an especially controversial but nonetheless sometimes relevant counsel Livernash observes that strikes (or wars) may be a means of *conflict resolution* as well as simply a manifestation of conflict. He suggests that some strikes were "turning points" in labor-management relations, leading to the resolution of old grievances. Obviously, we cannot ignore the damage which wars or strikes do, or the fact that by any reasonable measure they do not often result in compensating gains for the immediate participants and some discount rate must be applied to gains for future generations. Nor can we ignore the normative questions of justice which inevitably arise in any actual or attempted change of the status quo. But the possibility that both kinds of conflict can have their uses, especially if kept limited by tacit or explicit rules or by careful outside intervention, should not be forgotten either.[2]

●

[2] For a stimulating theoretical statement on this topic see L. A. Coser, *The Functions of Social Conflict* (New York: Free Press, 1956).

24

The Relation of Power to the Structure and Process of Collective Bargaining

E. R. Livernash

1. The Power Dimension of the Strike

From a relative point of view, one party or the other wins a strike by achieving settlement terms approximating its intended objectives. This is true even though the costs to both parties are large. But, as a general rule, management cannot win a short strike and can only win by means of a long strike. The typical management option is between settlement without a strike and taking a long strike. For rough purposes, a short strike may be thought of as one month's duration and a long strike of three months' duration.

Most strikes today are not accidents, and experienced negotiators do not stumble into strikes. As a strike deadline approaches, issues normally have been narrowed, but important differences remain. The parties typically must make one or more final concessions to achieve settlement without a strike. In making these concessions, management is, in effect, defining the terms on which it is willing to take a long strike. The union is, in turn, making concessions rather than risk a long strike. If these mutual concessions are not made and a strike takes place, the opportunity to achieve a "middle-ground" settlement may not be available as a consequence of a short strike.

Unions today typically have significant strike funds, and employee earnings and savings are such that one month without earnings is not a

Reprinted from the *Journal of Law and Economics*, **6**, pp. 14–34.

heavy burden. When these facts are coupled with the psychology of the commitment which takes place when a strike starts, it becomes clear that the short strike is rarely a meaningful option to management. In other words, once a strike starts, both sides become firmly committed to the positions held prior to the strike, and the union in particular is unlikely to make concessions to resolve the strike. The middle ground evaporates, and the settlement price remains at the terms set and held by the union. Management thus can usually make a better settlement without a strike than after one month of worker idleness.

There are four types of exceptions which should be made to this logic. In the first place, there is the case in which the internal political situation within the union makes it virtually impossible to settle without a strike. Various forms of "excessive democracy" and rival leadership or factionalism may make impossible the kind of rational settlement process previously assumed. Under these circumstances management may regard a reasonable final concession prior to a strike as futile, but may, depending upon how the political forces within the union develop, be able to settle for this offer after a short strike. Other variations on the theme of political instability may make at least a short strike inevitable, but severe political instability should be regarded as the exception and not the rule. This is not a situation in which a united union is opposing management.

A second exception involves government intervention other than mediation. The dilemma created is an extremely difficult one. The anticipation of government intervention tends greatly to reduce or to remove union fear of a long strike. The union expects, through government pressures to settle, no more than a short strike. At the same time the anticipation of intervention tends to frustrate bargaining. Neither party wishes to make concessions which will weaken its position in the intervention process. Mediation may possibly be successful in avoiding a strike, but the temptation to the union to try to achieve additional gains through the short strike, and the reluctance of management to make a full offer because additional concessions may be required to settle a possible short strike, create a very difficult negotiation atmosphere. The process of defining strike issues as a "credible deterrent" to strikes requires the free option of the long strike. The cost and consequences of the long strike to both parties, including the political consequences to union leadership of a lost strike, are the basic deterrents to strikes in free bargaining. Government intervention and its anticipation are very likely to increase the probability of the short strike, and to make the short strike pay off, by frustrating normal negotiation and removing the option of the long strike.

The third type of exception involves poor communication and assessment of position in negotiations. This introduces the possibility that settlement may be achieved with only a short strike when it becomes clear that one party is in fact willing to take a long strike contrary to the earlier belief of the other party. On the other hand, the commitment associated with the strike may convert issues on which a given party would have been flexible into stubborn ones. However, as earlier stated, experienced negotiators are less likely today to make major errors in communicating and assessing positions than in earlier years. Efforts to improve the process of negotiation, subsequently discussed, can be quite important in minimizing this exception.

Finally, there is the exception of the very weak party which cannot consider seriously the long-strike option. This is not an exception to the logic of the importance of the long strike, but may lead to some futile short strikes, as well as placing responsibility for settlement terms almost exclusively on the strong party.

It has been stated that management cannot normally win the short strike. Management can only win the long strike. Also, management frequently tends, in fact, to win the long strike. As a strike lengthens, it commonly bears more heavily on the union and the employees than on management. Strike relief is no substitute for a job. Even regular strike benefits, which few unions can afford, and which usually exhaust the union treasury quite rapidly (with some exceptions), are no substitute for a job. Certainly, many long strikes have been settled on terms approximating management's prestrike offer.

The previous paragraph requires qualification and exceptions. Neither managements nor unions are all equally situated as to their ability to sustain a long strike. Many particular variables, some of which are discussed subsequently, bear upon each party's willingness and ability to sustain a strike. It appears, for example, that managements have been substantially unable to take a long strike in over-the-road trucking and have been weak in construction. In both these industries the unions have been able to use a divide-and-conquer tactic with great effectiveness. Additionally, the particular issues in dispute, the strength of feeling of each side toward particular issues, the moral support received by each side in the community or nation, the particular relative impact of the strike on each party as the strike lengthens, the solidarity of the union, the character of the union-management relationship, and no doubt other variables influence both the timing and terms of settlement. Of great importance is attitude toward particular issues, and both unions and managements have won important issues through long strikes.

The suggestion has been made that the question of the outcome of long and short strikes, and the analysis of the long-strike option, should be tested by an examination of actual strikes, including an appraisal of their outcome. The question has also been raised whether or not the basic analysis of the long-strike option survives the exceptions.

It would be extremely interesting, but quite difficult, to make a detailed analysis of strikes. A large number of strikes would have to be studied closely to appraise the outcome. This cannot be done for this discussion. Some statistical data are available, however, and some illustrative strikes may at least be mentioned.

One would expect, if the logic of the long-strike option is correct, that increased experience in negotiation would lead to fewer strikes, but that such strikes as take place would be of increased duration. Strike statistics kept by the Bureau of Labor Statistics, covering almost all types and kinds of stoppages, are dominated by short, small strikes. But data with respect to these stoppages suggest a declining trend in time lost during the postwar years. The years 1960–1962 have been especially noteworthy in establishing a record low of lost time. And the average duration of strikes has been increasing (contrary to the statement in the report to the President from the Advisory Committee on Labor-Management Policy on free and responsible collective bargaining). Duration has advanced from 18.5 days in 1955 to 24.6 days in 1962. With respect to strikes involving more than 10,000 employees, and omitting strikes of 10 days and less (though this makes no meaningful difference in the figures), the proportion of strikes in excess of 50 days increased from 27 percent of the strikes during the years 1947–1952, inclusive, to 36 percent during the years 1953–1959, inclusive. Such data as exist do not appear to contradict the logic of the long-strike option.

Certainly, one can also find a significant number of illustrative long strikes won by management. A machine-tool company in 1949 under conditions of large inventory took a six-month strike. The strike involved a back-to-work movement. The employees returning to work were expelled from the union. The strike was not only settled on management terms, but the union has been very weak ever since. An electrical company in 1958 took a five-month strike and drastically revised the labor agreement in its favor. An agricultural implements company in 1952 took a long strike which was settled on management terms. While this company subsequently had difficult union-management relations for some years, the strike, in retrospect, was a turning point toward improved efficiency and better relations. In 1953 an aircraft company took a two-month strike which was settled on management terms. A machine-tool company in 1951 took a three-month strike which was a clear turning point toward improved union-management relations.

Clearly, there are numerous examples of long strikes won by companies. There are also shorter strikes won by companies, most notably when it is clear that the company is prepared to take a long strike. The 1960 General Electric strike, lasting 20 days, appears to be in this category. A multiplant paper company took a strike in one plant. It lasted only two weeks and was settled on management terms. Again, it was clear that management was able and willing to take a long strike.

Not all long strikes are company victories. Some are compromise settlements which are not clear "wins" by either party. There do not appear, however, to be easily discovered examples of long strikes which management has clearly lost, though perhaps some of the recent newspaper strikes might be so classified.

Management losses are clearest in short strikes, as argued earlier, and in situations where management was unable or unwilling to take a long strike. In 1954, management lost a New York trucking strike. Companies began signing on union terms very quickly, and the union had won within three weeks. The electrical strike in New York City which created the 25-hour week for the IBEW lasted seven days. The 1956 steel strike can be cited as a short-strike victory for the union.

A review of a number of strikes, including those used here as illustrations, tends to support the importance of the long-strike option in free bargaining. Companies do win, or make substantial gains, as a consequence of long strikes or the ability to take long strikes. The clearest instances of strong company positions are in single-plant bargaining by multiplant firms, but there is no obvious general company disadvantage in corporate bargaining arrangements.

Union power is clearest in instances of local labor market and product market control, especially in the construction and trucking industries. The particular vulnerability of these employers, coupled with what appears to be an inelastic product demand, makes the long strike largely unrealistic in these situations. Structural characteristics are considered subsequently.

A review of actual strikes emphasizes the unique features of each strike situation. Perhaps the earlier analysis, at least by implication, places too much emphasis on "rational" causes and results. This may reflect an emotional reaction against the "failure of collective bargaining" interpretation of strikes. But clearly, some strikes do meet hard issues realistically and do represent a defensible and constructive use of power. Some strikes do restructure relationships toward more realistic and responsible negotiation. Some strikes, which in and of themselves appear irrational, subsequently create changed attitudes and improved relations. On the other hand, constructive results as to issues or relationships cannot be claimed for all long strikes. It is to be hoped that an extensive study of strikes would demonstrate a gradual increase in the rational and constructive use of power. It does not appear, however, that irrational behavior and other exceptions refute the essential importance which the long-strike option plays in free bargaining in avoiding frequent strikes, facing hard issues, and building more responsible negotiation. And power in collective bargaining is the relative willingness and ability to strike or take a strike, however complex the variables may be which determine relative willingness and ability. . . .

2. Particular Conditions

The following four subjects will be discussed briefly under this heading: the willingness of a company to take a strike; the indirect consequences of a strike; negotiating as a pattern setter or pattern follower; and variations in the union-management relationship.

A. The Willingness of a Company to Take a Strike

The outsider is greatly impressed by the statements by almost all management officials of extreme reluctance to take a strike. This reluctance is found under widely varying circumstances. If a company is quite prosperous, then the issue, whatever it may be, is judged not to be worth taking a strike. Profits are too high to warrant a strike. If a company is not prosperous, then it is judged to be impossible to take the cost of a strike. Profits are too low to afford a strike.

Perhaps the vast proportion of concessions made by management rather than take a strike is wise management decision. But it is this question, rather than the concessions which management has made as a consequence of a long strike, which is the difficult one to answer in the assessment of union power. There is the suspicion that management often has made a short-run comparison of the costs and consequences of a strike relative to a concession and made concessions not warranted by longer-term appraisal.

If management makes this short-run type of comparison, it finds itself always bargaining from a position of weakness and taking the cumulative effects of a series of small concessions, particularly with respect to unwise contract clauses. This is not a question of ability or power to resist but of unwillingness to resist.

In more recent years, there has been a better balance between labor relations and sales in management decisions. In no small part, management has been a hard bargainer because of the increasing competitiveness of the economic environment, but many managements have had great difficulty in recovering from the effects of earlier concessions. Clearly, however, there are important differences among companies in the weight given to long-run labor relations considerations in top management decisions. Contrasts among companies in the effectiveness of labor relations administration are much greater than can be explained by relative power positions.

The discussion here of management willingness to take a strike has been general and has presented the difficult problem of decision in weighing concessions to settle without a strike and the costs of a long strike. But it is also true that different companies are in different positions with regard to ability to take a strike. At least the following variables are important:

1. The cash position of the company. Some companies cannot at times take the short-run cash drain a strike would entail or at least are unwilling to draw down working capital to the extent required.

2. The profitability of a company and its credit position.

3. Different consequences of a strike on the production of a company. This varies with the scope of the bargaining structure as previously noted, but there are other variables. Some utility and oil companies can continue to operate with supervision. A strike of insurance agents did not cut off a company's income, as individual policyholders crossed picket lines to continue to pay premiums on their insurance. In other words, a strike may or may not shut down completely the production of a company.

4. Some companies can maintain sales from inventory. Size of inventory then becomes important. Customers may even overbuy in anticipation of a longer strike than takes place. This only displaces sales in time and does not reduce total sales.

5. Service companies can, obviously, not sell from inventory and hence cannot hedge through anticipatory sales and production.

6. The greatest company fear is permanent loss of market. Some pipeline and supplier companies have great fear of permanent loss of business and feel that it is impossible for them to take a strike. Some consumer product companies greatly fear permanent loss of market. On the other hand, some companies have a sufficiently differentiated product or geographical market advantage to diminish greatly their concern over permanent loss of business.

It is clear that in assessing willingness to take a strike a company must consider its financial strength and the consequences to it of a strike at a particular time. Variations among companies in products, markets, and business conditions create significant differences in the consequences of strikes quite apart from bargaining structure. In addition, one of the greatest deterrents to taking a strike is the very uncertainty of the consequences. It is impossible to predict how long a strike will last, and the variables in the business picture are always complex. When the concession is something that can be "lived with," at least in the short run, there is a great temptation to make the concession and avoid the possible damages from the strike. As earlier noted, this whole question makes any easy assessment of union power most difficult. Nor can any law compensate for these complex differences.

This section has been written from a company point of view. Clearly those elements in bargaining structure or otherwise which strengthen a company also weaken the union. Each party in collective bargaining is conscious of its elements of weakness and of the power of the other party. But union ability and willingness to sustain a long strike, in addition to the inverse of the factors already mentioned and the ability to pay strike benefits, are particularly related to the solidarity of the union, the degree of support of union leadership, and the internal political impact of particular issues. Some issues have much stronger employee appeal than do others. While in any given negotiation most union leaders will be strongly supported on any issue, to remain in power union leaders must be discriminating as to issues and avoid lost strikes. The importance of employee attitudes as a long-term determinant of union militancy gives real hope for a continuing reduction in the power dimension of negotiation.

B. The Indirect Consequences of a Strike

The costs and consequences of a strike to the parties are one thing and the consequences to third parties something else. The social costs and inconveniences of a strike are the dimensions which attract greatest public attention. There is, in the first place, considerable difference in the inconvenience to the public of various strikes. Any industry which provides a direct and unique service to the public for which there is no easily available substitute is in a difficult position to take a strike, and a striking union is subject to widespread criticism. Transportation service is an obvious case in point. Interestingly, many public utilities, other than transportation, are today able to operate in spite of a strike of production workers. Shutting down food industries, particularly milk, can cause considerable inconvenience, if not some danger to health and safety. To some degree, different services and perishable commodities can be judged in terms of their "essentiality," and the more essential the service or good, the greater the public criticism of any strike which takes place.

In the second place, some strikes cause more secondary unemployment than other strikes. Subject to inventory qualifications, pipeline industries, particularly those distributing raw materials which are used widely in many other industries, may create widespread secondary unemployment. The possible consequences of such strikes can cause great public consternation.

Finally, as of today, the relation of a product or industry to national defense is the subject of great concern. Even though the *proportion* of man-hours lost from strikes at missile sites has never been at all high, the absolute figures look large, and any lost time at a missile site is judged to be a national crisis. Also the factor of "cost plus" in defense work may lead to excessive management concessions.

The indirect consequences of a strike in great part distort public judgment of the merits of the dispute. Government intervention is bound to be guided primarily by these considerations. These political dimensions of a strike, while to some extent related to social costs, are quite unrelated to the longer-run economic consequences of settlement.

C. Pattern Setting and Pattern Following

The pattern-setting employer is typically more dependent upon power bargaining than is the pattern follower. On the other hand, the pattern setter has the advantage of greater opportunity to get a *quid pro quo* for the economic concessions made. The pattern follower, while not subject to the power pressure of the setter, may have difficulty in avoiding a pattern-plus settlement and is in a most difficult position to initiate changes, without taking a strike, which do not conform with the terms of the pattern settlement.

While it is easy to critize the equity and economic appropriateness of pattern following, particularly when it conforms to broad union jurisdictions rather than true industry differences, it does diminish the direct use of power in collective bargaining. Most negotiation takes place in an environment in which the tacit basis for settlement of economic terms is fairly narrowly fixed. This is not to say that pattern following reduces the effects of union power or that some pattern followers have not been in a weak bargaining position. The only point being made is that pattern following reduces the open use of power.

D. The Union-Management Relationship

While the paper has its primary focus upon power, collective bargaining is greatly influenced by attitudinal considerations. Strikes in a certain sense are always nonrational. One party or the other, as most observers judge the issues, is being "unreasonable" even in terms of his own long-term interests. On the other hand, union-management relationships vary greatly in the degree of hostility exhibited and in the degree to which negotiation exhibits rational resolution of issues rather than the use of power. Historically, emotionalism is declining, and a larger and larger proportion of relationships can be described as exhibiting a reasonable degree of accommodation.

In many union-management relationships, negotiation takes place year after year with neither party giving serious consideration to the possibility of a strike. Since strikes make news, and big strikes or strikes with serious indirect consequences make big news, it is very easy to lose perspective as to the frequency of strikes in the totality of collective bargaining. For example, in Mark Perlman's study of the machinists' union the author reports with respect to this union's agreements for the years 1948, 1950, 1952, and 1956 that, respectively, .8, 1.6, 1.3, and 2.8 percent of the agreements (numbering in the various years from 3937 to 5125) were signed after a strike. A strike threat was used in 8.8, 7.8, 7.2, and 15.7 percent of the negotiations.[1] This type of data puts the strike in more realistic perspective. But, nevertheless, not only is an enlargement of the rational element of negotiation and a diminution of the power dimension an appropriate objective of the parties but it should be a major consideration of public policy. An important issue is how to achieve continued improvement in the process of negotiation....

3. The Process of Negotiation

The bargaining process is by no means simply a matter of power. The development of constructive policies and programs responsive to employee needs does count both within the negotiation context and as a determinant of employee attitudes. Management initiative and persuasion play important roles apart from power. Nor is it easy to judge the actual effects of union power. If we define the net effect of union power upon the company in terms of economic and noneconomic concessions which would not have been made except for union power, we are left with a very troublesome judgment as to what adjustments, over a period of years, management would, in fact, have made in the absence of union power. Management inclination is no doubt to understate the adjustments that would have been made on a unilateral basis.

What is clear, however, is that many companies increasingly have attempted to develop and be guided by labor relations policies rather than simply to resist union demands. As managements take this more constructive point of view, they develop labor relations objectives and goals:

[1] M. Perlman, *The Machinists* (Cambridge: Harvard University Press, 1961), p. 264.

to improve union-management and employee relations; to maintain competitive position; and to achieve certain specific long-run and short-run contract objectives. In pursuit of these goals, certain educational and communication objectives are necessarily developed.

The definition and pursuit of policy objectives require an almost continuous preparation for negotiation. A company must know how the clauses in its labor agreement, and its various personnel policies, are in fact working. From this continuous factual study, policies and procedures which are not working well are marked for change, and policies working well will and can be strongly supported. In addition to continuous study of existing policies and practices, studies must also be made of anticipated union demands and of the position which the company should take with respect to them.

Thinking historically of the management response to unionism, the approach presented here represents a substantial increase in management initiative in the labor relations area. This increase in management initiative tends to increase the rational process of resolution of issues in the bargaining process and to reduce the power dimension. It tends to increase the rational element in bargaining by its focus upon the appropriateness of policies as advanced by management and the union and by its emphasis upon what may be called factual bargaining.

Some managements, most notably General Electric, may be described as taking a maximum degree of management initiative in the bargaining procedure. This company tends to formulate a full proposal for settlement, to present this full proposal early in the negotiation, typically on an "effective-when-accepted" basis, to commit the company to the proposal by wide publicity, to be extremely reluctant to modify its position, and to indicate that the position taken will be supported in a long strike if necessary. The wisdom of this extreme degree of rigidity with respect to the bargaining process can be questioned. Carried too far, the procedure becomes a power play which cannot be said to encourage the mutual resolution of issues. On the other hand, it places a union in an extremely difficult position to strike against a substantial offer and, most significantly, has undoubtedly done a great deal to encourage other companies to assume greater initiative than would otherwise have been the case.

With a lesser degree of management initiative than that exhibited by General Electric, there remains an essential relation between management policy positions and making concessions because of a strike threat. By whatever series of steps management arrives at its final position prior to a strike, to the extent that this position rests on policy it must be supported by willingness to take a long strike. The long-term process of creating greater emphasis upon policy orientation in negotiation cannot duck the issue and reality of power, but must meet it by a policy-oriented willingness to take a long strike.

Management, through greater initiative in labor relations, is improving the process of negotiation. By taking positive policy-oriented positions on the substantive issues in negotiation and supporting this position by willingness to take a long strike, the power of the union is offset by the power of the company, and the rational process of policy formulation attains greater weight in the outcome of negotiation. This does not mean that a company makes no concessions which it would not have made in the absence of the union, but it does tend to contain in meaningful measure, and to make more rational, the power dimension of bargaining.

Unions also, in the author's judgment, have become more policy-oriented with the passage of time. While improvement in the process of negotiation, as mentioned, cannot eliminate power considerations, it should diminish the frequency of conflict, create a growing number of more constructive relationships, and contribute to the more rational use of power.

As has been suggested by comments on these views, greater policy orientation in negotiation, and greater experience in negotiation, may imply in considerable measure a reduction in the necessity continuously to test the power position of the other party rather than a reduction in the power dimension in negotiation. This is clearly an important point, but the constructive meeting of problems also resolves issues without a resort to power. Constructive policies also increase the effectiveness of power in that its exercise is less arbitrary.

Consider, for example, an instance in which a policy-oriented company became involved in one plant in a Teamster strike. The company was in a strong power position when the strike started in 1949, but began an intensive factual communication program which was of strategic importance. Every employee in the plant had full knowledge of the poor competitive position of the plant. A top official in the company had held a series of meetings with the entire employee group, beginning at the time the company took over the plant. Every employee was also aware of the company's personnel policies, including their stock-distribution plan. A strike settlement after two weeks and the voting out of the elected militant union officers were as much a policy and employee attitude victory as a power victory. The company's further progress in the plant is clearly the result of policy and communication leadership.

The concessions which Pittsburgh Steel achieved in their special 1959 settlement in relation to excessive incentive earnings, albeit coming subsequent to the industry strike, results from a combination of clear policy objectives, firmness, and an intensive factual communication program. It was not simply power which achieved the result. The effectiveness of the communication program with the employees and generally in the communities in which they operated was such as to undercut completely the local union leaders when the chips were down, and the union leaders readily admit this point.

The use of power by the unions must in the long run be sanctioned by employees and by the public. To the extent that companies create policies and conditions (and adequately explain their position to employees) which meet in large measure the needs of employees, unions will find it difficult to obtain sanction for the use of power.

The coming decade very probably will find companies giving greater emphasis to personnel policies. Many companies to date have been preoccupied of necessity in meeting the problems posed by unions. Personnel policies have been neglected. Some sharp contrasts can now be drawn between the personnel programs and policies of leading nonunion companies and equally prominent unionized companies. The challenge of the future is improved integration of personnel and labor relations policies. While there is no easy answer, and superficial emphasis upon "communication" can well be a snare and delusion, the most hopeful path toward an ultimate reduction in the use of union power appears to be through changed employee attitudes.

The "continuous bargaining" joint study approach clearly has meaning in reaching a higher degree of policy accommodation between unions and management. A meaningful agenda explored openly, off the record, and without commitment can clearly lead to improved negotiation. At the moment there is considerable bandwagon, fad, and panacea emphasis upon this process, but there is also real potential for improved negotiation. It also raises to new importance the extent of the legal duty to bargain collectively and the possible removal of such duty.

The history of union-management relations since the depression shows a growth of accommodation. The path to greater accommodation lies in improved employee relations policies and administration and in more widespread policy-oriented negotiation. The union movement can grow in numbers and status only by less, not more, militancy. The long-strike option is necessary to reinforce these trends and is not inconsistent with them. What can be accomplished through changes in the legal framework is less clear to the author.

4. Some Public Policy Considerations

A. The Preservation of Free Bargaining

Free bargaining is meaningfully inconsistent with any type of government intervention other than mediation, particularly if a long strike is assumed to be intolerable in any form. Also, mediation is not effective if it is to be followed by some more formal process of intervention.

Mediation can facilitate the settlement of disputes, and fundamentally for a very simple reason. The role of the mediator is such that he can frequently get each side privately to move from an existing position if the move implies settlement. This is so even though in face-to-face negotiation neither side will alter position because the new position has no guarantee of settlement and may simply imply a weakened bargaining position. The opportunity to work privately with each side is clearly what gives the mediator a constructive role in the settlement process. But mediation will not work unless and until each prefers settlement to continuation of the dispute. Private pressures for settlement must be working with the mediator. If positions are strongly held, the mediator may not be able to avoid a strike. Also, the mediator has no power to impose terms. He must work within the framework of the issues as privately defined.

Fact finding with recommendations is in some respects similar to mediation. If the dispute yields to a mediated settlement by the fact finders, then the recommendations will produce settlement and may have advantages to the parties in that responsibility for settlement terms can be placed on the fact finders. But if the dispute does not yield to a mediated settlement, recommendations may make subsequent settlement more difficult. Accepting or not accepting a recommendation becomes a matter of total victory or defeat for each party. Also, while "public opinion" is of minimal direct consequence, recommendations may be a lever to bring various governmental pressures upon the parties. On balance, fact finding with recommendations tends to turn the dispute from the private to the public domain while contributing nothing of consequence beyond mediation in facilitating private settlement.

Fact finding with recommendations requires straightforward analysis. It is typically regarded as a stronger form of intervention than mediation—stronger in its ability to avoid or terminate strikes. And the primary purpose of intervention in emergency disputes is to avoid or terminate a strike, hopefully on terms which do not offend outrageously notions as to the public interest. The recommendations seldom rally and never unite public opinion on controversial issues. The recommendations, however, give the executive branch of the government moral support in bringing pressure upon the parties to accept. The parties fully realize that pressure will be brought to accept recommendations. This is why the process frustrates private negotiation. The parties know full well that a long strike will be possible only by a degree of defiance of government. Government intervention can itself become an issue between the parties, because the union may see advantages in the short strike, though perhaps not consciously so, in the midst of frustrated negotiation.

The government cannot impose terms short of compulsory arbitration. Compulsory arbitration substitutes, in significant degree, the value judgments of the arbitrator for the value judgments of the parties. Generally acceptable standards are lacking. Compulsory arbitration does not eliminate strikes. The strike record in Australia is not demonstrably superior to that in the United States. It is probably a wasting asset, with defiance of decisions becoming more common with the passage of time. Decisions will be influenced by the desire to avoid defiance. Australia has not found an effective enforcement mechanism. Compulsory arbitration appears to be a rather peculiar institution. Strictly enforced (by police state methods, if necessary), it is inconsistent with free bargaining. Loosely enforced, it will bend to private pressures. It is by no means clear as to what its outcome would be if applied, for example, to the maritime industry.

The functioning of compulsory arbitration in Australia is instructive on at least two basic counts: (1) the reaction of private bargaining to compulsory arbitration has varied from industry to industry, with a few parties deliberately avoiding the process, but with most parties bringing almost all issues to the boards and (2) it is most difficult to arbitrate contract terms without arbitrating their detailed interpretation and application. Industries with continuing conflict and strikes have fundamental problems—technological and economic sources of extreme job insecurity, organizational instability, extreme incompatibility in management and union points of view—which are by no means solved by compulsory arbitration. Where most needed, the process tends not to work. We may well be tempted to try compulsory arbitration for selected industries, with the simplified notion that it solves industrial relations problems. Yet once adopted, it will be embedded in perpetuity in our institutional arrangements.

Fundamentally, any form of intervention which brings pressure to avoid a strike, and to restrict the long-strike option, is inconsistent with free bargaining. The role of the strike in free bargaining is not widely understood. The few strikes that take place are in a sense the cost of the strike option which produces settlements in the large mass of negotiations. Nor are strikes simply failures of negotiation. They may be necessary to face hard issues realistically. They may restructure relationships toward accommodation. The fact that all strikes do not have these positive results does not negate the fundamental role of the long-strike option.

Improvement in the process of free bargaining should be a primary objective of public policy. This requires an active nonintervention government policy. In contrast, an easy intervention policy will produce an increasing frequency of acts of intervention. Easy intervention creates a what-can-we-lose situation for unions, encourages short strikes which, typically, pay off, and frustrates bargaining.

Finally, even if no consensus is reached as to changes in public policy which will improve the process of free bargaining, the underlying trends are favorable. Surely, collective bargaining is working better today than in earlier years. While the expectations and aspirations with regard to how it should work appear to have increased even more than the process has improved, the resulting critical opinion brings pressure for reduced militancy and further improvement in the process.

B. *The Partial Injunction and Partial Operation*

An idea which holds some hope of contributing to the emergency dispute problem is the use by the government of an injunction to require partial operation to meet defense needs or to maintain essential services. The attractiveness of the idea, if a primary aim of public policy is to preserve free bargaining and if it be recognized that the major pressures for intervention are political rather than economic, as emphasized by Northrup and Bloom,[2] is the extent to which it meets the two basic criteria of (1) being difficult for the parties to induce and difficult for the politicians to invoke and (2) being capable of coping with a real emergency if it occurs.

The partial injunction (partial operation) procedure has the following advantages:

1. It has no associated settlement process and so would not be expected to frustrate negotiation.

2. It does not prohibit a strike, but, rather, by restricting the scope of a strike, protects the long-strike option and maintains private pressures to settle.

3. It appears reasonably even-handed as to its effects upon the parties.

4. It would not be embraced enthusiastically by either party, and its anticipation might thus add to the deterrent effects of a possible strike.

5. It could be made difficult to obtain by forcing the government to *pinpoint* the nature of the emergency.

The disadvantages are real but essentially impossible to specify in the present state of our knowledge. The difficulties relate to the practical problems and possibilities in using the technique and fall into three categories: (a) the economic and technical problems of partial operation

[2] Northrup and Bloom, *Government and Labor* (Homewood, Ill.; Richard D. Irwin, Inc., 1963), p. 434 and Ch. 15.

(units operated must meet reasonable tests of economic and technical efficiency); (b) the labor relations problems (both unions and companies would face problems, with some workers continuing to work while others were on strike); and (c) special administrative problems (administrative routines would have to be adapted to the special problems arising in a given situation).

In exploring these problems in steel, it appeared that neither management nor union officials wanted to face up to them. What plants get to operate, since most plants have facilities to supply the needed steel? Which customers get the nondefense steel? Which workers get to work? Yet, in spite of the obvious headaches involved, operating a selected 5–10 percent of steel capacity would more than remove any critical defense problem from steel strikes.

The important test for the idea of partial operation is with respect to transportation. It is impossible to say what a detailed study of the problems involved would reveal, but such a study should be made. Bargaining at present is so intermeshed with intervention in railroads and shipping that the primary result is frustration of all concerned. Perhaps no clear alternative will emerge, but the realities of creating a strike option should be studied. Northrup and Bloom state that there were thirty-nine instances of intervention flowing from the flight engineer issue when it appears probable that the union could not have held out in the wildcat strike for more than an additional one, two, or three weeks and certainly was counting on intervention to bail them out when they struck....

Our final selection for this part of the book is an article by Clark Kerr and Abraham Siegel in which the authors look at some empirical data about the propensity to strike in various industries and attempt to say something about the causes of strikes. In doing so they test some hypotheses that correspond rather closely to some of the propositions advanced by Livernash, and suggest some additional ones. Unfortunately, the detailed data are not presented; we do not have measures of the precise degree of association between various hypothesized conditions and the actual level of conflict that did occur, and we do not find sophisticated multivariate analyses of the interaction between conditions. The article is nevertheless useful, despite these limitations, for it further indicates the kind of relationships that an international relations scholar studying the causes of war should be alert to, and suggests also the extreme difficulty in finding powerful single-variable explanations.

The most powerful explanation discovered by the authors concerns the degree of isolation of the industry from the rest of the economic and social system. Industries like mining and lumbering they find to be particularly strike prone, especially where the parties—largely the workers—are tightly bound by many intragroup ties. Such a combination of isolation and intragroup integration is very likely to produce a belligerent and demanding union in contract negotiations; on the opposite side an industry where the workers are well integrated with the rest of the community is unlikely to be one that has been characterized by a high frequency of strikes. This recalls the familiar theoretical propositions in domestic and international relations about the virtues of cross-pressures for mitigating conflict, as well as the warnings about the dangers incurred when a particular nation or group of states is kept (or keeps itself) isolated from the rest of the world community.

While the explanation proves to be the authors' most effective one for identifying strike-prone *industries*, it leaves a good bit of conflict behavior unexplained even at that level. Furthermore, as essentially a system-level explanation, it says nothing about which *firms* within the industry will be more likely to experience strikes than will other firms. For further understanding of the causes of strikes they are forced to try a number of other hypotheses, some of which can be applied either at the system level or at a level of greater disaggregation, the individual firm or labor union. One of their hypotheses concerns the interaction process—the level of hostility generated by the bargaining process and the negotiating techniques employed—but this seems largely to be a derivative variable that can be traced back to other conditions. Similarly, they looked at the history of labor-management relations in the industry, noting those cases where the enterprise was in some sense born in conflict. They seem to find that a history of past conflict makes future conflict more likely—perhaps not a very surprising or profound finding, but one that does contradict some simple ideas about the integrative functions of conflict, and one where the empirical establishment of the details about the relationship would be well worthwhile.

Several other hypotheses are addressed to the specific characteristics of the decision-making units or of their components. One is the ideology most prevalent, and another they call the political environment; that is, the stability of the union's political system and the degree of opposition faced by its leadership. They also looked briefly at differences in the personalities and leadership styles of union officials, and, akin to national-character explanations in international politics, at the personality types who may be typical of workers in particular industries—belligerent lumberjacks, for example, or the kind of people willing to do very unpleasant work. Most of these explanations had little power in bivariate relationships, however, although personality type seemed to make some difference. This last is a bit surprising, in light of the fact that national character hypotheses have not proved very useful in international politics, but the hypotheses need further testing in both domains.[1]

[1] In addition to these two articles on labor-management relations, see R. E. Walton and R. B. McKersie, eds., *A Behavioral Theory of Labor Negotiation* (New York: McGraw-Hill, 1965).

25

The Interindustry Propensity to Strike—An International Comparison

Clark Kerr and Abraham Siegel

Are certain industries in democratic industrialized nations consistently strike prone, while others are consistently strike free?[1] If the facts give an affirmative answer to this question, then how can this social phenomenon be explained? How do several of the standard theories of industrial peace and industrial conflict fare in the light of these facts? Finally, if it were desired either to encourage or to discourage the propensity to strike in an industry, how best should it be attempted? These are the four questions to which this discussion is addressed.

1. The Similarity of Behavior

Table 1 gives a generalized grouping of industries. . . . This generalized grouping is possible because of the uniformity of behavior of certain industries in the eleven countries studied[2] (Australia, Czechoslovakia,

[1] Man-days lost due to strikes and lockouts are used as the measure of the propensity to strike. Thus an industry may have frequent small strikes of short duration and yet be shown with a lower propensity to strike than one with a few big strikes of substantial length. We are more concerned here with the significance of strikes than with their numerical occurrence.

[2] While the data disclose a substantial consistency of behavior, it should be kept in mind that they reflect the experience of only eleven countries over a limited period of time

Table 1
General Pattern of Strike Propensities

Propensity to strike	Industry
High	Mining
	Maritime and longshore
Medium high	Lumber
	Textile
Medium	Chemical
	Printing
	Leather
	Manufacturing (general)
	Construction
	Food and kindred products
Medium low	Clothing
	Gas, water, and electricity
	Services (hotels, restaurants, etc.)
Low	Railroad
	Agriculture
	Trade

Germany, Italy, the Netherlands, New Zealand, Norway, Sweden, Switzerland, the United Kingdom, and the United States)...

Manufacturing (general) is, of course, an omnibus description, and the grouping may turn up in the "medium" box only because quite divergent patterns cancel each other out. However, it seems more likely that general manufacturing (which includes, perhaps most importantly, metal working) is the significant standard case, and the question then becomes: Why are some industries more strike prone and others less than general manufacturing?

The industries in the "medium" box may be divided into two types: those which are quite consistently medium strike prone (general manufacturing, leather, and construction) and those which vary considerably from "high" or "medium high" to "medium low" or "low" (printing, chemical, and food and kindred products). Industries in the "medium" category are likely to be either under balanced environmental pressures toward both conflict and peace or under such little pressure in either direction that forces arising from other sources than the industrial environment are predominant.

---

and that the industrial breakdowns are not so numerous nor so comparable from one country to another, or even from one time period to another in the same country, as would be ideally desirable for the purposes of this analysis.

While the concern here is exclusively with industries, it is to be expected that individual firms in industries in the "medium" category should vary more widely one from another than firms in industries in the high-propensity or low-propensity categories. A medium-propensity industry is likely to give wide latitude for individual firm variations, while a high- or a low-propensity one is more likely to demand individual conformity,[3] and general observation attests that there is more uniformity in behavior among coal mines or government bureaus than among general-manufacturing plants.

Before turning to the question of whether there are any reasonable hypotheses to explain the apparently great impact of certain industrial environments on the propensity to strike, five exceptions to the uniformity of behavior should be noted:

Trade in Sweden (higher than usual).
Mining in Germany in the second period and in the Netherlands during the second period (lower than usual).
Machinery in Germany (higher than usual).
Automobiles in the United States in the second period (higher than usual).
Agriculture in Italy, in Australia during the second period, and in New Zealand in the first (higher than usual).

For the first two exceptions we have no explanation to offer; but comments on the last three will be made later on.

2. The Explanations

A. Hypothesis 1. The location of the worker in society

Is there any single theory which will largely explain the facts which we have found? Can we, at one and the same time, explain the high propensity to strike of miners, longshoremen, sailors, and loggers and the low propensity of government employees, grocery clerks, railroad employees, and garment workers? The first hypothesis is that the location of the worker in society determines his propensity to strike and that this location is heavily influenced by the industrial environment.

1. *The isolated mass.* The miners, the sailors, the longshoremen, the loggers, and, to a much lesser extent, the textile workers form isolated masses, almost a "race apart." They live in their own separate communities:

---

[3] This is not to suggest that a single firm cannot make a record for peace in a warlike industry or a record for conflict in a quiescent industry, but only that it is unlikely to do so.

the coal patch, the ship, the waterfront district, the logging camp, the textile town.[4] These communities have their own codes, myths, heroes, and social standards. There are few neutrals in them to mediate the conflicts and dilute the mass. All people have grievances, but what is important is that all the members of each of these groups have the same grievances: industrial hazards or severe depression unemployment or bad living conditions (which seem additionally evil because they are supplied by the employer), or low wages or intermittent work. And here is a case where the totality of common grievances,[5] after they have been verbally shared, may be greater than the sum of the individual parts. The employees form a largely homogeneous, undifferentiated mass—they all do about the same work and have about the same experiences. Here you do not have the occupational stratification of the metal or building crafts, of the hotel or restaurant, or of the government bureau.[6]

It is hard to get out of this mass. The jobs are specialized, and the workers come to be also. Skills are not transferable as they are for stenographers or electricians. Protest is less likely to take the form of moving to another industry and more the character of the mass walkout. Just as it is hard for these workers to move out, so also is it difficult for them to move up. To what higher occupational strata can the longshoreman or the coal

[4] Some of these communities, such as the coal towns, are geographically isolated, while others, such as waterfront districts, are socially isolated within metropolitan communities.

[5] The members of these groups not only have the same grievances, but they have them at the same time, at the same place, and against the same people. In the more peaceful industries their inevitable grievances are dispersed—by stratification of the workers (as in steel), by scattering of the employees (as in agriculture), by absorption of the workers into a mixed community (as in trade), by scattering of the targets (the employer, the landlord, the grocer, and the policemen being quite different people). The "mass grievance," not the individual grievance, is the source of the greater social difficulty. It may arise in the environment we are describing here, or may have a cross-industry content—for example, it may result from widespread unemployment, rapid inflation, general wage cuts. It is the mass grievance which leads to "class" action. The individual grievance can be more readily absorbed and managed by society. Industrial tranquillity depends on keeping grievances dispersed so that they may be handled one at a time. Proponents of social unrest are most successful in those places where, and at those times when, grievances are highly concentrated.

[6] Occupational stratification may be an unusually important aspect of the industrial environment, affecting the location of the worker in society and his propensity to strike. The iron and steel industry is often located in geographically isolated one-industry towns, and much of the work in it is arduous (see hypothesis 2), yet it is not particularly famous as a center of strike activity. Only three separate observations of this industry appear in our data, and they are too few for a confident generalization. The industry, however, seems to rank somewhat above the average ("high" in Germany in the second period and "medium" in the United States in the first period and "medium high" in the second). It might rank somewhat higher, nevertheless, were it not for the high degree of job differentiation which marks the industry and which both separates one worker from another and creates a ladder for each worker to climb.

miner or the logger rise in the natural course of events? Nor is he likely to be pulled from the mass in other ways. In these communities there are not the myriad of voluntary associations with mixed memberships which characterize the multi-industry town. The force of public opinion must seem rather weak to the logger in the camp or to the miner in the coal patch who never sees "the public"; and it is no more possible to cut trees than to mine coal with bayonets. The employer throws out few lines to these workers. He is usually an absentee owner who "cuts out and gets out" in the logging business or exhausts a mine and moves on or hires longshoremen on a casual basis or gets his views of personnel relations from the law on mutiny.[7] The worker is as detached from the employer as from the community at large.

The union becomes a kind of working-class party or even government for these employees rather than just another association among many. Union meetings are more adequately attended and union affairs more vigorously discussed; and, as one consequence, personal and ideological factionalism and rival unionism are more likely. Strife within and between unions is a sign that the union is important.

The strike for this isolated mass is a kind of colonial revolt against far-removed authority, an outlet for accumulated tensions, and a substitute for occupational and social mobility. The industrial environment places these workers in the role of members of separate classes distinct from the community at large, classes with their share of grievances. These individuals are not members of the ubiquitous middle class but of their own class of miners or longshoremen; and they do not aim to be more considerate of the general community than they think the general community is of them. Thus, the isolated mass in a classless society may become something like the isolated class in a class society, more or less permanently at odds with the community at large.[8]

[7] The industrial environment creates "bad" employers (just as it does strike-prone workers) who disregard the welfare of their employees because of the casual nature of their connection with them or who undertake to dominate their employees unduly, as landlord and policeman as well as employer, because they are the preponderant power in a one-industry community, or who do both.

[8] A third condition is necessary, in addition to the existence of a relatively homogeneous group of workers which is isolated from the general community, for an industry to be especially strike prone; but this condition is almost universally present when the other two are. This condition is the capacity of the group for cohesion. The existence of an identifiable group (such as the clothing workers) is not sufficient by itself nor is the fact of isolation (note the general lack of strikes by fishermen and oil-field workers) nor the two together, if cohesion is difficult for the isolated mass. The great hordes of agricultural harvest hands in the San Joaquin Valley of California have struck, but only with great difficulty, for they are such an inconstant, fluctuating, amorphous group. The capacity for cohesion is dependent on the fairly steady contact of the members of the group, which in turn creates the basis for permanent

2. *The integrated individual and the integrated group.* The opposite of
the isolated mass is the integrated individual or the integrated group.
"Integrated" is used here not in the psychological but in the sociological
sense: absorbed in and unified with society at large. The workers in the
industries at the other end of our scale—those in the industries where the
propensity to strike is low or medium low (railroad; trade; agriculture;
clothing; gas, water, and electricity; the services; and, we might add,
government, domestic services, and clerical)—are given an industrial role
to play which integrates them better into the general community. They are
more likely (with the exception of farm hands) to live in multi-industry
communities, to associate with people with quite different working
experiences than their own, and to belong to associations with heterogeneous memberships. In these communities their individual grievances
are less likely to coalesce into a mass grievance which is expressed at the job
level. There are many neutrals in any dispute, and this helps to assure the
impartiality of public officials.

In most of these cases the worker either can change his industry fairly
readily without losing the value of his skill or has access to higher skilled
jobs or managerial or even employer status. Generally also, the employer
is either not so remote or not so callous if remote. The industry has small-
scale employing units, or the employer-worker relationship is normally a
continuing one. And the community can bring pressure to bear to encourage peaceful conduct. The workers see and feel the general community:
in at least three cases (railroads, public utilities, and government) the
government asserts the supremacy of the public interest in continuity of
service; and in at least one other (clothing) the market for the products
makes steady production the sine qua non for both investment and jobs.
The union, except in the garment trades, where it runs the industry, and the
railroads, where it administers seniority, is not so wound into the lives of
the workers, and in no instance is it so much the chosen instrument for
protest, if it exists at all.

The workers in these industries are generally more dispersed in the
general community, more stratified in the hierarchy of jobs in each industry,

---

organization. Thus, the itinerant but occupationally specialized sheepshearers in the western
United States have long been organized, since they form a group of constant composition whose members have repetitive contacts with each other, while less specialized agricultural workers have not. An isolated mass can be kept from internal solidarity not only by
the turnover of its membership but also by racial, religious, and nationality barriers—a social
law on which certain American employers, particularly in earlier times, have founded their
recruiting practices. Hawaiian sugar-plantation workers did not become effectively organized
until they were "Americanized." See Mark Perlman, "Organized Labor in Hawaii," *Labor
Law Journal*, **3** (April 1952). Even agricultural workers strike when they move from a state of
individual isolation in an isolated mass to the state of a cohesive isolated mass.

more attached to their individual employers, more restrained by social pressures, and more able to escape job dissatisfactions without striking than are the workers in the high-propensity industries. The strike is against a known employer and affects a community of which the workers are a part. These workers are contained in society rather than maintained on its periphery.[9]

Several further notes are needed on the hypothesis that the location of the worker in society is the basic determinant of the interindustry propensity to strike. Agriculture in New Zealand, Australia, and Italy is, during certain periods, an exception to the rule of rural tranquility. Agriculture has also been an exception to this rule in California and Hawaii. These areas have in common large-scale agriculture. When agriculture moves from employing the single hired hand to large groups of socially isolated workers, it also moves from peace toward conflict. It is also instructive that the automobile and rubber industries, which rank so high in the second period in the United States, are predominantly localized in the special communities of Detroit and Akron, which were also the two homes of the sit-down strike. The experience of two additional industries, while the data on them is by no means conclusive, seems to support this hypothesis. Man-days lost due to strikes have been much above the average in the toy-manufacturing industry in Germany and in quarrying (stone, clay, and sand) and the fabricating activities associated with it wherever they are separately identifiable, and both these industries isolate groups of workers from the larger society.[10]

The location of industries in the "medium" box is not so readily elucidated by this hypothesis, although the occasional adventures into the conflict category of the printing and chemical industries might be laid to the well-developed sense of a common community which characterizes

[9] The industries ranked "low" or "medium low" may be divided into two distinct groups: (a) those in which the workers are relatively well integrated individually into the community (agriculture, trade, services), and (b) those in which the workers constitute collectively a recognizable group but where the group is under intense social pressure to settle its grievances peacefully (clothing, railroad, public utilities). In the two categories, the industries in the latter have demonstrated the greater inclination toward strikes. In either case, community integration, in contrast to mass segregation, is the key to the explanation of peaceful behavior. The farmhand living in his employer's family, however, is integrated into the community in quite a different fashion from the railroad workers whose union finds strikes socially unacceptable. The farm hands have no group cohesion, while the railroad workers have a great deal, but the pressure of society is against their making effective use of it through the strike. . . .

[10] A further illustration, not drawn, however, from the statistical data, is also instructive. Sailors working on oil tankers in the coastal trade of the United States, who are employed steadily by the same employer and have a more regularized family and community life than other seamen, are also less strike prone.

some printing trades and the frequent geographical isolation of chemical plants; and the consistently "medium" behavior of the general manufacturing, construction, and leather industries, to the balance of pulls toward both group and societal identification. The employees of these industries often form cohesive groups, but these groups are neither isolated from society, on the one hand, nor under strong social pressure to avoid strikes, on the other; and these employees, while they belong to unions, frequently have strong attachments in other directions as well.

In summary, this hypothesis may be stated as follows: (a) industries will be highly strike prone when the workers (i) form a relatively homogeneous group which (ii) is unusually isolated from the general community and which (iii) is capable of cohesion; and (b) industries will be comparatively strike free when their workers (i) are individually integrated into the larger society, (ii) are members of trade groups which are coerced by government or the market to avoid strikes, or (iii) are so individually isolated that strike action is impossible.

B. Hypothesis 2. The Character of the Job and the Worker

The second hypothesis is that the inherent nature of the job determines, by selection and conditioning, the kinds of workers employed and their attitudes, and these workers, in turn, cause conflict or peace. If the job is physically difficult and unpleasant, unskilled or semiskilled, and casual or seasonal, and fosters an independent spirit (as in the logger in the woods), it will draw tough, inconstant, combative, and virile workers, and they will be inclined to strike. If the job is physically easy and performed in pleasant surroundings, skilled and responsible, steady, and subject to set rules and close supervision, it will attract women or the more submissive type of man who will abhor strikes. Certainly, the bull of the woods and the mousy bank clerk are different types of people and can be expected to act differently. Certainly also, the community is more sympathetic with striking miners coming out of the ground than with school teachers abandoning their desks.

This hypothesis explains a good many of the facts, but not quite so neatly as the first. Sailors, longshoremen, miners, and lumberjacks are popularly accepted as being more vigorous and combative types than garment workers, grocery clerks, railway conductors, hotel maids, or cannery employees; they seem to strike more often, and their strikes are also more violent. But textile workers and printing craftsmen, who also strike with some frequency, are not classed as so forceful. Teamsters, farmhands, steelworkers, and construction tradesmen, who are not usually delicate individuals, do not strike with unusual frequency.

Several other elements of the industrial environment were examined, but they did not seem to lead to a general theory of the interindustry propensity to strike. They may, however, be important factors behind the behavior of individual industries, or they may explain the different records of the several plants within an industry. These factors are the following:

1. The sensitivity of the industry to the business cycle
2. The structure of the product market
3. The elasticity of demand for the product
4. Labor as a percentage of total cost
5. The profitability of the industry
6. The average size of plant
7. The state of technological change
8. The rate of expansion or contraction of the industry

Reference to any or all of these elements, as a careful examination of the characteristics of the industries ranked in Table 1 will make evident, is insufficient to explain the bulk of the facts.

We are left, then, with the two general hypotheses set forth here, of which the former seems the more consistent with the known facts. The two theories, however, have a uniting thread. Both of them are consistent with the thesis that strikes occur where they can occur, that is, where the working-class community is closely knit and the workers forceful and not where the workers are dispersed and subdued. This is not the same thing, however, as saying that strikes take place where strikes pay, for grocery clerks are probably in a better position to benefit from strikes, if they could develop them, than are textile workers; and railroad workers, than sailors.

The two hypotheses can be combined to state that strikes occur most severely in industries which (1) segregate large numbers of persons who (2) have relatively unpleasant jobs. Mass segregation by itself is not enough, for members of the "lower gentility" (telephone operators, bank clerks, and the like) would probably not strike frequently, in deference to their lower-middle-class psychology, even if they were put off by themselves in large groups; nor is unpleasant work enough by itself, for scavengers, sand-blasters, divers, and chimney sweeps have disagreeable jobs, but are so scattered that joint action is almost impossible. The polar cases then may be described as follows: (1) an isolated mass of persons doing unpleasant work and (2) dispersed individuals doing pleasant work.

3. Certain Theories Examined

Two explanations of the ranking of industries by the propensity of the workers to strike have been offered: the location of the workers in society and the character of the jobs and the workers, both of which explanations relate to what may be called the industrial environment; but there are many other theories which can be applied to these data, although not specifically devised to explain them. How adequate are these theories in explaining these particular data?[11]

1. *The economic environment,* which for these purposes we shall define as the market aspects of the larger industrial environment which was discussed previously, makes a contribution to an understanding of these data, but by itself is an inadequate explanation. The industries located at each extreme have quite various product- and labor-market structures. An elastic demand in the product market may encourage peace,[12] particularly where business may be lost to nonunion employers, and an inelastic labor-supply situation may lead workers to strike, since it reflects the fact that it is difficult for them to move out; but an elastic demand for the product may also cause trouble where a union is competing in a wage war with a rival union or is under pressure to match a pattern wage settlement and where the employer is handicapped in translating higher wage costs into higher prices for fear of losing volume, and an inelastic labor supply may encourage peace if it helps give rise to higher wage rates. Product-market and labor-market forces are, perhaps, more suited to explain variations among firms or between periods in the life of an industry than they are between industries over a span of time.

2. *The political environment,* particularly of the unions, has been persuasively adduced as the cause of industrial warfare or peace: the more secure the union and its leaders, the fewer the strikes; the less secure, the

[11] There are other tests of the validity of these theories for the explanation of industrial conflict and peace than those of how well they elucidate these data. If the theories fail this test, this does not mean they will not pass other tests or explain other phenomena.

[12] An elastic demand for the products of a firm or a group of firms and an elastic demand for labor have been advanced on occasion as a basic cause of labor-management cooperation. The employer faces stiff competition, and the union does not wish to injure his competitive position. The union, however, may not be so considerate if (a) any job reduction for this firm is matched by an increase in jobs somewhere else for members of the same union organization and, perhaps, even for the same workers (as may often happen in local trade and service industries) or if (b) the union or its leaders, for the sake of survival, must make certain wage gains regardless of the potential effects (which may be much delayed) on job opportunities. Union-management cooperation is most likely to result when disturbing actions by the union would cause a loss of jobs to areas outside its job territory *and* where its leaders are in a position to consider this effect as the dominant influence. An inelastic demand for the products is probably more generally conducive to peace since it gives the employer greater leeway in accommodating himself to the union. Then a gap is more likely to exist between the maximum which the employer can readily afford to pay and the minimum which the union can reasonably accept. . . .

more numerous. The unions of grocery clerks, government employees, and agriculture workers, however, have generally less institutional security than those of coal miners, printers, and longshoremen, yet they strike less. More jurisdictional and organizational rivalries usually face the construction and railroad unions than the unions of miners, yet they are more peaceful. In the United States the leader of the mine workers is popularly conceived to have a more secure position than the chief of the airline pilots' association, yet his union strikes more; and peace descended on the West Coast waterfront when the established union leaders became less secure. Certainly, the political environment of the union and its leaders is useful, even indispensable, in explaining certain situations at certain times,[13] but it does not provide a generally valid explanation of the interindustry propensity to strike.

Among the industries with a high propensity to strike, while unionism is usually most secure, union leaders and specific institutions may on the average be somewhat less secure than usual. This is consistent with the hypothesis that the "isolated mass" builds a strong union movement and that active memberships give rise to factionalism. Among the industries with a low propensity to strike, unionism finds its greatest uncertainty and factionalism its least assured market.

Employer associations are particularly strong where the industrial environment is coercive toward conflict (coal mining, logging, longshore, and maritime). While by increasing the ability to pay the individual employers, by increasing interemployer uniformity of terms and conditions of employment, and by lowering the level of the union's ultimate demands by raising the cost of strikes, multiemployer bargaining may encourage peace, it finds its origins, in part, in war.

Strikes may better be explained by looking not so much at the organization as at the membership. They occur most frequently not only in places where the membership is restless because of its industrial environment, as we have seen previously, but also at times of membership unrest.[14] It is to

[13] Ross and Irwin conclude that "differences in the frequency of strikes between one country and another can best be explained by differences in the position of the union and the union leader" and that "internal factionalism, like external competition, encourages the development and prosecution of grievances." See A. M. Ross and D. Irwin, "Strike Experience in Five Countries, 1927–1947: An Interpretation," *Industrial and Labor Relations Review*, **4**, 3 (April, 1951).

[14] "Frequent disputes are mainly caused by dissatisfaction among the workers; strikes from improvements are frequent when rising prices are not adequately met by rising wages, strikes against a worsening of conditions when the workers are menaced by cuts and especially by wage cuts not justified by a proportional fall in prices." K. Forschheimer, *Some International Aspects of the Strike Movement* (Oxford Institute of Statistics Bulletin 10, January 1948).

the reactions of the workers and not to the tactics of the leaders that we must turn for the more basic explanations.

3. *Human relations* at the face-to-face level are said by some to explain not only industrial but even international relations. Misunderstandings are not inherent in a situation but result from faulty communications. It may be true that face-to-face relations are worse between longshoremen and coal miners and their employers than between grocery clerks and theirs and that, if face-to-face relations were better between coal miners and their employers, there would be less conflict. But why are face-to-face relations often so unsatisfactory between coal miners and their employers? Is it because they always know less about semantics than construction workers and their employers, and is it only faulty communication systems which stand between them and ultimate harmony? And how are face-to-face relations to be improved? Can it be done by giving courses in group dynamics and introducing social engineers into the mines?

It seems more likely that some situations are structured against good face-to-face relations and that this structure is the more basic cause and the source of the more basic changes. The climate of face-to-face relations may be one way of testing and of describing the degree of conflict or cooperation in an industry, and there may be occasions when manipulation of these relations alone will bring great changes, but it seems unlikely that the peace in government agencies and the warfare on the waterfront are due primarily to the universal superiority in human-relations techniques of government bureaucrats over stevedoring contractors. Even if this were the case, it would still need to be explained why government draws to it a more skillful elite than the longshore industry. Labor relations may be a mirror in which the employer sees his own reflection—the decent employer may see decent relationships reflected back at him[15]—but why then are employers more decent in one industry than another? At this point some reference needs to be made to the industrial environment. *Causa causae est causa causati.*

4. *The trend of historical developments* varies considerably from one collective-bargaining system to another. In industries with a high propensity to strike, the origins have frequently been more violent and time has had less of a subduing effect. The printing trades tend to be among the earliest organized, as are the coal mines, but they both continue to be disposed toward conflict long after other industries have learned to tread a more peaceful path. The garment trades in the United States were organized in bitter struggles but, given an environment which was persuasive

[15] C. S. Golden and H. J. Ruttenberg, *The Dynamics of Industrial Democracy* (New York: Harper & Row, 1942). "Management as a general principle, gets the kind of union leadership it deserves. A tough management begets tough union leaders, while a patient, friendly, cooperative management begets a like type of union leadership...." (p. 58).

toward peace, soon established the standard for tranquil conduct. Both the nature of the birth and the trend of development must be explained by some common causes, for both have been quite uniform for the same industry from one country to another. More than historical accident is at work. The nature of the birth appears to be not purely accidental; so it is necessary to say more than that a bad start leads to poorer continuing relations than does a good one. Since time works fewer wonders with some industries than others, it is necessary to state more than that time smooths the wrinkles in the relationship.

5. *Dominant personalities* certainly leave an imprint on relations in an industry,[16] but why do the coal and longshore industries bring a John L. Lewis[17] and a Harry Bridges to the fore, and clothing, a Sidney Hillman, and why do coal and longshore and clothing industries perform about the same way in other countries without Lewis, Bridges, and Hillman?

6. *Adherence to ideological views* or merely to certain specific attitudes toward the other party profoundly affects bargaining relationships and the propensity to strike.[18] Communist-led unions probably cause more

---

[16] Several of the case studies in the National Planning Association series "Causes of Industrial Peace" emphasize the importance of dominant personalities in the shaping of peaceful relations. For example, "Perhaps the most important factor [determining the course of the relationship] is the president of the company. His philosophy and his personality have had a great deal to do with the ultimate development of health...." (Douglas McGregor and Joseph N. Scanlon, *The Dewey and Almy Chemical Company and the International Chemical Workers Union* (Washington: National Planning Association, 1948), pp. 63–64); or "A long and successful evolution has brought about these conditions, but what was the genesis of this evolution? Why did collective bargaining get off to a good start in this industry? The personality of Sidney Hillman played a dominant role. His constructive and honest approach was often an effective substitute for the picket line...." [D. B. Straus, *Hickey-Freeman Company and Amalgamated Clothing Workers* (Washington: National Planning Association, 1949), pp. 70–71.]

[17] John L. Lewis may very well have made a greater contribution to industrial tranquillity than Sidney Hillman, for he has channeled the ineluctable unrest of the miners into mass strikes called (usually) at a time of year (in the spring) when they cost the nation the very least. Hillman headed a union which has made a record for industrial peace in an industry which is almost always peaceful.

[18] See B. M. Selekman, "Varieties of Labor Relations," *Harvard Business Review*, **27**, 2 (March 1949). "Beyond any short-term changes in the bargaining program, accordingly, the ideological structure does constitute the most undeviating and ineradicable conflict pattern in present-day industrial relations. For the party-line leaders accept neither the system of free collective bargaining nor the American democracy of which it is a part. Manifestly, such an undivided focus on external goals means that the ideological structure of relationship possesses no innate potentialities for evolution toward a more accommodative structure of joint dealings. Consequently, the reliance on time and experience, which may prove helpful in other structures, in this one can become a source of actual danger. Only by ousting party-line leaders from positions of union leaderships, whether by legislation or by employer resistance or by intra-union action, may this source of conflict be minimized."

trouble and tough-minded employers invite more than do noncommunist-led unions and softhearted employers. Belligerent unions and reactionary employers seem, however, to be more effect than cause, for the citadels of union radicalism and the hotbeds of employer reaction are found in about the same industries from country to country.[19]

7. It is suggested, particularly by certain economists, that the *selection of good bargaining techniques* can prevent conflict, since strikes never pay and peace does[20]: but all the parties, regardless of industry, have access to the same storehouse and can draw from it the sword or the green table, as they wish. Better bargaining techniques can improve some situations, but it is not for lack of bargaining skill that so many strikes have occurred in the coal mines and on the waterfronts of the world....

4. Theories of the Trade-Union Movement

The trade-union movement is variously analyzed as moving toward "monopoly," "job control," "status" in its own trade-union society, "bureaucracy," "power accumulation," and "class consciousness." These are either the ascribed goals or contemplated ends, and it might be thought that, as individual unions reach the culmination of their development, some effect on their proneness to strike would be noticed—more peace in the first five cases and more conflict in the last one. What do the facts on the interindustry propensity to strike show? Generally, the industries at the conflict end of the ranking have unions with a greater monopoly in the labor market than have those at the other end of the range. Once job control is obtained by the teamsters, peace overwhelms the industry, but longshoremen continue their conflict after job control is seized. The garment workers have achieved a degree of status in a partially self-contained society of their own creation and seldom strike; typographical workers have also and are much less quiescent. The "iron law of oligarchy" has been confirmed by the coal miners' union in the United States without the dove of peace alighting on the coal tipple. Power has been accumulated by the unions of mine workers sufficient to make governments shake in the face of it, but the unions have not been satiated; but

---

[19] Not to be neglected is communist selection of certain strategic industries for infiltration, including coal mining and water transportation. These industries, however, were the locale of many strikes before the communists became active, but their efforts certainly have served to intensify the conflict in these already favorable environments.

[20] See J. R. Hicks, *The Theory of Wages* (New York, Peter Smith, 1948). "Under a system of collective bargaining ... the majority of actual strikes are doubtless the result of faulty negotiation.... The danger lies in ignorance by one side of the other's dispositions, and in hasty breaking-off of negotiations...." (pp. 146–147).

then the process of striving for power never comes to an end. The class-consciousness theory says that (1) workers are becoming more class minded and that (2), when they do, they are more inclined to violence against the surrounding society. While the first part of this theory is of doubtful truth, at least for the United States, the data seem to bear out the second part: workers strike most often and most violently when they are in an isolated mass with a strong sense of group, if not class, consciousness.

This suggests that some strikes have elements of a small-scale revolt against society rather than of bargaining tactics alone. There is a sense of a mass grievance against society and little sense of a community responsibility. The cost of striking is lowered, for there is more group support for the strike and less felt public pressure against it; and the gain in prospect is not alone a better contract but the release of accumulated tensions. The single equation of prospective economic cost against prospective economic gain (which will seldom show a positive surplus) is particularly inappropriate here, for cost and gain are calculated in more than the economic dimension. The revolt element is certainly not present in all strikes or even in many, but the industries where it may be present account for a substantial proportion of the man-days lost. In New Zealand, during the first period, over 80 percent of all man-days lost were in mining and water transport alone; in Germany, during the second period, mining alone accounted for over 40 percent of the total man-days lost; and in the United Kingdom, mining and quarrying accounted for almost 50 percent of the total man-days lost in industrial disputes during the three decades covered (exclusive of the 1926 losses). It was out of the isolated masses of coal miners in Great Britain and of longshoremen in San Francisco that two of the greatest strikes developed.

5. Summary

The most general explanation of the interindustry propensity to strike is the nature of the industrial environment and, particularly, its tendency to direct workers into isolated masses or to integrate them into the general community. This hypothesis elucidates the behavior of most of the industries surveyed for most of the time periods covered and does so better than alternative theories. However, it does not explain the ranking of all industries for all the time and is less effective in analyzing why industries are medium strike prone than why they are high or low; and thus other explanations are necessary too. We are dealing with complex phenomena and must resort to multiple causation: and, as we have seen, other theories are helpful or essential in explaining certain situations.

The hypothesis of the location of the worker in society is useful for the one task of explaining the interindustry propensity to strike. It has little to say about the behavior of individual firms, except that firms in industries located at the two extremes of the range are more likely to conform to the pattern of their industry than are firms in industries located in the middle of the range. At the level of the firm, many more factors than the industrial environment must be examined, particularly if the industrial environment is "neutral," as it appears to be for the bulk of manufacturing. The only explanation this hypothesis offers for the variation of the propensity to strike from one period of time to another is that the propensity will rise or fall in an industry or society as the workers become more isolated in masses or more integrated into society; and the only clues to the causes of international differences in the inclination to strike are that the industry mix of each nation is important, as is also the general integration of workers and their institutions into society. . . .

IV

Alternative Organizations for International Decision Making

●

For several decades, most notably since World War II, there has been a widespread if far from unanimous sense that the existing forms of international organization were grossly inadequate for the problems they were called upon to solve. This sense was partly manifested in the establishment of the UN, but certainly it did not stop there. Dissatisfaction has continued, and much of it is indeed directed precisely at the fact that the UN has not developed into a powerful supranational organization. The demand for new and for higher forms of global organization ebbs and flows somewhat, and perhaps has been rather quiescent since the achievement in the early 1960's of a seemingly stable balance of invulnerable deterrent forces between the superpowers. The condition of deterrent stability is unlikely to remain in its recent form over the long run, however; technological development of new weapons by the superpowers and the spread of existing weapons technology to the lesser powers are sure to produce new tensions and new problems that can be managed only with great difficulty by present institutional forms. In this concluding section we shall look at several pieces that suggest both some of the obstacles to devising appropriate new institutions for decision making among the world's peoples, and some of the potentials for devising new forms and the inadequacies of old ones that press us to search for new ways.

First, we shall examine two papers that, from quite different theoretical premises, suggest the virtues of existing structures which keep decision making at the relatively small and disaggregated level of the current nation-states rather than at a higher level requiring a more comprehensive overview of the entire global system and more frequent overt agreement on goals to be sought and the instruments for reaching those goals. The initial paper, by James M. Buchanan and Gordon Tullock, can be read as a conservative statement on the continued uses of the nation-state in the international system and the undesirability of transferring functions to a supranational organization. Their paper was, of course, not written with this specific conclusion in mind, and it is quite possible that the authors would want to modify it on the basis of other facts or assumptions than the ones discussed in their paper. My explicit extension of their argument for the international system is based only inferentially on their arguments, as is the case with the other articles in this section.

One of the primary reasons we have local units of governmental decision making is to take advantage of the flexibility such a system provides for experimentation—only a few people are injured if an experiment proves unproductive—and the flexibility it provides for dealing with peculiarly local conditions and difficulties that are not shared by people in the larger collectivity. Another common justification is in the sense of participation provided by small decision-making units, the sense that local government is the school of democracy. Buchanan and Tullock in addition provide another reason, one that is much less commonly advanced, in their argument that the costs of decision making, specifically the costs of bargaining among decision makers, are directly related to the *number* of decision makers who must be considered. More resources will be invested by each individual in the act of bargaining itself when he must bargain with many others. The authors do not provide empirical evidence for their argument, and this is unfortunate, because the implications for many very different circumstances are so great. But they make a major theoretical contribution simply by directing attention to the *costs of bargaining* at all, since this is a grossly neglected subject in both economic and political theory. We have some essays on *how* parties bargain and reach or fail to reach agreement, but virtually no data or even good theory on what determines the level of investment in bargaining—under what conditions great resources will be devoted to exploring one's own utility functions, to trying to ascertain the opponent's, and to searching for the most effective means of influencing his choices.[1]

If the costs of bargaining increase with the number of other decision makers whose actions must be taken into account, then clearly there are important diseconomies of scale and advantages to be reaped from making as many decisions as possible at a low level of aggregation. It would be better to make decisions within nation-states than with larger regional

[1] The closest, and limited, material is probably in E. Banfield, *Political Influence* (New York: Free Press, 1961), and R. A. Dahl, *Who Governs?* (New Haven: Yale University Press, 1961).

groupings, and better within international regions than on a global basis. Furthermore, the authors suggest that costs of bargaining increase with the *heterogeneity* of the decision makers; heterogeneity produces greater uncertainty about the tastes and bargaining skills of others, and, hence, requires greater effort to understand them. Again, the relatively homogeneous nation-state, or perhaps a not-too-heterogeneous regional institution, would have distinct cost advantages over worldwide arrangements. Nation-states would thus retain distinct utilities, perhaps as constituent federal units even within wider institutions, for they could deal efficiently with many issues.[2]

To balance these considerations at least three counter arguments should be borne in mind. First, a realistic assessment of large-scale decision-making systems must take into account the fact that a good deal of delegation and representation goes on; decisions are not made by all the component individuals acting collectively, but by representative bodies to which authority is delegated. Hence, more comprehensive bodies need not be larger in terms of the number of decision makers who play an active role in the process. Also, there may be some compensating mechanisms at work in a large unit (though not necessarily in a very heterogeneous one) to reduce decision-making costs. For instance, in recognition of the difficulties involved in detailed multilateral bargaining all of the parties may be much more ready to accept "prominent" solutions when they appear, and more assiduous in searching for them. Finally, external costs may be expected to vary inversely with decision-making costs, though not necessarily proportionately—presumably the investment in decision making has some uses. And, of course if one adds other considerations, such viewpoints as that of Michael Gort, presented in Section II, become relevant, suggesting that the stability of a market or system is positively related to the size of the largest firms or other units in the system.

[2] Anthony Downs has argued that individuals' ignorance of the full benefits they receive from public expenditures helps to keep the government budget smaller than it would be with better information. Since ignorance is likely to be greater with larger political units, Downs' argument would support Buchanan and Tullock's conclusion. See his, "Why the Government Budget is too small in a Democracy," *World Politics*, **12**, 4 (1960), pp. 547–561. Julius Mangolis, however, maintains that ignorance permits governments, by encouraging bargaining, to expand public services to a *higher* level than would otherwise obtain. See "Metropolitan Finance Problem: Territories, Functions and Growth," in *Public Finances: Needs, Sources, and Utilization; A Conference of the Universities-National Bureau of Economic Research* (Princeton: Princeton University Press, 1961). Some empirical evidence has been presented by Harvey J. Wheeler, without clearly supporting either side, in "Alternative Voting Rules and Local Expenditure: The Town Meeting vs. the City," *Papers in Non-Market Decision Making*, **2** (1967), pp. 61–70.

26

The Costs of
Decision Making

James M. Buchanan and
Gordon Tullock

1. Individual and Collective Decisions

When should an individual rationally stop considering the pros and cons of an issue and reach a decision? This question itself suggests that purely individual decisions involve costs. For this reason the individual typically "routinizes" many day-to-day choices that he makes: that is to say, he adopts or chooses a "rule" which dictates his behavior for many single choices. This method reduces the cost of individual decision making since it requires conscious effort, investment, only when an existing behavior rule is to be broken or modified in some way. Presumably, the rational individual himself goes through a "constitutional" choice process when he chooses this basic behavior pattern, and this process can in one sense be regarded as analogous to the more complex one examined in this book. The individual may be assumed to try to extend investment in decision making to the point where the marginal benefits no longer exceed the marginal costs.

There is no reason to expect that the individual's behavior in confronting political choices is fundamentally different from that which describes his purely private choices. In either case, he must reach a decision. The essential differences between individual choice and collective choice is that the latter requires more than one decision maker. This

Reprinted from J. M. Buchanan and G. Tullock, *The Calculus of Consent* (Ann Arbor: 1962), pp. 97–115, by permission of The University of Michigan Press. Copyright, 1962, by The University of Michigan Press.

means that two or more separate decision-making units must *agree* on a single alternative; and it is in the *reaching of agreement* among two or more individuals that the costs of collective decision making are reflected, which is the reason why these costs will tend to be more than the mere sum of individual decision-making costs taken separately. On a purely individual basis each party must decide on the alternative that is more "desirable"—most likely to further his own individual goals, whatever these may be. Only after these private decisions are made does the process of reconciling divergent individual choices, of reaching agreement, begin. . . .

This aspect of the political process has perhaps been neglected because of the implicit assumption that separate individuals, motivated by a desire to promote the "common good," will more or less naturally be led to agree quite quickly. However, if individuals should have different ideas about the "common good," or if, in accordance with the assumptions of our model, they seek to maximize their own utility, the costs of reaching agreement cannot be left out of account.

2. The Bargaining Range

If two or more individuals agree on a single decision, each of them must expect to be "better off" or at least "no worse off" as a result of the decision being carried out, with "better off" and "worse off" being defined in terms of revealed preferences in the political process. However, if all parties to an agreement expect to improve their individual positions, why is decision making costly? Decision-making costs arise here because normally a bargaining range will exist, and, recognizing this, each individual will seek to secure the maximum gains possible for himself while keeping the net gains to his partners in the agreement to the minimum. Each individual will be led to try to conceal his own true preferences from the others in order to secure a greater share of the "surplus" expected to be created from the choice being carried out. The whole gamut of strategic behavior is introduced, with the resulting costs of bargaining. From the point of view of the individual participant, some considerable investment in "bargaining" may be quite rational. This investment of time and resources in bargaining is not productive from a "social" point of view, because the added benefits that one individual may secure represent a reduction in the potential benefits of other parties to the agreement. Given a defined bargaining range, the decision-making problem is wholly that of dividing up the fixed-sized "pie"; the game is constant sum. Moreover, looking backward from a decision once made, everyone in the group will be able to see that he would have been better off had the investment in "bargaining" not taken place at all provided an agreement could have been reached in some manner without bargaining. This suggests that the individual may seek to devise means of eliminating needless and resource-wasting higgling, if possible. One method of eliminating bargaining costs is to delegate decision-making authority to a single individual and agree to abide by the choices that he makes for the whole group. If we look only at the costs of decision making (our second function), the most efficient rule for collective decision making is that of dictatorship. This provides the element of truth in the idea that dictatorial governments are more "efficient" than democratically organized governments. However, just as the rule of unanimity must normally be tempered by a recognition of decision-making costs, so must the dictatorship rule be tempered by the recognition that external costs may be imposed on the individual by collective decisions. If the individual feels that he might possibly disagree with the decisions of the dictator, that such decisions might cause him harm, he will never rationally support the delegation of important decision-making authority to a single unit.

This point presents an interesting paradox which seems worthy of mention, even though it represents a brief digression from our main argument. If the "public interest" or the "common good" is something that can be determined with relative ease, and if individual participants in collective choice act so as to promote this "common good" rather than their own interests, there seems to be little rational support for the many cumbersome and costly institutions that characterize the modern democratic process. Under such conditions the delegation of all effective decision-making power to a single decision maker, and an accompanying hierarchy, may appear perfectly rational. If some means can be taken to insure that the dictator will, in fact, remain "benevolent," the argument becomes even stronger. Moreover, this may seem to be insured by constitutional requirements for periodic elections of rulers or ruling groups. Much of the support for the growth of modern administrative government may be based on such reasoning as this, which seems to be a rather direct implication of the orthodox assumptions in much of the literature of political science.

A positive argument for democratic decision-making institutions, beyond the election of rulers periodically, must rest on the assumptions of individualist rather than idealist democracy. Individual interests must be assumed to differ, and individuals must be assumed to try to further these by means of political as well as private activity. Only on these assumptions can the costs of decision making be accepted as an inherent part of the process that will provide protection against the external costs that may be imposed by collective action.

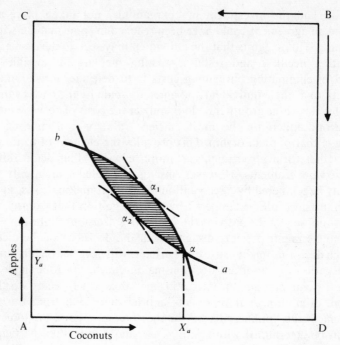

Fig. 1

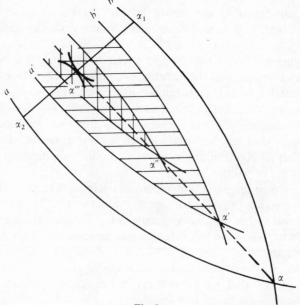

Fig. 2

3. A Simple Two-Person Bargaining Model

The actual bargaining process can best be described in terms of a model. For our purposes we may use the most simple of the many bargaining models. We assume two persons and two commodities (two "goods"). There is a given initial distribution of the two commodities between the two parties. This is illustrated in the Edgeworth box diagram of Fig. 1, a diagram familiar to all economists. The initial position, before trade or "agreement" is reached, is shown at α. Individual A, viewed from the southwest corners of the box, has in his possession AX_a of coconuts and AY_a of apples, coconuts and apples being used as labels for our hypothetical "goods." Individual B has in his possession the remaining amounts of the goods, DX_a of coconuts and CY_a of apples. The total amount of coconuts is shown by AD(CB) and the total amount of apples by AC(DB).

The initial combination of commodities will offer to each individual a certain amount, or level, of utility or satisfaction. Through point α we may draw indifference curves for A and B. Each point on the curve labeled *a* indicates the various combinations of commodities that provide A with the same level of satisfaction as that provided by the combination shown at α. Similarly, each point on *b* indicates combinations equally satisfactory to B. A whole family of such curves may be derived for each individual, and this family will fully describe the individual's tastes for the two goods. Moving in a northeasterly direction on the diagram, A's level of satisfaction increases; conversely, B's satisfaction increases as his position shifts in a southwesterly direction. The shaded area includes all of those combinations of the two commodities that will provide more utility or satisfaction to *both* parties (to both A and B) than is provided by the distribution shown at α. Gains from trade are possible.

The problem is that of reaching agreement on the terms of trade. Recognizing that a bargaining range exists, each individual will try to conceal his own "preference"; he will "bargain." If A can be wholly successful, he may be able to secure for himself the full amount of the "gain from trade": he may shift the distribution from α to α_1, keeping B not better off than he is without trade. Similarly, if B exploits his position fully, α_2 becomes a possible "solution." It can be anticipated that bargaining will continue until a final distribution somewhere along the line $\alpha_1\alpha_2$ is reached. This line is called the contract locus.

The shift from an initial position off the contract locus to a final position on this locus may be made in a single step or in a series of steps. Normally, the second method would be followed because of the ignorance of each party concerning his adversary's preferences. The process of trading may be illustrated in Fig. 2, which is an enlarged section of the earlier diagram. An initial exchange may be arranged which shifts the distribution of goods to that shown at α'. Both parties are better off than at α, A having moved to indifference curve a', and B to b'. Note that, at α', further mutually advantageous trades are possible, as is shown by the lightly shaded area. Note also, however, that the bargaining range has been substantially reduced by the initial exchange. The length of the possible contract locus has been reduced. Given this reduction in the potential gains from trade, the individual will have less incentive to invest resources in strategic moves designed to exploit his bargaining position.

Suppose now that a second exchange takes place, shifting the commodity distribution to α''. The bargaining range is again drastically reduced in size, and the distribution more closely approaches the contract locus. The chances of making gains from bargaining have almost disappeared. A final exchange may be considered to place the "solution" on the contract locus at α'''. In this last step there is little or no bargaining in the usual sense since the net gains are small. Both parties are forced into a relatively complete revelation of their true preferences. At the final or "equilibrium" position, the marginal rates of substitution between the two goods must be the same for both parties.

This extremely simple bargaining model can be of some help in the analysis of constitutional choice, since it suggests that the only means of reducing the profitability of individual investment in strategic bargaining is to reduce the size of the bargaining range—to reduce the gains to be expected from such investment. In a situation where substantial gains from mutual cooperation exist, this can only be accomplished by converting *total* decisions into *marginal* ones. This can best be illustrated by reference to the organization of decisions in the market economy.

4. Bargaining and Competitive Markets

The raison d'être of market exchange is the expectation of mutual gains. Yet insofar as markets are competitive, little scope for bargaining exists. Individuals have little incentive to invest scarce resources in strategic endeavor.... Competition among individuals does not characterize truly competitive markets, which are almost wholly impersonal in operation. The market mechanism converts all decisions into marginal ones by making all units marginal units. The conversion is effected by the diversibility of goods exchanged, which is, in turn, made possible by the availability of alternatives. The individual buyer or seller secures a "net benefit" or "surplus" from exchange, but the conditions of exchange, the terms of trade, cannot be influenced substantially by his own behavior. He can obtain no incremental personal gains by modifying his behavior because his partner in contract has available multiple alternatives. Thus, the buyer who refuses to pay the competitively established price for a good can expect no concessions to his "bargaining" efforts from the seller because the latter can sell at this price to other buyers. Similarly, the seller can anticipate no bargaining advantage from the buyer because the latter can turn to alternative sellers without undue costs.

An essential difference between market and political "exchange" is the absence of alternatives in the latter case. If we disregard the marketlike elements that may be introduced by a decentralized organization of political choice, which will be discussed later ... and concentrate on the collective action of a single governmental entity, the individual participants must, by definition, reach agreement with each other. It is not easy to withdraw from the ultimate "social contract," to turn to alternative "sellers of public goods," although the possibility of "out-migration" should never be completely left out of account. For our discussion it seems best to assume that the individual must remain in the social group. This almost guarantees that there will exist some incentive for the individual to invest resources in strategic behavior, in bargaining. . . .

5. Bargaining and "Efficient" Solutions

In a situation containing scope for bargaining, is there any assurance that an "efficient" solution will be reached at all? Will the contract locus be attained? All positions on the contract locus are defined to be "efficient" in the limited Pareto sense. Given a position on the locus, there is no other position to which a shift could be made without reducing the utility of at least one of the parties to the bargain. Thus, an "efficient" position in this sense is also an "equilibrium" position, since neither party to the bargain will have an incentive to propose further exchange. All gains from trade are secured once the contract locus is attained. The fact that mutual gains from trade will continue to exist until a solution on the locus is achieved would seem to insure that all parties will find it advantageous to continue to invest in bargaining effort until an "efficient" solution is attained. Initial investments may, of course, yield zero returns for both parties if both are stubborn and make errors in interpreting the true preferences of the other. Nevertheless, note that the failure of initial investment does not directly reduce the incentive for further investment. The possibility of mutual gains continues to exist. Moreover, failure to reach agreement may itself provide certain information to both parties which will tend to make further investments in bargaining more likely to yield returns. It seems reasonably certain, therefore, that the contract locus will be reached ultimately, if the parties are rational.

This is not to suggest that there may not be an overinvestment in bargaining, in decision making, which may more than offset the total gains from trade. In a larger sense, bargaining activity may involve "inefficient" resource usage, even though the contract locus is achieved as a result of each single bargaining process.

6. The Multiple-Party Bargain

In the simple two-party model, each individual has some incentive to invest in strategic maneuvering. Each party can, by refusing to agree and by remaining stubborn, prevent exchange (agreement) from being made. The "marginal value" of each individual's consent is the whole of the "gains from trade," but this consent is also required if the individual himself is to be able to participate in the division of the spoils. He can forestall all benefits to others by remaining recalcitrant, but the cost of so doing is the sacrifice of all private gain. Failure to reach agreement is his responsibility as well as that of his partner.

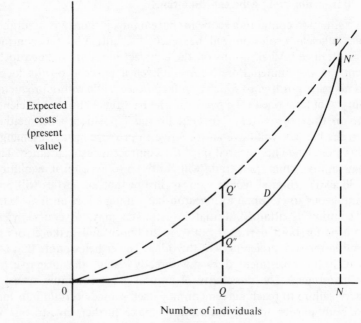

Fig. 3

If the size of the group is expanded, this aspect of the bargaining process is modified. Consider now a three-man, rather than a two-man, bargaining group. Here each party will realize that his own consent has a "marginal value," to the total group, equal to the full value of the total gains expected as a result of agreement or group action. Each of the three will also realize that his own consent is required for his own participation in any gain, but his private responsibility for attaining group agreement is less than in the two-man case. The single person will realize that, in addition to his own, the consent of *two others* is required. Greater uncertainty will be present in the bargaining process, and the single participant will be more reluctant to grant concessions. As in the two-party model, it seems clear that the contract plane will ultimately be reached; but it seems equally clear that the investment of each individual in decision making will be larger than in the two-party model.

As the size of the bargaining group increases beyond three, the costs of decision making for the individual participant will continue to increase, probably at an increasing rate. Everyday experience in the work of committees of varying size confirms this direct functional relationship between the individual costs of collective decision making and the size of the group required to reach agreement.

7. Multiple-Party Bargains within a Total Group of Fixed Size

We have just discussed the expected costs of decision making when all parties to the group are required to agree before the group action is taken. The dependence of the expected costs on the size of the total group is closely related to, but also quite distinct from, that which relates expected costs to the change in the number of persons required to agree *within a total group of defined size*. It is the second relationship that is important for the constitutional choice of rules, and it is in the difference between these two relationships that the explanation for much collective activity is to be found.

The distinction may be illustrated in Fig. 3. The V curve represents the expected costs, to the individual participant, as the size of the group is expanded, always under the requirement that *all* members of the group must give consent to group action taken: in other words, under the rule of unanimity. Thus, at QQ' it represents the expected costs of obtaining unanimous agreement among a specific group of Q persons, and at NN' the costs of obtaining unanimous agreement among N persons. By contrast, the D curve . . . relates the expected costs of decision making (to the individual) to the number of persons, *out of a group of N persons*, who are required by various decision-making rules to agree or consent before choices *for the whole group* are finally made. Thus, QQ'' represents the expected costs of obtaining the consent of a given percentage (Q/N) of the specified group N. At point N, of course, the two curves take on identical values. For any size group there may be derived a decision-rule curve similar to the unique curve D drawn with respect to a group of size N. Note that, for any group, the D curve rises as the proportion of the group required for decision increases, but this curve does not rise so rapidly as the unanimity curve V until N is approached, and the D curve remains below the V curve throughout its range.

The two curves increase for the same reason: the costs of securing agreement, *within the decision-making group*, increase as the size of the group increases. The D curve increases less rapidly than the V curve because the adoption of less-than-unanimity rules sharply restricts the profitability of individual investment in strategic bargaining. In a real sense, the introduction of less-than-unanimity rules creates or produces effective *alternatives* for the collective-choice process, alternatives which prevent decision-making costs from reaching prohibitive heights. Let us take an example in which all members of a total group of the size $(N/2 + 1)$, defined as equal to Q in Fig. 3, are required to agree unanimously. The costs of decision making expected by the individual participant may be quite significant (Q' in Fig. 3). Suppose we now consider the costs of decision making expected by the individual member of a group of size N when the rule of simple majority prevails (Q'' in Fig. 3). Note that this rule does not specify *which* individuals of the total population will make up the majority. The rule states only that a group of size $(N/2 + 1)$ must agree on decision. Here, the individual in the majority will have relatively little incentive to be overly stubborn in exploiting his bargaining position since he will realize that *alternative* members of the decisive coalition can be drawn from the minority. Bargaining within the majority group will, of course, take place. Such bargaining is a necessary preliminary to coalition formation. However, the bargaining range, and, hence, the opportunities for productive individual investment of resources in strategy, are substantially reduced.

Note that what is important here is the presence of alternative individuals outside the decision-making group who can potentially become members of the group. The D curve in Fig. 3 falls quite sharply as it moves to the left of N: that is, as the decision-making rule departs from absolute unanimity. A good practical illustration of this point is provided in the requirements for approval of zoning variances in some municipalities. In some places the "20 percent protest rule" prevails. Any 20 percent of property owners in the relevant area can raise objection to proposed departures from the zoning ordinance. Therefore, at least four-fifths of the property owners in areas adjacent to the property, the usage of which is to be modified, must consent implicitly or explicitly before a zoning variance can be granted. It is evident that this consent of 80 percent will be much easier to secure than the consent of 100 percent. In the latter case, the most stubborn of the group may hold out and try to secure the whole value of the "surplus" expected. However, under the 20 percent protest rule, even the stubborn property owner, if offered some compensation, will be reluctant to refuse consent when he fears that he will be unable to secure cooperation in making an effective protest.

This distinction between the two separate decision-making-costs functions provides an important link in our explanation for the collectivization of certain activities. If activities are left in the private sector, the securing of wholly voluntary agreements to remove existing externalities requires, in effect, that all, or nearly all, parties be compensated sufficiently to insure their consent. Such voluntary action is practically equivalent to a decision-making rule requiring unanimity for collective choice (note the coincidence of the curves V and D at N'). The bargaining costs that are involved in organizing such arrangements may be prohibitively high in many cases, with the result that, if left in the private sector, the externalities will be allowed to continue. On the other hand, the costs of organizing collective decisions under less-than-unanimity rules may be less than those expected from the continuation of the externalities. . . .

8. Bargaining Costs, Decision-Making Rules, and The Revelation of Preferences

The recognition, at the time of constitutional choice, of the costs that will be involved in securing the consent of the whole membership of the group on any single issue or set of issues is the only reason why the utility-maximizing individual will agree to place any activity in the collective sector, and, for activities placed there, will agree that operational decisions shall be made on anything less than consensus. Constitutional choices as to what activities to collectivize and what decision-making rules to adopt for these activities must depend on an assessment of the expected relative costs of decision making on the one hand, and of the operation of the activity on the other. To be able to make this assessment accurately, the individual needs to have an idea concerning the actual working of the various decision-making rules. . . . It is important to note here, however, that our theory of individual constitutional choice helps to explain many real-world institutions. The existence of externalities has long been used by scholars in welfare economics to justify collective action, but no one, to our knowledge, has satisfactorily provided any *economic* explanation for the general acceptance of less-than-unanimity rules for collective choice making.

In order to fully understand the theory, several separate issues relating to collective decision making must be kept quite distinct. We have repeatedly emphasized the necessity of distinguishing between individual choice *at the constitutional level*, where the choice is among rules, and individual choice of concrete and specific action, *within defined rules*. If attention is concentrated on collective decision making at the second, or action, level, the rule of unanimity is the only decision-making rule that is indicated by widely acceptable welfare criteria. Only under this rule will "solutions" be produced that are Pareto-optimal. The acknowledged fact that the inherent interdependence of individual choices in politics makes strategic behavior inevitable does not, in any way, invalidate this conclusion. Regardless of the number of persons in the choosing group, the contract surface will be achieved, if we assume rationality on the part of all members.

Modern welfare economics has been concerned primarily with collective action at the concrete level. Attempts have been made to devise criteria for judging specific policy measures. The reaching of unanimous agreement is the only possible test for improvement in the restricted Pareto sense, although this point has not been developed sufficiently. The recent theory of public expenditure, developed by Paul A. Samuelson and Richard A. Musgrave, represents an extension of welfare-economics models to the collective-goods sector. In this discussion the distinction between the failure to attain an "optimal" solution and the failure of individuals to reveal their "true" preferences does not seem to have been made clear. As we have emphasized, whenever a bargaining opportunity presents itself, the individual will find it profitable to invest resources in decision making, in bargaining. The two-person model presented here demonstrates, however, that the individual investment in strategy, which uses up resources, does not necessarily serve to reduce the attractiveness of further investment, unless shifts toward the contract locus are achieved. Bargaining ceases only during "equilibrium," that is, when the locus is attained.

In what sense does the presence of a bargaining opportunity cause individuals to conceal their "true" preferences? Each participant will try to make his "adversaries" think that he is less interested in "exchange" than is actually the case. However, in the only meaningful "equilibrium," the *marginal* evaluation of each individual must be fully revealed. On the contract surface the marginal rates of substitution among alternatives are equal for all individuals in the agreement. Note that this is the same revelation of preferences or tastes that market institutions force on the individual. There is nothing in the market process which requires the participating individual to reveal the extent of his "consumer's or seller's surplus." The market behavior of the individual reveals little information about his total demand schedule for a good; it does reveal his preferences at the appropriate *margins of decision* which he determines by his ability to vary the quantity of units that he keeps or sells. There exists, therefore, no fundamental difference between the market process, where bargaining opportunities are absent in the ideal case, and the political process, where bargaining opportunities are almost necessarily present, so far as the *revelation of individual preferences at the point of solution* is concerned. The difference in the two processes lies in the fact that bargaining opportunities afforded in the political process *cause the individual to invest more resources in decision making*, and, in this way, cause the attainment of "solution" to be much more costly.

The adoption of specific decision-making rules is required, therefore, not because bargaining opportunities force individuals to conceal their preferences or because bargaining can be expected to yield "imperfect" solutions in particular cases, but because of the relative "inefficiency" of the process. It is easy to see that, with a generally applicable rule of unanimity, there would be relative overinvestment in decision making. In this case the group would be devoting too much time and effort to the reaching of agreement relative to other pursuits. The possible overinvestment in collective decision making can be prevented only at the constitutional level. Once we are at the operational or action level, the decision-making costs will be related directly to the *rules* governing the choices. The "optimal" investment in decision making will, of course, vary from activity to activity since, as we have shown, these costs must be combined with expected external costs before an "optimal" rule can be chosen.

9. Group Size and Decision-Making Costs

The theory of individual constitutional choice, although developed in purely conceptual terms, is not wholly empty. Important implications of the theory have been suggested. Additional ones may be added as a result of the more careful consideration of the second basic functional relationship between costs and the number of individuals required for agreement. The costs that the individual expects to incur as a result of his own participation in collective decision making vary directly with the size of the deciding group in a given-sized total population. Significantly, these costs also vary directly with size of the total population. A concrete illustration may be helpful.

Let us suppose there are two collective units, one of which has a total voting population of one hundred citizens while the second has a voting population of one thousand citizens. If our hypotheses about the costs of collective decision making are valid, there may be several activities which the rational individual will choose to collectivize in the first "country" that he will leave under private organization in the second, and larger, political unit. The expected costs of organizing decisions, *under any given rule*, will be less in the smaller unit than in the larger, assuming that the populations of each are roughly comparable. For example, simple majority rule in the first "country" will require the assent of only 51 citizens to a decision. In the second "country" the assent of 501 citizens will be needed. The differences in the costs of organizing such majority coalitions may be significant in the two cases. On the other hand, if the two "countries" possess equal ultimate "sovereignty," the expected external costs of any given collective action may not be substantially different in the two units. From this it follows that, for those activities which are collectivized in both units, the smaller unit will normally have a more inclusive decision-making rule than the larger unit.

This is a very important implication which has normative value. As we have suggested, the costs of reaching agreement, of bargaining, are, from a "social" point of view, wasteful. One means of reducing these costs is to organize collective activity in the smallest units consistent with the extent of the externality that the collectivization is designed to eliminate.

10. The Optimum Size of Governments

On the basis of a theory of individual constitutional choice..., it is relatively straightforward to construct a theory for the optimum size of the collective unit, where this size is also subject to constitutional determinations. The group should be extended so long as the expected costs of the spillover effects from excluded jurisdiction exceed the expected incremental costs of decision making resulting from adding the excluded jurisdictions.

Suppose that an activity is performed at A (see Fig. 4); let us say that this represents the family unit and that the activity of elementary education. Clearly, the individuals most directly affected belong to the family unit making private decisions. It is acknowledged, however, that these decisions influence the other members of the group. Other members of the local community are most directly affected, as conceptually shown by the cross-hatched area enclosed by the circle B. Costs are also imposed

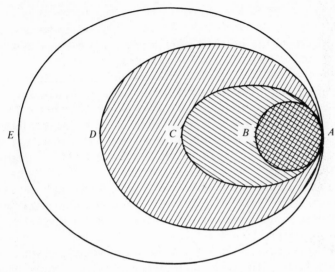

Fig. 4

on individuals living in the larger community, perhaps the municipal area, shown by *C*. Even for individuals living in other parts of the state, some external costs of educational decisions can be expected, as shown by the area *D*. Moreover, in a remote way, the family in Portland, Oregon, influences the utility of the family in North Carolina through its educational decisions. The question is: What is the appropriate size of the collective unit for the organization of elementary education, assuming that collectivization at some level is desirable? Conceptually, the answer is given by a comparison between the additional decision-making costs involved in moving from a lower to a higher level and the spillover costs that remain from retaining the activity at the lower level.

11. Decentralization and Alternatives for Choice

The preceding analysis follows directly from the theory of constitutional choice previously developed. In order to complete the picture, we must add one other element that is of significant importance. If the organization of collective activity can be effectively decentralized, this decentralization provides one means of introducing marketlike alternatives into the political process. If the individual can have available to him several political units organizing the same collective activity, he can take this into account in his locational decisions. This possibility of individual choice among alternative collective units limits both the external costs imposed by collective action and the expected costs of decision making. Insofar as the expected external costs of collective action are due to the anticipation of decisions adverse to the interest of the individual, the limit to damages expected must be the costs of migration to another collective unit. Similarly, the limit of individual investment in bargaining will be imposed by the costs of shifting to a more agreeable collectivity. In concrete terms, this suggests that the individual will not be forced to suffer unduly large and continuing capital losses from adverse collective decisions when he can move freely to other units, nor will he find it advantageous to invest too much time and effort in persuading his stubborn fellow citizens to agree with him.

The decentralization of collective activity allows both of the basic-costs functions to be reduced; in effect, it introduces elements into the political process that are not unlike those found in the operating of competitive markets.

Both the decentralization and size factors suggest that, where possible, collective activity should be organized in small rather than large political units. Organization in large units may be justified only by the overwhelming importance of the externality that remains after localized and decentralized collectivization.

12. Decision-Making Costs, External Costs, and Consensus on Values

The difficulties in reaching agreement will vary from group to group, even when all groups are assumed to contain rational individuals and no others. The second basic-costs function will be generally up-sloping for individuals in all groups, but the rate of increase will vary from one collective unit to another. The amount of investment in strategic bargaining that an individual can be expected to make will depend, to some extent, on his assessment of the bargaining skills of his fellow members in the group. It seems reasonable to expect that more will be invested in bargaining in a group composed of members who have distinctly different external characteristics than in a group composed of roughly homogeneous members. Increased uncertainty about the tastes and the bargaining skills of his fellows will lead the individual to be more stubborn in his own efforts. When he knows his fellows better, the individual will surely be less stubborn in his bargaining, and for perfectly rational reasons. The overall costs of decision making will be lower, given any collective-choice rule, in communities characterized by a reasonably homogeneous population than in those characterized by a heterogeneous population.

The implication of this hypothesis suggests that the more homogeneous community should adopt more inclusive rules for the making of collective decisions. However, the homogeneity characteristic affects external costs as well as decision-making costs. Thus the community of homogeneous persons is more likely to accept less restrictive rules even though it can "afford" more restrictive ones. By contrast, the community that includes sharp differences among individual citizens and groups cannot afford the decision-making costs involved in near-unanimity rules for collective choice, but the very real fears of destruction of life and property from collective action will prompt the individual to refuse anything other than such rules. Both elements of the costs of collective action remain very high in such communities.

The preceding discussion dealt with the relative costs involved in trying to reach agreements within large and small units; the next one concerns some of the reasons why, regardless of bargaining costs, the attempt to reach a comprehensive overview may be ill-advised. Though it does have serious implications about the virtues of keeping decision making on as disaggregated a level as possible it should not be read primarily as a defense of the nation-state or of other relatively small units per se. Its main thrust involves the difficulties of achieving major changes in any extant political or social system.

Dahl and Lindblom some time ago specified the virtues of "incrementalism" as a means of changing the goals or instruments of an organization, and stressed the obstacles, both of analytical comprehension and of institutional rigidities, that usually prevent sweeping change.[1] Here, Hirschman and Lindblom review several theories, including some of their own earlier efforts, that argue against the success of efforts to initiate large-scale planning. They identify problems of *complexity*; that is, planners' "inability to comprehend the present interrelatedness and future repercussions of certain social processes and decisions," special emphasis on *future uncertainty*; that is, the "inability to foresee the shape of technological breakthroughs"; and "the difficulty of mobilizing potentially available resources." According to this and similar less well-articulated but widely shared points of view, changes in the system of international organization must be brought about slowly and sweeping reforms are doomed to failure.

Their article is persuasive, but as the authors themselves point out, their thesis can be overdone. Particularly, incremental change is hardly an effective way to adapt to sharp discontinuous changes in the political environment. For example, if technological developments are sufficiently sudden and severe, incremental adjustment will not cope with them. A "system break" in a key environmental variable will likely demand an attempted "system break" in political controls. Any effort at comprehensive action and an overview, with forecasting, will involve great hazards, but if it is not tried the political system break may be forced, in very unwanted ways, on the decision makers. One obvious example is the change in the political system that would undoubtedly be produced even by a very limited exchange of nuclear weapons between the homelands of the two superpowers.

---

[1] R. A. Dahl and C. E. Lindblom, *Politics, Economics, and Welfare* (New York: Harper & Row, 1953).

27

Economic Development, Research and Development, Policy Making: Some Converging Views

Albert O. Hirschman and
Charles E. Lindblom

When, in their pursuit of quite different subject matters, a group of social scientists independently of each other appear to converge in a somewhat unorthodox view of certain social phenomena, investigation is in order. The convergence to be examined in this discussion is that of the views of Hirschman on economic development, Burton Klein and William Meckling on technological research and development, and Lindblom on policy making in general. These three independent lines of work appear to challenge in remarkably similar ways some widely accepted generalizations about what is variously described in the literature as the process of problem solving and decision making. Before discussing the interrelations of these views, we will give a brief description of each.

1. Hirschman on Economic Development

A major argument of Hirschman's *Strategy of Economic Development* (1958) is his attack on "balanced growth" as either a sine qua non of development or as a meaningful proximate objective of development policy.

Reprinted from *Behavioral Science*, 7, 2 (April 1962), pp. 211–222.

His basic defense of *unbalanced growth* is that, at any one point of time, an economy's resources are not to be considered as rigidly fixed in amount, and that more resources or factors of production will actually come into play if development is marked by sectoral imbalances that galvanize private entrepreneurs or public authorities into action. Even if we know exactly what the economy of a country would look like at a higher plateau, he argues, we can reach this plateau more expeditiously through the path of unbalanced growth because of the additional thrusts received by the economy as it gets into positions of imbalance.

Take an economy with two sectors that are interdependent in the sense that each sector provides some inputs to the other and that the income receivers of each sector consume part of the other sector's final output. With *given* rates of capital formation and increase in the labor supply, it is possible to specify at any one time a certain pair of growth rates for both sectors that is optimally efficient from the points of view of resource utilization and consumer satisfaction. This is balanced growth in its widest sense. Unbalanced growth will manifest its comparative initial inefficiency through a variety of symptoms: losses here, excess profits there, and concomitant relative price movements; or, in the absence of the latter, through shortages, bottlenecks, spoilage, and waste. In an open economy, a possible direct repercussion is a balance-of-payment deficit. In other words, sectoral imbalances will induce a variety of sensations— presence of pain or expectation of pleasure—in the economic operators and policy makers, whose reactions should all converge toward increasing output in the lagging sector.

To the extent that the imbalance is thus self-correcting through a variety of market and nonmarket mechanisms, the economy may be propelled forward jerkily, but also more quickly than under conditions of balanced expansion. Admittedly, the process is likely to be more costly in terms of resource utilization, but the imbalances at the same time *call forth* more resources and investment than would otherwise become available. The crucial, but plausible, assumption here is that there is some "slack" in the economy; and that additional investment, hours of work, productivity, and decision making can be squeezed out of it by the pressure mechanisms set up by imbalances. On the assumption of a given volume of resources and investment, it may be highly irrational not to attempt to come as close as possible to balanced growth; but without these assumptions there is likely to exist such a thing as an "optimal degree of imbalance." In other words, within a certain range, the increased economy in the use of given resources that might come with balanced growth is more than offset by *increased resource mobilization* afforded by unbalanced growth.

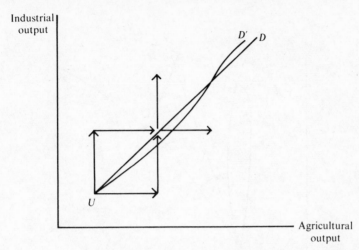

Fig. 1. Balanced versus unbalanced growth.

A simplified geometrical representation of balanced versus unbalanced growth is as follows : let there be two sectors of the economy, such as agriculture and industry, whose outputs are measured along the horizontal and vertical axes, respectively. Let point U be the point at which the underdeveloped economy finds itself and D or D' the goal at which it aims. At this stage, assume certainty and unanimous agreement about this goal. Balanced growth then aspires to a movement along such a line as UD or UD'. At the end of each investment period the economy would find itself producing outputs corresponding to successive points on such lines (See Fig. 1). Unbalanced growth means to strike out first in one direction (see arrows) and then, impelled by resulting shortages, balance-of-payments pressures, and other assorted troubles, in the other. Hirschman argues that by traveling along this circuitous route, which is likely to be more costly because of the accompanying shortages and excess capacities, the economy may get faster to its goal. Note that there are several varieties of unbalanced growth with varying degrees of pressure. For instance, to start by developing industry is likely to introduce more compelling pressures (because of the resulting food shortages, or, if food is imported, because of the balance-of-payments difficulties) than if the sequence is started by an expansion in agricultural output.

2. Klein and Meckling on Research and Development

Another apparently converging line is represented in the work of Klein and Meckling, who have for several years been studying military

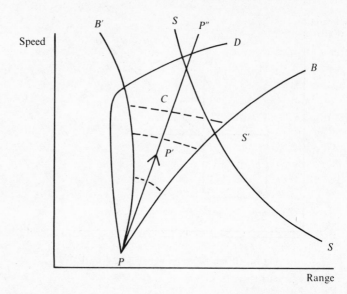

Fig. 2. Alternative paths of development of two performance characteristics.

experience with alternative research and development policies for weapons systems (Klein and Meckling, 1958; Klein, 1958, 1960). They allege that development is both less costly and more speedy when marked by duplication, "confusion," and lack of communication among people working along parallel lines. Perhaps more fundamentally, they argue against too strenuous attempts at integrating various subsystems into a well-articulated, harmonious, general system; they rather advocate the full exploitation of fruitful ideas regardless of their "fit" to some preconceived pattern of specifications.

Suppose a new airplane engine is to be developed and we know that it ought to have certain minimal performance characteristics with respect to, say, range and speed. A curve such as *SS* in Fig. 2 may represent this requirement. Is anything to be said here in favor of approaching the goal through an unbalanced path, rather than through shooting straight at the target?

The first and perhaps most important point made here by Klein and Meckling is that there is no single point to shoot at, but a great number of acceptable combinations of the two performance characteristics (shown in Fig. 2 by the set of all points lying to the northeast of the curve *SS*). It is perfectly arbitrary for anyone to pick out a point such as *S'* as *the* target to shoot at, even though this point may be in some sense the expected value of the desired technological advances. The argument then proceeds to show that because of this wide range of acceptable outcomes, and because of the uncertainty as to what is achievable, *any* advance in the northeasterly direction (such as PP') should be pushed and capitalized on rather than bent at great effort in the direction of any arbitrarily predetermined target.

The assumption here is that inventions and technical progress follow a "path of their own" to which we should defer : in other words, instead of getting upset at an early stage of development with the "lack of balance" between the two performance specifications (the engine that is being developed is all speed and very little range), we should go on developing it as best we can without reference to point S'. The simplest reason for this is that we may land anyway with a combination of the two characteristics that is acceptable for the purpose at hand : at P'' we have much more speed than we originally bargained for and enough range.

But then there may be other, more interesting reasons why "a wise and salutary neglect" of the balance between the two performance requirements may be desirable in the earlier stages of research and development. A second possibility is that, as an invention or technological advance matures and is fully articulated, possibilities of adjustment may appear that are not present earlier. In Fig. 2 we represent this phenomenon by two boundaries PB and PB' that limit the range within which trade offs between the two characteristics (along the dotted curves) are possible. If these boundaries diverge as shown in our figure, then we should postpone our attempt at trade offs until we reach the range of greater flexibility (point C).

Third, sometimes the new product that is being developed and which at one stage seemed to be so top-heavy with one of our two requirements will veer around along the path PD and, in the course of its "natural" development, will acquire the required amount of the second characteristic. To be sure, to assume that this will inevitably happen would require that one places his faith in some basic harmonies, similar to the Greek belief that the truly beautiful will possess moral excellence as well.

Most of what has been said for products with several characteristics applies also to systems with several complementary components. But some of the problems in which we are interested come into sharper focus when we deal with systems where individual components can be independently worked at and perfected. Here also, Klein and Meckling advocate full articulation of the components, even though this may mean uneven advances in their development and disregard for their overall integration into the system at an early stage.

Once again, a principal reason is uncertainty. The final configuration of the system is unknown, and knowledge increases as some of the subsystems become articulated. In the first place, knowledge about the nature of one subsystem increases the number of clues about the desirable feature of another, just as it is easier to fit in a piece of a jigsaw puzzle when some of the surrounding pieces are already in place. Second, if two pieces (subsystems) have been worked at independently, it is usually possible to join them together by small adjustments: what is important is to develop the pieces, even though they may not be perfectly adjusted to each other to start with.

Obviously, if the subsystems are being perfected fairly independently from one another, it is likely that one of them will be fully developed ahead of the others, a situation quite similar to that where one sector of the economy races ahead of another. Also, it is likely that even if they reach the point of serviceability together, some of them will be "out of phase" with the others, as in the case of a hi-fi system with an amplifier that is far too good for the loudspeaker.

3. Lindblom on Policy Making

A third converging line is represented in Lindblom's papers on policy-making processes (1958a, b, c, 1959, 1961). These papers aspire to fairly large-scale generalizations or to what, in some usages, would be called theory construction; while the points of departure of Hirschman and Klein and Meckling are two widely different, but still fairly specific, problem-solving contexts. The differences among the studies in this respect make the convergences all the more noteworthy.

Lindblom's point of departure is a denial of the general validity of two assumptions implicit in most of the literature on policy making. The first is that public-policy problems can best be solved by attempting to understand them; the second is that there exists sufficient agreement to provide adequate criteria for choosing among possible alternative policies. Although the first is widely accepted—in many circles almost treated as a self-evident truth—it is often false. The second is more often questioned in contemporary social science; yet many of the most common prescriptions for rational problem solving follow only if it is true.

Conventional descriptions of rational decision making identify the following aspects: (1) clarification of objectives or values, (2) survey of alternative means of reaching objectives, (3) identification of consequences, including side effects or by-products, of each alternative means, and (4) evaluation of each set of consequences in light of the objectives. However, Lindblom notes, for a number of reasons such a *synoptic* or comprehensive attempt at problem solving is not possible to the degree that clarification of objectives founders on social conflict, that required information is either not available or available only at prohibitive cost, or that the problem is simply too complex for man's finite intellectual capacities. Its complexity may stem from an impossibly large number of alternative policies and their possible repercussions from imponderables in the delineation of objectives even in the absence of social disagreement on them, from a supply of information too large to process in the mind, or from still other causes.

It does not logically follow, Lindblom argues, that when synoptic decision making is extremely difficult, it should nevertheless be pursued as far as possible. And he consequently suggests that in many circumstances substantial departures from comprehensive understanding are both inevitable and on specific grounds desirable. For the most part, these departures are familiar; and his exposition of them serves, therefore, to formalize our perceptions of certain useful problem-solving strategies often mistakenly dismissed as aberrations in rational problem solving.

These strategies, which we shall call "disjointed incrementalism," are the following:

A. Attempt at understanding is limited to policies that differ only incrementally from existing policy.

B. Instead of simply adjusting means to ends, ends are chosen that are appropriate to available or nearly available means.

C. A relatively small number of means (alternative possible policies) is considered, as follows from A.

D. Instead of comparing alternative means or policies in the light of postulated ends or objectives, alternative ends or objectives are also compared in the light of postulated means or policies and their consequences.

E. Ends and means are chosen simultaneously; the choice of means does not follow the choice of ends.

F. Ends are indefinitely explored, reconsidered, discovered, rather than relatively fixed.

G. At any given analytical point ("point" refers to any one individual, group, agency, or institution), analysis and policy making are serial or successive; that is, problems are not "solved," but are repeatedly attacked.

H. Analysis and policy making are remedial; they move *away* from ills rather than *toward* known objectives.

I. At any one analytical point, the analysis of consequences is quite incomplete.

J. Analysis and policy making are socially fragmented; they go on at a very large number of separate points simultaneously.

The most striking characteristic of disjointed incrementalism is (as indicated in I) that no attempt at comprehensiveness is made; on the contrary, unquestionably important consequences of alternative policies are simply ignored at any given analytical or policy-making point. But Lindblom goes on to argue that through various specific types of partisan mutual adjustment among the large number of individuals and groups among which analysis and policy making is fragmented (see J), what is ignored at one point in policy making becomes central at another point. Hence, it will often be possible to find a tolerable level of rationality in decision making when the process is viewed as a whole in its social or political context, even if at each individual policy-making point or center analysis remains incomplete. Similarly, errors that would attend overly ambitious attempts at comprehensive understanding are often avoided by the remedial and incremental character of problem solving. And those not avoided can be mopped up or attended to as they appear, because analysis and policy making are serial or successive (as in G).

While we cannot here review the entire argument, Lindblom tries to show how the specific characteristics of disjointed incrementalism, taken in conjunction with mechanisms for partisan mutual adjustment, meet each of the characteristic difficulties that beset synoptic policy making: value conflicts, information inadequacies, and general complexity beyond man's intellectual capacities. His line of argument shows the influence of pluralist thinkers on political theory, but he departs from their interest in the control of power and, rather, focuses on the level of rationality required or appropriate for decision making.

4. Points of Convergence

If they are not already obvious, specific parallels in the works reviewed are easy to illustrate. Compare, for example, an economy that is in a state of imbalance as the result of a sharp but isolated advance of one sector and a weapons system that is out of balance because a subsystem is "too good" in relation to the capacity of another system. Just as for a sector of the economy, it is possible that a completed subsystem is "too advanced" only in comparison with some preconceived notion, and that actually its unexpectedly high performance level is quite welcome, either because it improves upon overall system performance or because it happily compensates for the lag of some other component behind the norms originally set. On the other hand, a component can be "too advanced" in a real sense, as in a hi-fi set, where the performance of a component depends not only on its capacity but also on inputs from other components. This situation corresponds exactly to that of an economy in structural imbalance. The laggard components turn into bottlenecks for the full utilization of the avant-garde component's capacity. Yet even though such a system or economy represents in itself an inefficient utilization of inputs, it may, nevertheless, be a highly useful configuration if it is conceived as a stage in the development process. For it may be expected that attempts will be made to improve the weaker subsystems or sectors so that the capability of the stronger ones may be fully utilized. In the process, the weaker systems or sectors may be so improved that they become the stronger ones, and the stage thus set for a series of seesaw advances which may carry the overall "goodness" of our system or economy beyond what might have been achieved by maintaining balance.

For both economy and weapons system we are talking in terms of probabilities. There can be no certainty that with one avant-garde subsystem readied the others will dutifully be put in place or improved. The existence of the Maginot line along the French-German border failed to call forth a corresponding effort along the Belgian frontier to guard against the possibility of a German strategy aimed at circumventing the Line.

This example illustrates an important point: a "system" or economy is never quite finished. Today's system or economy-in-balance is likely to turn into tomorrow's subsystem or economy-out-of-balance, because of unforeseeable repercussions, newly emerging difficulties, unanticipated counterstrategies, changing tastes or techniques, or whatever other forces with which the system or economy has to deal. But these repercussions, difficulties, and counterstrategies could not possibly be fully visualized in advance. The transportation system consisting of highways, gasoline and repair stations, and automotive vehicles is found incomplete; first, because of inadequate accident prevention, and later also because of smog. The new system of defense against infections through antibiotics is suddenly "out of balance" because of the development of new varieties of drug-resistant microorganisms. In these cases, it would have been impossible to foresee the imbalance and incompleteness that emerged clearly only after the new system had been in operation for some time.

Once it is understood that a system is never complete or will never stay complete, the case against spending considerable effort on early integration and simultaneous development of subsystems is further stengthened. For if we do achieve early integration and simultaneity, we are much more likely to succumb to the illusion that our system is actually complete in itself and needs no further complements and watchfulness than if we had built it up as a result of seesaw advances and adjustments which do not provide for a natural resting place.[1]

---

[1] The examples of the Maginot line, of automobile traffic, and of antibiotics bring up an additional problem. In the latter two cases, the incompleteness of the system is forcefully brought to our attention through accidents and eye irritation, and through new types of infection. The trouble with some other systems that turn into subsystems is that the mutation

As another specific illustration of convergence, consider the sequence of moves in problem solving as described, on the one hand, in developmental terms by Hirschman, Klein and Meckling, and, on the other hand, in political terms, by Lindblom. Recall the picture of desired progress where we wished to move from one fixed point (the present) to another fixed point in a 2-dimensional diagram. From existing levels of output in industry and agriculture (or range and speed in aircraft) we wished to move to higher levels of both. Imagine a situation in which two parties with different preferences want to go off in two different directions. Lindblom argues that in this situation the best way to make progress is through "mutual adjustment," i.e., by a series of moves and counter-moves in the course of which a higher plateau can be reached even without prior agreement about the eventual goal. "Individuals often agree on policies when they cannot agree on ends. Moreover, attempts to agree on ends or values often get in the way of agreements on specific policies" (1958b, p. 534). Furthermore, it is possible, and even likely, that the value systems of the two parties will move more closely together once an advance that is tolerable to both has been achieved. "The decision-maker expects to learn about his values from his experiences and he is inclined to think that in the long run policy choices have as great an influence on objectives as objectives have on policy choices" (1961, p. 309).

Lindblom's reasoning reinforces the others. It parallels Klein and Meckling's emphasis on the inevitability of moving forward through move and countermove, in what appears an arbitrary, somewhat aimless fashion, rather than Hirchman's stress on the efficiency of such a sequence in

---

may not be so easily detected, or that it may be detected only when it is too late, as was precisely the case with the Maginot line.

There is real difficulty about the meaning of "too late." The imperfections of automobile traffic and antibiotics were discovered too late for the victims of accidents and new-type infections, but not too late, we hope, for the rest of us. The defects of the Maginot line were discovered too late to save France in 1940, although not too late to win the war against Hitler. This suggests that there may be cases where we cannot afford to do our learning about the imperfections and imbalances of a system through the failures, irritations, and discomforts that are the natural concomitants and signals of the imbalance. Such situations present us with a well-nigh insoluble task, similar to the one which would face a child who had to learn to walk without being permitted to fall. Here the temptation is particularly strong to prepare in advance a perfect theoretical solution. Yet we know from all that has been said that reliance on such a solution would be most likely to bring about the failure one is seeking to avoid. One way of dealing with situations in which we feel we cannot afford to learn the "hard way" is to develop institutions whose special mission it is to be alert to and to detect existing and developing system imbalances: in a democracy, some institutions of this kind are a free press and an opposition party. For national defense a certain amount of interservice rivalry may serve the same purpose, as each service has a vested interest in pointing out the "holes" in the other services' systems.

squeezing out additional resources. Nevertheless, the idea that unbalanced or seesaw advances of this kind are efficient in some sense is also present. Instead of focusing on the limited supply of decision makers and on the desirability of placing some extra pressures behind investment decisions, Lindblom emphasizes the limited supply of knowledge and the limited area of agreement that exists among the various powerholders, and visualizes a series of sequential adjustments as a way to maximize positive action in a society where ignorance, uncertainty, and conflict preclude not only the identification, but even the existence, of any "best" move.

But we can do better than illustrate parallels. We can explicitly identify the principal points of convergence.

1. The most obvious similarity is that all insist on the rationality and usefulness of certain processes and modes of behavior which are ordinarily considered to be irrational, wasteful, and generally abominable.

2. The three approaches thus have in common an attack on such well-established values as orderliness (cf. Hirschman's "model of optimum disorderliness" [1958, p. 80]), balance, and detailed programing; they all agree with Burke that some matters ought to be left to a "wise and salutary neglect."

3. They agree that one step ought often to be left to lead to another, and that it is unwise to specify objectives in much detail when the means of attaining them are virtually unknown.

4. All agree further that in rational problem solving, goals will change not only in detail but in a more fundamental sense through experience with a succession of means-ends and ends-means adjustments.

5. All agree that in an important sense a rational problem solver wants what he can get and does not try to get what he wants except after identifying what he wants by examining what he can get.

6. There is also agreement that the exploration of alternative uses of resources can be overdone, and that attempts at introducing explicitly certain maximizing techniques (trade offs among inputs or among outputs, cost-benefit calculations) and coordinating techniques will be ineffective and quite possibly harmful in some situations. In a sense more fundamental than is implied by theories stressing the cost of information, the pursuit of certain activities that are usually held to be the very essence of "economizing" can at times be decidedly uneconomical.

7. One reason for this is the following: for successful problem solving, all agree it is most important that arrangements exist through which decision makers are sensitized and react promptly to newly emerging problems, imbalances, and difficulties; this essential ability to react and to improvise readily and imaginatively can be stultified by an undue preoccupation

with, and consequent pretense at, advance elimination of these problems and difficulties through "integrated planning."

8. Similarly, attempts at foresight can be misplaced; they will often result in complicating the problem through mistaken diagnoses and ideologies. Since man has quite limited capacities to solve problems and particularly to foresee the shape of future problems, the much maligned "hard way" of learning by experiencing the problems at close range may often be the most expeditious and least expensive way to a solution.

9. Thus, we have here theories of successive decision making; denying the possibility of determining the sequence ex ante, relying on the clues that appear in the course of the sequence, and concentrating on identification of these clues.

10. All count on the usefulness for problem solving of subtle social processes not necessarily consciously directed at an identified social problem. Processes of mutual adjustment of participants are capable of achieving a kind of coordination not necessarily centrally envisaged prior to its achievement, or centrally managed.

11. At least Hirschman and Lindblom see in political adjustment and strife analogues to self-interested yet socially useful adjustment in the market.

12. All question such values as "foresight," "central direction," "integrated overview," but not in order to advocate laissez faire or to inveigh against expanded activities of the state in economic or other fields. They are in fact typically concerned with decision-making and problem-solving activities carried on by the state. In their positive aspects they describe how these activities are "really" taking place as compared to commonly held images; and insofar as they are normative they advocate a modification of these images, in the belief that clearer appreciation and perception of institutions and attitudes helpful to problem-solving activities will result.

Although many of these propositions are familiar, they are often denied in explicit accounts of rational decision making; and at least some of them challenge familiar contrary beliefs. Either the convergences are an unfortunate accident, or decision-making theory has underplayed the degree to which "common sense" rational problem-solving procedures have to be modified or abandoned. Account must be taken of man's inertia, limited capacities, costs of decision making, and other obstacles to problem solving, including uncertainty, which is the only one of the complicating elements that has been given sustained attention. And most investigations of uncertainty have been within the narrow competence of statistical theory.

5. Points of Difference

These similarities in approach, with their widely different origins, structures, and fields of application, are even better understood if their remaining points of difference are identified.

The basic justification for rejecting traditional precepts of rationality, planning, and balance is somewhat different for the three approaches here examined. For Lindblom it is *complexity*, i.e., man's inability to *comprehend* the present interrelatedness and future repercussions of certain social processes and decisions, as well as imperfect knowledge and *value conflicts*. For Klein and Meckling it is almost entirely *future uncertainty*, i.e., man's inability to *foresee* the shape of technological breakthroughs, or the desirability of letting oneself be guided by these breakthroughs if and when they occur, instead of following a predetermined sequence. For Hirschman it is the difficulty of mobilizing potentially available resources and decision-making activity itself; the *inadequacy of incentives* to problem solving, or, conversely, the need for *inducements* to decision making.

Although Klein's and Meckling's concern with future uncertainty could formally be viewed as a special case of Lindblom's problem of inadequate information, their treatment of the research and development problem is different enough from Lindblom's treatment of information inadequacies to argue against its being so viewed. Hirschman's concern with inducements to problem-solving activity is quite different from either Lindblom's or Klein's and Meckling's concern with limits on cognitive faculties. He argues not that men lack knowledge and capacity to solve problems in an absolute sense, but that there is always some utilized problem-solving capacity that can be called forth through a variety of inducement mechanisms and pacing devices. These different reasons for supporting the same conclusions make the conclusions more rather than less persuasive, for the reasons supplement rather than invalidate each other.

That they are complementary reasons is, of course, indicated by the overlap of the Lindblom and the Klein–Meckling approaches on the problem of imperfect information, and by some Hirschman-like concern for research and development *incentives* in the Klein–Meckling study. It is also true that Hirschman develops as a secondary theme the difficulties of ignorance and uncertainty in economic development. For instance, his partiality toward "development via social overhead capital shortage" is based in part on the position that shortages and bottlenecks remove uncertainty about the direction of needed overhead investments. Similarly, he emphasizes the importance of unforeseen or loose complementarity repercussions, such as "entrained wants" that arise in the course of development, and asserts that imports are helpful in inducing domestic production because they remove previous doubts about the existence of a market.

From the differences in the main thrust of the respective arguments, certain other major differences emerge, differences which do not deny the convergences, but which, on the other hand, ought not to be submerged by them. For example, Hirschman's argument that a very heavy reliance on central planning will often be inappropriate for underdeveloped countries looks superficially parallel to Lindblom's argument that *partisan* mutual adjustment can sometimes achieve efficiencies that could not be achieved through overambitious attempts at central omniscience and control. Yet, on closer scrutiny, Hirschman's cautions about centralism only second-arily refer to the *general* difficulties of managing complex affairs that strain man's incentives and intellectual capacities. Instead, he argues, that a conventional, centrally planned attempt to define and achieve a balance among many varied lines of development will be less helpful than a similarly central attempt to estimate and manage the critical linkages through which economic growth is forced or induced.

Hirschman's explicitly declared view of decision making for economic development is almost entirely one of central planning, or at least problem solving by persons—such as planning board managers or officials of international agencies—who assume general responsibility toward the economy as a whole, and whose point of view is, therefore, that of a central planner. Hirschman's policy maker or operator is, with only a few excep-tions, such a person or official; and Hirschman's prescriptions are always addressed to such a person. By contrast, Lindblom's policy maker is typically a partisan, often acknowledging no responsibility to his society as a whole frankly pursuing his own segmental interests; and this is a kind of policy maker for whom Hirschman, despite his between-the-lines endorsement of him, makes no explicit place in his formulation of the development process.

A further important point of difference between Hirschman and Lindblom appears to lie in Hirschman's emphasis on discovering and utili-zing the side effects and repercussions of development decisions, as compared to Lindblom's readiness to recommend at any given "point" neglect of such repercussions. It is, indeed, a major thesis of Hirschman that analysis of a prospective investment project should above all try to evaluate its effect on further development decisions instead of convention-ally concentrating on its own prospective output and productivity. Speci-fically, every decision should be analyzed to discover its possible "link-ages" with other decisions that might follow it. For example, a prospective decision to encourage the importation of some consumer goods, such as radios, should consider not simply the economy's need for these goods but the probability that their importation will in time lead to a decision by domestic investors to assemble them locally, as well as the "linkage effects" of such assembly operations on further domestic production decisions.

Hirschman's book (1958) is both an attempt to uncover such linkages and a prescription that developers seek to uncover them in every possible case. Lindblom suggests that this kind of by-product, the indirect conse-quences of a decision that flow from the decision's effect on still other decision makers, will often escape the analyst in any case; hence he should not try to always anticipate and understand it, but instead should deal with it through subsequent steps in policy making, if and when it emerges as a problem. Since, as Lindblom sees it, policy making is not only *remedial* and *serial* but also *fragmented*, both intentionally and accidentally neglected consequences of chosen policies will often be attended to either as a remedial next step of the original policy makers or by some other policy-making group whose interests are affected. Hence policy as a complex social or political process rises to a higher level of comprehensive-ness and rationality than is achieved by any one policy maker at any one move in the process.

The contrast between Hirschman and Lindblom on this point can be overdrawn, however. For one thing, Hirschman feels that calculations which purport to give greater rationality to investment planning may often interfere with development, because they typically do not and cannot take the "linkages" into account; whereas more rough-and-ready methods may be at least based on hunches about such linkages. Second, Hirschman's practical advice to policy makers is similar to Lindblom's when he tells them to go ahead with unintegrated and unbalanced projects on the ground that, in an interdependent economy, progress in some sectors will serve to unmask the others as laggards and will thereby bring new pressures toward improvement. In his general prescription, more implicit than explicit, that development planners try to move the economy wherever it can be moved, that is, seize on readiness to act wherever it can be found, Hirschman is endorsing Lindblom's suggestion that many consequences can best be dealt with only as they actually show themselves.

As a further point of difference, it is implicit in what has been said in the preceding paragraphs that Hirschman's thinking about secondary effects is preoccupied with possible bonuses to be exploited, Lindblom's with possible losses to be minimized. Again, the difference is easy to over-state: Hirschman too is at times concerned with possible losses, even if Lindblom has not explored at all the possibility of bonuses. Hirschman, however, relies on correct diagnosis of linkages for protection from damaging side effects; and his position is, therefore, parallel to his position on exploiting bonus effects. Only secondarily (1958, pp. 208 ff.) does he count on Lindblom's remedial, serial, and fragmented kind of process for minimizing losses.

6. Concluding Remarks

As Hirschman would now give uncertainty, complexity, and value conflict a more central place in justifying his conclusions on economic development policy, so also Lindblom's and Klein's and Meckling's analyses could be strengthened by taking into account the fact that the policies they defend could also be justified because they permit mobilization of resources and energies that could not be activated otherwise. Perhaps these latter analyses could go beyond the statement that the processes of research and development and of policy making are of necessity piecemeal, successive, fragmented, and disjointed; they could try to define typical sequences and their characteristics, similar to Hirschman's "permissive" and "compulsive" sequences. Once the intellectual taboo and wholesale condemnation are lifted from some of the policies Klein, Meckling, and Lindblom defend, it becomes desirable to have a closer look at the heretofore incriminated processes and to rank them from various points of view. It is useful to ask questions such as the following: as long as we know that a system is going to be out of balance anyway when the subsystems develop, what type of imbalance is most likely to be self-correcting? An answer to this question could affect the desirable distribution and emphasis of the research and development effort. Detailed descriptions of types of incremental meandering would also be interesting; perhaps this would more clearly differentiate between a sequence that leads to reform and another that leads to revolution.

One problem deserves to be mentioned again. The processes of economic development, research and development, and policy making must rely on successive decision making because they all break new, uncertain ground. Therefore, these processes must let themselves be guided by the clues that appear en route. Snags, difficulties, and tensions cannot be avoided, but must on the contrary be utilized to propel the process further. The trouble is that the difficulties are not only "little helpers" but may also start processes of disintegration and demoralization. An intersectoral imbalance set up a race between the catching-up, forward movement of the lagging sector and the retrogression of the advanced one. The greater the pressure toward remedial positive action, the greater is the risk if this action does not take place. There is a corresponding situation in systems development. The more a system is out of the balance, the greater will presumably be the pressure to do something about it, but also, the more useless is the system should no action be forthcoming.

All three approaches therefore have one further characteristic in common : they can be overdone. There are limits to "imbalance" in economic development, to "lack of integration" in research and development, to "fragmentation" in policy making which would be dangerous to pass. And it is clearly impossible to specify in advance the optimal doses of these various policies under different circumstances. The art of promoting economic development, research and development, and constructive policy making in general consists, then, in acquiring a feeling for these doses.

This art, it is submitted by the theories here reviewed, will be mastered far better once the false ideals of "balance," "coordination," and "comprehensive overview" have lost our total and unquestioning intellectual allegiance.

References

1. Hirschman, A. O., *The Strategy of Economic Development* (New Haven, Yale University Press, 1958).
2. Klein, B., "A Radical Proposal for R and D," *Fortune* (May 1958), p. 112.
3. Klein, B., "The Decision-Making Problem in Development." Paper No. P-1916 (Santa Monica, Calif.: The RAND Corporation, February 19, 1960).
4. Klein, B., and W. Meckling, "Application of Operations Research to Development Decisions," *Operations Research*, **6** (1958), pp. 352–363.
5. Lindblom, C. E., "Policy Analysis," *American Economic Reviews*, **48** (1958a), pp. 298–312.
6. Lindblom, C. E., "Tinbergen on Policy Making," *Journal of Political Economy*, **66** (1958b), pp. 531–538.
7. Lindblom, C. E., "The Handling of Norms in Policy Analysis," in M. Abramovitz, ed., *Allocation of Economic Resources* (Stanford: Stanford University Press, 1958c), pp. 160–179.
8. Lindblom, C. E., "The Science of 'Muddling Through.'" *Public Administration Review*, **19** (1959), pp. 79–88.
9. Lindblom, C. E., "Decision Making in Taxation and Expenditure," in Universities-National Bureau of Economic Research, *Public Finances: Needs, Sources, and Utilization* (Princeton: Princeton University Press, 1961).

The difficulties encountered in any attempt at comprehensive planning and forecasting for a complex political or economic system are certainly immense, and can easily be underestimated when a need for change seems pressing. And as Hirschman and Lindblom well pointed out, compared with what can be accomplished by more fragmented adjustment the need for comprehensive planning is often exaggerated. Nevertheless, the possibilities of obtaining an overview for predictive purposes are substantial, and show up most clearly in the success that economists have achieved in making both detailed and highly aggregated forecasts of income and production. They predict overall trends in gross national product and developments in its components (e.g., fixed capital formation) and, in particular, factors dependent on it (e.g., employment).

Econometrics, or the science of employing very sophisticated models to specify quantitative relationships among economic variables, has been especially well developed in the United States, but not only there. It has also made substantial strides in the Soviet Union. Efforts to plan production for an enormous industrial economy containing over 200 million people initially proved difficult in the extreme—failures of information on current production or in accurate forecasting of future needs and production led to bottlenecks and gross inefficiencies. Sometimes the result was simply a failure to produce enough goods of the right kind, other times it was one of distribution, where the needed goods were available, but not in the right place. The Soviet planning authorities had to make a number of concessions from their theoretical comprehensive planning efforts. The "fixer," for instance, usually was a man attached to an industrial enterprise, but who was something of an operator or entrepreneur in spirit; his job was to find the raw materials or equipment that his enterprise needed and make the appropriate barter arrangements, outside the comprehensive planning system, to get them and to keep the plant operating efficiently. In the late 1950's the Soviet government initiated a number of reforms in the direction of decentralization and greater autonomy for particular regions or industries. These and similar developments have been carried much further in other communist countries, the best known of these being the major moves toward free enterprise in Yugoslavia. Such moves *away* from comprehensive planning, however, have not been the only steps taken to make the Soviet economy more efficient. The planning system itself has been greatly improved by the use of econometric methods and the introduction of high speed computers. With modern methods of information retrieval and data processing it is now possible to achieve much greater success in economic forecasting even with all the complexities obviously present in the USSR.

In the following article Daniel B. Suits describes the econometric model which his group has refined over a number of years and which now gives predictions of short-term trends in the United States economy "well within the practical tolerances required for effective policy evaluation." It may seem highly elaborate, but as he notes, it is "only" a highly sophisticated method of observing the past operation of the economy and systematizing the information obtained. More importantly, for any assessment of the possible application of similar methods to *international relations*, it perhaps seems more formidable intellectually than it is, requiring "little more than a knowledge of elementary algebra to understand its nature." Now, of course, international politics theory and measurement efforts will for some time be far too primitive to permit the kind of results achieved by the econometricians. We are far less certain what the relevant variables are, what the functional relationships among them are, and how to gather valid and reliable data on them in any case. But various efforts in this direction are being undertaken, as manifested in several attempts to construct *computer* simulations either of national political systems or of the international system as a whole. In the long run it is likely to turn out that a systematic overview, which can be directed toward assessing the consequences of major induced changes in the system, will have distinct uses.

The detailed predictions and relationships in the following article will probably not be of direct interest to readers concerned primarily with international relations. I have left them in, however, so that the reader who wishes to do so may get an idea of the system by which the forecasts are made. The short-run policy multipliers shown in Section 3, C are interesting as an illustration of the way specific variables can be isolated as particularly subject to political control, while others are nearly autonomous, and how it is then possible to calculate in detail the overall effects of a given increase or decrease in spending on that particular item. A "multiplier," for instance, is simply an expression for the functional relationship, which can be written as a regression equation, between an increase in spending in one category and other income and production items. The computations can be carried throughout the system as the accumulated consequences take effect. The importance of the model is in identifying not only accounting identities, but *dynamic* relationships where spending on an item at time t is a function of spending on other items at $t - 1$, and the vulnerable *political choice points*. A variety of data—aggregative and special surveys—are employed. In international politics it is conceivable that we might eventually be able not only to calculate the effect of a decrease in one super-power's spending on armaments on its own economy or on the spending pattern of its rival, but to say by how much it affected the orientation of quite distant national political systems and the stability of the entire international system. And perhaps also, as knowledge improves, central-ized direction of the global political system will seem like a less formidable task.[1] Whether it would be desirable is yet another question whose answer depends in large part on how the decisions are reached. Even a "benevo-lent" world dictatorship would not necessarily reach decisions superior to those arrived at by bargaining.[2]

[1] An example of econometric methods on political phenomena, including the use of Markov chains with assumptions about the effect of past budgeting decisions on current ones, is O. A. Davis, M. A. H. Dempster, and A. Wildavsky, "A Theory of the Budgetary Process," *American Political Science Review*, **60**, 3 (September 1966), pp. 529–547. See also M. Shubik, *An Aggregate Socio-economic Simulation of a Latin American Country* (New Haven: Cowles Commission on Economic Research, 1966, Memorandum No. 203, mimeo).

[2] In addition to some of the materials employed elsewhere in this book, see I. M. D. Little, *A Critique of Welfare Economics*, (Oxford: Oxford University Press, 1951) on the impossi-bility of intersubjective comparisons of utility.

28

Forecasting and Analysis with an Econometric Model

Daniel E. Suits

Although an econometric model is the statistical embodiment of theoretical relationships that are every economist's stock in trade, its discussion has largely been kept on a specialized level and confined to the more mathematical journals. Models are rarely explored from the point of view of their usefulness to the profession at large, yet there is nothing about their nature or their application—aside, again, from a solid grasp of economic theory—that requires anything more than an elementary knowledge of school algebra. The compilation of an econometric model requires a certain degree of technical specialization, but once constructed, any competent economist can apply it to policy analysis and economic forecasting.

The purpose of this article is to present an actual econometric model of the US economy, to demonstrate its use as a forecasting instrument, and to explore its implications for policy analysis. To minimize the technical background required, the presentation is divided into two main parts. Section 1 deals with the general nature of econometric models, and, using a highly simplified schematic example, illustrates how forecasts are made with a model, how a model can be modified to permit the introduction of additional information and judgment, and how short-run and long-run policy multipliers are derived from the inverse of the model. Section 2 presents the 32-equation econometric model of the US economy compiled by the Research Seminar in Quantitative Economics....

Reprinted from *American Economic Review*, **52**, 1 (March 1962), pp. 104–132.

In Section 3 the outlook for 1962, as calculated and published in November 1961, is studied as an example of an actual forecast; and earlier forecasts of this kind that have been prepared by the Research Seminar annually since 1953 are compared with actual events as a demonstration of the potential of the method.

In Section 3 the inverse of the model is also presented and its application to policy evaluation is reviewed. Short-run and long-run multipliers are calculated for selected policy variables....

1. Econometric Models and Their Applications

The science of economics can be variously defined, but for the present purpose it is useful to think of it as the study of the relationships among a system of observable and essentially measurable variables: prices, costs, outputs, incomes, savings, employment, etc. These relationships derive from the complex behavior and interaction of millions of households, millions of firms, and thousands of governmental units, producing and exchanging millions of products. The relationships can be represented by a system of mathematical equations, but, unfortunately, a theoretically complete representation (e.g., a Walrasian system) would involve trillions of equations—surely millions for each household and firm. Moreover, these equations would be individually as complex as human behavior, and involve the elaborate interaction of numberless variables.

We have neither the time nor the resources to deal with such a vast system of equations; to proceed at all we must simplify and condense. Millions of individual households become a single "household sector," millions of products become a single item of expenditure, e.g., "durable goods." Moreover, complex mathematical relationships among thousands of variables become simple linear approximations involving two or three aggregates. An econometric model of the economy is obtained by confronting these highly simplified equations with data arising from the historical operation of the economic system and, by appropriate statistical techniques, obtaining numerical estimates for their parameters.

The minimum number of equations necessary for an adequate representation of the economic system depends on a number of considerations, but, clearly, the fewer the equations the greater must be the level of aggregation and the less accurate and useful the result. On the other hand, the larger the number of equations and the greater the detail shown in the variables, the more complicated it is to derive the individual equations, to manipulate the resulting system, and to see the implications of the model. Where modern computing facilities can be used the mere size of the model is no longer a serious barrier to its effective application, but for purposes of exposition the smaller and simpler the model the better.

A. A Simple Illustrative Example

To illustrate the principles of application, let us suppose that the statistical procedure gave rise to the following, purely schematic, model of four equations.

$$C = 20 + .7(Y - T) \tag{1}$$

$$I = 2 + .1Y_{-1} \tag{2}$$

$$T = .2Y \tag{3}$$

$$Y = C + I + G \tag{4}$$

According to Eq. (1), consumption (C) depends on current disposable income ($Y - T$). In Eq. (2), investment (I) depends on income lagged one period. The third equation relates taxes (T) to income, while the last defines income as the sum of consumption, investment, and government expenditure G.

While this model is small, it illustrates most of the properties of the larger model. The single consumption function in Eq. (1) corresponds to the set of four Eqs. (01), (02), (03), and (04) that describe the behavior of the consumer sector in Section 2. The investment behavior represented in (2) corresponds to Eqs. (05) through (10). The single tax Eq. (3) corresponds to a combination of the eleven tax and transfer equations, while the relationship of production to income embodied in Eq. (4) is indicated in much greater detail by Eqs. (11) through (20).

The econometric model approximates the economy by a system of equations in which the unknowns are those variables—income, consumption, investment, and tax yield—whose behavior is to be analyzed. The "knowns" are government expenditure and lagged income. When projected values for the "knowns" are inserted in the equations, the system can be solved to forecast the values of the unknowns.

Quotation marks are used advisedly on the word "knowns." For, while some economic variables move so slowly along secular trends that their future values can be projected with considerable accuracy, others —for example new government expenditures—are unknown in advance of their occurrence, even in principle. Moreover, even the values of lagged variables are unknown at the time of the forecast, since a useful forecast must be made some months before the end of the preceding year. For example, each of the forecasts shown in Table 3 was made during the first week of November of the preceding year. To make such forecasts, lagged variables are estimated from data for the first three quarters of the year, with the third quarter given double weight.

At any rate, suppose we expect next year's government expenditure to be 20, and the preliminary estimate of this year's income is, say, 100. Substituting $G = 20$ and $Y_{-1} = 100$ into the equations just presented and solving gives $C = 86.2, I = 12, T = 23.7, Y = 118.2$.

B. Introducing Outside Information

It may appear from the foregoing that this kind of forecasting is a blind, automatic procedure; but while an econometric model looks like a rigid analytical tool, it is actually a highly flexible device, readily modifiable to bring to bear additional information and judgment. For example, the investment equation in our little model is surely an unreliable predictor of capital formation. If no other information were available, the equation would have to serve the purpose. But suppose we have available a survey of investment intentions reported by business. An estimate derived from a such a survey is clearly superior to any that Eq. (2) could produce. To introduce the information into the forecast we simply remove Eq. (2) from the model and, in the remaining equations, set I equal to the survey value. Forecasts made from the Research Seminar model have frequently involved use of a figure for gross investment in plant and equipment derived from the McGraw-Hill Survey of Investment Intentions rather than from Eq. (05) of the model.

Information can also be used to modify individual relationships short of replacing them entirely. For example, a prospective improvement in consumer credit terms—a variable that does not appear in our schematic model—would be expected to stimulate consumption expenditure. It is often possible to set an upper limit to this stimulating effect, and by increasing the constant term in the consumption function by this amount, to set an upper limit to the forecast economic outlook. An adjustment of this kind was applied to Eq. (01) to allow for the probable influence of the compact car on the outlook for automobile sales during 1960. For the same forecast, a similar modification of the housing starts Eq. (06) was made in anticipation of activity of the Federal National Mortgage Association.

Using the flexibility to full advantage permits the forecaster to explore any desired number of alternative sets of projections and modifications, and to bring to bear all information and judgment he possesses. The econometric model is not, therefore, a substitute for judgment, but rather serves to focus attention on the factors about which judgment must be exercised, and to impose an objective discipline whereby judgment about these factors is translated into an economic outlook that is consistent both internally, and with the past observed behavior of the economic system.

C. The Inverse Matrix

In principle, the exploration of a range of alternative projections and other modifications of the model consists of inserting each set of alternatives in turn as "knowns" in the equations and solving for the resulting forecast. The process is greatly expedited by further simplifying the model and by the use of the inverse matrix. Simplification of the model is made possible by the fact that one of the unknowns, I, depends only on knowns. I helps to determine the current values of C, T, and Y, but the latter do not, in turn, feed back into the determination of the current value of I. As a result, once the knowns are given, I can be directly calculated from (2) without reference to any other part of the model, and hence, as far as the remaining equations are concerned, I can be treated as a known in the sense used previously. (Indeed, it is this fact that enables us to replace Eq. (2) with survey values for I.)

The process of solving the system of equations can then be divided into two parts. First: using the values of the knowns, calculate the value of I. Second: substitute the knowns (now including I) into the remaining equation, and solve for the other unknowns.

The inverse matrix facilitates the second step. For those unfamiliar with matrix manipulations the following will help clarify the nature and use of this table. Since I is now considered as known, the model is reduced to the system of three Eqs. (1), (3), and (4). By transferring all unknowns to the left side, and representing the right sides by P_1, P_3, and P_4, these equations can be expressed as:

$$C - .7Y + .7T = 20 = P_1 \tag{1}$$

$$-.2Y + 1.0T = 0 = P_3 \tag{3}$$

$$-C + Y = I + G = P_4 \tag{4}$$

Now using any convenient method to solve this system for C, Y, and T in terms of P_1, P_3, and P_4 will yield:

$$C = 2.273P_1 - 1.591P_3 + 1.273P_4$$
$$T = .445P_1 + .682P_3 + .455P_4$$
$$Y = 2.273P_1 - 1.591P_3 + 2.273P_4$$

That is, the value of each unknown is obtained as a specified weighted total of P_1, P_3, and P_4. Where a large number of equations is used, and a lot of calculating is to be done, it is convenient to display the weights used for each unknown as a column of numbers in a table, with the detail of the P's shown in a separate column at the right:

Equation No.	C	T	Y	P
(1)	2.273	.455	2.273	20
(3)	-1.591	.682	-1.591	0
(4)	1.273	.455	2.273	$I + G$

To make a forecast we first substitute Y_{-1} into Eq. (2) and solve for I. Then I and G are substituted in the P column of the table and the values of P_1, P_3 and P_4 calculated. These values, weighted by the numbers shown in the C column of the inverse and summed, give the forecast value of consumption; use of the weights in column Y gives the forecast for income, etc.[1] For example, if we set $Y_{-1} = 100$ and $G = 20$, we first find, from (2), $I = 12$. Substituting these values in column P of the table gives the forecast values: $C = 86.2$, $T = 23.7$, $Y = 118.2$.

D. Short-Run Policy Multipliers

It is an obvious step from economic forecasting to short-run policy analysis. To investigate any specified set of prospective government actions, we insert them in the proper place in column P and solve for the forecast implied by these assumptions. The analysis is expedited if we first calculate short-run multipliers for the individual components of government action. These can then be applied in any desired policy mixture.

Short run multipliers for any policy variable are readily calculated by inserting $+1$ for the variable everywhere it appears in column P, and then (ignoring all terms that do not contain the variable in question) extending a forecast using the columns of the inverse. For example, to calculate the government expenditure multiplier, set $G = 1$ in row (4) of column P. This makes $P_4 = 1$. To find the effect of this value on G on, say, income, multiply this value of P_4 by the weight in row (4) of the Y column to get $Y = 1 \times 2.273 = 2.273$. That is, the income multiplier on government expenditure is 2.273. Likewise, $T = 1 \times .455 = .455$. That is, the tax-yield multiplier on government expenditure is .455. In other words, for every dollar of additional government expenditure, tax receipts rise by nearly 46 cents. A corollary is that—according to our

---

[1] As those with matrix algebra will recognize, the inverse matrix is tabulated here in its transposed form, and goes into the P vector at the right column by column.

schematic model—an increase in government expenditure of 1 with no change in tax legislation will generate an increase in deficit of only:

$$G - T = 1 - .46 = .54$$

In addition to changing the value of exogeneous variables like government expenditure, government policy can produce changes in the equations themselves. An extensive change—e.g., a substantial alteration in tax rates—can only be studied by replacing the old tax equation by a new one, but less extensive changes can be studied as shifts in the levels of existing equations, the coefficients being unaltered.

Multipliers for such shifts are easily determined by placing $+1$ in the row of column P that corresponds to the equation being shifted. The extensions are then made as before. For example, to calculate the multipliers on a $+1$ shift in the level of the tax equation, we put $+1$ in the row marked (3) of column P, since the tax equation is (3). The multiplier effect of this shift is then calculated by multiplying this 1 by the weight in the corresponding row of the appropriate column, as shown previously. For example for income:

$$Y = 1 \times (-1.591) = -1.591$$

For consumption:

$$C = 1 \times (-1.591) = -1.591$$

In other words, the multipliers associated with the shift of any equation are merely the weights in the row of the inverse corresponding to that equation.

Note that according to our simplified model, the tax-yield multiplier is .682. That is, an upward shift of \$1 billion in the tax *schedule* actually increases *yield* by only \$682 million. The difference is due to the decline in income arising from the shift in the tax schedule.

The small size of our illustrative model limits the policy variables to government expenditure and the level of taxes. In the more extensive model presented later, policy is given considerably more scope; a number of individual tax and transfer equations can be shifted, and a number of different kinds of expenditure altered. The number of possible combinations of action is correspondingly very large; but one important advantage to a linear system lies in the fact that once multipliers for the individual components have been calculated, the economic implications of a complete policy "package" can be estimated by summing the effect of the individual components.

For example, an increase of \$1 in government expenditure coupled with an upward shift of \$1 in the tax schedule would generate a change in income given by the sum of the two individual multipliers:

$$Y = 2.273 - 1.591 = .682$$

This is what might be called an "ex-ante-balanced" government expenditure multiplier. That is, the change in the law is such as to increase tax yield at the *existing* level of income by enough to balance the planned expenditure, but the budget will not necessarily be balanced ex post. The tax and expenditure program will alter income, and hence will change tax yields. Analysis of the complete fiscal impact of the operation requires the examination of all revenue and outlay items combined. Adding together the two tax-yield multipliers, we find that the additional expenditure of $1 is offset by a tax yield of:

$$.682 + .455 = 1.137$$

That is, the ex-ante-balanced expenditure of $1 billion would, in our example, be accompanied by an increase of $1.137 billion in tax yield and give rise to an ex-post surplus of $137 million.

E. Dynamics and Long-Run Multipliers

An increase in government expenditure of 1.0 will increase income by 2.273 the same year. But the long-run effect of expenditure sustained at this level will differ from this. According to Eq. (2), an increase in income this year will generate an increase in investment next year. This will again raise income and add further stimulus the following year, etc. Once the inverse has been tabulated, however, the sequence can easily be calculated by inserting the forecast values of one year as the "knowns" of the next. Thus, an initial increase in G of 1 will raise Y by 2.273. This will raise I by $.2 \times 2.773 = .455$ the following year. The value of P_4 is then $G + I = 1.455$ and the second year income rises to 3.307 above its initial value, etc. The 5-year sequence of values would be:

Year	1	2	3	4	5
Income	2.273	3.307	3.775	3.989	4.087

This means, for example, that if government expenditure is increased by 1 in 1961, and sustained at that new level, the level of income in 1965 will—other things equal—be 4.087 higher than it was in 1960.

Similar sequences can be worked out for other policy variables. For example, a shift of 1 in the tax schedule in year 1 would imply the following sequence of annual income values:

Year	1	2	3	4	5
Income	−1.591	−2.314	−2.643	−2.793	−2.862

Like short-run multipliers, these long-run multipliers can be combined by simple addition. For example, a permanent rise of 1 in government expenditure coupled with an ex-ante shift of 1 in the tax schedule would raise income by $2.273 - 1.591 = .682$ the first year. After 5 years, however, income would be $4.087 - 2.862 = 1.225$ higher than its initial level.

Although the discussion has been focused on a highly simplified example, the principles developed apply equally to any linear econometric model. The presentation of the actual Research Seminar model in Section 2 will follow the same pattern as the illustration of Section 1.

2. The Model of the U.S. Economy

The model developed by the Research Seminar in Quantitative Economics consists of 32 equations, most of them least-squares linear regressions fitted to annual first differences [i.e., the value of 1 year less the equivalent sum for the previous year] in the variables.... Figures in parentheses are the standard errors of the regression coefficients.

A. *Aggregate Demand*

1. Consumption

Automobiles and parts:

$$\Delta A = .177\Delta(Y - X_u - X_f - X_s) - .495A_{-1} + .260\Delta L_{-1} + 4.710 \quad (01)$$
$$\quad\quad (.806) \quad\quad\quad\quad\quad\quad (.168) \quad\quad (.082)$$

Consumer expenditure for new and net used automobiles and parts (ΔA) depends on disposable income (Y), net of transfers for unemployment compensation (X_a), and other federal (X_f) and state (X_s) transfers. These transfers are deducted on the ground that they are unlikely to find their way into the automobile market. Servicemen's insurance dividends (X_{GI}) are not deducted from disposable income. In addition, automobile demand depends on the stock of cars on the road (A_{-1}) and on the real value of consumer liquid assets at the end of the preceding year (ΔL_{-1}). For this purpose liquid assets are defined as household holdings of currency and demand deposits plus fixed-value redeemable claims as estimated by the Federal Reserve Board. The sizeable constant term in the equation probably reflects replacement demand.

Demand for other durables:

$$\Delta D = .176\Delta Y - .0694D_{-1} + .0784\Delta L_{-1} + .262 \quad (02)$$
$$\quad\quad (.015) \quad\quad (.029) \quad\quad\quad (.016)$$

This equation relates ΔD, consumer expenditure for durables (other than automobiles and parts) to disposable income (ΔY), the accumulating stock of durables (D_{-1}) and liquid assets.

Demand for nondurable goods:

$$\Delta ND = .224\Delta Y + .205\Delta ND_{-1} + .143\Delta L_{-1} - .149 \tag{03}$$
$$ (.060) \quad\quad (.135) \quad\quad\quad (.059)$$

Nondurable expenditure depends on disposable income, liquid assets, and last year's nondurable expenditure (ΔND_{-1}). Notice the difference between this and the foregoing equations. In (01) and (02) the lagged values were undifferenced representing accumulation of stock. In this equation the difference itself is lagged, representing a dynamic adjustment in nondurable expenditure: an initial rise in level is followed by a subsequent secondary rise.

Demand for services:

$$\Delta S = .0906\Delta Y + .530\Delta S_{-1} + .0381\Delta L_{-1} + .363 \tag{04}$$
$$ (.029) \quad\quad (.170) \quad\quad\quad (.029)$$

This equation is similar to (03) and relates expenditure for services (ΔS) to disposable income, liquid assets, and lagged service expenditure. It should be remembered that service expenditure is here defined to exclude imputed items.

These four equations constitute the demand sector. Note that the aggregate marginal propensity to consume can be estimated by summing the income coefficients in the four equations. The sum, .67, is an estimate of the marginal propensity to consume, at least as an initial impact. The lagged terms in the individual equations, however, generate a dynamic response of consumption to income. As the equations show, the long-run response of nondurables and services tends to be greater, and that of automobile and durables less, than the initial impact. The implications of this fact for the calculation of multipliers will appear later.

2. Gross Capital Expenditure

Plant and equipment expenditure:

$$\Delta PE = .605\Delta(P^{*}_{-1} - T_{fc-1} - T_{sc-1}) - .124PE_{-1} + 4.509 \tag{05}$$
$$ (.238) \quad\quad\quad\quad\quad\quad\quad\quad\quad (.216)$$

ΔPE, expenditure for new plant and equipment, includes producers' durables, nonfarm nonresidential construction, and all farm construction. It is related to the preceding year's corporate profits (P^{*}_{-1}) after federal (T_{fc}) and state (T_{sc}) corporate income taxes and to its own lagged, undifferenced value (PE_{-1}). The latter represents growth in the stock of plant and equipment. As in (01), the large constant term probably represents replacement.

Housing starts:

$$\Delta HS = 19.636\Delta\left(\frac{FHA + VA}{2} - Aaa\right) - .702HS_{-1} + 66.147 \quad (06)$$
$$\quad\quad (17.0) \quad\quad\quad\quad\quad\quad\quad\quad (.312)$$

This equation, which applies only to the postwar period, relates the number of nonfarm residential housing starts (ΔHS), measured in thousand of units per month, to the gap between the simple average of the *FHA* and *VA* ceiling interest rates on the one hand, and the *Aaa* bond yield on the other (both expressed in percentage points). This interest rate differential reflects the substantial influence of credit availability on the volume of *FHA* and *VA* financed residential construction. It can function, however, only in the presence of a strong underlying housing demand. With the accumulation of a large stock as a consequence of construction in recent years, this interest rate differential may lose its role in the model. The term HS_{-1}, the lagged undifferenced value of housing starts, only partially represents the effect of this accumulation, and Eq. (06) is probably due for revision.

Housing expenditure:

$$\Delta H = .125\Delta HS + .024\Delta HS_{-1} + 6.580\Delta C + .083 \quad\quad (07)$$
$$\quad (.013) \quad\quad (.012) \quad\quad\quad (5.42)$$

Expenditure on housing, (ΔH), depends on the rate at which residential construction is carried forward, and, thus, on current and lagged starts. In addition, it depends on construction costs. The term ΔC is the ratio of the index of construction costs to the *GNP* deflator.

Durable goods inventory:

$$\Delta ID = .291\Delta(A + D) + .591\Delta PD + .305\Delta M_{+1} - .669ID_{-1} \quad\quad (08)$$
$$\quad (.100) \quad\quad\quad (.157) \quad\quad (.085) \quad\quad (.109)$$

Accumulation of durable inventories, ΔID, depends on sales of consumer durables, producers durables ΔPD, and the stock of inventory already accumulated ID_{-1}. In addition, an important component of inventory is associated with government military orders. Production on such orders appears in the national accounts as goods in process, and exerts a strong impact on the economy long before delivery of the finished product materializes as government expenditure. A wide variety of arrangements and lead times are involved in this process. As a proxy for such orders in any given year, we use ΔM_{+1}, federal military purchases from private industry the following year.

The equilibrium sales-inventory ratio implied by this equation compares favorably with that observed from other data.

Nondurable goods inventory:

$$\Delta IND = .427 \Delta ND - 1.121 IND_{-1} \tag{09}$$
$$\quad\quad (.111) \quad\quad\quad (.248)$$

Accumulation of nondurable inventory, ΔIND, depends on consumer sales of nondurables and the stock already on hand, IND_{-1}.

Imports:

$$\Delta R = .0602 \Delta G^* + .369 \tag{10}$$
$$\quad (.03)$$

This relates the aggregate level of imports to the private GNP (G^*).

3. Private Gross National Product

$$\Delta G^* = \Delta(A + D + ND + S) + (\Delta F - \Delta R) + \Delta ID + \Delta IND$$
$$+ \Delta PE + \Delta H + \Delta g \tag{11}$$

Private GNP is defined as the sum of its parts, including net exports ($\Delta F - \Delta R$) and government purchases from private firms (Δg).

B. Income and Employment

Wage and salary workers, private sector:

$$\Delta E = .068 \Delta G^* \tag{12}$$

This production function, relating ΔE, the number of full-time equivalent employees in the private sector (measured in millions of persons) to the private GNP, applies specifically to the forecast of 1962 and is based on the first three quarters recovery experience during 1961.

Unemployment:

$$\Delta U = \Delta LF - \Delta E_0 - \Delta E_G - \Delta E \tag{13}$$

Unemployment is the difference between labor force (ΔLF), on the one hand, and, on the other hand, the number of self-employed and unpaid family workers, (ΔE_0), government workers, including armed services (ΔE_G) and employees of private industry (ΔE).

Average annual earnings:

$$\Delta w = -.0216\Delta U + .00436P^*_{-1} - .0743$$
$$(.0076) (.0025)$$

$\quad$(14)

Δw, average annual earnings (including wages and salaries plus "other labor income," and measured in thousands of dollars) is related to unemployment and last year's profits. This relationship reflects two facts. First, and probably more important, annual earnings are heavily influenced by overtime pay, which varies inversely with the level of unemployment. Secondly, pressure of union demands varies directly with profits and inversely with the level of unemployment. The undifferenced level of profits is used since the *existence* of profits acts as a target for wage demands.

Private wage bill:

$$\Delta W = \Delta(wE) = w_{-1}\Delta E + E_{-1}\Delta w \quad (15)$$

By definition the wage bill is the product of average earnings and employment. To keep the model linear, this nonlinear relationship is replaced by the linear approximation shown.

Depreciation:

$$\Delta Dep = .0456\Delta G^* + .763 \quad (16)$$

Property income:

$$\Delta P = \Delta G^* - \Delta W - \Delta Dep - \Delta T_{fe} - \Delta T_{cd} - \Delta T_{bp}$$
$$- \Delta T_{ss} - \Delta T_{os} - \Delta SI_r \quad (17)$$

Property income (ΔP) is a residual from the GNP after deducting wage costs, depreciation (ΔDep), employer contributions for social insurance (ΔSI_r), and indirect business taxes: federal excises (ΔT_{fe}), customs duties (ΔT_{cd}), business property (ΔT_{bp}), state sales (ΔT_{ss}), and other state taxes on business (ΔT_{os}).

Corporate profits:

$$\Delta P^* = .902(\Delta P - \Delta P_f) - 1.027 \quad (18)$$

This relates profits (ΔP^*) to total property income net of farm income (ΔP_f). There is, of course, no strong theoretical basis for the particular distribution of corporate business found in the US economy. This equation is an empirical representation of the distribution of property income under existing institutional arrangements.

Dividends:

$$\Delta Div = .229\Delta(P^* - T_{fc} - T_{sc})$$
$$(.064)$$
$$+ .0198(P^* - T_{fc} - T_{sc} - Div)_{-1} - .0191 \qquad (19)$$
$$(.052)$$

Current dividends (ΔDiv) depend on current profits after federal (T_{fc}) and state (T_{sc}) corporate profits taxes, and on last year's level of undistributed profits.

Disposable income:

$$\Delta Y = \Delta W + \Delta W_G + (\Delta P - \Delta P^*) + \Delta Div + \Delta i_G + \Delta X_u + \Delta X_f + \Delta X_s$$
$$+ \Delta X_{GI} - \Delta T_{fy} - \Delta T_{sy} - \Delta T_{eg} - \Delta T_{op} - \Delta SI_e + \Delta T_{ref} \qquad (20)$$

Disposable income is the sum of wages, including government wages (W_G), noncorporate property income ($\Delta P - \Delta P^*$), dividends, government interest payments (i_G), plus transfers, less personal taxes: federal (ΔT_{fy}), and state (ΔT_{sy}) income, estate and gift (ΔT_{eg}), other personal taxes (ΔT_{op}), and personal contributions for social insurance ΔSI_e, all net of tax refunds ΔT_{ref}.

C. Taxes and Government Transfers

1. Federal Taxes
Federal corporate profits tax:

$$\Delta T_{fc} = .500\Delta P^* \qquad (21)$$

Federal personal income tax receipts:

$$\Delta T_{fy} = .111(\Delta W + \Delta W_G) + .150(\Delta P - \Delta P^* + \Delta i_G) + .195\Delta Div \qquad (22)$$

This equation relates income tax receipts in the form of withholding, quarterly payments on estimated tax, and final tax payment to the several income components. The coefficients reflect both variation in income shares by tax bracket and the effect of the dividend tax credit.

Federal personal income tax liability:

$$\Delta T_{fy}^* = .100(\Delta W + \Delta W_G) + .114(\Delta P - \Delta P^* + \Delta i_G) + .154\Delta Div \qquad (23)$$

Tax receipts commonly exceed liability. The difference (ΔT_{ref}) appears as a tax refund the following year.

Federal excise taxes:

$$\Delta T_{fe} = .099\Delta A + .011\Delta D + .003\Delta ND + .010\Delta G^* + .015\Delta Y \qquad (24)$$

Customs duties:

$$\Delta T_{cd} = .083\Delta R + .012 \tag{25}$$

State and Local Taxes

State corporate income taxes:

$$\Delta T_{sc} = .019\Delta P^* \tag{26}$$

State and local sales taxes:

$$\Delta T_{ss} = .033(\Delta A + \Delta D + \Delta ND + \Delta S) \tag{27}$$

State and local personal income taxes:

$$\Delta T_{sy} = .010(\Delta W + \Delta W_G + \Delta P - \Delta P^* + \Delta Div + \Delta i_G) \tag{28}$$

3. Social Insurance Programs

Private employer contributions for social insurance:

$$\Delta SI_r = .149\Delta E \tag{29}$$

Personal contributions for social insurance:

$$\Delta SI_e = .129(\Delta E + \Delta E_G) + .050(\Delta P - \Delta P^*) \tag{30}$$

Covered unemployment:

$$\Delta U_c = .675\Delta U - .140(\Delta LF - \Delta LF_{-1}) \tag{31}$$

The relationship of unemployment covered by compensation programs (ΔU_c) to total unemployment varies with the rate of increase in the labor force. When the labor force is growing rapidly, new entrants, not yet covered, make up a larger proportion of total unemployment.

Unemployment compensation:

$$\Delta X_u = 1.77\Delta U_c + .101 \tag{32}$$

3. The Model as a Forecasting Instrument

A. The Forecast of 1962

The unknowns of the model are the 32 variables like automobile demand, disposable income, private GNP, etc., that stand on the left side of the equations. The knowns are variables like government purchases from private firms, labor force, household liquid assets, etc., that appear only on the right side of the equations, and whose values must be projected or assigned before the unknowns can be forecast.

The forecast of 1962, calculated and presented in November 1961, employed the projected values shown in Table 1. The most important

Table 1
Projections Underlying Forecast of 1962

Equation

(01) $A_{-1} = 14.3$ $\Delta L_{-1} = 16.9$ $X_f = \Delta X_s = 0$
(02) $D_{-1} = 27.3$ $\Delta L_{-1} = 16.9$
(03) $\Delta ND_{-1} = 1.2$ $\Delta L_{-1} = 16.9$
(04) $\Delta S_{-1} = 3.4$ $\Delta L_{-1} = 16.9$
(05) $\Delta PE = 1.3^a$
(06) $\Delta Aaa = +.02$ $\Delta\left(\dfrac{FHA + VA}{2}\right) = -.06$ $HS_{-1} = 93.1$
(07) $\Delta HS_{-1} = 3.2$ $\Delta C = 0$
(08) $\Delta PD = .7^a$ $\Delta M_{+1} = 1.0$ $ID_{-1} = 0.0$
(09) $IND_{-1} = 1.7$
(10) —
(11) $\Delta F = 0$ $\Delta PE = 1.3^a$ $\Delta g = 6.9$
(12) —
(13) $\Delta LF = 1.2$ $\Delta E_0 = .2$ $\Delta E_G = .6$
(14) $P^*_{-1} = 39.6$
(15) $w_{-1} = 4.38$ $E_{-1} = 46.9$
(16) —
(17) $\Delta T_{bp} = .730$ $\Delta T_{os} = .087$
(18) $\Delta P_f = 0$
(19) —
(20) $\Delta X_f = \Delta X_s = \Delta X_{GI} = 0$ $\Delta W_G = 1.5$ $\Delta i_G = .1$ $\Delta T_{op} = .35$ $\Delta T_{eg} = .08$
     $\Delta T_{ref} = 0$
(21) —
(22) $\Delta W_G = 1.5$ $\Delta i_G = .1$
(23) $\Delta W_G = 1.5$ $\Delta i_G = .1$
(24) —
(25) —
(26) —
(27) —
(28) $\Delta W_G = 1.5$ $\Delta i_G = .1$
(29) —
(30) $\Delta E_G = .6$
(31) $\Delta LF = 1.2$ $\Delta LF_{-1} = 1.0$
(32) —
(Addendum) Δ Imputed Services $= 1.5$

<hr>

[a] Based on McGraw-Hill survey showing 4 percent increase in plant and equipment expenditure.

single item was the \$16.9 billion increase in consumer holdings of liquid assets. A few of the other key items were: a \$6.9 billion projected increase in government purchases from private firms; an increase of .6 million in government employment; increase in government way payments of \$1.5 billion; and a \$1 billion rise in military orders. Note that investment in plant and equipment is projected directly on the basis of the McGraw-Hill survey rather than from Eq. (05). All monetary values are in 1954 dollars.

When the projections of Table 1 were inserted in the equations, the solution gave the outlook for 1962 shown in Table 2. The first two columns

Table 2

Review of 1961 and Outlook for 1962

(monetary figures, except column 5, are billions of 1954 dollars)

	1961			Forecast 1962	
	Forecast	Actual	Forecast increase	(1954 prices)	(1962 prices)
Gross national product	450.1	446.8	27.5	474.3	559.9
Consumer expenditures					
Automobile and parts	14.6	14.3	4.5	18.8	21.2
Other durables	25.1	24.8	1.9	26.7	28.7
Nondurables	144.7	142.7	5.3	148.0	163.6
Services	119.9	119.6	5.5	125.1	147.9
Private gross capital expenditure					
Plant and equipment	39.0	37.3	1.3	38.6	48.1
Residential construction	19.9	17.7	0.1	17.8	21.4
Inventory investment					
Durables	2.4	0.0	2.6	2.6	2.8
Nondurables		1.7	0.4	2.1	2.3
Imports	24.8	22.2	1.9	24.1	24.8
Exports	24.6	26.4	—	26.4	28.7
Government expenditure on goods and services	84.7	84.5	7.8	92.3	120.0
Corporate profits	40.3	39.6	5.1	44.7	52.5
Dividends	12.4	12.3	0.7	13.0	15.3
Civilian labor force					
Millions of persons	71.3	71.6	0.9	72.5	
Private wage and salary					
Workers		46.9	1.7	48.6	
Government employees (civilian)	67.0	8.8	0.3	9.1	
Self-employed		11.0	0.2	11.2	
Unemployed					
Number (millions)	4.3	4.9	−1.3	3.6	
Percent of civilian labor force	6.0	6.8	—	5.0	

Table 3
Review of Past Forecasts

	1953[a]		1954[a]		1955[a]		1956[a]		1957[b]	
	Forecast	Actual	Forecast	Actual	Forecast	Actual	Forecast	Actual	Forecast	Actual
Gross national product	177.4	178.6	174.8	173.9	176.4	188.5	191.6	191.2	337.0	335.2
Consumption expenditure	114.4	115.9	117.3	116.7	118.6	125.1	127.4	128.5	226.3	226.1
Private gross capital formation	24.2	24.9	22.7	23.6	25.2	25.9	28.7	26.3	47.2	44.4
Employee compensation	80.4[f]	79.8[f]	82.3[f]	83.0[f]	81.2[f]	89.5[f]	107.1	104.3	196.5	196.3

	1958[c]		1959[d]		1960[e]	
	Forecast	Actual	Forecast	Actual	Forecast	Actual
Gross national product	432.7	432.5	456.7	475.7	432.0	439.2
Consumption expenditure	282.1	287.3	295.4	310.7	287.1	296.8
Automobiles	—	—	—	—	16.7	15.6
Other durables	—	—	—	—	25.2	25.2
Nondurables	—	—	—	—	138.9	141.9
Services	—	—	—	—	106.3	113.7
Private gross capital expenditure	61.9	53.7	61.2	70.4	62.4	60.5
Plant and equipment	—	—	44.0	43.0	40.5	39.3
Residential construction	—	—	17.8	21.6	19.7	18.0
Inventory	—	—	-.6	5.8	2.2	3.2
Government purchase of goods and services	88.8	90.5	100.1	94.6	83.7	80.3
Net exports	—	—	—	—	-1.3	1.6
Employee compensation	254.3	251.8	261.0	273.4	236.3	257.1
Corporate profits	39.5	36.5	47.7	45.8	42.7	38.7
Dividends	—	—	—	—	12.2	12.2
Civilian employment	66.4	66.5	66.0	65.6	65.5[g]	66.7[h]
Unemployment	4.8	4.7	3.4	3.8	4.4[g]	3.9[h]

[a] 1939 prices.
[b] 1947 prices.
[c] 1957 prices.
[d] 1958 prices.
[e] 1954 prices.
[f] Private sector only.
[g] Excludes Alaska and Hawaii.
[h] Includes Alaska and Hawaii.

contain a detailed comparison of the forecast of 1961 with the preliminary actual values. The middle column contains the solutions obtained from the equations. These are in first differences and are expressed as increases over 1961. When the forecast increase is added to the preliminary actual level for 1961 the result is the forecast level of 1962 shown in the fourth column. In the last column this forecast has been translated into approximate 1962 prices.

The forecast entails substantial increases in consumption expenditure, especially for automobiles. The forecast level of $18.8 billion for this sector constitutes a record level of automobile sales, exceeding the $17.9 billion reached in 1955. This large increase derives primarily from the high level of consumer liquidity and the small addition to stocks of cars during 1961.

Aside from the consumer sector the main stimulus to the economy derives from the projected increases in government outlays, associated with the trend of state and local expenditures and federal defense expenditure. In preparing the forecast no allowance was made for the possible effect of a steel strike during 1962. Inventory accumulation in anticipation of interruptions of steel supplies will probably accelerate inventory accumulation in the first half of the year and depress it in the second half. There is no indication that this will alter the overall level for the year.

The forecast increase in production is adequate to absorb more than the growth of the labor force, and the outlook concludes by showing a reduction of 1.3 million in unemployment, reducing the average for the year to 3.6 million or 5 percent of the civilian labor force.

B. Review of Past Forecasts

The Research Seminar in Quantitative Economics has been making annual forecasts since 1953, each a matter of record published in advance of the year forecast. The econometric model has been revised and improved several times over this period (the version presented here was first used for the 1962 forecast), but the review of past forecasting performance in Table 3 will illustrate the general reliability of the method. Each forecast is shown as it was presented, and compared with the actual outcome.... The increasing elaboration of the model is evident in the table.

As plotted in Fig. 1, the general accuracy of these forecasts speaks for itself. The direction of movement was correctly forecast each year, and the levels were generally well predicted. The recession of 1954 was forecast with considerable precision. The recovery of 1955 was likewise forecast, but the magnitude of the boom that developed was grossly

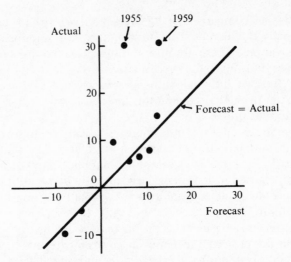

Fig. 1. Comparison of forecast with actual changes in GNP (1953–1961) in billions of 1954 dollars.

underestimated. The fact that the error of the 1955 forecast is concentrated in the consumer sector lends support to the idea that this was a consumer-generated movement. The recession of 1958 was well predicted. The recovery of 1959 was somewhat underestimated.

In many respects the forecast of 1960 was the most interesting of all. Made in November 1959 at the height of business optimism, and amidst general anticipation of the "soaring sixties," its pessimistic outlook for 1960 was greeted with almost complete skepticism, but it proved to be more exact that any other forecast placed on record in advance.

C. Short-Run Policy Multipliers

Simplification of the model is carried out as illustrated in Section 1. Inspection shows that in Eq. (05), plant and equipment expenditure (ΔPE) depends only on "known" values: last year's profits after taxes, and the stock of plant and equipment available at the beginning of the year. Similarly, in Eqs. (06) and (07), housing starts (ΔHS) and expenditure for nonfarm residential construction (ΔH) depend only on credit availability, construction costs, last year's starts, and the stock of houses at the beginning of the year. To make a forecast, therefore, we use the knowns to estimate ΔPE, ΔHS, and ΔH via Eqs. (05), (06), and (07), and then use these values, together with the other knowns, to solve the remaining equations. The inverse of the model is shown in Table 4. This is merely an enlarged version of the little table shown earlier for the illustrative model of Section 1, and is used in the same way. For example, if the projected values of Table 1 are inserted in column P of Table 4, multiplied by the weights in the "automobile" column and summed, the result is 4.5, the forecast increase in automobile demand shown in Table 2. Short-run multipliers for any policy variable are readily calculated as before by inserting 1 for the variable everywhere it appears in column P and then (ignoring all terms that do not contain the variable in question) extending a forecast using the columns of Table 4.

For example, to find the multiplier on government purchases from private firms, set $\Delta g = +1$ everywhere it appears in column P. The term Δg is found in only one place: in row (11) it is multiplied by 1. To find the effect of $\Delta g = \$1$ on, say, private GNP, we multiply the weight in row (11) of the GNP column by 1:

$$\Delta G^* = 1 \times 1.304 = 1.304$$

That is to say, the short-run multiplier on government purchases is about 1.3. Similarly, the effect on, say, automobile demand is given by

$$\Delta A = 1 \times .092 = .092$$

i.e. the short-run "automobile demand multiplier" on government purchases from the private sector is .092.

In working out a policy multiplier, care must be taken to include changes in *all* exogenous variables affected by the policy action. For example, an increase in government employment involves hiring additional people [ΔE_G in rows (13) and (30)] and paying them wages [ΔW_G in rows (20), (22), and (28)]. At an average annual wage of \$5000, an addition of \$1 billion to the government wage bill will hire .2 million additional employees. To find the multipliers on government wages, therefore, we set $\Delta E_G = .2$. This gives $-.2$ in row (13) and .0258 in row (30) of column P. We also set $\Delta W_G = \$1$ to get 1 in row (20), .111 in (22), and .010 in row (28) of column P. The impact of additional government employment on private GNP is then found by extending these figures by the weights in the corresponding rows of the GNP column:

$$\begin{aligned} \Delta G^* &= -.2 \times .167 + 1 \times 1.119 - .111 \times 1.119 - .010 \times 1.119 \\ &\quad -.0258 \times 1.119 \\ &= .692 \end{aligned}$$

To find the effect of the action on total GNP, we must add in the additional value added by government (i.e., government wages and salaries). Thus:

$$\text{Total GNP} = .692 + 1 = 1.692$$

Table 4

Equation	ΔA	ΔD	ΔND	ΔS	ΔID	ΔIND	ΔR	ΔG^*	ΔE
01	1.113	.089	.113	.046	.350	.048	.100	1.660	.113
02	.117	1.092	.118	.048	.351	.050	.101	1.676	.114
03	.130	.103	1.130	.053	.068	.483	.112	1.854	.126
04	.091	.072	.091	1.037	.047	.039	.078	1.298	.088
08	.092	.073	.093	.037	1.048	.040	.078	1.304	.089
09	.092	.073	.093	.037	.048	1.040	.078	1.304	.089
10	−.095	−.076	−.097	−.040	−.050	−.041	.921	−1.318	−.089
11	.092	.073	.093	.037	.048	.042	.078	1.304	.089
12	.884	.623	.793	.321	.439	.339	.192	3.205	1.218
13	−.118	.091	.116	.047	−.008	.049	.010	.167	.011
14	8.621	8.030	10.220	4.133	4.845	4.364	2.283	37.929	2.579
15	.184	.171	.218	.088	.103	.093	.049	.809	.055
16	−.040	−.037	−.047	−.019	−.022	−.020	−.012	−.175	−.012
17	.040	.037	.047	.019	.022	.020	.012	.175	.012
18	−.179	−.166	−.212	−.086	−.100	−.090	−.047	−.786	−.053
19	.202	.188	.240	.097	.114	.102	.054	.890	.061
20	.254	.237	.302	.122	.143	.129	.067	1.119	.076
21	−.046	−.043	−.055	−.022	−.026	−.024	−.012	−.204	−.014
22	−.254	−.237	−.302	−.122	−.143	−.129	−.067	−1.119	−.076
24	−.040	−.037	−.047	−.019	−.022	−.020	−.012	−.175	−.012
25	−.040	−.037	−.047	−.019	−.022	−.020	−.012	−.175	−.012
26	−.046	−.043	−.055	−.022	−.026	−.024	−.012	−.204	−.014
27	−.040	−.037	−.047	−.019	−.022	−.020	−.012	−.175	−.012
28	−.254	−.237	−.302	−.122	−.143	−.129	−.067	−1.119	−.076
29	−.040	−.037	−.047	−.019	−.022	−.020	−.012	−.175	−.012
30	−.254	−.237	−.302	−.122	−.143	−.129	−.067	−1.119	−.076
31	.101	.391	.498	.201	.143	.213	.088	1.461	.099
32	.058	.221	.281	.114	.081	.120	.050	.825	0.56

Projections

01	$4.710 - .495A_{-1} + .260\Delta L_{-1} - .177\Delta X_f - .177\Delta X_s$
02	$.262 - .0694D_{-1} + .0784\Delta L_{-1}$
03	$-.149 + .205\Delta ND_{-1} + .143\Delta L_{-1}$
04	$.363 + .530\Delta S_{-1} + .0381\Delta L_{-1}$
08	$0 + .591\Delta PD + .305\Delta M_{+1} - .669ID_{-1}$
09	$0 - 1.121IND_{-1}$
10	$.369$
11	$0 + \Delta F + \Delta PE + \Delta H + \Delta g$
12	0
13	$0 + \Delta LF - \Delta E_0 - \Delta E_G$
14	$-.0743 + .00436P^*_{-1}$
15	0
16	$.763$
17	$0 - \Delta T_{bp} - \Delta T_{os}$

Inverse Matrix

ΔW	ΔP^*	ΔDiv	$\Delta(P - P^*)$	Federal tax receipts	State and local tax receipts	Social ins. contr.	ΔX_u	ΔY
.609	.694	.076	.076	.585	.066	.035	−.135	.506
.615	.780	.085	.084	.545	.068	.036	−.136	.525
.680	.875	.096	.096	.600	.072	.040	−.151	.583
.476	.606	.066	.066	.414	.060	.028	−.105	.407
.478	.638	.070	.069	.432	.028	.028	−.106	.414
.478	.638	.070	.069	.432	.028	.028	−.106	.414
−.483	−.719	−.079	−.078	−.546	−.030	−.029	.107	−.431
.478	.638	.074	.069	.458	0.30	.030	−.106	.438
6.568	−3.586	−.395	−.390	−1.002	.076	.319	−1.455	3.539
−.952	.997	.109	.109	.430	.016	.009	1.181	.516
60.808	−25.478	−2.806	−2.767	−4.726	1.091	.579	−3.082	45.619
1.297	−.543	−.059	−.060	−.101	.023	.012	−.066	.973
−.064	−.980	−.107	−.107	−.544	−.026	−.009	.014	−.211
−.064	.980	.107	.107	.544	.026	.009	−.014	.211
−.288	.651	.075	−1.038	.106	−.021	−.067	.064	−.946
.326	.395	1.040	.043	.497	.045	.019	−.072	1.070
.410	.496	.040	.054	.378	.045	.024	−.091	1.346
−.075	−.090	−.238	−.010	.886	−.010	−.004	.017	−.245
−.410	−.496	−.040	−.054	.622	−.045	−.024	.091	−1.346
−.064	−.980	−.107	−.107	.456	−.026	−.009	.014	−.211
−.064	−.980	−.107	−.107	.456	−.026	−.009	.014	−.211
−.075	−.090	−.238	−.010	−.114	.990	−.004	.017	−.245
−.064	−.980	−.107	−.107	−.544	.974	−.009	.014	−.211
−.410	−.497	−.040	−.054	−.378	.955	−.024	.091	−1.346
−.064	−.980	−.107	−.107	−.544	−.026	.991	.014	−.211
−.410	−.497	−.040	−.054	−.378	−.045	.976	.091	−1.346
.535	.661	.072	.072	.486	.059	.031	1.651	2.224
.303	.374	.041	.041	.274	.033	.018	.932	1.256

Projections

18	$-1.027 - .902\Delta P_f$
19	$-.0191 + .0198(P^* - T_{fc} - T_{sc} - Div)_{-1}$
20	$0 + \Delta W_G + \Delta i_G + \Delta X_f + \Delta X_s + \Delta X_{GI} - \Delta T_{op} - \Delta T_{eg} + \Delta T_{ref}$
21	0
22	$0 + .111\Delta W_G + .150\Delta i_G$
24	0
25	$.012$
26	0
27	0
28	$0 + .010(\Delta W_G + \Delta i_G)$
29	0
30	$0 + .129\Delta E_G$
31	$0 - .140(\Delta LF - \Delta LF_{-1})$
32	$.101$

Table 5
Selected Multipliers

| | Multiplier for impact on: | | | | | | | | | | |
| | GNP | | Employment | | Tax receipts | | Social insurance | | Government surplus or deficit (−) | | | |
Multiplicand	Private	Total	Private	Total	Federal	State and local	Contri-butions	Transfers	Federal	State and local	Social insurance	Total
Plant and equipment[a]	1.690	1.690	.115	.115	.586	.058	.038	-.137	.586	.058	.175	.819
Federal purchases from firms	1.304	1.304	.089	.089	.458	.030	.030	-.106	-.542	.030	.136	-.376
Federal employment[b]	.692	1.692	.063	.263	.209	.016	.044	-.314	-.791	0.16	.358	-.417
Federal personal income tax shift	-1.119	-1.119	-.076	-.076	.622	-.045	-0.24	.091	.622	-.045	-.115	.462

[a] Additional expenditure of **$1** billion of which half is spent for producers' durable equipment.
[b] Additional expenditure of **$1** billion in government wages to hire .2 million new workers.

We also recall that government tax policy can be expressed by shifts in the equations themselves. As shown in Section 1, these shift multipliers are equal to the weights found in the row of the inverse matrix that corresponds to the equation being shifted. Thus, we see from the -1.119 in row (22) of the GNP column that a $1 billion shift in the federal personal tax function will reduce private GNP by $1.1 billion, etc. Note again [row (22) of the federal tax column] that an upward shift of $1 billion in the federal income tax *schedule* increases federal tax *yield* by only $622 million due to the decline in personal income and expenditure associated with the rise in taxes.

Some multiplier effects of a selection of government actions are given in Table 5. As before, once the multipliers are worked out they can be combined in any desired proportions. Thus, an increase in government purchases of $2 billion coupled with additional government wages of $.5 billion and an upward shift of the personal tax schedule of $1.3 billion would produce a total change in GNP of $(2 \times 1.304) + (.5 \times 1.692) + (1.3 \times -1.119) = \$2$ billion. The same program would raise total employment by .211 million, and add $.67 billion to the federal deficit. ...

D. Dynamic Responses and Long-Run Multipliers

As shown in Section 1, dynamic responses are studied by iteration. Among the initial impacts of any program, we must find the effects on automobile demand, inventory accumulation, plant and equipment, and other variables whose values reenter the system with a lag. These form a set of additional knowns for the next year. Using these values in turn gives rise to another set, etc. Repeating this operation enables us to follow the implications of a given program over as long a period as desired. It appears, however, that the dynamic elements stabilize by the end of the fifth year, and the system can be treated as in equilibrium after five iterations.

A complete study of the dynamic behavior of each variable in response to each possible policy action cannot be presented here, but Table 6 shows the response of the GNP and its components to a permanent increase of $1 billion in government expenditure. The tabulated figures are the value of the variables measured as deviations from their levels as of year 0 before the shift in expenditure policy.

In response to increased government expenditure, the GNP rises by $1.3 billion the first year and under the stimulation of the dynamic factors climbs to a maximum of $1.6 billion over its initial level. It declines thereafter under the back pressure of accumulating stocks. The behavior of the individual components is in keeping with their respective natures.

Table 6

Dynamic Responses to a Permanent Increase of $1 Billion in Government Expenditure
(tabulated figures are deviations from initial levels)

			Year		
	1	2	3	4	5
Gross national product[a]	1.304	1.619	1.582	1.545	1.335
Automobiles and parts	.092	.088	.050	.042	.014
Other durables	.073	.104	.113	.117	.104
Nondurables	.093	.159	.193	.215	.213
Services	.037	.075	.104	.126	.134
Plant and equipment	0.	.186	.173	.133	.082
Inventory					
Durable goods	.048	.079	.017	−.010	−.031
Nondurable goods	.040	.023	.012	.008	−.002
Net foreign investment	−.078	−.101	−.103	−.103	−.098
Government purchases	1.	1.	1.	1.	1.

[a] Detail may not add to total because of rounding.

Automobile demand rises immediately to its maximum and declines slowly as the stock of cars on the road accumulates. Consumer expenditure for durables rises sharply and levels off, while outlays on nondurable goods and services continue to rise throughout the period, although at declining rates.

Investment in plant and equipment spurts in response to the immediate improvement in corporate profits and tapers off as the new plant becomes available. Inventory accumulation occurs at a high rate, but durable inventory overshoots and the rate of accumulation is forced somewhat below the year 0 level.

4. Conclusion

To approximate the behavior of a complex economy by a set of 32 linear approximations is a heroic simplification. Yet experience has shown the statistical model to be a useful and flexible device for economic forecasting. Moreover, while the system of equations is small in relation to the vast structure of pure theory, it is considerably more elaborate than other devices that can be brought to bear on a practical level. Indeed, if an econometric model is nothing else, it is a highly sophisticated method of observing the past operation of the economy and systematizing the information obtained.

Yet, once the technical work of constructing the model is completed, a competent economist needs little more than a knowledge of elementary algebra to understand its nature, or to apply it to a wide range of analytical problems. Properly used, the model provides quantitative estimates of economic responses to specific changes in conditions. It goes without saying that the accuracy of these estimates is below the level that might be inferred from the precision of their statement in the text. But they show the proper order of magnitude involved and fall well within the practical tolerances required for effective policy evaluation.

We mentioned earlier that incremental, disjointed adjustment processes were ill-suited to meeting sharp step-level changes in the environment of politics. But even in the absence of step-level changes that make
special demands on the political system, the consequences of uncoordinated adjustments will not always be in the desired direction. In the
final selection of this book Alfred E. Kahn considers some of the dangers
inherent in a failure occasionally to take a comprehensive overview of
individual decisions and to develop the means for a continuous overall
monitoring. Big changes, he says, "occur as an accretion of moderate-sized
steps, each of them the consequence of 'small' purchase decisions—small
in their individual size, time perspective, and in relation to their total,
combined ultimate effect." That a kingdom may be lost for want of a nail
will hardly be news to any sophisticated analyst, but Kahn then specifies
in a stimulating way some of the particular circumstances that may
produce conflict between the desires that lead to the small decisions and
their ultimate consequences.

One such set of circumstances of course applies to our discussion,
in Section I of the book, about public goods and externalities; the consequences of a decision made by a particular group will apply to others
far beyond it. An appropriate example is the decision of a nation to
acquire nuclear weapons, for the encouragement this gives to the spread
of such weapons to other states can produce a dangerously unstable
world, despite the immediate gains it brings to the nuclear power. Not
only will it make the other states worse off, it may well even work to the
net loss of the initial proliferator. Often these consequences, such as
the external costs of air pollution, simply are not foreseen at the time,
so that they cannot be taken into account in the initial calculations.

Another and probably equally dangerous category derives from
"failures of competition," especially where economies of scale or temporary phenomena like excess capacity offer a seller a choice between
lowering prices and the opportunity to engage in nonprice competition,
such as to undertake substantial advertising without needing to raise
prices. Many forms of nonprice competition offer entirely illusory
"savings" accruing to the customer. As an example he gives the widespread
distribution of trading stamps. For certain large firms in oligopolistic
industries with excess capacity the stamps may be provided without
raising prices, and so seem to consumers to be free goods. They are not
that at all in an overall sense, however, since they merely divert trade
from other firms (until they also adopt stamps) and substitute for the
reduction of prices that would take place in a fully competitive market.

The result is a real increase in the price consumers must pay for groceries, gasoline, and other products because of the addition of costs for the trading stamp industry and the limitations on free consumer choice inherent in the stamps, which are less freely negotiable than cash.

A political analogy to this outcome might be the permanent expansion of the military and the arms industry in the United States as a result of every wartime exertion. From 1871 to 1898 the American armed forces numbered fewer than 50,000; after the Spanish American war they never again dropped below 100,000. The aftermath of World War I saw a leveling off to about 250,000, but the World War II mobilization left 1,400,000 as the permanent floor. Since the Korean War, the United States military establishment has never numbered fewer than about 2,500,000 men.[1] This phenomenon can be "explained" in a variety of ways—including objective needs and Parkinson's law—but the mechanism Kahn describes also may be relevant. After wars nations may have "excess" military capacity, but because there is often insufficient pressure to reduce that capacity, they then continue to compete at a high level of defense expenditure. Worldwide propaganda competition directed by the great powers to small states represents a similar phenomenon, closer in its functional manifestation to the advertising competition that he considers.

The danger from all of these unforeseen consequences is not that they occur, but that they may be *irreversible*. The wilderness, once ravished, cannot be replaced. The nuclear genie, once out of the bottle, cannot be recaptured. The military-industrial complex, once built, probably can never be totally disarmed. Hence small decisions, taken without at least an attempt to comprehend their larger consequences, may lead to a system transformation that we would never have chosen. An attempt to drift indefinitely with the present international system is unlikely to maintain current levels of stability and control over the long run. Trying to muddle through will merely insure our ultimate entrapment in a muddle.

[1] US Bureau of the Census, *Historical Statistics of the United States, Colonial Times to 1957* (Washington: US Government Printing Office, 1958) and US Bureau of the Census, *Statistical Abstract of the United States, 1967* (Washington: US Government Printing Office, 1967).

29

The Tyranny of Small Decisions: Market Failures, Imperfections, and the Limits of Econometrics

Alfred E. Kahn

The perennial problem of the appropriate role of government in economic life has been subjected to increasingly intense consideration by American economists in recent years, as part of the active political controversy over the proper balance of resource allocation between 'private wants and public needs'.[1] In particular, strenuous efforts have been made on the one hand to identify and analyze defects in the resource allocation effected by an unregulated market, such as might be remedied by government intervention; and, on the other, to devise economic criteria for allocating resources, alternatively, via government spending. The present essay falls in the former category: it defines and analyzes a particular inherent characteristic of the market, not to my knowledge hitherto identified as such, that is capable under certain circumstances of producing a defective or possibly objectionable allocational result.

Reprinted from *KYKLOS*, **19**, 1 (1966), pp. 23–46.

[1] This is the title of a very useful compendium of readings edited by E. S. Phelps, (New York: Norton, rev. ed., 1965). See also Francis M. Bator, *The Question of Government Spending* (New York: Harper & Row, 1960).

1. The Phenomenon Defined

A market economy makes its major allocation decisions on the basis of a host of "smaller" decisions—smaller in size and time dimension—recorded in individual market transactions. These smaller transactions themselves vary greatly in their size and scope—in the amount of resources they affect and the period of time they cover. The short- and long-run determinations by businessmen are governed by decisions of customers involving a corresponding range in size and time perspective—to buy a single candy bar, a camping trip, an automobile, a house, or to enter a rental contract of short or long duration. Still, the "size" or importance of the individual choices by customers is typically less than of those made by the businessman, so that each of the latter's decisions reflects a prospective adding up of the consequences of a large number of customer actions taking place over a period of time.

A critical task in appraising the allocative efficiency of such an economy, then, is to determine whether and under what conditions the total effect of these small decisions will be optimal. The "tyranny of small decisions" suggests that it may not be, *merely because* the decisive determinations are individually too "small," in the sense just indicated. It suggests that if one hundred consumers choose option x, and this causes the market to make decision X (where X equals $100\,x$), it is not necessarily true that those same consumers would have voted for that outcome if that large decision had ever been presented for their explicit consideration. If this is true, *the consumer can be victimized by the narrowness of the contexts in which he exercises his sovereignty.*

Now, welfare economists have long ago exposed various reasons why, indeed, these individual decisions may not add up to a collective microeconomic optimum. These reasons fall essentially into two categories: (a) market imperfections and (b) market failures. The significance of imperfections of competition is obvious: if even the individual choices are short of optimal, because, let us say, of consumer ignorance or monopoly, there is no reason to expect their total to be optimal. As for (b), it is by now commonplace that even perfectly competitive markets may fail to achieve Pareto-optimal results in the presence of such phenomena as externalities (economies or diseconomies, unpaid social costs, privately inappropriable social benefits) or internally increasing returns (when a price equated to marginal cost, as the Pareto optimum would require, will not be adequately remunerative to a private entrepreneur).[2] In addition, economists have long recognized the possibility of objections to consumer

---

[2] See, e.g., Bator, "The Anatomy of Market Failure," *Quarterly Journal of Economics,* **72** (August 1958), pp. 351–379.

sovereignty itself, on "noneconomic" grounds. This category of possible objections to the functioning of the market, in contrast with the first two, questions or rejects the value judgments underlying Pareto's definition of optimality, and raises considerations generally deemed to lie outside the particular competence of economics.

The "tyranny of small decisions" does not add a fourth category to this list. As the ensuing discussion will show, its manifestations fall some-times in one, sometimes in another of the familiar three; and the defect of, or possible basis for objection to, the private market that it identifies can in principle be conceived of in one or another of those familiar terms. Thus Section 2 will consider situations in which it may cause authentic market failure. The problems analyzed in Sections 3–5 will prove to involve mixtures of all three categories: sometimes the real culprit proves to be an imperfection of competition; sometimes what seem to be involved are dynamic consequences of the market that welfare economics is simply incapable of appraising.

But in all instances, I believe, the "smallness" of the governing deci-sions is in one way or another an additional explanatory element. It seems in some instances to illuminate the problem better than the more familiar market failures or imperfections; and it sometimes seems to have the virtue of more clearly suggesting the necessity of looking at the process in broader terms than does the market, and possibly substituting a "large" for a piecemeal accumulation of "small" decisions, if the results of the market are to be intelligently appraised or effectively improved.

2. The Phenomenon as an Instance of Market Failure

The event that first suggested the phenomenon to this writer was the disappearance of passenger railroad service from Ithaca, a small and comparatively isolated (since that time, even more so!) community in up-state New York. It may be assumed the service was withdrawn because over a long enough period of time the individual decisions travelers made, for each of their projected trips into and out of Ithaca and the other cities served, did not provide the railroads enough total revenue to cover incremental costs (defined over the same period). Considering the com-parative comforts and speeds of competing media, those individual deci-sions were by no means irrational: the railroad was slow and uncomfort-able.

What reason, then, was there to question the aggregate effect of those individual choices—withdrawal of the service? The fact is the rail-road provided the one reliable means of getting into and out of Ithaca in all kinds of weather; and this insufficiently exerted option, this inadequately used alternative was something I for one would have been willing to pay something to have kept alive. This way of looking at the result suggests a simple, though unfortunately subjective and hence not necessarily practical, test of whether the railroad's closing was economically correct: let each traveler or potential traveler have asked himself[3] how much he would have been willing to pledge regularly over some time period, say, annually, by purchase of prepaid tickets, to keep rail passenger service in Ithaca. So long as the amount he would have declared (to himself) would have exceeded what he actually paid in that period—and my own introspective experiment shows it would—then to that extent the disappearance of passenger service from Ithaca was an incident of market failure.

The cause of the failure was the discrepancy between the time perspective of the choices I was given an opportunity to make—deciding, each time I planned to travel, whether or not to go by train—and the relevant decision of the railroad, which was a long-run, virtually all-or-nothing and once-for-all decision, to retain or abandon passenger service. When each traveler or potential traveler chose between the local airline, his own automobile, and the railroad, his individual choice had an only negligible effect on the continued availability of the latter; it would therefore have been irrational for him to consider this possible implication of his decision. The fact remains that each selection of *x* over *y* constitutes also a vote for eliminating the possibility thereafter of choosing *y*; if enough people vote for *x*, *each time necessarily on the assumption that y will continue, y* may, in fact, disappear. And its disappearance may constitute a genuine deprivation that customers might willingly have paid something to avoid. The only choice the market offered us travelers to influence the longer-run decision of the railroad was thus shorter in its time perspective, and the sum-total of our individual purchases of railroad tickets necessarily added up to a smaller amount than our *actual combined interest* in the continued availability of rail service. We were victims of the tyranny of small decisions.

But if most of the travelers who felt a sense of loss at the railroad's demise had, in fact, patronized it, though infrequently, when it was still available, could not the railroad company have tested their evaluation of

[3] If instead he *had been* asked by someone else—say the railroad company—he might not have answered honestly. This is because the mere *availability* of railroad service to a community is what P. A. Samuelson has termed a public good: so long as the railroad remains, it costs nothing additional to keep it available for *B* as well as *A*; and as long as it is available to *A*, it is automatically available also to *B*. This is the kind of situation in which each person approached to contribute to its continued availability is under systematic temptation to understate the intensity of his demand, in hope that the pledges of others will suffice to preserve the option for him anyhow. "The Pure Theory of Public Expenditure," *Review of Economics and Statistics*, **36** (November 1954), pp. 388–389.

its continuation in service by charging them higher fares than it did on those few occasions? It might have tried, and to some extent succeeded: apart from administrative and regulatory inconveniences, railroads could, for example, charge higher passenger fares on rainy days, when the airplanes are grounded, or in the winter, and in this fashion appropriate a share of the consumer's surplus derived from their continued availability for just such emergencies.[4] But such a policy could not escape the basic difficulty. At each such time, the individual traveler would still be deciding whether or not to pay the higher price on the basis of the costs, pains, and benefits facing him *in that particular instance*. The higher fare might cause him simply to postpone his trip. He would still have no opportunity to express or convey to the railroad—and, on the contrary, would still have an incentive to conceal—his full appraisal of the value to him of having the service available at all times.

As has already been suggested, this instance of the tyranny of small decisions can be conceived in more familiar terms. As has frequently been noted, when some of the economic effects of individual transactions do not enter into the calculations of the transacting parties, the total effect of individual optimizing decisions may fall short of a collective optimum. The essential flaw is precisely the one emphasized here: the individual transaction is "too small" if it has external, unconsidered effects. Conversely, if, as in the present instance, the larger result, representing a summation of smaller decisions, is not optimal, it must mean that the component transactions involved external economies or diseconomies.

The specific externality involved here has been very clearly identified by Burton A. Weisbrod.[5] Weisbrod's argument concerns the possible failure of the market to provide services part of the demand for which is the desire of potential customers to keep open the possibility or option of enjoying them, when (a) the option is not (or not always), in fact, exercised, (b) revenues from actual purchasers are or become insufficient to cover the costs of continued operation, and (c) "expansion or recommencement of production at the time [in the future] when occasional purchasers wish to make a purchase . . . [is] difficult or impossible."[6] As Weisbrod points out, provision of the option to nonusers is a costless (external) by-product of supplying actual users; underallocation of resources to this endeavor occurs only when condition (b) prevails. So the external benefit in our example is the mere availability of the service to

---

[4] On some of the difficulties, see B. A. Weisbrod, "Collective-Consumption Services of Individual Consumption Goods," *Quarterly Journal of Economics*, **78** (August 1964), pp. 475–476.

[5] *Op. cit.*, pp. 471–477.

[6] *Ibid.*, p. 474.

nonusers, the continued ability to satisfy as-yet unexerted "option demand," as he terms it.[7]

The concept of externalities is, however, in some situations inadequately descriptive of what we have in mind here. Thus, it has not until Weisbrod (to my knowledge) suggested to economists the tendency of the market to underrate option demand. While Milton Friedman recognizes that because of their great "neighborhood effects" city parks would be supplied in inadequate quantities by the private market alone, he rejects this case for governmental initiative in the provision of national parks. Surely, he reasons, the only people benefited by the latter are those who actually travel to them: distant, unseen parks can generate no external benefits. Why not then leave it to the market to ascertain by a system of user charges to what extent the users or potential users are willing to pay the opportunity costs of providing these services?[8] The point is, however, that there are other, economically interested parties who would not be consulted in this determination—the people who may never travel to the parks, yet for whatever reason derive satisfaction from their availability, and who would feel a loss if they were to disappear. The wilderness is a particularly apt example, because it most clearly meets the previously given irreversibility requirement, (c): once "production" has ceased it cannot ever be resumed!

So in our railroad example: externalities are usually understood to refer to the effects of a transaction on other parties, or on the transactors in other roles. In the present situation it is in large measure the interests of the same parties, railroad passengers as such, that are inadequately considered. The offenders are also the unwitting—or, if witting, nonetheless helpless—victims. One might, of course, still maintain that the potential rail passenger on a wintry night when planes are grounded is in economic terms a different person than the one who decides to take the plane on a sunny June day. The effect of the latter's decision on his own welfare in the former situation is an authentic externality. But it has a special character. Whereas it would never pay the individual that imposes external costs on others to alter his course of conduct unless compelled or bribed to do so, it *would* pay travelers and commuters to take into account, and be influenced in their travel choices by, the "external" effect—on themselves—of their combined actions, if only the market gave them the opportunity.

[7] The simplest case of the Weisbrod phenomenon is where the option demand is not exercised at all during the period over which revenues must cover cost if service is to be continued. But, as he recognizes (*op. cit.*, p. 476) and our foregoing discussion demonstrates, the problem may arise also if the option demand is merely exercised infrequently—insufficiently for the revenues from users, on the one hand, to cover costs, on the other hand, fully to reflect consumers' aggregate evaluation of the continued availability of the service.

[8] *Capitalism and Freedom* (Chicago: University of Chicago Press, 1963), p. 31.

3. Invention as the Mother of Necessity

The philosopher Morris R. Cohen, I have been told, used to challenge his classes with something like the following question: "Suppose, seventy-five years ago, some being from outer space had made us this proposition: 'I know how to make a means of transportation that could in effect put 200 horses at the disposal of each of you. It would permit you to travel about, alone or in small groups, at 60 to 80 miles an hour. I offer you this knowledge; the price is 40,000 lives per year.' Would we have accepted?" If there is a possibility we might have refused the offer, thus presented—a "big" decision—then our having reached the same result gradually, unwittingly, by a series of individual purchases could represent a product of the tyranny of small decisions. It may be instructive to sift out the various possible reasons why, or criteria according to which, the market may not have produced optimal results in this historical process.

First, who are the "we" in this experiment? The way in which the question is posed would seem to require some sort of collective determination, ending in a simple "yes" or "no" response, rather than—as the market does it—x yeses and y nos, perhaps at the cost of an equivalent proportion of 40,000 lives. If one feels "we" as a collectivity—rather than as a simple aggregation of separate individuals—would have been better off had we had the opportunity to make the ("big") decision, politically, on an all-or-none basis, one may, of course, be simply rejecting the standards of welfare economics. This view, while defensible, is one about which the economist has comparatively little to say.

But perhaps the implication is, instead, that individual consumers may have made the wrong decisions, in the sense that at least some of them would have decided otherwise had they known the risks. Then we have a simple case of market imperfection—inadequate knowledge. This interpretation would be valid, of course, only if the risks (and other costs) were costs to the motorist alone. To the extent that the decision of X to buy a car increases the risks of injury or lung cancer to Y, whether or not Y buys a car, we have an external cost and genuine market failure, though of a familiar kind, and not particularly reflective of the tyranny of small decisions.[9]

The spread of the automobile takes on the peculiar quality of the phenomenon expounded here if, as well may be the case, there is some *threshold level* of traffic density or air pollution below which there are no such risks, or beyond which these external costs mount disproportionately with subsequent individual purchases. It then takes a cumulation of small,

[9] Except in the special sense, already suggested, that any decision from consideration of which external costs are excluded is ipso facto too "small."

individually riskless or comparatively riskless additions to the automobile population to develop a major external cost. Any possible consequent market failure would still be the result of the externality, however: if the interests of all affected parties, perpetrators and potential victims together, were to be consulted in each consecutive small decision, the sharply mounting social costs of consecutive automobile purchases would be adequately reflected in the price, and no market failure need occur.

One moves beyond the familiar externalities, however, when one traces the cumulative effects of individual purchase decisions on the structure of consumer wants themselves. Pigou long ago identified envy as an external cost of consumption, and saw that it was a possible source of market failure. Y may want a car merely because X and Z have purchased one; and Z may then want a newer model because B has one. But such externalities are not confined to envy, the "demonstration effect," or vicarious or altruistic pleasure.[10] Y may have to have a car because more and more of his friends are enabled by the cars they have purchased to live on the outskirts of town, and he wants to be able to continue visiting his friends; or because grocery stores have moved to shopping centers; or he may feel impelled to move to the suburbs himself because now the schools are better than in town. Invention, Veblen noted, is the mother of necessity. And the process is gradual and cumulative: it takes the moving of more than one friend or one grocery store to require the abandoned Y to move too and fall victim to the garageman and the plumber who charges portal-to-portal; and Y's move adds its small part to the pressure on W. So what we have is a situation in which a series of apparently free, individually welfare-maximizing purchase decisions, made in the context of a given way of life and given alternatives, has such a cumulative effect on those parameters that subsequent choices can no longer be made in the same atmosphere (literally, as well as figuratively: the very atmosphere in town is polluted by cars). In a real sense the decision is less free than it was. The invention has bred a need; and to the cumulative process of creating new needs and then satisfying them one cannot apply the traditional welfare-maximization criteria constructed on the basis of the assumption that that economy serves best that best satisfies wants that are given and unchanging—or, if changing, that change under influences exogenous to the economic system that satisfies them. It would seem we have two distinct phenomena here: one, market failure, within the criteria of welfare economics; and second, a change in tastes that welfare economics is incapable of adjudging.

[10] A. C. Pigou, *The Economics of Welfare* (New York, Macmillan, 4th ed., 1960), p. 191; E. J. Mishan, "A Survey of Welfare Economics, 1939–59," *The Economic Journal*, **70** (June 1960), pp. 246–248.

The process of converting inventions into necessities by changing the parameters of individual choice consists in part in the setting in motion of a great threshold cost destruction of alternatives. The rise of the automobile gradually undermined the profitability of the passenger (and commuter) railroads, making it progressively more difficult for the latter to attract either capital or enterprising managers. The comfort and convenience of rail service therefore deteriorated, both absolutely and relative to emerging alternatives. This, in turn, made it progressively more rational to prefer the latter, and these choices in turn gave another twist to the screw. (This process is far advanced 'in the United States; I do not know whether Europe has begun to experience it as yet, or is on the verge of doing so.) Even, then, if some of the newer alternatives began to involve mounting costs—congestion on city streets, long trips to and from airports —travelers and commuters might still prefer these options to the deteriorated rail service. So long as the deterioration of the latter proceeded more rapidly than the disutilities of the former, the process would not have reversed itself.

In these circumstances, it is entirely conceivable that the total process may not have involved optimization at all. If some fraction of the total resources put into autos, highways and air travel could have been equally available to invest in improving (and research in improving) the railroads (or some other mass transit), consumers might individually have chosen the latter in sufficient quantity to produce quite a different mix from the one that has emerged. Here then, is a possible case for large public investment in such a renovation, justified partly by the imperfections of the private capital market,[11] partly by externalities,[12] and partly by the necessity of extramarket intervention to offset the tyranny of small decisions. It may take a major, discrete step, breaking the market-determined

[11] If such an investment were economically justified, why would not the market provide it? Why is the process irreversible in the absence of government intervention? In part, because management apparently considers internally generated capital lower-cost than external and is more likely to invest in risky ventures like research and product innovation with the one than with the other; and railroads have relatively little of such capital available to them. In part because this is not a purely competitive industry: the effort can hardly be mounted, except by existing railroad companies. And suppliers of any new capital to the railroads, whatever its marginal revenue product, would have to pool that revenue product with the meager returns from past investment, and so receive only a diluted benefit—whereas if new entry were feasible all the profits of successful innovation would accrue to the new investors. Also for this reason the marginal efficiency of investment is reduced: for established firms, in contrast with new entrants, new equipment would be competing with the old for passengers they are already serving.

[12] Private investors in improved mass transit would not reap all the benefits—for example, of reduced congestion in city streets.

spiral of history, to offer consumers the full range of economically feasible alternatives required for rational choice.

4. Skimming the Cream and the Destruction of Associated Services

In the transportation field particularly, the argument is often made for restrictions on competition, and particularly on entry, that otherwise aggressive competitors would "skim the cream" of the traffic, and in so doing make it impossible for the established, common carriers to continue the less lucrative services—conducting regularly scheduled operations in bad seasons as well as good, on thin as well as rich routes. A similar case is often made for resale price maintenance: that unrestricted price competition on popular, fast-moving brands (best-selling books, whiskies, toothpastes, or appliances) would drive out of business the small, conveniently situated, low-volume retailer, the merchandiser who offers service, the diversified bookstore, the neighborhood pharmacist, all of whom, it is alleged, survive in part because of the protected margins on the former items.

These arguments find an important part of their support in the fact of consumer ignorance and the threat of destructive competition, familiar market imperfections, and to this extent do not concern us here.[13] But they also implicitly or explicitly invoke the principle we have been expounding. If unrestricted competition prevailed, it would be irrational for each consumer to choose where to make each of his individual purchases on any basis except price and convenience, and, where these considerations so dictated, to buy his toothpaste and whiskey at the supermarket, his best sellers at a discount by mail, his appliances from the discount house, to travel on a nonscheduled airline if it offered bargain rates during the peak season. His individual, small decision to do otherwise would not in itself make a significant contribution to keeping the corner drug-, book-, or liquor store in business, or the off-peak flights on the schedule. And yet, the total effect of these individual decisions might be to kill off not only the rejected alternative but the auxiliary services it alone provides—options that buyers might, if given the explicit opportunity, have been willing to pay something to keep alive.

The problem can be illuminated, though not resolved, by the economics of integration. The drugstore, scheduled airline, and maritime

---

[13] That is, they involve a contention that the consumer is often deceived when he turns to what seems to him a cheaper source of supply: the discount house may turn out to give inadequate service on his appliance, the tramp freighter to carry inadequate insurance against loss of cargo, and so on.

shipping conference member are integrated firms, purveying a variety of products or services. There are only two possible effects of this integration on the ability of these firms to compete with interlopers or price competitors who confine themselves to skimming the cream.

1. It may give them an advantage—in which event, it would seem, they can make no case for protection. The telephone company needs no artificial barriers against the entry of specialist firms seeking to take away its apparently more lucrative daytime, long-distance telephone business, in order to ensure its continued provision of nighttime service. Its rates for the former would have to be even higher than they are were it not also in a position, with the same equipment, to supply off-peak, nighttime service at rates in excess of incremental costs. Indeed, in such a situation it is in a sense impossible to say which part of the business is the "cream," which part the "skimmed milk," because the bulk of the costs are common. No competitor could survive on the cream alone, unless the incumbent company is inefficient, or charging extortionate rates, or using an outmoded technology—no one of which reasons constitutes a social justification for limitations on entry.

2. The integration may *not* confer an advantage in the lucrative part of the business sufficient to offset the advantages potential entrants may enjoy (perhaps because of their enterprise, abilities, volume of operations, of their particular kind of integration), in which event, it would appear, they still deserve no protection. Suppose, for example, some firm outside the Bell System found a new way to transmit long-distance telephone messages using the rays of the sun—i.e., during the daytime only—at total unit costs less than current daytime rates. Would the incumbent company then deserve protection against the undermining of those high rates on the ground that otherwise night telephone service would disappear? The correct answer is that no class of customers should be required to pay more than the total cost of serving it alone. Whether by competition or by regulation, the daytime rates should be brought down at least to the total unit costs under the new technology. If this requires higher nighttime rates for the joint service to continue, then night rates should go up, possibly to the point where this business covers the bulk of the common costs. The advantages of integration may then still suffice to keep the old, established telephone company in business, perhaps retaining its monopoly—this would be our case 1. Or they may no longer suffice—our case 2—in which event night telephonic communication is no longer economically feasible, and should disappear.

The policy issues here under consideration would seem to involve case 2 rather than case 1 situations. It is evidently possible without competitive handicap to sell whiskey and not delivery service, toothpaste and not the filling of prescriptions, New York to Miami and not New York to Ithaca flights, appliances and not quick repairs. The cream and the skimmed milk are separable; that is why purveyors of both ask to be protected in the former part of their business. In these circumstances, it would seem, competition ought to be allowed to drive the prices of the separable services down, and up, to their respective long-run marginal costs. Otherwise, purchasers of cream are being forced to subsidize devotees of skimmed milk.

And yet—over and above the possibly excessive imperfections of competition in the real world—there remains the germ of validity to the opposing case already suggested in this essay. May not many of the patrons who shift to the cheaper, sun-powered, daylight telephone service later regret—that is, experience a sense of loss they would willingly have paid something to avoid—the disappearance of night service that results from these individually rational, small decisions? To this consideration it would seem a sufficient response, in most cases, that the market *will* ordinarily give customers the opportunity to keep the skimmed milk flowing. The price will have to rise to a truer reflection of its opportunity cost, and if enough patrons are willing to pay the price, it will flow; if they are not, it ought not.[14] If prices are not correctly adjusted, we have market imperfection, not market failure.

In what circumstances, then, may such an outcome reflect authentic market failure? As Weisbrod suggests, two conditions have to be met: (a) it must be infeasible to charge the required price for the separate service, and (b) resumption of service, once suspended, must be difficult (i.e., costly) or impossible.[15] But these conditions are rarely absolute; different markets will satisfy them in varying degrees. Whether, then, we may have market failure because of the tyranny of small decisions in bookstores as well as railroads, drugstores, or local-service airlines as well as national parks, is a question of fact to be confronted in each situation separately.

As for condition (a), for example, it is impossible for public parks to levy charges on patrons who never actually visit them. This is the extreme

[14] It should, perhaps, be reemphasized that the kind of market failure considered in this essay is not the only possible kind. There may be external benefits flowing from a continued provision of service that may justify its continuation even if sales revenues prove insufficient.

[15] *Op. cit.*, p. 476. The reader will recognize the relevance of the second consideration in another situation of possible market breakdown, destructive competition. One of the main circumstances in which unrestricted price rivalry may be undesirable is in the presence of temporary excess capacity, where a tendency for price to be driven to out-of-pocket costs of some producers (and below those of others) may cause the dismantling or inadequate maintenance of productive capacity and going organizations that will in time be needed, and can at such times be reconstituted only at markedly higher cost.

case. But even when the option is sometimes exercised, it may be infeasible to collect the entire consumer's surplus generated by preservation of the alternative. We have already suggested why this might be so for passenger railroads. Similarly, it may be infeasible for the well-stocked bookstore to charge for the privilege of browsing. On the other hand, it is difficult to see why druggists cannot charge to the filling of prescriptions as much of the common costs as competition in toothpastes and patent medicines requires; why liquor stores cannot charge separately for delivery; and why feeder airlines cannot charge the travelers and communities they serve the full costs of that service.

Finally, even if competitive skimming of the cream did, in fact, cause the disappearance of desired associated services, we would have a case for government intervention only if condition (b) were met as well. It is very questionable that most of the cases discussed in this section meet this test nearly as well as those analyzed previously, in Section 2. The wilderness, once despoiled, can never be a wilderness again. The closing down of a neighborhood drug- and liquor store, diversified bookstores, even feeder airline service on thin routes, on the other hand, probably do not represent such "large" decisions that they cannot be reversed in the future, should demand warrant it. For these cases, then, the social costs of restricted competition probably outweigh the costs of eventually rectifying market failure, when and if necessary. Whatever case can be made for fair trade, for maritime shipping conferences, and for restricted entry into airline transport must, therefore, be based on the imperfections of unregulated competition rather than, importantly, on the tyranny of small decisions.

5. Product Inflation

The phenomenon that J. M. Clark has termed "product inflation" has certain characteristics very similar to those of the tyranny of small decisions. What Clark refers to is the possibility that in highly concentrated industries—he refers particularly to American automobiles—competition may take the form principally of cost-inflating and largely specious quality improvements.[16]

In confronting the knotty problem of evaluating product competition, the welfare economist usually settles for asking whether consumers continue to be provided with sufficient, technologically feasible price-quality combinations, and have sufficient ability to judge product quality, so that each can register a free and tolerably well informed monetary appraisal of quality differentials and changes. Product inflation could by this test be said to have occurred only if quality competition had operated in such a

[16] *Competition as a Dynamic Process* (Washington: Brookings, 1961), pp. 252–257.

way as to eliminate or to fail to develop lower quality-price combinations that consumers would willingly have purchased (or continued to purchase) in quantities sufficient to cover the cost of providing them. The question from the standpoint of this essay would then be: may there be something in the process of day-by-day or year-by-year choosing among quality-price combinations, each choice typically involving rather modest differences—i.e., a "small" decision—such that while consumers make the proper (from their standpoint) individual short-term choices, in so doing they pay an aggregate cost over time that they would have deemed excessive had they ever been given the opportunity to make such an overall assessment? Or such that the total effect of these decisions is eventually to produce a range of choice from which desired and economically feasible lower price-quality combinations have either disappeared or have failed to appear? The answer to these questions may be yes; product inflation could, therefore, be a manifestation of the tyranny of small decisions. But, the subsequent discussion will attempt to show, it is not principally an evidence of market failure: the principal culprit seems to be imperfections of competition.

There are two aspects of product inflation that may, indeed, cast doubt on the optimality of the competitive market outcome; having already been discussed, they need detain us but briefly. One is the tendency quality variations have of generating external diseconomies of consumption—envy. The other is their contribution to the process of want creation: the mere appearance of new models inculcates in consumers dissatisfaction with the ones they have. These two effects can involve households in a self-defeating spiral of model changes, each at one and the same time creating dissatisfaction and (temporarily) removing it, at a cost that buyers might well deem excessive if the question were ever put to them on something other than a piecemeal, family-by-family, year-to-year basis. This is not to say one can be sure consumers would necessarily have had it any other way, whether in automobiles, refrigerators, women's dresses, or books. First, they would undoubtedly appraise many of the quality changes as unequivocal and unidirectionally improvements, and willingly pay their cost, even if offered the choice over a much longer period of time. Second, they might derive sufficient pleasure from the process itself of buying, discarding, and buying again, and willingly pay its costs (consider, for example, the changing "models" of books).

But, apart from the two foregoing considerations, it is ineffective competition that must be blamed for product inflation. The difficulty is not that consumers, *offered the relevant short-term alternatives*, make rational choices setting in motion a course of development that produces a less-than-optimal end result, for which they would not vote if given the opportunity: that would be market failure. It is that an inadequately competitive market often fails to present them in the first place with the proper small choices. They are often not offered a choice between unchanged and changed models at a price differential fully reflecting the cost saving made possible by sticking to the former. The recognition among oligopolists that competition probing the price elasticity of industry demand tends to be self-defeating, whereas "quality" competition that moves that curve to the right is mutually beneficial, tends to make the choice rather between a new model of seller *A* and an unchanged model of seller *B at the same price.* The consumer is thus deceived about the social cost of satisfying his taste for variety and change, and hence votes to satisfy that taste more often than he would in a market characterized by more effective price competition.

It is concentrated oligopoly with high barriers to entry that makes the leading American automobile manufacturers comparatively uninterested in aggressively developing and promoting economy—of initial purchase, operation, and repair—durability, or safety. Another market imperfection reinforcing this tendency, also mentioned by Clark, is the difficulty consumers have in appraising, hence their slowness in shifting their patronage in response to, claims along these lines.

Similarly, it is oligopoly plus the limitations on entry and discouragement of price competition in passenger air transport, domestic and international, that have caused competition to take forms—notably emphasizing newer and faster equipment, frequency of scheduling, inflight entertainment, and luxurious meals—that adjust costs upward toward price rather than price down toward cost—another instance of product inflation. Or, to take a homelier but possibly more irritating example, it is significant that when the A & P company at last succumbed to the competitive pressure to introduce trading stamps, it stated it did not expect to have to raise prices because it anticipated the increased volume resulting "without corresponding increases in fixed costs" would absorb the added costs. It is not clear whether the company rejected the alternative competitive tactic of reducing prices because it felt (a) such a competitive move would have been less perceptible to customers, or (b) more quickly matched by its competitors, or (c) consumers really prefer stamps to equivalent price reductions. But if the reason for this significant incident in our national reversion to barter was either of the first two, then this further spread of trading stamps was an instance of product inflation attributable to market imperfection.

In each of these instances, the consumer may have been offered an excessively small range of choice, unreflective of all the consequences of this or that decision—to phone the airline with the more or the fewer flights scheduled, to patronize the grocery offering trading stamps or the one that did not, in both cases with no apparent price differential between the rival suppliers. Naturally, in each instance he chose the former, in numbers sufficient to force competitors to "improve" their service in the same way, at mounting costs all around.[17] To consider the latter example alone, it remains an interesting question how shoppers would now respond if they were given a once-and-for-all choice for or against trading stamps, in terms clearly setting forth how much groceries and gasoline would cost with and without them. Whether through market imperfection or market failure, we may here again have been victims of the tyranny of small decisions.

6. Conclusion

It is an inherent characteristic of a consumer-sovereign, market economy that big changes occur as an accretion of moderate-sized steps, each of them the consequence of "small" purchase decisions—small in their individual size, time perspective, and in relation to their total, combined, ultimate effect. Because change takes place in this fashion, it sometimes produces results that conflict with the very values the market economy is supposed to serve. In some instances, this seems to be because certain kinds of economically significant votes never get taken in the ballot box of the marketplace. In others, of which economists have long been aware, because the individual transactions have consequences extending beyond the transacting parties themselves, so that the sum total of economic costs and benefits do not get calculated by the market. In others, not because of inherent defects of the market system itself, but because of imperfections of competition. All have these characteristics in common: that "large" changes are effected by a cumulation of "small" decisions; that consumers never get an opportunity to vote with their dollars on the large changes as such; and if they were given the opportunity, they might not approve what they have wrought.

[17] There is a clear analogy here to the case of competitive and self-defeating advertising. It pays each individual company to advertise, whether aggressively or defensively; and the expectation of a favorable customer response and the presence of either excess capacity or economies of scale may permit the advertised product to be offered at the same price as the unadvertised one. Yet the net effect of such a cycle of competitive moves and responses may be nothing more than higher costs for all. If consumers are never presented with a clear-cut choice between advertised and unadvertised brands at prices reflecting their respective costs, or are deterred by ignorance from choosing the cheaper, unadvertised brand we have a case of product inflation attributable to market imperfection. So, of course, even if A & P's anticipation of higher sales and hence no-higher total unit costs were justified—and in fact it was not, universally; some A & P stores did in fact raise prices when they introduced stamps (*Wall Street Journal*, September 17, 1963)—that anticipation would not have been correct for the industry as a whole.

Index